THE MODERN VERSION
INCURSION

- Assaults Accuracy
- Assaults Doctrinal Purity
- Assaults Finality
- Assaults Total Truth
- Assaults Spiritual Stability

747 verses assailed equals 747 reasons to mistrust the modern versions!

Dr. Ken Matto

ISBN 978-1-64140-869-1 (paperback)
ISBN 978-1-64140-870-7 (digital)

Christian Faith Publishing, Inc.
832 Park Avenue
Meadville, PA 16335
www.christianfaithpublishing.com

PREFACE

Three of the most conspicuous characteristics of the modern Bible versions are the following:

1. The omission of complete Bible verses
2. The omission of key parts of many verses
3. The altering of the English words, thus changing or reversing the meaning of the verse completely

When one uses a modern version, they are using a seriously corrupted version that has been handed down to modern-day scholarship by the Gnostics of the second and third century. These modern versions are counterfeits and have brought nothing but confusion into the church and the Christian. A Christian who uses multiple versions for their study is basing their study on corrupted versions. I want to focus on the egregious omissions in the modern versions. If you have a modern version, I urge you to make the comparison between your modern version and the King James Bible. You will see that what is missing in your modern version is not missing in the King James Bible. Who is the author of confusion? "For God is not the author of confusion, but of peace, as in all churches of the saints" (1 Corinthians 14:33, KJV).

According to this verse, it definitely is not God, so then why would you want to use a counterfeit version devised by the enemy of Christ? You will see changes, omissions, and additions that range from the very small to the very large, yet they are unauthorized changes that are nothing more than attacks on the Bible. Even though there are many changes listed here, there are many others; and with each new version that is produced, the message of the Bible will be harder and harder to find. Plus, there will be more omissions, changes, and additions.

People are becoming saved every day, and that will happen until the last day. Once a person becomes saved, they normally attach themselves to a church. If that church is using a modern version, then it would follow that the new Christian would be given the modern version they use. This would mean that the new believer will not even know that there are serious problems and deficiencies in the modern versions unless they compare the affected verses to the King James Bible. That is what this book is all about. It shows the effect the omissions, deletions, and additions have on doctrinal truths taught plainly in the King James Bible. This work was done by me over a twelve-and-a-half-year period when I sent these out weekly to about a thousand people online.

The format for this book will be easy. I will place the King James verse in its entirety, and then I will place in italics the part that is left out or changed in the modern versions, and then I will state which doctrine is being assaulted. You will then have the ability to make the comparison with your modern version, and you will see firsthand the corruption in the modern versions. It must be noted that not every corruption will be present in all the modern versions, but there are verses that will be corrupted across the majority of them. All you need to do is make the comparison between your version and the King James Bible.

> Thou shalt keep them, O LORD, thou shalt preserve them from this generation for ever. (Psalm 12:7, KJV)

We are told that verse 7 speaks about the poor being preserved by God; however, that would be teaching that salvation is by economic status. Whenever the word *for ever* is used, we need to look at eternal matters, and that is the eternal Gospel. If we believe that God preserves the poor people for ever, then we have to ask, where are these preserved people today? Why aren't they around? It is because they died, which means God is preserving something else that is eternal.

> LAMED. For ever, O LORD, thy word is settled in heaven. (Psalm 119:89, KJV)

What was preserved in heaven according to Psalm 119:89?

The Hebrew word *natsar*, which is used for *settled* in Psalm 119:89, carries with it the meaning of "guard, preserve, or established." So we see that the words of God are preserved forever because they are established forever. In both verses, we see the eternality of the word of God.

> Heaven and earth shall pass away, but my words shall not pass away. (Matthew 24:35, KJV)

Christ said that His words will never pass away, and He is the one who gave the words of scripture to be penned by the prophets and apostles. This also shows the eternality of the word of God, which harmonizes with Psalm 12:7 and Psalm 119:89. The reason that modern-version proponents do not like to see these truths is because the modern versions take the word of God and make it subjective to man and his "science." If the modern-version editors truly believed that God's word was settled or established in heaven forever, they would not have written twenty-eight versions of Nestle-Aland Greek and five versions of the UBS Greek, which is just as corrupt as the Roman Catholic Nestle-Aland texts.

Many times, the modern-version-only proponents like to call those of us who use only the King James Bible a cult. Those who accuse us of being King James only would have a hard time making that moniker apply to the seventeenth, eighteenth, and nineteenth centuries when the King James Bible was the primary and, in the majority of cases, the only Bible in use. The first attempt to subvert the King James Bible Greek text was done by John Mill, who created a critical text in 1707. Even when 1881 rolled around, the Hort-Westcott counterfeit text did not make much of an impact till we hit the twentieth century. Once the twentieth-century scholars got their hands on a few old manuscripts, that is when Satan made his move to try and replace the true word of God with counterfeits starting with the 1901 ASV, and then it was a slide downhill. The modern-version proponents like to refer to us as a cult while all the time it is their modern-version-only mind-set that has invaded the church. Just like the cults that try to take Christians away from the local church, it is akin to the modern versions that try to draw Christians away from the true preserved word of God. It is not those of us who use and stick to the King James Bible; it is the modern-version-only crowd that has sown discord among the brethren. Church history is on the side of the King James Bible.

The problem with placing your faith in modern-version-only theologians, especially those on the radio, instead of God is that you come away with the mistaken notion that you do not have an infallible Bible by a perfect God. It impugns the character of God to claim that He could not preserve His word. The modern-version-only cult walks by sight and not by faith. They have to hold the manuscripts in their hand whereas those of us who trust the Lord in this area do not need those critical text crutches. The word of God is settled in heaven. The word *settled* carries with it the meaning of "established" or "fixed" as we previously saw. "LAMED. For ever, O LORD, thy word is settled in heaven" (Psalm 119:89, KJV)

It is a shame that so many once-truthful and faithful churches are now using Satan's counterfeits to try and ascertain truth. So many Protestant churches like the Presbyterian, Reformed, Baptist, Methodist, and other churches and denominations serve the Vatican through the Roman Catholic modern versions. Their oldest and best manuscripts are Roman Catholic in origin. The Vaticanus, which has been dated to the fourth century, has no history before 1475. The King James translators had access to it and rejected it because of its massive corruptions. The Sinaiticus has now been overwhelmingly proven to be a nineteenth-century counterfeit. On these two manuscripts, plus forty-three others, sits the basis for the modern versions while the King James sits on the basis of over five thousand that are in agreement. The Vaticanus and Sinaiticus contradict each other in 3,036 places in the four gospels alone. It is a dangerous foundation to build on! The Holy Spirit inspired the Bible and preserved the words, as well as the inspiration of the King James Bible. How inspired can a Bible be that is based on Roman Catholic manuscripts and counterfeits?

The Greek text of the New Testament has been horribly attacked. Seventeen years after Hort and Westcott came out with their revised version, Eberhard Nestle created his first edition of the Novum Testamentum Graece in 1898. Nestle took the three leading scholarly editions of the Greek New Testament at that time by Tischendorf, Westcott-Hort, and Weymouth as a basis. (After 1901, he replaced the Weymouth with Bernhard Weiss's 1894/1900 edition.) The Nestle-Aland critical Greek text has just published its twenty-eighth edition in 2012. Along with these editions is the United Bible Societies critical Greek text, which is now in its fifth edition, which means, since 1898, the Greek critical text has undergone thirty-three revisions. Every time the archaeologist's spade turns up a new papyrus or another manuscript, then immediately, it is included in the newest edition. The danger here is that the modern Greek text, which underlies all the modern versions, is never established or settled; they are always changing. What is correct today may be wrong tomorrow, thus leaving the Christian in a state of confusion as to what is the word of God and what isn't. One of those who worked on the Novum Testamentum Graece critical text was Jesuit cardinal Carlo Martini (1927–2012), a Roman Catholic. He also worked on the United Bible Societies fourth edition of the Greek critical text. Below is a quote from the twenty-seventh edition of the Nestle-Aland critical Greek text, where they come right out and state that modern versions are made under the supervision of the Vatican.

> *The text shared by these two editions was adopted internationally by Bible Societies, and following an agreement between the Vatican and the United Bible Societies it has served as the basis for new translations and for revisions made under their supervision* [emphasis mine]. This marks a significant step

with regard to interconfessional relationships. It should naturally be understood that this text is a working text (in the sense of the century long Nestle Tradition): it is not to be considered as definitive, but as a stimulus to further efforts toward defining and verifying the text of the New Testament. For many reasons, however, the present edition has not been deemed an appropriate occasion for introducing textual changes. (Page 45, third paragraph)

The Roman Catholic Church could not destroy the line of Bibles leading to the King James Bible, so instead they decided to go in league with them in the area of Bible translations in hopes to neutralize the true message of the Bible. Since 1881, there have been well over two hundred translations of the Bible, especially the New Testament, and all using the critical text to subvert and supplant the King James Bible by claiming they are easier to read and understand. Whenever you tell some Christians that there is an easier way or it is the path of least resistance, they will, without doing any investigation, accept it because of ease. Biblical truth does not come at an easy and cheap price; in fact, claiming ease is Satan's way of doing things. God tells us in 2 Timothy 2:15 (KJV), "*Study* to shew thyself approved unto God, a *workman* that needeth not to be ashamed, rightly dividing the word of truth." The word *study* in Greek carries with it the idea of "laboring, being earnest or being diligent, to make effort." The word *workman* carries with it the idea of "toiling or labor." In both cases, we see that coming to biblical truth comes from study and toiling in the Bible. There is no such thing as instant understanding!

The King James Version used in this book is the 1900 Cambridge Text printed by Cambridge University Press. It is available through Sword Searcher by Brandon Staggs and is obtainable online at www.swordsearcher.com.

I will be showing corruption in 747 verses and will offer commentary on them. What I want to do is to show the conspicuous attacks on the cardinal doctrines of the faith so you may see how corrupt your modern version really is! If this book puts a crimp in Satan's scheme to corrupt the word of God and make Christians accept counterfeits, then this book has achieved its goal!

Many books have been written concerning the corruption of God's word and contain much history. In this book, I want to go directly to the many verses I have researched to show plainly without much wording how corrupt these modern versions really are. Modern-version publishers do not care about your spiritual growth, nor do they care about whether you go to heaven or hell. If they did, then they would not publish these counterfeits called Bibles, and neither would your pastor or favorite media ministry push them unless they have an agenda. And normally, that agenda is personal profit and gain.

Generally speaking, these are the modern versions that, when compared to the King James Bible, will show their corruptions. These Bible versions can be located online so you can instantly compare and see the verse distortions.

Modern Bible Version List

Amplified Bible, 2015 (AMP)
American Standard Version of 1901 (ASV)
Common English Bible, 2010 (CEB)
Contemporary English Version (CEV)
Christian Standard Bible, 2017, revision of the Holman Christian Standard Bible (CSB)
Darby Version, 1867, 1872–1884 (DARBY)
Douay-Rheims, 1899, American edition (Roman Catholic version)
Easy to Read Version, 2006 (ERV)
English Standard Version, 2001 and 2016 (ESV)
Good News Bible, 1992 (GNB)
Holman Christian Standard Bible, 2003 (HCSB)
J.B. Phillips New Testament in Modern English, 1962 (PHILLIPS)
The Message by Eugene Peterson, 2002 (MSG)
New American Bible of the Roman Catholic Church (NAB)

New American Standard Version, 1995 (NASV)
New Century Version, 2005 (NCV)
Dan Wallace's online version, 2006
New International Reader's Version, 1998 (NIRV)
New International Version, 1984 and 2011 (NIV)
New King James Version, 1982 (NKJV)
New Life Version, 1969 (NLV)
New Living Translation, 2004 (NLT)
New Revised Standard Version, 1989 (NRSV)
New World Translation of the Jehovah's Witnesses, 1961 (NWT)
Revised Version of Hort and Westcott of 1881 (RV)
Revised Standard Version, 1946–52 (RSV)
Today's New International Version, 2002 (TNIV)
The Voice, 2012 (VOICE)

THE OLD TESTAMENT

Genesis 12:19

> Why saidst thou, She is my sister? so I *might*
> have taken her to me to wife: now therefore
> behold thy wife, take her, and go thy way.
> (Genesis 12:19, KJV)

"I might have taken her" is changed to "I took her."

This is one of the subtler yet major abominations in the modern versions. In the KJV, we read the single word in verse 19 *might*. This means that Pharaoh did not yet take Sarah to be one of his wives. The modern versions omit the word *might* and teach that Pharaoh took Sarah to be his wife, which would make Sarah an adulteress. This would also mean that the plagues that God sent on the house of Pharaoh would have been fruitless (verse 17). The reason that God sent those plagues was to prevent Pharaoh from taking her as his wife. According to the KJV, Pharaoh did not take Sarah as wife and returned her to Abraham, who was rebuked by Pharaoh for lying about Sarah. When one little qualifying word is omitted, it changes the entire meaning of the passage, which also affects the teachings of other passages and the continuity of the flow of scripture. All the modern versions above use the word *took*, which means that the action of taking Sarah as wife had already been completed, as the word *took* is the past tense of the word *take*. The CEV states plainly that Pharaoh married her.

A quick English lesson:

I may take the one on sale. (It means the possibility exists that I may take the item on sale.)

I took the one on sale. (This means that a definite action on my part has already taken place.)

This is the seriousness of the change in Genesis 12:19.

Exodus 26:14

> And thou shalt make a covering for the tent of rams' skins dyed red, and a covering above of *badgers'* skins. (Exodus 26:14, KJV)

Badgers is changed to "sealskins," "porpoise or dolphin," "beaded leather," "fine leather," "violet-color skins," "goat skins," "manatee," "tahash," "strong leather," "durable leather," "sea cow hides."

Hebrew Word in Question

The Hebrew word used for "badger" is *techashim*, which is translated "badger" or "badgers" fourteen times in the Hebrew scriptures. It is not translated any other way until you get to the modern versions. Sometime ago, I authored an article titled "Multiple Version Disorder," which is available at the end of the book. It basically surrounds the theme of each of the modern versions saying something different concerning a single verse of scripture. Well, here is one of those scriptures. Exodus 26:14 is very clear that badger skins were to be used on the tabernacle. If I were to use multiple versions on this verse, I would be thoroughly confused. Let's look at the multiplicity of translations of the word for "badger":

Sealskins
Porpoise or dolphin skins
Beaded leather
Fine leather
Violet-colored skins

Goatskins
Manatee
Tahash
Strong leather
Durable leather
Sea cow hides

Here, you have twenty-five modern versions and ten different translations of the word for "badger." So which one is yours? So if I used only modern versions, then how would I know which word to choose? Stay with the King James; there is no guesswork!

Deuteronomy 23:18

> Thou shalt not bring the hire of a whore, or the price of a *dog*, into the house of the LORD thy God for any vow: for even both these are abomination unto the LORD thy God. (Deuteronomy 23:18, KJV)

Dog is changed to "male prostitute."

The word behind "dog" in the Hebrew is the word *kelev*, and it is translated thirty-two times in the Old Testament as "dog" and nothing else. Here are two examples:

> And Hazael said, But what, is thy servant a dog, that he should do this great thing? And Elisha answered, The LORD hath shewed me that thou shalt be king over Syria. (2 Kings 8:13, KJV)

> His watchmen are blind: they are all ignorant, they are all dumb dogs, they cannot bark; sleeping, lying down, loving to slumber. (Isaiah 56:10, KJV)

What the modern translators did was not to translate the word but make an interpretation. This is a very dangerous practice because it places the meaning of the verse in subjection to the translator/

interpreter instead of granting that privilege to the Holy Spirit, where it belongs, when a Christian is doing a study in that verse; plus, it limits it to one application.

1 Samuel 6:19

> And he smote the men of Beth-shemesh, because they had looked into the ark of the LORD, even he smote of the people *fifty thousand and threescore and ten men*: and the people lamented, because the LORD had smitten many of the people with a great slaughter. (1 Samuel 6:19, KJV)

The number *50,070* is changed to "70."

The text states *shivim ish chamishim eleph ish*, which translates literally, "seventy men fifty thousand men." The modern versions above reduce the severity of looking into the ark by omitting the fact that, in addition to the seventy who perished, another fifty thousand perished. Remember how God struck Uzzah when he steadied the ark. Remember when the Philistines took the ark and placed it next to Dagon? Dagon kept falling to the floor. The ark was a very holy symbol and was not to be touched by anyone. Here, God shows the severe penalty for men attempting to violate His holiness. So the *50,000* number is definitely in the text but is omitted in the modern versions.

When we look further into this verse, we find corroborating evidence in the King James Bible itself. The "modern versionaires" tell us that the town of Beth-shemesh was not big enough to validate the 50,070 number. Well, let us once again show how the King James Bible is its own interpreter. Check out the following verses:

> And Ain with her suburbs, and Juttah with her suburbs, and Beth-shemesh with her suburbs; nine cities out of those two tribes. (Joshua 21:16, KJV)

And Ashan with her suburbs, and Beth-shemesh
with her suburbs. (1 Chronicles 6:59, KJV)

In both these verses, we see that Beth-shemesh was not a stand-alone city but had suburbs that made them part of the city itself. There are many cities around the world that have a business district and many suburbs making them part of the city itself. So it would definitely not be out of the question that Beth-shemesh would have been set up the same way: a business district and outlying communities. Take New York City for example. The borough of Manhattan is where the main business district is, as you can easily see by the number of skyscrapers. There are also four outlying boroughs: the Bronx, Brooklyn, Queens, and Staten Island. When you combine all five of them, you have a population of ten million.

2 Samuel 21:19

And there was again a battle in Gob with the Philistines, where Elhanan the son of Jaare-oregim, a Beth-lehemite, *slew the <u>brother</u> of Goliath* the Gittite, the staff of whose spear was like a weaver's beam. (2 Samuel 21:19, KJV)

"Slew the brother of Goliath" changed to "slew Goliath."

This is one of those modern-version quagmires that needs very little commentary. The question arises, *who killed Goliath?* "And David put his hand in his bag, and took thence a stone, and slang it, and smote the Philistine in his forehead, that the stone sunk into his forehead; and he fell upon his face to the earth" (1 Samuel 17:49, KJV). David was the one who killed Goliath as the scriptures so plainly teach, but as we see in the modern versions, they say that Elhanan killed Goliath, especially in the 1984 edition of the NIV. How do they arrive at that? In the King James Bible, we see the words *the brother of* in italics, which gives clear meaning to the verse and causes no confusion but continuity of the scriptures concerning the death of Goliath's brother. The modern-version edi-

15

tors did not believe it was necessary to keep these words to allay any confusion. Instead of including them, they omitted them and have caused confusion in the biblical narrative about Goliath and his brother. Now here is an interesting addition to the confusion that anyone who uses a modern version will encounter. The parallel verse to 2 Samuel 21:19 is 1 Chronicles 20:5, which reads:

> And there was war again with the Philistines; and Elhanan the son of Jair slew Lahmi the brother of Goliath the Gittite, whose spear staff was like a weaver's beam. (1 Chronicles 20:5, KJV)

Psalm 10:4-5

> The wicked, through the pride of his countenance, will not seek after God: God is not in all his thoughts. His ways are always *grievous*; thy judgments are far above out of his sight: as for all his enemies, he puffeth at them. (Psalm 10:4–5, KJV)

Grievous is changed to "prosperous" or "prosper."

The word for "grievous" in Psalm 10:5 is the Hebrew word *chil*, which is a verb that carries with it the meaning of "having labor pains, be in pain, or writhing." It is used fifty-one times in the Masoretic Text. Some examples are below:

> This day will I begin to put the dread of thee and the fear of thee upon the nations that are under the whole heaven, who shall hear report of thee, and shall tremble, and *be in anguish* because of thee. (Deuteronomy 2:25, KJV)

> So Esther's maids and her chamberlains came and told it her. Then was the queen exceedingly *grieved*; and she sent raiment to clothe Mordecai,

and to take away his sackcloth from him: but he received it not. (Esther 4:4, KJV)

The wicked man *travaileth with pain* all his days, and the number of years is hidden to the oppressor. (Job 15:20, KJV)

And they shall be afraid: pangs and sorrows shall take hold of them; *they shall be in pain* as a woman that travaileth: they shall be amazed one at another; their faces shall be as flames. (Isaiah 13:8, KJV)

I have included verse 4 to give context. The beginning of verse 5 is definitely building on what was said in verse 4. The scripture teaches that the way of the wicked is grievous, and we have seen that the word that underlies it in Hebrew has only a negative meaning, which includes "pain" and "suffering." The verse is teaching that the way of the wicked is a painful, writhing way. However, when we look at the modern versions, it states exactly the opposite. It shows that the ways of the wicked are "prosperous," "secure," and "firm." The modern versions are actually endorsing living a sinful life because it produces a prosperous life. We read nowhere in scripture that sinful living can bring security. Security from what? Death? Pitfalls?

Now we know there are verses that teach that there is pleasure in sin for a season. "Choosing rather to suffer affliction with the people of God, than to enjoy the pleasures of *sin for a season*"_(Hebrews 11:25, KJV). This speaks of enjoying the pleasures of sin for a season, which is a short length of time; in fact, the word means "temporary." It does not speak of the essence of the pleasure as the modern versions do. God states that the way of sin is hard and grievous, but the modern versions actually turn the meanings completely around and claim that a sinful lifestyle can give you security and prosperity. The word *chil* in the Hebrew no way intimates any definition related to security or prosperity. This is another change in the false Hebrew text to mislead Christians. If God says that sinful living creates a grievous situation, then we better not change it to appease the religious sinners in the church.

Psalm 60:4

Thou hast given a banner to them that fear thee,
that it may be displayed because of *the truth*.
Selah. (Psalm 60:4, KJV)

The truth is changed to "bow," "archers," "escape destruction," or "attack."

The word for "the truth" in Psalm 60:4 is the Hebrew word *qô shet*. It is used only one time in the Masoretic text. It is a noun, and it means "truth." It is a variant spelling of the word *qô sht*, which is also a noun and used only once in the text. "That I might make thee know the *certainty* of the words of truth; that thou mightest answer the words of truth to them that send unto thee?" (Proverbs 22:21, KJV). Some of the modern versions translate it as "bow," "archers," "escape destruction," "attack." They no doubt took this interpretation from the Septuagint.

Psalm 68:11

The Lord gave the word: great was the *company*
of those that published it. (Psalm 68:11, KJV)

Company is changed to "women."

There are two Hebrew words that must be looked at. The first is the word for "company," and that is the word *tsava*, which can be translated "host" or "army." It is a noun in the masculine gender and singular. The next word for "those that published" is *hamvasseroth*, which means to "bring news or report." This word is a verb in the piel stem, participle, feminine plural. The piel stem is an intensive active that intensifies the action of the verb. In this case, it is speaking of the company that published it as an intensified action or strengthened or increased in the activity of publishing. If you will notice the way the modern versions have added "the" or "of women" after "company" or after the first clause of the verse. The normal Hebrew word for women is *ishsha*, which is not used here. The modern translators took liberty with the feminine gender of the word *hamvasseroth* and added "of women," which is not in view in the text. Now, when looking at this verse, do we take a cultural look, or do we take a scriptural look?

Psalm 138:2

I will worship toward thy holy temple, and praise thy name for thy lovingkindness and for thy truth: *for thou hast magnified thy word above all thy name.* (Psalm 138:2, KJV)

"For thou hast magnified they word above all they name" is changed to various readings in modern versions

In this verse of scripture, God is making it very plain to us that His word can be trusted. In fact, He enforces that by stating that He has magnified His word above His name. This gives us great assurance that whatever God has written in His word will surely come to pass, and none of it is written without reason, even though we may not understand many passages. Remember, it was through the word of God that Jesus overcame the three temptations that Satan placed before Him, and that is the great power of the word. God wants us to know that it is the same word that carries the same power today to bring us into victory in any circumstance. The modern versions tend to dilute this truth that God is pointing out to us by equating His name with His word.

Proverbs 13:11

Wealth gotten by vanity shall be diminished: but he that gathereth *by labour* shall increase. (Proverbs 13:11, KJV)

"By labour" is changed to "little by little."

Proverbs 13:11 is a continuation of the theme of those who work versus those who are lazy. Those who attempt to be wealthy by methods that are vain will see that their funds will eventually diminish. They will not be able to keep their wealth. Sometimes this happens when a person becomes wealthy too quickly, and they start going on a spending spree, and soon they look around and find that their funds have been diminished. However, the person who labors for their money will see an increase in their money because they will realize they worked hard for it. Instead of them buying everything in sight, they will make proper investments and control their spending. This way, they are handling their money with wisdom and will increase instead of going bankrupt.

There is also a spiritual application to this verse. Those who study the scriptures will increase in biblical knowledge and wisdom as the Holy Spirit implants the truths into them. Those who just listen to others and never do their own studies will diminish in understanding because they will find it hard to bring to mind the sayings of others. The modern versions omit the fact that instead of seeking quick wealth, when one works for their money, they are able to budget properly and build their wealth. The modern versions just claim that "little by little" will increase, but they omit how that "little by little" is to be accomplished. God's plan for man is to work for their wages: "In the sweat of thy face shalt thou eat bread, till thou return unto the ground; for out of it wast thou taken: for dust thou art, and unto dust shalt thou return" (Genesis 3:19, KJV). The word in the Hebrew for "by labor" can also mean "by a hand," which denotes that a person is to be working with their hands in some form of labor. "Little by little" is not a proper translation of the word *al-yadh*.

Ecclesiastes 8:10

And so I saw the wicked buried, who had come and gone from the place of the holy, and *they were forgotten* in the city where they had so done: this is also vanity. (Ecclesiastes 8:10, KJV)

"They were forgotten" is changed to "receive praise" or "were praised."

The following verse from Proverbs shows us that these modern versions in their praise of the wicked is a total error. "The memory of the just is blessed: but the name of the wicked shall rot" (Proverbs 10:7, KJV). By praising the wicked, these modern versions are celebrating their eternal destruction in hell. "Say unto them, As I live, saith the Lord GOD, I have no pleasure in the death of the wicked; but that the wicked turn from his way and live: turn ye, turn ye from your evil ways; for why will ye die, O house of Israel?" (Ezekiel 33:11, KJV). Yet the modern versions that scholars claim to be the word of God are saying exactly opposite of what God had declared in Ezekiel 33:11.

Are you seeing in just these few verses that the modern versions tend to reverse meanings of words? The modern scholars claim they have more tools available to them than the King James translators did, but what kind of intellects will reverse a meaning of a word? To me, a very incompetent one! How is reversing the meaning of words here going to improve the Christian walk when these modern versions tend to glorify and deify the life of sin? The life of sin is never praised in the true Bible but is condemned and judged. Seeing these kind of horrible word translations, how can anyone trust these modern versions, even minimally, since they take such liberties to completely obscure and reverse meanings of the words of God?

Isaiah 9:1

> Nevertheless the dimness shall not be such as was in her vexation, when at the first he lightly afflicted the land of Zebulun and the land of Naphtali, and afterward did more *grievously afflict* her by the way of the sea, beyond Jordan, in Galilee of the nations. (Isaiah 9:1, KJV)

"Grievously afflict" is changed to "made it glorious" or "honored."

The Hebrew word behind "grievously afflict" is the word *kavedh*, which carries with it the meaning of "to be heavy, to glorify, grievously afflict." Now this word is the type that is used according to context. For example,

> And the LORD said, Because the cry of Sodom and Gomorrah is great, and because their sin is very grievous. (Genesis 18:20, KJV)

> And I will harden Pharaoh's heart, that he shall follow after them; and I will be honoured upon Pharaoh, and upon all his host; that the Egyptians may know that I am the LORD. And they did so. (Exodus 14:4, KJV)

How did the King James translators know which word to use? In Isaiah 9:1, the context of the verse is speaking about the destruction of the northern kingdom. Now Shalmaneser took the ten tribes into Assyria, and they were never to be heard from again. Since the Assyrians took the northern kingdom, there would have been no one left at that time for a "more grievous affliction," and that is why it is looking toward the final destruction. What is in view here is the further destruction of Galilee that happened about four to five years after the destruction of Jerusalem. Then in Isaiah 9:2, he speaks of the coming of the Messiah, which is the great light, but verse 1 is speaking about the further destruction that region would face about AD 75. Therefore, the King James translators have it right, and the modern versions do not.

Isaiah 14:12

> How art thou fallen from heaven, O *Lucifer*, son of the morning! how art thou cut down to the ground, which didst weaken the nations! (Isaiah 14:12, KJV)

Lucifer is changed to "morning star."

The words for "O Lucifer, son of the morning" in Isaiah 14:12 is *helel, ben shachar.* The modern versions substitute the name "morning star" for "Lucifer," and this is not what the Hebrew is teaching. In the Hebrew, the word *kokhav* is the word God uses for "star" thirty-six times. The word does not appear in Isaiah 14:12; therefore, it has been interpolated. In Job 38:7, we read, "When the morning stars sang together, and all the sons of God shouted for joy?" The words *morning stars* are the words *kokhve voqer.* Neither of these Hebrew words shows up in Isaiah 14:12. In Job 38:7, we know that this verse is speaking of the physical stars in the universe because it is being used in the plural.

Now, when we look at the way the modern versions portray Satan in this verse, we see them using the term *morning star* and *day star.* Now we get into the outright arena of blasphemy. Both of these terms are attributed to the Lord Jesus Christ, but the modern versions give these names to Satan. In his early days, Brooke F. Westcott took on the study of Mormonism, and he studied the book of Mormon. The reason I bring this to light is because in Mormon belief, Jesus and Satan were brothers. Both presented their salvation plans to God the Father, and God chose the one presented by Jesus. Keep in mind that the influence of Hort and Westcott is still very heavy upon modern theologians and Bible translators. So it would follow that if Westcott believed Mormonism, then some of that belief would have trickled down through the false seminaries and into the belief systems of translators.

Look at the following verse from Revelation:

> *I Jesus_*have sent mine angel to testify unto you these things in the churches. *I am* the root and the offspring of David, and the bright and *morning star.* (Revelation 22:16, KJV)

Based upon this one verse, we see that the Lord Jesus is given the title of the morning star. Satan is not given this title in scripture at all. It is applied to Satan by unbelieving theologians.

Look at the following verse in 2 Peter:

> We have also a more sure word of prophecy;
> whereunto ye do well that ye take heed, as unto
> a light that shineth in a dark place, until the
> day dawn, and the *day star* arise in your hearts.
> (2 Peter 1:19, KJV)

Here is another allusion to the person of the Lord Jesus Christ. He is called the "day star" in this verse. The verse speaks of light shining in a dark place. "Then spake Jesus again unto them, saying, I am the light of the world: he that followeth me shall not walk in darkness, but shall have the light of life" (John 8:12, KJV). "And he shall rule them with a rod of iron; as the vessels of a potter shall they be broken to shivers: even as I received of my Father. *And I will give him the morning star*" (Revelation 2:27–28, KJV).

Here is a salvation verse that those who are the elect of God will receive the "morning star," who is the Lord Jesus Christ. "And I give unto them eternal life; and they shall never perish, neither shall any man pluck them out of my hand" (John 10:28, KJV).

> I shall see him, but not now: I shall behold him,
> but not nigh: there shall come a *Star out of Jacob*,
> and a Sceptre shall rise out of Israel, and shall
> smite the corners of Moab, and destroy all the
> children of Sheth. (Numbers 24:17, KJV)

Who is the star that came out of Jacob? That star is the Lord Jesus Christ, who came from the lineage of Jacob through the nation of Israel. The star is not Satan.

The modern versions and their translators prove once again that they are wrong when it comes to the reality of scripture. To give the same name to both the Lord Jesus Christ and to Satan shows that the modern translators lack the necessary knowledge to be translators, and they have shown the height of blasphemy. In Revelation 22:16, where it plainly says that Jesus is the morning star, the name Jesus could be replaced by the name Satan, and this could be corroborated by the evil mistranslation of Isaiah 14:12 in the modern versions. I wonder if they will do that when the next "accurate" version is thrown on to the market and endorsed by theologians.

Once again, the King James Bible has shown itself to be the superior work of godly men by giving us the proper translations of words. Just seeing how the false versions highly esteem Satan, this alone would cause me to run from them. Don't give up your King James, for you hold in your hand the only true word of God.

Jeremiah 17:9

> The heart is deceitful *above all things, and desperately wicked*: who can know it? (Jeremiah 17:9, KJV)

Desperately wicked is changed to "sick."

Here is another case of using the wrong English word that lowers the reality and severity of the verse. The Hebrew word in question is *anash*, which carries with it the meaning of "sick, incurable, wicked, or feeble." Jeremiah 17:9 is the only place that this word is translated "wicked." It is used nine times in the Hebrew scriptures, and the other eight times, it is translated "sick or incurable." The following two verses give alternate uses of *anash*.

> And Nathan departed unto his house. And the LORD struck the child that Uriah's wife bare unto David, *and it was very sick.* (2 Samuel 12:15, KJV)

Second Samuel 12:15 is a proper use of the word *anash* because it is speaking of the baby as one who is physically sick, so the word is translated properly and according to context.

> Why criest thou for thine affliction? thy sorrow *is incurable* for the multitude of thine iniquity: because thy sins were increased, I have done these things unto thee. (Jeremiah 30:15, KJV)

Jeremiah 30:15 is a proper use of the word *anash* because it too speaks of the sorrow being incurable, so the word is translated properly and according to context.

Now we come to Jeremiah 17:9, where the word is translated "wicked." "The heart is deceitful above all things, and desperately wicked: who can know it?" (Jeremiah 17:9, KJV). Jeremiah 17:9 is not speaking of a physical situation but a spiritual situation. When Adam sinned, it was the soul that became wicked, at enmity with God; and therefore, the King James translators got it right by translating the word *anash* as "wicked." The other eight usages in the Hebrew scriptures deal with physical situations. The modern versions have reduced the severity of the wicked heart to a sickness. When Adam sinned, he did not become physically sick but spiritually dead. "Sick, incurable, corrupt" is more of a moderation or reduction in severity of what happened when Adam sinned and before regeneration in Christ and does not belong in Jeremiah 17:9.

Daniel 3:25

> He answered and said, Lo, I see four men loose, walking in the midst of the fire, and they have no hurt; and the form of the fourth is like the *Son of God*. (Daniel 3:25, KJV)

"*Son of God*" is changed to "son of the gods."

Some of the modern versions have translated the words behind "Son of God" as follows, and we wonder why Christians are so confused or why there can never be agreement in any single congregation. Here are five different renditions of the same words from twenty-five Bible translations.

> "son of the gods"
> "one of the gods"
> "a god"
> "an angel"
> "a divine being"

Another criticism that the modern-version-only proponents (MVOP) level against the King James Bible is found in Daniel 3:25. The question concerning this verse is, should it be singular as *God*, or should it be plural as *gods*? The MVOP claim that Nebuchadnezzar was a polytheist, and there is no way that he would have understood that the Lord Jesus Christ was the one in the fire with Shadrach, Meshach, and Abednego. Now a question must be asked. Did God write the Bible according to the belief systems of the people mentioned therein, or did He write the Bible according to His own wisdom? Once we get into the text, we will see that the King James Bible has rendered the word properly as "God" and not "gods" as the modern versions do.

The Aramaic words found in the statement are as follows, *da^mēh lebar 'ela^hi^yn* ("Son of God"). The last word corresponds to the word *elohim* in the Hebrew, which shows the plurality of God. In other words, it does not signify three gods but is used to show *three distinct persons* as one Godhead. Now the Aramaic word *elahiyn* may be translated "gods" or "God," and the usage is determined by the context.

> Thus shall ye say unto them, The *gods* that have not made the heavens and the earth, even they shall perish from the earth, and from under these heavens. (Jeremiah 10:11, KJV)

> But if not, be it known unto thee, O king, that we will not serve thy *gods*, nor worship the golden image which thou hast set up. (Daniel 3:18, KJV)

> Let the work of this house of *God* alone; let the governor of the Jews and the elders of the Jews build this house of *God* in his place. (Ezra 6:7, KJV)

Jeremiah 10:11 is the only place outside of Daniel where the word *elahiyn* is translated "gods." In the book of Ezra, it is translated

"God" forty-three times. So we see that the word is definitely used according to context as many words in scripture are.

When we look at the modern versions that say "son of the gods," it is basically claiming *son* (singular) but *gods* (plural), so which son of which god in the pantheon of gods of Babylon was he? The plural word *gods* does not fit the context of the immediate statement that it is in. It is like five men standing next to one another, and a little boy is brought out and introduced as a son of the men. It does not make grammatical sense because the boy can only be the son of one of the men. Now let us go further in the context.

> Then Nebuchadnezzar came near to the mouth of the burning fiery furnace, and spake, and said, Shadrach, Meshach, and Abednego, ye servants of the most high God, come forth, and come hither. Then Shadrach, Meshach, and Abednego, came forth of the midst of the fire. (Daniel 3:26, KJV)

Notice verse 26 that Nebuchadnezzar came by the furnace and spoke into the furnace, calling the three men servants of the Most High God, not gods. So the context of verse 25 would demand that the word *God* be used to make proper sense out of the narrative. Let us look at a verse that precedes the actual furnace scene.

> If it be so, our God whom we serve is able to deliver us from the burning fiery furnace, and he will deliver us out of thine hand, O king. (Daniel 3:17, KJV)

Notice the three Hebrew boys state that the God they serve can deliver them. So they told Nebuchadnezzar about the God they serve, which is in keeping with the context of the following verses of the furnace scene. There would have been no need on Nebuchadnezzar's part to change it to a plural *gods* since he was seeing a miracle and

would have remembered they spoke of them serving only one God and not many. Now, finally, we look at two more verses in this chapter.

> Then Nebuchadnezzar spake, and said, Blessed be the God of Shadrach, Meshach, and Abednego, who hath sent his angel, and delivered his servants that trusted in him, and have changed the king's word, and yielded their bodies, that they might not serve nor worship any god, except their own God. Therefore I make a decree, That every people, nation, and language, which speak any thing amiss against the God of Shadrach, Meshach, and Abednego, shall be cut in pieces, and their houses shall be made a dunghill: because there is no other God that can deliver after this sort. (Daniel 3:28–29, KJV)

Four times in the closing verses of this chapter, Nebuchadnezzar mentions God (same word as in verse 25); and in all four mentions, not one is made in the plural. Therefore, in verse 25, the word *God* stands as the correct rendering that fits the context of the entire narrative in this chapter.

Then the modern-version-only people level another charge concerning the word *son*. If you notice in verse 25, it is capitalized as *Son*. When the King James translators saw this verse and knew that the word *elahiyn* would be singular in this case because of context and not plural, then they knew that this was a Christophany, which is a pre-Bethlehem appearance of Christ. Therefore, armed with that knowledge, they capitalized Son in respect to the Lord Jesus Christ.

> I will declare the decree: the LORD hath said unto me, Thou art my Son; this day have I begotten thee. (Psalm 2:7, KJV)

> Kiss the Son, lest he be angry, and ye perish from the way, when his wrath is kindled but a little.

Blessed are all they that put their trust in him.
(Psalm 2:12, KJV)

If you notice in Psalm 2, in verses 7 and 12, the word *Son* is capitalized because it is directly referencing the Lord Jesus Christ. I have yet to this day come across anyone who rejects the capitalization of those two words, yet the MVOP attempt to make a claim that it should not be capitalized in Daniel 3:25, when it is also referencing the Lord Jesus Christ. So there you have it, more confusion untangled by the King James Bible.

Hosea 10:1

Israel is an *empty* vine, he bringeth forth fruit unto himself: according to the multitude of his fruit he hath increased the altars; according to the goodness of his land they have made goodly images. (Hosea 10:1, KJV)

Empty is changed to "luxuriant."

This is one of those verses that is reversed in meaning in the modern versions. In the King James Version and the 1611 King James Version, the word *empty* is properly translated. The word for "empty" in the Hebrew is *baqaq*, which means "to empty or lay waste." The word in no way can be translated "luxuriant or lush." God was chiding Israel for their idolatry, and this verse is no way a positive reassuring verse that God is favoring what they are doing. The word *baqaq* is translated elsewhere in the following manner:

Behold, the LORD *maketh* the earth *empty*, and maketh it waste, and turneth it upside down, and scattereth abroad the inhabitants thereof. (Isaiah 24:1, KJV)

And *I will make void* the counsel of Judah and Jerusalem in this place; and I will cause them

to fall by the sword before their enemies, and
by the hands of them that seek their lives: and
their carcases will I give to be meat for the fowls
of the heaven, and for the beasts of the earth.
(Jeremiah 19:7, KJV)

For the LORD hath turned away the excellency
of Jacob, as the excellency of Israel: for *the emp-
tiers have emptied them out*, and marred their vine
branches. (Nahum 2:2, KJV)

These verses contain the word *baqaq* exactly as it is used in
Hosea 10:1. So we see that this word is never used in a positive light
concerning the prophecies about Judah and Israel. Once again, the
modern versions reverse the meaning of a verse by using the wrong
English words, or we are seeing inept translators at work. I think it
is quite funny that the modern translators tend to believe they have
more insight than the KJV translators had. I think we are seeing just
the opposite.

Haggai 2:7

And I will shake all nations, and the *desire* of all
nations shall come: and I will fill this house with
glory, saith the LORD of hosts. (Haggai 2:7, KJV)

Desire is changed to "precious things" or "treasure."

The Hebrew word *chemdath* is used for the word *desire* in the
Masoretic Text. It means "something desirable or something valuable." It is a singular noun.

Septuagint Reading

The modern versions, instead of properly interpreting the word
chemdath, followed the Septuagint reading and turned a singular
word into a plural word with the wrong definition. "For thus saith
the Lord Almighty; Yet once I will shake the heaven, and the earth,

and the sea, and the dry land; and I will shake all nations, and the choice *portions* of all the nations shall come: and I will fill this house with glory, saith the Lord Almighty" (Haggai 2:7–8, Septuagint).

The singular word *chemdath* is a prophecy of the coming of the Lord Jesus Christ. The word is used sixteen times in the Old Testament and never once translated plural or, as the modern versions have translated it—rather, interpreted it—as material goods or precious items. The Voice interprets it as "all that is valuable in the eyes of the world." What is valuable in the eyes of the world? Is it the Lord Jesus Christ? No, it is riches and material goods, which the modern versions have focused on.

It is also a very subtle way to once again remove another reference to the Lord Jesus Christ. "Behold, I will send my messenger, and he shall prepare the way before me: and the Lord, whom ye seek, shall suddenly come to his temple, even the messenger of the covenant, whom ye delight in: behold, he shall come, saith the LORD of hosts" (Malachi 3:1, KJV). The "desire of all nations" is a continued fulfillment of God's promise to Abraham: "And I will make of thee a great nation, and I will bless thee, and make thy name great; and thou shalt be a blessing: And I will bless them that bless thee, and curse him that curseth thee: and in thee shall all families of the earth be blessed" (Genesis 12:2–3, KJV). The modern versions focus only on worldly things and remove the true focus on the Lord Jesus Christ.

THE NEW TESTAMENT

Matthew 1:25

And knew her not till she had brought forth her *firstborn* son: and he called his name Jesus. (Matthew 1:25, KJV)

Firstborn is omitted; some versions replace with *a*.

The Greek word for "firstborn" is omitted in both Vaticanus and Sinaiticus. By removing this word in the modern versions, it endorses the Roman Catholic doctrine of the perpetual virginity of Mary. The word *firstborn* automatically indicates that Mary did have other children, and the Bible tells us that she did in the following scriptures:

> And when the sabbath day was come, he began to teach in the synagogue: and many hearing him were astonished, saying, From whence hath this man these things? and what wisdom is this which is given unto him, that even such mighty works are wrought by his hands? Is not this the carpenter, the son of Mary, the brother of James, and Joses, and of Juda, and Simon? and are not his sisters here with us? And they were offended at him. (Mark 6:2–3, KJV)

By removing the word *firstborn*, it can also set up erroneous beliefs that Mary had children before she had Jesus. That word *firstborn* is pivotal to the doctrine of the virgin birth. The removal of this word is a serious breach of truth and can lead to the denial of the virgin birth of Christ. If Christ was not born of a virgin, then we will still be in our sins and bound for hell. The modern versions, along with the Jehovah's Witness version, all agree with the Roman Catholic institution's teaching that Mary was a perpetual virgin. For someone to say that the modern versions do not stem from Roman Catholic manuscripts is willful denial of the truth. Keep in mind that the two manuscripts that omit *firstborn*, the Vaticanus and Sinaiticus, were in the hands of the Roman Catholic Church, yet they have become the primary manuscripts underlying the modern versions.

So when your pastor reads the narrative about the birth of Jesus from the book of Matthew in a modern version, then realize he is perpetuating the Roman Catholic error of the perpetual virginity of Mary, which has caused many true Christians to be put to death under their inquisition because they refused to believe what was false in light of Mark 6:1–3.

Matthew 4:18

> And *Jesus*, walking by the sea of Galilee, saw two brethren, Simon called Peter, and Andrew his brother, casting a net into the sea: for they were fishers. (Matthew 4:18, KJV)

Jesus is changed to "he."

Here is another verse where the Lord Jesus is omitted in favor of the nebulous *he*, which could be anybody. They changed a proper masculine noun to a pronoun. When the Bible names Jesus specifically, the name is to stand. The modern versions want to do away with the deity of the Lord Jesus Christ in any way they can, and chipping away at His name a little in each new version will eventually cause Him to be deleted from the very book that is about Him. Keep in mind that the Gnostics did not believe that Jesus was deity, so they removed all or part of his name, which we will also see in other verses.

Matthew 5:22

> But I say unto you, That whosoever is angry with his brother *without a cause* shall be in danger of the judgment: and whosoever shall say to his brother, Raca, shall be in danger of the council: but whosoever shall say, Thou fool, shall be in danger of hell fire. (Matthew 5:22, KJV)

"*Without a cause*" is omitted.

"Be ye angry, and sin not: let not the sun go down upon your wrath" (Ephesians 4:26, KJV). Ephesians 4:26 teaches us to be angry but to sin not. According to the modern versions, if we are angry, then we are in sin and heading for hell. So according to the modern versions, how do you homogenize oil and water? Here we have another dilemma. The modern versions tell us that if I am angry with my brother, then I am in danger of heading for hell, which leaves no place for the eternal security of the believer, thus exalting works. In fact, the NIV, NCV, HCSB tells us that we will be subject to judgment. Now we have an additional dilemma because in Matthew 23, the Lord Jesus Christ really let go on the Pharisees. Now, according to the modern versions, Jesus has sinned. If He sinned, then His sacrifice to pay for our sins has been made null and void; and therefore, we are still in our sins without any possibility of salvation. Let us look at the contradictory nature of the modern versions:

> *In your anger do not sin*: Do not let the sun go down while you are still angry. (Ephesians 4:26, NIV)

> *But I tell you that anyone who is angry with his brother will be subject to judgment.* Again, anyone who says to his brother, "Raca," is answerable to the Sanhedrin. But anyone who says, "You fool!" will be in danger of the fire of hell. (Matthew 5:22, NIV)

Be angry and do not sin. Don't let the sun go down on your anger. (Ephesians 4:26, HCSB)

But I tell you, everyone who is angry with his brother will be subject to judgment. And whoever says to his brother, "Fool!" will be subject to the Sanhedrin. But whoever says, "You moron!" will be subject to hellfire. (Matthew 5:22, HCSB)

How contradictory the modern versions are. Either I am to abstain from being angry, or I am to control my anger and properly channel it. Which is it? According to the modern versions, there is no definite answer because the modern versions void themselves of absolutes in many areas.

When we look at Matthew 5:22 in the King James, we are told that we are not to have anger against a brother *without a cause.* Christians are permitted to be angry, but that anger must never become rank hatred. If I am counseling a Christian who has been delivered from alcohol and then I find out that he went to a bar and got drunk, then I am permitted to be angry with him because his actions give me cause. The anger is then properly channeled at the sin and at the brother who committed the sin. Then proper and more stringent steps can be taken for his restoration. So when the modern versions leave out that vital phrase, they are completely distorting the meaning of what the Lord was teaching, which is typical for the modern versions. The King James teaches that anger is proper, but only if it has a legitimate cause and the effect will be the rectifying of the situation that caused the anger. Once again, the King James leaves nothing to guesswork, and that is the way it should be.

Matthew 5:27

Ye have heard that it was said *by them of old time,* Thou shalt not commit adultery. (Matthew 5:27, KJV)

"By them of old time" is omitted.

Jesus continues His Sermon on the Mount focusing on sins of the heart being as dangerous as the physical acting out of those very same sins. "Thou shalt not commit adultery" (Exodus 20:14, KJV). Jesus continues with another of the Ten Commandments that the people would have been familiar with, like the Christian being familiar with John 3:16. He speaks about the time Moses received the commandments and mentions adultery. That sin must have been running rampant back then as it is today so people would have been familiar with it, whether it was they or someone they know partaking in it. Adultery is responsible for the breaking up of many marriages and homes, and the family is the basic unit of society, just as much back then as it is today. When the modern versions remove "by them of old time," they remove the reference to the Ten Commandments, which are in view here as Christ is teaching on them. "Thou shalt not commit adultery" (Exodus 20:14, KJV). This means Jesus is giving His approval of the Old Testament.

Matthew 5:44

But I say unto you, Love your enemies, *bless them that curse you, do good to them that hate you*, and pray for them which despitefully use you, and persecute you. (Matthew 5:44, KJV)

"Bless them that curse you, do good to them that hate you" is omitted.

This verse contains some instructions to the true child of God concerning their witness, which is evidence of their transformation. First of all, when someone is cursing us, which means they are wishing evil against us, we are not to return evil for evil. Instead, we are to show them kindness in words. We do not curse them; we bless them and seek their best and not their worst. There are those who are going to hate us because of our testimony for Christ. Instead of us thinking up vengeful acts against them, we are to do good to them. How many times has a person hated us, and sometimes they might need a little help, and the Lord may engineer their circumstances so that you are the only one who can help them. Then there are those who will despitefully use us. The word *despitefully* carries with it the meaning of "mistreat us." How many times have believers been used by those in the world to advance themselves while the believer is left behind? This happens every day.

Sometimes the world uses our talents or money and makes believe they are appreciative when, in reality, they are just using us. The Lord Jesus Christ makes sure that we will take no acts of vengeance against anyone who does these things. Instead, we are to bless them, pray for them, do good for them, and finally love them. No one says it is going to be easy. When the Gnostics left out these words by chopping up the verse, they were acting on their own mind-sets. In the academic world, there is cutthroat competition to be the tops in the field. What kind of a person would earn the respect of their colleagues if it looked like they were being walked upon? Arrogance and pride were at the heart of the butchering of this verse, and it is a shame that the modern translators have allowed the arrogance of the Gnostics to have survived. Sixteen words have been removed from the verse.

Matthew 5:47

> And if ye salute your brethren only, what do ye more than others? do not even the *publicans* so? (Matthew 5:47, KJV)

Publicans is changed to "Gentiles."

The word *telônai* is the Greek word for "publican or revenue officer." In the New Testament, it is used twenty-three times in twenty-two verses and is always translated "publican" or "publicans." In Matthew 5:46, we read, "For if ye love them which love you, what reward have ye? do not even the publicans the same?" Jesus is specifically referencing the publicans in verse 46 that they only greet or deal with those who love them or are friends with them. Jesus had just finished speaking about the fact that Christians are to love those who persecute and abuse them; then He references the publicans by basically asking, how can you show a difference as a child of God if you only love the way the world loves—that is, those who love you back? We are to love those who do not love us; that is, our enemies. He shows the difference between the way the publicans love and the way the Christians love. Then Jesus continues His comparison in verse 47:

> And if ye *salute* your brethren only, what do ye
> more *than others?* do not even the publicans so?
> (Matthew 5:47)

Salute means "embraced, cherished or greeted." One who salutes only their own brethren are no better than the unbelieving publicans who socialize with their own kind. The true believer is to show they are more than just a mere religious group and to show compassion and love to those who are not of their social strata. The publicans would never socialize with someone who is lame or sick because they were considered the outcasts or the dregs of society, and it would not look good if they were seen with those who were outcasts. Let's bring it up to today. When was the last time a multimillionaire came to your house? When was the last time some CEO of some company looked at you as his equal? These people only salute those of like status and wealth. Jesus is saying that we must have a different outlook and realize the fact that within every person, wealthy or not, is an eternal soul, and their social status will mean nothing at the judgment seat of Christ. Their social standing means nothing in the kingdom of God either because we are all equal at the foot of the cross. If we salute only those of like status, then everyone will make an assessment that Christians are just like the rest of the world.

The modern versions change the word from *publican* to "Gentiles" or "heathens." When they do this, they break the continuity of the two verses that complement each other on how true Christians are to show true love. The publicans were hated because they represented the Roman Empire as their tax collectors, and the publicans would always collect more than required so they would be able to increase their own wealth. The Romans did not care because they set an amount, and when that was reached, anything left over the publican could take. It is like Jesus is using a Hebrew parallelism in that He is coming to the same truth from two different examples. So by replacing *publican* with "heathen" or "Gentile," it breaks continuity of the teaching; plus, the publicans were normally taken from among the Jews, so they would not be Gentiles. It completely destroys the example that Jesus is emphasizing.

Matthew 6:4

That thine alms may be in secret: and thy Father which seeth in secret *himself* shall reward thee *openly*. (Matthew 6:4, KJV)

Himself and *openly* are omitted.

This verse has been the given the unbeliever's penknife twice. Both are important to understand the true principle of giving. The first omission removes a major principle, and that is God Himself will do the rewarding; and the second omission removes the second reward of true giving, and that is God rewarding the true giver openly, in front of others. When we do our alms in secret, it shows that we have no desire to be praised for what we have done. We engage our giving with the right spirit. Giving is not done as a personal achievement but out of love for the Lord. If giving is done in the right spirit, then God will reward the giver, and He will do it openly. The word *openly* in the Greek may also be understood as "visible," "clear, or "plain."

This is probably done for two reasons. The first is to show the world that God keeps all of His promises, and the second is to provoke cheap Christians into giving by showing them that giving is not just giving but is an eternal investment in the kingdom of God. This verse shows that God is personally involved in the giving by His children, whether it be money, time, or material goods. To remove the fact that God Himself does the rewarding is to remove a great act of God on behalf of His children. Then to remove the fact that God will reward His children openly for giving secretly removes the proper attitude of giving. If God rewarded only in secret, then the world and the Christian would lose a great perspective on God's faithfulness. God is not cheap when it comes to His children having the proper attitude about giving. It is a shame how the modern versions mutilate this great passage of promise.

Matthew 6:13

And lead us not into temptation, but deliver us from evil: *For thine is the kingdom, and the power, and the glory, for ever. Amen.* (Matthew 6:13, KJV)

"For thine is the kingdom, and the power, and the glory, for ever. Amen" is omitted.

In the Lord's Prayer, the Lord Jesus Christ is exalting His Heavenly Father by stating that His is the kingdom, which is the kingdom of God; plus, God is the rightful owner of the entire universe. Then the Lord states that He has the power, the very power that created the universe and the earth. Then the Lord Jesus states by reason of God being God, He is entitled to all the glory and all the praise for all eternity. For it is the hand of God that created us and saved us, so we give Him all the glory. It is unfortunate that the modern versions remove this section of scripture because it is a fitting end to the prayer by our Lord. This is another vicious attack on the person of God the Father. Instead of the modern versions bringing glory to Him, they omit Him. Woe unto them on judgment day!

Matthew 6:15

But if ye forgive not men their *trespasses*, neither will your Father forgive your trespasses. (Matthew 6:15, KJV)

Trespasses is omitted.

The word *trespasses* in the Greek is the word *paraptoma*, which carries with it the meaning of "misdeeds, trespasses, or offences." It does not carry a meaning of "sins." That is because we cannot forgive sins; only the Lord Jesus Christ can forgive sins. That concept would play right into the teachings of the Roman Catholic Church, where they believe the priests can absolve a person from their sins. The right teaching is that those who commit trespasses against us or misdeeds are whom we forgive. If they are children of God, then their sins are already forgiven. One of the characteristics of the unsaved is an unforgiving spirit. If they are hurt in some manner, the world's way is to exact revenge upon the other person and get even. That type of spirit shows that a person has not become saved, and in essence, God has not forgiven their sins. If they never become saved, then the Father has not forgiven their trespasses, and they will die unsaved. A true believer always exhibits a spirit of forgiveness. We have been forgiven much, and therefore we forgive others who trespass against us, whether they are saved or unsaved. Even the 1828 *Webster Dictionary* does not equate *trespasses* with *sins*. Another blunder by the modern versions.

Matthew 6:18

> That thou appear not unto men to fast, but unto thy Father which is in secret: and thy Father, which seeth in secret, shall reward thee *openly*. (Matthew 6:18, KJV)

Openly is omitted.

They were not to appear in public in a religious show as the Pharisees did. When they fasted about a certain situation or need, they were to appear in public like they were not fasting; in other words, clean and presentable. The same situation exists here as it did with praying. If one is fasting about something in their lives and they are sincere and not doing it for show, then if their fasting is in accord with the will of God for their life, then God will reward them openly. God is not afraid to reward openly and in front of others. When He rewards openly, He is allowing others to see that He is always faithful to His word. There is another kind of fast that we find in the

Scriptures. In Isaiah 58:5–7, we see the type of fast that God desires from His people.

> Is it such a fast that I have chosen? a day for a man to afflict his soul? is it to bow down his head as a bulrush, and to spread sackcloth and ashes under him? wilt thou call this a fast, and an acceptable day to the LORD? Is not this the fast that I have chosen? to loose the bands of wickedness, to undo the heavy burdens, and to let the oppressed go free, and that ye break every yoke? Is it not to deal thy bread to the hungry, and that thou bring the poor that are cast out to thy house? when thou seest the naked, that thou cover him; and that thou hide not thyself from thine own flesh? (Isaiah 58:5–7, KJV)

It is the fast of neglecting your own life for the purpose of sending forth the Gospel. It is giving your life to the service of the Lord rather than fasting for some personal reason. The fast is performed like this. If you go to the streets and hand out tracts for five hours, then you have fasted for five hours because you gave those five hours for the purpose of sending forth the Gospel instead of doing something else. Let us expand the meaning a little larger. Your entire Christian life is to be a life of fasting; that is, of sending forth the Gospel and ministry. Many people are under the mistaken notion that you fast until you receive what you are asking God for. That is erroneous, and let me give you an example. I became saved at the age of twenty-seven. What if I started praying for a Christian wife? What if I physically fasted until God sent me one? I am sixty-four right now and still single, which means no food or water for thirty-seven years. So you see, the Christian fast is not one of neglect of food and water; it is a life of sacrificial service. While the majority of Christians are watching football games on Sunday afternoon, you are out witnessing. You are fasting, but the others are not.

Matthew 6:27

Which of you by taking thought can add one *cubit* unto his stature? (Matthew 6:27, KJV)

Cubit is omitted or changed to "hour." *Stature* is changed to "span of life."

Here is another case of the modern-version translators making an interpretation instead of a translation. What time is it? It is one foot and six inches! That is about the way the "experts" have confused this verse. A cubit is approximately eighteen inches. So when we look at some of the modern versions, how can one add eighteen inches to the length of their life? It is confusing time with measurement. Now, the Greek word behind the term *stature* is the word *hlikia*, and it is translated two ways in the New Testament. The first way is in Matthew 6:27 and Luke 12:25, where it speaks of a person's stature, which is a person's natural height. The second way is "age," which would represent time, and we see this in the modern versions. "But by what means he now seeth, we know not; or who hath opened his eyes, we know not: he is of age; ask him: he shall speak for himself" (John 9:21, KJV).

So we see that the meaning of this word is determined by the context. In John 9:21, we read the parents of the blind man made to see were speaking of the age of the man. In Matthew 6:27 and Luke 12:25, we interpret it as height because the word *stature* is connected to the words *one cubit*. The Greek word behind *cubit* is *pêchus*, which is used four times in the New Testament and always means a unit of measurement. *One cubit* is a term of physical measurement and not of time. What we have here in the modern versions again is the neglect of context. If we ignore and neglect context, then we will always come up with an erroneous conclusion just like the modern versions have.

Matthew 6:33

But seek ye first the kingdom *of God*, and his righteousness; and all these things shall be added unto you. (Matthew 6:33, KJV)

Of God is omitted.

When seeking the kingdom, the modern versions leave it up to you as to what kingdom to seek. The King James Bible makes it clear that we are to seek the kingdom of God. In today's confused society, there are many false religions, like New Age, who would have you seek the universe or seek some ascended master in some mythical kingdom like Shangri-La. For salvation, we must seek the kingdom of God, and there is no other kingdom to seek. There are only two kingdoms on this earth: the kingdom of God and the kingdom of Satan. If you are not seeking the kingdom of God, then you are seeking the kingdom of Satan. Once again, the King James Bible points us to the correct teaching.

Matthew 8:15

> And he touched her hand, and the fever left her: and she arose, and ministered unto *them*. (Matthew 8:15, KJV)

Them is omitted.

> And he stood over her, and rebuked the fever; and it left her: and immediately she arose and ministered unto them. (Luke 4:39, KJV)

> And he came and took her by the hand, and lifted her up; and immediately the fever left her, and she ministered unto them. (Mark 1:31, KJV)

Both times this event is written about, it states that when Peter's mother-in-law was healed by Jesus, she had immediately began to minister to them, which means Jesus and all those who were with Him. Even the modern versions in the above two accounts state that she ministered to *them* and not just Jesus alone. This is just another mutilation in the modern versions because in the King James Bible, all three accounts are in harmony, stating *them*. Only the modern versions damage the harmony by exchanging *them* for *him*, implying that there is disharmony in the scriptures.

Matthew 8:29

> And, behold, they cried out, saying, What have
> we to do with thee, *Jesus*, thou Son of God? art
> thou come hither to torment us before the time?
> (Matthew 8:29, KJV)

Jesus is omitted.

Here is another attack on the deity of the Lord Jesus Christ. His name *Jesus* has been omitted from the three basic corrupted manuscripts, and no reason is given for this omission. In fact, there is nothing mentioned as to why his name was omitted. This omission attempts to detach the Lord Jesus Christ from His divine title as "Son of God." This verse is one of approximately 125 verses in the New Testament in which the modern versions omit some part of His divine title. The demons knew exactly who He was since they were up in heaven with Him before the rebellion of Satan and their expulsion from heaven. This is why they specifically mentioned Him by name, and they also knew that they were heading for eternal judgment, and that is why they questioned Him on that subject.

Matthew 8:31

> So the devils besought him, saying, If thou cast
> us out, *suffer us to go away* into the herd of swine.
> (Matthew 8:31, KJV)

"Suffer us to go away" is changed to "send us away."

In this verse, we read that the Lord Jesus Christ has just healed two men from devil possession. Close by, there are about two thousand swine; and in the King James Bible, the devils are asking Jesus permission if He will allow them to go into the herd of swine. In the modern versions, the devils are commanding Jesus and telling Him where they want to go. There is no way that any devil will ever command the Lord Jesus Christ in any situation. The proper understanding of this verse is that the devils are servant to Christ, not the other way around.

Matthew 9:8

But when the multitudes saw it, they *marvelled*,
and glorified God, which had given such power
unto men. (Matthew 9:8, KJV)

Marvelled is changed to "fear" or "afraid."

The modern versions changed *marvelled* to "afraid" or "awe." When the people saw Jesus heal the man with the palsy, there was astonishment or marveling. Marveling is a wonder with admiration, which causes a person to arrest their attention and causes a person to stare. There would have been more joy than there would have been fear or awe, which is reverence mixed with fear.

Matthew 9:13

But go ye and learn what that meaneth, I will
have mercy, and not sacrifice: for I am not come
to call the righteous, but sinners *to repentance*.
(Matthew 9:13. KJV)

"To repentance" is omitted.

When the Lord Jesus came to earth, He came to call sinners to repentance; that is, to salvation. "In meekness instructing those that oppose themselves; if God peradventure will give them repentance to the acknowledging of the truth" (2 Timothy 2:25, KJV). The King James Bible makes no bones about who is being called and for what purpose. The modern versions omit the fact that the Lord is calling people to salvation. This, of course, plays right into the belief system of the Gnostics, who disbelieved that Jesus was God in the flesh and therefore could call no one to repentance or salvation. However, the truth coming from the King James Bible refutes the fact that Jesus was just a good teacher and that He was divinely able to call sinners to repentance, a.k.a. salvation. Once again, the King James Bible does not leave us wondering why Jesus was calling the sinners. In the modern versions, you could take this verse to mean that the sinners were being called for dinner or for some other reason than salvation. Let us stay with the King James Bible for truth untarnished.

Matthew 9:14

Then came to him the disciples of John, saying, Why do we and the Pharisees fast *oft*, but thy disciples fast not? (Matthew 9:14, KJV)

Oft is omitted.

Apparently, even after John was thrown into prison, some of his disciples had stayed together in a group. "And the disciples of John and of the Pharisees used to fast: and they come and say unto him, Why do the disciples of John and of the Pharisees fast, but thy disciples fast not?" (Mark 2:18, KJV). This little feast in Matthew's house had probably been planned on a day of fasting when both the Pharisees and the disciples of John would fast. The Pharisees would fast on Monday and Thursday, so this even may have occurred on one of those days. The disciples of John had approached Jesus directly on the question of fasting. They wanted to know why they and the Pharisees fast often, but His disciples do not fast. It is the difference between freedom in Christ and a religious system. The Pharisees had made fasting a part of the ceremonial law and expected people to keep it. Fasting was voluntary on the part of the believer. The modern versions make it sound like the followers of Jesus never fast, will fast, or have ever fasted.

Matthew 9:18

While he spake these things unto them, behold, there came a certain ruler, and *worshipped* him, saying, My daughter is even now dead: but come and lay thy hand upon her, and she shall live. (Matthew 9:18, KJV)

Worshipped is changed to "knelt or bowed."

Here is a case of the translators' choice of words. The word *pro-skuneo* in the Greek is translated as "worship" in every instance in the New Testament. The word is used to show the proper respect for the Lord Jesus Christ as deity. The King James translates it as "worship" while the modern versions reduce the intent of the word to "kneel down" or just "bowing." Now, you can kneel down before a king or head of state as a sign of obeisance or recognition of their title, but you would not worship him. These people who came to the Lord Jesus Christ worshipped Him, and He accepted that worship because He was God in the flesh. The modern versions, in their incessant attack on the deity of Christ, tend to always bring His position of deity down to that of just a man. These people worshipped Him and did not just bow down. They, no doubt, bowed down or knelt in front of Him, but that was their position of worship. For the modern versions to omit the fact that people worshipped Jesus is to omit the fact that Jesus is God and deserves worship. "That at the name of Jesus every knee should bow, of things in heaven, and things in earth, and things under the earth" (Philippians 2:10, KJV). Someday the whole world will worship Jesus, even the modern Bible translators. Let us stay with the King James as it places the Lord Jesus where He belongs: as God in the flesh and not just a man.

Matthew 9:35

> And Jesus went about all the cities and villages, teaching in their synagogues, and preaching the gospel of the kingdom, and healing every sickness and every disease *among the people.* (Matthew 9:35, KJV)

"Among the people" is omitted.

The opposition of the Pharisees ("But the Pharisees said, He casteth out devils through the prince of the devils" [Matthew 9:34, KJV]) did not stop Jesus one bit. In fact, if you look at this verse, Jesus really increased His ministry along with the increase in miracles. What is a miracle to us is a normal day's activity for the Lord Jesus Christ because when He is on the scene, diseases and the devils must flee. Jesus not only went to the main cities, but He also went to the smaller villages, which teaches us that we should not neglect areas of smaller ministry because the souls in those areas are just as important as those in the big city.

What I want to focus in on is the villages and cities. These are specific areas where the Lord Jesus Christ was ministering, and the KJV text states that He healed every sickness and disease from "among the people." The modern versions omit this phrase, making it seem like when Jesus went into a town or city, He healed every disease or sickness in the entire town, maybe including any animal sicknesses. He healed those who came to Him in the crowds, denoting the personal ministry of Jesus. His ministry was not random and universal, but He specifically dealt personally with those He healed. His ministry was always among the people.

Matthew 9:36

> But when he saw the multitudes, he was moved with compassion on them, because they *fainted*, and were scattered abroad, as sheep having no shepherd. (Matthew 9:36, KJV)

Fainted is changed to "distressed," "confused," or "harassed."

The word *faint* in the Greek in the King James Bible means "to weaken, languid, or exhausted." The main context is that the crowds who were following Jesus had followed Him for so long that they began to become tired and weary. If you notice the words the modern versions exchange it for—"distressed," "harassed," "skinned," "troubled," "confused," "beaten down," "bewildered," "miserable," "worried," "aimless," and "hurting"—not one of these words would be a proper replacement for the word *faint*. We have all been tired and weary, but does that mean we are aimless, confused, distressed, etc.? Let's approach it from another angle. If we were weakened, a good rest along with some good food would revive us. Would good rest and food stop confusion or being harassed? The answer is no. The crowd was suffering from fatigue from following Jesus and were not being skinned or harassed or bewildered.

Matthew 10:3

> Philip, and Bartholomew; Thomas, and Matthew the publican; James the son of Alphaeus, and *Lebbaeus, whose surname was* Thaddaeus. (Matthew 10:3, KJV)

"Lebbaeus, whose surname was" is omitted.

Lebbaeus the name means "courageous." He was also called Judas Lebbaeus. He was probably the brother of James mentioned in Luke 6:16. "And Judas the brother of James, and Judas Iscariot, which also was the traitor" (Luke 6:16, KJV). He was also called *Thaddeus*, which means "praise." It was not uncommon for people to have more than one name. The father-in-law of Moses had three names:

> Now Moses kept the flock of *Jethro* his father in law, the priest of Midian: and he led the flock to the backside of the desert, and came to the mountain of God, even to Horeb. (Exodus 3:1, KJV)

> And when they came to *Reuel* their father, he said, How is it that ye are come so soon to day? (Exodus 2:18, KJV)

> And Moses said unto *Hobab*, the son of Raguel the Midianite, Moses' father in law, We are journeying unto the place of which the LORD said, I will give it you: come thou with us, and we will do thee good: for the LORD hath spoken good concerning Israel. (Numbers 10:29, KJV)

The modern versions only mention the third name of *Judas*, brother of James, thus leaving out a vital piece of information. If a census was taken like in the time of Ezra, the name *Thaddeus* would not appear in the lineage of Israel, but the name *Judas* would. It would cause confusion in trying to prove that Judas was a true Israelite.

Matthew 11:2

Now when John had heard in the prison the works of Christ, he sent *two* of his disciples. (Matthew 11:2, KJV)

Two is omitted.

Here is another open-ended verse. While John was in prison, he specifically sent two of his disciples to Jesus. The way the modern versions read, it could look like he sent 520 disciples to Jesus or any other number. God does things in order, and here we have a specific number of two disciples. Remember, when Jesus sent out His disciples, it was two by two. "And he called unto him the twelve, and began to send them forth by two and two; and gave them power over unclean spirits" (Mark 6:7, KJV). In Luke 7:19, we have Luke's account of the disciples of John going to Jesus. "And John calling unto him two of his disciples sent them to Jesus, saying, Art thou he that should come? or look we for another?" (Luke 7:19, KJV). In Luke 7:19, the modern versions correctly contain the number two. One of the principles of interpreting scripture is to compare scripture with scripture. In the KJV, these two verses perfectly harmonize and cause no problem; but in the modern versions, there is no harmony.

Matthew 11:19

The Son of man came eating and drinking, and they say, Behold a man gluttonous, and a winebibber, a friend of publicans and sinners. But wisdom is justified of her *children*. (Matthew 11:19, KJV)

Children is changed to "works or deeds."

This is another amazing change. There are thirteen manuscripts that use the word *teknon* for children. There are only two manuscripts that use the word *ergon* for "works." Isn't it amazing that they accept the reading of the two manuscripts over the thirteen? If this isn't Satan's handprints all over this, I don't know what is. You can see the satanic agenda alive and well by the acceptance of a minority amount of readings versus overwhelming evidence for the King James reading. It is a change that should not have happened because the evidence is not supporting it, yet there it is.

Jesus states that wisdom is justified of her children. Children are a direct issue from the parents, and that means true wisdom is justified by her children or the direct results. Wisdom begets wisdom as parents beget children, and this is why Jesus used children as an example of wisdom. Wisdom does not do works nor deeds. Wisdom is given to those who do the works and deeds. When one is given wisdom and it is used in a situation, then the wisdom will be seen by the results. The world may believe that the wisdom of God looks odd, but nevertheless, when the final analysis is made, one cannot argue with the wisdom of God because it accomplishes what God sets it out to do, despite the unbelieving world and their nonunderstanding. What the Pharisees failed to see was that Jesus changed the group; He was not changed by them, a very important principle when witnessing in the midst of rank sinners.

Matthew 11:29

> Take my yoke upon you, and *learn of me*; for I
> am meek and lowly in heart: and ye shall find rest
> unto your souls. (Matthew 11:29, KJV)

"Learn of me" is changed to "learn from me."

This exposé concerns a single word switch that has a dramatic effect upon the meaning of this verse. In the five translations below, you will see the same rendering as we have in the King James Version. The Wycliffe Bible, which was printed in 1384, predates the King James Bible by 227 years. The Revised Version of 1881 and the

American Standard Version of 1901 use the phrase "learn of me" instead of "learn from me." For 631 years of English language translations, the true scriptures read "learn of me."

> Wycliffe (1384): "Take ye my yok on you, and lerne ye of me, for Y am mylde and meke in herte; and ye schulen fynde reste to youre soulis."

> Tyndale Bible (1526): "Take my yoke on you and lerne of me for I am meke and lowly in herte: and ye shall fynd rest vnto youre soules."

> Matthews Bible (1537): "Take my yoke on you, and learn of me; that I am meek and lowly in heart: and ye shall find rest unto your souls."

> RV (1881): "Take my yoke upon you, and learn of me; for I am meek and lowly in heart: and ye shall find rest unto your souls."

> ASV (1901): "Take my yoke upon you, and learn of me; for I am meek and lowly in heart: and ye shall find rest unto your souls."

The Greek word in question is *ap*, which may be translated "from" or "of." So then, what is the problem if the word can be legitimately translated "from"? If you notice that in the Bibles leading up to and including the King James Bible—plus the false versions of the RV, ASV, and 1881 Revised Version—they are telling us that we are to learn *of* the Lord Jesus. The modern versions, probably from the RSV on, are telling us to learn *from* the Lord Jesus.

The problem is that you can learn from anyone, including atheists, religious unbelievers, questionable radio and TV preachers, etc. In today's society, there is a plethora of people with opinions ready to disseminate them. However, when we hear those opinions and set out to "learn of them," we will uncover facts about them, which will cause us to separate ourselves from them. If someone listens to the late Robert Schuller or late Norman Vincent Peale, their message may have sounded good; but when we investigate them further, we would find that they were mostly psychology- and New Age–based, which are both antithetical to true Christianity. Hence, the difference about learning *from* and learning *of.*

Now enter the Lord Jesus Christ. When we look at the four Gospels, we read much teachings and acts of compassion on His part. However, when we investigate Him or learn of Him, we find that He is God, He is our Savior, He is our Redeemer, He is our Friend, He is the Great I Am of Sinai, the Son of God, the Way, the Truth, the Life, the Narrow Way, the Head of the Church, etc. This is what the modern theologian fears that Christians will study the Lord Jesus and find that He is the only way to heaven. Many modern theologians believe there is more than one way to heaven, especially by adding works to grace. So if one learns *from* the Lord Jesus Christ, then they will emulate the good works that He did. Good works are at the source of salvation plans for many different denominations and world religions. Pure grace is hated by the modernist, for they feel they must add something to ensure their salvation. But the problem is that many believe that they have no assurance of salvation, even with their own works included.

This word switch is a very subtle way of bringing the Lord Jesus down from deity to the human position of just a teacher, where the New Age places Him. Even the unbelievers and the New Age crowd give credence to the good works and teachings of Jesus. It is when we study Jesus and find that He is God that the road splits, and the Gnostics, New Agers, and unbelievers reject Him. This is why this word change is important to unbelievers because good works are part of the equation of a man-based salvation plan while pure grace is of the heavenly based salvation plan. A very big difference! Those of us who are saved can learn from Jesus, but not without knowing *of* Jesus.

> *And I will give them an heart to know me*, that I
> am the LORD: and they shall be my people, and I

will be their God: for they shall return unto me
with their whole heart. (Jeremiah 24:7, KJV)

But let him that glorieth glory in this, *that he
understandeth and knoweth me, that I am the* LORD
which exercise lovingkindness, judgment, and
righteousness, in the earth: for in these things I
delight, saith the LORD. (Jeremiah 9:24, KJV)

Notice these two verses from Jeremiah are stating that the Lord
is going to give a heart to His people that they may "know Him."
Notice it does not say that they will know about Him or from Him
but that we will know Him. That lines up perfectly with the believer
learning *of Him* rather than learning *from Him.* Notice Jeremiah
9:24, which states that we will know that He *is* the LORD. What a big
difference one word makes and how it changes the whole complex-
ion of the verse.

Matthew 12:4

How he entered into the house of God, and did
eat the *shewbread,* which was not lawful for him
to eat, neither for them which were with him,
but only for the priests? (Matthew 12:4, KJV)

Shewbread is changed to "bread of presence" in CEB, ESV, RSV,
NRSV, 1899 Douay Rheims American Edition.

Here, we see in this term *bread of presence* a very Roman Catholic
term denoting transubstantiation, where Catholics believe that after
consecration, the bread and wine turn into the body and blood of
Christ. We see this very openly in the ESV, which is a very popular
version in many churches today. Below are some Roman Catholic
websites that speak of the "presence."

http://www.newadvent.org/cathen/05573a.htm

From the Roman Catholic Catechism: http://
www.vatican.va/archive/ccc_css/archive/cate-
chism/p2s2c1a3.htm. Look at sections 1376,
1377, and 1378.

Matthew 12:8

For the Son of man is Lord *even* of the sabbath
day. (Matthew 12:8, KJV)

Even is omitted.

In the Greek, the word *kurios* ("Lord") begins the statement
that which is in the nominative case, making it the subject. What is
in view here is that the Lord Jesus Christ is superior or Lord over the
law, and that includes the sabbath. He is the master, and the law is
His servant. The law will judge all unbelievers on the last day. The
authority over the law belongs only to Jesus and no one else. The way
the modern versions have it written, they make Jesus as Lord of the
sabbath, only thus leaving out the fact that He is the Lord of all, and
all authority has been given unto Him, including being Lord of the
sabbath. That is why the word *even* is very important and must not
be minimized or omitted.

Matthew 12:15

But when Jesus knew it, he withdrew himself
from thence: and great *multitudes* followed him,
and he healed them all. (Matthew 12:15, KJV)

Multitudes is omitted.

The Greek word in question is *ochlos*, which carries with it the
meaning of "multitude, throng, or crowd." The King James Bible
translates that word correctly, denoting the fact that after Jesus
healed the man with the withered hand, He withdrew; but a great
multitude of people followed Him, and He healed them all. Does
one think that after a notable miracle has taken place like that, it
would draw only twenty-five or fifty or even one hundred? The

word would spread like wildfire, and anyone in that town with some kind of malady would have shown up to be healed. This was near Capernaum, and that would have been a populated area with approximately 1,500–2,000 living there. It would not surprise me if the majority of the town came out not only to be healed but to see Jesus. The modern versions always seem to reduce the intensity and scope of the miracles of Jesus simply because they make man increase while Jesus decreases.

Matthew 12:35

> A good man out of the good treasure *of the heart* bringeth forth good things: and an evil man out of the evil treasure bringeth forth evil things. (Matthew 12:35, KJV)

"Of the heart" is omitted.

Jesus makes the comparison that those who are saved and have a heart that is filled with light will bring forth the good things such as salvation, eternal life in Christ, the indwelling of the Holy Spirit. Those who have an evil heart will be deprived of knowing the truth, and this will result in blasphemous teachings, lies, hatred, and false accusations. "A new heart also will I give you, and a new spirit will I put within you: and I will take away the stony heart out of your flesh, and I will give you an heart of flesh" (Ezekiel 36:26, KJV).

The essence of this verse is that when a person becomes saved, their heart will change. God will give a heart of flesh for a heart of stone, and out of the new heart will come good things and not evil things, which pour out of the heart of the unregenerate. Many of the modern versions omit the part concerning the heart, which is a very important part of the new life in Christ. Some of the modern versions make it sound like you bring something good of a treasury, like a bank account or physical treasury, like rich people had in those days where they stored their wealth. The wealth of the believer is the new heart from where all our actions begin.

Matthew 13:36

Then *Jesus* sent the multitude away, and went into the house: and his disciples came unto him, saying, Declare unto us the parable of the tares of the field. (Matthew 13:36, KJV)

Jesus is changed to "he."

Here is another case of Jesus being omitted from His own scriptures. They take a proper name and replace it with a pronoun. *He* can be anyone, making it subjective to the reader.

Matthew 13:51

Jesus saith unto them, Have ye understood all these things? They say unto him, Yea, *Lord*. (Matthew 13:51, KJV)

"Jesus saith unto them" and *"Lord"* are omitted.

Here is a verse that has been subjected to both sides of the Gnostic hatchet. In the first part of the verse, Jesus is asking the question to His disciples if they understood the parables that He just taught them. Their response was, "Yes, Lord." If you notice, some of the versions have left out "Jesus said unto them." This identifies Jesus as the one asking the question. Then they all omit "Lord," which is His title of deity, by which His disciples are addressing Him. The Gnostics did not believe that Christ was the Lord from heaven, so they have deleted His divine title in this verse. "Jesus saith unto them" identifies the fact that Jesus is the "Lord." Once again, the King James Bible gives us the complete picture and leaves nothing to speculation, and that is how the word of God should be, not chopped up according to unbelievers.

Matthew 14:25

And in the fourth watch of the night *Jesus* went unto them, walking on the *sea*. (Matthew 14:25, KJV)

Jesus is changed to "he," and some modern versions replace *sea* with "lake."

The modern versions replace *Jesus* with "he," which is just another attack on Christ. Here, Jesus comes to His disciples in the midst of a storm on the sea. The modern versions, by replacing *sea* with "lake" or "water," minimize the ferocity of the storm the disciples were facing. The Sea of Galilee was more than a lake or just water; it was a sea where storms could come up in a moment's notice. The Greek word for "sea" is *Thalassa*, which is translated "sea" throughout the entire New Testament. The word *lake* is used ten times in the New Testament and is never translated from this word. The specific name of Jesus also appears in the Greek text but was replaced in the critical text.

Matthew 14:30

> But when he saw the wind *boisterous*, he was afraid; and beginning to sink, he cried, saying, Lord, save me. (Matthew 14:30, KJV)

Boisterous is omitted.

Some of the modern versions omit the term *boisterous* or "strong" when describing the wind that Peter came in contact with. Some just say "he saw the wind." Well, seeing the wind does not necessarily mean that the wind was strong or boisterous. One can see a wind that is not blowing strongly. This word is important because it adds depth to the story that Peter was really facing a major storm when he went out of the boat, not just "a wind," which could have been less fierce.

Jesus saved Peter from a fierce storm and not just a casual wind. It shows that no matter what fierce problems we face in life, Jesus will always be there to help and to bring us through. "When thou passest through the waters, I will be with thee; and through the rivers, they shall not overflow thee: when thou walkest through the fire, thou shalt not be burned; neither shall the flame kindle upon thee" (Isaiah

43:2, KJV). Once again, the King James Bible keeps the narrative intact and delivers the entire teaching.

Matthew 14:33

> Then they that were in the ship *came and* worshipped him, saying, Of a truth thou art the Son of God. (Matthew 14:33, KJV)

"Came and" is omitted.

Once Jesus had calmed the sea, the disciples, who were probably in all different places around the ship, had gotten up from where they were hunkered down and came to where Jesus was and began to worship Him. The modern versions have it looking like they all stayed in their places and worshipped there. The King James Bible has it correct that by the disciples getting up and coming to Jesus, it tells us the storm was completely over according to the command of Jesus, and the sea was calm, making it possible for the disciples to move around the boat without any fear of being cast overboard by a wave.

Matthew 15:6

> And honour not his father *or his mother*, he shall be free. Thus have ye made the *commandment* of God of none effect by your tradition. (Matthew 15:6, KJV)

"Or his mother" is omitted. *Commandment* is changed to "word."

This verse received the Gnostic ax in two places. First of all, the fifth commandment includes the mother. "Honour thy father and thy mother: that thy days may be long upon the land which the LORD thy God giveth thee" (Exodus 20:12, KJV). The modern versions have seen fit to omit the *mother*. The second place is when the modern versions replace the word *commandment* with the word *word*. They are the Ten Commandments, not the "ten words." When God gives a commandment, it is to be obeyed.

Matthew 15:8

This people *draweth nigh unto me with their mouth*, and honoureth me with their lips; but their heart is far from me. (Matthew 15:8, KJV)

"Draweth nigh unto me with their mouth" is omitted.

"Wherefore the Lord said, Forasmuch as this people draw near me with their mouth, and with their lips do honour me, but have removed their heart far from me, and their fear toward me is taught by the precept of men" (Isaiah 29:13, KJV). The Lord takes a quote directly out of Isaiah 29:13, but if you notice, the modern versions omit the part where the people draw nigh unto Him with their lips. In Isaiah's time, God was indicting Israel that they were keeping all the rituals of the law, but their heart was far from the Lord. In other words, they were doing the works of the law, but in their unbelief, they were as far from God as a person can get.

Now, Jesus indicted the scribes and Pharisees that they were doing the same thing. They worked out all the rituals of the law, and by the time the Lord came on the scene, they had added much more to the law of God, but their hearts were far from the Lord. In fact, He stated that their worship was in vain (useless) because they were teaching the doctrines of men for the doctrines from the scriptures.

The phrase that is left out of the passage is important to us today, for there are many who stand in churches every Sunday and are vain in their worship. That phrase is a warning to us that we may draw close to the Lord with our mouths because of ritual, but it is more important that we draw close to the Lord because of being saved. Those who are truly saved worship in Spirit and not ritual, and we all need a cudgel to make sure we do not worship the Lord in ritualistic ways. Once again, the King James Bible makes sure we examine ourselves so that we can be sure if we are in the faith.

Matthew 15:14

Let them alone: they be blind leaders *of the blind*.
And if the blind lead the blind, both shall fall
into the ditch. (Matthew 15:14, KJV)

"Of the blind" is omitted.

Jesus was instructing His disciples concerning the Pharisees, who were upset at what Jesus had been teaching. Jesus had instructed His disciples to leave them alone, for they were blind leaders of the blind. In other words, they did not know the scriptures and were teaching them to those who did not know so they could make no discernment on the teaching. As a matter of fact, what was taught more than the scriptures was the Babylonian Talmud, which was nothing but collective Rabbinical commentary dating from the time of the Babylonian captivity. This commentary was and is much in opposition to the scriptures. When one chooses to study commentaries and not the actual scriptures, they are studying the works of man and not the words of God. The phrase "of the blind" was removed by Hort and Westcott for no reason, but maybe they looked at the scriptures and became convicted that they too were blind leaders of the blind.

Matthew 15:30

And great multitudes came unto him, having with
them those that were lame, blind, dumb, maimed,
and many others, and cast them down at *Jesus'*
feet; and he healed them. (Matthew 15:30, KJV)

Jesus' is changed to "his."

Once again, Jesus has been omitted from the text. Jesus was healing great multitudes, and the scripture is being specific that it is Jesus doing the healing and no one else. When a proper name is replaced with a pronoun, that also means that the person in view could be replaced by anyone.

Matthew 16:3

And in the morning, It will be foul weather to day:
for the sky is red and lowring. *O ye hypocrites*, ye
can discern the face of the sky; but can ye not discern the signs of the times? (Matthew 16:3, KJV)

"O ye hypocrites" is omitted.

In Matthew 16, the Pharisees and Sadducees had tried to tempt
the Lord Jesus into giving them a sign as to whether He was who
He said He was. The religious leaders continued to hound the Lord
Jesus, and in verse 3, the Lord called them hypocrites. They were not
really concerned as to whether the Lord was who He claimed to be,
and that is why they were called hypocrites. A hypocrite is a person
who says one thing and does another. They live contradictory life-
styles. It is like many today who are church leaders on Sunday and
live like the world the rest of the week. Religious on Sunday for show
and worldly when no one is looking. I guess there is a little hypocrite
in each of us being humans.

The modern versions omit the term *hypocrites*, which accurately
described these religious leaders. They were the leaders of Israel and
should have had a very good grasp on the scriptures, resulting in
knowing who the Lord Jesus was since His coming was prophesied
many times in the Old Testament. Removing the term *hypocrite*
removes the divine assessment of how bad these religious leaders
really were and the parallel we see today with many of the religious
leaders in the churches, which also serves as a warning for us. Many
claim to be pastors but are more concerned with worldly endeav-
ors. Once again, the King James gives us the true assessment of false
leaders.

Matthew 16:4

A wicked and adulterous generation seeketh after
a sign; and there shall no sign be given unto it,
but the sign of *the prophet* Jonas. And he left
them, and departed. (Matthew 16:4, KJV)

"The prophet" is omitted.

The Pharisees and Sadducees were once again heckling Jesus, and this time, they wanted another sign that He was who He said He was. Jesus told them that they would not be given a special sign but one that is already familiar to them. They would be given the sign of the prophet Jonah. Jesus is confirming the fact that Jonah was indeed a prophet of God and that his writings are scripture and therefore worthy to be quoted. The modern versions omit the phrase "the prophet," thus reducing the ministry of Jonah from prophet to preacher. Jesus quoted Jonah because his words were scripture and given under the inspiration of the Holy Spirit, giving credence to the Old Testament. The modern versions, by omitting this fact, omit the fact that Jonah was a prophet. It makes Jesus quoting a preacher instead of one of the prophets, thus reducing the impact of His declaration to the Pharisees.

Matthew 16:20

> Then charged he his disciples that they should
> tell no man that he was *Jesus* the Christ.
> (Matthew 16:20, KJV)

Jesus is omitted.

Here is another attack upon the Lord Jesus Christ as they remove His name from being the Christ or the Messiah. The Gnostics did what they could to remove any allusion to deity, and the modern versions have done what they could to perpetuate those errors with the help of the Christian intellectual hit squads known as theologians.

Matthew 17:4

> Then answered Peter, and said unto Jesus, Lord,
> it is good for us to be here: if thou wilt, *let us make*
> here three tabernacles; one for thee, and one for
> Moses, and one for Elias. (Matthew 17:4, KJV)

"Let us make" is changed to "I will make" (plural to singular).

Here is a case of the plural *let us* being changed to singular *I* for no reason at all. Peter, James, and John were on the Mount of Transfiguration, and Peter wanted to prolong this tremendous experience as I am sure that he wanted to pose many questions to Moses and Elijah. However, there were bigger things in view here than Peter's desire to stay on the mount. While he was speaking, the cloud overshadowed them, and God the Father had spoken, stating that they were to hear His Son. This took the focus off Moses, Elijah, Peter, James, and John. "God, who at sundry times and in divers manners spake in time past unto the fathers by the prophets, Hath in these last days spoken unto us by his Son, whom he hath appointed heir of all things, by whom also he made the worlds" (Hebrews 1:1–2, KJV).

In these last days, which commenced at the cross, we are to hear from Jesus and not the apostles or the prophets. Hebrews 1:1 states that we heard from the prophets in times past, which means that time is over, and now we hear from the Lord Jesus, not audibly but through the scriptures. There is no reason for the scripture to be changed from plural to singular. I am sure if they would have built tabernacles, all three would have built them for Jesus, Moses, and Elijah. This change may have been an attempt to focus on the Roman Catholic belief that Peter was the first pope and that he was the one who would have built the tabernacle, being the vicar of Christ on earth. The tabernacle would have represented the Church of Rome, which they claim is the true church. This might have been another effort to make Peter the central figure, a.k.a. the first pope.

Matthew 17:20

> And *Jesus* said unto them, Because of your *unbelief*: for verily I say unto you, If ye have faith as a grain of mustard seed, ye shall say unto this mountain, Remove hence to yonder place; and it shall remove; and nothing shall be impossible unto you. (Matthew 17:20, KJV)

Jesus is changed to "he." *Unbelief* is omitted.

Here is a very subtle change that can be passed over without notice. If you will notice in the King James, the Lord tells the disciples that because of their unbelief, they could not cast out the demon from the boy. Now, the word in the Greek is *apistian*, which means "no faith." When you have the alpha privative in front of a word, it means "no." For example, in English, a person who is an atheist states there is no God. The word broken down is *a*, which refers to "no," and *theist*, which refers to "God." So we see in our verse that Jesus was chiding the disciples because they had no faith. In the modern versions, they state that they have little faith.

There is a great difference between none and little. If I have no money, it means I am totally broke. If I have one dollar, it means I have little money, but I am not totally broke. Now here is a confusing scenario that appears in this verse in the modern versions. Jesus accuses the disciples of having little faith but then goes on to say that if you have faith the size of a mustard seed, then you can move mountains. He just got done telling them they have little faith and then tells them if they have small faith like a mustard seed. Well, don't they already possess the small faith needed to move mountains?

In the King James, Jesus is telling them they have no faith, and if they had faith the size of a mustard seed, they could move mountains. Which scenario removes the confusion? It is the King James because the faith goes from unbelief (no faith) to small faith, which shows a progression in their faith. The modern versions go from little faith to small faith—well, which direction is the progression of faith? I don't know! Once again, the King James Bible removes the confusion and shows a proper growth in faith from none to little.

Matthew 17:21

> Howbeit this kind goeth not out but by prayer
> and fasting. (Matthew 17:21, KJV)

The entire verse is omitted.

When the Lord speaks of fasting and prayer in this verse, He is emphasizing intense prayer and that if one fasts and prays in certain situations, they must realize that their dependence is totally upon God, and it is not their actions that will work in their situation. "For that ye ought to say, If the Lord will, we shall live, and do this, or that" (James 4:15, KJV). Every believer lives within the Lord's will for their lives, and sometimes, even when we go into intense prayer, God may choose to say no to our request. Keep in mind that no is an answer to prayer as well as yes.

The modern versions omit this verse, and it has a great lesson that Christians need to be in intense prayer, not only in certain situations but in all of life since we live in perilous times. There is no reason why the modern versions should omit this verse. Fasting and praying went together in the old days as well as today. Fasting is designed to keep our eyes upon the Lord and not to be interrupted with the cares of this life. There is a great verse in the Old Testament that speaks of fasting:

> Is it such a fast that I have chosen? a day for a man to afflict his soul? is it to bow down his head as a bulrush, and to spread sackcloth and ashes under him? wilt thou call this a fast, and an acceptable day to the LORD? Is not this the fast that I have chosen? to loose the bands of wickedness, to undo the heavy burdens, and to let the oppressed go free, and that ye break every yoke? (Isaiah 58:5–6, KJV)

In Isaiah 58:5-6, we see that the fast in the Christian's life is not one of food but of being involved with sending forth the Gospel. When we engage in the Lord's work, we are, in essence, fasting or giving up our own pleasures for the sake of the Gospel. "He that findeth his life shall lose it: and he that loseth his life for my sake shall find it" (Matthew 10:39, KJV). We are using up the time on earth for the Gospel's sake, and that is the fast that the Lord has in view as we read in Matthew 10:39. As we lose our life (get involved with kingdom work), we are finding our true life, and that is Christ. "When Christ, who is our life, shall appear, then shall ye also appear with him in glory" (Colossians 3:4, KJV).

As we read in Colossians 3:4, Christ is our life, so we see that fasting is much more than giving up a meal or two; it is basically for a lifetime. In Matthew 17:21, when it speaks of demon possession and that casting them out comes by prayer and fasting, it is basically pointing to the fact that when a person becomes saved, the Holy Spirit lives in them and the devils no longer can reside in that person. "And they come to Jesus, and see him that was possessed with the devil, and had the legion, sitting, and clothed, and in his right mind: and they were afraid" (Mark 5:15, KJV). Probably the best verse showing this is Mark 5:15 that the Gadarene demoniac was delivered from all the indwelling devils and was in his right mind. This is a great picture of salvation, the transition from the kingdom of Satan to the kingdom of God. Once again, the modern versions rob the Christian of a great teaching.

Matthew 18:2

And *Jesus* called a little child unto him, and set him in the midst of them. (Matthew 18:2, KJV)

Jesus is omitted.

Here is another attack upon the person of the Lord Jesus Christ. The name of Jesus was omitted from the text.

Matthew 18:11

For the Son of man is come to save that which was lost. (Matthew 18:11, KJV)

The entire verse is omitted.

This verse describes the mission of the Lord Jesus Christ. This verse also met its death in the second century. The Gnostics believed that knowledge was the key to immortality, so therefore they would have to delete this verse since it is by knowledge that someone can attain eternal life. This concept was well accepted into the nineteenth century by a man named Frederick Dennison Maurice, who claimed that eternal life was having the knowledge of God. F. D. Maurice was the principle man whom Satan used to inculcate Unitarianism, Communism, and Universalism into Christianity; and with the insertion of these beliefs, a new Bible had to be produced whereby the ideas of these three systems could be implanted in the pages in a very subtle way. Hort was a student of Frederick Dennison Maurice. The new Bible had to be man-centered, which the modern versions are.

This verse is missing in the Vaticanus and the Sinaiticus and "L," which is the Regius manuscript (AD c. 750), so Hort and Westcott had regarded this verse as a "rejected reading." After all, if man was going to save himself by his own abilities, then the mission of the Lord Jesus Christ was no longer needed. The problem is that Matthew 18:11 is surrounded by a great cloud of witnesses for its authenticity. It is confirmed by the Old Latin Vulgate (AD c. 90–150), the entire Universal Eastern Church, the Peshitta, the Coptic, Armenian, Ethiopic, Georgian, and Slavonic Versions, plus the entire line of manuscripts leading up to the King James Bible. It is also witnessed by Tertullian, Ambrose (fourth century), and Augustine.

Matthew 18:11 is in the majority of both cursive and uncial manuscripts that contain the book of Matthew or fragments thereof. To remove this verse when it belongs there is to remove the reason the Lord Jesus came to earth. The reason for his death, burial, and resurrection was for the eternal salvation of His people as stated in Matthew 1:21. Bring this belief system up to day, the New Age system believes that a person can be promoted to the higher spiritual planes without any outside help; and therefore, the New Age system rejects the efficacious sacrifice of the Lord Jesus Christ, as does the Unitarian. Matthew 18:11 belongs in the Bible, and woe unto those who take it out.

Matthew 18:22

Jesus saith unto him, I say not unto thee, Until seven times: but, Until *seventy times seven.* (Matthew 18:22, KJV)

"Seventy times seven" is changed to "seventy-seven."

The adverb *hebdomêkontakis* above carries with it the meaning of "seventy times," not "seventy." The word *hepta* at the end of the sentence is translated "seven," and it is in cardinal form; meaning, it is a stand-alone number showing a specific number. In this case, it is seven. These are two separate words *seventy times* and *seven*; they are not one word meaning "77" or "seventy-seven." Once again, the King James grammar shows its superiority over these modern versions.

Matthew 18:29

And his fellowservant fell down *at his feet*, and besought him, saying, Have patience with me, and I will pay thee *all*. (Matthew 18:29, KJV)

"At his feet" and *"all"* are omitted.

This verse has suffered two swipes of the Gnostic ax. The first hit is the place where the man fell to beg for more time to pay the puny debt in contrast to the outstandingly large debt that was forgiven by the king. "The rich ruleth over the poor, and the borrower is servant to the lender" (Proverbs 22:7, KJV). It was at the feet of his fellow servant that was exactly the same thing the other servant did before the king. By leaving this phrase out, it could seem the man fell in some other place rather than at his feet, which was a sign of deference.

The second hit was the removal of the word *all*, which is a very important word in this verse. The servant who fell down before the king would have been unable to pay all the debt, but this man had such a small debt that amounted to about one hundred days' work. Jesus is telling a parable of a servant and his king in the area of forgiveness. Forgiveness is a key trait of the Christian life, and being able to forgive others should not be difficult for the Christian, especially since we have received forgiveness for the multitude of sins that God will no longer ever hold against us; and therefore, we should never hold any sins against other Christians because they too have received the same total forgiveness.

Matthew 18:35

So likewise shall my heavenly Father do also unto you, if ye from your hearts forgive not every one his brother *their trespasses*. (Matthew 18:35, KJV)

"Their trespasses" is omitted.

Here, we have the story of the wicked servant who was forgiven ten thousand talents and was very grateful to the master for forgiving him his debt. However, this servant, instead of rejoicing, thought he would make a little extra money, so he found a person who owed him one hundred pence, which would be approximately equal to about nine dollars in American money or about three pounds in the United Kingdom. This story delivers a very powerful salvation message. The servant was forgiven for the debt that he owed his master, but even though he was forgiven this debt, he proved that this forgiveness fell on stony ground. "Some fell upon stony places, where they had not much earth: and forthwith they sprung up, because they had no deepness of earth" (Matthew 13:5, KJV).

If this servant was truly saved, he would have forgiven the one who owed him a mere pittance in comparison to what he owed his master. Instead of forgiving the small debt, he tried to exact it; but as the scriptures teach, our sins will find us out. "But if ye will not do so, behold, ye have sinned against the LORD: and be sure your sin will find you out" (Numbers 32:23, KJV). The result is that the wicked servant was thrown to the tormentors until he should pay the entire debt; in other words, it is an eternal debt. This is akin to those who die unsaved and will be in hell, eternally paying for their sins.

Now to verse 35. It seems like Jesus is saying that our salvation depends upon our forgiving others their trespasses. However, this could not be because this would make it salvation by works, and salvation is by grace. What is in view here is the fact that this servant is called a "wicked servant." This means that he was never saved. This is why he was handed over to the tormentors until he should pay every cent of his debt, which would be akin to an unbeliever paying for their sins. Verse 35 is pointing to the unbelievers in the crowd who do not have the spirit of forgiveness that accompanies salvation.

If a person is truly saved, then they will possess the spirit of forgiveness and will forgive people for their trespasses many times. When people sin against us, it is like the one hundred pence; but as they continue to sin against God, it is like the ten thousand talents that make it unpayable. Unless a person becomes saved, they will be thrown to the tormentors, which means they will be sent to hell for their sins. The modern versions leave out the fact in verse 35, we are to forgive concerning trespasses. When someone sins against us, we who are saved must show the spirit of forgiveness. It is the ones who are unsaved who hold to the spirit of vengeance, just like the wicked servant. Whenever a salvation lesson is in view, then we must speak about the fact that we are forgiven all our sins, and those who are not saved still retain all their sins. Even if we forgive a person's trespass against us, it does not guarantee their salvation, but it does present a good testimony on our part that our salvation is real.

Matthew 19:9

And I say unto you, Whosoever shall put away his wife, except it be for fornication, and shall marry another, committeth adultery: *and whoso marrieth her which is put away doth commit adultery.* (Matthew 19:9, KJV)

"And whoso marrieth her which is put away doth commit adultery" is omitted.

One of the most egregious sins of the church and many Christians is to remarry after divorce or to marry another who is divorced. The Bible is very clear on this matter.

And he saith unto them, Whosoever shall put away his wife, and marry another, committeth adultery against her. And if a woman shall put away her husband, and be married to another, she committeth adultery. (Mark 10:11–12, KJV)

Whosoever putteth away his wife, and marrieth another, committeth adultery: and whosoever marrieth her that is put away from her husband committeth adultery. (Luke 16:18, KJV)

For the woman which hath an husband is bound by the law to her husband so long as he liveth; but if the husband be dead, she is loosed from the law of her husband. So then if, while her husband liveth, she be married to another man, she shall be called an adulteress: but if her husband be dead, she is free from that law; so that she is no adulteress, though she be married to another man. (Romans 7:2–3, KJV)

The wife is bound by the law as long as her husband liveth; but if her husband be dead, she is at liberty to be married to whom she will; only in the Lord. (1 Corinthians 7:39, KJV)

These verses clearly indicate that if a man or woman divorces their spouse and remarries another, whether they be Christian or not, they are committing adultery. The church has become a haven for remarrying divorced people, and this practice is in absolute contradiction to the teaching of the scriptures. This means that the church is an active participant in aiding Christians to sin. It is highly hypocritical for the church to speak out against committing adultery and then turning around and sanctioning an entire life of adultery. "Thou shalt not commit adultery" (Exodus 20:14, KJV). The seventh commandment is very clear that we are not to commit adultery, and that means adultery in any form. Why then is the church condoning approved adultery under the umbrella of marriage? An adulterous marriage is as sinful in God's sight as a marriage of a Christian and a nonbeliever.

One of the reasons the church is so quick to endorse this sinful practice is if they use a modern version and come to Matthew 19:9—the prohibition of remarriage after divorce has been removed. This omission paves the way for remarriage after divorce in direct disobedience to the other scriptures that deal directly with this matter.

Matthew 19:9 has been abused because of the so-called exception clause. Countless numbers of Christians have used Matthew 19:9 to seek a divorce so they can remarry somebody else. When we look at Matthew 19:9, we see the words "except it be for fornication." Now, the question we must ask is, what type of fornication? Is it physical fornication, or is it spiritual fornication? This means that if a person commits physical fornication, then they are guilty. Then what happens if a person commits spiritual fornication? What if that person happens to believe a false teaching? Then according to Matthew 19:9, they are allowed to divorce. What happens if a spouse has an evil thought? That too is spiritual fornication, and they are guilty. Do you see where this leads? Any woman who listens to a false teaching or has an evil thought may be put away by their husband. This abuse of Matthew 19:9 has cheapened the marriage institution. It is no longer "till death do we part"; it should now be "till you have an evil thought do we part." What human does not have evil thoughts on a recurrent basis? Everyone does! Matthew 19:9 is not an excuse for divorce and remarriage; rather, it is a testing ground for the marriage.

> But I say unto you, Love your enemies, bless them that curse you, do good to them that hate you, and pray for them which despitefully use you, and persecute you. (Matthew 5:44, KJV)

> But I say unto you which hear, Love your enemies, do good to them which hate you. (Luke 6:27, KJV)

What do these two verses teach us? If we are to forgive and love our enemies, then how is it that we hate our spouses so fast to divorce them? It is the evil, sensual nature of sin that causes us to want to divorce the spouse so quickly. If we are to love our enemies, why then can we not love our spouses, even if they sin? Did the Lord Jesus divorce you when you sinned? How many times in the previous day have you sinned against God? Did God send you away, or did He still remain true to His vow? "All that the Father giveth me shall come to me; and him that cometh to me I will in no wise cast out" (John 6:37, KJV).

Matthew 19:9 must be looked on as a testing program for the believer and not an excuse for the practice of revolving-door marriages. Matthew 19:9 must be compared with the other verses that deal with divorce and remarriage, and when all are taken in the proper context, you will see that Matthew 19:9 is boundary or a testing program for the true believer. Let us stay with the King James and remain faithful.

Matthew 19:17

> And he said unto him, Why callest thou me good? there is none good but one, *that is, God*: but if thou wilt enter into life, keep the commandments. (Matthew 19:17, KJV)

"*That is, God*" is omitted.

By the modern versions removing the reference to God in this verse, they are removing a vital part of the verse. The rich young ruler came to the Lord Jesus Christ and asked Him how he could inherit eternal life. In his approach to the Lord Jesus, he calls Him "Good Master." Then the Lord Jesus gives him a very puzzling answer, "Why callest thou me good?" Now we know that the Lord Jesus Christ is good, but why this answer to this man? The reason is that the man is looking at Jesus as a man and not the Savior. The Bible tells us that there is not one good man upon earth.

> They are all gone out of the way, they are together
> become unprofitable; there is none that doeth
> good, no, not one. (Romans 3:12, KJV)

The Lord Jesus was diverting his attention from man to God. In other words, because this man was looking at Jesus as a man rather than God in the flesh, Jesus wanted to teach him that there is no good man on earth, and only God is good. The reason for this is that this understanding will stem the desire for preacher worship. This is something the modern translators love. They love to be seen by men with all their PhDs, but when the phrase "that is God" is left intact, it then teaches the believer that man is not to be trusted, especially those who have the innate arrogance to change the word of God without conscience.

> It is better to trust in the LORD than to put confi-
> dence in man. It is better to trust in the LORD than
> to put confidence in princes. (Psalm 118:8–9, KJV)

So when the modern versions leave God out of this verse, they completely ruin and shroud the meaning of this verse. By replacing God with "one," it can allow a person to place anyone in that category such as dead saints of Rome or New Age avatars. Once again, the King James shows its superiority by removing all doubt as to whom we are to focus our spiritual eyes on.

Matthew 19:20

> The young man saith unto him, All these things
> have I kept *from my youth up*: what lack I yet?
> (Matthew 19:20, KJV)

"From my youth up" is omitted.

Here is a young man who had learned the commandments from his parents and was telling Jesus that he had kept them all from the time he was a youth. What this conveys is that a person can keep the letter of the law their entire life and neglect the fact that sin is part of the human nature. Every person is a sinner, even the ones who claim they have kept the law perfectly (but that is the outward keeping of the law, which cannot save). If the parents were saved, they would have taught the child spiritual truths that works cannot save; only grace can save, and that is why we must teach our children to seek the Lord early in their life. Good works can never negate the sin nature we inherited from Adam. We can teach our children that good works are acceptable, but they cannot save, no matter how many good works a person does. In fact, the Bible refers to good works only after a person is saved. "For we are his workmanship, created in Christ Jesus unto good works, which God hath before ordained that we should walk in them" (Ephesians 2:10, KJV). Notice that the believer is created in Christ unto good works.

"The sacrifice of the wicked is abomination: how much more, when he bringeth it with a wicked mind?" (Proverbs 21:27, KJV). Proverbs 21:27 teaches that the sacrifice of the wicked is an abomination unto the Lord, and it worsens it when he brings it with a wicked mind. Of course, he is speaking of the animal sacrifices under the Mosaic system, but the principle is applicable to those who think they are righteous in their own eyes. The modern versions, by leaving out the phrase, make it sound like the young man kept those laws only for a short time instead of his entire life. This is important because a lifetime of good works does not earn anyone salvation. Once again, the King James Bible delivers another timeless, namely, eternal truth.

Matthew 19:29

> And every one that hath forsaken houses, or brethren, or sisters, or father, or mother, *or wife*, or children, or lands, for my name's sake, shall receive an hundredfold, and shall inherit everlasting life. (Matthew 19:29, KJV)

"Or wife" is omitted.

Here, Jesus is giving a teaching that those who have forsaken all the things that they love and are familiar with for His sake will receive a hundredfold more in this life. The amount "hundredfold" is an open-ended number, and the Lord is basically stating that the blessings of the Christian life are without number. When the Lord speaks of forsaking family, He is not advocating leaving without any communication with their earthly family, but He is stating that the Christian must seek the eternal family above the earthly family. If they are the only ones saved in that family, then their outlook on life is going to be different than the unsaved ones, and their worldly outlook must also be forsaken. If you notice in the text, the Lord also mentions forsaking a wife. This does not mean that a man is to forsake his wife because that would be in violation of the scriptures. What is in view here is a man forsaking the institution of marriage, exchanging the married life for the life in service to Christ. "For there are some eunuchs, which were so born from their mother's womb: and there are some eunuchs, which were made eunuchs of men: and there be eunuchs, which have made themselves eunuchs for the kingdom of heaven's sake. He that is able to receive it, let him receive it" (Matthew 19:12, KJV).

Matthew 20:7

> They say unto him, Because no man hath hired us. He saith unto them, Go ye also into the vineyard; *and whatsoever is right, that shall ye receive.* (Matthew 20:7, KJV)

"And whatsoever is right, that shall ye receive" is omitted.

Verse 7 is the beginning of a parable that shows the equality of all believers regardless of when a person becomes saved. Those who went to work in the vineyard in the early part of the day thought they were going to get much more than those who went to work in the vineyard in the late part of the day. Well, everyone received the same wages. This lesson is for those who think they will receive some great rewards for their service, but the lesson here is that all the children of

God receive the same. "But he shall receive an hundredfold now in this time, houses, and brethren, and sisters, and mothers, and children, and lands, with persecutions; and in the world to come eternal life" (Mark 10:30, KJV). Eternal life is the great gift that God gives His children.

In this parable, the modern versions leave out the phrase "and whatsoever is right, that shall ye receive." It is apparent that the Gnostics did not want that part of the verse in because maybe they were fearful that when judgment day came, they would receive what is right. That is, they would receive according to their works. Anyone who tampers in any way with the word of God will receive the punishment of eternal damnation, according to Revelation 22:18–19. When the Lord is telling these people that they will receive what is right, He is showing that all the true believers are equal and receive what is right, which is eternal life based upon the merits of Christ. This part of the verse shows the fairness of Christ as He will give what is right, and that is based upon His work on Calvary. This parable is a very important parable because it brings back to earth those who feel they hold a more important position than other Christians in the body of Christ. Wait until we get to heaven and find out the greatest ones were the praying people found in nursing homes, hospitals, and places like that. Let us stay with the King James because it tells us what is right!

Matthew 20:16

So the last shall be first, and the first last: *for many be called, but few chosen.* (Matthew 20:16, KJV)

"For many be called, but few chosen." is omitted

The second part of this verse is the qualifier for God's salvation plan. When that portion is removed, it gives the indication that there is going to be universal salvation. The Bible teaches very clearly that God is the one who chooses His elect for salvation. "But we are bound to give thanks always to God for you, brethren beloved of the Lord, because *God hath from the beginning chosen you to salva-*

tion through sanctification of the Spirit and belief of the truth" (2 Thessalonians 2:13, KJV). The Gospel call goes out through all the world, and many hear the Gospel, but only those who are chosen from the foundations of the world will respond to the Gospel and become saved. So when the second part of this verse was removed, it also removed the method whereby God will be accomplishing His salvation plan until the last day.

"For many be called but few chosen" means we send forth the Gospel to everybody we can, but only those whom God has qualified to hear the Gospel and be saved will become saved. Universal salvation or universal atonement is never taught in the Bible. The removal of the qualifier does not negate the truth that it omits.

Matthew 20:22

> But Jesus answered and said, Ye know not what ye ask. Are ye able to drink of the cup that I shall drink of, *and to be baptized with the baptism that I am baptized with?* They say unto him, We are able. (Matthew 20:22, KJV)

"And to be baptized with the baptism that I am baptized with?" is omitted.

James and John were looking forward to Jesus ruling in Jerusalem, and despite the constant reminders by Jesus that He was going to Jerusalem to be crucified, their mother requested that one sit on his right and one sit on his left. Jesus told her that she did not realize what she was asking because those positions were given to someone by the Father. Jesus asked them if they were able to drink of the cup He was going to drink and the baptism that he was going to undertake. In their quickness to reply, they told Jesus that they are able.

In verse 23, Jesus went on to tell them that they would drink of the cup and would be baptized with His baptism. "Then said Jesus unto Peter, Put up thy sword into the sheath: the cup which my Father hath given me, shall I not drink it?" (John 18:11, KJV). The cup that the Father gave Him was to be crucified and pay for the sins of all God's elect. Every true believer has a cup that the Father gives them, which represents the suffering they will do for the kingdom of God and what they are to accomplish in spite of that suffering.

In Luke 12:50, Jesus speaks of His coming baptism. "But I have a baptism to be baptized with; and how am I straitened till it be accomplished!" (Luke 12:50, KJV). That baptism was His coming bloody death on Calvary. "Know ye not, that so many of us as were baptized into Jesus Christ were baptized into his death?" (Romans 6:3, KJV). Each true believer is baptized into the death of Christ, which symbolizes our being dead to the things of the world. No longer does the world hold any attraction for us because a crucified person is a dead person, and as Christians, we are to be dead to the things of this world. I am not speaking about the ocean or the Grand Canyon or the parks because God gave those things to us to enjoy. I speak of the allurements of the world such as gambling, sexual attractions, drinking, etc.—the things that go against the believer's transformed lifestyle.

The modern versions leave out the part about Christ's baptism, and that is a very integral part of the scriptures concerning His death for the believers. The cup was His dying for the elect, and the baptism was the method that was used to accomplish the essence of the cup. The modern versions leave out a very important part of the verse, which is not surprising because these modern versions are not Christ-glorifying. Rather, they are hostile to Christ.

Matthew 20:23

> And he saith unto them, Ye shall drink indeed of my cup, *and be baptized with the baptism that I am baptized with*: but to sit on my right hand, and on my left, is not mine to give, but it shall be given to them for whom it is prepared of my Father. (Matthew 20:23, KJV)

"And be baptized with the baptism that I am baptized with" is omitted.

The cup that the Lord Jesus Christ was about ready to drink from was His crucifixion for the sins of His people. "And he went a little farther, and fell on his face, and prayed, saying, O my Father, if it be possible, let this cup pass from me: nevertheless not as I will, but as thou wilt" (Matthew 26:39, KJV). Then Jesus went on to state that He was going to undergo the baptism. "But I have a baptism to be baptized with; and how am I straitened till it be accomplished!" (Luke 12:50, KJV). This was not the baptism at the Jordan River where Jesus was baptized with water. This baptism was His sufferings, which were total. As one is submersed in baptism, Jesus was about to be totally immersed in suffering to the point of death. This baptism meant that He was totally committed to what was about to happen and that He was going to face total suffering and humiliation for His people.

The disciples answered Jesus very flippantly, not realizing the kind of baptism Jesus was speaking of. The modern versions omit the fact that Jesus was to undergo suffering to the point of death for His people. Once again, the downplaying of His sufferings because the Gnostics did not believe that in His deity.

Matthew 21:4

All this was done, that it might be fulfilled which
was spoken by the prophet. (Matthew 21:4, KJV)

All is omitted.

The word *all* is the Greek word *holon*, which carries with it the meaning of "whole, entire, or complete." By using the word *all*, the King James Bible is correctly stating that all the events leading up to this point was prophesied by the prophet Zechariah. However, Zechariah only states the culmination of these several events while we are given the details by Matthew of how the colt was procured. "Rejoice greatly, O daughter of Zion; shout, O daughter of Jerusalem: behold, thy King cometh unto thee: he is just, and having salvation; lowly, and riding upon an ass, and upon a colt the foal of an ass" (Zechariah 9:9, KJV). So the word *all* conveys the series of events in procuring the colt, plus the triumphal entry into Jerusalem.

By the modern versions omitting *all*, it makes it sound like only the last command was done to fulfill what the prophet spoke of. The Old Testament prophets many times prophesied events that would take place in the life of Christ, but details are not given till the actual events are recorded in the New Testament, such as in this case. The word *all* tells us that there was not just a partial fulfillment of the prophecy but a complete fulfillment, giving credibility to the Old Testament prophecies of the Lord Jesus Christ.

Matthew 21:12

> And Jesus went into the temple *of God*, and cast out all them that sold and bought in the temple, and overthrew the tables of the money-changers, and the seats of them that sold doves. (Matthew 21:12, KJV)

"Of God" is omitted.

The modern versions omit a very important phrase: "of God." This shows specifically that the temple that Jesus entered was the temple of God. Jesus quotes from both Isaiah and Jeremiah concerning the reason for the temple.

> Even them will I bring to my holy mountain, and make them joyful in my house of prayer: their burnt offerings and their sacrifices shall be accepted upon mine altar; for mine house shall be called an house of prayer for all people. (Isaiah 56:7, KJV)

> Is this house, which is called by my name, become a den of robbers in your eyes? Behold, even I have seen it, saith the LORD. (Jeremiah 7:11, KJV)

The temple of God was to be a house of prayer for all people, but the temple leaders had turned it into a personal business. This is why Jesus quotes from Jeremiah 7:11 that the temple had become a den of robbers. Then Jesus commenced to toss out the money changers. God specifically calls the temple "mine house" and "this house which is called by my name." That is exactly what the scripture in Matthew 21:12 is specifically alluding to when it states the temple of God because this is a fulfillment of prophecy. By omitting "of God," one can place any temple in this verse, even a pagan temple; but the King James Bible retains "of God," thus teaching us that the money changers were a fulfillment of prophecy.

Matthew 21:44

And whosoever shall fall on this stone shall be broken: but on whomsoever it shall fall, it will grind him to powder. (Matthew 21:44, KJV)

Included in text but attacked in the footnotes of the 1881 RV, CEV, ERV, ESV, GNB, HCSB, ISV, NABRE, NCV, NIV, NLT, NRSV, RSV, TLV, VOICE.

Those who hear the Gospel preached and do not respond to it will eventually face eternal damnation, and this is why the modern versions will place this verse in the text and then place doubt about it in the footnotes. There is more manuscript evidence for this verse than against it, and yet the modern-version editors follow the lesser evidence. According to Nestle-Aland twentieth edition, the two main manuscripts it is missing from is D 05, Bezae Cantabrigiensis (fifth century); and 33 Minuscule (ninth century). There are eight major codices that they are contained in, including Vaticanus and Sinaiticus. So to choose the lesser amount of manuscripts shows that there seems to be a consensus among the modern-version translators that hell and judgment should be omitted.

Matthew 22:13

Then said the king to the servants, Bind him hand and foot, *and take him away*, and cast him into outer darkness; there shall be weeping and gnashing of teeth. (Matthew 22:13, KJV)

"And take him away" is omitted.

In ancient times, to be taken away or sent away from a meal was a disgrace. Not being properly washed and in proper clothing was also an insult to the host. This is why the king had him punished. This has another meaning, and that is on the last day, those who thought that they were properly clothed—that is, they did everything their church told them, and they stuck to all the rituals, and they thought those things had clothed them in righteousness—will become shocked that they had never become saved. Then the angels will be told to "take them away," meaning to a place of damnation. The phrase also means that the place of damnation is separated from the place of eternal life. The modern versions remove the phrase, making it sound that the place of torment is right there where the Lord is sitting and judging.

Matthew 22:30

> For in the resurrection they neither marry, nor are given in marriage, but are as the angels *of God* in heaven. (Matthew 22:30, KJV)

"Of God" is omitted.

There are two types of angels that are listed in the Bible. There are the angels of God who did not rebel with Satan; these are known as the elect angels. "I charge thee before God, and the Lord Jesus Christ, and the elect angels, that thou observe these things without preferring one before another, doing nothing by partiality" (1 Timothy 5:21, KJV). Then there are the angels who did rebel with Satan, and these are the fallen angels. By the modern versions removing "of God" as an identifier of which angels, it can cause confusion for new Christians. The angels of God who did not follow Satan will live forever in heaven, but those evil angels who fell with Satan will be cast into the lake of fire for eternity. Jesus is specifically identifying the believers as being like the angels of God who will live eternally in glory.

Matthew 22:32

I am the God of Abraham, and the God of Isaac, and the God of Jacob? *God is not the God of the dead, but of the living.* (Matthew 22:32, KJV)

"God is not the God of the dead, but of the living" is changed to, "He is not the God of the dead, but of the living."

Not only is the Lord Jesus Christ attacked in the modern versions, but so is God the Father. Here we have a major statement that God is not the God of the dead but of the living. Look at the passage very carefully. "I am the God of Abraham, and the God of Isaac, and the God of Jacob? God is not the God of the dead, but of the living" (Mathew 22:32, KJV). If you notice, the passage does not say, "I was the God of..." This is because Abraham, Isaac, and Jacob are alive in heaven at the present time. The modern versions replace the proper name *God* with the personal pronoun *he*. Once again, a personal pronoun can be turned into anyone the reader wants it to be, but here, it is so wrong because the Bible is telling us plainly that *God* is the "God of the living" in no uncertain terms.

This verse is a verse of encouragement for the believer because if Abraham is alive for over four thousand years in heaven, then we as contemporary believers are looking for that blessed hope in that we may be alive forever more. "In hope of eternal life, which God, that cannot lie, promised before the world began" (Titus 1:2, KJV). We read in Titus 1:2 that God himself is making the promise of eternal life for the believer, and that harmonizes beautifully with Matthew 22:32 that God is the God of the living. It is a shame that there is no fear of God among modern Bible translators because they turn God into a personal pronoun on the say-so of two occultists, Hort and Westcott. Let us stay with the King James Bible because it is the Bible that honors God the Father and God the Son.

Matthew 23:8

But be not ye called Rabbi: for one is your
Master, *even Christ*; and all ye are brethren.
(Matthew 23:8, KJV)

"Even Christ" is omitted.

The Pharisees had loved titles, and *rabbi* was one of the titles they coveted. It meant "my master." The Lord Jesus Christ had told them not to be called rabbi because they too had a master in heaven, and that was the Lord Jesus Christ. The modern versions omit the specific reference to Christ as being "the Master." This opens the door for anyone to claim the title of master. That title belongs to the Lord Jesus Christ alone and not to any earthly person. The title *rabbi*, at first, was one of respect; but as time went on, it became the title for one who was in charge of a synagogue. Christ had forbidden His disciples to look to an earthly man as their master since Christ was their Master. Once again, the modern versions omit the name of Christ, robbing Him of His title as Master. The King James once again proves its superiority by proclaiming Christ as Master of His redeemed children.

Matthew 23:14

Woe unto you, scribes and Pharisees, hypocrites!
for ye devour widows' houses, and for a pretence
make long prayer: therefore ye shall receive the
greater damnation. (Matthew 23:14, KJV)

Entire verse omitted.

This is one of those verses that could come right back at the false clergy as they do the same things in modern churches that the false teachers did to the ancient people. There is no reason why this verse has been omitted in its entirety, but it is another example of how the modern versions omit or bracket according to the dictates of the early Gnostics, who would have also lorded it over the people. Of course, this verse speaks about these people getting the greater damnation, and that is one subject that every false teacher desires to stay away from. Let us stay with the King James Bible as it continues to guide us into truth.

Matthew 23:19

> Ye *fools and* blind: for whether is greater, the gift, or the altar that sanctifieth the gift? (Matthew 23:19, KJV)

"Fools and" is omitted.

Jesus asked them a question concerning which is of more value, the gift or the altar? The altar has more value because it sanctifies the gift and gives it its value. Jesus called them fools because, in their mind, the gift was worth more because of the fact that they loved money and that was their god. The altar had consecrated the gift, but the only thing the Pharisees had their minds on was wealth. This is why Jesus called them fools because their money would soon perish with them. "Professing themselves to be wise, they became fools" (Romans 1:22, KJV). They were looking at this completely backward because their theology was backward.

Matthew 24:2

> And *Jesus* said unto them, See ye not all these things? verily I say unto you, There shall not be left here one stone upon another, that shall not be thrown down. (Matthew 24:2, KJV)

Jesus is changed to "he."

Here is another case of the proper name of Jesus being changed to a pronoun. It is another attempt to shroud the person of Jesus by omitting His name and replacing it with a pronoun.

Matthew 24:6

> And ye shall hear of wars and rumours of wars: see that ye be not troubled: for *all* these things

must come to pass, but the end is not yet.
(Matthew 24:6, KJV)

All is omitted.

Not only will there be those pretending to be the Messiah (24:5) before the terrible destruction of Jerusalem, but there are going to be wars and rumors of wars. These are not signs of the end because wars have always been around. The disciples are not to be troubled when the war drums sound or if they hear a rumor that some type of war is coming. "But when ye shall hear of wars and commotions, be not terrified: for these things must first come to pass; but the end is not by and by" (Luke 21:9, KJV). Luke adds to the scenario with the words "but the end is not by and by," which means the end is not immediate.

The verse in Matthew uses the word *all*, which is very important. Jesus is stating that all things must happen first before the end will come. This is important because too many build prophecy doctrines on single events that are separated from the rest of the events, thus creating wild stories and fantasies. Here, Jesus gives us the reality that the end will come after *all* these things happen. The modern versions omit *all*, thus making it sound like only the events in verses 4 and 5 will have to come to pass, but Jesus is looking at all the signs, not just these few. I remember when the Gulf War of 1990 happened; everyone was looking for the return of Christ. Every time Israel gets into a war, the prophecy pundits sell more books. At present, war is not a sign of the end as it was not a sign of the end in the time of the disciples. In fact, the text even states that it is necessary for these things to happen.

Matthew 24:7

For nation shall rise against nation, and kingdom against kingdom: and there shall be famines, *and pestilences*, and earthquakes, in divers places.
(Matthew 24:7, KJV)

"And pestilences" is omitted.

One of the most premier signs right before the Lord returns is that of pestilences. Pestilences are plagues or diseases. No one can deny that the human race is in the middle of many diseases. The more medicines that are created, the more people die of diseases. Some of the top killing diseases in the world are heart disease, lower respiratory infections, stroke, lung cancer, COPD, AIDS/HIV, diabetes, tuberculosis, etc. No one can deny that there are more diseases today than ever before, and many of these diseases have mutated. For the modern versions to omit pestilences in Matthew 24:7 is to deny reality. There is no rational reason for it to be omitted in Matthew 24:7 since it has sufficient manuscript evidence.

Matthew 24:36

But of that day and hour knoweth no man, no,
not the angels of heaven, but my Father only.
(Matthew 24:36, KJV)

"Neither or nor the Son" is added to the English text.

Matthew 24:36 in the modern versions is in violation of Revelation 22:18. "For I testify unto every man that heareth the words of the prophecy of this book, If any man shall add unto these things, God shall add unto him the plagues that are written in this book" (Revelation 22:18, KJV). In this week's verse, we have an addition to the text. Apparently, whoever made this addition was trying to match the verse with Mark 13:32. "But of that day and that hour knoweth no man, no, not the angels which are in heaven, neither the Son, but the Father" (Mark 13:32, KJV). Nevertheless, it was not part of Matthew 24:36 and therefore is a violation of scripture by addition.

Matthew 24:42

Watch therefore: for ye know not what *hour* your
Lord doth come. (Matthew 24:42, KJV)

Hour is changed to "day."

The Lord Jesus is going to return at a very specific time, and obviously it will be a day. Here, the Lord Jesus Christ is narrowing the time frame by stating "hour" instead of "day." This would cause Christians to be ready every hour of the day and not just in a generic time period of twenty-four hours. The word *hour* also fits the context of the portion of scripture. Verses 40 and 41 speak about people working, which would be in hours and not days. In verse 43, Jesus speaks about the "watch" in which there were four watches in the night. Verse 44 speaks about being ready in an "hour" when ye think not the Son of man cometh. The hour means that both the believer and the unbeliever will not have any advance warning beyond "be ready" when the Lord will return. "But the day of the Lord will come as a thief in the night; in the which the heavens shall pass away with a great noise, and the elements shall melt with fervent heat, the earth also and the works that are therein shall be burned up" (2 Peter 3:10, KJV). Once again, the modern versions break context and distort the flow of truth.

Matthew 25:6

> And at midnight there was a cry made, Behold,
> the bridegroom *cometh*; go ye out to meet him.
> (Matthew 25:6, KJV)

Cometh is omitted.

This verse lies right in the middle of a discourse on the return of Christ. It is pointing to the fact that the bridegroom (Christ) is coming for his prepared virgins (the redeemed). The word *cometh* signifies the fact that Christ is keeping His promise of returning for His children. "And if I go and prepare a place for you, I will come again, and receive you unto myself; that where I am, there ye may be also" (John 14:3, KJV). The modern versions omit it, making it like it is the Christian's responsibility to go to meet Christ instead of the other way around.

Matthew 25:13

Watch therefore, for ye know neither the day
nor the hour *wherein the Son of man cometh.*
(Matthew 25:13, KJV)

"Wherein the Son of man cometh" is omitted.

This verse is teaching us that we need to watch, to be vigilant in our Christian walk because we do not know when the Lord is going to return; plus, He does not want us slacking off. This is why we are given this warning. The modern versions omit the most important part of this verse, which is the reason we are to be watching. The modern versions just tell us that we don't know the day nor the hour. Day or the hour for what? Our favorite TV program? Suppertime? Without the omitted part, this verse really makes no sense. The King James Bible warns us to be on the alert and not to slack off in our Christian walk because we do not know when the Lord Jesus Christ is going to return. Christians must remain watchful in these last days. The modern versions warn us of nothing and keep their readers guessing.

Matthew 25:31

When the Son of man shall come in his glory, and
all the *holy* angels with him, then shall he sit upon
the throne of his glory. (Matthew 25:31, KJV)

Holy is omitted.

Here is one of the verses that make a distinction between the holy angels of God and the evil angels who followed Satan. The passage teaches that when the Lord Jesus Christ returns to earth, He is going to come with the holy angels from heaven. When the modern versions remove the word *holy*, it removes the distinction as to which angels will be accompanying the Lord Jesus Christ on His return. It seems the modern versions want to combine all the angels, both holy and evil, into one crowd, as if there is a possible chance that the unholy angels can be saved. Those angels who followed Satan in the rebellion became devils and are already sentenced to eternal damnation with Satan. "Know ye not that we shall judge angels? how much more things that pertain to this life?" (1 Corinthians 6:3, KJV).

Whatever part the believer plays in the judgment of angels, the outcome will be the same. Mark 8:38 and Luke 9:26 also speak of the "holy angels," but this is the only one of the three verses where *holy* is omitted. This is typical of the modern versions. They mutilate one verse, and a similar verse they leave alone for the present.

Matthew 25:44

> Then shall they also answer *him*, saying, Lord, when saw we thee an hungred, or athirst, or a stranger, or naked, or sick, or in prison, and did not minister unto thee? (Matthew 25:44, KJV)

Him is omitted.

Here is the section of scripture where the Lord has all the believers and unbelievers before Him, and He contrasts them by stating that the believers had ministered to people while on earth. Then He comes to the unbelievers in verses 42 and 43, telling them that they did no ministry, and as a result, their lack of works shows their true spiritual condition, which results in them being sentenced to an eternity in hell.

In verse 44, the pronoun *him* is used to denote a response to the Lord Himself, who makes the statement to the unbelievers. That word *him* shows that there is going to be a direct judgment with many questions. Those responses the unbelievers give are directly in response to the Lord's queries. When the modern versions omit *him*, they have no source for the questions, and in essence, they are denying the personal judgment of the unbelievers by the Lord Himself. "For the Father judgeth no man, but hath committed all judgment unto the Son" (John 5:22, KJV). I am definitely sure that the unbelievers who corrupted this verse would love nothing more than to omit the reality that there is a coming personal judgment of all unbelievers.

Matthew 26:3

Then assembled together the chief priests, *and the scribes*, and the elders of the people, unto the palace of the high priest, who was called Caiaphas. (Matthew 26:3, KJV)

"And the scribes" is omitted.

The storm clouds are gathering as the Sanhedrin has met to try and see if they might seize Jesus and kill Him. The Sanhedrin consisted of Pharisees, Sadducees, and scribes. The scribes were those who kept the written journals of the meetings. It might be that the scribes were left out of this passage to make it a meeting that never took place since the scribes were not there to keep a record of it. The scribes were members of the Sanhedrin as well as the others. There is no reason to omit them from the meeting.

The scribes also were responsible for interpretation of the law and teaching of it. Where there was no specific law concerning something, they sat down and studied and came up with a near law. This is how basically the tradition of the elders was born, and by the time of Christ, it was considered equal authority with the law of God. There is no legitimate reason for the scribes to be omitted from this passage since they were as guilty of plotting against Christ as the rest of the leaders of Israel.

Matthew 26:28

For this is my blood of the *new* testament, which is shed for many for the remission of sins. (Matthew 26:28, KJV)

New is omitted.

"And Moses took the blood, and sprinkled it on the people, and said, Behold the blood of the covenant, which the Lord hath made with you concerning all these words" (Exodus 24:8, KJV). When the modern versions leave out the word *new*, the verse can be misconstrued to mean a continuation of the covenant of Sinai, which we read here in Exodus 24:8. The Lord Jesus Christ went to the cross and instituted the *new* covenant or testament. It was totally different than the Old Testament. "Behold, the days come, saith the Lord, that I will make a new covenant with the house of Israel, and with the house of Judah" (Jeremiah 31:31, KJV).

The new covenant was a fulfillment of numerous Old Testament passages of scripture such as Jeremiah 31:31. When the modern versions omit *new*, it leaves grace out of the equation. The new covenant is the only way a person can become saved because under the law of the Old Testament, it was called a curse since no one could ever keep the law for salvation. "For as many as are of the works of the law are under the curse: for it is written, Cursed is every one that continueth not in all things which are written in the book of the law to do them" (Galatians 3:10, KJV).

Jesus was the new Passover lamb that was foreshadowed under the old covenant by the lambs that were sacrificed on the altar in the tabernacle and temple. "And to Jesus the mediator of the new covenant, and to the blood of sprinkling, that speaketh better things than that of Abel" (Hebrews 12:24, KJV). Jesus was the mediator of *the new* covenant, not just *a* covenant. There needs to be a specific rendering so a difference between the old and new can be recognized. Once again, the modern versions bring nothing but confusion and wrong teachings. It is better to stay with the King James Bible and avoid these confusion traps.

Matthew 26:42

> He went away again the second time, and prayed, saying, O my Father, if this *cup* may not pass away *from me*, except I drink it, thy will be done. (Matthew 26:42, KJV)

"*Cup*" and "*from me*" are omitted.

This verse received the Gnostic ax twice. The first one was the removal of the word *cup*. "But Jesus said unto them, Ye know not what ye ask: can ye drink of the cup that I drink of? and be baptized with the baptism that I am baptized with?" (Mark 10:38, KJV). Jesus likened His coming payment for sins as a cup that He must drink. "Then said Jesus unto Peter, Put up thy sword into the sheath: the cup which my Father hath given me, shall I not drink it?" (John 18:11, KJV). To drink something means the entire body is permeated with it. To drink freshwater is to refresh the entire body; to drink poison would be to kill the entire body. The coming crucifixion, death, and resurrection of Christ would engulf His entire body, soul, and spirit. It was a total sacrifice for the sins of His people.

Then the next ax was the fact that Christ was paying for the sins Himself. The modern versions omit "from me," which teaches us that Christ was taking on all the sins of those He came to save. "Who being the brightness of his glory, and the express image of his person, and upholding all things by the word of his power, when he had by himself purged our sins, sat down on the right hand of the Majesty on high" (Hebrews 1:3, KJV). Christ alone took our sins on the cross, and the King James Bible tells us that here while the modern versions omit it.

Matthew 26:59

Now the chief priests, *and elders*, and all the council, sought false witness against Jesus, to put him to death. (Matthew 26:59, KJV)

"And elders" is omitted.

The phrase that is omitted in the modern versions, "the elders," speaks of the three groups of the Sanhedrin who were the highest Jewish legal authorities. Jesus had to appear before the entire Sanhedrin who at this time had assembled themselves in the house of Caiaphas. All the religious leaders had a hand in the trial of Jesus, especially the Sanhedrin, who had pronounced a sentence of death upon Him. The modern versions may have left them out here, but they will not be left out at the great white throne of judgment.

Matthew 26:60

> But found none: yea, though many false witnesses came, *yet found they none*. At the last came two *false witnesses*. (Matthew 26:60, KJV)

"Yet found they none" is omitted, and "false witnesses" is omitted.

In the sham trial of the Lord Jesus Christ, the chief priests, elders, and council had sought to find false witnesses against Jesus. Their chief aim was to find something bad enough to have Him executed because, if you remember, the leaders feared that Rome would come and take their country and remove them from their lofty positions. As we read in the King James Bible, the verse directly speaks to the fact that they failed to find anything against the Lord Jesus worthy of capital punishment. Though they had found many false witnesses, their stories did not corroborate and therefore were dismissed.

Then later, two false witnesses had arrived, and one of them spoke, saying that Jesus was going to destroy the temple of God and rebuild it in three days. Of course, the false witnesses had heard these words, but they did not understand them. Jesus spoke of the temple of His body. It was required in the law that there be two witnesses to accuse someone. "At the mouth of two witnesses, or three witnesses, shall he that is worthy of death be put to death; but at the mouth of one witness he shall not be put to death" (Deuteronomy 17:6, KJV). The modern versions leave out the fact that the false witnesses had failed to corroborate their stories. Then they leave out the fact that the last two who appeared were false witnesses. Once again, the King James Bible shows its superiority in giving us the true account of the Lord's accusers.

Matthew 27:2

> And when they had bound him, they led him away, and delivered him to *Pontius* Pilate the governor. (Matthew 27:2, KJV)

Pontius is omitted.

Here is another one of those name-cutting verses. They omit *Pontius*, which is the first name of the governor. There is no logical reason for this name to be omitted.

Matthew 27:4

Saying, I have sinned in that I have betrayed *the* innocent blood. And they said, What is that to us? see thou to that. (Matthew 27:4, KJV)

The *the* before "innocent blood" is omitted.
This verse has been attacked from two ways:

1) In the Greek, the word *athoon* means "innocent." In the Hort-Westcott Critical Text, the word was changed to *dikaion*, which means "righteous." The modern versions continue to translate this word as "innocent," which tells me they follow the text when it makes their case. If they were to translate *dikaion* properly, it would say "righteous" in the text. The only one who translates it "righteous" is the Jehovah's Witness Bible. Even though the Greek text has been changed, the translators left the word *innocent* in the English text. What they did was use the wrong English word for the wrong Greek word. This means they interpreted instead of translating it. This is what makes the modern versions dangerous because not only is the text corrupt, the translators have created further corruptions by mistranslating the words that are there. This leads, of course, to a false translation, but it also puts the reader at the mercy of the bias of the translator.

2) The second way this verse was attacked was by omission of an English word. In Greek, the word *hoi* means "the." It is a definite article that points to something specific. In this case, in this verse, it is pointing to the innocent blood of the Lord Jesus Christ. This is why it states "the innocent blood" and not just a generic "innocent blood."

Throughout the ages, innocent people have been betrayed and put to death. This would make the generic "innocent blood" applicable.

However, when we deal with a definite article, *the* is pointing to only one person who had true innocent blood, and that was the Lord Jesus Christ. His was the ultimate innocent blood in that it was never infected by original sin of Adam's fall. When they leave out *the*, this places Jesus on a level with all the other innocent people of Adam's fallen race (not innocent before God). This is why *the* is so important and needs to be there in the English text because it places the Lord Jesus Christ as unique and on a level above the rest of the human race. This omission of *the* in the English text was intentional because *hoi* is in both the Hort-Westcott Critical Text and the Textus Receptus Traditional Text. This shows another very subtle but hostile attack on the Lord Jesus Christ by making Him a martyr on the level of created human beings. *The* innocent blood was shed for those He came to save.

Matthew 27:16

And they had then a notable prisoner, called Barabbas. (Matthew 27:16, KJV)

Jesus is added to both the Greek text and English. It is placed before the name *Barabbas*.

Based upon a few corrupted manuscripts, some of the modern versions claim that the first name of Barabbas is Jesus. This may be because the name *Barabbas* means "son of the father," so they erroneously associated it with the Lord Jesus Christ. There is no evidence given that the first name of Barabbas was Jesus. This was a corruption and was added by some manuscripts corrupter in antiquity. The earliest manuscript it is found in is seventh century while the Byzantine text predates it by 250 years, which means it was added between the fifth and seventh centuries. Even the corrupt Alexandrinus from the fifth century does not have that addition in it. The name *Barabbas* is mentioned ten times, and only here in Matthew 27:16 and 17 is the name *Jesus* applied. Barabbas is also mentioned in Mark, Luke, and John with no reference to the name *Jesus*.

Matthew 27:24

When Pilate saw that he could prevail nothing, but that rather a tumult was made, he took water, and washed his hands before the multitude, saying, I am innocent of the blood of this *just* person: see ye to it. (Matthew 27:24, KJV)

Just is omitted.

At the trial of the Lord Jesus Christ, Pilate had done everything he could to release Jesus because he knew that Jesus had done nothing wrong to warrant execution. So finally, after some time, Pilate finally acquiesced to the crowd and then washed his hands off the situation. However, Pilate made the statement that Jesus was a just or righteous person. The modern versions have omitted this revelation by Pilate. Even Pilate knew that Jesus was a just man and not deserving of the treatment he received by the people. It seems even Pilate had more insight than the modern-version editors and translators.

Matthew 27:34

They gave him *vinegar* to drink mingled with gall: and when he had tasted thereof, he would not drink. (Matthew 27:34, KJV)

Vinegar is changed to "wine."

The word for vinegar in the Greek is *oxos*, which is translated seven times in the Gospels only as "vinegar." The modern versions change the word to *oinos*, which means "wine," something totally different. The vinegar would have made the Lord Jesus Christ thirstier, thus increasing his sufferings. Wine would have acted like a painkiller, and the Romans were not humane in that way. If you went into a restaurant and ordered a glass of grape wine and they brought you vinegar instead, you would definitely know the difference between *oxos* and *oinos*. Once again, the King James shows its superiority in telling the whole story.

Matthew 27:35

And they crucified him, and parted his garments, casting lots: *that it might be fulfilled which was spoken by the prophet, They parted my garments among them, and upon my vesture did they cast lots.* (Matthew 27:35, KJV)

"That it might be fulfilled which was spoken by the prophet, they parted my garments among them, and upon my vesture did they cast lots" is omitted.

Matthew 27:35 is a fulfillment of the prophecy of Psalm 22:18. "They part my garments among them, and cast lots upon my vesture" (Psalm 22:18, KJV). By removing the twenty words in the Greek, which in turn deletes the twenty-five English words, it denies the literal fulfillment of the prophecy of Psalm 22 at the crucifixion of Christ. By removing the fulfilling part of the verse, they are, in essence, trying to convey to us that the Bible is not a prophetic book and is incapable of being fulfilled. The crucifixion of Christ had fulfilled about three hundred prophecies in one day. When any of these are attacked by elimination, the verity of the event is truncated, and then the rest of the prophecies are open for attack.

Where does it end? If biblical prophecies are questioned and eliminated, then that begins to chip away at the supernatural character of the Bible. The second-century Gnostics and the modern theologians have attempted to make the Bible just another secular religious book akin to the book of Mormon or the Vedic writings. One of the greatest hopes the Christian has is to read the many prophecies that have come to pass, which piles hope upon hope for future prophecies to be fulfilled. When the unbelieving theologians and publishers remove passages like this, they also make God out to be a liar in that He has not fulfilled the prophecies of scripture. The modern versions remove hope from the pages of holy writ, but the King James Bible retains it. Which would you rather have in your time of need? A counterfeit version or the preserved word of God?

Matthew 27:42

> He saved others; himself he cannot save. *If* he be the King of Israel, let him now come down from the cross, and we will *believe him*. (Matthew 27:42, KJV)

"If" and *"believe him"* are omitted.

This verse has been corrupted in two places. The first place is where the modern versions omit the word *if*, turning the question into a declarative statement. "Then said the chief priests of the Jews to Pilate, Write not, The King of the Jews; but that he said, I am King of the Jews" (John 19:21, KJV). The Jews did not see Jesus as the king of the Jews, and for those at the cross to make a declaration that He was king of the Jews does not fit the context of this verse nor the mind-set of those who had Him crucified.

Then the second place where there is corruption is where the modern versions change *him* into "in him." This verse is not a question of salvation, but it is a question of, "if Jesus comes down from the cross, then we will believe Him that He is the Son of God." The modern versions turn this into a works salvation, that if Jesus does a miracle by coming down from the cross and saving Himself, then those who are present will claim to be saved by believing in Him. No one is saved in that manner, and those at the crucifixion did not have salvation on their mind; it was the last thing they would have thought of.

Matthew 27:54

> Now when the centurion, and they that were with him, watching Jesus, saw the earthquake, and those things that were done, they feared

greatly, saying, Truly this was *the* Son of God.
(Matthew 27:54, KJV)

The *the* before "Son of God" is attacked in the footnotes of the 1881 RV, 1901 ASV, ESV, LB, NASV, NRSV, RSV.

Both the Traditional and Critical Text agree on this verse. However, in the following manuscripts, two words are reversed, causing the footnotes of these versions to state "a son."

B 03, Vaticanus (fourth century)
D 05, Bezae Cantabrigiensis (fifth century)
33, Minuscule (ninth Century)

In the regular text, the term "the son of God" is written as following θεου υιος, but in these three manuscripts, the words are reversed υιος θεου. These seven modern versions follow the three manuscripts. B 03 and D 05 are known to be two of the most corrupt extant manuscripts, and yet they were followed by those seven versions. This is why it is so important that Christians know exactly what they are using in their spiritual walk.

Matthew 27:64

Command therefore that the sepulchre be made sure until the third day, lest his disciples come *by night*, and steal him away, and say unto the people, He is risen from the dead: so the last error shall be worse than the first. (Matthew 27:64, KJV)

"By night" is omitted.
One of the fears that the Pharisees had was that the disciples would come by night and steal away the body of Jesus and then claim He was resurrected. They remembered the resurrection of Lazarus, and unlike the Sadducees, they believed in a future resurrection. This is why they went to Pilate and asked for a guard. They knew that His disciples would not come by day because there would be too many

who would see them; plus, they were all in hiding for fear of the Jews. "Then the same day at evening, being the first day of the week, when the doors were shut where the disciples were assembled for fear of the Jews, came Jesus and stood in the midst, and saith unto them, Peace be unto you" (John 20:19, KJV). This is why the night would have been a better time if they could have overtaken the guards. There is no reason why the words *by night* should have been removed.

Matthew 28:2

And, behold, there was a great earthquake: for the angel of the Lord descended from heaven, and came and rolled back the stone *from the door*, and sat upon it. (Matthew 28:2, KJV)

"From the door" is omitted.

Here, we have the narrative of the women going to the tomb to finalize the proper burial custom for the body of the Lord Jesus Christ. However, when they arrived at the tomb, they were about to experience a life-changing event. The Lord Jesus Christ had already arisen. When the women arrived at the tomb, there had been a great earthquake, and an angel of the Lord had descended from heaven and rolled the stone away from the door of the tomb.

The tomb was not opened so the Lord Jesus could come out; the tomb was opened so the people could go in to see for themselves that the Lord Jesus Christ had arisen from the dead, and the angel was there to confirm that fact to the women. Just as the tomb could not hold the Lord Jesus Christ, so it will be that those who died in Christ throughout history will not be hindered from their resurrection by any situation, whether it is disintegration of their body or being buried in a grave. Death has no power, and resurrection has no hindrance for those given eternal life by the Lord Jesus Christ.

Now, back to the verse above, God included the phrase "from the door" in the text of the Greek. It is obvious from the context that it is referring to the stone that sealed the tomb. It is important to realize that context never supersedes text. If God has written it in the text of the Greek, it is not to be omitted and left up to context to figure out what is in view. That would be tantamount to *assumptive hermeneutics*. We are never to leave to assumption what God has given in clarity of text. However, the modern versions cause their adherents to consistently use assumptive hermeneutics, and this method has resulted in the massive amounts of false teachings that began to prevail in the churches ever since Satan began publishing the counterfeit versions of the Bible.

"And, behold, I send the promise of my Father upon you: but tarry ye in the city of Jerusalem, until ye be endued with power from on high. And he led them out as far as to Bethany, and he lifted up his hands, and blessed them" (Luke 24:49–50, KJV). Luke 24:49 is another mutilated verse whereby the modern versions left out the words "of Jerusalem." When we look at verse 50, we see that the Lord led them as far as Bethany where He ascended into heaven. Now, Bethany was about two to three miles to the east of Jerusalem, so if we leave out the term "of Jerusalem" and invoke assumptive hermeneutics, then we could come to the conclusion that the Lord wanted them to remain in Bethany since that was where they were at the time.

Luke 24:49–50 (ASV)

> And behold, I send forth the promise of my Father upon you: but tarry ye in the city, until ye be clothed with power from on high. And he led them out until they were over against Bethany: and he lifted up his hands, and blessed them.

Luke 24:49–50 (NIV)

> "I am going to send you what my Father has promised; but stay in the city until you have been clothed with power from high." When he had led them out to the vicinity of Bethany, he lifted up his hands and blessed them.

I would caution anyone who uses a modern version that when you must assume something when the King James gives a specific word about something, abandon that modern version. If anyone thinks specifics are unimportant, they need to read again the guidelines that God gave for the building of the tabernacle, temple, and ark of the covenant, never mind the specific ways in which the priests were to prepare and offer sacrifices. Just as Nadab and Abihu (Leviticus 10) offered strange fire before the Lord, so likewise the modern versions are also offering strange fire before the Lord.

> In those days *there was* no king in Israel: every
> man did *that which was* right in his own eyes.
> (Judges 21:25, KJV)

Let me paraphrase the above verse concerning the modern versions. "Everyone read what was right in their own minds." Stay with the King James Bible, and God will not leave you wondering and wandering as these modern versions do.

Matthew 28:6

> He is not here: for he is risen, as he said. Come, see
> the place where *the Lord* lay. (Matthew 28:6, KJV)

"The Lord" is omitted and changed to "he" or "him."

Here is another case of an attack on the Lord Jesus Christ at the time of His resurrection. The Gnostics could not deny the resurrection, but they could deny specifically who was raised from that tomb. The Bible specifically states "the Lord," but the modern versions turn a noun into a pronoun, making it an undefined person. If God deals in specifics, it must remain specific.

Matthew 28:9

> *And as they went to tell his disciples*, behold, Jesus
> met them, saying, All hail. And they came and

held him by the feet, and worshipped him.
(Matthew 28:9, KJV)

"And as they went to tell his disciples" is omitted.

When the Lord Jesus Christ had risen from the dead, the women who went to anoint His body for proper burial met an angel at the tomb who told them that He was risen from the dead. They then received instruction to go and tell His disciples, and verse 9 states that they were following the instructions they received and were proceeding to go and tell the disciples. Then Jesus met them while they were going and told the women exactly where He would meet with the disciples: in Galilee. By removing these eight words, the modern versions eliminate the obedience of the women to go and tell his disciples.

The great principle of obedience is shown in these eight words, just as Paul obeyed the same type of heavenly command.

> Whereupon, O king Agrippa, I was not disobedient unto the heavenly vision: But showed first unto them of Damascus, and at Jerusalem, and throughout all the coasts of Judaea, and then to the Gentiles, that they should repent and turn to God, and do works meet for repentance. (Acts 26:19–20, KJV)

The true believers are to be obedient to the heavenly directives that we receive. Paul received it in a vision, and the women at the tomb received it by means of an angel. We receive our heavenly directive from the word of God. When the modern versions continue to chop away at the great teachings in scripture, they cause Christians to be disobedient to the heavenly directives in scripture. However, Christians who use these modern versions are creating their own disobedience by not investigating the source of the versions they are using. Every true Christian has a message of hope to bring to the world, and that message is the resurrection of Christ. Let us not neglect the urgency of going and telling, but let us go and tell with the proper tool, the King James Bible, the true word of God.

Matthew 28:20

Teaching them to observe all things whatsoever I have commanded you: and, lo, I am with you alway, even unto the end of the world. *Amen.* (Matthew 28:20, KJV)

Amen is omitted.

The word *amen* is very familiar to the Christian because we end our prayers with it. The word means "truly, surely, so let it be, indeed." It is also at the end of all four Gospels, which means God is giving each Gospel His commendation that each one is truth. The word in the Greek for *amen* is also used many times in the Gospels as "verily." "Jesus answered and said unto him, *Verily, verily*, I say unto thee, Except a man be born again, he cannot see the kingdom of God" (John 3:3, KJV).

We understand *verily* to mean "in truth, in fact, or certainty." It is also a word of affirmation. So the word *amen* at the end of the Gospel of Matthew is also an important word because it is stating that the Gospel of Matthew is ending at verse 20, and the contents of it are true, factual, and certain. The modern versions omit *amen* at the end, thus taking away God's affirmation of the Gospel. In fact, the modern versions omit it from Mark 16:20, Luke 24:53, and John 21:25. I guess the modern versions have a low opinion of the four Gospels.

Mark 1:2

As it is written in the *prophets*, Behold, I send my messenger before thy face, which shall prepare thy way before thee. The voice of one crying in the wilderness, Prepare ye the way of the Lord, make his paths straight. (Mark 1:2–3, KJV)

"The prophets" is changed to "Isaiah the prophet."

The words in the Greek for "the prophets" have been changed to "Isaiah the prophet." The verse in question is not a quotation from a single prophet but is a quotation from two prophets. This is why the King James uses the plural *the prophets*. It is a combined quotation from Malachi in verse 2 and Isaiah in verse 3.

> Behold, I will send my messenger, and he shall prepare the way before me: and the Lord, whom ye seek, shall suddenly come to his temple, even the messenger of the covenant, whom ye delight in: behold, he shall come, saith the LORD of hosts. (Malachi 3:1, KJV)

> The voice of him that crieth in the wilderness, Prepare ye the way of the LORD, make straight in the desert a highway for our God. (Isaiah 40:3, KJV)

> [*Malachi*] As it is written in the prophets, Behold, I send my messenger before thy face, which shall prepare thy way before thee. [*Isaiah*] The voice of one crying in the wilderness, Prepare ye the way of the Lord, make his paths straight. (Mark 1:2–3, KJV)

Isn't it amazing that none of those who translated the modern versions knew the difference between a quote from Malachi and a quote from Isaiah? This is just another subtle deception found in the modern versions. The interesting thing is that they never correct any of these errors. Instead, they just perpetuate them, and then in the prefaces of these modern versions, they proclaim how inaccurate the King James Bible is. In the opening statement of the preface in the seventh paragraph in the Revised Standard Version, it states this: "Yet the King James Version has grave defects." If you look above, you will see the RSV is one of those that claim the Mark 1:2 quote is from Isaiah. Sounds to me like the RSV is the one that has the grave defects. Once again, the King James Bible shows its superiority by giving the proper translation to Mark 1:2.

Mark 1:14

> Now after that John was put in prison, Jesus came into Galilee, preaching the gospel *of the kingdom of God*. (Mark 1:14, KJV)

"Of the kingdom" is omitted.

"And saying, The time is fulfilled, and the kingdom of God is at hand: repent ye, and believe the gospel" (Mark 1:15, KJV). Verse 14 removes a very important phrase: "of the kingdom." In Mark 1:15, the verse teaches that the kingdom of God is at hand; in other words, it had come, not in the future but now. The Lord Jesus Christ was the entrance to the kingdom of God, and that was a major teaching point of John the Baptist. It is the teaching of the kingdom of God that sets Christianity apart from the world's religions. If verse 14 is left as is in the modern versions, then it opens the door for the belief that false religions can speak truth about God.

In every religion in the world, the name *God* is used throughout. It is the name of Jesus that is anathema to world religions. The Hindu believes that they can teach about God. The Buddhist believes they can teach about God. The Roman Catholic believes they can teach about God. The New Ager believes they can teach about God. Of course, in the New Age, man is considered divine and called God. Judaism believes they can teach about God.

Many world religions think they can teach about God, but the reality is that not one of them know God because one comes to know God only through the Lord Jesus Christ, and world religions reject Him and even attempt to reject His divinity, thus bringing him down to a human level. The kingdom of God is totally associated with Christ, and those in Christ who have become saved through Him are in the kingdom of God. "For the kingdom of God is not meat and drink; but righteousness, and peace, and joy in the Holy Ghost" (Romans 14:17, KJV).

The kingdom of God is not of the physical realm but is only for those who have the Holy Spirit, and those are the saved ones whom the Holy Spirit indwells eternally in salvation. The modern versions leave the door open for false religions to claim God, but the reality is that only those who are in Christ are in the kingdom of God.

Mark 1:31

And he came and took her by the hand, and lifted her up; and *immediately* the fever left her, and she ministered unto them. (Mark 1:31, KJV)

Immediately is omitted.

This verse not only teaches that Jesus healed the sick when He was here on earth, but a verse like this has a parallel meaning. When the Lord Jesus Christ healed the sick, it typified what happened when He saves a person.

But he was wounded for our transgressions, he was bruised for our iniquities: the chastisement of our peace was upon him; and with his stripes we are healed. (Isaiah 53:5, KJV)

Who his own self bare our sins in his own body on the tree, that we, being dead to sins, should live unto righteousness: by whose stripes ye were healed. (1 Peter 2:24, KJV)

Both of these verses state that we are healed by his stripes; that is, we are healed from the sickness of sin. These verses in no way teach that we are healed from physical sickness, although if it is according to God's will, He does heal, and He even heals the unbelievers. If these verses taught that physical healing is part of the atonement, then why do churches have cemeteries? The charismatic churches teach healing as part of the atonement, and if that is true, then why do most of the charismatic preachers wear glasses and their churches have cemeteries? They should be able to heal their eyes so they will not need glasses and heal their people so they will not die. Of course, their next comment is that people are sick and die because they do not have enough faith.

> And, behold, they brought to him a man sick of the palsy, lying on a bed: and Jesus seeing their faith said unto the sick of the palsy; Son, be of good cheer; thy sins be forgiven thee. (Matthew 9:2, KJV)

> When Jesus saw their faith, he said unto the sick of the palsy, Son, thy sins be forgiven thee. (Mark 2:5, KJV)

Matthew 9:2 speaks about some friends who bought a man who had the palsy for Jesus to heal him. Mark 2:5 speaks about four friends who disassembled a roof to let down their friend so Jesus would heal him. Both of these verses have a common thread running through them. In both instances, Jesus did not speak of the faith of the one who was sick, but He responded to the faith of the people who brought them to Him. So it was not the faith of the sick people but of their friends that moved Jesus to heal them. Maybe there isn't enough faith in these charismatic congregations to heal their own sick, and that is why they need glasses and cemeteries.

I threw that in for free, so let us go back to Mark 1:31. The keyword omitted in this verse is *immediate*, and that is important. When Jesus healed Peter's mother-in-law, she was healed immediately. There was no process or time lapse between Jesus lifting her and her healing. This gives us an important lesson concerning salvation. The moment a person becomes saved, they are totally saved with the indwelling Holy Spirit. Salvation is immediate, just as the healing of Peter's mother-in-law. This is why when the word *immediate* is omitted, anyone can claim there is a time lapse between a person being called and being saved. Instantly, our sins are forgiven, and we are then in the kingdom of God; and like Peter's mother-in-law, we can

113

begin serving the Lord Jesus Christ. We need not wait many years to start serving because *immediately* we become saved, and then we can start working in the kingdom. How nice the King James maintains the parallel picture of a person's salvation.

Mark 1:41

> And Jesus, *moved with compassion*, put forth his hand, and touched him, and saith unto him, I will; be thou clean. (Mark 1:41, KJV)

"Moved with compassion" is omitted in the CEB, ERV, LEB, NIRV, NIV.

The word *splanchnistheis* in the Greek is translated "compassion" all twelve times it is used in the New Testament. It carries with it the meaning of "have compassion, feel sympathy, or have mercy." I remember when the 1984 NIV was being revised in 2011 by Biblica (formerly International Bible Society) and the president and CEO of Biblica made the following statement: "And we'll make sure we get it right this time." Here is how bad they still did:

> "Filled with compassion…" (1984 NIV)
> "Jesus was indignant…" (2011 NIV)

After they revised their version, they went from correct to incorrect, so how did they get it right? *They didn't!*

Here are the definitions of the words used by the modern versions above from the 1913 *Webster's*. Quite different than the Greek word in the Textus Receptus.

> *Indignant.* Affected with indignation; wrathful; passionate; irate; feeling wrath, as when a person is exasperated by unworthy or unjust treatment, by a mean action, or by a degrading accusation.

Incensed. Angered; enraged. (2) Represented as enraged, as any wild creature depicted with fire issuing from mouth and eyes.

Once again, the modern versions take a Greek word with a specific meaning and translation throughout the New Testament and apply their own meaning to it. The worst part about it is that the word is translated with a definition that is completely opposite of what the word means. This is why the modern versions are so dangerous because you never know when they have taken a word and translated it wrongly. They do this so they can get a new copyright because to gain a copyright, you must have a certain amount of changes. So they make changes, not even concerning themselves with your spiritual growth.

Mark 1:42

And as soon as he had spoken, immediately the leprosy departed from him, and he was cleansed. (Mark 1:42, KJV)

"And as soon as he had spoken" is omitted.

A leper had come to Jesus to be healed, and Jesus was willing to heal him. He had commanded him to stretch out his hand, and then Jesus touched his hand and said, "Be thou clean," so immediately the leprosy had left him. The modern versions omit the fact that Jesus spoke this disease out of the leper just as Jesus spoke the creation into existence. The modern versions remove the fact that Jesus has the ability to command a disease to leave a body. These healings are also pictures of salvation. When Jesus saves a person, it is not a long-drawn-out affair such as progressive salvation, but it is instantaneous. When Jesus saves a person, they are saved from the moment that He declares them saved. The modern versions omit a great lesson on salvation; plus, they attack the words of the Lord Jesus in that as soon as He commands, whatever He commands, obeys.

Mark 2:2

And *straightway* many were gathered together, insomuch that there was no room to receive them, no, not so much as about the door: and he preached the word unto them. (Mark 2:2, KJV)

Straightway is omitted.

Jesus had come back to Capernaum, and as soon as the word was published, a crowd gathered immediately at the house where He was teaching. This shows how spiritually hungry the people were and leads to a great faith lesson in that they wasted no time in getting to the house where Jesus was. This means that the people were anxious to see Jesus. The modern versions omit this word *straightway*, which means "immediately." The way the modern versions put this incident, you could suppose the crowd took several hours or even days to gather at the house. ("For he saith, I have heard thee in a time accepted, and in the day of salvation have I succoured thee: behold, now is the accepted time; behold, now is the day of salvation" [2 Corinthians 6:2 KJV].) Now is the time of salvation, not later.

Mark 2:15

And it came to pass, that, as *Jesus* sat at meat in his house, many publicans and sinners sat also together with Jesus and his disciples: for there were many, and they followed him. (Mark 2:15, KJV)

Jesus is changed to "he."

Here is another attack upon the name of the Lord Jesus Christ by changing a proper name to a pronoun.

Mark 2:17

When Jesus heard it, he saith unto them, They that are whole have no need of the physician, but

they that are sick: I came not to call the righteous,
but sinners *to repentance*. (Mark 2:17, KJV)

"To repentance" is omitted.

The Lord Jesus Christ came to earth for the purpose of saving
His elect. In this verse, we are being told that He came to call the
sinners to repentance. The term *repentance* is a synonym for *salvation.* "In meekness instructing those that oppose themselves; if God
peradventure will give them repentance to the acknowledging of the
truth" (2 Timothy 2:25, KJV). God is the one who takes a sinner
and makes them into a saint. The modern versions omit the reason
that Christ came, which is to call sinners "to repentance." Without
those words being there, this call could be construed as Jesus calling
the sinners to the supper He was attending. Those who are healthy
do not need a physician but only those who are sick. In like manner,
those who are sinners need to be saved, and that was the purpose of
Christ's coming to earth. He came to save His people from their sins,
as Matthew 1:21 proclaims.

Obviously, the Gnostics did not believe that Christ was God
and that he had no power or authority to call someone to repentance,
so they omitted those words. And just like good clones, the modern
theologians have maintained the omission, which would make them
suspect of their own salvation if they do not believe that Jesus can
save. Let us stay with the King James Bible and avoid the personal
pitfalls of the modern theologians.

Mark 3:5

And when he had looked round about on them
with anger, being grieved for the hardness of their
hearts, he saith unto the man, Stretch forth thine
hand. And he stretched it out: and his hand was
restored *whole as the other*. (Mark 3:5, KJV)

"Whole as the other" is omitted.

This verse shows Jesus as the Creator and Healer. The verse tells us that the hand was restored as whole as the other one. The modern versions leave off the last phrase that his arm was now made whole "as the other," which shows Jesus restoring the arms as not only healing the man but as the Creator who creates the human body. Jesus designed our arms, and here He restores the man's arms as a whole pair. Omitting the last part does not give information concerning the fact that the arms were now healed and equal. A surgeon can restore an arm, but that does not mean it is as good as if it was never injured. By omitting that important part, Jesus is denied the glory as our Creator. There is no reason as to why that phrase has been omitted in the modern versions. It just basically seems like another attack on the Lord Jesus Christ.

Mark 3:15

And to have power *to heal sicknesses, and* to cast out devils. (Mark 3:15, KJV)

"To heal sicknesses, and" is omitted.

Here, we read a verse in which the twelve disciples were chosen by the Lord Jesus Christ for the purpose of preaching the Gospel and to heal sicknesses and exorcise devils from people. "And these signs shall follow them that believe; In my name shall they cast out devils; they shall speak with new tongues" (Mark 16:17, KJV). At this point in the infant ministry of the disciples, Jesus had given them the authority to heal the sick and cast out devils. The purpose of this is not to start a denomination of signs and wonders, but it was to confirm the ministry of the Lord Jesus Christ. "And they went forth, and preached every where, the Lord working with them, and confirming the word with signs following. Amen" (Mark 16:20, KJV).

When John sent his disciples to Jesus to find out if Jesus truly was the Anointed One, Jesus sent back the following answer: "Jesus answered and said unto them, Go and show John again those things which ye do hear and see: The blind receive their sight, and the lame walk, the lepers are cleansed, and the deaf hear, the dead are raised up, and the poor have the gospel preached to them" (Matthew 11:4–5, KJV). We read in these verses that the sick were being healed as a sign that the kingdom of God was now among them. The healing of people was a miracle that represented the difference between one who is laden with the sickness of sin, and after healing, they show what it is like to be saved. "Who his own self bare our sins in his own body on the tree, that we, being dead to sins, should live unto righteousness: by whose stripes ye were healed" (1 Peter 2:24, KJV). By the modern versions omitting the portion of scripture that speaks of the healing of physical disease, they remove a great picture of salvation.

Mark 3:16

And Simon he surnamed Peter. (Mark 3:16, KJV)

"He appointed the Twelve" is added to the English text.

"He appointed the twelve" is not in the traditional Greek text. Here is an addition made to the Greek text as far back as the fourth century in violation of Revelation 22:18. "For I testify unto every man that heareth the words of the prophecy of this book, If any man shall add unto these things, God shall add unto him the plagues that are written in this book" (Revelation 22:18, KJV). Westcott and Hort placed it in the margins of their text, and the modern versions placed it in their text, thus continuing the violation. Can God bless a translation that violates His commands?

Mark 3:29

But he that shall blaspheme against the Holy Ghost hath never forgiveness, but is in danger of eternal *damnation*. (Mark 3:29, KJV)

Damnation changed to "sin."

The Lord Jesus had taught that those who blaspheme the Holy Spirit will never have forgiveness, which means they will be condemned for eternity in hell. The Gnostics had changed the word *damnation* to the word *sin*. Since they did not believe that the Holy Spirit was a truly eternal God, they lowered the penalty for blaspheming Him. This exchange is just another example of how the modern versions disrespect the person of the Holy Spirit. The Lord stated that anyone who blasphemes Him will be subject to eternal damnation, but the modern versions have removed that penalty by exchanging words.

> Wherefore I say unto you, All manner of sin and blasphemy shall be forgiven unto men: but the blasphemy against the Holy Ghost shall not be forgiven unto men. And whosoever speaketh a word against the Son of man, it shall be forgiven him: but whosoever speaketh against the Holy Ghost, it shall not be forgiven him, neither in this world, neither in the world to come. (Matthew 12:31–32, KJV)

> And whosoever shall speak a word against the Son of man, it shall be forgiven him: but unto him that blasphemeth against the Holy Ghost it shall not be forgiven. (Luke 12:10, KJV)

As we can plainly see in the parallel verses, anyone who blasphemes the Holy Spirit will be subject to eternal damnation. The changing of words in the modern versions show us the contempt they have for the teaching of the Lord Jesus Christ. Here is a specific sin with a specific judgment attached to it, and the modern versions reduce the intensity of it by changing the words. It looks like the modern-version editors really care nothing for the souls of their readers. To remove a warning of this caliber is to show contempt for the teachings of Jesus.

Mark 4:4

> And it came to pass, as he sowed, some fell by the way side, and the fowls *of the air* came and devoured it up. (Mark 4:4, KJV)

"Of the air" is omitted.

The fowls of the air represent Satan who steals the truth of the scriptures from those who are hearing it and steals it before there is any understanding. "And these are they by the way side, where the word is sown; but when they have heard, Satan cometh immediately, and taketh away the word that was sown in their hearts" (Mark 4:15, KJV). Satan is called the prince of the power or the air, and as we read in this verse, it is the fowls of the air that steal the word. "Wherein in time past ye walked according to the course of this world, according to the prince of the power of the air, the spirit that now worketh in the children of disobedience" (Ephesians 2:2, KJV). It looks like the reason that phrase was omitted was because it was a direct reference to satanic activity concerning the dissemination of the Gospel.

Mark 4:9

> And he said *unto them*, He that hath ears to hear,
> let him hear. (Mark 4:9, KJV)

"Unto them" is omitted.

Here is another case of another dative personal pronoun that has been omitted. The dative case is the case of the one being addressed, and the Lord is specifically addressing the group on the seashore. The modern versions turn this into a generic address when it is to a specific group. We will see this scenario in Revelation when John is being addressed, and the specifics were turned into a generic statement.

Mark 4:11

> And he said unto them, Unto you it is given *to
> know* the mystery of the kingdom of God: but
> unto them that are without, all these things are
> done in parables. (Mark 4:11, KJV)

"To know" is omitted.

Here is another example of the meaning of a verse being mutilated. The King James states that unto the Christian it is "given them to know" the mysteries of the Kingdom and that would be by means of the indwelling Holy Spirit. The modern versions state that they would be given the mystery of the Kingdom. There is a big difference between being given something and knowing something. For example, someone gives me a radio and then tells me that I will know how the radio operates versus someone just giving me a radio. Once again the inferiority of the modern versions shines through.

Mark 4:24

And he said unto them, Take heed what ye hear: with what measure ye mete, it shall be measured to you: *and unto you that hear* shall more be given. (Mark 4:24, KJV)

"And unto you that hear" is omitted.

The Lord Jesus Christ just finished speaking a parable to a great crowd about sowing the Gospel. He then proceeds to warn them about the fact that everything they have done will be made manifest; that is, will be revealed. No one can hide sin from God. He then warns them that they should take heed as to what they hear, for those who hear the Gospel and reject it are those who will face a greater judgment because they had more light given to them. Then the Lord states that to those who hear will more be given—that is, this group are the saved; and the more they hear the Gospel and study the scriptures, the more they will increase in the faith.

The word *hear* carries with it the meaning of "understanding." The only ones who understand are those who have become saved. This word is in the present tense and active voice, which means the people who are saved will continue to hear, understand, and receive more insight into the Gospel through the indwelling of the Holy Spirit. The modern versions remove the phrase "and unto you that hear," which means the modern versions turn this verse into a judgment-only verse, but that is incorrect. Jesus is speaking to a large crowd, and within that crowd will be those who become saved, so He is including them concerning their growth in the Gospel because of their hunger for God's word. "If any man have ears to hear, let him hear" (Mark 4:23, KJV). Verse 23 speaks about those who have ears to hear, and that is not speaking of physical ears but spiritual ears of the saved, as He continues the thought in verse 24.

Mark 5:6

But when he saw Jesus afar off, he ran and *worshipped* him. (Mark 5:6, KJV)

Worship is changed to "fell, bow, or knelt."

The word in question is the word *proskuneo*. The word is used sixty times in the New Testament with various inflections (twenty-four in the book of Revelation alone) and is always translated "worship" or "worshipped" in the King James Bible. The modern-version translators, with their incessant desire to lower the status of the Lord Jesus Christ to that of just a mere human leader, have taken that word and lessened the meaning of it. The healing of the Gadarene demoniac is very important because the demons that indwelled the man knew who the Lord Jesus was because they were in heaven with Him before the rebellion of Satan and knew that the Lord Jesus Christ is God.

In Mark 5:7, the devils knew who He was and even admitted they knew who He was. They knew He had the power to throw them into hell immediately, and that is why they asked Him if He would send them into the herd of swine instead. The modern versions lessen the lordship of Christ by claiming that the man just kneeled or fell down before Him. This man was partaking in the act of worship with many trembling devils in his body until the Lord Jesus Christ freed him from these devils. The modern versions just about treat this narrative as one that is reforming rather than transforming. This is why we need to stick with the King James Bible because it teaches correctly about the Lord Jesus Christ, whereas His person is at the mercy of the biased translators of the modern versions.

Mark 5:13

And *forthwith Jesus* gave them leave. And the unclean spirits went out, and entered into the swine: and the herd ran violently down a steep place into the sea, (they were about two thousand;) and were choked in the sea. (Mark 5:13, KJV)

"Forthwith Jesus" is omitted. *Jesus* is changed to "he."

The word *forthwith* carries with it the meaning of "immediate, at once, without delay, or interval." Jesus gave a command to the devils, and they immediately obeyed. The modern versions make this a low-level command by stating "he gave." They make it a command that could be obeyed at their leisure.

Mark 5:19

Howbeit *Jesus* suffered him not, but saith unto him, Go home to thy friends, and tell them how great things the Lord hath done for thee, and hath had compassion on thee. (Mark 5:19, KJV)

Jesus is changed to "He" in the NASV, ASV, ESV, HCSB, RSV.

Once again, the modern versions attempt to omit Jesus as He gives a specific command to the Gadarene demoniac after he became saved.

Mark 5:36

As soon as Jesus *heard* the word that was spoken, he saith unto the ruler of the synagogue, Be not afraid, only believe. (Mark 5:36, KJV)

"As soon as" and *"heard"* is changed to "ignored" or "overheard."

The way this verse has been corrupted makes the Lord Jesus Christ out to be one who does not care nor hears what His people say. Some of the servants of Jairus came to him and told him that his daughter had died. Jairus had previously asked the Lord Jesus if He would come to his house and lay his hands on her that she might live. The Lord Jesus had begun to go toward the house when the woman with the issue of blood had touched His garment and was healed. In the meantime, the daughter of Jairus had died, and the servants came to Him and told Him.

Now, in the KJV, it states that "as soon as Jesus heard the word." Jesus had told him not to be afraid but to believe. This death was to the glory of God, just as the raising of Lazarus was. Some of the modern versions claim that Jesus had ignored what the servants said. This is ridiculous because if He ignored what they said, then why, in response to the news, did He tell Jairus to believe? Then some of the modern versions state that Jesus overheard what the servants told Jairus. This too is ridiculous because Jesus does not overhear any conversation or prayer of His people. To overhear means that someone is hearing a conversation without the knowledge of the speaker, and if someone is speaking with Jesus, He is not overhearing.

Now, in the King James Bible, we read that as soon as the words were spoken, Jesus responded. "Then said he unto me, Fear not, Daniel: for from the first day that thou didst set thine heart to understand, and to chasten thyself before thy God, thy words were heard, and I am come for thy words" (Daniel 10:12, KJV). Just as Daniel's prayer was immediately heard, so were the words of the servants. Jesus did not waste time but told Jairus to have faith. In the King James, the word *heard* carries with it the meaning of "hearing with understanding." That means that Jesus immediately knew the situation, and now He was ready to raise the girl and give a lesson for us all.

The modern versions exchange the word *heard* with a word that carries with it the meaning of "refuse to listen," "overhear," or "hear imperfectly." Does Jesus hear us imperfectly, or does He ignore us? The answer is no because the Bible is replete with examples that show that God answers the prayers of His people. Sometimes the answer is no, and it may seem like He did not answer, but no is an answer. So the modern versions use this verse as an attack upon the Lord Jesus Christ and that He is not listening to the prayers of His people.

Mark 6:11

And whosoever shall not receive you, nor hear you, when ye depart thence, shake off the dust under your feet for a testimony against them. *Verily I say unto you, It shall be more tolerable for Sodom and Gomorrha in the day of judgment, than for that city.* (Mark 6:11, KJV)

"Verily I say unto you, It shall be more tolerable for Sodom and Gomorrha in the day of judgment, than for that city" is omitted.

This is another one of those severely mutilated verses. There are twenty-three words omitted from this verse in the modern versions, and we are supposed to accept the propaganda that the modern versions are better and more accurate. How many would buy a car if twenty-three components were missing from the engine? I don't think so, yet we are supposed to accept this grammatical rape of the true Bible.

In this verse, the Lord Jesus Christ is teaching a tremendous lesson; and as usual, the modern-version translators fail to see it. But then again, you must be saved to see spiritual truth. The Lord is saying that wherever He sends His witnesses in the world, and if the message of the true Gospel is rejected by those to whom it was sent, then it will be more tolerable for Sodom and Gomorrha in the day of judgment. Why? Because Sodom and Gomorrha did not have the extensive witness of the true Gospel light as we have today. When the Lord Jesus Christ was on earth, He was the walking witness and the truth personified. Sodom and Gomorrha will be judged on the basis of the light that was given to them. The unbelievers who scoff and mock the Gospel will be judged more harshly because they will have been given much more Gospel witness than Sodom and Gomorrha.

If we look at the United States, there is hardly any town where there are no church steeples dotting the landscape. Even if the church is a dead one, from the outside, it still holds a religious implication and is a reminder that there is a God in heaven. Even when one passes by a cemetery, it is a reminder of the fact that "life's transient dream" will end someday. Churches are reminders to the unbelievers of something that is not of this world, which means that they are reminders of the light of the Gospel. Those who scoff will give a greater account than Sodom and Gomorrha with their limited light. If the translators of the modern versions would see that they are nothing more than prostitutes for the kingdom of Satan, they might realize how much of a role they are playing to confuse the body of Christ. Once again, the King James Bible gives us the complete story while the modern versions have just done Satan's bidding.

Mark 6:14

> And king Herod heard of him; (for his name was spread abroad:) *and he said*, That John the Baptist was risen from the dead, and therefore *mighty works* do shew forth themselves in him. (Mark 6:14, KJV)

"And he said" is changed to "people were saying," and *"mighty works"* is changed to "miraculous powers."

King Herod was making a statement that John the Baptist was risen from the dead. Herod made this statement, not a group of people. "Mighty works" is also much different than "miraculous powers" because the mighty works being done were done by the power of the Holy Spirit, whereas someone given miraculous powers would be doing the miracles out of their own power. It removes the working power of the Holy Spirit and makes it man-centered.

Mark 6:16

> But when Herod heard thereof, he said, It is John, whom I beheaded: he is risen *from the dead*. (Mark 6:16, KJV)

"From the dead" is omitted.

Herod had put John to death, and when he heard of the miracles of Jesus, he thought, mainly through superstition, that John was raised from the dead. The modern versions leave out the part of the fact that John was dead. There are many religions who believe in only spiritual resurrection and not physical resurrection. Here, Herod believed that John was physically back from the dead. No doubt he had guilty feelings from having him beheaded. The modern versions omit the fact that John was physically dead. By Herod believing that John was alive, it is also a lesson that the true believers will be raised physically on the last day to the resurrection of life. The modern versions omit some of the best lessons for the true believer.

Mark 6:20

> For Herod feared John, knowing that he was a just man and an holy, and observed him; and when he heard him, *he did many things*, and heard him gladly. (Mark 6:20, KJV)

"He did many things" is omitted.

In the King James Bible, Herod had many conversations with John; and in response to each conversation, Herod seemed to be doing some type of good work according to the phrase "he did many things." Maybe John was instructing him in the law of Moses, and that was why Herod had heard him gladly. The Herod clan were not Jewish but were of Edomite ancestry, and John may have been instructing him in the Hebrew scriptures. Herod did fear John in that he knew that John was a prophet of God, and yet he heard him gladly. The modern versions make out what John was telling Herod was causing him to be perplexed or filled with anxiety. This would be an oxymoron because, on one hand, Herod is hearing him gladly; but on the other hand, he is filled with anxiety over hearing John. It does not make sense. How could you listen to someone gladly when they cause you much anxiety?

Mark 6:33

> And the people saw them departing, and many knew *him*, and ran afoot thither out of all cities,

and outwent them, *and came together unto him.*
(Mark 6:33, KJV)

"Him" and *"and came together unto him"* are omitted.

In this verse, we are seeing the running of a marathon. The modern versions are stating that the people recognized the disciples and had outrun them, and that is where the story stops. The sad fact is that there are two mutilations in this verse. The first one is that people had recognized the Lord Jesus Christ, "and many knew him." The modern versions eliminate this specific identification and take the singular word *him* and change that singular word to a plural word *them.* In the Textus Receptus, the word is singular; and in the Hort-Westcott text, it is changed to a plural word.

What the modern versions have done is to group together the Lord Jesus Christ with His disciples. In other words, they lost Him in the crowd. "That I may know him, and the power of his resurrection, and the fellowship of his sufferings, being made conformable unto his death" (Philippians 3:10, KJV). The Bible teaches that we are to know *Him* and not the disciples for our salvation. The modern versions and their translators do not seem to understand this.

The second mutilation was the omission of the reason that the people had outrun the Lord Jesus and His disciples. They outran them to catch up to them so they could gather themselves unto Him, as is seen in the last part of the verse. The modern versions just give us a rendition of some kind of footrace without meaning.

Mark 6:44

And they that did eat of the loaves were *about* five
thousand men. (Mark 6:44, KJV)

About is omitted.

The King James Bible states that "about" five thousand men had eaten of the five loaves and two fishes. The modern versions state that five thousand is a specific number. "The number of the men who had eaten was five thousand" (Mark 6:44, NIV). In the parallel account in Matthew 14, in verse 21, we read that the modern versions retain *about*. "And they that had eaten were about five thousand men, beside women and children" (Matthew 14:21, KJV). "The number of those who ate was about five thousand men, besides women and children" (Matthew 14:21, NIV).

In the Luke account in Luke 9, the modern versions also retain *about*. "For they were about five thousand men. And he said to his disciples, Make them sit down by fifties in a company" (Luke 9:14, KJV). "About five thousand men were there. But he said to his disciples, 'Have them sit down in groups of about fifty each'" (Luke 9:14, NIV).

So once again, the modern versions cause confusion by using a specific number in the Mark account and an approximate number in Luke and Matthew.

Mark 6:51

And he went up unto them into the ship; and the wind ceased: and they were sore amazed in themselves *beyond measure, and wondered.* (Mark 6:51, KJV)

"Beyond measure and wondered" is omitted.

Both phrases in the Greek are in the imperfect tense, which gives a great insight into the mind-set of the disciples. When the Lord Jesus Christ entered the boat after coming to them by means of walking on the water, the winds had ceased, and the disciples not only saw the miracle of the loaves and fishes; now they saw that Jesus had complete authority over the weather by means of Him quelling the wind. Here is the mind-set: the modern versions just have the disciples being amazed at what happened, but the King James Bible teaches us that not only were they amazed at what they saw, but the imperfect tense teaches us that they had begun to ponder or to think out what was happening at that time.

The imperfect tense portrays the action as it unfolds. This is why we have the disciples wondering or marveling at what took place. They were not satisfied just seeing the winds stop, but they wanted to know how it stopped and to know more about Jesus and His authority. The modern versions stop at the point of their amazement, but the authorized Bible continues to give us the whole story. The phrases are also in the indicative mood, which means the disciples were doing the pondering over this latest miracle by Jesus. The imperfect tense does not give a certain length of time, which means they could have been discussing this for quite a long time. At this time, verse 52 states that their hearts were still hardened, so we do not know how in-depth they discussed the matter.

Mark 7:2

> And when they saw some of his disciples eat bread with defiled, that is to say, with unwashen, hands, *they found fault.* (Mark 7:2, KJV)

"They found fault" is omitted.

The disciples had eaten bread, but the Pharisees had complained that they did not wash their hands. This was not in reference to dirty hands, but the disciples had violated one of the man-made requirements started by the Pharisees. The Pharisees had often washed their hands according to the tradition of the elders, which we read in verse 3. The disciples had not violated any biblical commandment. "For Aaron and his sons shall wash their hands and their feet thereat: When they go into the tabernacle of the congregation, they shall wash with water, that they die not; or when they come near to the altar to minister, to burn offering made by fire unto the LORD: The washing that God required was of those who were ministering in the Tabernacle" (Exodus 30:19–20, KJV).

So the tradition of the elders continued to lay this law down on anyone. There was no tabernacle at this time, and the disciples were not ministering in the temple, so there was no requirement for them to wash their hands. This is a good example of being legalistic, and this is why Jesus chided them in Mark 7. The disciples did not wash, yet the Pharisees had found fault with them because they did not wash.

Ceremonial washing before eating was not required. The Pharisees were always looking to find fault with Jesus and His disciples and tried every method they could to entrap them. However, no violation of the law of God had taken place, and the Pharisees knew it. Yet they found fault with the disciples. The modern versions leave out the fact that the Pharisees found fault with them for violating the law of the Pharisees. They did not care what how they would trap Jesus and His disciples because they were out to kill Him. The modern versions fail to indict the Pharisees on legalism and man-made tradition.

Mark 7:8

> For laying aside the commandment of God, ye hold the tradition of men, *as the washing of pots and cups: and many other such like things ye do.* (Mark 7:8, KJV)

"As the washing of pots and cups: and many other such like things ye do" is omitted

Here, the Lord Jesus is bringing to light one of the additions that the religious leaders had added to the law of God. The Lord Jesus was showing the people what type of things the leaders had added to the law of God that caused them to twist the law. The Pharisees had added many such things to the law of God, and when one adds things to the law of God, it blurs the distinctions between the law of God and the additions of man.

The Lord Jesus was chiding the leaders and trying to show the people that adding to the word of God causes only confusion and never leads to salvation. The more things the leaders added to the law, the harder it was to keep the law. God gave 618 commandments in the law, but that was greatly enlarged by the time the Lord Jesus came on the scene. It is like the false religions of today that place many burdens upon their followers. The modern versions leave off this very important portion about the additions to the law of God. He was trying to show that the washing of cups and pots was nothing but a man-made law and had nothing whatsoever to do with the law of God. Once again, the King James brings out the truth and does not leave anything to speculation.

Mark 7:16

If any man have ears to hear, let him hear. (Mark 7:16, KJV)

Entire verse is omitted. The NASV places verse in brackets.

This verse is in the midst of the chapter that deals with the word of God versus the traditions of men. This chapter is one of the most hated by "works gospels." The statement that the Lord Jesus Christ makes, "If any man have ears to hear, let him hear," is focused upon those who are truly saved. All human beings are born with ears, and those who heard the Lord Jesus had physical ears; but what is in view here are those who can understand spiritual truths, those with spiritual ears. The Gnostics did not believe in the Holy Spirit as being the third Person of the Trinity and therefore did not believe that He indwells the true believer, giving to them the spiritual ears that have the ability to understand the spiritual truths of the Bible.

This is also one of the ways a person can tell if they are saved: by the way they respond to spiritual truths. If they can understand them, then they have spiritual ears; but if they are just heard with unsaved ears, then the spiritual truths are not understood. Once again, the modern versions place doubt upon a great spiritual truth of the Bible. If we remain with the King James Bible, our faith remains intact rather than being fragmented in doubt and disbelief, which spews from the modern versions.

Mark 7:24

And from thence he arose, and went into the borders of Tyre *and Sidon*, and entered into an house, and would have no man know it: but he could not be hid. (Mark 7:24, KJV)

"And from thence" and *"and Sidon"* are omitted.

Jesus was ministering in Galilee, and verse 24 marks His departure from Galilee into the area of Tyre and Sidon. It is here where He ministers to a Syrophoenician woman whose daughter was possessed by a devil. There is no logical reason why "and from thence" and "and Sidon" should have been omitted from the modern versions.

Mark 7:27

> But *Jesus* said unto her, Let the children first be filled: for it is not meet to take the children's bread, and to cast it unto the dogs. (Mark 7:27, KJV)

Jesus is omitted in some and changed to "he" in some.

This is another attack upon the Lord Jesus Christ as He is giving a great lesson of faith to the Syrophoenician woman whom the Lord declared had great faith.

Mark 8:25

> After that he put his hands again upon his eyes, *and made him look up*: and he was restored, and saw every man clearly. (Mark 8:25, KJV)

"And made him look up" is changed to "looked intently.'"

This man had just began to see, so he would have been unable to look intently; plus, he was no doubt prostrate in front of Jesus, which would mean he would have to look up. There is no reason that this verse should be changed.

Mark 8:26

> And he sent him away to his house, saying, Neither go into the town, *nor tell it to any in the town*. (Mark 8:26, KJV)

"Nor tell it to any in the town" is omitted.

Jesus had just healed a blind man and told him that he should go straight home, maybe this was told to him so he could share this miracle with his family, and together, they would glorify God. He did not want this man to go into Bethsaida because Jesus did many miracles there. "Woe unto thee, Chorazin! woe unto thee, Bethsaida! for if the mighty works had been done in Tyre and Sidon, which have been done in you, they had a great while ago repented, sitting in sackcloth and ashes" (Luke 10:13, KJV). The problem was that the people of Bethsaida were filled with unbelief concerning Christ. This is why the man was told not to go into the town of Bethsaida. Then Jesus told him, in addition to not going into the town, not to tell anyone associated with the town of Bethsaida. He did this because a miracle of this caliber would stir up the leaders and could cause much problems.

The part that is omitted in the modern versions is important because the man was not to go into the city, nor tell anyone from Bethsaida. There were people travelling all the time, and if the man ran into someone from Bethsaida, then he was not to say anything about the healing. Jesus had withheld this from them because of their unbelief and hardness of heart, and Jesus did not want the town coming after Him for the wrong reason. Once again, the King James Bible keeps the continuity in the passage for clarity and truth.

Mark 9:23

Jesus said unto him, If thou canst *believe*, all things
are possible to him that believeth. (Mark 9:23, KJV)

Believe is omitted.

If thou canst *what*? The modern versions omit one of the most vital words in the Bible, and that is *believe*. Jesus is setting a major principle of faith. First, if one can believe; then secondly, if you can believe, then all things are possible. But first, you must believe. It is important as the first principle segues right into the major principle in that verse without any guessing as to what.

Mark 9:24

And straightway the father of the child cried out,
and said with tears, Lord, I believe; help thou
mine unbelief. (Mark 9:24, KJV)

"And said with tears, Lord" is omitted.

In this verse, the father of the possessed boy had come to Jesus
for help to cast out a devil that held his son in its power. Jesus had
said to him that "if you believe, all things are possible." In other
words, if you truly believe in Christ, then all things are possible, even
the casting out of this devil. The father responded with such emotion
that he was in tears because he believed that Jesus could cast out the
devil, yet his belief was wavering, probably because he kept his eye
on the situation his son was in and did not look beyond it to Christ,
who could remove the devil from his son. The father believed in Jesus
because he called Him Lord, and *Lord* is a title of deity.

I think this man is a picture of many of us believers who know
that Christ can do something, yet there is breach in our faith when it
comes to full belief. The modern versions remove two main elements
from this verse: First, they remove that fact that the man recognizes
Jesus as deity by calling Him Lord. Secondly, they leave out the fact
that the father was in such consternation over his son that his emotions made him erupt in tears for the situation his son was in. The
Gnostics did not believe that Jesus was God in the flesh, so every
time they thought they could get away with it, they deleted the title
of *Lord*, and the modern versions make it sound like this father was
asking his friends to help him increase his faith. Once again, the King
James gives us the full story and does not attack the deity of the Lord
Jesus Christ.

Mark 9:29

And he said unto them, This kind can come
forth by nothing, but by prayer *and fasting.*
(Mark 9:29, KJV)

"And fasting" is omitted.

First fact is that the manuscript evidence for inclusion of "and fasting" is literally ten to one, so what do the modern translators follow? The one corrupt manuscript (Vaticanus) where it is missing. The parallel verse is Matthew 17:21. Jesus tells them about this kind of devil, which teaches us that some of the devils are much more wicked than others. "Then goeth he, and taketh with himself seven other spirits more wicked than himself, and they enter in and dwell there: and the last state of that man is worse than the first. Even so shall it be also unto this wicked generation" (Matthew 12:45, KJV). The type of devil that had this boy was of the type who stayed in the person for a long period of time and was of the evilest type in that his goal seemed to want to kill that boy.

What seemed lacking with the disciples was their faith, and since they were in unbelief, they would also have had very weak prayers, if they prayed at all. Then Jesus added fasting in there, which means they would have denied themselves food and water until the devil had left the boy. The fast means they would have been more concentrated on the situation at hand rather than praying for him and then taking lunch.

Then there is the other kind of fast that the Bible speaks about, and that is a spiritual fast.

> Is it such a fast that I have chosen? a day for a man to afflict his soul? is it to bow down his head as a bulrush, and to spread sackcloth and ashes under him? wilt thou call this a fast, and an acceptable day to the LORD? Is not this the fast that I have chosen? to loose the bands of wickedness, to undo the heavy burdens, and to let the oppressed go free, and that ye break every yoke? Is it not to deal thy bread to the hungry, and that thou bring the poor that are cast out to thy house? when thou seest the naked, that thou cover him; and that thou hide not thyself from thine own flesh? (Isaiah 58:5–7, KJV)

The fast that the believer must partake in goes back to the principle of the believer utterly denying themselves for the purpose of following Christ. A Christian denies the self to help bring the Gospel to others, and when they become saved, they are freed from any satanic oppression.

Mark 9:42

And whosoever shall offend one of these little ones that believe *in me*, it is better for him that a millstone were hanged about his neck, and he were cast into the sea. (Mark 9:42, KJV)

"In me" is omitted in NASV.

The NASV omits a very important phrase, and that is "in me." Jesus is stating that those little ones who believe in Him are protected by Him, and there will be a judgment on those who hurt any of those believers. By omitting "in me," they leave open the door for a person to believe in anything they want, even dead religion.

Mark 9:44, 46

Where their worm dieth not, and the fire is not quenched....Where their worm dieth not, and the fire is not quenched. (Mark 9:44, 46)

Both verses were entirely omitted or placed in brackets.

There are three verses that repeat themselves in this chapter, and that is verses 44, 46, and 48. However, verses 44 and 46 have met its fate by being removed from the Greek text. It is missing in Aleph and B and was therefore left omitted by Hort and Westcott and today's intellectual hit squads. These two verses speak of the horrors of hell and have been removed since the Gnostics in the second century and the modern liberal unbelieving scholars of today disbelieve in hell. These two verses are part of the triple warning the Lord Jesus Christ gave concerning our actions in life. God carried this idea over from Isaiah 66:24: "And they shall go forth, and look upon the carcases of the men that have transgressed against me: for their worm shall not die, neither shall their fire be quenched; and they shall be an abhorring unto all flesh" (Isaiah 66:24, KJV).

They speak of eternal damnation based upon the sinful life that people lead. In verse 43 and 45, we read that the Lord Jesus is giving the warning that we are to abandon anything that causes us to stumble, and He uses the hands and the feet as examples of two body members that can get us into much trouble.

> An heart that deviseth wicked imaginations, *feet that be swift in running to mischief.* (Proverbs 6:18, KJV)

> A proud look, a lying tongue, and *hands that shed innocent blood.* (Proverbs 6:17, KJV)

The admonition of the Lord is twofold: First, He speaks to His children and teaches them to avoid all sinful situations that will cause us to ruin our lives. Secondly, He speaks to the unbelievers that all their actions are sinful and need to be lopped off. The only way to use the hands and the feet for good is for a person to become saved because the consequences will be eternal hell.

Hort and Westcott and the second-century Gnostics believed in shortening the text, so what they have here is a triple warning by God that hell is very real; and unless a person becomes saved, then they will go there. Instead of keeping it in the text, they took out the first two verses and left verse 48 intact. When we read the Bible, we can see that God definitely uses repetition as a teacher. Let us take a look at an example:

> They are all gone aside, they are all together become filthy: there is none that doeth good, no, not one. (Psalm 14:3, KJV)

> Every one of them is gone back: they are altogether become filthy; there is none that doeth good, no, not one. (Psalm 53:3, KJV)

> They are all gone out of the way, they are together become unprofitable; there is none that doeth good, no, not one. (Romans 3:12, KJV)

As we can see, here is an example of God repeating Himself three times, which means that God intentionally uses this method in His word. What the Gnostics have done is dammed themselves to hell by subtracting from God's Word. "And if any man shall take away from the words of the book of this prophecy, God shall take away his part out of the book of life, and out of the holy city, and from the things which are written in this book" (Revelation 22:19, KJV). The sorry situation is that Christians who use these modern versions are giving approbation to the corrupted texts.

Now something interesting surfaced in this study that should be of interest to all those who claim that the Jehovah's Witness Bible is not translated from the same corrupted manuscripts as the modern versions. In the NWT, they mention that these two verses are not found in (B) Vaticanus, (a) Sinaiticus, and "C," which is the fifth-century manuscript Ephraemi Rescriptus. These three manuscripts are part of the forty-five that make up the Hort-Westcott text, which lies behind every modern version used in the Protestant Church. So when you pick up your NIV, RSV, or ESV, you are using the same version the Jehovah's Witnesses bring to your door to try and pry you away from the Lord Jesus Christ. Then we wonder why the power of the church has waned.

The NASV and NKJV keep the two verses in the text; however, the NASV places brackets around them and then, in the footnotes, questions their authenticity. They claim they are not found in the early manuscripts. What manuscripts do they mean? Their statements are so nebulous yet are taken as so credible. The NKJV is also a subtle deceiver. They claim they used the Textus Receptus in translating it, yet Dr. D. A. Waite of the Bible for Today has a detailed listing of two thousand departures from the Textus Receptus. When we come to Mark 9:44 and 46, the center column in the NKJV states that the NU text omits these verses. The NU text is, "N," the Nestle-Aland Text, which has twenty-eight updates; and the "U," the United

Bible Societies text, which has five revised editions. That is a combined total of thirty-three revisions as of 2012. Has God changed His word thirty-three times? God wrote one Bible, and that was it.

If they are using the Textus Receptus, then why are they referencing the corrupted Gnostic texts? The 1881 Revised Version and the 1901 American Standard Version both state that these verses are omitted by the best ancient authorities. Those ancient authorities are Sinaiticus and the Vaticanus, two corrupted Roman Catholic manuscripts. Can anything from Rome be in the best interest for the Protestant Christian?

Mark 9:45

> And if thy foot offend thee, cut it off: it is better for thee to enter halt into life, than having two feet to be cast into hell, *into the fire that never shall be quenched*. (Mark 9:45, KJV)

"Into the fire that never shall be quenched" is omitted.

Here is a detailed description of hell stating that it is fire that will never be quenched. Just as verses 44 and 46 received Jehoiakim's penknife (Jeremiah 36:23), this verse was also mutilated. It seems those who chopped up this verse had a fear of hell and did not want to face the reality of what hell is. Some claim hell is only the grave, but how many grave sites have you seen with fire coming out of them? Hell is the lake of fire, and it is a never-ending punishment. Many cults such as Jehovah's Witnesses have removed the true teaching of hell and its characteristics, but there is one place they can't remove it from, and that is the true word of God found in the King James Bible.

"LAMED. For ever, O LORD, thy word is settled in heaven" (Psalm 119:89, KJV). Psalm 119:89 speaks about the word of God being settled in heaven. The word *settled* carries with it the meaning of "established." The reason that the modern versions cannot remove the things they do not like is because the true word of God is forever settled or established. The "Bible babblers" may change the words, but they can never change what God has already decreed and established. The modern versions are nothing more than deceptions and diversions and are setting millions up for a shock on judgment day.

Mark 9:47

And if thine eye offend thee, pluck it out: it is better for thee to enter into the kingdom of God with one eye, than having two eyes to be cast into hell *fire*. (Mark 9:47, KJV)

Fire is omitted after *hell*.

"And if thy right eye offend thee, pluck it out, and cast it from thee: for it is profitable for thee that one of thy members should perish, and not that thy whole body should be cast into hell" (Matthew 5:29, KJV). In Matthew 5:29, Jesus speaks about plucking out the right eye, just as he did the hands and feet, but He is not saying one should do this literally because the Bible forbids mutilation of the body. In other words, if your eyes see something that offends the regenerated spirit within you, then you are to turn away and immediately reject what you have seen before it becomes a stronghold of lust in your life. This offense can come from a myriad of places such as the Internet, TV, movies, sexual conversations, or whatever source that may titillate someone. Reject looking at whatever causes you to sin, or else you could be on the receiving end of the chastising hand of God if you are a believer. If you are an unbeliever, it will mean eternal damnation.

The eye is the receptor and is the first cause of sin in a person's life. A person can easily see sinful things around them, but if they continue to gaze upon them, then those sightings will turn into desires, and that is when we engage the hands and the feet. Jesus makes the same observation that just as a person plucks out their eye and can no longer see, then we must be blind to the things that will cause us to stumble. When we are in the supermarket line and there are magazines with scantily dressed people looking at us, we must turn away and refuse to look. If one has a problem in that area, they might even want to stay away from the shore because bathing suits aren't suits anymore. Basically, what Jesus is teaching is that we must give up what comes between us and our obedient Christian walk.

Mark 9:49

For every one shall be salted with fire, *and every sacrifice shall be salted with salt.* (Mark 9:49, KJV)

"And every sacrifice shall be salted with salt" is omitted.

Those whom the Lord was speaking about in the previous verses are those who are unsaved, and if they remain unsaved, they shall be cast into eternal hell. The fact that they will be salted with fire means they will be tormented in the flames of eternal damnation. Then the Lord uses the same analogy, but a different group of people are in view. The first half of the verse deals with unbelievers whom He previously spoke of, but now there is a different application for the same principle. "That the trial of your faith, being much more precious than of gold that perisheth, though it be tried with fire, might be found unto praise and honour and glory at the appearing of Jesus Christ" (1 Peter 1:7, KJV). Every true believer is considered a sacrifice. "I beseech you therefore, brethren, by the mercies of God, that ye present your bodies a living sacrifice, holy, acceptable unto God, which is your reasonable service" (Romans 12:1, KJV). As the unbeliever in hell is salted with the fire of judgment, the believer as a living sacrifice is salted with the fire of trials as we read in 1 Peter 1:7 and 1 Peter 4:12. "Beloved, think it not strange concerning the fiery trial which is to try you, as though some strange thing happened unto you" (1 Peter 4:12, KJV).

As salt is used as a preservative, as believers, we have the salt of the Gospel within us. "All the heave offerings of the holy things, which the children of Israel offer unto the LORD, have I given thee, and thy sons and thy daughters with thee, by a statute for ever: it is a covenant of salt for ever before the LORD unto thee and to thy seed with thee" (Numbers 18:19, KJV). In Numbers 18:19, God speaks of a covenant of salt, but that covenant is one of eternal nature. The only covenant that lasts throughout eternity is the covenant of grace.

So here, in Numbers 18:19, the covenant of salt has foreshadowed the covenant of grace in that it is an eternally preserving covenant.

"Jude, the servant of Jesus Christ, and brother of James, to them that are sanctified by God the Father, and preserved in Jesus Christ, and called" (Jude 1:1, KJV). Jude 1 speaks about those who are sanctified by God, and that would be the believers. Then the verse goes on to say that they are preserved in Jesus Christ, and that is exactly what the second half of Mark 9:49 is speaking about when it speaks about every sacrifice being salted with salt. So when the modern versions leave off the second half of Mark 9:49, they are omitting a great promise that Christians will be preserved in Christ Jesus forever.

Mark 10:7

For this cause shall a man leave his father and mother, *and cleave to his wife*. (Mark 10:7, KJV)

"And cleave to his wife" is omitted in the NASV, NET Version, AMP, and HCSB places it in brackets.

Mark 10:7 is a direct quote from Genesis 2:24: "Therefore shall a man leave his father and his mother, and shall cleave unto his wife: and they shall be one flesh" (Genesis 2:24, KJV). What these four versions have done is not only cast doubt upon the scripture in Mark 10:7 but have mutilated the direct quote from Genesis 2:24, thus removing a portion from scripture in violation of the scriptures.

Mark 10:21

Then Jesus beholding him loved him, and said unto him, One thing thou lackest: go thy way, sell whatsoever thou hast, and give to the poor, and thou shalt have treasure in heaven: and come, *take up the cross*, and follow me. (Mark 10:21, KJV)

"Take up the cross" is omitted.

One of the most important distinctive principles of being a true disciple of Christ is the fact that one must take up their cross. The taking up of the cross means that the true believer is to give their life totally to the service of the Lord. It means that we are to deny ourselves and give unceasingly of ourselves unto the Lord. The cross was an instrument of execution, but it also symbolizes the follower of Christ being dead to themselves and alive unto God. In other words, our lives are to be walking gospels here on earth.

By removing the phrase "take up the cross," the verse is reduced to just writing a check, and that is the extent of our commitment; plus, it states that if you give to the poor, then automatically you are saved. You cannot follow Christ by giving only of your worldly goods. Following Christ demands a total commitment that is not only our earthly goods but also our very lives. When the verse teaches that we are to sell whatever we have and give to the poor, it does not mean that we are to sell everything we own and walk around in poverty and rags. It means that we are to use all our earthly goods for the advancement of the Gospel of the Lord Jesus Christ. If I was a millionaire and gave all my money and possessions to feed the poor, what would that accomplish? It would accomplish nothing for the kingdom of God. But if I took that money and began to give to missions, supply tracts and Bibles, help other Christians in their ministries, then I would be selling all I have and giving to the poor—that is, the spiritually poor—to reach the world with the Gospel.

There are many today who believe they are following Christ simply because they write a check to some organization or if they are in a religious establishment. To follow Christ, we must follow the principle found in Colossians 3:4: "When Christ, who is our life, shall appear, then shall ye also appear with him in glory" (Colossians 3:4, KJV).

Christ *is our life*, not a part of it. The essence of true discipleship is to follow the Lord Jesus Christ right to the end. Those who removed the part of the verse that speaks of taking up their cross have created an easy discipleship program. All you have to do is give something to the poor, and then you are following Christ and will have treasures in heaven. There is no such thing as an easy life following Christ. We are constantly facing persecution and prejudice every day, and a life of service is not an easy thing. One only needs to look at the martyrs who followed Christ. They suffered all kinds of cruelties and tortures because they took up the cross and followed Christ.

The modern versions do not believe in earnest discipleship as they reduce the reality of Christianity to the mere giving of a few dollars to the poor. Is it wrong to give to the poor, to help someone out? No, it isn't, but if your ministry is only centered around the things of the earth such as food and clothing, then you do not have a ministry worthy of the Lord Jesus Christ. The true ministry concerns itself with the salvation of souls and the spiritual growth of the Christian. Don't be taken in by the easy and false belief systems that the modern versions proclaim because they are part of the system of the beast. "And I beheld another beast coming up out of the earth; and he had two horns like a lamb, and he spake as a dragon" (Revelation 13:11, KJV).

The second beast is the false prophet who deceives the world with false religions, which means that false Bibles are also part of his plan. Notice that the beast has two horns like a lamb. This beast tries to imitate the Lord Jesus Christ who is the true Lamb of God. The beast comes as one that offers a salvation plan that looks like the real thing but is not. As we saw in the false versions, giving to the poor constitutes works, and no one gets to heaven by works. This is a grave deception by the beast, which, unfortunately, is accepted by many in the Christian community.

Mark 10:24

> And the disciples were astonished at his words. But Jesus answereth again, and saith unto them, Children, how hard is it *for them that trust in riches* to enter into the kingdom of God! (Mark 10:24, KJV)

"For them that trust in riches" is omitted.

Jesus is giving a discourse concerning riches and the kingdom of heaven. He is basically teaching His disciples that those who own much riches rarely ever give a thought to spiritual things because their thoughts are how they can make more money. So Jesus tells His disciples that those who trust in riches will have a harder time entering into the kingdom of heaven. Now, it is not that a rich man cannot become saved because there have been many rich men who have become saved. "And Jesus looking upon them saith, With men it is impossible, but not with God: for with God all things are possible" (Mark 10:27, KJV). The lesson that Jesus is giving is that those who are rich concern themselves with riches and not with the fact of their mortality.

This verse has been so mutilated that the modern versions are actually teaching that it is hard to enter the kingdom of heaven. The omission can be taken to mean that one must work very hard to get into heaven. The way the modern versions are wording this verse is that they are teaching a works gospel. There is no such thing as working our way to heaven. Our salvation was given to us by *free grace*, and if we attempt to add works, then we are adulterating the grace of God in salvation. Of course, the disciples would be astonished to hear that it is hard to get into heaven because if it would be by works, then who could get in? The answer would be that nobody could unless it was by the grace of God.

This verse would play perfectly into religions like Roman Catholicism, which require that their adherents partake in works to satisfy the church's requirement for salvation; and if that is not bad enough, when they die, they have to go to purgatory for many years. So according to Roman Catholicism, it is hard to get into heaven. All one has to do is read about the monastic life of Roman Catholic orders, and you will read the impossibility to attain heaven by their requirements. Once again, the King James Bible gives us a clear picture about what is in view and does not lead us into an erroneous direction. This is definitely a matter of affecting the doctrine of salvation, yet the modern-version proponents claim modern versions do not attack doctrine!

Mark 10:26

And they were astonished out of measure, saying *among themselves*, Who then can be saved? (Mark 10:26, KJV)

"Among themselves" is omitted. AMP, ESV, RSV, Voice change this to "saying to him."

Some of the modern versions change this to "saying to him." The disciples were speaking among themselves, and no doubt Jesus was with them, but they were not directly addressing Him as they posed the question of, "Who then can be saved?"

Mark 10:29

> And Jesus answered and said, Verily I say unto you, There is no man that hath left house, or brethren, or sisters, or father, or mother, *or wife*, or children, or lands, for my sake, and the gospel's. (Mark 10:29, KJV)

"Or wife" is omitted.

Here, Jesus is giving a teaching that those who have forsaken all the things that they love and are familiar with for His sake will receive an hundredfold more in this life (v. 30). The amount "hundredfold" is an open-ended number, and the Lord is basically stating that the blessings of the Christian life are without number. When the Lord speaks of forsaking family, He is not advocating leaving without any communication with their earthly family, but He is stating that the Christian must seek the eternal family above the earthly family. And if they are the only ones saved in that family, then their outlook on life is going to be different from the unsaved ones, and their worldly outlook must also be forsaken.

If you notice in the text, the Lord also mentions forsaking a wife, which is omitted in the modern versions. This does not mean that a man is to forsake and divorce his wife because that would be in violation of the scriptures. This would have two possible meanings: The first is a man forsaking the institution of marriage, exchanging the married life for the life in service to Christ. The second meaning would be that the husband takes on a ministry that causes him to be separated from his wife for long periods of time. For example, Peter was married, but he left his wife at home while he pursued ministry with the Lord, which took him away from home for long periods of time. Throughout history, there have been many gospel widows who did not see their husbands for long periods of time. The modern versions remove that word *wife*, which also removes a great promise to those married people who become separated from each other for long periods of time for the sake of the Gospel.

Mark 10:52

And *Jesus* said unto him, Go thy way; thy faith hath made thee whole. And immediately he received his sight, and followed Jesus in the way. (Mark 10:52, KJV)

Jesus is changed to "he" or "him" in the NASV, ASV, ESV, HCSB, RSV, NRSV.

Once again, this is another attack upon the person of the Lord Jesus Christ by omitting His proper name and referring to Him as "he" or "him."

Mark 11:10

Blessed be the kingdom of our father David, *that cometh in the name of the Lord*: Hosanna in the highest. (Mark 11:10, KJV)

"That cometh in the name of the Lord" is omitted.

"And they that went before, and they that followed, cried, saying, Hosanna; Blessed is he that cometh in the name of the Lord: Blessed be the kingdom of our father David, that cometh in the name of the Lord: Hosanna in the highest" (Mark 11:9–10, KJV). As the Lord entered Jerusalem, the Jews began to shout, "Blessed is He that cometh in the name of the Lord," but then they shouted an appendage to that found in verse 10. Not only was He who came in the name of the Lord, but they also shouted, "Blessed is the kingdom of our Father, David, who came in the name of the Lord."

It was at this time that the Jews in Jerusalem were expecting Jesus to restore the kingdom of Israel as it was in the days of David. However, they were really rejoicing because the Lord Jesus Christ was about ready to establish the kingdom of God on earth, but not the type of kingdom that was expected. He was a few days from the cross, and after His crucifixion, resurrection, and ascension, he sent the Holy Spirit to begin the task of indwelling the true believers. Those true believers are now in the kingdom of God, but it is not a political kingdom but a spiritual kingdom. "And when he was demanded of the Pharisees, when the kingdom of God should come, he answered them and said, The kingdom of God cometh not with observation: Neither shall they say, Lo here! or, lo there! for, behold, the kingdom of God is within you" (Luke 17:20–21, KJV).

The kingdom of God does not come with observation—that is, there is no fanfare or bells and whistles when someone becomes saved. If you look at a group of people, you could not tell who is saved and who isn't until you personally get to know them. Not only did Christ come in the name of the Lord, but His kingdom comes in the name of the Lord; that is, it is God's kingdom, and it is identified by the name of God. Omitting the phrase "that cometh in the name of the Lord" removes the kingdom identification, and the true believers are identified with only one kingdom, and that is God's kingdom.

Mark 11:14

And *Jesus* answered and said unto it, No man eat fruit of thee hereafter for ever. And his disciples heard it. (Mark 11:14, KJV)

Jesus is changed to "he."

Once again, we see another attack on the specific name of the Lord Jesus Christ, being changed from a proper name to a pronoun. Are you starting to see how much the modern versions despise the Lord Jesus Christ?

Mark 11:19

And when even was come, *he* went out of the
city. (Mark 11:19, KJV)

He is changed to "they" (third-person singular is changed to
third-person plural).

At the close of each day, the gates of the city would be closed,
and this would be for safety purposes. But Jesus and His disciples
would not stay in the city, so they would leave and go out of the city.
The Lord Jesus had just overturned the tables of the money changers
in the temple, and at the end of the day, the scripture states that *He*
went out of the city. Many times, He went to the Mount of Olives,
and sometimes He stayed in Bethany. At this time, the focus was specifically on Jesus and not the disciples. It was Jesus who overturned
the tables of the money changers; the disciples would not have been
that bold to do something like that. Therefore, the entire set of passages is focused specifically on Jesus.

The word in the Greek for "he went" in the King James is in
the third-person singular, but in the Hort and Westcott text, it was
changed to third-person plural. In the Greek language, person and
number agree with the subject of the sentence. The focus of the sentence is the Lord Jesus Christ; therefore, it would follow that the
statement about Him leaving the city would be singular since it was
still focusing on Christ alone. To include the disciples here would
give the impression that they too had something to do with over-
turning the tables in the temple, and that is not a true impression.
If anything, the disciples, being Jews, would have feared the action
the Lord took at that time concerning the desecration of the temple.
Once again, in the modern versions, we see the downgrading of the
action of the Lord Jesus Christ and credit being given to those who
did nothing. The King James has it right when it keeps the entire
focus on the Lord Jesus Christ.

Mark 11:26

But if ye do not forgive, neither will your Father which is in heaven forgive your trespasses. (Mark 11:26, KJV)

The entire verse omitted or placed in brackets.

This verse is an indicator as to whether a person is saved or not. As Christians, we know that we have been forgiven for every single sin in our life. "And you, being dead in your sins and the uncircumcision of your flesh, hath he quickened together with him, having forgiven you all trespasses; {14} Blotting out the handwriting of ordinances that was against us, which was contrary to us, and took it out of the way, nailing it to his cross" (Colossians 2:13–14, KJV). Since we have been forgiven of all our sins, it should be part of the makeup of a Christian to forgive others who have sinned against us. As God forgave us based upon the merits of Christ on Calvary, then based upon our total forgiveness, we need to forgive others. If a person refuses to forgive, then that shows a hard heart, which is an indicator that the person who refuses to forgive may be unsaved.

There may be a time when a Christian may have a hard heart toward someone temporarily, but the Lord eventually softens it. But a person with a continual hard heart is one who is unsaved. We can confirm this by realizing that if the believer has had every single sin paid for, then what sin could God possibly not forgive in this verse? Because of Calvary, the slate has been wiped clean for the believer. On the other hand, the religious unbeliever, who has not had their sins paid for, still has them; and if they do not become saved, then God will not forgive their sins. An unforgiving attitude will be another sin that they must pay for on the last day.

Apparently, the Gnostics did not believe in forgiving others who sinned against them, and they were probably fearful of the implications of this verse, and that is why it was omitted in the Hort-Westcott Critical Text. Keep in mind also that Hort and Westcott were both Roman Catholics and believed that forgiveness came through confession and penance, so they would definitely remove this verse if God would forgive sins without the intervention of a pagan priest. Let us stay with the King James Bible and get the whole word of God.

Mark 12:4

> And again he sent unto them another servant; *and at him they cast stones*, and wounded him in the head, and sent him away shamefully handled. (Mark 12:4, KJV)

"And at him they cast stones" is omitted.

By leaving out this phrase, the modern versions omit a major truth from the New Testament. This verse has to do with the treatment the believer will experience as they attempt to bring the Gospel. "They were stoned, they were sawn asunder, were tempted, were slain with the sword: they wandered about in sheepskins and goatskins; being destitute, afflicted, tormented" (Hebrews 11:37, KJV). Hebrews 11:37 states that "they were stoned," and that is what the Lord Jesus Christ is prophesying in this verse. Stoning was also a common method of execution in Old Testament Israel. "And Joshua said, Why hast thou troubled us? the LORD shall trouble thee this day. And all Israel stoned him with stones, and burned them with fire, after they had stoned them with stones" (Joshua 7:25, KJV).

Achan was stoned to death along with his family for violating God's command to not touch the gold and silver. In the New Testament, both Stephen and Paul were stoned. "And they stoned Stephen, calling upon God, and saying, Lord Jesus, receive my spirit" (Acts 7:59, KJV). "And there came thither certain Jews from Antioch and Iconium, who persuaded the people, and, having stoned Paul, drew him out of the city, supposing he had been dead" (Acts 14:19, KJV).

Mark 12:23

> In the resurrection *therefore, when they shall rise*, whose wife shall she be of them? for the seven had her to wife. (Mark 12:23, KJV)

"Therefore, when they shall rise" is omitted.

Many of the false versions omit "when they shall rise" because the Gnostics did not believe in a physical resurrection but in a spiritual resurrection, and the modern versions follow suit. This is where the Jehovah's Witnesses get their disbelief in a physical resurrection. Many in the New Age believe only in a spiritual resurrection. But the great promise to the believer, written in many parts of the Bible, is the fact of the physical resurrection of the believer on the last day when they will receive their glorified spiritual bodies, so we will be able to be in the presence of God without being consumed. "It is sown a natural body; it is raised a spiritual body" (1 Corinthians 15:44, KJV). There is a natural body, and there is a spiritual body. No amount of Gnostic deception will ever deprive the believer of that great hope.

Mark 12:29

> And Jesus answered him, The first *of all the commandments* is, Hear, O Israel; The Lord our God is one Lord. (Mark 12:29, KJV)

"Of all the commandments" is omitted.

"And one of the scribes came, and having heard them reasoning together, and perceiving that he had answered them well, asked him, Which is the first commandment of all?" (Mark 12:28, KJV). In verse 28, a scribe asks Jesus which is the first commandment of all? In Mark 12:28 and 29, the Greek word behind "first" is the word *protos*, and carries with it the idea of "foremost" or "most important." This is important because Jesus and the scribe are referring to the first of *all* the commandments and not just a certain section of them. The modern versions omit the section where it says "of all the commandments."

Jesus is emphasizing the fact that the Lord our God is one in essence, one in unity, one in purpose, one in truth, one in love, one in judgment, and one in holiness; and for a person to realize this, it will then become apparent as to the reasons for the other hundreds of other laws that will fall under the umbrella of this first and foremost law. It is a shame that these modern versions omit this very important part because this verse and verse 30 are very important to understand the rest of the law.

Mark 12:30

And thou shalt love the Lord thy God with all thy heart, and with all thy soul, and with all thy mind, and with all thy strength: *this is the first commandment*. (Mark 12:30, KJV)

"This is the first commandment" is omitted.

Jesus completes the first commandment in this verse. He reiterates at the end of the verse that this is the first commandment. Now, the word *first* is in the ordinal form (understood as first, second, third, etc.) instead of the cardinal form (one, two, three, etc.). This is important because it is showing us that the first commandment is not just one of the commandments (cardinal). The ordinal form is showing us that this commandment is before all the rest—that is, it is the first one, and the rest are ancillary.

As you can read in verse 31, Jesus speaks of a second commandment that is also in the ordinal form; meaning, it follows in importance after the first commandment. It is a shame that the modern versions leave out this important piece of information, but what else could you expect from counterfeiters? If we stay with the King James Bible, we will definitely know the first and second commandments, which come from the heart of the Lord.

Mark 12:32

And the scribe said unto him, Well, Master, thou hast said the truth: *for there is one God*; and there is none other but he. (Mark 12:32, KJV)

"For there is one God" is changed to "God is one."

In the King James Bible and its lineage, it states that there is one God. It is taught throughout the Bible that there is one God in three distinct persons: the Father, the Son, and the Holy Ghost. The Hebrew uses the word *elohim* for God, which denotes "three." So we see, even in the Hebrew scriptures, there speaks of a plurality within one God. However, when we look at the way the modern versions have rewritten this verse, it carries with it the idea of *modalism*. Modalism is the false teaching that there is only one God in three manifestations. The manifestations are the Father in the Old Testament, the Lord Jesus Christ coming to earth, and presently, He is the Holy Spirit. Modalism teaches that there are not three distinct personalities in the Godhead but only one, who manifests Himself differently at different times, as we read above.

Modalism is also known as *oneness* and is taught by some churches and theologians. As you can plainly read, there is a vast difference between "There is one God" and "He is One." If the modern versions stated that He is one in three persons, then it would make sense, but they word it in such a manner that it reeks with oneness. With these modern versions permeating Christianity, no wonder there is a rise in modalism and the denial of the biblical Trinitarian doctrine.

Mark 12:33

> And to love him with all the heart, and with all the understanding, *and with all the soul,* and with all the strength, and to love his neighbour as himself, is more than all whole burnt offerings and sacrifices. (Mark 12:33, KJV)

"And with all the soul" is omitted.

In this verse, we see a strategic part of the verse omitted. If you will notice, the part that is omitted deals with the soul of man. The soul of man is a very interesting and significant part of the makeup of the born-again believer. The word for "soul" in the New Testament is the word *psuchê*, which carries with it the meaning of "soul, life, heart, person, or self." It carries a wide set of definitions while holding to a very narrow yet important part of the makeup of man. In the Old Testament, the word *soul* carries with it the idea of "person, soul, or life" in the Hebrew word *nephesh*. It is also synonymous with the Hebrew word *ruach*, which is translated "spirit."

Now, when Adam was created, he was made a living soul (nephesh). Adam was also spiritually alive when he was created. He was spiritually alive in both soul and spirit. When Adam sinned, he was warned by God that he would die. Upon the first sin came the sentence of death, yet Adam still lived many years beyond that judicial pronunciation. This was because Adam had died spiritually, and instead of his soul remaining regenerated, it was reduced to physical life only because he became spiritually dead. Now, the whole human race has inherited Adam's penalty. When a person is born, they still receive the soul, which is basically their life given them by God; but at that point, it is only dealing with the physical part of the body. "And the Lord God formed man of the dust of the ground, and breathed into his nostrils the breath of life; and man became a living soul" (Genesis 2:7, KJV).

When a person becomes born again, the Holy Spirit indwells them, and here is a mystery. The soul of man is also regenerated, which makes that soul a conduit between the spiritual and the physical. It enables the regenerated believer to not only understand spiritual things but allows the believer to physically put into practice the faith that they receive upon regeneration. When the modern versions omit the phrase about the soul, they are asking the believer to be less than totally committed to the Lord Jesus Christ. This is why the scribe had given the Lord Jesus a tremendous answer concerning the responsibility of the believer.

It is interesting that the modern versions leave out the soul, which is a very significant part of the tripartite being. It is the very thing God uses to give life to a body upon its creation and the very thing to connect the living physical body to the regenerating Spirit of God, thus creating the fully furnished born-again believer. When the soul is regenerated, it becomes spiritually alive and directs the believer toward their spiritual life and away from the worldly life because now it is alive and causes us to focus upon the Lord Jesus Christ through the indwelling of the Holy Spirit. Its regeneration motivates the believer to obedience and service. Isn't it wonderful how the King James Bible continues to bring the real light of the truth concerning the greatness of our salvation. For many years, I had believed that the soul and the spirit were synonymous, but it is very interesting how God points out that there are three parts to man in scripture.

> And the very God of peace sanctify you wholly; and I pray God your whole spirit and soul and body be preserved blameless unto the coming of our Lord Jesus Christ. (1 Thessalonians 5:23, KJV)

> For the word of God is quick, and powerful, and sharper than any twoedged sword, piercing even to the dividing asunder of soul and spirit, and of the joints and marrow, and is a discerner of the thoughts and intents of the heart. (Hebrews 4:12, KJV)

Mark 12:40

> Which devour widows' houses, and for a pretence make long prayers: these shall receive *greater damnation.* (Mark 12:40, KJV)

"Greater damnation" is changed to "condemnation, punishment, severer judgment."

The modern versions once again attack the ultimate punishment of the unbeliever, which is damnation. Here, Jesus states that those who trouble the most vulnerable people in society while acting religious and pious in public will receive a greater damnation. What that entails remains to be seen but will be revealed on judgment day.

Mark 13:8

> For nation shall rise against nation, and kingdom
> against kingdom: and there shall be earthquakes
> in divers places, and there shall be famines *and*
> *troubles*: these are the beginnings of sorrows.
> (Mark 13:8, KJV)

"And troubles" is omitted.

The word *troubles* in this verse gives a very important sign of the beginning of the end of time. It speaks of a "stirring up (of something or people), disturbance, or tumult." We see this occurring in every country in the world. It does not necessarily mean that an entire country is being stirred up, but certain groups within the country are being stirred up. In the USA, we see groups like animal activists, political groups, environmental groups, global-warming groups, the mainstream media, and it is the groups like these who are stirring up the people and causing troubles among them. Terrorists abound in many countries and are stirring up the people by killing. These things are a sign that we are in the end-times. "And there shall be signs in the sun, and in the moon, and in the stars; and upon the earth distress of nations, with perplexity; the sea and the waves roaring" (Luke 21:25, KJV).

One of the major signs of the end-times is that nations are going to be in perplexity. It means filled with uncertainty or puzzlement, full of difficulty. I don't think there is one country in this world that does not fit that description. This is why when the modern versions omit the word, they are omitting a great sign of the end-times.

Mark 13:11

> But when they shall lead you, and deliver you
> up, take no thought beforehand what ye shall
> speak, *neither do ye premeditate*: but whatsoever
> shall be given you in that hour, that speak ye:
> for it is not ye that speak, but the Holy Ghost.
> (Mark 13:11, KJV)

"Neither do ye premeditate" is omitted.

The admonition not to premeditate or study beforehand to give an answer is important because they would not know what the accusations would be or the central theme beforehand. The answers were to be given to them by the Holy Spirit at the moment they needed it so they could take no credit for the answers. The answers given will be fit perfectly for the accusations. This admonition is not to discourage proper Bible study, but it is for those extreme times of trial when God promises a proper answer to those who come against the believer. The modern versions omit this phrase and therefore could make man the center of any type of confrontation because it seems like premeditation in study was acceptable in those particular situations when it is not.

Mark 13:14

> But when ye shall see the abomination of desolation, *spoken of by Daniel the prophet*, standing where it ought not, (let him that readeth understand,) then let them that be in Judaea flee to the mountains. (Mark 13:14, KJV)

"Spoken of by Daniel the prophet" is omitted.

Omitting the portion that states "spoken of by Daniel the prophet" removes a vital link as to where the passage in Mark is taken from. The book of Daniel is closely tied to events that will occur in the last days (probably the most prophetic book in the Old Testament), and to remove such vital information removes the bond with the book of Daniel. The key to understanding the Bible correctly is to compare scripture with scripture, and that can only be done when we know where to compare certain scriptures to. This section of Mark is a brother to Matthew 24 and Luke 21. Any portions that are omitted can lead the Bible student down a wrong path. Mark 13:14 is related to Daniel 9:27; 11:31; and 12:11. The omission of this portion of scripture is an attack on the doctrine of the Bible and of prophecy.

Mark 13:33

Take ye heed, watch *and pray*: for ye know not
when the time is. (Mark 13:33, KJV)

"And pray" is omitted.

"Pray without ceasing" (1 Thessalonians 5:17, KJV). First
Thessalonians 5:17 commands the believer to pray without ceasing. This means we are to pray about everything in our life, which
includes both the spiritual and the physical. We are to make our petitions known to God, and of course, He already knows them before
we even approach Him. Prayer is our communication between us
and our Heavenly Father. Here, in Mark 13:33, the modern versions
omit the second half of the command of the Lord Jesus Christ, which
is not only to watch but to pray along with that watching.

Mark 13 is a chapter that contains information about the return
of the Lord Jesus Christ. We are commanded not only to watch,
which can be understood as "keep awake or remain vigilant," but
along with that vigilance, we are to pray. Since Mark 13 is a prophetic chapter, there is much being published today by people and
groups concerning the Lord's return, and we must not only pray to
remain focused on the Lord's return, but we are to pray to remain
aloof from false and unbiblical teachings about His return. If we are
not careful, we can fall for everyone who has a prediction about the
return of Christ, which can take us out of the Bible and into the evil
habit of following a man and his teachings.

So many books have been published, and so many have set dates
for the return of Christ that there will be mass confusion if we choose
to divert from scripture and follow the fanciful teachings of someone. The Holy Spirit will guide us into all truth, but it behooves us
to pray about what we seek to learn. It seems the modern versions do
not want us to pray about such matters, and that is why there are so
many views and false teachings surrounding the Lord's return. People
are simply creating belief systems and are not praying for guidance.
We must remain extremely vigilant in prayer and true Bible study
because as we progress in time, many teachings will get more and

more false with the ability to draw us in. That is why we are not only to watch but to pray—they go together.

Mark 14:19

And they began to be sorrowful, and to say unto him one by one, Is it I? *and another said, Is it I?* (Mark 14:19, KJV)

"And another said, is it I?" is omitted.

The phrase left out of this verse is an important one because it points to Judas who betrayed the Lord Jesus. The word *another* denotes something different. We find that usage in Galatians 5:10. "I have confidence in you through the Lord, that ye will be none *otherwise* minded: but he that troubleth you shall bear his judgment, whosoever he be" (Galatians 5:10, KJV). Each of the disciples had asked concerning the betrayal of Christ, "Is it I?" Then the verse states, "And another said is it I?" Who was the only one who was different than the rest among the twelve disciples? "Jesus answered them, Have not I chosen you twelve, and one of you is a devil?" (John 6:70, KJV). It was Judas, and that is why that phrase is important because it separated Judas from the other disciples who became saved and carried on the ministry.

Mark 14:22

And as they did eat, *Jesus* took bread, and blessed, and brake it, and gave to them, and said, Take, *eat*: this is my body. (Mark 14:22, KJV)

Jesus is changed to "he," and *eat* is omitted.

I am the living bread which came down from heaven: if any man eat of this bread, he shall live for ever: and the bread that I will give is my flesh, which I will give for the life of the world. The Jews therefore strove among themselves, saying, How can this man give us his flesh to eat? Then Jesus said unto them, Verily, verily, I say unto you, Except ye eat the flesh of the Son of man, and drink his blood, ye have no life in you. Whoso eateth my flesh, and drinketh my blood, hath eternal life; and I will raise him up at the last day. (John 6:51–54, KJV)

In John 6, the Lord Jesus Christ gave a discourse on the eating of His flesh and drinking of His blood. This, of course, was a symbolic gesture. For if he meant it literally, then after He went back to Heaven, how could anyone else get saved? So He meant this in a symbolic way. "For we are members of his body, of his flesh, and of his bones" (Ephesians 5:30, KJV). Ephesians 5:30 states that we are members of His flesh and bones. Well, if Christ is in heaven and we are on earth, then how can we be members? Again, it is a symbolic message. Basically, what the Lord Jesus is intimating is that His children are so much a part of Him that we are like members of His physical body. This can be seen in marriage when the two become one flesh. When we become saved, we are married to Christ as we become His bride, and therefore, we become one flesh with Him.

In Mark 14:22, at the Last Supper, the Lord was giving a symbolic fulfillment of what He taught in John 6. The disciples were eating the bread, which symbolized His body, as we read in John 6:51, which was the bread that came down from heaven. Then they drank the grape juice that symbolized the blood of Christ. "For the life of the flesh is in the blood: and I have given it to you upon the altar to make an atonement for your souls: for it is the blood that maketh an atonement for the soul" (Leviticus 17:11, KJV). Just as the Lord gave the blood of the animals under the Mosaic system to atone for the sins of the people, this foreshadow is of the blood of the Lord Jesus Christ making atonement for our sins and cleaning our souls of every vestige of sin. "But if we walk in the light, as he is in the light, we have fellowship one with another, and the blood of Jesus Christ his Son cleanseth us from all sin" (1 John 1:7, KJV).

This is why it is important in Mark 14:22 that the word *eat* is left in because the command was to ingest symbolically the body and blood of the Lord Jesus Christ for eternal life. When the modern versions leave out the word *eat*, they leave it up to the individual as to what to do with the bread; and also, it does not fulfill the teaching of John 6, which specifically speaks about eating the body of Christ. The modern versions really destroy the meaning and fulfilling nature of Mark 14:22 by omitting *eat*. They have also turned the name *Jesus* into "he," thus removing who it was breaking the bread.

Mark 14:24

> And he said unto them, This is my blood of
> the *new* testament, which is shed for many.
> (Mark 14:24, KJV)

New is omitted.

This mutilated verse is an attack upon the New Testament. As far back as Jeremiah, we were told that God was going to make a new covenant with the house of Israel.

> Behold, the days come, saith the LORD, that I will
> make a new covenant with the house of Israel, and
> with the house of Judah. (Jeremiah 31:31, KJV)

The Lord Jesus was about ready to go to the cross for His people and told the disciples that His blood was the blood of the New Testament. The modern versions omit *new*, and by doing this, we are not told what covenant the Lord was fulfilling. Was it the Abrahamic covenant? Was it the covenant of salt? Was it the covenant of Sinai? The covenant He was fulfilling was the covenant whereby *free grace* would be imparted to the true believers. This was the covenant of grace that would be given to the many, which is the elect of God.

Omitting the term *new* obliterates the line between the Old and New Testament. It does not tell the reader that Christ's sacrifice was for the purpose of the new but could be misconstrued that this was the continuation of the old covenant. Once again, the modern versions create confusion, and once again, the King James removes any doubt and confusion concerning the blood of the Lord Jesus Christ being shed for the *new* covenant or testament.

Mark 14:27

And Jesus saith unto them, All ye shall be offended *because of me this night*: for it is written, I will smite the shepherd, and the sheep shall be scattered. (Mark 14:27, KJV)

"Because of me this night" is omitted.

This verse is teaching that the disciples are going to be offended, which carries with it the idea of stumbling because the Lord was going to the cross, and they did not understand that He had to die for the sins of His people. The modern versions omit the part that the reason they stumbled was because of the Lord Jesus, and Jesus tells them plainly that they will be offended. This verse as written in the King James Bible also reveals a fulfillment of prophecy. "Awake, O sword, against my shepherd, and against the man that is my fellow, saith the LORD of hosts: smite the shepherd, and the sheep shall be scattered: and I will turn mine hand upon the little ones" (Zechariah 13:7, KJV).

Mark 14:27 identifies Jesus as being the Shepherd of His sheep, thus fulfilling Zechariah 13:7. The modern versions omit the identification of Jesus as being the Shepherd and thus robs another fulfillment of prophecy in the life of the Lord Jesus. It is very important to note that the centrality of the attacks by modern versions is on the Lord Jesus Christ. Each modern version attacks the deity of the Lord Jesus Christ, thus lowering Him to the level of just another teacher, which is what the Gnostics originally thought of Christ. The modern versions reduce Him while simultaneously elevating man. We can be thankful that God gave us His word in the King James Bible.

Mark 14:68

> But he denied, saying, I know not, neither under-
> stand I what thou sayest. And he went out into
> the porch; *and the cock crew.* (Mark 14:68, KJV)

"And the cock crew" is omitted.

"And Jesus saith unto him, Verily I say unto thee, That this day, even in this night, before the cock crow twice, thou shalt deny me thrice" (Mark 14:30, KJV). Mark 14:68 is a fulfillment of the prophecy of Mark 14:30. Peter was being his usual self in proclaiming that he would never forsake the Lord Jesus Christ, but in Mark 14:30, the Lord had told Peter that before the rooster will crow twice, he will have denied Him three times. Upon the third denial of Christ, Peter went out on to the porch, and the cock crew, and Peter remembered the Lord's words. Some of the modern versions omit this very important fact where it shows a fulfillment of the prophecy of the Lord Jesus to Peter. Now, another ruination of this verse comes when some of the other modern versions use the words "a rooster crowed."

The term in the King James "the cock" is in the nominative case. The nominative is the case used to show the subject of a sentence or a clause. In Mark 14:68, the term "the cock" is the subject of the clause. The modern versions translate it as one of the roosters crowing, but the Lord Jesus Christ told Peter that "the cock will crow twice." Mark 14:68 in the KJV and its predecessors all use the word *the*, making it the specific rooster that Christ had ordained to crow at that time. Am I being picayune? The answer is no because this principle is laid out in another verse.

> Notwithstanding, lest we should offend them,
> go thou to the sea, and cast an hook, and take
> up the fish that first cometh up; and when thou
> hast opened his mouth, thou shalt find a piece of
> money: that take, and give unto them for me and
> thee. (Matthew 17:27, KJV)

If you notice in Matthew 17:27, is the Lord speaking of finding a piece of money in a fish? No! In *the* fish which first cometh up! He is prophesying that a specific fish would have the money in its mouth. Just as He prophesied that a specific rooster would crow when Peter denied Him the third time. Did the rooster sit there and count the number of times Peter denied the Lord? Of course not. That rooster was ordained by the Lord to crow when the Lord commanded Him to. Very, very important principle and action. If the Lord can command the sea and the waves to be cease, He can surely ordain an animal to do His bidding. How wonderful the King James keeps this intact and gives us the principle. It truly is God's real word!

Mark 14:70

> And he denied it again. And a little after, they
> that stood by said again to Peter, Surely thou art
> one of them: for thou art a Galilaean, *and thy
> speech agreeth thereto.* (Mark 14:70, KJV)

"And thy speech agreeth thereto" is omitted.

"And after a while came unto him they that stood by, and said to Peter, Surely thou also art one of them; for thy speech bewrayeth thee" (Matthew 26:73, KJV). Mark 14:70 and Matthew 26:73 are confirming verses that it was the dialect or accent that caused the people around Peter to know that he was a Galilean. The word for "speech" in the Greek is *lalia* and carries with it the alternate meanings of "dialect," "accent," or "pronunciation." Mark 14:70 states that the people knew Peter was from Galilee by the means of his accent or pronunciation. As there are different accents or dialects in almost every language, these accents can allow you to know where a person comes from. If a person has a Scottish accent, then you know they are from Scotland. If they have an English accent, you know they are from England. So the part that is left out by the modern versions is very important because the people around Peter knew he was a Galilean by means of his accent. Otherwise, if you read the modern versions, how would the people around him know he was a Galilean?

How do people know we are Christians? They know by our actions and our words. Mark 16:17 states that Christians will speak with new tongues; that is, before salvation, our words were always talking worldly things, but the new tongues of salvation cause us to speak spiritual things. By these words, people will know that we are identified with Jesus. That is a very important principle that is omitted from the modern versions in Mark 14:70. Once again, the King James Bible keeps together a very important spiritual principle.

Mark 15:3

And the chief priests accused him of many things:
but he answered nothing. (Mark 15:3, KJV)

"But he answered nothing" is omitted.

Here, we have another omission of a prophecy. "He was oppressed, and he was afflicted, yet he opened not his mouth: he is brought as a lamb to the slaughter, and as a sheep before her shearers is dumb, so he openeth not his mouth" (Isaiah 53:7, KJV). Mark 15:3 is a fulfillment of Isaiah 53:7 in that Jesus did not answer any of the false accusations brought against Him. Once again, the modern versions omit a very important phrase, linking it to a prophecy that was about 750 years old.

Mark 15:8

And the multitude *crying aloud* began to desire him to do as he had ever done unto them. (Mark 15:8, KJV)

"Crying aloud" is omitted.

The crowd was starting to sound out in an uproar, and their voices were very loud. The words "crying aloud" denote a very loud yelling. The modern versions say the people were going up to Pilate, but the people were already assembled in front of him. They were crying out for Pilate to perform the custom that he did every Passover, and that was to release a prisoner. They were yelling because they wanted Barabbas to be released instead of Jesus. The way the modern versions put it, it is like they were going up to Pilate's hall to deliver him a petition. This crowd was anything but calm, and they wanted the blood of Jesus. No doubt, there were probably many of the friends of Barabbas in the crowd who wanted him released, so they were not going to demand his release in a quiet manner.

Mark 15:28

And the scripture was fulfilled, which saith,
And he was numbered with the transgressors.
(Mark 15:28, KJV)

The entire verse is omitted or placed in brackets.

This verse attacks the Lord Jesus Christ concerning His sacrifice. Mark 15:28 is a fulfillment of Isaiah 53:12:

Therefore will I divide him a portion with the great, and he shall divide the spoil with the strong; because he hath poured out his soul unto death: *and he was numbered with the transgressors*; and he bare the sin of many, and made intercession for the transgressors. (Isaiah 53:12, KJV)

By removing this verse or bracketing it (same mind-set), the modern Bibles are denying that the Lord Jesus Christ fulfilled the prophecy of Isaiah 53:12 on the cross. The Lord Jesus Christ had to be made sin for the elect. "For he hath made him to be sin for us, who knew no sin; that we might be made the righteousness of God in him" (2 Corinthians 5:21, KJV). The Lord Jesus Christ Himself was innocent of any sin, but because He took on Himself the sins of all the elect, He was therefore guilty before God of all the sins He was bearing. Therefore, He could rightly be called a transgressor but for the sake of the elect. This is why the Lord Jesus had asked if God had forsaken Him because this was the first time in all eternity that the Father and the Son were separated. God could not look upon sin, but

He greatly accepted the sacrifice of the Lord Jesus Christ on behalf of the elect; and because of that, every true believer is now fitted for Heaven.

So when the modern Bible rewriters remove this verse, they are removing one of the greatest teachings on the sacrifice of Christ. Isn't it a shame that so many Christians accept these false versions and do not realize that Satan is selling them a bill of goods? One of the biggest cries from the modern-version camp is that no doctrine is missing from the modern versions. Well, quite frankly, to remove a verse that has specific teachings on the crucifixion of Christ is to remove a part of the doctrine of Christ. A person who orders a steak in a restaurant and receives only half of it still has steak, but half is missing. When a Christian goes to a bookstore and buys a modern version, they are paying full price for a partial Bible. Not too smart, huh?

Mark 16:8

And they went out *quickly*, and fled from the sepulchre; for they trembled and were amazed: neither said they any thing to any man; for they were afraid. (Mark 16:8, KJV)

Quickly is omitted.

As soon as they received the word from the angel to go tell His disciples, they departed quickly from the tomb with a combination of fear and with great joy. The word in the Greek behind "quickly" carries with it the meaning of "swiftly" or "without delay." They did not just walk or walk fast after they departed from the tomb, but they had run from the tomb, for they knew that the disciples would have wanted to know as soon as possible. The women had fled from the sepulcher in both amazement and trembling. The experience would have been a time of mixed emotions for anybody, but it seemed that the great joy had overshadowed the fear. They did not stop to speak to anyone but went right to the disciples as the angel had commanded them to do. The women were obedient to the angel when they quickly departed the tomb. This fact is missing in the modern versions.

Mark 16:9–20

Because of the length of this scripture, I will only include the comments here, but you can look at your modern version and see the doubt it casts upon it. This passage is placed in brackets, and its authenticity is questioned in the footnotes. This section of scripture has many ancient witnesses and is found either in full or part in 618 extant manuscripts, along with early patristic evidence such as Justin Martyr, Irenaeus, and Tertullian of the second century.

Many preachers and theologians make false claims that Mark 16:9–20 is not found in any old manuscripts. Once again, when a person does not do real studies, which can yield truth, they remain ignorant as anyone can be. Mark 16:9–20 is found in many ancient manuscripts; in fact, 618 of them. A very partial list is below.

Byzantine Text (AD 450–1450)
A 02, Alexandrinus (fifth century)
C 04, Ephraemi Rescriptus (fifth century)
D 05, Bezae Cantabrigiensis (fifth century)
K 017 (ninth century)
Q 026 (fifth century)
W 032 (fourth/fifth century)
X 033 (tenth century)
Delta 037 (ninth century)
Theta 038 (ninth century)
PI-041 (ninth century)
28, Minuscule (eleventh century)
33, Minuscule (ninth century)
137, Minuscule (twelfth century)
138, Minuscule (eleventh century)
565, Minuscule (ninth century)
700, Minuscule, (eleventh century)
892, Minuscule (ninth century)

1010, Minuscule (twelfth century)
1110, Minuscule (eleventh century)
1210, Minuscule (eleventh century)
1215, Minuscule (thirteenth century)
1216, Minuscule (ninth century)
1217, Minuscule (AD 1186)
1221, Minuscule (eleventh century)
1582, Minuscule (AD 948)

Early Patristic Evidence

Second century. Justin Martyr, Irenaeus, Tertullian

Third century. Hippolytus, Vincentius at the Seventh Council of Carthage (AD 258); Acta Pilati, Apostolical Constitutions

Fourth century. Eusebius, Macarias Magnes, Aphraates, Didymium, the Syriac Acts of the Apostles, Epiphanius, Leontius, Ambrose, Chrysostom, Jerome, Augustine

Fifth century. Leo, Nestorius, Cyril of Alexandria, Victor of Antioch, Patricius, Marius Mercator

Sixth century. Gregentius, Prosper, John of Thessalonica, Hesychius, Gregentius, Modestus, Bishop of Jerusalem

Early Bible Versions That Contain Mark 16:9–20

Second century. Old Latin and Peshitta Syriac versions, Tatian's Diatessaron

Third century. Coptic and Sahidic versions

Fourth century. Curetonian Syriac and Gothic versions, Syriac table of canons

Fifth century. Armenian version (some copies), Philoxenian Syriac

Sixth and seventh centuries. Georgian and Ethiopic versions

Open your modern version and notice the words that these false versions use concerning their corrupted manuscripts: "authorities," "witnesses," "early," "ancient," and "oldest." If I were a new Christian, these words, when used so convincingly, would cause me to instantly question as to whether Mark 16:9–20 is really part of the book of Mark. They speak of the oldest Greek manuscripts, but there are Textus Receptus readings going back to the first and second century in the form of church lectionaries.

This questioning of Mark 16:9–20 is also stating that God was unable to preserve and protect His word since man was able to add anything they wanted. This is really an attack on the character of God. The Bible would definitely come in second place when you have the church of Rome, which places tradition and ritual much higher than scripture. So for them, the adding of words by scribes would not be something catastrophic. However, for the true Bible-believing Christian, it is catastrophic because if scribes down through the ages were able to add anything they desired, then we would have no way of knowing what God's word really says in contrast to what was added by man.

However, God has not left His children without reliable witnesses. He allowed 618 manuscripts to remain extant so that we may know that Mark 16:9–20 is indeed part of the inspired canon. God knew very well that His word was going to be attacked by the Gnostics and the intellectual community down through the ages, including the times we live in right now. We can choose to believe that God was able to preserve His word for 1,800 years, or we can believe that the word of God did not exist until two Roman Catholic occultists put together a perversion with less than 1 percent of the available manuscripts. As a matter of fact, the actual percentage is .0085632 of the existing manuscript evidence.

When we use the King James Bible, we are confident that we have the preserved word of God. He preserved it in the Masoretic Text (Ben Chayyim text) and the Textus Receptus. We do not need the approval of some unsaved apostate to tell us that we do not have the word of God in the KJB. It's interesting that in the prefaces of the modern versions, they are always comparing it to the King James Bible but never to the other modern versions. It smells like a well-orchestrated attack on the King James Bible by every modern version. Gee, I wonder why.

One quick question that needs to be asked: You needed a heart valve replacement. The cardiologist, while in school, was required to study several books on this technique, and the pages came to 5,255. But he did not think that the information in 5,210 of those pages were necessary, so he only studied 45 pages of the material. How confident would you be in his abilities to perform that operation? Think about it!

Mark 16:20

And they went forth, and preached every where, the Lord working with them, and confirming the word with signs following. *Amen.* (Mark 16:20, KJV)

Amen is omitted.

It is bad enough the modern-version editors disbelieve the authenticity of Mark 16:9–20, but they remove *amen* in verse 20. This also reveals something that if *amen* was removed, that means Mark 16:20 was around in the past. So if it didn't exist, then how was *amen* removed from the text? These modern-version translators seem to be clueless when dealing with reality. Mark 16:20 is found in manuscript C 04, Ephraemi Rescriptus (fifth century). The *amen* was removed from Mark 16:20 in manuscript A 02, Alexandrinus (fifth century). So if Mark 16:9–20 has no historical manuscript evidence, then how could two manuscripts from the fifth century have Mark 16:20 in them?

Luke 1:28

And *the angel* came in unto her, and said, Hail, thou that art highly favoured, the Lord is with thee: *blessed art thou among women.* (Luke 1:28, KJV)

"The angel" and *"blessed art thou among women"* are omitted.

The angel Gabriel had approached Mary and told her that she was highly favored and that the Lord was with her. Then he went on to tell her that she was blessed among women. At that moment, she did not know what this greeting and blessing meant. The promise of the Messiah was a major prophetic understanding in the ancient nation of Israel, and every woman had the hope that she would bear the promised Messiah. Well, that long-awaited privilege came to Mary, and the resulting greeting was that she was blessed among women. The great privilege of bearing the Messiah came to her alone, and that is why Gabriel said to her that she was blessed among women.

I do not profess to know the reason that the Gnostics left this out, but it could be that since they did not believe that divinity could dwell in human flesh, they might have decided to omit this part that Mary was blessed among women because she carried the sinless Messiah in her womb. It is another attempt by the modern versions to suppress important information. This part of the passage speaks specifically about Mary carrying the Messiah. The modern versions tend to turn specifics into ambiguities for the purpose of compromising biblical truth till Christianity is just one of the major world religions with its own holy book.

Luke 1:29

And *when she saw him*, she was troubled at his saying, and cast in her zmind what manner of salutation this should be. (Luke 1:29, KJV)

"When she saw him" is omitted.

The angel from the Lord was just about to make the announcement to Mary that she was going to bear the Messiah. The King James Bible makes it clear that the angel was definitely visible and speaking specifically to Mary. The modern versions make it look like she was just hearing a voice without seeing anyone specifically speak to her. The King James uses the word *she* in reference to Mary. Ten modern versions insert the proper name *Mary*, which is not found in this verse. The word for "Mary" in the Greek is *Maria* and is not found in this statement. They literally have added to the word of God.

Luke 2:14

Glory to God in the highest, and on earth peace, *good will toward men.* (Luke 2:14, KJV)

"Good will toward men" is changed to the idea that God is well-pleased with man.

If that was the case, then why did Christ have to die for the elect? "God judgeth the righteous, and God is angry with the wicked every day" (Psalm 7:11, KJV). Psalm 7:11 sure does not sound like God is pleased with man.

Luke 2:22

And when the days of *her purification* according to the law of Moses were accomplished, they brought him to Jerusalem, to present him to the Lord. (Luke 2:22, KJV)

"Her purification" is changed to "their purification."

This is one of the subtlest changes in the New Testament. This change actually attacks the sinless nature of the Lord Jesus Christ. If you will notice, all the modern versions state that the days had come to purify them after the birth of Jesus. The modern versions have changed *her* to *them*, which does not fit the biblical pattern of the Old Testament.

And when the days of her purifying are fulfilled, for a son, or for a daughter, she shall bring a lamb of the first year for a burnt offering, and a young pigeon, or a turtledove, for a sin offering, unto the door of the tabernacle of the congregation, unto the priest: Who shall offer it before the LORD, *and make an atonement for her;* and she shall be cleansed from the issue of her blood. *This is the law for her* that hath born a male or a female. And if she be not able to bring a lamb, then she shall

> bring two turtles, or two young pigeons; the one
> for the burnt offering, and the other for a sin offer-
> ing: *and the priest shall make an atonement for her,*
> and she shall be clean. (Leviticus 12:6–8, KJV)

According to the law of Moses, when a woman gives birth to a male, she had a time for purifying of forty-one days. She had him circumcised on the eighth day and then was to continue her purification for another thirty-three days. "And she shall then continue in the blood of her purifying three and thirty days; she shall touch no hallowed thing, nor come into the sanctuary, until the days of her purifying be fulfilled" (Leviticus 12:4, KJV). If you will notice in these Levitical scriptures, there is nothing stated concerning an offering for both child and mother. The sin offering and burnt offering were specifically for the mother, not mother and child.

By the modern versions' changing *her* to *them* or *their,* they are teaching that Christ was born with a sin nature. I have looked at some commentaries concerning Luke 2:22, and I was appalled at what some of them accept. Some claim that the word *their* is fine since Christ was to bear the sins of His people. It is true that He was to bear the sins of His people, but not at that time. He began his suffering in the garden of Gethsemane; and when He was on the cross, he bore the full brunt of God's justice in fulfilling the requirements of God's holy law. There is no way that Christ was born with sin, for then He could not have been the sinless Savior but would have been just another human being born in the lineage of Adamic sin. Christ was the second Adam, and that is what set Him apart from the sinful human race.

Christ did not need to have a sin offering for Him at birth because He was born sinless. Do you see how subtle this major attack on the sinless nature of the Lord Jesus Christ is written in the text? If you were not looking for it, you would glean right over it. Leviticus refutes the teaching in the modern versions that Christ needed to have an atonement made for Him. The Bible teaches in 1 Corinthians 2:13 that we are to compare scripture with scripture. "Which things also we speak, not in the words which man's wisdom teacheth, but which the Holy Ghost teacheth; comparing spiritual things with spiritual" (1 Corinthians 2:13, KJV). The scripture does not compare in the modern versions either. Let us look at Leviticus 12:6–8 in the NIV.

> "When the days of *her purification* for a son or daughter are over, she is to bring to the priest at the entrance to the Tent of Meeting a year-old lamb for a burnt offering and a young pigeon or a dove for a sin offering. He shall offer them before the LORD to make atonement for her, *and then she will be ceremonially clean from her flow of blood." These are the regulations for the woman* who gives birth to a boy or a girl. If she cannot afford a lamb, she is to bring two doves or two young pigeons, one for a burnt offering and the other for a sin offering. In this way the priest will make *atonement for her, and she will be clean.* (Leviticus 12:6–8, NIV)

> When the time of *their* purification according to the Law of Moses had been completed, Joseph and Mary took him to Jerusalem to present him to the Lord. (Luke 2:22, NIV)

So if you compare scripture with scripture in the NIV, you will see there is no harmony between the scriptures of Leviticus and that of Luke 2:22. This shows a very serious deficiency in the accuracy of the NIV, and this is only one example from this hideous book.

In the Greek Textus Receptus, which underlies the King James Bible, the word is *autes*, which is strictly in the feminine gender (but it was changed in the Hort-Westcott text to *auton*, which can be used as a masculine, feminine, or neuter), "autes" is singular while *auton* is plural. It is plural because it ends in omega nu. So we see it was changed from feminine singular to the plural to make the case of the

Gnostics that Jesus was not born sinless but became the Christ at His baptism.

This attack on the Lord Jesus Christ finds agreement in the Roman Catholic and Jehovah's Witness Bible. If you use a modern version, you are in bad company. "Be ye not unequally yoked together with unbelievers: for what fellowship hath righteousness with unrighteousness? and what communion hath light with darkness?" (2 Corinthians 6:14, KJV). If you use a modern version, you are unequally yoked with unbelievers by means of their translations, which means you are in violation of the scriptures! It is a shame that the majority of Christians will research a mutual fund they want to invest in, check out the history of a car they want to buy, research a neighborhood to live in, but when it comes to God's word, they couldn't care less what they use. This is a sorry indictment upon many Christians, and then they ask why God won't bless them. Think about it!

Luke 2:33

And *Joseph* and his mother marvelled at those things which were spoken of him. (Luke 2:33, KJV)

Joseph is changed to "father."

If you notice something about the modern versions, they change *Joseph* to "father." These modern versions have complete agreement with the Roman Catholic and Jehovah's Witness Bibles. In the Textus Receptus, the proper name *Joseph* is written; but in the Hort-Westcott Greek, the term was changed to "father," which comes from the Sinaiticus manuscript. The effect of changing *Joseph* to "father" will teach that Jesus had an earthly father, which completely voids the cardinal doctrine of the virgin birth of Christ. If Joseph was the earthly father of the Lord Jesus, then He would have had to inherit the sin nature that was passed down from Adam. Gnostics teach that all flesh is evil, and there is no way that a holy God could dwell in sinful flesh.

By removing verses that support the virgin birth, it brings Jesus down to the level of just a human being. If Jesus was born with a sin nature, then He was an unqualified candidate for atonement for the sins of His people, and therefore, we Christians are still in our sins. In the second century, a heretic named Marcion disqualified Matthew, Mark, and John as being legitimate gospels and held only that Luke was authentic. However, he tended to make changes in the book of Luke to fit his Gnostic beliefs and may have been the one who changed the text from *Joseph* to "father."

Nevertheless, whoever changed it, it remained that way for sixteen hundred years, resurrected in the nineteenth century and has been accepted by unbelieving modern scholarship and given credence by Christians who use these modern versions without doing any investigation of the version they use.

When trying to understand the subject of the corruption of the modern versions, you must understand it as thousands of small corruptions, such as the one we just saw, rather than a few large corruptions. If Satan used large and obvious corruptions, then Christians would not accept it, but Satan knows that the easiest way to corrupt and derail Christianity is by subtlety, through the back door. It is easier to make smaller encroachments through the back door than a major frontal assault. The NIV and ESV are the most corrupted of the modern versions, yet is used by more Christians and churches than ever before.

Luke 2:40

> And the child grew, and waxed strong *in spirit*, filled with wisdom: and the grace of God was upon him. (Luke 2:40, KJV)

"In spirit" is omitted.

The modern versions omit the words "in spirit," which means anything could be substituted for those words. Those words are important because they tell us that as the Lord Jesus Christ was growing in the Spirit, it was by the Spirit that He gained wisdom daily.

Christ, being divine in nature, was also human in His nature and attained wisdom daily, although He never ceased to be God. It is another one of those great mysteries.

Luke 2:43

And when they had fulfilled the days, as they returned, the child Jesus tarried behind in Jerusalem; and *Joseph and his mother* knew not of it. (Luke 2:43, KJV)

"Joseph and his mother" changed to "parents."

This verse is brother to Luke 2:33. "And Joseph and his mother marvelled at those things which were spoken of him" (Luke 2:33, KJV). It is very important to understand that God has written the Bible very meticulously, and nothing is there that does not belong there. God specifically makes a point in Luke 2:33 and 43 that Joseph was not the earthly father of the Lord Jesus Christ. If Joseph was the earthly father of the Lord Jesus Christ, that would completely nullify the virgin birth, and that would also mean the Lord Jesus Christ was not born sinless and therefore would be disqualified as being the Savior. The modern versions all claim that Joseph was the father of Jesus in Luke 2:33, and in this verse, they lump Joseph and Mary as His parents.

Jesus was born totally apart from any earthly father. The Holy Spirit came upon Mary, and she conceived, and thus the virgin birth of Christ. The modern versions, because of Gnostic influence, have attempted to diminish the reality of the virgin birth, which was absolutely necessary for salvation to be effectual. Do not fall for the idea that words in the Bible are not important and that only concepts are. God wrote the Bible in words, not concepts. Whenever words are tampered with in any venue, meanings become changed and clouded. This is what leads to nebulous Bible passages with ill-defined understanding instead of the very specifics that God wrote that engenders clear understanding. "I will worship toward thy holy temple, and praise thy name for thy lovingkindness and for thy truth:

for thou hast magnified thy word above all thy name" (Psalm 138:2, KJV). Once again, the King James brings glory to God.

Luke 2:49

> And he said unto them, How is it that ye sought me? wist ye not that I must be *about my Father's business*? (Luke 2:49, KJV)

"About my Father's business" is changed to "in my father's house."

Since this verse is not corrupted in the Hort-Westcott text, it is subject to the translators, and they just followed whatever the previous version said without even looking at the text. The word for "house" is not in the Greek text and therefore is not the focus of this verse. The Lord Jesus Christ was twelve years old in this portion of scripture. He had remained behind in Jerusalem, and when Mary and Joseph found Him, He was in the temple sitting with all the theologians discussing biblical things.

Jesus had come to earth to die for His people, saving them from eternal damnation. Jesus was in the temple, but that is not the focus of this verse. "Jesus saith unto them, My meat is to do the will of him that sent me, and to finish his work" (John 4:34, KJV). Jesus was doing the will of God and to finish the work. The modern versions focus wrongly on the place where Jesus was. The King James Bible focuses on the reason that Christ was there; plus, the words "my Father's business" shows that, at twelve years old, Jesus already knew that He was the Son of God. This is a phrase that shows the deity of the Lord Jesus Christ and His relationship with His Father. Jesus knew that He came to earth for a purpose, and even at twelve years old, He was preparing for the time when He would be revealed and start His earthly ministry.

Luke 4:4

> And Jesus answered him, saying, It is written, That man shall not live by bread alone, *but by every word of God*. (Luke 4:4, KJV)

"But by every word of God." is omitted.

The affected part of this verse is not found in either (B) Vaticanus or (a) (Aleph) Sinaiticus. These are just deleted without reason. The removal of this part of scripture gives the impression that every word of God is not important. The Christian is to live by the word of God in contrast to the world that lives only by its five senses. The editors of the modern versions make it clear that their concern is not that Christians read the Bible in its entirety, without any deletions or omissions, but they truncate the word of God according to the Westcott-Hort belief system.

If these editors of the modern versions were serious about giving the Christians a complete Bible, they would not allow tampered versions to be placed into the hands of Christians. Their unconcern is obvious when they impeach the verity of the scriptures by even removing the reminder to Christians that we are to live by every word of God, and where is the word of God found? In the Holy Bible!

There is a total of 140,521 words in the Greek text of the New Testament. The Hort-Westcott text differs from the Textus Receptus in 5,604 places for a total of 9,970 words. That is 7 percent of the entire New Testament in Greek. That would be approximately 15.4 words per page in the New Testament Greek. That is a copious amount of corruption, yet Christians claim that their modern version is more accurate than the King James! Dr. Jack Moorman has researched and found that 2,886 words have been eliminated from the Greek Textus Receptus. This is the equivalent of removing 1 and 2 Peter from the New Testament.

By removing the requirement for Christians to live by the word of God, it opens the doors for false churches and cults to fill in that gap with their own teachings and rituals. If we do not live by the word of God, then what do we live by? Is it the teachings of apostate Protestantism? Is it the superstition of the Roman Catholic institution? Is it the phony love gospel as found in many cults? When the command of scripture to live by scripture is removed, it opens the door for Satan's people to fill in that gap.

That part of the verse is very important because God had promised to preserve His words and not the concepts or teachings. "The words of the LORD are pure words: as silver tried in a furnace of earth, purified seven times. Thou shalt keep them, O LORD, thou shalt preserve them from this generation for ever" (Psalm 12:6–7, KJV). Not only has God promised to preserve His words, but this passage is a quotation from the Old Testament.

> And he humbled thee, and suffered thee to hunger, and fed thee with manna, which thou knewest not, neither did thy fathers know; that he might make thee know that man doth not live by bread only, but by every word that proceedeth out of the mouth of the LORD doth man live. (Deuteronomy 8:3 KJV)

In Deuteronomy, God had told the Israelites that man does not live by only bread but by the word of God. The Israelites were in the wilderness for forty years, and throughout their sojourn, was it only the physical food that kept them going? It was God's guidance, and His guidance came through the written and spoken word. So when these modern Gnostics remove any part of scripture, they are denying true guidance for the Christian from the words of God Himself. Do the modern intellects actually believe they have more knowledge and wisdom than God so that they can sit in judgment of His holy word?

The modern versions disregard the very words of God in the Bible and take the liberty of removing what they do not want. The second-century Gnostics attacked the scriptures, and the intellects of today claim superior knowledge to what they had back then and yet have chosen to agree with the Gnostics by perpetuating the evil attacks on the scriptures. So how then do today's version pundits hold superior knowledge when they are doing the same things the unbelieving Gnostics did and accepting all their corruptions? That would be like a medical doctor who holds a degree from Johns Hopkins University or Harvard University but who still uses second-century medical techniques. Could the seminaries be putting out religious Gnostics rather than true Bible-believing Christians? Guess what?

Whatever school uses the Hort-Westcott text, that school is a descendant of the school of Alexandria, a.k.a. Gnosticism. Then we wonder why our churches are overrun with false gospels. False versions cannot expose or expunge false gospels, not when they themselves are a false gospel.

Luke 4:8

And Jesus answered and said unto him, *Get thee behind me, Satan*: for it is written, Thou shalt worship the Lord thy God, and him only shalt thou serve. (Luke 4:8, KJV)

"Get thee behind me Satan" is omitted.

In this verse, the Lord Jesus had dialogued with Satan in His temptations. However, at this point, the temptations had finished, and Jesus was now rebuking and sending Satan away in a very effective manner. The Lord Jesus had rebuked Satan because He had successfully endured the temptations, and now Jesus is specifically telling Satan to go. "Submit yourselves therefore to God. Resist the devil, and he will flee from you" (James 4:7, KJV). The principle is given to us in James 4:7 that if you resist the devil and his temptations, he will flee from you. It does not mean that he will never return to tempt.

This portion of Luke 4:8 is very important because it tells us who is truly behind the temptation of the Saints. Jesus quotes a passage from Deuteronomy 6:13 in His rebuffing of Satan's temptations. It tells us that the key to overcoming temptation is the scriptures themselves. When we have them memorized and Satan begins to attack in a moment of weakness, then we can be like the apostle Paul who became strong in weakness. "Therefore I take pleasure in infirmities, in reproaches, in necessities, in persecutions, in distresses for Christ's sake: for when I am weak, then am I strong" (2 Corinthians 12:10, KJV). It is a shame that the modern versions omit the part where the Lord directly rebukes Satan and commands him to leave. It is important to know who our archenemy is and the secret to defeat him. This is probably why we have so many modern versions and simultaneously an escalation in sin among Christians.

Luke 4:18

> The Spirit of the Lord is upon me, because he hath anointed me to preach the gospel to the poor; he hath sent me *to heal the brokenhearted*, to preach deliverance to the captives, and recovering of sight to the blind, to set at liberty them that are bruised. (Luke 4:18, KJV)

"To heal the brokenhearted" is omitted.

> The spirit of the Lord God is upon me; because the Lord hath anointed me to preach good tidings unto the meek; he hath sent me to bind up the brokenhearted, to proclaim liberty to the captives, and the opening of the prison to them that are bound. (Isaiah 61:1, KJV)

Luke 4:18 is a quote of Isaiah 61:1. The Lord Jesus Christ was in the synagogue on the sabbath day, and He was handed the scroll of Isaiah. He read Isaiah 61, which was the description of His own ministry. In Isaiah 61:1, the phrase "bind up the brokenhearted" carries with it the meaning of "to wrap firmly or gird about those who are destroyed or broken." It carries with it the idea that the Messiah will bring salvation to those who are downtrodden. That can be applied to every human being in this world as depression runs high, and people can put on a happy exterior, but inside they may be crushed.

Luke 4:18 carries the same meaning that Christ is going to heal or make whole those who are broken or shattered in the heart. He is not speaking of a physical sickness but a depressed spirit, which can lead to physical sickness. Instead, what is in view here is the healing of salvation. Christ makes us whole through salvation.

> Afterward Jesus findeth him in the temple, and said unto him, Behold, thou art made whole: sin no more, lest a worse thing come unto thee. The man departed, and told the Jews that it was Jesus, which had made him whole. And therefore did the Jews persecute Jesus, and sought to slay him, because he had done these things on the sabbath day. (John 5:14–16, KJV)

This is the whole essence of what is in view in Isaiah 61:1–3 and Luke 4:18. Why this section was omitted in the modern versions is a mystery. Apparently, the Gnostic mutilators did not think that Christ could heal the brokenhearted through salvation. They did not think of Him as deity, so any way they could put a doubt on His ministry, they would. He was the complete fulfillment of Isaiah 61:1.

Luke 4:41

> And devils also came out of many, crying out, and saying, Thou art *Christ* the Son of God. And he rebuking them suffered them not to speak: for they knew that he was Christ. (Luke 4:41, KJV)

Christ is omitted.

The divine title for the Lord Jesus Christ is *Christ*. This verse leaves out the witness that the devils had for the Lord Jesus Christ. They knew exactly who He was because before the rebellion of Satan and the fallen angels, they were up there with Him. The Lord Jesus had rebuked them and commanded them to stop speaking because the testimony of who the Lord Jesus is was not to come from the mouth of devils but from the mouth of His children. "That I may show forth all thy praise in the gates of the daughter of Zion: I will rejoice in thy salvation" (Psalm 9:14, KJV). The modern versions leave out the fact that the devils knew who He was, and this is import-ant because it speaks of the pre-Bethlehem existence of the Lord Jesus

Christ; in other words, His eternal nature. This is just another attack upon the divine nature of the Lord Jesus Christ.

Luke 4:44

And he preached in the synagogues of Galilee. (Luke 4:44, KJV)

Galilee is changed to "Judean" or "Judea."

Jesus was in the area of Galilee at this point in His ministry. In fact, Capernaum was His base of operations; and from there, Jesus ministered to the other cities in Galilee. He was also a guest at the house of Peter while He was in this area. "And he arose out of the synagogue, and entered into Simon's house. And Simon's wife's mother was taken with a great fever; and they besought him for her" (Luke 4:38, KJV). Judea was south of Galilee. Jesus had ministered in the Galilee area for over a year. Just another example of the confusion the modern versions bring to the table. The modern translators need to study geography.

Luke 5:33

And they said unto him, *Why do* the disciples of John fast often, and make prayers, and likewise the disciples of the Pharisees; but thine eat and drink? (Luke 5:33, KJV)

"Why do" and the question mark *(?)* are omitted, thus changing the verse from a question to a declarative statement.

Here is a very visible case of turning a question into a declarative statement. The scribes and Pharisees asked Jesus why His disciples ate and drank while John's disciples fasted often and prayed? The modern versions take this question and turn it into a declarative statement that the disciples of Jesus did not fast and pray but only ate and drank. The modern versions make the disciples out to be a bunch of party people while the King James Bible turns the scenario into a question for the sake of finding out why there is a difference between the disciples of Jesus and the disciples of John. It is totally inconsistent with proper grammar, but then again, the modern versions are inconsistent with truth.

Luke 5:38

But new wine must be put into new bottles; *and both are preserved.* (Luke 5:38, KJV)

"And both are preserved" is omitted.

Neither do men put new wine into old bottles: else the bottles break, and the wine runneth out, and the bottles perish: but they put new wine into new bottles, and both are preserved. (Matthew 9:17, KJV)

And no man putteth new wine into old bottles: else the new wine doth burst the bottles, and the wine is spilled, and the bottles will be marred: but new wine must be put into new bottles. (Mark 2:22, KJV)

And no man putteth new wine into old bottles; else the new wine will burst the bottles, and be spilled, and the bottles shall perish. But new wine must be put into new bottles; and both are preserved. (Luke 5:37–38, KJV)

In the above three verses, we read the parable of putting new wine into new bottles. Jesus took this picture from a familiar part of daily life. In Matthew 9:16, Jesus warned that an old garment could not be patched up with a new patch of cloth. "No man putteth a piece of new cloth unto an old garment, for that which is put in to fill it up taketh from the garment, and the rent is made worse" (Matthew

9:16, KJV). Verse 16 is basically stating in parabolic language that the new life, the Christian life, could not be used to fill in the breaches of Pharisaic Judaism. If that were to take place, the gospel patches would not fit into the garment of law, and that would cause a bigger rip. The gospel of grace was totally different than the Mosaic law and therefore could not be combined because either a person is saved by grace, or they are saved by keeping the law perfectly, without violation of a single law, minor or major.

Then Jesus continued on in His parable about the new life. We see the same lesson but in different language. He was stating in parabolic language that the new wine of the Gospel cannot be placed in old bottles. It says that the gospel of grace cannot be found within the confines of the law. A person becomes saved by grace without keeping the law. The grace would be the new wine, and the old bottles would be the Mosaic law. The principle is thus: if new wine was placed in an old bottle, the fermentation process would cause the old bottles to swell, and then they would burst. What was done and still is done in the Middle East is that the wine is placed into new leather flasks made of either goatskin or sheepskin, and the fermentation process would be slowed and the leather flasks would not burst.

The making of wine is not in view in this parable, but just like the new cloth on an old garment, the new wine of the Gospel must stand alone and not be mixed with the Mosaic law. If someone tried to mix grace and law, they would burst because they would not know what laws to keep and what laws to neglect under grace. The *new wine* of the Gospel makes a person holy, alive unto God, having faith, and spiritually alive. The law does not accomplish these things, and that is why Jesus said the new wine must be in the wineskin of the Gospel because grace stands on its own and is never earned or mixed with law. When a person becomes saved, they have the new regenerated soul, and this is where the Gospel fits perfectly; and because of it, both the gospel and the person receiving it are preserved eternally. This is another great truth that the modern versions omit. How can anyone build their faith on what is omitted in the Bible?

Luke 6:10

And looking round about upon them all, he said unto the man, Stretch forth thy hand. And he did so: and his hand was restored whole *as the other*. (Luke 6:10, KJV)

"As the other" is omitted.

This verse shows Jesus as the Creator and Healer. The verse tells us that the hand was restored as whole as the other one. The modern versions leave off the last phrase that his arm was now made whole "as the other," which shows Jesus restoring the arms as not only healing the man but as the Creator who creates the human body. Jesus designed our arms, and here He restores the man's arms as a whole pair. Omitting the last part does not give information concerning the fact that the arms were now healed and equal. A surgeon can restore an arm, but that does not mean it is as good as if it was never injured. By omitting that important part, Jesus is denied the glory as our Creator. There is no reason as to why that phrase has been omitted in the modern versions. It just basically seems like another attack on the Lord Jesus Christ. Remember, it was the heretic Gnostic Marcion (circa AD 85–160) that butchered the Gospel of Luke, and I would not doubt for a minute that this was his handiwork.

Luke 6:16

And *Judas the brother of James*, and Judas Iscariot, which also was the traitor. (Luke 6:16, KJV)

"Judas the brother of James" is changed to "Judas the son of James."

Judas (not Iscariot) had three names just like the father-in-law of Moses. Judas was the brother of James, who wrote the epistle of Jude. Judas was not the son of James. James and Judas were the sons of Alphaeus. Judas was known also as Thaddeus and Lebbaeus. By the modern versions calling him the son of James, they cause confusion and give another erroneous verse that hinders true Bible study.

The modern versions cannot be relied upon for accuracy. This is just one of many examples.

Luke 6:48

> He is like a man which built an house, and digged deep, and laid the foundation on a rock: and when the flood arose, the stream beat vehemently upon that house, and could not shake it: for it was *founded upon a rock*. (Luke 6:48, KJV)

"Founded upon a rock" is omitted.

Once again, the modern versions attack and remove a tremendous reference to the Lord Jesus Christ. In the Old Testament, God is spoken of as a rock:

> O come, let us sing unto the LORD: let us make a joyful noise to the rock of our salvation. (Psalm 95:1, KJV)

> But the LORD is my defence; and my God is the rock of my refuge. (Psalm 94:22, KJV)

> And they remembered that God was their rock, and the high God their redeemer. (Psalm 78:35, KJV)

These three verses will suffice to show us that in Luke 6:48, the Lord Jesus Christ was not speaking about a house that was well-built. This was far from a structural engineering lesson. The teaching here is that those who are on the Lord Jesus Christ—namely, those who are saved—are like a house that can never be affected by any of the harsh elements because of its foundation. Our foundation is in the Lord Jesus Christ. "For other foundation can no man lay than that is laid, which is Jesus Christ" (1 Corinthians 3:11, KJV). The true believer is safe upon the Lord Jesus Christ, and the modern versions hide this great and comforting fact. God is our rock and our salvation, and to remove the part in Luke 6:48 about being founded on a rock is to distort this beautiful truth.

Luke 7:10

And they that were sent, returning to the house, found the servant whole *that had been sick.* (Luke 7:10, KJV)

"That had been sick" is omitted.

Here is the story of the centurion who sent people to the Lord Jesus Christ to heal his servant. He did not feel worthy for the Lord Jesus to come under his roof, but he had such faith that he believed that all Jesus had to do was to say the word, no matter what distance He was from the centurion's home, and his servant would be healed. Jesus saw this as great faith, and because of that faith, Jesus healed his servant from a distance.

In verse 10, we read a very important part to the narrative that is found in the last phrase: "that had been sick." The modern versions omit this phrase and therefore reduce the visible effect of both the miracle of healing Jesus did and the faith that the centurion had in Christ. The whole essence of this narrative is the faith of the centurion and the deity of Christ showing through with the ability to heal at a distance. The modern versions leave out the fact that the servant was previously sick, and it just makes the verse look like he was well when visitors came to him. The whole idea was that Christ healed him, and those who saw him saw that he was well, and they knew that he was previously ill. Once again, the modern versions rob the Lord Jesus Christ of glory for His divine healing of the centurion's servant.

Luke 7:22

Then *Jesus* answering said unto them, Go your way, and tell John what things ye have seen and heard; how that the blind see, the lame walk, the lepers are cleansed, the deaf hear, the dead

are raised, to the poor the gospel is preached.
(Luke 7:22, KJV)

Jesus is changed to "he."

Here, Jesus was directly answering the disciples of John who inquired if He was the expected Messiah, or should they look for another? Jesus answered according to the works He had done, which would give John sufficient evidence that Jesus was indeed the Messiah. When they change *Jesus* to "he," it could look like one of the disciples was giving the answer instead of Jesus Himself.

Luke 7:28

For I say unto you, Among those that are *born of women* there is not a greater *prophet* than John *the Baptist*: but he that is least in the kingdom of God is greater than he. (Luke 7:28, KJV)

"Prophet" and *"the Baptist"* are omitted.

On this particular verse, different modern versions omit different parts of this verse. Some of these leave out the part "born of women." This shows the humanity of John and that he was born of Elizabeth, who was the cousin of Mary, the mother of Jesus. Then some omit his title "the Baptist." That part of his name revealed his ministry as the forerunner of the Lord Jesus Christ. "Behold, I will send you Elijah the prophet before the coming of the great and dreadful day of the LORD" (Malachi 4:5, KJV).

John had baptized people in the Jordan River as he preached the coming kingdom of God. They all omit his office of being a "prophet." John was the last of the Old Testament prophets. This showed his official standing as equal to Isaiah or Jeremiah, even though he did not pen any books. Nevertheless, his ministry was prophetic and ordained from heaven. Once again, we see the modern versions mutilating a portion of scripture; plus, they all do it differently based upon the preference of the translators. There is no reason why the phrase "born of women" should be omitted from these versions since it is in the Hort-Westcott text, but again, it goes back to the preferences and prejudices of the translators.

Luke 7:31

And the Lord said, Whereunto then shall I liken the men of this generation? and to what are they like? (Luke 7:31, KJV)

"And the Lord said" is omitted.

Here, we have another attack upon the Lord Jesus Christ. It is He who was making the above statement, but the modern versions based upon the Gnostic manuscripts chose to omit this fact. Since the Gnostics did not believe that the Lord Jesus Christ could be both a man and God in the flesh, they chose to omit the direct reference to the fact that He is being called *the Lord*. The Gnostics believed that flesh was evil, and based upon that fact, deity could not exist in a physical body. However, this is just another intellectual attack on the deity of the Lord Jesus Christ, which is made so plain in this verse. Once again, the King James Bible shows itself superior to the modern versions by not denying the lordship of Christ. That denial plays beautifully into the doctrinal belief system of the Jehovah's Witnesses, which has total commonality with the modern versions.

Luke 8:43

And a woman having an issue of blood twelve years, *which had spent all her living upon physicians*, neither could be healed of any. (Luke 8:43, KJV)

"Which had spent all her living upon physicians" is omitted.

The omitted part teaches that the woman had spent all that she had on physicians to help her stanch her blood flow. Since she had tried all human attempts and failed, she had faith enough just to touch the hem of Christ's garment and be healed. Her faith was proven correct because she was healed instantly. This verse teaches us that not all of man's ways will help our problem, but when we trust the Lord to intervene in our problems, we can expect great results, as this woman did.

Luke 8:45

And Jesus said, Who touched me? When all denied, Peter *and they that were with him* said, Master, the multitude throng thee and press thee, *and sayest thou, Who touched me?* (Luke 8:45, KJV)

"And they that were with him" and *"and sayest thou, Who touched me?"* are omitted.

This verse has been attacked in two places by the scissor of the unbeliever. The first place it is attacked is when Jesus had asked who touched Him. There was a great crowd around Him, and the woman who had the issue of blood touched Him, and she was instantly healed. All those around Him had denied that they touched Him; maybe some out of fear, and others were telling the truth. This statement perplexed the disciples because there was a great crowd around Jesus, and many were touching Him.

If you notice, the KJV text states that it was Peter and those who were with him. This was shortened to "Peter" alone. Now this would fall right into Roman Catholic theology as Peter was heralded as the first pope. So if the text only shows Jesus and Peter and not the others, then it would show a distinct relationship only between Christ and Peter. However, this could not be true because the real text states that the others also inquired of Jesus, which means that Jesus was not speaking only to Peter.

The second hit this verse took is when the disciples quoted Jesus about asking who touched Him. This portion of the verse is an emphasis on the fact that even though a person is in a crowd, Jesus knew exactly who His sheep are. "I am the good shepherd, and know my sheep, and am known of mine" (John 10:14, KJV). It did not matter if there was a great multitude of people; Jesus dealt with each individual believer on an individual basis. This is omniscience at work, where Jesus has personal knowledge of every one of His sheep.

The disciples did not understand at this point the divine nature of the Lord Jesus Christ. This should be a great comfort to Christians as Jesus knows every one of their hurts, needs, and desires and how unique each is to each person. It is not like earthly government where a king or president rules, and they make some kind of law that affects everyone, whether good or bad. Jesus sees each of His children as individuals, and no one has greater standing before Jesus than another.

Luke 8:48

And he said unto her, Daughter, *be of good comfort*: thy faith hath made thee whole; go in peace. (Luke 8:48, KJV)

"Be of good comfort" is omitted.

The woman who was afflicted with the issue of blood for twelve years would have been an outcast, and according to the law, she was unclean and was disallowed from going to the synagogue. She had enough faith to approach the Lord Jesus Christ, and when she touched the hem of His garment, she was instantly healed. Now, because she was unclean and knew the law, she had feared that she had broken the law by coming in contact with another, especially a rabbi. Jesus had known that virtue or power had gone out from Him, and when the woman knew that she was found out, she had feared. However, Jesus did not chide her but commended her for her faith in Him, and she was made well, so He told her to be of good comfort, so she would not fear.

The modern versions omit this important phrase because when a person has sinned tremendously in their life and God calls them, they need not fear coming to the Lord for salvation. Christ will clean up every person whom He saves, and He will take that cringing fear from them and turn that emotion into love for God and their fellow man. When the Lord tells this woman to be of good comfort, it is a statement that belongs to all Christians, especially if we sin. We can have confidence in bringing those things to the Lord. It is a shame that those who use the modern versions will never know of that comforting phrase. Christians who use modern versions are truly missing out on many great spiritual truths.

Luke 8:54

And he put them all out, and took her by the hand, and called, saying, Maid, arise. (Luke 8:54, KJV)

"And he put them all out" is omitted.

Here, Peter, James, and John had the privilege to witness another miracle of the Lord Jesus Christ. The daughter of Jairus was sick unto death, and while the Lord Jesus was coming to his house, Jesus had stopped to deal with the woman who had the issue of blood. It was during this time that Jairus sent word to the Lord Jesus that the girl had died. This is a similar situation to that of Lazarus. Jesus had delayed His coming, and Lazarus had died, but it was for a purpose to show the people that the Lord Jesus had power over death, thus confirming His deity. Here, Jesus delayed His coming, and the girl had died, but He sent word back to Jairus that he needed to have faith and believe, and she would be made whole. Jesus came into the house and saw the wailing. He told them that she was not dead but was sleeping. The reaction turned instantly from sadness to laughter.

The problem is that when we see something from man's point of view and then neglect God's point of view, it can be disastrous. It is like going to the funeral of a Christian. We see a body in a casket that is dead, but we do not see from God's vantage point that they are in heaven, more alive than they were here.

Then we come to verse 54, where Jesus takes all the unbelievers and puts them out of the room because of their mocking unbelief. "And he could there do no mighty work, save that he laid his hands upon a few sick folk, and healed them. And he marvelled because of their unbelief. And he went round about the villages, teaching" (Mark 6:5–6, KJV). These unbelievers did not believe that Jesus could cure her, and therefore, because of their unbelief, Jesus sent them away. If they would have shown faith, Jesus might have let them stay to witness the miracle of resurrection.

The modern versions leave out the part where the unbelievers were cast out of the room, and this is a very integral part of the narrative. As we read in Mark 6:5–6, Jesus could do no mighty works because of the unbelief of the people. "But without faith it is impossible to please him: for he that cometh to God must believe that he is, and that he is a rewarder of them that diligently seek him" (Hebrews 11:6, KJV). We find the principle in Hebrews 11:6 that those who come to God must believe that He is, and He is to be approached with faith. This is why Jesus had to put the unbelievers out of the room because they did not believe God, and they did not approach Him in faith. The King James Bible gives us the complete narrative by keeping that portion of scripture in. It helps teach us that we must never come to God without faith, or we must never adopt a mocking spirit because of viewing things from only our point of view.

Luke 9:1

> Then he called *his* twelve *disciples* together, and gave them power and authority over all devils, and to cure diseases. (Luke 9:1, KJV)

His is changed to "the," and *disciples* is omitted.

Here, in Luke 9:1, the Lord Jesus had called His twelve disciples together for the purpose of sending them on to continue His ministry when he went back to heaven. This was a test for them to see how well they would perform their ministry duties. Jesus called His disciples together for this task. If you will notice in the modern versions, it speaks about Jesus calling the twelve together and leaves out the fact that He called His disciples. This is a very horrible omission because in New Age thinking, the council of twelve are spirit guides who theoretically assist their seekers in healing and shifts of consciousness. This is nothing more than channeling devils, and the modern versions can leave one thinking that Jesus summoned the twelve or the council of twelve to go to earth and heal. This was the mission of His twelve disciples at this time: to heal. So the parallel is frightening because the modern versions play right into that New Age teaching and belief.

Jesus, in summoning His twelve disciples, represents the fact that He summons all His earthly disciples to bring the Gospel to the entire earth. He summons those who are His, and He does not send any unbeliever or devil to do the work of the Lord. "Saying, Let us alone; what have we to do with thee, thou Jesus of Nazareth? art thou come to destroy us? I know thee who thou art, the Holy One of God. And Jesus rebuked him, saying, Hold thy peace, and come out of him" (Mark 1:24–25, KJV). Jesus healed the man with a devil in the synagogue, and they said to Him that they knew Him as the Holy One of God, but Jesus rebuked the devils and told them to hold their peace. This is because Jesus will not accept any adulation from devils, never mind Him summoning them to do His evangelistic work.

Luke 9:35

And there came a voice out of the cloud, saying, This is my *beloved* Son: hear him. (Luke 9:35, KJV)

Beloved is omitted.

Here is another attack upon the Lord Jesus Christ. On the Mount of Transfiguration, Peter was speaking about building tabernacles for Moses and Elijah; and while he was speaking, God from heaven spoke and told all that Jesus is His beloved Son, and we are to hear Him. The word that is omitted in the modern versions is *beloved*. This word is in the singular, meaning God was speaking about Jesus alone. The word *beloved* means "to be dearly loved," and that is what God is saying: that He dearly loves His Son. The Gnostics did not believe that Jesus was the Son of God, and therefore, in disbelief, questioned how Jesus could be beloved of God? So in keeping with their belief system, they removed it. It is another example of Gnostic butchering.

Luke 9:43

And they were all amazed at the mighty power of God. But while they wondered every one at all things which *Jesus* did, he said unto his disciples. (Luke 9:43, KJV)

Jesus is changed to "he" in the NASV, ASV, HCSB, NRSV, RSV.

Once again, a proper name is changed to a pronoun to remove the name of Jesus from this scripture.

Luke 9:50

And Jesus said unto him, Forbid him not: for he that is not against *us* is for *us*. (Luke 9:50, KJV)

Us and *us* is changed to "you" and "you."

The way the modern versions change the word *us* to "you" makes it seem like they are teaching that Jesus is detaching Himself from the disciples. By using the word *us* in the King James Bible, Jesus is including Himself with those who will be hated by the world. "If the world hate you, ye know that it hated me before it hated you" (John 15:18, KJV). Jesus has always identified Himself with His people who have suffered persecution for Him. "And he fell to the earth, and heard a voice saying unto him, Saul, Saul, why persecutest thou me?" (Acts 9:4, KJV). Here is the full spiritual pecking order. "He that receiveth you receiveth me, and he that receiveth me receiveth him that sent me" (Matthew 10:40, KJV). Those who receive the believers are receiving the person of Christ, and those who receive Him are receiving the Father. You and me are different people, but the word *us* reveals we are together, just as Jesus is with His children.

Luke 9:54

And when his disciples James and John saw this, they said, Lord, wilt thou that we command fire to come down from heaven, and consume them, *even as Elias did?* (Luke 9:54, KJV)

"Even as Elias did" is omitted.

And Elijah answered and said to the captain of fifty, If I be a man of God, then let fire come down from heaven, and consume thee and thy fifty. And there came down fire from heaven, and consumed him and his fifty. (2 Kings 1:10, KJV)

And Elijah answered and said unto them, If I be a man of God, let fire come down from heaven, and consume thee and thy fifty. And the fire of God came down from heaven, and consumed him and his fifty. (2 Kings 1:12, KJV)

James and John were furious over the fact that the Samaritans would not let Jesus go into their village, so they had asked the Lord if they should command fire to come down from heaven and consume them. Now, they did not ask this off-the-cuff, but they asked if they should be like Elijah when he commanded fire to come down and consume the first two companies of fifty men. Some think this is where James and John received the name *sons of thunder*. They were probably looking at a total destruction like Sodom and Gomorrha. James and John did not realize that this was a different situation than in the time of Elijah.

Ahaziah had suffered a serious injury when he fell through a lattice, and instead of sending for Elijah to inquire of the Lord for him, he had chosen to inquire of Beelzebub, the god of Ekron. So Elijah told his messengers that because he chose to inquire of Beelzebub instead of the God of heaven, he was going to die in his bed. Then Elijah left the messengers, and they returned to Ahaziah to deliver the message. Then Ahaziah inquired as to who this was, and immediately he knew it was Elijah. Then Ahaziah dispatched a company of fifty men to bring Elijah back, and the fifty men were there to bring him back by force. But instead Elijah stated that if he was a man of God, then fire would come down and consume the company of men. This happened a second time. What was being shown here was that God was the God who could command fire to consume the enemies of His people; plus, He was showing Ahaziah that he was the real

God with the real power, who should have been consulted first about his condition.

The third company of soldiers came, but the commander spoke nice to him, and God told Elijah to go with them, but he delivered the same message to Ahaziah that he did to his messengers: that he would die in his bed because he chose to seek the god of Ekron. We see here that the word of God to Ahaziah did not change even when delivered directly to him or to his messengers; the message was the same. It is like the King James Bible, which does not change the message with every new version that comes off the publisher's printing presses. The modern versions omit the part about this verse going back to the time of Elijah, and this results in Christians missing out on the background.

Jesus did not come to destroy the lives of people, but the problem was that James and John were still living with the idea of instant judgment as seen in the Old Testament. Jesus was weaning them off this type of thinking by stating that they were not of the spirit of revenge or wrath, but they would receive the Holy Spirit who will make them meek and loving, a total difference from the instant-destruction mind-set.

Luke 9:55–56

> But he turned, and rebuked them, and said, *Ye know not what manner of spirit ye are of. For the Son of man is not come to destroy men's lives, but to save them.* And they went to another village. (Luke 9:55–56, KJV)

Verse 55, *"and said, Ye know not what manner of spirit ye are of,"* is omitted. Verse 56, *"for the Son of man is not come to destroy men's lives, but to save them,"* is omitted.

These are two of the most destroyed verses in the New Testament of the modern versions. Between the two verses, in the Greek, twenty words have been omitted, making twenty-eight less words in the English. Let us look at the context of these verses.

And it came to pass, when the time was come that he should be received up, he steadfastly set his face to go to Jerusalem, And sent messengers before his face: and they went, and entered into a village of the Samaritans, to make ready for him. And they did not receive him, because his face was as though he would go to Jerusalem. And when his disciples James and John saw this, they said, Lord, wilt thou that we command fire to come down from heaven, and consume them, even as Elias did? But he turned, and rebuked them, and said, Ye know not what manner of spirit ye are of. For the Son of man is not come to destroy men's lives, but to save them. And they went to another village. (Luke 9:51–56, KJV)

Looking at the context of these verses, we will see that the deletion of those twenty-eight words are an important part that gives us under-standing of two vital biblical truths: the nature of the Holy Spirit and the mission of the Lord Jesus Christ. Jesus had sent some messengers before him as He was ready to go to Jerusalem, but since the Samaritans were not accepted by the Jews, the Samaritans did not accept Jesus. So the disciples, in hopeful retribution, had remembered what Elijah did to the prophets of Baal on Mount Carmel and to the two compa-nies of men who were messengers of the king of Samaria, whom Elijah destroyed by bringing fire down from heaven on them (2 Kings 1). They wanted to repeat that action by calling fire down from heaven to destroy these Samaritans. As usual, the disciples did not under-stand what was happening. They were looking at vengeance on the Samaritans, but Jesus corrected their attitude for three major reasons:

1) All sin will be judged at the last day and not now. "Let both grow together until the harvest: and in the time of harvest I will say to the reapers, Gather ye together first the tares, and bind them in bundles to burn them: but gather the wheat into my barn" (Matthew 13:30, KJV).

2) The Holy Spirit is not a vengeful spirit. He was going to guide them into a new way of thinking. No longer would they think vengeance; instead, they were to think mercy, truth, and love. "Howbeit when he, the Spirit of truth, is come, he will guide you into all truth: for he shall not speak of himself; but whatsoever he shall hear, that shall he speak: and he will show you things to come" (John 16:13, KJV). This is why the Lord was emphasizing the fact that they did not know what Spirit they were of. Satan is the destroyer; the Holy Spirit is the life giver.

3) The mission of the Lord Jesus is to save the souls of His elect. "And she shall bring forth a son, and thou shalt call his name JESUS: for he shall save *his* people from their sins" (Matthew 1:21, KJV). Some of those elect were probably among the Samaritans, and Jesus did not come to destroy them but to save them. The disciples did not understand this yet. They had to be made aware that their primary responsibility was to be witnesses for the Lord Jesus Christ and not to return evil for evil.

The modern versions hold a consistency in their attacks on the Lord Jesus. Matthew 18:11 is omitted in the modern versions: "For the Son of man is come to save that which was lost" (Matthew 18:11, KJV).

In this verse, we see the mission of the Lord Jesus. If you notice, the teaching is parallel to that of Luke 9:56, of which that part is omitted from the text. Gnosticism attacked the idea of Christ being God in the flesh and the idea of Him being the Savior, so it follows that they would destroy whatever teachings there were concerning the salvation mission of the Lord Jesus Christ. It is a shame that the editors and writers of the modern versions agree wholeheartedly with the Gnostics. A major principle emerges here. In Genesis 1, we see a principle of creation.

> And God said, Let the earth bring forth the living
> creature after his kind, cattle, and creeping thing,
> and beast of the earth after his kind: and it was

> so. And God made the beast of the earth after his kind, and cattle after their kind, and every thing that creepeth upon the earth after his kind: and God saw that it was good. (Genesis 1:24–25, KJV)

When we look at these verses, we see that like begets like. Cattle do not bring forth baby monkeys, and vice versa. That principle is important when we look at Bible versions. True Christians brought forth true Bible versions. Unbelievers brought forth false versions. This means that those who bring forth these corrupted versions are unsaved people. Why would a true Christian choose to deceive another true Christian, unless the one deceiving is a Christian in name only?

There were two manuscript lines. The bottom line is that both cannot be correct.

Luke 9:55–56 is mutilated in the Sinaiticus manuscript and the Alexandrinus manuscript. The first part of verse 56 is also missing in the Vaticanus manuscript. All the other manuscripts that contain the Gospel of Luke include these verses in its entirety. It is found in the Old Latin Vulgate (c. AD 150) and the Peschito (c. AD 150), plus the Armenian, Coptic, Georgian, Slavonic, and Ethiopic versions; plus many church fathers such as Tertullian. The Eastern Church reads this portion of scripture after the day of Pentecost.

Westcott and Hort relegated these two verses to their pile of "rejected readings." Westcott and Hort were two closet Catholics, but Hort came out as early as 1847 in hatred of the Textus Receptus and his adoration of Mary. Today Protestant scholars laud these two men as great Christians. It is obvious that they do not know of what spirit they were of! As true Christians, we must choose this day whom we will serve, either the dedicated Roman Catholic deceivers who continue to give us these false versions or the true Christians who literally bathed the lineage of the King James Bible in blood to keep the words of God for subsequent generations. I guess there must be some reason that the Vatican hates the King James Bible but has no opposition to the modern versions. Think about it!

Luke 9:57

And it came to pass, that, as they went in the way,
a certain man said unto him, *Lord*, I will follow
thee whithersoever thou goest. (Luke 9:57, KJV)

Lord is omitted.

This unnamed disciple wanted to follow Jesus wherever He
went. This man knew who He was and addressed Him as *Lord*,
which the modern versions omit, thanks to their Gnostic corrupters.

Luke 9:59

And he said unto another, Follow me. But he
said, *Lord*, suffer me first to go and bury my
father. (Luke 9:59, KJV)

Lord is omitted.

Here is another case of a follower of Jesus who knew who He
was and addressed Him as *Lord*, but the Gnostics disbelieved that
Jesus could be deity, so they omitted *Lord*.

Luke 10:1

After these things the Lord appointed other *seventy
also*, and sent them two and two before his
face into every city and place, whither he himself
would come. (Luke 10:1, KJV)

"*Seventy also*" is changed to "seventy others." *Seventy* is also
changed to "seventy-two" in the NIV, CEB, CEV, ERV, ESV, GNB,
NCV, NET.

This verse has been attacked in two places. The first place is
when they change *seventy* to "seventy-two." "Seventy-two" holds
absolutely no significance and is not found in the King James Bible.
They would have been sent out by two for two basic reasons: the first
was for companionship, and the second was for legal reasons (the

law required two witnesses). The number seventy (70) was symbolic because there were seventy on the Sanhedrin, seventy nations listed in Genesis 10, all the souls that came from the loins of Jacob were seventy, seventy years of captivity in Babylon, Peter having to forgive seventy times seven. The sending of the seventy was kind of a precursor of the time when the Gospel would go forth throughout all the world.

The second place they attack this verse is by omitting the word *also*. While it seems like an insignificant word, if there is one thing we have learned, it is that every word in the Bible has significance. The word also looks back to the dispatching of the twelve, who were also given the authority to heal and to cast out devils. The word means "in like manner" or "likewise." "Then he called his twelve disciples together, and gave them power and authority over all devils, and to cure diseases. And he sent them to preach the kingdom of God, and to heal the sick" (Luke 9:1–2, KJV).

Luke 10:17

> And the *seventy* returned again with joy, saying, Lord, even the devils are subject unto us through thy name. (Luke 10:17, KJV)

Seventy is changed to "seventy-two" in the NIV, CEB, CEV, ERV, ESV, GNB, NCV, NET.

"After these things the Lord appointed other seventy also, and sent them two and two before his face into every city and place, whither he himself would come" (Luke 10:1, KJV). At the beginning of this chapter, the Lord sent out seventy disciples, and therefore seventy should return and not seventy-two.

Luke 10:21

> In that hour *Jesus* rejoiced in spirit, and said, I thank thee, O Father, Lord of heaven and earth, that thou hast hid these things from the wise and prudent, and hast revealed them unto babes: even

so, Father; for so it seemed good in thy sight.
(Luke 10:21, KJV)

Jesus is changed to "he."

The Holy Spirit is not in view in this verse. This is why the
King James translators did not capitalize *spirit*, as they do in every
other place when referencing the Holy Spirit. "And grieve not the
holy Spirit of God, whereby ye are sealed unto the day of redemption" (Ephesians 4:30, KJV). Jesus rejoiced in his spirit when the
seventy came back reporting a successful missionary venture. Now,
it is true that the Holy Spirit gives the true believer joy, but in this
verse, the spirit of Jesus was in view. It would be like going to a Bible
conference and coming away refreshed in the "spirit." It does not
mean the Holy Spirit is refreshed because He is the one who does the
refreshing. In other words, their successful missionary venture gave
Jesus much joy. The modern versions also changed *Jesus* to "he," thus
reducing Him to a nameless character and removing the connection
this verse makes between Jesus and God the Father.

Luke 10:35

And on the morrow *when he departed*, he took
out two pence, and gave them to the host, and
said unto him, Take care of him; and whatsoever
thou spendest more, when I come again, I will
repay thee. (Luke 10:35, KJV)

"*When he departed*" is omitted.

This Samaritan did not just drop the man off at the inn and
then go on his way but stayed with him all night to care for him.
Then when the next day came, he probably saw that the man was
stable and on the mend, so he went to the innkeeper and told him to
take care of the man; and if he incurred any more expenses beyond
the two denarii that the Samaritan gave him, then on his return trip,
he would reimburse the man for whatever he spent out of pocket.
This Samaritan showed not only compassion but trust. He was gen-

erous to the man who was recovering from his wounds, and he was trusting that the innkeeper would not just pocket the money.

In those times, innkeepers were notorious for being dishonest, and Rome dealt heavily with those people if they were caught. This story gives Christians a good understanding to show kindness to people whenever they have the opportunity, even if it costs them something.

The phrase "when he departed" is important because it sets up the scenario of faith that the good Samaritan had. He had to depart first before he could return and check up on the injured man. When handing the two denarii to the innkeeper, he addressed him personally by using the phrase "unto him," which is in the dative case, showing that the Samaritan dealt specifically with the innkeeper.

Luke 10:39

And she had a sister called Mary, which also sat at *Jesus'* feet, and heard his word. (Luke 10:39, KJV)

Jesus' is changed to "Lord's."

Once again, we see an attack on the Lord Jesus Christ by the modern versions. In the King James Version, it is very specific whose feet Mary had sat at. She sat at the feet of Jesus. The modern versions change it to "Lord." He is the Lord, but when they remove a specific name and replace it with another noun that does not specify who the Lord is, then that person could be thought to be anybody they please. The principle taught in the New Testament is specifically that we are to listen to the Lord Jesus Christ. Here are two examples of that:

While he yet spake, behold, a bright cloud overshadowed them: and behold a voice out of the cloud, which said, This is my beloved Son, in whom I am well pleased; hear ye him. (Matthew 17:5, KJV)

On the Mount of Transfiguration, Peter wanted to make three tabernacles; but as he spoke, he was overshadowed by the voice of the Father from heaven that we are to listen to His beloved Son.

> God, who at sundry times and in divers manners spake in time past unto the fathers by the prophets, Hath in these last days spoken unto us by his Son, whom he hath appointed heir of all things, by whom also he made the worlds. (Hebrews 1:1–2, KJV)

Then in Hebrews 1:1–2, the writer tells us that in these last days, God the Father has spoken to us by His Son. The last days has commenced at the cross and will end on the last day. So the responsibility of the Christian is to listen to Jesus, just as Mary did, since this principle was further enunciated in the New Testament. Sitting at Jesus's feet was not just a onetime event but a major biblical principle for the believer.

Luke 11:2–4

> And he said unto them, When ye pray, say, *Our* Father *which art in heaven*, Hallowed be thy name. Thy kingdom come. *Thy will be done, as in heaven, so in earth*. Give us day by day our daily bread. And forgive us our sins; for we also forgive every one that is indebted to us. And lead us not into temptation; *but deliver us from evil*. (Luke 11:2–4, KJV)

Verse 2, "*Our...which art in heaven...Thy will be done, as in heaven, so in earth*" are omitted. Verse 4, "*but deliver us from evil*," is omitted

These verses have multiple attacks upon them, and each one is a significant hit. We will look at each one individually.

Our Father Which Art in Heaven

This is a significant deletion because two major points are in view:

1) The term *our* means that this model prayer is only to be used by Christians and not unbelievers. Christians have the right to claim God as their Father, but the unbeliever does not. It shows the personal relationship between the Christian and God the Father.

2) Then they omit "which art in heaven." This is another significant omission. Our Father is in heaven and not on the earth. The Roman Catholic Church calls the pope *holy father*, which means that there are two fathers in view. The pope is tied to an apostate system and is revered as a father, but the true Father of the Christian is the Father in heaven. So a possible reason for this omission is to get the Christian to look to the pope as their father instead of God the Father. Thanks to the ecumenical movement, many are doing just that!

Thy Will Be Done, As in Heaven, So in Earth

The Christian desires that God's will is to be done on the earth just as His will is prevalent in heaven. The Christian is part of the kingdom of God and desires that the same environment in heaven will become part of the kingdom work here on earth. The Christian desires to have God's will as the rule in their life since probably the most important part of the kingdom on earth is doing the will of God. This part could also have been omitted since many are slaves to the will of false religious leaders throughout history, and omitting this part keeps Bible readers aloof of the truth that we must seek God's will on earth and not ours or somebody else's.

But Deliver Us from Evil

One of the great promises of scripture was that the Lord Jesus Christ came to destroy the works of the devil. "He that committeth sin is of the devil; for the devil sinneth from the beginning. For this purpose the Son of God was manifested, that he might destroy the works of the devil" (1 John 3:8, KJV). Another great promise of scripture is found in 1 Corinthians 10:13 in that God will not allow us to be tempted beyond what we are able to endure. Probably the greatest promise for the believer is that someday the Lord Jesus Christ is going to return and bring us home to glory, and with that residence transfer, the true Christian will never again see any evil and will never again have to face any evil temptations from Satan.

It is a shame that the modern versions leave out such tremendous promises of scripture for the true believer. The bigger shame is that Christians will actually accept these perverted versions without even checking into them to see what is missing and what is twisted.

Luke 11:11

If a son shall ask bread of any of you that is a father,
will he give him a stone? or if he ask a fish, will he
for a fish give him a serpent? (Luke 11:11, KJV)

"If a son shall ask bread of any of you" and *"will he give him a stone?"* are omitted.

Here, Jesus is giving a lesson on faith, and the modern versions have chopped it up to a point that it makes no sense. This verse speaks about two staple foods that a son asks for. They are fish and bread. Now, do you remember what two miracles Jesus performed concerning the fish and bread (loaves)?

And he commanded the multitude to sit down
on the grass, and took the five loaves, and the
two fishes, and looking up to heaven, he blessed,
and brake, and gave the loaves to his disciples,

and the disciples to the multitude. And they did all eat, and were filled: and they took up of the fragments that remained twelve baskets full. And they that had eaten were about five thousand men, beside women and children. (Matthew 14:19–21, KJV)

And his disciples answered him, From whence can a man satisfy these men with bread here in the wilderness? And he asked them, How many loaves have ye? And they said, Seven. And he commanded the people to sit down on the ground: and he took the seven loaves, and gave thanks, and brake, and gave to his disciples to set before them; and they did set them before the people. And they had a few small fishes: and he blessed, and commanded to set them also before them. So they did eat, and were filled: and they took up of the broken meat that was left seven baskets. (Mark 8:4–8, KJV)

When Jesus had taken the fishes and loaves in both cases and blessed them, He was able to feed literally thousands. In Luke 11:11, He is giving a lesson on faith among family members. He is asking the fathers among them if their child would ask for fish and bread, would they give them a stone, something that would be of no value since it could not be eaten; or give them a serpent, something that could kill them? An earthly father would not do this, especially one who is sinful (v. 13), will give good gifts to their children and not hurt them. Then He goes on to say in verse 13 that the Holy Heavenly Father would never do anything like that, which would be an absurd assumption.

The Lord deals with two contrasts here: The first is that He compares the actions of an earthly father to those of the Heavenly Father. God the Father can be expected to supply more to His children than an earthly father can for his. The second is that an earthly father can only supply the physical needs, but the Heavenly Father can give the Holy Spirit, who can minister to all our spiritual needs in this life and the next. As the Lord gave the fish and bread to the multitudes, the Heavenly Father gives the Holy Spirit to the multitude of the body of Christ.

We must be careful not to insist that Luke 11:13 is stating that the Holy Spirit is given to every human. He only indwells those who become saved. However, there are many who do partake of the benefits of the Holy Spirit who are not saved. "For it is impossible for those who were once enlightened, and have tasted of the heavenly gift, and were made partakers of the Holy Ghost, And have tasted the good word of God, and the powers of the world to come" (Hebrews 6:4–5, KJV). Those who sit in churches each week and hear the beautiful hymns or those who are in hospitals built by Christians are two groups who have benefited from those who are saved. What about Christians who help those unbelievers in disasters or personal trials in their life? They too are tasting the good word of God and partakers of the Holy Ghost yet are not indwelled through salvation. There is no good reason why the modern versions have chopped this verse up.

Luke 11:29

> And when the people were gathered thick together, he began to say, This is an evil generation: they seek a sign; and there shall no sign be given it, but the sign of Jonas *the prophet.* (Luke 11:29, KJV)

"*The prophet*" is omitted.

Jonah was a bona fide prophet of the Lord, and his ministry was a sign to the Ninevites that there was a judgment coming unless there was repentance. In the same manner, the Lord Jesus Christ was also a sign to the generation that He was born into. They had sought a sign as to His authenticity, but He told them to look at the ministry of Jonah. Jonah had preached that if Nineveh did not repent, then there would come a total judgment upon them. So everyone in Nineveh had repented in sackcloth and ashes; therefore, the judgment of God was delayed upon Nineveh for 135 years when we read about their pending destruction in the book of Nahum.

The Lord Jesus was teaching the same thing that if there was no repentance, then judgment would fall upon the present generation. The end of Judah came in AD 70 when Titus ravaged the city of Jerusalem. That destruction symbolized the end of the temple sacrificial system and the feasts since the Lord Jesus had already fulfilled them in AD 33 by His death and resurrection.

The modern versions leave out the fact that Jonah was a prophet of the Lord and that he was speaking directly for God to Nineveh. He was not just an itinerant preacher who was on a mission of evangelism; he was declaring the imminent judgment of God. This is why Jesus pointed the Pharisees to Jonah because they were now facing the same situation. The rejection of Jesus meant that the nation of Judah would be destroyed by the coming judgment of God upon it. Jonah, being a prophet of God, was at the same par with Isaiah, Jeremiah, Ezekiel, and others. This omission in the modern versions lessens the authority by which Jonah had ministered. Once again, we see the modern versions dumbing down the scriptures by erasing valuable information that is part of the real Bible.

Luke 11:34

> The light of the body is the eye: therefore when thine eye is *single*, thy whole body also is full of light; but when thine eye is evil, thy body also is full of darkness. (Luke 11:34, KJV)

Single is changed to "healthy, clear, or sound."

The word *single* in the Greek is only used twice in the New Testament. The other verse is Matthew 6:22 (KJV): "The light of the body is the eye: if therefore thine eye be single, thy whole body shall be full of light." It is the word *haplous* and carries with it the idea of "sincere, generous, sound, or free from wrong motives" in a positive way. As the verse states, the light of the body is the eye; and if the eye is single in purpose, then the whole body shall be filled with light. It speaks of a disciple who is single in purpose, and that purpose is to be sold out to the Lord Jesus Christ and the propagation of the Gospel. If one focuses their life on the kingdom of God, then they are living in total light and wish to fulfill the fact the we are the light of the world. "Ye are the light of the world. A city that is set on an hill cannot be hid" (Matthew 5:14, KJV). This would refer only to a true believer who invests their life in the kingdom of God.

A true believer who still walks with the world will never give evidence they are the light. The modern versions make this verse sound like the physical eye is in view when in reality it is the spiritual single eye of the believer who has only one focus in their life, and that is the Gospel. "For I determined not to know any thing among you, save Jesus Christ, and him crucified" (1 Corinthians 2:2, KJV). The true believer has a single eye or focus in their life, and that is service in the Lord's body. In the modern versions, it is not always what they leave out but how they misinterpret words that causes the verses to derail the true context of or meaning of passages.

Luke 11:44

Woe unto you, *scribes and Pharisees, hypocrites!* for ye are as graves which appear not, and the men that walk over them are not aware of them. (Luke 11:44, KJV)

"Scribes and Pharisees, hypocrites!" is omitted.

In this verse, the Lord Jesus Christ is specifically addressing the scribes and Pharisees and calling them hypocrites. They pretended to be so religious, and they were the furthest thing from true piety, and that is why Jesus is indicting them as hypocrites. Religious people are an affront to the true Gospel, but religious hypocrites are more dangerous because they claim to be something in public that they are not in private. Once again, the modern versions protect the guilty religious hypocrites by omitting this part and making it a generic pronouncement. Jesus specifically gave a list of their hypocrisies in

Luke 11, and that is why the section is preceded by the defining term *hypocrite*. Jesus was focusing on the leaders because as the leaders go, so goes the flock. Once again, the King James Bible shines through with the truth.

Luke 11:53

And as he said these things unto them, the scribes and the Pharisees began to urge him vehemently, and to provoke him to speak of many things. (Luke 11:53, KJV)

"And as he said these things unto them" is changed to "Jesus leaving," "Jesus left," or "He left."

The King James states that as Jesus was saying these things, that is when the scribes and Pharisees began to provoke Him to start speaking about many matters. Some of the modern versions state that after Jesus left, that is when they started to question Him. Now I have a question. How do you question someone who has left the scene? If you look at the continuation of this scene in Luke 12, Jesus began to teach the people. If he left, then how did He teach an innumerable amount of people.

Laying wait for him, and seeking to catch something out of his mouth, that they might accuse him. (Luke 11:54, KJV)

In the mean time, when there were gathered together an innumerable multitude of people, insomuch that they trode one upon another, he began to say unto his disciples first of all, Beware ye of the leaven of the Pharisees, which is hypocrisy. (Luke 12:1, KJV)

This is just another terrible mutilation of the New Testament.

Luke 11:54

Laying wait for him, *and seeking* to catch something out of his mouth, *that they might accuse him.* (Luke 11:54, KJV)

"And seeking" and *"that they might accuse him"* are omitted.

The Lord was chiding the Pharisees and the lawyers in this chapter for their ungodly conduct, and they were trying to get the Lord to make comments whereby they could bring some type of accusation against Him. The modern versions omit the part of why the leaders were engaging the Lord. They wanted to accuse Him of something so they could have Him executed, and then they would be rid of Him so they could continue in their corruptness without a verbal conscience, awakening the people to their evils.

This is the same scenario that happens in many churches when those who teach the truth are normally escorted out, which is a type of being killed, so you cannot bring any more Gospel conscience that sometimes forces Christians to think, a lost art in the body. The modern versions want to protect the Pharisees and lawyers by omitting the real reason for engaging the Lord, and that was entrapment. The King James gives the reason and teaches us how evil a heart can be, even of religious leaders who attempt to manifest piety, as false as it may be. Probably one of the reasons that the King James Bible has been thrown out of many churches is because of its convicting authority. So if you throw out the authority, you throw out the conviction, and all things can continue in a sanctified stupor.

Luke 12:25

And which of you with taking thought can add to his *stature* one cubit? (Luke 12:25, KJV)

"Stature one" is changed to "one hour or single hour."

What time is it? It is one foot and six inches! That is about the way the "experts" have confused this verse. A cubit is approximately eighteen inches, so when we look at some of the modern versions, how can one add eighteen inches to the length of their life? It is confusing time with measurement. Now, the Greek word behind the term *stature* is the word *hlikia*, and it is translated two ways in the New Testament: The first way is in Luke 12:25, where it speaks of a person's stature, which is a person's natural height. The second way is "age," which would represent time, and we see this in the modern versions. "But by what means he now seeth, we know not; or who hath opened his eyes, we know not: he is of *age*; ask him: he shall speak for himself" (John 9:21, KJV). So we see that the meaning of this word is determined by the context.

In John 9:21, we read the parents of the blind man made to see was speaking of the age of the man. In Luke 12:25, we interpret it as height because the word *stature* is followed by the words *one cubit*. One cubit is a term of physical measurement and not of time. The modern versions removed the Greek word for *one*, which I have underlined in the Hort-Westcott Critical Text. So what we have here in the modern versions again is the neglect of context. If we ignore and neglect context, then we will always come up with an erroneous conclusion just like the modern versions have.

Luke 12:31

> But rather seek ye the kingdom *of God*; and all these things shall be added unto you. (Luke 12:31, KJV)

"Of God" is omitted.

One of the major characteristics of the modern versions is that they tend to go from the specific to the general. In this verse, we are told to seek the kingdom of God, but in the modern versions, we are told to seek "his" kingdom. The problem is that when you reduce the meaning of something from a specific to the nebulous, it always engenders questions. What kingdom are we to seek? There are two spiritual kingdoms on this earth: one is the kingdom of God, and the other is the kingdom of Satan. Within the kingdom of Satan, there are many subkingdoms, and we find them in the New Age, false religions, false teachings, etc. Each cult is their own little kingdom. All the cults together are a kingdom.

Some years ago, Walter Martin wrote a book called *The Kingdom of the Cults*, which was a fitting title since each false religion has its own set of teachings and rules, especially in the area of salvation. Each one will define their own method of salvation. This is why it is absolutely crucial for the words of the Bible to be left in specifics, as God wrote it, and not turned to generalizations.

In 2006, I went on medication for high blood pressure. My doctor told me that there are many blood pressure medications on the market. Can you imagine me giving a prescription to the pharmacist and written on the prescription was "blood pressure medication"? Which one would he give me out of the many that are out there? Do you see the importance of being specific? I gave the prescription with the name of the drug to the pharmacist and got the proper medication. Specifics to generalizations are a degenerative property of the modern versions.

Luke 12:39

And this know, that if the goodman of the house had known what hour the thief would come, *he would have watched*, and not have suffered his house to be broken through.

"He would have watched" is omitted.

The Lord Jesus gives a lesson to the Christian and the church that they must be ready for the return of the Lord Jesus Christ. If a person has become saved, they are ready for His return. However, the Lord is beginning a discourse that the steward must be faithful; that is, the Christians are not to live a sloppy life but live a disciplined life in anticipation of the Lord's return. The portion omitted in verse 39, "he would have watched," is important because the Lord expects His children to be watching for His return. And while we are watching, we are to be busy with kingdom business, which is sending forth the Gospel, training new Christians, and just being a testimony. We do not know when the Lord is returning, and that is why there are quite a number of verses teaching us that we are to be ready by being busy. In verse 43, the Lord says that He commends the servant who is doing these things when He returns. "Redeeming the time, because the days are evil" (Ephesians 5:16, KJV). The modern versions seem to think that being busy in the Lord's work is not a necessity, or else they would have left that verse intact.

Luke 13:2

> And *Jesus* answering said unto them, Suppose ye that these Galilaeans were sinners above all the Galilaeans, because they suffered such things? (Luke 13:2, KJV)

Jesus is changed to "he."

Who is he? It could be any of the apostles who were with Jesus at the time. Once again, the modern versions attack the proper name of Jesus by replacing it with a pronoun.

Luke 13:19

> It is like a grain of mustard seed, which a man took, and cast into his garden; and it grew, and waxed a *great* tree; and the fowls of the air lodged in the branches of it. (Luke 13:19, KJV)

Great is omitted.

The black mustard tree in Israel grows to a height of ten to twelve feet. The seed of that tree is very small, and that is why the Lord used it in His teaching. The modern versions omit the word *great*, and that reduces the immensity of the story being told. If one plants a seed to be a mustard tree, then obviously, it is going to grow up to be a mustard tree, and this is what the modern versions convey. The King James Version states that the tree that will grow will be a great tree. This was in response to the question about the kingdom of God. The Lord was stating that it was going to be like a great tree, and that great tree represented the fact that the kingdom of God will eventually be all over the world as the Gospel goes out and people become saved in all the countries of the world.

So the King James is looking forward to a worldwide dissemination of the Gospel while the modern versions just see a nominal growth. It is really a shame that the modern versions do not see the kingdom of God as being "great" since we see Christianity in every country in this world. But then again, the modern versions are no friend of the kingdom of God, and they prove it right here.

Luke 13:25

> When once the master of the house is risen up, and hath shut to the door, and ye begin to stand without, and to knock at the door, saying, Lord, *Lord*, open unto us; and he shall answer and say unto you, I know you not whence ye are. (Luke 13:25, KJV)

Second *Lord* is omitted (some versions omit both).

When people were invited to the home of an important host and the appointment was for a very specific hour, the invited person needed to be on time. In those days, the host had the right to bolt the door at a specific hour, and after that, no one was allowed to enter. When we look at this verse, we see an urgency in the invited guest's voice, "Lord, Lord, open unto us." The use of the word *Lord* twice adds to that urgency. Jesus tells this small parable that represents salvation and the kingdom of God. ("For he saith, I have heard thee in a time accepted, and in the day of salvation have I succoured thee: behold, now is the accepted time; behold, now is the day of salvation" [2 Corinthians 6:2, KJV].) Now is the time to seek the Lord for salvation because there will come a time when it will be too late.

"Many will say to me in that day, Lord, Lord, have we not prophesied in thy name? and in thy name have cast out devils? and in thy name done many wonderful works?" (Matthew 7:22, KJV). Matthew 7:22 speaks of a time when people will be at the white throne judgment of Christ giving a list of their works, and they will be in an urgent state because they too use the phrase "Lord, Lord." The modern versions omit the second *Lord*, making it a casual conversation when it is anything but. Some of the counterfeit versions change the word to *sir*. Luke never uses the word *sir* in either the book of Luke or Acts. I seriously doubt the people will be calling Jesus *sir* at the white throne judgment.

Luke 13:35

> Behold, your house is left unto you desolate: and *verily* I say unto you, Ye shall not see me, until the time come when ye shall say, Blessed is he that cometh in the name of the Lord. (Luke 13:35, KJV)

Verily is omitted.

Jesus is affirming to these people that their house is now left unto them desolate. He is confirming to them by saying *verily* that they shall not see Him until they actually accept Him by claiming, "Blessed is He that cometh in the name of the Lord." In other words, they will be affirming the fact that He is the Messiah. The Greek word behind *verily* is also the word for *amen*, which means "finally," "confirmed," or "it is established." The modern versions leave this important word out.

Luke 14:5

> And answered them, saying, Which of you shall have an *ass* or an ox fallen into a pit, and will not straightway pull him out on the sabbath day? (Luke 14:5, KJV)

Ass is changed to "son."

Here, we have a complete word switch. The word for "donkey" or "ass" in Greek is *onon*, and the word for "son" is *huios*. So there is no way that each word can be interpreted any other way. Now, in Classical Greek, the term *huios* can be considered an offspring of an animal. Classical Greek was common in Greece about the time period of ninth to the fourth century BC, which predates the Greek Text of the Bible by over four hundred years. The Bible was written in Koine Greek, which was the standard language that predated Modern Greek. It was also known as Common or New Testament Greek. It seems those who originally corrupted this verse as early as the third century had borrowed the word from a language that had been dormant for four hundred years. As with any language that was in the state of development, one cannot count on a present definition of a word taken from a four-hundred-year-old language.

In 1611, when the King James Bible was written, the English language was also in a period of development, and the translators would not have borrowed word meanings from four hundred years prior. That means while the country was speaking early modern English, the meanings would have been taken from Middle English. As words develop, their meanings will follow suit. This is why the modern-version translators should not have followed the meanings of Classical Greek because the New Testament was not written in Classical Greek. It would be like writing a book in German and taking the word meanings from French. There may be some similarities, but there may also be many differences, which could give the wrong meaning and thus the wrong interpretation. The New Testament was written in Koine Greek, and the King James Bible stays with it for the proper interpretation of its words.

Luke 17:3

Take heed to yourselves: If thy brother trespass *against thee*, rebuke him; and if he repent, forgive him. (Luke 17:3, KJV)

"Against thee" is omitted.

The modern versions omit "against thee" and make it a general rebuke for any sin. If we have a friend or a relative who has sinned, of course, we tell them and rebuke them for it so they will not do it again. However, in this verse, Jesus tells us that if our brother sins against us, we are to rebuke him; and if he repents and is truly sorry, then we are to forgive him. Let us ask, what is the difference between the two? Let's use an illustration. If your brother takes a can of spray paint and paints up the neighbor's car, then we need to rebuke him so he will not do it again. If he takes that can of spray paint and paints your car all up, will it be as easy to forgive him as it was if he sinned against someone else and didn't cause you the problem? That is the difference. It is easier to rebuke a person who has sinned against someone else, but if they sin against us, it becomes harder to forgive because it becomes personal. This is why the Lord is personalizing the Christian response.

The words *rebuke* and *forgive* are in the imperative mood, making them commands and not suggestions. So if someone sins against you and you do not rebuke and forgive, then you are as guilty of disobedience against the word of God as the one who has sinned against you. This verse is also speaking of a Christian brother or sister. This is why the phrase "against thee" is so important because it completes the reason for the command to rebuke and forgive. Once again, the modern versions omit a strategic piece of scripture.

Luke 17:9

Doth he thank that servant because he did the things that were commanded *him? I trow not.* (Luke 17:9, KJV)

"Him? I trow not" is omitted.

The removal of *him* takes away the object of who is being commanded. Then when "I trow not" is omitted, it removes the bridge to the next verse. "Doth he thank that servant because he did the things that were commanded him? I trow not. So likewise ye, when ye shall have done all those things which are commanded you, say, We are unprofitable servants: we have done that which was our duty to do" (Luke 17:9–10, KJV). The servant is required by their masters to prepare their dinner for them. This was part of their daily routine and was expected of them. The master was not going to go out of his way and thank the slave for doing what he was supposed to be doing.

This example segues right into the Christian life. We are supposed to be witnessing, giving, and being a testimony to the world. Should the Lord thank us for what we should be doing as a natural part of the Christian life? Jesus is not being cruel when He uses this illustration because that was the master-servant relationship back then. It is the same today. Do wealthy people thank the servants they are paying for to do what they are getting paid to do? On your job, does your boss come to you and thank you for what you should be doing anyway? I think not. These verses are showing the responsibility of the believer, and we must have the same mind-set that as we go on in ministry, serving the Lord. We are not going to be getting a special thank-you or some type of special gifts. We must have the mind-set of the servant that we know what our responsibility is as believers, and we are to engage our lives in the service of the Lord, not looking for a handout.

Luke 17:36

Two men shall be in the field; the one shall be taken, and the other left. (Luke 17:36, KJV)

The entire verse is omitted or placed in brackets.

This verse is part of a trilogy of verses describing the condition of the earth when the Lord Jesus Christ returns. It will basically be business as usual.

I tell you, in that night there shall be two men in one bed; the one shall be taken, and the other shall be left. Two women shall be grinding together; the one shall be taken, and the other left. Two men shall be in the field; the one shall be taken, and the other left. (Luke 17:34–36, KJV)

If we look closely at all three verses, they teach us that when the Lord Jesus Christ returns, it will be at one time, and the whole world will be affected. In the first group, we have two men in one bed, which means that part of the world will be in darkness and will be asleep. The next group are those who are grinding at the mill, and this would probably represent the morning as the women grind to make the bread for the day. Then the third group would be those in the field, which would mean that there would be people working in the daytime and through the day. When these three verses are combined, they teach us that when the Lord Jesus Christ returns, there will be a separation of those who are close friends and those who are workers and those who are in families. One will go to judgment, and the other will go to heaven. "Marvel not at this: for the hour is coming, in the which all that are in the graves shall hear his voice, And shall come forth; they that have done good, unto the resurrection of life; and they that have done evil, unto the resurrection of damnation" (John 5:28–29, KJV).

So when the modern versions leave out verse 36, what they are doing is leaving out a vital piece of the prophetic picture that God is giving to us. Stay with the King James Bible, and you will have the entire scenario.

Luke 19:5

> And when Jesus came to the place, he looked up, *and saw him*, and said unto him, Zacchaeus, make haste, and come down; for to day I must abide at thy house. (Luke 19:5, KJV)

"And saw him" is omitted.

In this verse, we have the scene with Zacchaeus. Zacchaeus wanted to see Jesus, but he was short and probably did not come up to the shoulders of the people in the crowd. I know about that. I am only five foot two myself. So Zacchaeus had climbed into a sycamore tree so he could see Jesus as He passed by, and it was this time that Zacchaeus became saved. When Jesus came to the tree, he looked up and saw Zacchaeus and told him to come down because He was going to stay at his house. Now these words "and saw him" are very important because these words are describing the faith that Zacchaeus had exercised to see Jesus. The reason why these words are important is because a similar situation had happened previously to Jesus.

> And, behold, men brought in a bed a man which was taken with a palsy: and they sought means to bring him in, and to lay him before him. And when they could not find by what way they might bring him in because of the multitude, they went upon the housetop, and let him down through the tiling with his couch into the midst before Jesus. And when he saw their faith, he said unto him, Man, thy sins are forgiven thee. (Luke 5:18–20, KJV)

Do you remember the men who brought their friend to see Jesus in hopes that he would heal them? What was the pivotal statement in that scene? It was in verse 20 when Jesus *saw* the faith of the friends of this paralytic. Then what happened? The first thing was, the man became saved; and secondly, Jesus healed him. This also shows that physical healing is ancillary to salvation. Jesus saw the faith of the friends of the paralytic, and he became saved. The same word describes Jesus when He saw Zacchaeus in the tree. Zacchaeus had made a faith-based effort to see Jesus, and Jesus saw that faith. This is an important principle in the Christian walk. Our faith must be seen by God and others so they know that Christianity is not just a talking religion but a walking faith. The modern versions, by leaving out that phrase, deny one of the most living truths of the Bible, and that is faith with shoes on.

Luke 19:45

> And he went into the temple, and began to cast out them that sold therein, *and them that bought*. (Luke 19:45, KJV)

"And them that bought" is omitted.

Here we have a verse that is a fulfillment of another prophecy.

> Is this house, which is called by my name, become
> a den of robbers in your eyes? Behold, even I have
> seen it, saith the LORD. (Jeremiah 7:11, KJV)

> Behold, I will send my messenger, and he shall
> prepare the way before me: and the Lord, whom
> ye seek, shall suddenly come to his temple, even
> the messenger of the covenant, whom ye delight
> in: behold, he shall come, saith the LORD of
> hosts. (Malachi 3:1, KJV)

The Lord came to the temple and cast out the thieves who were making the temple a business. The verse states that the Lord had cast out those who were selling. These were the ones who would sell the animals for sacrifice. If someone brought their own animal for sacrifice, it would be inspected and then rejected. This would mean the people who brought the animal was forced to buy another one from the temple stock. This was orchestrated by the leaders of the temple, and they made great gain on it. Then the other ones who were tossed out were those who bought. This group probably also worked for the leaders in buying animals at a discount for resale to the people at a much higher price. This is just speculation, but it would not surprise me if they took the animals from the people and, after they sold them another one, would turn around and sell that animal to different people.

Thieves are thieves and have all angles worked out for their benefit. A second thought on those who bought: it might be those who were too lazy to bring their own animal and did not care what they sacrificed, so they would buy whatever was available. In other words, they were not concerned about pleasing the Lord, only getting it over with. The ones who "bought" have been omitted in the modern versions, and we can see they were an integral part of the scam that was going on in the temple. It is important that both groups be mentioned because both are culpable for defiling the temple.

Luke 20:5

And they reasoned with themselves, saying, If we shall say, From heaven; he will say, Why *then* believed ye him not? (Luke 20:5, KJV)

Then is omitted.

The word *then* in the Greek is a conjunction. A conjunction connects two phrases or two sentences or two thoughts. The religious leaders did not answer Jesus immediately when He posed the question to them concerning the origin of John's baptism. Instead, they reasoned among themselves and set up a scenario that if they said it was "from heaven" (thought 1), then "why didn't they believe it" (thought 2)? Without the conjunction, it is just a straight question with no pondering or comparative thought.

Luke 20:23

But he perceived their craftiness, and said unto them, *Why tempt ye me?* (Luke 20:23, KJV)

"Why tempt ye me?" is omitted.

This verse teaches us that Jesus knew how wicked these scribes were along with the chief priests. Jesus knew their intent, and that is why He said to them, "Why tempt ye me?" This verse teaches us that Jesus had omniscience because He knew what their intent was. They wanted to catch Him in some type of treason against Rome. Omniscience is a character of deity. The word *tempt* also carries with it the idea of "putting one to a test." "Ye shall not tempt the LORD your God, as ye tempted him in Massah" (Deuteronomy 6:16, KJV). The scribes would have been familiar with Deuteronomy 6:16 about tempting the Lord, and Jesus here is asking why they were tempting Him. That phrase "why tempt ye me?" is also another way of Jesus claiming to be God. The modern versions go along with the

Gnostic belief that Jesus was not God, and this is just another verse to prove their disbelief, which they subtly pass on to their unsuspecting readers.

Something to Note

I think it is interesting that there is are four corrupted manuscripts versus ten that agree with the Receptus readings. Look which ones they go to. They speak of manuscript evidence, and here, the ratio is *ten* for and *four* against, and they go with the *four*. They are not concerned with manuscript evidence because these modern versions are satanic in nature and are bent on attacking the Lord Jesus Christ in any way they can.

Luke 20:30

And the second *took her to wife, and he died childless.* (Luke 20:30, KJV)

"Took her to wife" omitted in some; *"and he died childless"* is omitted in all.

In this discourse, the Sadducees had tried to give the Lord Jesus Christ a question that would trip Him up. First of all, it must be noted that the Sadducees did not believe in the resurrection, so this was also an attempt to discredit it. Yet they put forth this question. Starting in verse 29, they asked a question about a woman who was married seven times, and they specified that the first husband died without children, and then the second husband died, and he too without children, up to seven husbands. They wanted to know whose wife she would be in the resurrection.

When the Sadducees started asking this question, they built up the scenario by stating specifically that the first and second husband died childless, and then in like manner, the other ones also died. There is absolutely no reason for the modern versions to omit the last part of verse 30 where it states the husband died childless since the manuscript evidence is *nine* in favor of the reading against *four* that omit it. The modern-version translators and editors claim that manuscript evidence is most important, but here we have a case where the proper reading has the majority of manuscripts including it, yet they go with the two most corrupt manuscripts that omit it. This is why textual criticism is dangerous because it is subjective. It puts the Bible at the whim of every critic.

Luke 21:4

For all these have of their abundance *cast in unto the offerings of God*: but she of her penury hath cast in all the living that she had. (Luke 21:4, KJV)

"Cast in unto the offerings of God" is omitted.

The modern versions omit the most important reason that Christians give. We give unto the Lord. The widow gave her two mites, and Jesus took notice of it. The rich were putting in out of their abundance. As rich folks, they knew that their needs were supplied for, so they gave from their surplus. The widow gave out of her poverty, probably not knowing where her next meal was coming from. The widow had a good understanding of who God was, and she did not fear giving her money unto God. When the modern versions leave out "cast in unto the offerings of God," they omit the reason that Christians give. In our day, there are many organizations seeking the funds of the Christian. As Christians, it is our responsibility to discern what organizations we want to donate to. Just because an organization claims to be Christian does not necessarily mean they are.

As Christians, this verse is giving us insight that we are to make sure that when we give, it is given unto a reputable Christian organization. It does not even have to be an organization, but it can be a person too. I got hoodwinked some years ago. A fellow came to our church, and he was dressed like a homeless person, yet he was a regular attendee. So I thought that he really had needs, so I slipped him a few shekels. Later on, I came to find out he worked for the railroad and made a big salary; plus, I saw him smoking. This man should not have taken the money, but human nature being what it is, he took it.

Never again would I give to a person until I knew they were really in need. I was not going to subsidize the tobacco companies (we have the government for that). The principle is that Christian giving is to be focused upon the Lord and His ministry, not our feelings based on guilt, manipulating mailings that we all receive. Once again, the King James Bible keeps our mind focused on the Lord; and when our minds are focused on the Lord, our giving will also be focused.

Luke 21:8

> And he said, Take heed that ye be not deceived: for many shall come in my name, saying, I am *Christ*; and the time draweth near: go ye not *therefore* after them. (Luke 21:8, KJV)

Christ and *therefore* are omitted.

The first hit this verse took is that the modern versions have replaced *Christ* with "he." Now, neither the word *Christ* nor the word *he* is in the text, which means it is the editors who decide which word to use. The King James uses the word *Christ*, making it a specific reference to Jesus as the Christ. The word *Christ* is a noun, and the word *he* is a pronoun. The word *he* makes it a very nebulous choice as to whom Jesus was speaking about, but when the King James uses *Christ*, there is no guessing as to who is in view. Using the noun *Christ* also names Jesus as the Messiah.

The second hit is when the modern versions omit the word *therefore*, which means that we are to look at the prior reasons given as to why we should not go after those who claim to be Christ. *Therefore* points us to a specific part of scripture as our authority as to why we do not believe these false teachers.

Luke 21:36

> Watch ye therefore, and pray always, that ye may *be accounted worthy* to escape all these things that shall come to pass, and to stand before the Son of man. (Luke 21:36, KJV)

"Be accounted worthy" is omitted.

The final admonition of Jesus on this subject is to always watch that we do not get snared into the world's temptations, and we are to pray and seek God to give us the wisdom to avoid those things that could ensnare a person. The only way a person is accounted worthy is if they are saved through the grace of God in Christ. We will be here till the last day and will experience what the world will experience in the realm of natural things when the Lord begins to wind this world and universe down. The true Christian will know what is happening and will not be part of all the anxiety and fears that the rest of the unbelieving world will face. The unbelievers will not be able to stand before the Lord in the sense that they will be found guilty of their sins because they have no savior. The true believer will be able to stand because their sins have been paid for, and Christ's salvation makes them worthy and accepted because they have already been judged in Christ and found not guilty.

The modern versions place personal strength (man-centered) instead of salvation to come through the end-time events in Luke 21. Personal strength will not help a person in overcoming the judgments to fall.

Luke 22:14

And when the hour was come, he sat down, and
the *twelve* apostles with him. (Luke 22:14, KJV)

Twelve is omitted.

The word *twelve* tells us that all the apostles were present at the beginning of the Last Supper. The hour had come for the last Passover, which would be followed immediately by the bread and the juice, symbolizing the Lord's blood and body that was broken for us. At the end of the Last Supper, there were only eleven disciples because Judas had already left to betray the Lord. The modern versions omit the number *twelve* and just use a generic saying "the apostles," not giving any specifics, especially since Judas betrayed the Lord at the Last Supper. The manuscript evidence is overwhelming, twelve to thirteen for the inclusion of the number *twelve*, and yet the modern-version editors go with the witness of the least amount, which is the very thing they accuse the King James Bible of—that there were not a sufficient amount of manuscripts in 1604. And now that there are many more, they go with the least amount. Smells a little like hypocrisy to me.

Luke 22:31

And the Lord said, Simon, Simon, behold, Satan hath desired to have you, that he may sift you as wheat. (Luke 22:31, KJV)

"And the Lord said" is omitted.

The portion that was omitted gives us the source of the quote. The Lord was telling Peter that Satan desired to have him and sift him like wheat, which would be to persecute him to the point that he would be unable to continue in his future ministry. But the Lord not only prayed for Peter. He prophesied that he would have a ministry that would strengthen other believers. Here, in verse 31 and 32, we are being specifically told that the Lord Himself was praying not only for Peter but for all the disciples. It gives us an insight into the intercessory ministry of the Lord Jesus Christ for all His children. With the omission of that portion in scripture, it can be concluded that anyone present could be praying for Peter. It is important that we know that the Lord Himself prays for His own. Once again, the modern versions omit a very vital part of scripture that gives details into the intercessory ministry of Christ, and the King James gives us clear insight into that ministry.

Luke 22:44

And being in an agony he prayed more earnestly: and his sweat was as it were *great* drops of blood falling down to the ground. (Luke 22:44, KJV)

Great is omitted.

These two verses have been attacked and removed from the Greek text even though there is sufficient manuscript evidence to prove that they are genuine. Hort and Westcott omitted both verses 43 and 44 from their Greek text and placed them in the margin. This is why they are bracketed in some of the counterfeit versions. Then those modern versions that included the two verses have removed the word *great*. It is the Greek word *thromboi*, which is behind "great drops." No one will ever know the anxiety the Lord Jesus was suffering in the garden. It was so intense that He was dripping great drops of blood. It is a medical condition that can happen to a person under great stress. Small capillaries can break because of coagulated blood and exit through the pores. Thrombosis is a condition of blood clots. The word *great* is very good because it describes well the blood loss that was commensurate with the stress the Lord Jesus Christ was under because of His impending crucifixion. The modern versions just make it sound like a normal condition under normal circumstances. The Lord Jesus was about to be separated from His Heavenly Father for the first time in eternity and was about to take upon Him all the sins of God's elect, from Adam to the last one who will become saved. The word *great* is a proper description of the Lord's bleeding through His pores.

Luke 22:57

And he denied *him*, saying, Woman, I know him not. (Luke 22:57, KJV)

Him is omitted.

Once Peter heard the accusation, he immediately went into denial. The King James states openly that Peter had denied the Lord Jesus Christ. The word behind "him" in the Greek is a personal pronoun in the masculine gender and should never be translated as "it"; otherwise, it would be neuter. It is also in the accusative case, which means it is the receiver of the action of the verb. The verb is *denied*, and *him* in the accusative case is showing that it was Christ who was denied by Peter. It is also singular, which means one person is receiving the action, and that would be Christ. This is another example of the agreement of the critical text and the modern versions. The essence of the denial by Peter was the denial of him being with Christ and not the denial of the accusation the girl made. The modern versions focus on the latter while the King James Bible keeps the focus where it belongs.

Luke 22:60

And Peter said, Man, I know not what thou sayest. And immediately, while he yet spake, *the cock* crew. (Luke 22:60, KJV)

"*The cock*" is changed to "a rooster."

Verse 60 is a fulfillment of the prophecy made by Jesus back in Luke 22:34: "And he said, I tell thee, Peter, the cock shall not crow this day, before that thou shalt thrice deny that thou knowest me" (Luke 22:34, KJV). Jesus was speaking of a specific rooster that would crow upon the third denial of Christ by Peter. When Peter made his third denial, then Jesus looked at him when the cock crew. The modern versions exchange a definite article for an indefinite article, giving it the notion that it was a coincidence that a rooster crowed just at the right time. As with the donkey on which Jesus rode into Jerusalem, it was a specific donkey, not just any one they could find. "Saying unto them, Go into the village over against you, and straightway ye shall find an ass tied, and a colt with her: loose them, and bring them unto me" (Matthew 21:2, KJV). As with the donkey, so it was with the rooster, a specific one. Everything was planned in advance by Jesus, and there was nothing left to chance as the modern versions intimate.

Luke 22:64

And when they had blindfolded him, *they struck him on the face*, and asked him, saying, Prophesy, who is it that smote thee? (Luke 22:64, KJV)

"They struck him on the face" is omitted.

In Luke 22:64, we have another attack upon the Lord Jesus Christ. This time, they have attacked and removed the part where the Lord Jesus Christ began to suffer at the hands of the people. We are told here that they had blindfolded Him and struck Him on the face. According to Matthew 26:67–68, after the rulers of the Jews had examined Jesus, they began to spit on Him, hit Him with their fists, and struck Him on the face. All of this was even before He was delivered unto Pilate. To remove the section of scripture in Luke where we read that Jesus was being struck in the face is to remove part of the suffering He underwent for the sins of His people.

Probably, this portion of scripture was removed in the second century by a man named Marcion, who was a heretic and had a copy of the book of Luke that he mutilated until it fit the pattern of the Arian and Gnostic beliefs. Once again, we are seeing that the modern versions are descendants of the Arian and Gnostic views. Unfortunately, the modern-version editors heartily agree with these antichrists of the second century as they have continued to include their ungodly attacks. Luke 22:64 is a fulfillment of two Old Testament prophecies, so not only are they attacking the sufferings of Christ; they are also attacking the verity of scripture.

> I gave my back to the smiters, and my cheeks to them that plucked off the hair: I hid not my face from shame and spitting. (Isaiah 50:6, KJV)

> Now gather thyself in troops, O daughter of troops: he hath laid siege against us: they shall smite the judge of Israel with a rod upon the cheek. (Micah 5:1, KJV)

How can anyone who uses a modern version actually think they are using a "holy Bible" since they have been engineered to fit world belief systems outside of Christianity?

Luke 22:68

And if I also ask you, ye will not answer me, *nor let me go*. (Luke 22:68, KJV)

"Nor let me go" is omitted.

Jesus was taken before the Sanhedrin to answer charges, and they asked Him straight out as to whether He was the Christ or not. Jesus knew that no matter what he responded, they would not accept it. So He turned the tables and said to them that if he asked them a question, they would not answer Him, nor would they let him go. Their desire was to find something to accuse Him of so they could pass Him off to the Roman authorities and then have Him killed so they would be rid of Him. The modern versions leave off the part where Jesus stated they would not have let Him go. Jesus knew that they were determined to have Him executed no matter what, and that is why that phrase is important because it basically reveals their plans and that they were not interested in truth.

Luke 23:6

When Pilate heard *of Galilee*, he asked whether the man were a Galilaean. (Luke 23:6, KJV)

"Of Galilee" is omitted.

As soon as Pilate heard the region of Galilee, he then inquired as to whether Jesus was a Galilean. There were many Galileans who had come to the feast, and it was these who stayed in the Mount of Olives and other outdoor places. These were the same ones who welcomed Jesus in His triumphant entry into the city. They had thought Jesus to be a Galilean because He spent so much time ministering in that region, but the fact is that He was born in Bethlehem of Judah. "But thou, Bethlehem Ephratah, though thou be little among the thousands of Judah, yet out of thee shall he come forth unto me that is to be ruler in Israel; whose goings forth have been from of old, from everlasting" (Micah, 5:2 KJV). God is being very specific here because with the mention of Galilee, Pilate thought that he could rid himself of the problem and send Jesus to Herod Antipas, who ruled Galilee. The modern versions omit the first *Galilee* and replace it with a nebulous "it" or "this."

Luke 23:17

> For of necessity he must release one unto them at the feast. (Luke 23:17, KJV)

The entire verse is omitted or placed in brackets.

This verse probably met the knife of Marcion, who mutilated the book of Luke. This verse is found in the other three gospels and is in the Byzantine text (AD 450–AD 1450), which means it was removed by someone. It speaks of the freeing of Barabbas and the fact that Pilate had to release a prisoner at the Passover. It was more of a custom than a right, but if he did not do it, there would have been much more of an uproar, and his position as governor would have been in jeopardy if he could not keep a stable peace in that region. This verse is a connector that gives the reason why Pilate released one prisoner. Pilate was hoping that they would call for the release of Jesus, but it backfired, and they chose Barabbas.

There is no reason why this verse should have been omitted. The fact that it is in the Byzantine text tells us it is a valid verse because the Byzantine text postdates P 75 by about two hundred years and Vaticanus by about one hundred years and was probably contemporary with Alexandrinus. Once again, the evidence surfaces for the existence of two manuscript lines: one underlying the King James Bible and the other underlying the modern versions.

Luke 23:23

> And they were instant with loud voices, requiring that he might be crucified. And the voices of them and *of the chief priests* prevailed. (Luke 23:23, KJV)

"And *of the chief priests*" is omitted.

It seems that the modern versions are giving the chief priests a pass. The modern versions omit the fact that the chief priests were also part of the crowd who were calling for the crucifixion of Jesus. They were chief instigators in wanting to see Christ killed. God specifically points out the chief priests were also among the crowd yelling. That is why God states it the way He does as "and of the chief priests." He is letting us know that from the chief priests to the citizens, they all were calling for the death of Christ. There was no one innocent in the crowd; all partook, and all were guilty. It seems the modern versions want to protect the chief priests from culpability.

Luke 23:25

And he released *unto them* him that for sedition and murder was cast into prison, whom they had desired; but he delivered Jesus to their will. (Luke 23:25, KJV)

"Unto them" is omitted.

When the Lord Jesus Christ was on trial, the Jews had desired that Barabbas be given to them; we read that Barabbas was released unto them as they had requested. This brings up a major principle that we have seen throughout all the history of Israel. "But lusted exceedingly in the wilderness, and tempted God in the desert. And he gave them their request; but sent leanness into their soul" (Psalm 106:14–15, KJV). All throughout their history, Israel had continually rebelled against God, which caused God to judge them. Their final major act of rebellion was when they delivered up the Lord Jesus Christ to be crucified. They always thought that they knew what was good for them, but they did not. That is why, many times, God gave them their way; but at the same time, He sent leanness into their souls. This means they were spiritually starving. They had physical food but not spiritual food.

The way the verse reads in the King James shows us that the leaders of Israel were specifically responsible for choosing Barabbas over Jesus because it includes the phrase "unto them," which is missing in the modern versions. This omission makes it read like Barabbas was released and went his way. He didn't. He was released unto the leaders of Israel, showing they preferred a murderer; and as a result, God sent more leanness into their souls until finally, in AD 70, it spelled the end of Israel.

Luke 23:33

> And when they were come to the place, which is called *Calvary*, there they crucified him, and the malefactors, one on the right hand, and the other on the left. (Luke 23:33, KJV)

Calvary is changed to "Golgotha" or "place of a skull."

The word *kranion* in the Greek can be translated as skull. It is translated that way in the following:

> And when they were come unto a place called Golgotha, that is to say, a place of a skull. (Matthew 27:33, KJV)

> And they bring him unto the place Golgotha, which is, being interpreted, The place of a skull. (Mark 15:22, KJV)

> And he bearing his cross went forth into a place called the place of a skull, which is called in the Hebrew Golgotha. (John 19:17, KJV)

These three usages of *kranion* are in the genitive case (*kraniou*), which is the case of possession. In other words, the place where they crucified Jesus was a place where other executions had taken place, and that is why it would be in the possessive case. However, when we come to the book of Luke, we see that the word *Calvary* is used. In Luke 23:33, the word *kranion* is in the nominative case. The nominative case points to the subject. This is why the KJV translators used *Calvary* instead of *skull*. Calvary is the subject and the focus of the verse. Calvary comes from Latin and has been used as far back as Wycliffe's 1388 Bible, which makes it 626 years that the book of Luke was pointing to Calvary. The Roman name for the place was called *Calvarius*, which is Latin for "skull." Calvary has come to be identified more with the crucifixion of Christ than skull.

The name *Calvary* has become part of the Christian language as many hymns that we sing speak of Calvary:

"At Calvary" (William Newell and Daniel Towner)

"Calvary Covers It All" (Mrs. Walter Taylor)

"I Believe in a Hill Called Mt. Calvary" (Bill and Gloria Gaither, Dale Oldham)

"Arise My Soul Arise," third stanza (Charles Wesley)

"Jesus Has Loved Me," second stanza (J. W. MacGill)

"Hallelujah to the Lamb," chorus (Isaac Watts)

"In My Heart There Rings a Melody," second stanza (Elton M. Roth)

"I Will Sing the Wondrous Story," first stanza (Francis Rowley)

"Singing I Go," first stanza (Eliza Hewitt)

"My Jesus I Love Thee," second stanza (William Featherston)

Remember, it is not the place of the skull that we focus on, as the modern versions do; it is what took place on that hill to warrant the name *Calvary*. These ten classic hymns are the tip of the iceberg. We sing about Calvary because Christ was crucified on Calvary; we don't sing about the place itself. Take these hymns and replace *Calvary* with skull and see if they make sense. I think not. The modern versions obliterate *Calvary*.

Luke 23:34

Then said Jesus, Father, forgive them; for they know not what they do. And they parted his raiment, and cast lots. (Luke 23:34, KJV)

Included in modern versions but bracketed in the CEV, HCSB, NET, NIV, NRSV, VOICE. Majority of modern versions attack this verse in their footnotes

Luke 23:34 contains probably the greatest example of forgiveness the human race has ever known. That is why Satan wanted it thrown out of the Bible. These footnotes not only cast doubt on the scriptures but also the content. Satan's normal mode of operation is revenge, but the Lord's is forgiveness. The manuscripts that included this entire verse are twelve, and the ones that did not are only six, and yet the modern translators go with the lesser amount. It is almost like they too are in agreement that this verse on forgiveness should be removed. Then again, what can you expect from Satan's workers?

One of the highest forms of love is forgiving someone who has hurt you, especially when they do it intentionally. To say to one who hurts you that you forgive them usually shocks them into apologizing to you for their misdeeds. Unconditional forgiveness is one of the highest characteristics of true Christianity, which can be manifested by a believer. It is with this trait that you may win people to Christ. We must be realistic. Many times, we hear people telling us to forgive and forget; only God is capable of forgetting. We will remember what people have done to us because Satan will not let us forget, so we must learn how to deal with those memories so we don't fall into Satan's snare of dredging up past hurts and conflicts.

Luke 23:38

And a superscription also was *written* over him
in letters of Greek, and Latin, and Hebrew, THIS IS
THE KING OF THE JEWS. (Luke 23:38, KJV)

"Written" and *"in letters of Greek, and Latin, and Hebrew"* are omitted.

Whenever a person was crucified for crimes against Rome, their crimes were written on a board and placed on the cross. Since the Lord Jesus Christ was not guilty of any crimes against anyone or Rome, they placed above Him a written message that stated that He was King of the Jews. No doubt an authority higher that Pontius Pilate allowed these words to be placed on the cross. For at that time, there was no king but Caesar. Now, the Bible points out specifically that the inscription was written in three different languages. Latin was the official language of the Roman Empire. Greek was used because it was a local language that was also used since the time of the conquests of Alexander the Great and would have been easily read by the Hellenistic Jews; and Hebrew, which would have been the language of Israel at that time. It was written in these three contemporary languages so there would be no doubt as to what was written. It was basically a derisive message probably aimed at the Jews who wanted Him dead. There is no reason given why these words were omitted in the modern versions. They simply denote the people who were in Jerusalem at the time of the Passover when Christ was crucified. Once again, the King James Bible gives us the accurate information concerning the suffering of the Lord Jesus Christ.

Luke 23:42

And he said unto Jesus, *Lord*, remember me when
thou comest into thy kingdom. (Luke 23:42, KJV)

Lord is omitted.

In the modern versions, this verse attacks the Lord Jesus Christ as being Lord by removing the word *Lord*. It goes one step further, and it destroys the testimony of the salvation of the thief on the cross. "Wherefore I give you to understand, that no man speaking by the Spirit of God calleth Jesus accursed: and that no man can say that Jesus is the Lord, but by the Holy Ghost" (1 Corinthians 12:3, KJV). According to 1 Corinthians 12:3, no one can truly call Jesus is Lord unless it is given them by the Holy Spirit. Removing *Lord* removes biblical proof that the thief on the cross was truly saved and went to heaven. These modern versions not only attack the Lord Jesus Christ, but they remove the hope of the Christian.

Luke 23:45

And the sun *was darkened*, and the veil of the temple was rent in the midst. Luke (23:45, KJV)

"*Was darkened*" is changed to "sun stopped shining" or "sun failed."

Here, we have another attack upon the supernatural events surrounding the death of the Lord Jesus Christ on Calvary. The KJV states that the sun "was darkened." The words "was darkened" are in the passive voice in the Greek. It is one word, and because it is in the passive voice, it means that the sun is receiving the action. The sun was being supernaturally darkened by God. God did the darkening, and the sun received the action of that darkening. When we compare this to the modern versions, the underlying Greek word used there is the one we get the word *eclipse* from. The word *eclipse* actually means "to omit, fail, of have some mind of defect." Basically, what the modern versions are teaching is that the sun was eclipsed or had failed. They take the supernatural action of God on the sun and reduce it to a natural occurrence such as an eclipse. They reduce another significant aspect of the crucifixion of Christ. The Gnostics did not want to see Jesus as God, so they have done everything to reduce Him to just another teacher. This is why the modern versions are dangerous because if Jesus is not God, then none of us reading this post can ever be saved.

Luke 24:1

Now upon the first day of the week, very early
in the morning, they came unto the sepulchre,
bringing the spices which they had prepared, *and
certain others with them.* (Luke 24:1, KJV)

"And certain others with them" is omitted.

"It was Mary Magdalene, and Joanna, and Mary the mother
of James, and other women that were with them, which told these
things unto the apostles" (Luke 24:10, KJV). Verse 1 and verse 10
confirm each other that there was a number of women who went
to the tomb beside the three named in verse 10. There is no reason
why the phrase "and certain others with them" should have been
removed from the text since it was confirmed in verse 10. Now,
here may be a reason why the Gnostics removed this phrase. The
word in Greek *tines* for "certain others" is actually a masculine pronoun, so there may have been some men who went to the tomb
along with the women. It is possible that they were brought along
to remove the stone because of its weight. It is also interesting that
God does not mention who they were but focuses the passage on
the women.

In Judaism, a woman's testimony on legal matters was excluded,
but now they were being the first ones to witness to the resurrection of Christ. I believe God is now saying that the old gender
bias of Judaism is now over, and women are now equal to men in
Christianity. God had elevated the women to a new status unheard
of in Judaism. "There is neither Jew nor Greek, there is neither
bond nor free, there is neither male nor female: for ye are all one in
Christ Jesus" (Galatians 3:28, KJV). There must have been quite a
number of those who initially went to the tomb, but since Gnostics
only believed in a spiritual resurrection rather than a physical one,
the modern versions have also done what they can to attack the
resurrection.

Luke 24:4

And it came to pass, as they were *much* perplexed thereabout, behold, two men stood by them in shining garments. (Luke 24:4, KJV)

Much is omitted.

The word used in the modern versions carries with it the meaning of "perplexed" or "doubt." The group that came to the tomb on Sunday morning to properly prepare the body of Jesus for permanent burial had seen that the stone was rolled away. So they entered in and saw the two angels in shining apparel. This caused them to be "much perplexed," which is beyond the meaning of the word in the modern versions. If you walked into a tomb and saw two men sitting there in shining apparel, you would be way beyond perplexed; you would definitely be much perplexed. Their wonderment and questions were very soon to be answered because when they had gone into the tomb, they had seen what looked like two men dressed in shining garments. It must have been a shock to them to see that Jesus was gone, but these two men who were actually radiating a glow were there instead.

The words *much perplexed* carries with it the meaning of "going through all possible solutions but finds no way out." In other words, the women had gone over every possible scenario in their minds and could not come to a solution as to what happened to the body of Jesus or who the two men were. The words *much perplexed* in English is actually one word in the Greek. What the modern-version editors did was to actually truncate the true meaning of this word by leaving the word *much* out.

Luke 24:42

And they gave him a piece of a broiled fish, *and of an honeycomb*. (Luke 24:42, KJV)

"And of an honeycomb" is omitted.

Honey was a very popular item in Israel and was something that was eaten as a common item. It was not expensive because bees were plentiful, and that made honey very plentiful. In fact, John the Baptist had eaten wild honey. "And the same John had his raiment of camel's hair, and a leathern girdle about his loins; and his meat was locusts and wild honey" (Matthew 3:4, KJV). I do not know why this portion was omitted from the modern versions. Maybe the answer may be found in Proverbs 16:24. "Pleasant words are as an honeycomb, sweet to the soul, and health to the bones" (Proverbs 16:24, KJV).

In the verses following Luke 24:42, the Lord Jesus Christ made many great promises to the disciples and opened their understanding of the scriptures so they would know why everything had to happen the way it did. When the scriptures are opened to the believer, they are sweet to the soul because they feed the saved soul. When a soul is at rest in the Lord, it even brings a calmness to the body, which creates health. The bones are in our bodies to give us the strength to be able to stand, and the words of Jesus act like bones, giving us the strength to stand in the face of an evil world. The world runs around in anxiety, but the believer lives on the honeycomb of the truth of the scriptures.

Luke 24:49

> And, behold, I send the promise of my Father upon you: but tarry ye in the city *of Jerusalem*, until ye be endued with power from on high. (Luke 24:49, KJV)

"Of Jerusalem" is omitted.

Here, the Lord was giving a specific command that when He went back to heaven, the promise of the Holy Ghost would become fulfilled. The Lord gave them an order to wait in the city of Jerusalem for the receiving of the Holy Ghost. In the modern versions, we read that the disciples were to wait "in the city." What city? Bethlehem? Bethsaida? Jerusalem? The modern versions keep everything in a very ill-defined position. The Lord gave them a specific place to wait so there would be no question where they were to wait. If the Lord just told them "the city," a discussion could have arisen among them concerning where they were to wait. God deals in specifics and does not cause His children to guess. Once again, the King James Version gives us specific information, but the modern versions keeps one guessing. That alone should convince someone that the source of these modern versions are not God but man.

Luke 24:53

And were continually in the temple, *praising* and blessing God. *Amen.* (Luke 24:53, KJV)

Praising and *amen* are omitted.

All the modern versions have omitted the word *amen*. It carries with it the meaning of "be firm or be established, so be it." It signifies that all that has been previously written has been established. Then the modern versions omit the word for *praising* and use the word *eulogountes* for both words "blessing" and "praising." The problem is that *eulogountes* is translated forty-seven times in the New Testament as "blessed," "bless," or "blessing." Only one time is it translated "praising," and that is in Luke 1:64, where what follows is a great eulogy of blessing by Zechariah upon announcing the birth of John the Baptist.

John 1:14

And the Word was made flesh, and dwelt among us, (and we beheld his glory, the glory as of the only *begotten* of the Father,) full of grace and truth. (John 1:14, KJV)

Begotten is omitted in the CEV, ERV, ESV, GNB, HCSB, LB, MESSAGE, NCT, NET, NLV, NLT, NRSV, RSV.

The Greek word behind *begotten* is *monogene* □. It is contained in both the Textus Receptus and the Hort Westcott manuscripts. The word carries with it the meaning of "unique" or "one of a kind." The word is used to denote the difference between the Lord Jesus Christ, who is in unique relationship with the Father, and the born-again Christians, who are also called sons and daughters of God.

John 1:18

No man hath seen God at any time; the only begotten *Son*, which is in the bosom of the Father, he hath declared him. (John 1:18, KJV)

Son is changed to "God." *Son* is changed to "One and Only" in some versions.

When *Son* is changed to "God" instead of keeping with the teaching that God is one God in three Persons, which is the doctrine of the Trinity, it alludes to the false teaching of two different Gods. It endorses the belief of multiple gods instead of keeping to the correct teaching of one God in three Persons.

John 1:27

He it is, who coming after me *is preferred before me*, whose shoe's latchet I am not worthy to unloose. (John 1:27, KJV)

"Is preferred before me" is omitted.

In this portion of scripture, John the Baptist is speaking to the delegation sent by the Pharisees to inquire as to whether John was the prophesied Messiah or not. John, being a very strong and true prophet, did not point the men to himself. He stated that he came before the Lord Jesus Christ, and his ministry had started before the ministry of Jesus, but the Lord Jesus Christ was the one whom he was the forerunner for. This is why under the inspiration of the Holy Spirit, he made the statement that Christ was preferred before him. This pointed the representatives of the Pharisees toward Christ and away from John. The King James Bible keeps our spiritual eyes focused on the coming of the Lord Jesus Christ and not John. John was being a humble man because he stated that he was not even worthy to untie the shoes of the Lord Jesus.

The modern versions remove that portion that points to the Lord Jesus Christ. After all, if you were an intellectual Gnostic, would you want to point people to another rather than yourself? Let's bring it down to today. If you were a PhD, would you want to point people to others rather than yourself? By continually removing the phrases that lead us to the Lord Jesus Christ from scripture, the modern versions tend to push us into the hands of the intellectual clergy and their psychology-based counseling ministries. The Holy Spirit is the one who leads us into all truth, but the modern versions keep chipping away at the truths of scripture and leave more and more to conjecture rather than written truth. If more churches would keep the King James Bible and preach from it, there would be no need for psychobabble or "purpose-driven" nightmares. Once again, the King James proves itself faithful while the modern versions attack the Lord Jesus Christ.

John 1:42

> And he brought him to Jesus. And when Jesus beheld him, he said, Thou art Simon the son of Jona: thou shalt be called Cephas, which is by interpretation, *A stone.* (John 1:42, KJV)

"A stone" is changed to "Peter."

In this verse, we read that Peter is at the center. The Lord changed his name from *Simon* to *Cephas.* The verse gives us the interpretation of the word *Cephas*, which means "stone." The Greek word is *petros*, which is translated as Peter throughout the entire New Testament. The only place where it is translated "stone" is here in John 1:42. There is a major reason why it is translated "stone" and not "Peter."

One of the primary teachings of the Roman Catholic institution is that Peter was the first pope, and this is based upon Matthew 16:18. "And I say also unto thee, That thou art Peter, and upon this rock I will build my church; and the gates of hell shall not prevail against it" (Matthew 16:18, KJV). They claim that the Lord Jesus Christ had stated in Matthew 16:18 that He was going to build His church upon Peter, whom they call the rock. Now, the word for "rock" in the Greek is *petra*, which is only translated "rock" sixteen times in the New Testament. It is never translated "Peter," nor does it ever reference him.

This word *petra* is translated "rock" in reference to the Lord Jesus Christ.

> And did all drink the same spiritual drink: for they drank of that spiritual *Rock* that followed them: and that *Rock* was Christ. (1 Corinthians 10:4, KJV)

The reason why John 1:42 interprets *Cephas* as "stone" is to show that Peter is no higher than any other true believer. "Ye also, as lively stones, are built up a spiritual house, an holy priesthood, to offer up spiritual sacrifices, acceptable to God by Jesus Christ" (1 Peter 2:5, KJV). All those who are saved are called "lively stones," and look who is writing that—it is Peter, the stone. While the Roman Catholics glorify Peter, the Bible is stating that he is no more important than any other true believer. All believers are stones that are building up the spiritual house of God. While the word *petros* is translated "Peter" everywhere in the New Testament, it is very important to know why it was translated as "stone" here in John 1:42. The modern versions completely omit and destroy that reason, and that is because their two primary manuscripts, Vaticanus and Sinaiticus, are Roman Catholic manuscripts.

John 1:51

> And he saith unto him, Verily, verily, I say unto you, *Hereafter* ye shall see heaven open, and the angels of God ascending and descending upon the Son of man. (John 1:51, KJV)

Hereafter is omitted.

The word *hereafter* is a specific point of time that Jesus is referring to. He is telling Nathanael that hereafter or from this moment on, "you will see the heavens opened." The modern versions do not give a specific time reference when this will occur. They only claim that they "will see," but no starting time is given.

John 2:22

> When therefore he was risen from the dead, his disciples remembered that he had said this *unto them*; and they believed the scripture, and the word which Jesus had said. (John 2:22, KJV)

"Unto them" is omitted.

Jesus had expunged the money changers from the temple and made the statement that the Pharisees did not understand. Jesus said, "Destroy this temple, and in three days, I will raise it." Since Jesus was at the physical temple, the Jews had thought He made reference to the physical temple, but He was speaking about his body, which would be resurrected from the dead on the third day. John states in 2:22 that the disciples had remembered that Jesus spoke this unto the Pharisees, and then they believed the scriptures and the word that Jesus spoke. They normally did not understand these types of sayings as they were walking with Jesus from town to town, but after the final events occurred, they remembered what was said to them as the Holy Spirit opened up the scriptures to them.

By leaving out "unto them," the word in the Greek behind these words is in the dative case, which means the statement that Jesus made about His body was directed at the Jews. By omitting that phrase, the modern versions make it a general statement to all, which is incorrect since Jesus directed that statement to the leaders. Understanding was given only to His disciples after the resurrection.

John 3:13

> And no man hath ascended up to heaven, but he that came down from heaven, even the Son of man *which is in heaven*. (John 3:13, KJV)

"Which is in heaven" is omitted.

Here is an attack upon the omnipresence of the Lord Jesus Christ. Omnipresence is a characteristic of God. In this John 3 discourse, Jesus was speaking with Nicodemus and was telling him that He had descended from heaven, yet at the same time, He was in heaven. This is a revelation of the omnipresence of Christ that at the same time He was on earth, He was still in heaven. Deleting "which is in heaven" removes the testimony of deity from Christ. As eternal God, He still had authority in heaven while still on earth.

The Gnostics did not believe that Christ was God because they taught that flesh was evil and that deity could not dwell in sinful flesh. They neglected the understanding of the virgin birth that disallowed the sin nature to be passed to Him. When Christ was on earth, He never ceased to be God. If He did, then He would never have been qualified to be our sin substitute. The word *is* is in the present tense, which means that Christ was signifying that while He was on earth, He was still in heaven. This is one of those great mysteries beyond the comprehension of the human mind, and that is why the Gnostics chose to remove it since they could not explain it.

John 3:15

That whosoever believeth in him *should not perish*, but have eternal life. (John 3:15, KJV)

"Should not perish" is omitted.

In removing the words "should not perish," there is a denial of the literalness of hell. Eternal damnation for sin has long been held by liberals and apostates as a false teaching. This is why it is not surprising that both the second-century Gnostics of Alexandria, Egypt, and the modern-day theologians have both agreed that this true biblical doctrine must go. The idea of accountability with consequences to a holy God has been anathematized over the centuries, and in our day of great "enlightenment" through intellectualism, culpability has been excised. With many apostates in the pulpits and the Christians afraid to ask questions or to question the validity of these versions, this creates a perfect environment for deception. The modern versions are sources for disbelief, doubt, and doctrinal attacks and must be avoided at all costs.

John 3:16

> For God so loved the world, that he gave his *only begotten Son*, that whosoever believeth in him should not perish, but have everlasting life. (John 3:16, KJV)

"Only begotten son" is changed to "one and only son."

The Greek word behind *begotten* is *monogene*. It is contained in both the Textus Receptus and the Hort-Westcott manuscripts. The word carries with it the meaning of "unique" or "one of a kind." The word is used to denote the difference between the Lord Jesus Christ, who is in unique relationship with the Father, and the born-again Christians, who are also called sons and daughters of God. In the modern versions, we read that Jesus was the *only* Son of God. This is a misnomer because when you change the word to *only* from *begotten*, you are attacking two major teachings in the scripture: first, the unique relationship the Lord Jesus had with the Father by means of Him coming to earth and dying for His elect and paying the complete price for their sins. The second teaching is that when a person becomes truly born again, they become a son or daughter of God. The modern versions make it sound like there are no other sons or daughters, and this is proven incorrect by the following scriptures.

> And will be a Father unto you, and ye shall be my *sons and daughters*, saith the Lord Almighty. (2 Corinthians 6:18, KJV)

> I will say to the north, Give up; and to the south, Keep not back: *bring my sons* from far, *and my daughters* from the ends of the earth. (Isaiah 43:6, KJV)

> Behold, what manner of love the Father hath
> bestowed upon us, *that we should be called the
> sons of God*: therefore the world knoweth us not,
> because it knew him not. (1 John 3:1, KJV)

> That ye may be blameless and harmless, *the sons
> of God*, without rebuke, in the midst of a crooked
> and perverse nation, among whom ye shine as
> lights in the world. (Philippians 2:15, KJV)

The importance of the word *begotten* shows the difference between those who have become sons and daughters of God by adoption and the Lord Jesus Christ, who has always been with the Father throughout all eternity. "To redeem them that were under the law, that we might receive the adoption of sons" (Galatians 4:5, KJV). In the Greek, there is a perfectly good word that God could have used if He wanted to convey Jesus as His *only* Son, and that word is *monon*, which is used sixty-seven times in the New Testament and is translated "only" or "alone."

> Neither pray I for these *alone*, but for them also
> which shall believe on me through their word.
> (John 17:20, KJV)

> And not for that nation *only*, but that also he
> should gather together in one the children of God
> that were scattered abroad. (John 11:52, KJV)

So in the book of John, there is a usage of the word *monon* and the word *monogene*, which shows us that there is a difference in the meanings and their usage. It is also interesting to note that the word *begotten* is included in the English text of the 1881 Hort-Westcott Revised Version and the 1901 American Revised Version, which is a clone of the 1881 RV. This means that the deletion of the word *begotten* is of recent origin. The translation of the Revised Standard

Version was approved in 1937 by the National Council of Churches, and the New Testament was completed in 1946. So the change of *begotten* to *only* probably was done around that time. It seems apparent that the modern theologians are no better than their second-century Gnostic colleagues.

John 3:18

He that believeth on him is not condemned: but he that believeth not is condemned already, because he hath not believed in the name of the only *begotten* Son of God. (John 3:18, KJV)

Begotten is changed to "one and only" and "only." See commentary on John 3:16.

John 3:25

Then there arose a question between some of John's disciples and the *Jews* about purifying. (John 3:25, KJV)

Jews is changed to "a Jew" (plural in Greek).

"Then said he to the multitude that came forth to be baptized of him, O generation of vipers, who hath warned you to flee from the wrath to come?" (Luke 3:7, KJV). The modern versions make it sound like there was only one Jew who was challenging John's disciples when we read in Luke 3:7 that a multitude of people had come to see John when he was baptizing. The word in the Greek text is plural (*Jews*) but was changed to a singular (*Jew*) in the modern versions. There were many who came to John, and therefore, there would have been much discussion among many of them and not just one. John drew many people because they wanted to know if he was the Messiah or not.

John 3:36

> He that believeth on the Son hath everlasting life: and he that *believeth not* the Son shall not see life; but the wrath of God abideth on him. (John 3:36, KJV)

"Believeth not" is changed to "obey not, rejects, disobeys."

"And they said, Believe on the Lord Jesus Christ, and thou shalt be saved, and thy house" (Acts 16:31, KJV). The apostle Paul states that a person must believe on the Lord Jesus Christ to be saved, and we see that in the first part of John 3:36. But the second part turns it into a works gospel that one must obey the Lord Jesus Christ, or you will not be saved. Obedience is a work and is one that is done by believers after they become saved, not before. Here is John 3:36 in the 1901 ASV: "He that believeth on the Son hath eternal life; but he that obeyeth not the Son shall not see life, but the wrath of God abideth on him."

John 4:16

> *Jesus* saith unto her, Go, call thy husband, and come hither. (John 4:16, KJV)

Jesus is changed to "he."

Once again, the name of Jesus has been omitted from the scriptures and replaced with a pronoun, making the person speaking subjective to the reader.

John 4:42

> And said unto the woman, Now we believe, not because of thy saying: for we have heard him ourselves, and know that this is indeed *the Christ*, the Saviour of the world. (John 4:42, KJV)

"The Christ" is omitted.

Once again, the modern versions based upon the Gnostic man-uscripts have stripped the Lord Jesus of His divine title of being the Christ. The name *Christ* means "anointed" or "Messiah" and is the predominant name by which we know Him. It describes Him as being the specific Christ of God. When this direct appellation is removed, then anyone in any religion can make any man their "savior." The King James tells us in no uncertain terms that the Lord Jesus Christ is the Savior of the world while the modern versions deny it in this passage.

There is a major but subtle pattern to these omissions. In describing the Lord Jesus Christ, when descriptive words and titles are removed, then each removal, even if it is only one word in a verse, strips away at the overall picture of the Lord Jesus Christ in scripture. Every verse that describes Him teaches us something else about Him, and the Bible tells us that we are to learn of Him. "Take my yoke upon you, and learn of me; for I am meek and lowly in heart: and ye shall find rest unto your souls" (Matthew 11:29, KJV). How could we possibly learn of Him if the modern versions keep chipping away at His descriptive divine title. Once again, the King James proves superior in how it handles the descriptions of the Lord Jesus Christ. It honors Him and does not attempt to obliterate Him.

John 4:46

So *Jesus* came again into Cana of Galilee, where he made the water wine. And there was a certain nobleman, whose son was sick at Capernaum. (John 4:46, KJV)

Jesus is omitted and replaced with "he."

Once again, the name of the Lord Jesus is omitted from scrip-ture and replaced with "he." The modern versions do not even have the courtesy of capitalizing *he*.

John 5:3–4

In these lay a great multitude of impotent folk, of blind, halt, withered, waiting for the moving

of the water. For an angel went down at a certain season into the pool, and troubled the water:
whosoever then first after the troubling of the
water stepped in was made whole of whatsoever
disease he had. (John 5:3–4, KJV)

Verse 3, "waiting for the moving of the water," is omitted. The
entirety of verse 4 is omitted or placed in brackets.

The removal of this verse is one of the most blatant denials of
the doctrine of angels, when you add the fact that an angel came
down and stirred the water so the first one who stepped in would
become well. The corruption of these verses goes back as far as AD
200, which means that the Gnostic corruption is still adhered to
today. These two verses are the prelude to the real focus of this section, and that is the healing of the sick man of thirty-eight years by
the Lord Jesus Christ. These two verses are needed to lay the ground-
work for the miracle that the Lord Jesus Christ was going to do.
These two verses are in Tatian's Diatessaron, dated about AD 175,
which predates the corruption. It was also found in the Old Latin
Vulgate dated between AD 90–150, which predates the corruption.
Tertullian in AD 200 also referred to these two passages, which
means that these verses were intentionally corrupted to destroy the
continuity of the message of the miracle that the Lord performed.

Others who confirmed the authenticity are Gregory of
Nazianzus (AD 390), Ambrose (AD 340–397), Chrysostom (AD
390) and Didymus (AD 379), Ammonius (third century), Hilary
(fourth century), Ephraem the Syrian (c. AD 306–373), Nilus (died
c. AD 430), Jerome (AD 347–420), Cyril of Alexandria (c. AD
376–444), Augustine (AD 354–430), and Theodorus Studita (AD
759–826). Other Bible translations that include the two verses in full
are Wycliffe (1384), Tyndale (1526), Coverdale (1535), the Great
Bible (1540), Matthew's Bible of 1549, the Bishops' Bible (1568),
the Geneva Bible (1560 and 1599), Wesley's New Testament (1755).
The modern versions continue to hold to the Gnostic corruption,
but the King James delivers the truth without any hesitation simply
because it is God's preserved word.

John 5:16

And therefore did the Jews persecute Jesus, *and sought to slay him*, because he had done these things on the sabbath day. (John 5:16, KJV)

"And sought to slay him" is omitted.

Jesus was being accused of being a sabbath breaker because he healed the man with the disease for thirty-eight years. The religious leaders had reviled him for breaking the sabbath; plus, they wanted to take it to the next level and slay Him. The modern versions omit the part where the religious leaders sought to slay the Lord Jesus Christ, either by bringing charges against Him before the council or some other way. This portion shows the hostility those leaders had toward the Lord Jesus Christ, and the principle is important because those of us who are Christians can expect the religious establishment to hate us also.

Religion has always been the enemy of Christianity, and there have been many attempts down through the ages to amalgamate the two, but water and oil cannot be homogenized. This verse is a warning to Christians that not only would we be persecuted for our faith but that persecution can also include our well-being. We may be silenced by either being told to be quiet and keep our views to ourselves, or we may be physically killed. That is why this is an important part of the verse and should not have been omitted because it keeps the true Christian on their toes.

John 5:29

And shall come forth; they that have done good, unto the resurrection of life; and they that have done evil, unto the resurrection of *damnation*. (John 5:29, KJV)

Damnation is changed to "judgment or condemned."

The unbelievers who are raised on the last day will indeed go into judgment, but that is not their final destination. The final destination of the unbelievers will be eternal damnation, which is denied here in the modern versions. "Having damnation, because they have cast off their first faith" (1 Timothy 5:12, KJV).

John 5:30

I can of mine own self do nothing: as I hear, I judge: and my judgment is just; because I seek not mine own will, but the will of *the Father* which hath sent me. (John 5:30, KJV)

"The Father" is changed to "him."

Here is case where a noun has been replaced by a pronoun, but this time, the attack is against the Father. The word *Father* has been expunged from the modern versions and replaced with "him." The word *Father* is important because it tells us that Jesus always wanted to seek the Father's will, which is a lesson for the believer that we are always to seek the Father's will in life. "For that ye ought to say, If the Lord will, we shall live, and do this, or that" (James 4:15, KJV). In the modern versions, a person can seek the will of the one who sent him; that is, the human who sent him or her to do something. It creates another nebulous teaching by removing the specific teaching from that verse. If Jesus sought to do the Father's will, then we believers must follow that example and seek the will of the Father for our lives. Once again, the modern versions deliver confusion and vagueness into a person's life.

John 6:11

And Jesus took the loaves; and when he had given thanks, *he distributed to the disciples, and the disciples* to them that were set down; and likewise of the fishes as much as they would. (John 6:11, KJV)

"He distributed to the disciples, and the disciples" is omitted.

Here is one of those verses that contain a historical event that points to the responsibility of all believers. Jesus took the physical loaves of bread and gave thanks for it. (I wonder what bread tasted like in those days without all the preservatives.) He then proceeded to give the bread to the disciples for distribution. The Lord followed the same procedure with the fish. This verse shows a great example of how the believers get the Gospel out to the world. The Lord gives us the word, and we, in turn, give the word to others.

Now, with the crowd being five thousand, it becomes obvious that the disciples also needed help in distribution so all in attendance were able to eat. Wait a minute! Did I say five thousand? Let us look at this again. It says five thousand men. This would mean that the five thousand number would probably be doubled because of women and children accompanying their husbands and fathers. So it becomes more obvious now that the disciples received more help to distribute the miracle lunch to everyone who was seated. Now, with the disciples needing help, this shows us that as the Lord saves people, and they grow in the faith. Then they, in turn, give the Gospel to others. This verse shows that the believers have a great responsibility in the Great Commission.

Surely, no one can doubt that if Jesus can feed thousands with a small lunch, He would have the ability to distribute it without human help, but He does not do that. "Then said Jesus to them again, Peace be unto you: as my Father hath sent me, even so send I you" (John 20:21, KJV). As the Father sent Jesus, He sends us. As Jesus distributes the bread to the crowd, the believers distribute the word to others. As with the bread that did not run out, the bread of life never becomes empty, and we send out as much Gospel into the world as we can. I hope we will make this a priority.

As we can plainly see, the modern versions have completely omitted the involvement of the believer in worldwide evangelism. This is because the same intellectual elite that have corrupted the manuscript lines are the same ones who think the "little people" are not important nor trained enough to bring the Gospel. For many years and still today, the Roman Catholic Church has believed and published that Bible interpretation is best left to those who are

DR. KEN MATTO

trained to do it. This same mind-set unfortunately exists in many Protestant churches too, where the pastor is basically the king of the congregation, and all must fall in line with his teachings or else. This mind-set leaves out one major element, and that is that every true believer is indwelled with the Holy Spirit, and one can neither add nor subtract from the salvation through either ignorance or education. It is a shame that the modern versions leave out the believers in their role in evangelism, but we can thank the Lord for the King James Bible, which shows that the believer has a very strategic role to play in evangelism until the last day.

John 6:22

> The day following, when the people which stood on the other side of the sea saw that there was none other boat there, save that one *whereinto his disciples were entered,* and that Jesus went not with his disciples into the boat, but that his disciples were gone away alone. (John 6:22, KJV)

"Whereinto His disciples were entered" is omitted.

This verse teaches us that where Jesus was, there was only one boat, and that was the one that the disciples had entered earlier. Jesus did not enter the boat because He was sending the multitudes away; plus, He had planned two great miracles to occur on the sea. The people did not know where Jesus went since the disciples had gone over to the other side in the boat by themselves; plus, Jesus was also found on the other side of the sea. The two great miracles are found in Matthew 14, where Jesus came to them in the midst of the roaring sea by means of walking on the water, and Peter left the boat to walk on the water with Jesus.

The modern versions leave out a very important part of this verse because it sets up the scenario for the two great miracles. If there was no boat there except the one that the disciples used, then Jesus would have to have walked on the water across the sea to Capernaum; or else, if he walked around the shore of the lake, it would have taken

266

Him much longer to arrive. But we know He walked on the water right across the lake.

John 6:28

> Then said they unto him, What shall we do, that we
> might work the works of God? (John 6:28, KJV)

The word *requires* is added, making it sound like God requires certain works for salvation.

"Then they asked him, 'What must we do to do the works God requires?'" (John 6:28, NIV). God requires no work for salvation since salvation is all of the Lord.

John 6:33

> For the bread of God *is he* which cometh down
> from heaven, and giveth life unto the world.
> (John 6:33, KJV)

"Is he" is changed to "is that" in the NASV, ASV, NIV, NRSV, RSV. When the modern versions replace *he* with "that," they are taking away from the fact that the Lord Jesus Christ came down from heaven. It sounds like actual bread came down instead of a person.

John 6:39

> And this is the *Father's* will which hath sent me,
> that of all which he hath given me I should lose
> nothing, but should raise it up again at the last
> day. (John 6:39, KJV)

Father's is changed to "him."

Throughout the ministry of Jesus, He was stating that He came to do the will of the Father. In John 6:39, He states a great truth that is comforting to the believer. The Father's will is that all the believers whom God gives Him, He will not lose one; that is, no one will lose their salvation because you cannot slip out of the Savior's hand. You did not work for salvation, and you cannot work to lose it. The Father's will is that the believers are secure. The modern versions remove *Father* and replace it with "Him." Jesus always told us His Father was involved in salvation, and to leave Him out removes the eternal bond between the Father and the Son. This is an attack on the Father as the text goes from a noun to a pronoun. The Gnostics tried to remove every connection between Jesus and the Father as best as they could, and the modern versions continue that satanic practice.

John 6:47

Verily, verily, I say unto you, He that believeth *on me* hath everlasting life. (John 6:47, KJV)

"On me" is omitted.

In the KJV Greek, we see the word *eme*, which has seven different inflections. The word comes from *ego*. In every instance, it is a first-person singular personal pronoun. This word denotes the focus of a specific belief of a person. In the English text of the KJB in John 6:47, we see the words "on me," which teaches that those who believe specifically on the Lord Jesus will have everlasting life. The footnote in the United Bible Societies under this verse shows that these words are missing from Vaticanus and Sinaiticus, which are the two primary manuscripts that underlie all the modern versions. The NIV and the NASB are in total agreement with the NAB (New American Bible [Roman Catholic]) and NWT (New World Translation of the Jehovah's Witnesses). This is because the same manuscripts that the rewriters of the NIV and NASB used are the same ones that underlie the cult bibles.

When the words "on me" are removed, the statement loses its specificity of belief. With the modern versions claiming that all you have to do is believe, it sets up the person to believe what they want. The Roman Catholic can freely believe in Mary as their co-redemptrix simply because the passage says "he who believes." A New Ager can believe in their astral planes because it says "he who believes." By removing "on me" in the text, it also removes the unique redemptive nature of the Lord Jesus Christ. It is only through Him that a person will become saved and have everlasting life. "Neither is there salvation in any other: for there is none other name under heaven given among men, whereby we must be saved" (Acts 4:12, KJV).

To remove "on me" removes the only path of true salvation and opens the doors for any and all adherents of whatever religion suits a person. Some may say, "Well, we know what the Bible means when it say *believes*." The only reason that people know what that means is because when they were growing up, they used the King James Bible and are remembering it. What about a new believer who goes to the bookstore and asks for a Bible and the store manager sells them an NIV or ESV? That new believer is starting their Christian life with a false version and no prior knowledge of the KJB. Beginning a Christian life with a "Bible" that is the same as what the Roman Catholics and Jehovah's Witnesses use is building on a sandy foundation and will lead to a consistent weakness in their Christian life. Try and witness to a JW with an NIV; it is like using their NWT to try and prove them wrong.

John 6:58

> This is that bread which came down from heaven:
> not as your fathers did eat *manna*, and are dead:
> he that eateth of this bread shall live for ever.
> (John 6:58, KJV)

Manna is omitted

Here is a direct link to the Old Testament when the manna came down from heaven, which was a representation of the Lord Jesus Christ. Many of the modern versions omitted the word *manna* and replaced it with "bread." They were two totally different things by means of their ingredients. The Greek has a perfectly good word for "bread," and it is *artos*, which is totally different from the Greek word "manna." They were also different because one was made with earthly ingredients, which was bread, but the manna was a heavenly blessing created daily by the Lord. By removing the word *manna*, the modern versions also break context. Here is John 6:49 from two modern versions that include *manna* but remove it in verse 58:

> Your fathers ate the manna in the wilderness, and they died. (John 6:49, ASV [1901])

> Your fathers ate the manna in the wilderness, and they died. (John 6:49, RSV)

> So there is no real reason why the word *manna* should be removed from verse 58 when it was perfectly suitable for verse 49.

John 6:65

> And he said, Therefore said I unto you, that no man can come unto me, except it were given unto him of *my* Father. (John 6:65, KJV)

My is changed to "the."

In the King James Bible, we read in this verse that Jesus is specifically stating that no one can come to Him unless by His Father. Jesus emphasizes the relationship that God is His Father by using the personal pronoun *my*. The modern versions change this to an article that is devoid of the connection between the Lord Jesus Christ being the Son of the Father in heaven. The early Gnostics did what they could to separate the two because they disbelieved that divinity could dwell in sinful flesh. If they would have done their homework a little, they would have realized that Christ did not have sinful flesh. For a group of people who prided themselves on having great knowledge, they sure did not possess much of it!

John 6:69

> And we believe and are sure that thou art *that Christ, the Son of the living* God. (John 6:69, KJV)

"That Christ, the Son of the living" is changed to "Holy one."

This verse is one of the most mutilated verses in the modern versions with a heavy New Age slant added to it. The first to meet the blade of the Gnostic knife is "that Christ."

> And we believe and are sure that thou art *that Christ*, the Son of the living God. (John 6:69, KJV)

The word *that* in the Greek is a definite article that means that the Lord Jesus Christ is the Christ, and because there is no indefinite article in the Greek, this means that this verse is pointing specifically to the Lord Jesus Christ and no other as being the Savior.

The second part to meet the blade of the Gnostic knife is *Son*.

> And we believe and are sure that thou art that Christ, the **Son** of the living God. (John 6:69, KJV)

The Lord Jesus Christ is spoken of as the "Son" of the living God." In Genesis 1, we read the principle that like begets like. If Jesus is the Son of the living God, that would make Him God, and the Gnostics and the Arians both believed that He was a created being. Obviously, the modern-version editors believe the same thing since they left it alone to read that way.

The third part to meet the blade of the Gnostic knife is *living*.

> And we believe and are sure that thou art that Christ, the Son of the *living* God. (John 6:69, KJV)

This omission that God is living would have played perfectly in the realm of thought of Friedrich Nietzsche, who was the father of the "God is dead" movement. Well, Nietzsche is dead, and God is still living. "It is a fearful thing to fall into the hands of the living God" (Hebrews 10:31, KJV). Maybe Hebrews 10:31 scared the Gnostics, and that is why they took out the fact that God is a living God. On judgment day, they will know how alive and well God is. The term *living God* appears thirty times in the scriptures, which means God is emphasizing the fact that He isn't going anywhere. It also tells us that since God is living, Jesus is also a living Savior who rules and reigns today.

The term *Holy One* does not appear in the Greek Textus Receptus in this verse but was changed in the Hort-Westcott Text to read as such. There is nothing in this verse that specifically ties the Lord Jesus Christ to being the Holy One in view. The KJV tells us specifically who we are reading about, and that is the Lord Jesus, who is the Son of the living God. Any New Ager can use this generic verse to refer to any of their avatars or ascended masters on the fourth or seventh plane, according to their belief system. The Holy Spirit penned this verse to teach us that Jesus is the son of the living God and to teach us that God is living. Once again, we see the modern versions agreeing with the second-century Gnostics and the unbelief of the modern-version translators and editors. True Christians need to stay away from modern versions because of the many deceptions contained within their pages.

John 7:8

Go ye up unto this feast: I go not up *yet* unto this feast; for my time is not yet full come. (John 7:8, KJV)

Yet is omitted.

As you can plainly see in the King James Bible, the Lord makes the statement that He is not yet going up to the feast. In the modern versions, they say that the Lord is saying that he is *not* going up to the feast. There is a great difference in both statements. One says that He is going at a later time, and the other one states that He is not going.

The modern versions make the Lord Jesus a liar because in John 7:10, the Bible states that He did go up to the feast. "But when his brethren were gone up, then went he also up unto the feast, not openly, but as it were in secret" (John 7:10, KJV). Even these modern versions state that the Lord Jesus went up to the feast in John 7:10:

> But when his brethren were gone up unto the feast, then went he also up, not publicly, but as it were in secret. (ASV)

> But after his brothers left for the festival, Jesus also went, though secretly, staying out of public view. (NLT)

> But after his brothers had gone up to the feast, then he also went up, not publicly but in private. (RSV)

On one hand, the modern versions are claiming that the Lord Jesus was not going to the feast, but then a few verses later, they say He had gone up to the feast. It is changed from *oupo* to *ouk* in Aleph (Sinaiticus). In the United Bible Societies text fourth edition, the Greek word *oupw* (*oupo*) is changed to *ouk* (*ouk*). The difference in the words are vast. *Ouk* means "not" or "no." It is used five times in the New Testament in Matthew 5:37, Matthew 7:29, Matthew 13:29, and Luke 14:33.

> But let your communication be, Yea, yea; *Nay, nay*: for whatsoever is more than these cometh of evil. (Matthew 5:37, KJV)

> For he taught them as one having authority, and *not* as the scribes. (Matthew 7:29, KJV)

The word *oupo* is used twenty-nine times in the New Testament. The word *oupo* means "not yet."

> Jesus saith unto her, Touch me not; for I am *not yet* ascended to my Father: but go to my breth-

ren, and say unto them, I ascend unto my Father, and your Father; and to my God, and your God. (John 20:17, KJV)

And there are seven kings: five are fallen, and one is, and the other is *not yet* come; and when he cometh, he must continue a short space. (Revelation 17:10, KJV)

There is absolutely no logical or grammatical reason to change the words since the context states that the Lord Jesus Christ did go up to the feast, but at a later time. The only reason that can be given is that this is another attack upon the character of the Lord Jesus Christ. The subtlety of these changes is a serious thing and should not be accepted by any true Christian. What is the spiritual advantage of having a version that teaches that the Lord Jesus Christ was a liar? It is another satanic attack on the Lord and on the truths of the word of God.

John 7:26

But, lo, he speaketh boldly, and they say nothing unto him. Do the rulers know indeed that this is the *very* Christ? (John 7:26, KJV)

Very is omitted

The people wanted to know if the rulers had switched positions and have accepted the fact that Jesus was the true Messiah. The word that the modern versions omit, *very*, carries with it the meaning of "truly" or "really." It enforces the fact that Jesus was the true Messiah because there were many who proclaimed themselves to be Messiah. This was one reason why Jesus did miracles: to set Himself apart from those false messiahs. There were many false messiahs, especially during the time of the Roman destruction of Jerusalem beginning in AD 66. By the modern versions omitting *very*, they place Jesus in with the group of those who claim to be messiah when there can only be one true Messiah.

John 7:29

But I know him: for I am from him, and he hath sent me. (John 7:29, KJV)

But is omitted.

The modern versions omit the word *but*, which is the Greek word *de*. It is a conjunction that normally shows a contrast between two clauses. In this case in verse 28, Jesus is telling those in the temple that they do not know Him that sent Him. "Then cried Jesus in the temple as he taught, saying, Ye both know me, and ye know whence I am: and I am not come of myself, but he that sent me is true, *whom ye know not*" (John 7:28, KJV). Then the conjunction begins verse 29 by Jesus stating, "But I know Him," showing the difference between the temple leaders who do not know God but think they do and Jesus, who actually knows God the Father since He came from Him. The conjunction is a small but important word because here it shows the spiritual standing in reference to the Father of the temple leaders versus Jesus and His relationship with the Father.

John 7:33

Then said Jesus *unto them*, Yet a little while am I with you, and then I go unto him that sent me. (John 7:33, KJV)

"*Unto them*" is omitted.

Here is another example of the modern versions leaving out an important word. The Pharisees and chief priests sent officers to see what Jesus was up to since the people were asking, "Can another person do more miracles than Jesus? Would He not be the Messiah?" So the officers approached Jesus, and He directly addressed them. The word that was left out, *unto them*, is one word in the Greek that is in the dative case, showing that these officers were the ones who received the action of Jesus's words. It was not a general addressing but specifically to these officers.

John 7:39

> But this spake he of the Spirit, which they that
> believe on him should receive: for the *Holy* Ghost
> was not yet given; because that Jesus was not yet
> glorified. (John 7:39, KJV)

Holy is omitted.

Here is another case of the modern versions reducing deity. The word *holy* before "Ghost" is the word that shows the difference between the Holy Spirit, who is the third Person of the Godhead, and the word *spirit* alone, which could be speaking about anything such as the "spirit of the age." In fact, in both the Byzantine text and the Stephanus text, the word in the Greek for "holy" is capitalized to show that it is speaking of the Holy Spirit and not just a generalized use of the word *spirit* as it appears in the modern versions. It is specifically speaking of the Holy Spirit.

John 7:50

> Nicodemus saith unto them, (he that came to Jesus
> *by night,* being one of them). (John 7:50, KJV)

"By night" is omitted.

"The same came to Jesus by night, and said unto him, Rabbi, we know that thou art a teacher come from God: for no man can do these miracles that thou doest, except God be with him" (John 3:2, KJV). The modern versions omit the fact that Nicodemus came to Jesus by night. They make it sound like he just saw Him a few minutes ago by leaving out that portion. Nicodemus came by night because he feared the other members of the Sanhedrin. The spiritual lesson here is that we all come to Jesus by night, and when He saves us, He turns our night to day.

John 7:53–8:11

And every man went unto his own house. (John 7:53, KJV)

Jesus went unto the mount of Olives. And early in the morning he came again into the temple, and all the people came unto him; and he sat down, and taught them. And the scribes and Pharisees brought unto him a woman taken in adultery; and when they had set her in the midst, They say unto him, Master, this woman was taken in adultery, in the very act. Now Moses in the law commanded us, that such should be stoned: but what sayest thou? This they said, tempting him, that they might have to accuse him. But Jesus stooped down, and with *his* finger wrote on the ground, *as though he heard them not.* So when they continued asking him, he lifted up himself, and said unto them, He that is without sin among you, let him first cast a stone at her. And again he stooped down, and wrote on the ground. And they which heard *it,* being convicted by *their own* conscience, went out one by one, beginning at the eldest, *even* unto the last: and Jesus was left alone, and the woman standing in the midst. When Jesus had lifted up himself, and saw none but the woman, he said unto her, Woman, where are those thine accusers? hath no man condemned thee? She said, No man, Lord. And Jesus said unto her, Neither do I condemn thee: go, and sin no more. (John 8:1–11, KJV)

These verses are placed in brackets, and doubt is placed upon it in the footnotes. This section has much evidence for its authenticity going back to the originals. The Old Latin Vulgate Bible (AD

157), the Greek Vulgate Bible (AD 150), and the Byzantine text (AD 450–1450) all contain these passages. Manuscript D 05 from the fifth century contains it. It is included in the following versions:

KJV
KJV (1611)
Geneva Bible (1587)
Bishop's Bible (1568)
Great Bible (1539)
Matthews Bible (1537)
Coverdale Bible (1535)
Tyndale Bible (1526)
Wycliffe Bible (1382)

John 7:53–8:11 is the narrative concerning the woman caught in adultery. For some reason, the Gnostic butchers did not see fit to include this account in their manuscripts and had intentionally omitted it. If you look at the modern-version footnotes, they claim that the most ancient authorities do not contain it. They have denied three other ancient authorities that contain the passage: the Old Latin Vulgate Bible (c. AD 157), the Greek Vulgate Bible (c. AD 150), and the Byzantine text, which reigned from AD 450–1450. Even D 05 from the fifth century contains it. The evidence that this passage of scripture is authentic is great. The two primary manuscripts where it is missing is Sinaiticus and Vaticanus. These two manuscripts differ from each other in 3,036 places in the Gospel alone. This passage of scripture has been preserved by God from the originals to the King James Version we have today.

Contained in the following manuscripts:

D 05, Bezae Cantabrigiensis (fifth century)
K 017 (ninth century)
M 021 (ninth century)
U 030 (ninth century)
036, Majuscule (tenth century)

28, Miniscule (eleventh century)
700, Miniscule (eleventh century)
Byzantine text (AD 450–1450)
Stephanus (AD 1550 AD)

John 8:9

And they which heard it, *being convicted by their own conscience*, went out one by one, beginning at the eldest, even unto the last: and Jesus was left alone, and the woman standing in the midst. (John 8:9, KJV)

"Being convicted by their own conscience" is omitted.

The true Gospel pricks the conscience, and here Jesus speaks something that would give even the greatest moral person something to think about. Those who are without sin let him cast the first stone. In other words, anyone could be in that woman's position if our sin closets were opened. The older people had become pricked in their conscience because, being older, they knew that they had committed more sins and therefore were convicted. And after them, the younger ones know that they too could be convicted of their sins if found out.

The modern versions make it sound like these people just didn't like what they heard, but it went much deeper than that. The reason they left was because they were convicted of their own sins and knew it would be hypocrisy if any of them cast the first stone. The gospel affects the inner man, and here is a great example of that, but the modern versions remove this great insight. In fact, the word *heard* in the Greek carries with it the meaning of "hearing with understanding." So the crowd understood the fact that they too have sinned in their life and could not, in good conscience, condemn someone else when they knew they were just as guilty.

John 8:10

When Jesus had lifted up himself, *and saw none but the woman*, he said unto her, Woman, where are those thine accusers? hath no man condemned thee? (John 8:10, KJV)

"And saw none but the woman" is omitted.

Jesus made the challenge to the crowd that those who were without sin should cast the first stone at her, but one by one, they were convicted and had left. And when Jesus lifted Himself up, He saw only the woman and not those who brought her to Him. The modern versions leave out that most important part that her accusers had been convicted by their own consciences and had left the scene.

John 8:20

These words spake *Jesus* in the treasury, as he taught in the temple: and no man laid hands on him; for his hour was not yet come. (John 8:20, KJV)

Jesus is omitted.

Once again, Jesus is omitted from the scriptures and replaced with a pronoun, allowing anyone to fill in any name.

John 8:28

Then said Jesus unto them, When ye have lifted up the Son of man, then shall ye know that I am he, and that I do nothing of myself; but as *my* Father hath taught me, I speak these things. (John 8:28, KJV)

My is changed to "the."

Changing *my* to "the" destroys the Father-Son relationship. It looks like Jesus is speaking about God the Father who is detached from Him rather than Him being His Heavenly Father. It shows a coldness in the relationship rather than a family relationship.

John 8:59

Then took they up stones to cast at him: but
Jesus hid himself, and went out of the temple,
going through the midst of them, and so passed by.
(John 8:59, KJV)

"Going through the midst of them, and so passed by" is omitted.

In verse 58, Jesus had just claimed to be "I Am," which is the way God had described Himself to Moses on Mount. Sinai. Therefore, the Jews would have been familiar with this saying. According to the law, blasphemers are to be stoned to death. Jesus was claiming that He is the "I AM" of Sinai, and claiming to be God would have been blasphemy in the ears of the Jews. In verse 59, the crowd was so incensed at Jesus that they had already begun to pick up stones to kill Him. Then we are told that He hid Himself and went out of the temple. Here is the interesting part of the verse: He passed right through the midst of them. Does anyone else see a great miracle here? The crowd was totally against Jesus to the point of wanting to kill Him, but Jesus passed right through their midst, and no one saw Him?

You can be sure they would have been looking for Him, and someone would have spotted Him and called the crowd to that location. But it seems a divine blindness had fallen over the crowd, and Jesus was able pass through their midst without them seeing or apprehending Him. This blindness was on the same level of the blinding of the people of Sodom who wanted to try and take Lot, but the angels intervened. Here in John, we have a notable miracle that took place; and the modern versions, with their secular view of Jesus, have omitted this miracle. This was not the time for Jesus to be apprehended, so therefore, He escaped the crowd through a divine miracle. It is a shame that the modern versions have omitted this miracle because it is a comfort for Christians to know that we can never be taken one day before God has decreed our homecoming. Once again, the King James Bible proves itself as the only truth bearer among the many versions.

John 9:4

I must work the works of him that sent me, while
it is day: the night cometh, when no man can
work. (John 9:4, KJV)

I is changed to "we."

The word *I* in John 9:4 has been changed in the modern versions to "we." They have taken a singular word and exchanged it for
a plural one. In John 9:4, the Lord was in the middle of a discourse
with his disciples. He was about to open the eyes of a blind man,
and He made the statement that "I must work the works of him that
sent me." The opening of the blinded eyes was symbolic for a person
becoming saved and having their spiritual eyes opened. Blind eyes
cannot let in the light, only eyes that work.

If we follow the leading of the modern versions, then it was not
only the Lord Jesus Christ who opened the eyes of the blind man,
but the disciples did it too. Now this is an important replacement
because it is basically telling us that man has a part in his salvation,
and this is incorrect. Man can do nothing to procure salvation. It is
all of the Lord. "For as the Father raiseth up the dead, and quickeneth them; even so the Son quickeneth whom he will" (John 5:21,
KJV). Does it say that the Lord and the disciples will quicken, or just
the Lord will quicken?

It is true that the Lord will eventually hand over all evangelism to
His followers, but here in this verse, He is telling us that it is He who
opens the eyes of the blind; in other words, it is He who does the saving. Further in John 9, when the man was examined by the religious
rulers, he did not claim that the disciples had anything to do with his
healing, only the Lord. So the testimony of the singular word pointing to the Lord Jesus alone follows the true context of this narrative.

The singular *I* is found back in the oldest versions of the Bible
in the line of the King James. It actually antedates the corrupted
Alexandrian manuscripts. It is found in the pre-Gothic manuscripts
of AD 350 and before. Here is the verse written in the Wycliffe Bible.
If you notice, it too states that it is Jesus doing the works.

It bihoueth me to worche the werkis of hym
that sente me, as longe as the dai is; the nyyt
schal come, whanne no man may worche.
(Wycliffe Bible of 1382–89)

John 9:11

He answered and said, A man that is called Jesus
made clay, and anointed mine eyes, and said
unto me, Go to *the pool of* Siloam, and wash:
and I went and washed, and I received sight.
(John 9:11, KJV)

"The pool of" is omitted.

Here is another example of a confusing verse. When Jesus
placed the clay on the man's eyes, He told him to go to the pool of
Siloam to wash, and then he would be able to see. The modern versions leave out the important part that he was to go to the pool of
Siloam. Siloam was a community, and without the specific directions
of Jesus, where would the man go in Siloam? Was he supposed to go
to some inn? Was he to go to someone's home? The problem is that
Jesus gave a specific destination to affect the healing of his eyes. If he
would have gone somewhere else, then he would have been disobedient and would not have regained his eyesight. The modern versions
are very nebulous in many of their passages. If Jesus commands a
specific thing and that is left out of the modern version, then a person will be in disobedience. It seems the modern versions endorse
disobedience. It also seems they want to elevate the intellect of man
while reducing the deity of Christ, a very Gnostic technique.

John 9:35

Jesus heard that they had cast him out; and when
he had found him, he said unto him, Dost thou
believe on the Son of *God*? (John 9:35, KJV)

God is changed to "Man."

The word *Theou* ("God") is changed to *anthropou* ("man") in the following corrupted manuscripts: Aleph (Sinaiticus), B (Vaticanus), D (Bezae Cantabrigiensis, fifth century), W (four–fifth century). Both D and W manuscripts contains the four Gospels and the book of Acts alone.

The TR plainly calls Jesus the "Son of God," but the modern versions reduce him to son of man. In the New Testament, the term *Son of Man* is used to describe the Lord Jesus eighty-eight times in eighty-four verses, so there is ample allusion to this earthly title of the Lord Jesus Christ identifying Him as coming in the flesh. The term *Son of God* is used forty-seven times in forty-six verses. It is used ten times in the book of John, seven times in the book of 1 John, and one time in the book of Revelation.

Some may ask, "What is the problem with the term *Son of Man?*" Well, there is nothing wrong with that term since it is used copiously in the New Testament, but the problem is that in this particular verse, God did not use the word for "man"; instead, He originally used the word for "God." This word was surreptitiously changed for no reason except another attack on the deity of the Lord Jesus Christ. If you look at the context in which this verse occurs, it is where Jesus had given sight to the blind man. If you look in John 9:38, you will read a very important clause:

> And he said, Lord, I believe. *And he worshipped him.* (John 9:38, KJV)

The man who received his sight was having a dialogue with the Lord Jesus, and the culmination of that dialogue was that the man had worshiped the Lord Jesus.

> Then saith he unto me, See thou do it not: for I am thy fellowservant, and of thy brethren the prophets, and of them which keep the sayings of this book: *worship God.* (Revelation 22:9, KJV)

In the context of this verse in Revelation, John began to worship at the feet of the angel who was showing him these things, but the angel told him to worship God.

> And Jesus answered and said unto him, Get thee behind me, Satan: for it is written, *Thou shalt worship the Lord thy God*, and him only shalt thou serve. (Luke 4:8, KJV)

Satan had tried to get the Lord Jesus Christ to worship him in exchange for world domination, but the Lord Jesus told him and told us that we are to worship the Lord our God. Now back to John 9:35. If we follow the modern versions and keep the changed term as *son of man*, then we will have this man worshipping a mere human being. The modern versions keep John 9:38 intact with the term *worship*. The problem with the context of this dialogue in John 9 would look like this in the modern versions. We will use the NIV.

> Jesus heard that they had thrown him out, and when he found him, he said, "Do you believe in the Son of Man?" (John 9:35, NIV)

> Then the man said, "Lord, I believe," and he worshiped him. (John 9:38, NIV)

Instead of the man worshipping the Son of God, he would be worshipping the son of man! A very, very big difference! If God wrote *Theou* ("God"), then it is to be translated and read "God" and not changed to "man" by the Gnostic theologians of the second century nor endorsed by the contemporary church. We see this principle of identification revealed to us in Matthew 19:16–17:

> And, behold, one came and said unto him, Good Master, what good thing shall I do, that I may have eternal life? And he said unto him, Why callest thou me good? there is none good but one,

that is, God: but if thou wilt enter into life, keep the commandments. (Matthew 19:16–17, KJV)

This is the narrative of the rich young ruler who came to Jesus and called Him *Good Master*. Jesus rejected the title *Good Master* in this dialogue, but why? The young ruler was looking at Him as a human being and not as God. This is why Jesus said to Him that there is none good except God.

> As it is written, *There is none righteous, no, not one*: There is none that understandeth, there is none that seeketh after God. They are all gone out of the way, they are together become unprofitable; *there is none that doeth good, no, not one.* (Romans 3:10–12, KJV)

So by changing *God* to "man," we would be seeing man worshipping man.

> Who changed the truth of God into a lie, *and worshipped and served the creature more than the Creator,* who is blessed for ever. Amen. (Romans 1:25, KJV)

Do you see how important just one word can be? Stick to the King James and let the Lord bless you by giving you more understanding than those who hold to the modern versions because some unbelieving scholar says so. Don't worship the creature, worship the Creator! The modern versions have changed the truth of God into a lie!

John 9:38

And he said, Lord, I believe. And he worshipped him. (John 9:38, KJV)

And he said, Lord, I believe. And he worshipped him. (John 9:38, ASV)

Footnote in 1901 ASV (Unitarian edition) states that Christ was a created being: "The Greek word denotes an act of reverence, whether paid to a creature (as here) or to the Creator."

If you notice, the verse appears the same in both the King James Bible and in the American Standard Version of 1901. However, the footnote attached to this verse in the Unitarian edition of the ASV is stating openly that Jesus is not the Creator but that He is the creature. This is another footnote attack on the deity of Christ. The 1901 ASV is the forerunner of the Revised Standard Version of 1946 and 1952 of the National Council of Churches. The majority of the corruptions were done in the second century by Gnostics who disbelieved the deity of Christ.

Here, we see that the attitude that prevailed in Alexandria, Egypt, is still prevalent in the modern versions. You can see the Gnostic influence in any modern version by doing a parallel study of the verses in the King James that contain the phrase "Lord Jesus Christ" and whatever translation you use, and you will see this divine title is chopped up to make Christ as only an enlightened teacher and not God. One of the most open characteristics of the modern versions are the attacks on the divinity of the Lord Jesus Christ.

The ASV of 1901 (Unitarian edition) straightly teaches that Christ was not God in the footnotes. The footnotes in the modern Bibles are just as dangerous as the rewriting of the text. Some of the notables on the revision committee of the 1901 ASV were J. Henry Thayer, Philip Schaff, Ezra Abbott, who was a Unitarian. Unitarians deny the deity of Christ and the Trinity. There was a Unitarian on the Revision committee of 1881 also. His name was G. Vance Smith. Christians must do a historical study of the Bibles they use, or else the great possibility exists that their version was written by unbelievers who are or were hostile to true Christianity.

Philip Schaff was behind the 1893 Parliament of World Religions, which was also called the debut of the New Age movement. Conference speakers were heralding the New Age movement. There were many Hindus who spoke at this event. There were also Brahmins, Buddhists, Wicca (witches), members of the New

Jerusalem Church of Swedenborg, and many pagans. Schaff wanted to see a complete unification of the world's religions. The next time you read Schaff's writings, know that he was anything but saved and be alert. Isn't it amazing that this is the caliber of men rewriting the Bible and trying to convince you that their version is the best and is better than the King James? Schaff was the general director of the entire ASV committee. In looking at the qualifications of the King James translators, I did not find anyone involved in witchcraft or spiritism. Would a holy God give His word to men like this to correct it?

John 10:26

> But ye believe not, because ye are not of my sheep, *as I said unto you.* (John 10:26, KJV)

"As I said unto you" is omitted.

Jesus was reiterating what he told the Pharisees in John 10:4. "And when he putteth forth his own sheep, he goeth before them, and the sheep follow him: for they know his voice" (John 10:4, KJV). The sheep of Jesus know His voice, and they follow Him. Jesus told the Pharisees that they would not follow Him because they were not of His sheep. He repeated that in verse 26 because the Pharisees were discussing whether Christ was the Messiah since only God could open the eyes of the blind. Even though they discussed it among themselves, they were still not the sheep of Christ and would not follow Him. This was the second time they gathered to Him, and Jesus was reminding them they would not follow Him. The modern versions make it sound like this was the first and only time Jesus told this to the Pharisees.

John 10:29

> My Father, which gave them me, is greater than all; and no man is able to pluck them out of *my* Father's hand. (John 10:29, KJV)

My is changed to "the."

Here is one of those verses where a word in the Greek is completely omitted. It is the word *mou* and is a personal pronoun in the genitive case. Genitive is the case of possession. Jesus was speaking of the disciples that no one can pluck them out of His Father's hands. The word *my* also states that Jesus was identifying Himself with His Father. Wouldn't it sound strange if I was standing next to my father and said, "Hi, I am Ken, and this is the father." That would make no sense. Instead, it is more appropriate to say, "Hi, I am Ken, and this is my father." Now you have an understanding of who the man is next to me and my relationship to him.

By Jesus stating that God was His Father, He was identifying Himself as the Son of God and revealing His relationship to Him. Bit by bit, the modern versions continue to chip away at the deity of Christ and His relationship with His Father, which further identifies Him as deity. Once the modern versions reach their goal of completely stripping the Lord Jesus Christ off His deity, then they will have reduced Him to a teacher on par with Buddha or Confucius. The King James Bible is a safe haven for truth for true Bible believers, and we must never abandon it.

John 10:32

> Jesus answered them, Many good works have I
> shewed you from *my* Father; for which of those
> works do ye stone me? (John 10:32, KJV)

My is changed to "the."

There is no reason given as to why this was changed in the Vaticanus manuscript. However, we do know that this is another attack on the fact that the Lord Jesus Christ is God the Son. By changing *my* to "the," it also gives the impression that God is the spiritual Father of all creation. Jesus was telling us here that God is His Father, but removing *my* also removes the revealing of the relationship of Jesus to God. With the use of *the*, any group on earth can claim that God is their Father. In the eighth chapter of John, Jesus was debating the Pharisees when they had claimed that God was their Father.

> Ye do the deeds of your father. Then said they to him, We be not born of fornication; we have one Father, even God. Jesus said unto them, If God were your Father, ye would love me: for I proceeded forth and came from God; neither came I of myself, but he sent me. Why do ye not understand my speech? even because ye cannot hear my word. Ye are of your father the devil, and the lusts of your father ye will do. He was a murderer from the beginning, and abode not in the truth, because there is no truth in him. When he speaketh a lie, he speaketh of his own: for he is a liar, and the father of it. (John 8:41–44, KJV)

Here, we see a perfect example of a group claiming to have God as their Father. The Jewish leaders had claimed that God was their Father, but Jesus quickly corrected them in telling them that if they were truly of God, then they would have known who He was and would love Him. He then went on to tell them that they were of their father, the devil. Let me repeat: by using the word *the*, any group can claim that God is their Father. The only group on earth who can legitimately claim that God is their Father is the body of Christ who was redeemed by the blood of Christ, who is God the Son. The word *mou* in the Greek is a personal pronoun in the genitive case. The genitive case shows possession, and that is why the Lord Jesus said "*my* Father" and not "the Father."

John 10:38

> But if I do, though ye believe not me, believe the works: that ye may know, and *believe*, that the Father is in me, and I in him. (John 10:38, KJV)

Believe is changed to "understand."

Many of the modern versions change "and believe" to "understand." There is a vast difference between them. Look at the verse. It states that the Father is in Jesus, and Jesus is in the Father. Let me see a show of hands. Who can understand the Trinity? As finite people, it is impossible for us to know the inner workings of the Trinity, and that is why we take it on faith through belief. Belief is the verb form of faith; in other words, it is that action of belief that is built upon faith. We understand with our senses. I understand the principle of electricity or the principles of economics, but who can understand the Trinity so deeply that they can claim they understand it fully?

John 11:41

Then they took away the stone *from the place where the dead was laid*. And Jesus lifted up his eyes, and said, Father, I thank thee that thou hast heard me. (John 11:41, KJV)

"From the place where the dead was laid" is omitted.

This mutilated verse is right in the important account of the raising of Lazarus. The omitted portion is very important because it specifically states that Lazarus was in the place where the dead was laid. This portion of scripture is a confirmation that Lazarus was indeed dead and was not in a state of physical sleep or just being sick. This part of scripture is vital because it leads up to the point when the Lord Jesus Christ raised Lazarus from the dead. To omit this portion of scripture allows the readers of the modern versions to create a belief that Lazarus was not dead and that Jesus did not have any authority over death. This would make it an attack on the deity of Christ. It also takes away the hope of the believer that if they physically die before the return of Christ, there would be no resurrection. The omitted part of scripture is a great part that brings comfort that death has no authority over the Lord Jesus Christ, and because of that, it has no authority over the Christian either. Once again, the

King James Bible brings forth a great comfort for the true believer while the modern versions omit a great truth.

John 12:1

> Then Jesus six days before the passover came to Bethany, where Lazarus was *which had been dead,* whom he raised from the dead. (John 12:1, KJV)

"Which had been dead" is omitted.

The raising of Lazarus from the dead is probably the most widely known miracle of Jesus. Lazarus was dead for four days, and his body started to decay, and Jesus raised him from the dead. John 12:1 makes it certain that we know that Lazarus was dead. The modern versions omit the fact that Lazarus was dead by omitting the phrase "which had been dead." God is emphasizing the fact that Lazarus was dead and that Jesus had raised him from the dead. This is an attack on the greatest miracle that Jesus performed because it is a foreshadowing of the great day when Jesus will raise every believer who has died. The modern versions are always attempting to neutralize the reality of the deity of Christ.

John 12:41

> These things said Esaias, *when* he saw his glory, and spake of him. (John 12:41, KJV)

When is changed to "because."

Both words, *because* and *when,* are conjunctions. *When* is also used as a noun, adverb, and pronoun. John 12:40–41 ties into Isaiah 6, where Isaiah sees the glory of God in His temple.

> And he said, Go, and tell this people, Hear ye indeed, but understand not; and see ye indeed, but perceive not. Make the heart of this people fat, and make their ears heavy, and shut their eyes; lest they see with their eyes, and hear with

their ears, and understand with their heart, and convert, and be healed. (Isaiah 6:9–10, KJV)

John 12:41 is pointing to the fact that Isaiah was in the presence of the Lord and recorded his commission to go to Israel and preach the truth. Isaiah received this commission to be a prophet to Israel when he was in the presence of the Lord and not because of it. The word *when* shows that Isaiah was present when the Lord spoke to him, but the word *because* could be deemed a reaction by Isaiah where he would not necessarily have been present. The word *when* shows that Isaiah received his commission from the mouth of the Lord, and *because* can show a delayed reaction to the calling and can also open the door for a third-party commission, thus lessening Isaiah's authority. For example, God spoke to X, and X told Isaiah; and because he was told by X, he became a prophet by proxy. However, the word *when* tells us that Isaiah was in the presence of the Lord just like John was in Revelation. When God commissioned a prophet, He did it personally when they were in His presence.

John 12:45

And he that seeth me seeth *him* that sent me. (John 12:45, KJV)

Him is changed to "the one." The One is also used as a New Age term. The term "the one" is used 126 times in 119 verses throughout the Bible and is never used in reference to God the Father or God the Son. The Greek words behind both English words are totally different. The word behind "him" is *autos*, and the word for "one" is *heis*.

John 13:2

And supper being ended, the devil having now put into the heart of Judas Iscariot, Simon's son, to betray him. (John 13:2, KJV)

"And supper being ended" is changed to "during or while supper was being served."

The word in the Greek behind "during supper" in the modern versions is a present-tense verb. In the King James, it is an aorist verb denoting a past action. It was right after supper when the Lord Jesus Christ got up from the table and began to wash the feet of His disciples. He would not have done this in the middle of the meal but when it was ended.

John 14:15

> If ye love me, keep my commandments.
> (John 14:15, KJV)

"Keep my commandments" is changed to "you will keep my commandments." It changes it from a command to a statement.

In the Textus Receptus (King James), the word *keep* is a commandment from the Lord Jesus Christ. It is in the imperative mood. The modern versions, by adding the word *will* to *keep*, makes it a future action on behalf of the people Jesus is speaking with. Jesus gives a commandment to His followers that if they love Him, they are to keep His commandments. The modern versions make it sound like there is no possibility that Jesus's followers will ever accidentally overlook His commandments.

As fallen creatures, even though we are saved, we are still imperfect in following the Lord Jesus Christ. To make a declarative statement that His followers "will" keep His commandments can build discouragement and even depression if a Christian does not follow the future prophecy of the statement of Jesus as written in the modern versions. We all have feet of clay and are imperfect in our following and obedience. The modern versions make it sound like a Christian will be perfect in obedience.

John 14:28

> Ye have heard how I said unto you, I go away, and
> come again unto you. If ye loved me, ye would

rejoice, because I said, I go unto the Father: for *my* Father is greater than I. (John 14:28, KJV)

My is changed to "the."

Here, Jesus is specifically stating that God is His Father by using the genitive pronoun *my*. It shows the relationship between them. The modern versions use the generic *the*, which does not show a relationship between Jesus and His Father. It is like someone saying that they are going to the parents for a visit rather than saying, "I am going to my parents for a visit."

John 15:7

If ye abide in me, and my words abide in you, *ye shall* ask what ye will, and it shall be done unto you. (John 15:7, KJV)

"Ye shall" is omitted.

The King James keeps the teaching of Jesus specifically geared toward His disciples by including the phrase "ye shall" instead of the generic "ask," which the modern versions use. It sounds like anyone can ask Jesus for anything, including unbelievers, by using the generic term. Only those who are truly saved and indwelled by the Holy Spirit will ask the Lord according to His will because the Holy Spirit will guide us to seek and pray in the will of God.

John 16:3

And these things will they do *unto you*, because they have not known the Father, nor me. (John 16:3, KJV)

"Unto you" is omitted.

In John 16:3, Jesus is making it very plain to the disciples that the persecutions that He spoke about in verse 2 will happen to them. "They shall put you out of the synagogues: yea, the time cometh, that whosoever killeth you will think that he doeth God service"

(John 16:2, KJV). The modern versions make it sound like these people will do these things in some type of random fashion, but the persecution will be aimed at the disciples and all followers of the Lord Jesus Christ. This verse is a warning to all Christians throughout the ages.

John 16:10

Of righteousness, because I go to *my* Father, and
ye see me no more. (John 16:10, KJV)

"My Father" is changed to "the Father."

The Lord Jesus Christ always had a unique relationship with His Father. In this verse, He leaves nothing to speculation as He states plainly that God is His Father by using the personal pronoun *my*. The modern versions remove that unique relationship by using the generic *the*.

John 16:16

A little while, and ye shall not see me: and again,
a little while, and ye shall see me, *because I go to
the Father*. (John 16:16, KJV)

"Because I go the Father" is omitted.

This omission is another attack on the ascension of the Lord Jesus Christ and the fact that He is the Son of God. The Gnostics did not believe that Jesus was the Son of God, so it would naturally follow that they would remove this important part of the verse that deals with His ascension and His relation to God the Father. There is no reason given in the modern Greek text as to why this was left out, but there is a notation that Origen was the one who had it removed. As you recall, Origen was a Gnostic pagan.

When that phrase was taken out, verse 16 made no sense. It sounds like the Lord is rambling when He says that in a little while, they will see Him, and in a little while, they will not. "Because I go to the Father" is the phrase that gives the statement its proper meaning.

It explains why they will not see Him in a little while and the fact that they will see Him again when they go to heaven. Leaving this phrase out also removes the heavenly witness of the Lord Jesus Christ and the reunification of all the believers in heaven.

Once again, the modern versions create a confusing situation in the context of these verses:

> A little while, and ye shall not see me: and again, a little while, and ye shall see me, *because I go to the Father.* Then said *some* of his disciples among themselves, What is this that he saith unto us, A little while, and ye shall not see me: and again, a little while, and ye shall see me: and, *Because I go to the Father?* (John 16:16–17, KJV)

> "In a little while you will see me no more, and then after a little while you will see me." Some of his disciples said to one another, "What does he mean by saying, 'In a little while you will see me no more, and then after a little while you will see me,' and *Because I am going to the Father*'?" (John 16:16–17, NIV)

> "A little while and you will no longer see Me; again a little while and you will see Me." Therefore some of His disciples said to one another, "What is this He tells us: 'A little while and you will not see Me; again a little while and you will see Me'; and, '*because I am going to the Father*'?" (John 16:16–17, HCSB)

In verse 17, the disciples ask the question among themselves concerning the statement the Lord made in verse 16 that He was going to the Father. But wait, in the modern versions, they are concerning themselves with a statement that the Lord never made. In verse 17, they are questioning the phrase about Him going to the Father when He did not make that statement according to the modern versions. So once again, it seems like they added the phrase "because I am going to the Father" instead of it being part of the flow of the context of the surrounding verses. Once again, the King James shows its superiority in dispelling confusion while the modern versions once again create it because they go to their father.

John 17:11

> And now I am no more in the world, but these are in the world, and I come to thee. Holy Father, keep through thine own name *those whom* thou hast given me, that they may be one, as we are. (John 17:11, KJV)

"Those whom" is omitted.

"All that the Father giveth me shall come to me; and him that cometh to me I will in no wise cast out" (John 6:37, KJV). We read in John 6:37 that all those whom the Father gives to the Lord Christ for salvation will come to Him. In His high-priestly prayer in chapter 17, the King James Bible reveals that the Lord Jesus Christ is specifically praying for all the believers as evidenced in the phrase in verse 11, "those whom thou has given me," which harmonizes perfectly with John 6:37 above. The modern versions remove that phrase and replace it with "name," thus taking away a great truth out of the Lord's Prayer for His people.

John 17:12

> While I was with them *in the world*, I kept them in thy name: those that thou gavest me I have kept, and none of them is lost, but the son of perdition; that the scripture might be fulfilled. (John 17:12, KJV)

"In the world" is omitted.

"She saith unto him, Yea, Lord: I believe that thou art the Christ, the Son of God, which should come into the world" (John 11:27, KJV). The Lord Jesus Christ came into the world. This was the incarnation of the Son of God. When the manuscript corrupters remove the portion "in the world," it denies the incarnation of the Lord Jesus Christ. We see in John 11:27 that the Lord Jesus Christ was to come into the world. He entered the world to die for the sins of the elect, and to deny that He came into the world, like the modern versions do in this verse, is to deny the very mission of the Lord Jesus Christ. Once again, the modern versions deny a cardinal doctrine of the Bible, the Incarnation, without which no one could be saved.

John 17:17

Sanctify them through *thy truth*: thy word is truth. (John 17:17, KJV)

First *"thy truth"* is changed to "the truth."

The word that the modern versions omit is important because it specifically names the fact that the truth that the believers will be sanctified by is God's truth. The word *thy* is genitive, which means the truth is owned by God; and also, it is a second-person singular personal pronoun, which means Jesus is specifically addressing God the Father that it will be His truth that will sanctify the believer. The modern versions use the generic *the*, which can be applied to any truth anyone wishes and does not specifically teach that the truth in view is possessed by God—another step in the direction of making the Bible a generic book by removing all specifics and making it acceptable to world religions.

John 17:20

Neither pray I for these alone, but for them also which *shall* believe on me through their word. (John 17:20, KJV)

Shall is omitted.

The word *shall* is in the future tense. Jesus widens that prayer request to go beyond the scope of the disciples. He now prays for all those who will become saved through the hearing of the word of God by all the elect down until the last day. Jesus is praying that Christians in our day will continue to sanctify themselves for the task of sending forth the Gospel. Those who become saved through our ministries will go forth with the Gospel, and others will become saved. And then they will go out and proclaim the Gospel, and this will continue in this fashion until the last day. In our day, the apostasy is definitely entrenched in Christianity, and there only seems to be a remnant of Christians sanctified unto the Great Commission who have not compromised with the world.

John 19:16

> Then delivered he him therefore unto them to be crucified. And they took Jesus, *and led him away.* (John 19:16, KJV)

"And led him away" is omitted.

Pilate handed Jesus over to the soldiers, and there was no time lapse as it looks like in the modern versions. They immediately took Him away to be crucified.

> Then delivered he him therefore unto them to be crucified. And they took Jesus, and *led him away.* (John 19:16, KJV)

> And when they had mocked him, they took off the purple from him, and put his own clothes on him, *and led him out* to crucify him. (Mark 15:20, KJV)

> And as they *led him away,* they laid hold upon one Simon, a Cyrenian, coming out of the country, and on him they laid the cross, that he might bear it after Jesus. (Luke 23:26, KJV)

John 19:38

And after this Joseph of Arimathaea, being
a disciple of Jesus, but secretly for fear of the
Jews, besought Pilate that he might take away
the body of Jesus: and Pilate gave him leave.
He came therefore, and took the body *of Jesus.*
(John 19:38, KJV)

The third use of *"of Jesus"* is omitted in this verse.

There is no legitimate reason that the third usage of "of Jesus"
should be omitted and replaced with "his." Nevertheless, they
replaced it.

John 20:29

Jesus saith unto him, *Thomas,* because thou
hast seen me, thou hast believed: blessed are
they that have not seen, and yet have believed.
(John 20:29, KJV)

Thomas is omitted.

Here is another case of a specific that was removed from the
text. Thomas had just made his declaration in the previous verse that
the Lord Jesus Christ was his Lord and God. Then Jesus addressed
Thomas specifically in response to his declaration. This is a very
important principle because we see Jesus responding to individuals on
many occasions and not groups. The apostles were gathered together
the first time when Jesus appeared, but Thomas was not among
them. It is the same principle that happened when Lazarus became
sick, and Jesus was not there to heal him. He came to Bethany after
Lazarus died for the purpose of raising him from the dead. Thomas
was absent the first time, but now he was among the disciples when
Jesus appeared to them again. He made a major declaration like Peter
did when he said that Jesus was the Christ, the Son of the living God
(Matthew 16:16).

Jesus turned to him and said, "Blessed are you, Simon Barjona." Jesus responded in kind to individuals. It is an important principle for Christians today that Jesus responds to us as redeemed individuals. He turned to Thomas and told him that because he saw, he believed. Then He went on to say that blessed are those who did not see and yet believed. Jesus was also introducing a faith principle that we believe even though we do not see.

Christians, for two thousand years, have believed, yet they have not seen. Every Christian is responded to individually and according to their needs. When the modern versions leave out *Thomas*, it is not just an incidental omission of a name, but it conveys the personal attention that Jesus gives to all His children. Once again, the King James continues to keep everything intact so the Christian's faith can be increased and not attacked.

John 21:3

> Simon Peter saith unto them, I go a fishing. They say unto him, We also go with thee. They went forth, and entered into a ship *immediately*; and that night they caught nothing. (John 21:3, KJV)

Immediately is omitted.

As soon as Peter stated that he was going fishing, others joined him, and they immediately got into the boat and fished. However, that night, they caught nothing, which set the stage for another miracle by the Lord when He told them to cast the nets on the right side of the boat. The word *immediately* is important because it shows that there was no time span between Peter's declaration and the beginning of them going fishing. It shows they were out there all night and not just a short time since they commenced fishing immediately.

John 21:25

> And there are also many other things which Jesus did, the which, if they should be written every one, I suppose that even the world itself could

not contain the books that should be written. *Amen.* (John 21:25, KJV)

Amen is omitted.

This corruption may seem very small in comparison to other verse corruptions in the modern versions. The word *amen* is a very important word, especially when the scriptures use it. It carries with it the meaning of "truly, surely, so let it be, be it firm or be established." It is important because that small word tells us that the word of God is established and firm without change. The modern versions are always changing the words and sentences because they do not believe they have a copy of the true word of God, so their modern versions are always in flux.

"LAMED. For ever, O LORD, thy word is settled in heaven" (Psalm 119:89, KJV). Psalm 119:89 speaks about the word of God being settled in heaven. The word *settled* carries with it the meaning of "established." So when the scriptures use the word *amen*, it is speaking of the established, nonchanging word of God that gives us confidence that we have the word of God that will never change. Those who believe in the modern versions are always changing their words because their Bibles are not settled, and that is why they are counterfeits and why those who use them have very weak testimonies and churches.

Acts 1:14

These all continued with one accord in prayer *and supplication*, with the women, and Mary the mother of Jesus, and with his brethren. (Acts 1:14, KJV)

"And supplication" is omitted.

The word *supplication* was omitted in the modern versions, and it means that the disciples and the others who were gathered in the upper room were not only in one accord in prayer but were making specific petitions or earnest requests within those prayers. They had just returned from the ascension of the Lord, and now was a time of waiting for the coming of the Holy Spirit. But they did not know it would be ten days, so they were specifically petitioning the Lord and no doubt concerning the coming of the Comforter.

Acts 2:1

And when the day of Pentecost was fully come, they were all with *one accord* in one place. (Acts 2:1, KJV)

"One accord" is omitted.

Here is another case of the modern translations completely giving a different meaning than the King James verse. The Greek word *homothumadon*, which is omitted in the modern versions, gives a primary meaning to this verse. It carries with it the meaning of "united in purpose or united in spirit." The fact that the apostles were gathered together does not convey their purpose for being together. They were together, but they were united in purpose and spirit. There was a unity among them. This word is used eleven times in the book of Acts. Two examples are below, which convey the meaning and importance of this word:

Then they cried out with a loud voice, and stopped their ears, and ran upon him with *one accord*. (Acts 7:57, KJV)

And the whole city was filled with confusion: and having caught Gaius and Aristarchus, men of Macedonia, Paul's companions in travel, they rushed with *one accord* into the theatre. (Acts 19:29, KJV)

In Acts 7:57 and 19:29, the words "one accord" shows the single purpose they had when they rushed upon Stephen and Paul's companions. Their single purpose was to destroy these Christians.

In Acts 2:1, the singular purpose of the Christians who gathered was in obedience to Christ's command for them to tarry in the city until they receive the promised Holy Spirit. The modern versions just say they were all together but omit the reason they were together. Once again, the King James Version gives us the truth while the modern versions omit it.

Acts 2:7

And they were *all* amazed and marvelled, saying *one to another*, Behold, are not all these which speak Galilaeans? (Acts 2:7, KJV)

"All" and *"one to another"* are omitted.

In Acts 3, as Peter and John were going to the temple, they had encountered a crippled man who sat by the gate Beautiful that was at the entrance to the temple. He sat there begging for money from those who were on their way to prayer time, which was about 3:00 p.m. Peter and John approached, and this beggar asked for alms. Peter looked at him and told him that silver and gold they did not have, but what they had, they would give him. Peter commanded the crippled man to rise and walk in the name of Jesus of Nazareth. The man literally leapt up, springing to his feet, and walked around with a spring in his step. Very soon after this happened, word had spread that a great miracle had taken place. Now all the people who attended the temple knew that it was the crippled man who was now walking because they were all familiar with him, seeing him every day.

The King James uses the words *all* and *one to another* to emphasize the fact that this word spread not only to a small portion of the attending crowd but to every single person who was there. As we would say today, the news of that healing went "viral." The modern versions remove the reality that this word spread like wildfire and that every person was speaking about it. Everyone present was discussing among themselves the reality of this notable miracle. The modern versions tend to reduce the excitement of the crowd and thus reduce the scope of the miracle. This, the King James Bible does not do!

Acts 2:23

> Him, being delivered by the determinate counsel and foreknowledge of God, ye *have taken,* and by wicked hands have crucified and slain. (Acts 2:23, KJV)

"Have taken" is omitted.

The modern versions omit a very important phrase from this verse. Before there could have been a crucifixion, there had to be an arrest. The Jews had taken Jesus and delivered Him up to Pilate to be crucified. "And straightway in the morning the chief priests held a consultation with the elders and scribes and the whole council, and bound Jesus, and carried him away, and delivered him to Pilate" (Mark 15:1, KJV). It was the consensus of all in attendance, except for Nicodemus and Joseph of Arimathaea, to deliver Jesus to Pilate for crucifixion.

The King James includes this phrase "have taken" because it is a stated part of the scriptures in all four of the Gospels. Just because this was God's plan does not remove the culpability of the hatred of the Jews toward Jesus and their desire to be rid of Him. The King James Bible does not omit this section because it is the word of God, and God is no respecter of persons, and neither should we. "Then Peter opened his mouth, and said, Of a truth I perceive that God is no respecter of persons" (Acts 10:34, KJV).

Acts 2:30

> Therefore being a prophet, and knowing that God had sworn with an oath to him, that of the fruit of his loins, *according to the flesh, he would raise up Christ to sit on his throne.* (Acts 2:30, KJV)

"According to the flesh, he would raise up Christ" is omitted.

> And when thy days be fulfilled, and thou shalt sleep with thy fathers, I will set up thy seed after thee, which shall proceed out of thy bowels, and I will establish his kingdom. He shall build an house for my name, and I will stablish the throne of his kingdom for ever. (2 Samuel 7:12–13, KJV)

> The LORD hath sworn in truth unto David; he will not turn from it; Of the fruit of thy body will I set upon thy throne. (Psalm 132:11, KJV)

By removing "according to the flesh, he would raise up Christ," the translators violate the scriptures in three ways: First, they once again remove the name of the Lord Jesus Christ; and by doing that, they remove the specific name of the one who was to fulfill the prophecy found in the above two verses. The Lord Jesus Christ is the one who fulfilled the prophecy and promise that God made to David. Secondly, they have removed another reference to the resurrection. "He would raise up Christ" seems to indicate a reference to the resurrection when the Lord Jesus Christ would rise from the dead, ascend into heaven, and then take His rightful place as the eternal King of the body of Christ, of which David was a member. Thirdly, they remove a reference to the incarnation of Christ: "according to the flesh." This verse teaches that Christ did not appear as some type of spirit but came in the flesh, according to the prophecy of many scriptures.

By removing these nine words, the modern versions have attacked and removed three cardinal doctrines of the Christian faith; and they attacked, once again, the person of the Lord Jesus Christ, who is the head of the church. Of course, the second-century Gnostics did not believe that Christ was God come in the flesh, so they removed this reference to Him. The modern translators have also followed the same line of thinking because if they disagree with the Gnostics, then they would have left the verse intact, but they didn't.

Acts 2:41

Then they that *gladly* received his word were baptized: and the same day there were added unto
them about three thousand souls. (Acts 2:41, KJV)

Gladly is omitted.

Do you remember when you were a young Christian and how you heard the message of salvation? Then do you remember how joyful you were when you were a young Christian? That was because life in Christ was new to you, and there was so much to learn and know. Life on earth now took on a perspective. As these people gathered at the temple, they were hearing the message of the true Gospel from the 120 who were gathered together, waiting for the Promise that had finally arrived. Peter had now begun to preach the true Gospel, and God had prepared the hearts of the people. On that day, three thousand were saved. The people who were gathered had known about the same old rituals of their religion, but now Peter was speaking the words of eternal life through the Lord Jesus Christ, and the people *gladly* heard him.

The word *gladly* in the Greek means "joyfully." Joy is one of the great tenets of the Christian faith. In fact, it is one of the fruits of the Holy Spirit. "But the fruit of the Spirit is love, joy, peace, long-suffering, gentleness, goodness, faith" (Galatians 5:22, KJV). When the Lord Jesus spoke to the crowds, it is written that the common people heard Him gladly. "David therefore himself calleth him Lord; and whence is he then his son? And the common people heard him gladly" (Mark 12:37, KJV). There is even joy in the presence of the angels when a person becomes saved. "Likewise, I say unto you, there is joy in the presence of the angels of God over one sinner that repenteth" (Luke 15:10, KJV). It is a shame that the modern versions omit the one word that describes the mood of the crowd who heard Peter speak and the way they received the word of God. Then again, there is no joy in the false religion of Gnosticism, which the modern versions follow.

Acts 2:47

Praising God, and having favour with all the people. And the Lord added *to the church* daily such as should be saved. (Acts 2:47, KJV)

"To the church" has been changed to "to them or being saved."

Here is an attack on the doctrine of the church in the modern versions. In the King James Bible, the word for church is *ekklesia*, which means "a called-out assembly." When God saves a person, He takes them from the uncalled assembly, which is the whole human race, and places them into the called-out assembly, which is the body of believers, and sets them apart. It goes far beyond just adding to their numbers. God takes a person from a state of spiritual death, makes them alive, and then transfers them to the church, which is the eternal body of believers. It is much more than a numbers game.

Acts 3:6

Then Peter said, Silver and gold have I none; but such as I have give I thee: In the name of Jesus Christ of Nazareth *rise up and* walk. (Acts 3:6, KJV)

"Rise up and" is omitted.

The words *rise up* in the Greek is one word, and it is in the imperative mood. This means that it is a command. Peter was commanding this man to rise and walk in the name of the Lord Jesus Christ. This means that it was not Peter's voice but the power of Christ that was giving this man the ability to walk. This man was lame from the time he was born and was carried to the gate every day. Then all of a sudden, here came Peter telling him he had no gold or silver but giving him what he had and then commenced to command him in the name of Jesus. And then the man became healed and started walking. In fact, in verse 8, it states that he leaped and went right into the temple with them. Verses 6 and 8 are a beautiful couple. Jesus healed the man's legs, and he not only stood up, but he leaped. What a beautiful picture of salvation. When Jesus saves us, we are no longer lame in our souls, but we now have such life that we leap to the glory of God.

The lame man is a picture of the unbeliever who can do nothing to save himself, and Peter is a good picture of the believer in evangelism. The majority of believers in this world do not have much gold and silver, but we give the world what we have, and that is the Gospel. Gold and silver supplies may run low or run out, but that will never happen with the true Gospel because it is always plentiful. When the modern versions remove the command to "rise up," it takes away from the momentum of the narrative because when Jesus saves us, instantly we become saved, and we get up and start walking. "How beautiful upon the mountains are the feet of him that bringeth good tidings, that publisheth peace; that bringeth good tidings of good, that publisheth salvation; that saith unto Zion, Thy God reigneth!" (Isaiah 52:7, KJV). The feet that were once lame and useless now are beautiful because they bring the true Gospel so others may get up and leap to eternal life.

Acts 3:11

> And as the *lame man which was healed* held Peter and John, all the people ran together unto them in the porch that is called Solomon's, greatly wondering. (Acts 3:11, KJV)

"Lame man which was healed" is omitted.

In these opening verses of Acts 3, Peter performed a miracle of healing on a man who was lame from birth. This man was so grateful for being healed that he was walking and leaping all around praising God that He healed him. Verse 11 in the modern versions leave out a tremendous piece of information. In the modern versions, it sounds like the man was not healed since they left out the phrase "which was healed." It sounds like the man was clinging to Peter and John to stabilize himself so he could stand. The modern versions deny a great miracle had taken place, which denies Christ the glory due Him.

This man was totally healed, and he clung to Peter and John out of joy, not out of necessity.

Acts 3:20

And he shall send Jesus Christ, *which before was preached* unto you. (Acts 3:20, KJV)

"*Which before was preached*" is changed to "appointed or prepared."

What is in view in the King James Bible is the fact that from Genesis to Malachi, the Lord Jesus Christ had been preached (word in Greek means "proclaimed") to the nation of Israel. Peter is not speaking to this crowd by the temple claiming that Christ was proclaimed to them only a short time ago, but the scarlet thread runs through the entirety of the Hebrew scriptures. This is the point that Peter is making, that Israel had 1,500 years to identify and receive their Messiah. Since they were very scripturally ignorant, they could not identify Him and therefore had rejected Him. But here Peter is telling them that they could receive Christ as personal Savior.

Jesus Christ would come to them, not in person but in the person of the indwelling Holy Spirit. While it is true that Jesus was the ordained Messiah, what is in view in this verse is the fact that He did not just show up on the scene unexpectedly. Israel had 1,500 years of warning and depending upon when the book of Job was written, maybe even longer. "For I know that my redeemer liveth, and that he shall stand at the latter day upon the earth" (Job 19:25, KJV). It is believed that Job was a contemporary with the time of Abraham. If that was the case, then Israel had a pre-Pentateuch writing that mentioned the fact that the Redeemer would live on the earth in the latter days. The modern versions omit these great truths by just pointing to the fact that Christ was the ordained Messiah, but not pointing to the fact that He was possibly prophesied for two thousand years, fifteen hundred for sure.

Acts 3:21

Whom the heaven must receive until the times of restitution of *all* things, which God hath spoken by the mouth of all his holy prophets since *the world began*. (Acts 3:21, KJV)

"All" is omitted. *"The world began"* is changed to "ancient times."

The term "ancient times" gives a very vague time frame and can be applied to any past era, but the phrase "since the world began" gives a precise time frame, teaching us that God has always had a witness in this world from the beginning of the world and not starting at some late time.

Acts 3:25

Ye are the children of the prophets, and of the covenant which God made with *our* fathers, saying unto Abraham, And in thy seed shall all the kindreds of the earth be blessed. (Acts 3:25, KJV)

Our is changed to "your."

This is another example of a subtle change from the first-person plural to the second-person plural. The way the modern versions word it, it is as if the apostles were outsiders coming to the Jews instead of them being part of the Jewish nation. If it was a case of a situation like Jonah going to Nineveh, which was a Hebrew prophet going to Assyria, then the word *your* would be appropriate since Jonah was not a citizen of their country but a visiting stranger. It is like the modern versions are making the apostles out to be from another country when they were as much a part of Israel as the ones they were preaching to.

The Apostles were definitely included in the Abrahamic covenant. "And if ye be Christ's, then are ye Abraham's seed, and heirs according to the promise" (Galatians 3:29, KJV). Peter had included himself and the other apostles as children of the Abrahamic covenant. Those who would become saved on that day were also part of the Abrahamic covenant, just as much as those who would become saved in the future until the last one is saved.

Acts 3:26

> Unto you first God, having raised up his *Son Jesus*, sent him to bless you, in turning away every one of you from his iniquities. (Acts 3:26, KJV)

"Son Jesus" is changed to "servant."

In Acts 3:26, we have a double corruption. First, the modern versions have removed the name of Jesus from the English text because the Gnostics removed from the Greek text. The New King James Version retains the name of Jesus, but it errors in the description that places it in the category of a corrupted version. Secondly, they have reduced the Lord Jesus Christ from "Son" to "servant."

> To you first, God, having raised up His *Servant* Jesus, sent Him to bless you, in turning away every one *of you* from your iniquities. (Acts 3:26, NKJV)

The word in question is the Greek word *paida*, and it is one of the Greek words that contain several meanings. The root word is actually *pais*, and it may mean "servant, child, son or daughter." This word defines human relationships and relationship to God. Nowhere in the King James Version is this word, when referencing the Lord Jesus Christ, ever translated "servant."

> When God raised up his *servant*, he sent him first to you to bless you by turning each of you from your wicked ways. (Acts 3:26, NIV)

> God raised up His Servant and sent Him first to you to bless you by turning each of you from your evil ways. (Acts 3:26, HCSB)

When we look at both the NIV and HCSB, we read the verses with the question, "Who is the servant in view?" They completely remove the name of Jesus and replace it with the term *servant*. The NKJV is identical in translation in the above verses in the NIV, NASV, NLT, ESV, ASV, HCSB, NAB, and NWT. This means that they followed the false translations and corrupted meanings. The word *paida* could have been translated as "Son" in the modern versions, but since the modern-version editors think lowly of Christ, as we have seen previously, they decided to translate the word as "servant," making Him equal to a household servant instead of exalting Him as the Son of God.

Acts 4:24

> And when they heard that, they lifted up their voice to God with one accord, and said, Lord, *thou art God*, which hast made heaven, and earth, and the sea, and all that in them is. (Acts 4:24, KJV)

"Thou art God" is omitted.

The threats and the warnings that the Christians had received did not deter them one bit nor cause any discouragement. In fact, they had gone into a time of praising God and worshipping Him. They were extolling the fact that God was the Creator of heaven and earth and had the power to direct His creation any way He saw fit, including the fact that He can heal those who are beyond help in human terms, as was the lame man who was healed. There was great harmony of mind and understanding as they praised the Lord. These words are a great testimony of the sovereignty of God and His power that can control everything that is contained in heaven, earth, and the seas. The apostles and those with them were making a confession that the Lord, "thou art God." This was a phrase used to extol God also found in the Hebrew scriptures.

David

For thou art great, and doest wondrous things: *thou art God* alone. (Psalm 86:10, KJV)

And now, LORD, *thou art God*, and hast promised this goodness unto thy servant. (1 Chronicles 17:26, KJV)

Moses

Before the mountains were brought forth, or ever thou hadst formed the earth and the world, even from everlasting to everlasting, *thou art God*. (Psalm 90:2, KJV)

Elijah

And it came to pass at the time of the offering of the evening sacrifice, that Elijah the prophet came near, and said, LORD God of Abraham, Isaac, and of Israel, let it be known this day that *thou art God* in Israel, and that I am thy servant, and that I have done all these things at thy word. (1 Kings 18:36, KJV)

So we see that the modern versions remove a great confession by children of God who acknowledge Him as the great God of the universe who had created all things. The modern versions reduce the glory of God to more of a delivery of information rather than extolling the glory of God.

Acts 5:21

And when they heard that, they entered into the temple early in the morning, and taught. But the high priest came, and they that were with him, and called the council together, and all the senate of the children of Israel, and sent to the prison to have them brought. (Acts 5:21, KJV)

"And when they heard that" omitted in the CEB, CEV, GNB, HCSB, LB, NIV, NLT.

The apostles who were in prison were responding to the command by the angel who set them free to go to the temple and preach the Gospel. When they heard the command, they responded accordingly and immediately.

Acts 5:23

Saying, The prison truly found we shut with all safety, and the keepers standing *without* before the doors: but when we had opened, we found no man within. (Acts 5:23, KJV)

Without is omitted.

The apostles were thrown into prison for preaching the Gospel. When the temple soldiers came to get them, they found the guards standing outside; but when they went in, the apostles were not there. After the angel released them, they went back to the temple to teach the people. The fact that the text states that the guards were outside the prison tells us that they were also doing a perimeter search for the prisoners when they did not find them inside the prison. From this vantage point, they would have seen the apostles escaping form the prison, but they did not. The modern versions make it sound like they just stood at the doors of the prison rather than being on the outside where they could have spotted them escaping. The King James shows a total escape by the apostles because of where the guards were stationed on the outside of the prison rather than the inside.

Acts 5:24

Now when *the high priest* and the captain of the temple and the chief priests heard these things, they doubted of them whereunto this would grow. (Acts 5:24, KJV)

"*The high priest* and" is omitted.

The high priest had been involved heavily with both the condemnation of the Lord Jesus Christ and now with the apostles. He was as guilty as the rest of the rulers in the temple. There is no reason why he should have been omitted here by the modern versions. They seem to want to hide his culpability.

Acts 5:25

Then came one and told them, *saying*, Behold, the men whom ye put in prison are standing in the temple, and teaching the people. (Acts 5:25, KJV)

Saying is omitted.

The word *saying* in the King James Bible is in the present tense active voice indicative mood. This means that the apostles were preaching actively while the man came and reported their escape from the jail. The indicative mood tells us that it was a certainty that the apostles were preaching the Gospel when they should have been in prison. They continued to preach until they were once again rearrested. *Saying* in this form means that the man was actively speaking while the apostles were continuing to preach.

Acts 5:34

Then stood there up one in the council, a Pharisee, named Gamaliel, a doctor of the law, had in reputation among all the people, and commanded to put the *apostles* forth a little space. (Acts 5:34, KJV)

Apostles changed to "men."

The King James Bible tells us that as the Sanhedrin was beginning to discuss the problem of evangelism by the apostles, that Gamaliel had ordered the apostles to be removed from the place where they were discussing the situation. The modern versions just state *men*, which could be applied to any group that was in attendance. It was the apostles who were threatening the luxurious existence of the leaders, and they were determined to end this threat. God specifically named the apostles as the object of the hatred of these leaders.

Acts 5:42

And daily in the temple, and in every house, they ceased not to teach and preach *Jesus Christ*. (Acts 5:42, KJV)

"Jesus Christ" is changed to "Jesus is" or "as the Christ."

The apostles were preaching the Lord Jesus Christ everywhere in Jerusalem, whether it was the temple or in houses of believers. Their only subject was not only that He was the promised Messiah but that salvation only comes through Jesus Christ. So they would have preached many subjects concerning Jesus.

Acts 6:3

Wherefore, brethren, look ye out among you seven men of honest report, full of the *Holy Ghost* and wisdom, whom we may appoint over this business. (Acts 6:3, KJV)

"Holy Ghost" is changed to "the Spirit."

This is an attack upon the Holy Spirit. The Gnostics did not believe that spirit could ever indwell a human body because of the filthiness of the flesh. Now, the fact that they omitted the term *holy* gives evidence of their disbelief in the Holy Spirit being the third Person of the Triune God. In Gnosticism, "Sophia" is the spirit of wisdom and is portrayed this way in the Gnostic writing called Wisdom of Solomon. This Sophia is referred to as *a* holy spirit that penetrates the all and is even referred to as the spouse of the Lord.

Wisdom of Solomon was written in Alexandria, Egypt, which was the center of Gnosticism.

Gnosticism removes the Holy Spirit of God and replaces Him with a mythical female spirit called Sophia. This is one of the reasons why these modern versions are so dangerous because they carry Gnostic teachings right into the church and the mind of the Christians. It is important that the word *holy* is left in the text because, otherwise, it endorses the Gnostic teachings of Sophia. Christians should be livid about omissions like this in the Gnostic modern versions.

Acts 6:8

> And Stephen, full of *faith* and power, did
> great wonders and miracles among the people.
> (Acts 6:8, KJV)

Faith is changed to "grace."

The change from *faith* to "grace" in the modern versions is a major blunder. All Christians are endowed with the full grace of God, but not all build their faith in God to the point that Stephen did. In fact, many Christians operate more out of fear than they do faith. A few verses back in Acts 6:5, we read that Stephen was chosen as a deacon because he was full of faith. "And the saying pleased the whole multitude: and they chose Stephen, a man full of faith and of the Holy Ghost, and Philip, and Prochorus, and Nicanor, and Timon, and Parmenas, and Nicolas a proselyte of Antioch" (Acts 6:5, KJV). Verse 8 confirms the fact that Stephen was filled with faith. "And Stephen, *full of faith* and power, did great wonders and miracles among the people" (Acts 6:8, KJV).

Stephen's faith was so strong in the Lord Jesus Christ that he defended the true Gospel and the Lord Jesus Christ to the same group of Sanhedrin that condemned Jesus. His great faith caused him to be stoned to death for the sake of the Gospel. Only one who had great faith in the Lord Jesus Christ would not cower in the face of that sentence.

Acts 6:13

And set up false witnesses, which said, This man ceaseth not to speak *blasphemous* words against this holy place, and the law. (Acts 6:13, KJV)

Blasphemous is omitted.

This is another strange omission because the word *blasphemous* is included in verse 11 in the modern versions, and yet they omit it in verse 13. It seems that the modern versions are trying to mollify the accusations brought by the false witnesses. In the King James, they stated that Stephen was speaking blasphemy against Moses and the temple. In the modern versions, they claim he "spoke against," not specifying what was spoken. Blasphemy is a specific charge while "speaking against" is a nebulous charge that can even be something positive.

However, in this case, the charges were trumped up that Stephen was a blasphemer, and blasphemy would be a capital offense, especially if someone was preaching truth about a false system, which Stephen was definitely doing in chapter 7. So there was no reason to omit the false accusations that the false witnesses brought concerning Stephen. It is just another effort by the modern versions to protect those guilty ones who persecute Christians.

Acts 7:30

And when forty years were expired, there appeared to him in the wilderness of mount Sina an angel *of the Lord* in a flame of fire in a bush. (Acts 7:30, KJV)

"Of the Lord" is omitted.

And mount Sinai was altogether on a smoke, because the LORD descended upon it in fire: and the smoke thereof ascended as the smoke of a furnace, and the whole mount quaked greatly. And

> when the voice of the trumpet sounded long, and waxed louder and louder, Moses spake, and God answered him by a voice. And the LORD came down upon mount Sinai, on the top of the mount: and the LORD called Moses up to the top of the mount; and Moses went up. And the LORD said unto Moses, Go down, charge the people, lest they break through unto the LORD to gaze, and many of them perish. (Exodus 19:18–21, KJV)

Acts 7:30 is taken out of the narrative from Exodus 19:18–21. In Exodus 19:18–21, we read that it was God Himself who came to Moses on Mount. Sinai. The term "Angel of the Lord" is used as a synonym for God Himself. As we see in the narrative from Judges 13 where the parents of Samson were visited by an "Angel of the Lord." When we read further into the scriptures, we read in Judges 13:22 that Manoah thought he and his wife would die because they saw God.

> And the angel of the LORD said unto Manoah, Though thou detain me, I will not eat of thy bread: and if thou wilt offer a burnt offering, thou must offer it unto the LORD. For Manoah knew not that he was an angel of the LORD. (Judges 13:16, KJV)

> And Manoah said unto his wife, We shall surely die, because we have seen God. (Judges 13:22, KJV)

Manoah and his wife surely would not have been fearful of losing their lives if they just saw an angel. The King James Bible keeps the phrase "of the Lord" intact in Acts 7:30 because it is speaking of God Himself visiting Moses on Sinai. The modern versions omit "of the Lord," thus reducing God to a mere created angel. The hard thing to understand is that the proponents of the modern versions claim that no doctrines are affected. Here, we see plainly in Acts 7:30 in the modern versions that God is reduced to a created angel. If that is not a doctrine affected by the modern versions, then I don't know what is! God is the Creator of the angels and can never be identified as an angel without the qualifier "of the Lord" attached, so we know who we are specifically speaking of. Once again, the King James Bible shows it is a God-glorifying Bible as it gives God his rightful place as sovereign of the universe while the modern versions reduce Him to an angel.

Acts 7:37

> This is that Moses, which said unto the children of Israel, A prophet shall the Lord your God raise up unto you of your brethren, like unto me; *him shall ye hear.* (Acts 7:37, KJV)

"Him shall ye hear" is omitted.

> The LORD thy God will raise up unto thee a Prophet from the midst of thee, of thy brethren, like unto me; unto him ye shall hearken. (Deuteronomy 18:15, KJV)

> I will raise them up a Prophet from among their brethren, like unto thee, and will put my words in his mouth; and he shall speak unto them all that I shall command him. (Deuteronomy 18:18, KJV)

Acts 7:37 is a quote from Deuteronomy 18:15–18. This, of course, is a prophecy of the Lord Jesus Christ who would appear on the scene about 1,440 years later. It is the Lord Jesus Christ whom we are to listen to.

> While he yet spake, behold, a bright cloud overshadowed them: and behold a voice out of the cloud, which said, This is my beloved Son, in whom I am well pleased; hear ye him. (Matthew 17:5, KJV)

Here, we read a quote from God the Father at the mount of transfiguration that the disciples are to be quiet and listen to the Lord Jesus Christ. We also read this same principle in Hebrews 1:1–2:

> God, who at sundry times and in divers man-
> ners spake in time past unto the fathers by the
> prophets, Hath in these last days spoken unto
> us by his Son, whom he hath appointed heir of
> all things, by whom also he made the worlds.
> (Hebrews 1:1–2, KJV)

God speaks to us through His Son and no longer through any prophets since the word of God is now completed. So when the Gnostics removed "him shall ye hear" from Acts 7:37, they removed a major prophecy; plus, they removed the specific implication of whom Moses was speaking of. By removing that section of scripture, anybody can now step into those shoes and claim to be a prophet or the prophet as so many cult leaders have done already.

This portion of scripture is also very important because Moses is literally relinquishing his authority by stating that they are going to hear that other prophet. This is because grace came through the Lord Jesus Christ, and the law came through Moses. Those who become saved will have fulfilled, through the Lord Jesus Christ, all the demands of God's righteous law, meaning that the law of Moses no longer has any judicial effect upon them. In other words, the law no longer can exact any penalty from a true believer. Those who still listen to Moses are under the condemnation of death because they are still under the law. "For the law was given by Moses, but grace and truth came by Jesus Christ" (John 1:17, KJV).

Acts 8:18

> And when Simon saw that through laying on of
> the apostles' hands the *Holy* Ghost was given, he
> offered them money. (Acts 8:18, KJV)

Holy is omitted.

Here, Simon thought that he would be able to purchase the Holy Spirit with money, not realizing that the Holy Spirit is given to the true believer, and He is not purchased with money. Peter gave him a severe rebuke that his money should perish with him. Isn't it interesting that Peter rebuked Simon, who tried to buy salvation for money? The Roman Catholic institution sees Peter as the first pope, and instead of following Peter's example, they sold indulgences to get people out of purgatory and into heaven. So if he was their first pope, then why did they disobey him and try to sell salvation? I threw that in for nothing.

The modern versions omit the fact that the Holy Spirit is in view, and the lesson is that God cannot be bought with money or anything man has. To omit *holy* is to attack the doctrine of the Holy Spirit. We live in a day when there are many spirits. Everyone you speak to is spiritual such as New Agers or occultic or whatever. It is important that the word *holy* be included when speaking of the Holy Spirit so an instant distinction can be made about whom is in focus.

I think it is also interesting that the manuscript evidence favors including *hagios* at ten in favor and two against. So they go with the two most corrupt manuscripts that omit it instead of including it because of overwhelming evidence. I have been studying this issue since 1986, and I still marvel at the way the theologians trash the real Bible in favor of their counterfeits. The scary thing is that these same "experts" are the ones who teach the next generation of preachers and missionaries.

Acts 8:37

And Philip said, If thou believest with all thine heart, thou mayest. And he answered and said, I believe that Jesus Christ is the Son of God. (Acts 8:37, KJV)

The entire verse is omitted or placed in brackets.

Acts 8:37 is another verse that met its doom in the second century. It is omitted in the Vaticanus and Sinaiticus. It is also omitted in the NIV, ESV, RSV, NWT, and NAB. The NASB and the NKJV are subtler in the way they attack this verse. The NASB places brackets around the verse and then states without any qualifying evidence that "early manuscripts do not contain this verse." This statement is very vague and really means nothing since all manuscripts are early. What is the definition of early? First century, second century, fifth century?

The NKJV (New King James Version) is also very subtle in its attack. The center column of the NKJV is Satan's playground, and on this verse it states, "NU-Text and M-Text omit this verse. It is found in Western texts, including the Latin tradition." The NU Text they are referring to is the Nestle-Aland Text (N) and the United Bible Societies Text (U), both of which are heavily based on the Vaticanus and Sinaiticus. So the NKJV claiming to be a revision of the King James is another false version that, according to Dr. D. A. Waite in his research (which I have in my possession), departs from the Textus Receptus in two thousand plus places.

Now, the second half of their claim. What Western texts? What is the Latin tradition? Is it referring to Jerome's corrupt Latin Vulgate of the fourth century? Is it the Old Latin Vulgate (c. AD 90–150)? Or is it Roman Catholic tradition?

There are 5,255 extant manuscripts, and unless one studies the manuscript issue, they will never know that statements such as "oldest and best" or "early manuscripts" refer to the two corrupted manuscripts, Sinaiticus and Vaticanus. In fact, the modern translations are based on only forty-five manuscripts, which are less than 1 percent of all manuscripts. This means that the modern versions have completely and intentionally disregarded over 99 percent of the manuscripts. Christians must begin to question these things; it is necessary that they do.

Acts 8:37 is another testimony that Jesus is the Son of God. By the Ethiopian eunuch using the word *is* (present tense in Greek) instead of *was*, he was stating a fact that Jesus is alive. His resurrection was doubted by many, but here the scripture is stating that He is alive; plus, it is another scriptural testimony of Jesus being the Son of

God, a title of divinity. This is why the Gnostics would have ripped it out of the text, simply because they did not believe that God, being good, could dwell in a sinful, corrupted human body. They did not believe that Jesus was the Son of God, only a good human being; plus, that He only became Christ at His birth without preexistence. This verse is in the Old Latin Vulgate of AD 90–150, which was a direct copy from the original autographs.

Acts 9:5–6

And he said, Who art thou, Lord? And the Lord said, I am Jesus whom thou persecutest: *it is hard for thee to kick against the pricks. {6} And he trembling and astonished said, Lord, what wilt thou have me to do? And the Lord said unto him*, Arise, and go into the city, and it shall be told thee what thou must do. (Acts 9:5–6, KJV)

"It is hard for thee to kick against the pricks" is omitted in verse 5. *"And he trembling and astonished said, Lord, what wilt thou have me to do? And the Lord said unto him"* is omitted in verse 6.

Here, we have one of the accounts of the conversion of the apostle Paul. In verse 5, the Lord Jesus is telling Paul that it is hard for thee to kick against the pricks. In other words, the Lord Jesus was telling Paul that to fight the Gospel is like continually kicking a cactus with large thorns. All that will happen is that your foot will become bloody, and you will never win over the cactus. Those who fight against the Gospel are in the same boat since they might win a skirmish, but they will never win the war because the Lord had stated that the Gospel will be preached to the ends of the earth, and then He will return.

Then in verse 6, the apostle Paul was trembling before the Lord and asked Him what he should do, and the Lord gave him instruction what to do. Paul was very arrogant, thinking that by putting Christians to death, he would be able to stem the tide of Christianity;

but when he came face-to-face with the Lord, that arrogance and pride turned to fear, which manifested itself in tremors and astonishment.

The modern versions leave out these vital parts of the verses, which shows the deity of the Lord Jesus Christ and how people tremble in His holy presence. Since the Gnostics did not believe that Jesus was deity, they apparently thought that it was unnecessary to include the parts about the Lord Jesus being deity and causing a mere human to tremble in His presence. This account of Paul's conversion shows him having direct dialogue with the Lord Jesus from heaven. The modern versions make it sound like a casual conversation, as if Paul was just stopping to ask for directions. The King James Bible retains the awesome nature of the encounter between Jesus and Paul, but the modern versions make it sound like a street-corner conversation with nothing special about it. In these two verses alone, thirty words have been removed.

Acts 9:29

And he *spake boldly in the name of the Lord Jesus,*
and disputed against the Grecians: but they went
about to slay him. (Acts 9:29, KJV)

"Spake boldly in the name of the Lord Jesus, and" is omitted.

Here is the beginning testimony of the apostle Paul after he was first given the introduction to the apostles by Barnabas. The apostle Paul was speaking boldly in the name of the Lord Jesus. The word behind "spake boldly" in the Greek carries with it the meaning "to speak fearlessly and openly." Paul's fearlessness did not come from himself but came because of the authority the believer has in Christ and the commission to send forth the true Gospel without fear into the whole world. There is a great spiritual principle in this verse, and that is that the believer's fearlessness to proclaim the Gospel comes from our relationship with the Lord Jesus Christ, who placed the Holy Spirit in us to complete the task of world evangelization.

It is the Lord who gave the spirit of fearlessness to the early martyrs and then those who were murdered in the Inquisition in the Middle Ages by the Roman Catholic institution. It is this spirit of fearlessness that catapulted the great missionary movement of the nineteenth century, which is still going on today. The boldness of the believer, even today, comes from the fact that we speak in the name of the Lord because we have been given that right and authority. "For he taught them as one having authority, and not as the scribes" (Matthew 7:29, KJV). Jesus taught as one having authority, and since we have the word of God today in the King James Bible, we are also able to teach as one having authority, and this is what the modern versions do away with. But they have to because there is no authority in those counterfeits.

Acts 9:31

> Then had the *churches* rest throughout all Judaea and Galilee and Samaria, and were edified; and walking in the fear of the Lord, and in the comfort of the Holy Ghost, were multiplied.

"*The churches*" is changed to "the church."

The Roman Catholic institution refers to itself as "the church," believing that they are the one and only true church. In this verse, we see that the word in the Greek text was changed from plural to singular. The word is properly written *ekklesiai*, which denotes plurality of churches or assemblies. The word has been replaced in the critical Greek text with *ekklesia*, which shows a single church. The idea of a single church plays right into Roman Catholic teaching. However, the text of verse 31 records three separate sections in Israel denoting plurality because there were multiple churches in those areas, so the singular would not fit the context. It is important to look at the small changes because they too affect the meaning of passages.

Acts 10:6

> He lodgeth with one Simon a tanner, whose house is by the sea side: *he shall tell thee what thou oughtest to do.* (Acts 10:6, KJV)

"He shall tell thee what thou oughtest to do" is omitted.

Cornelius the centurion saw a vision sent from God, but he did not understand the vision. So an angel of the Lord came to him and instructed him to go and see Peter, and Peter would give him certain instructions. However, this scenario became a test for Peter also. He had considered Cornelius an unclean Gentile and would have no dealings with him. Then God allowed Peter to see a vision that contained unclean animals, which Peter claimed he had never eaten in obedience to the law. However, God had told Peter that these animals were now clean; and Cornelius, being a true believer, was also cleaned by the same blood of Christ that cleansed him. It is a lesson for us also that if there is a brother or sister we do not like, we must realize that they are cleansed by the same blood of Christ as we are, and we must never look down on them.

Cornelius was specifically told to see Peter and that Peter would explain to him what he must do. Here we have a case of a person being given a specific divine order, yet the modern versions omit it. Cornelius was not to visit Peter for a social visit but was to visit him for a specific reason. The modern versions leave out the reason for the visit of Peter by Cornelius. Once again, the King James Bible supplies the entire text and does not leave us wondering why Peter was sent for.

Acts 10:21

> Then Peter went down to the men *which were sent unto him from Cornelius*; and said, Behold, I am he whom ye seek: what is the cause wherefore ye are come? (Acts 10:21, KJV)

"Which were sent unto him from Cornelius" is omitted.

Cornelius was a godly man, and he had a vision. He was also commanded to send for Peter so he may receive understanding of the vision. Cornelius, being a centurion, would have charge of one hundred soldiers. So in response to the command to send for Peter, he dispatched some men to Joppa to bring Peter to him. The King

James Bible specifically states that the men Peter had come to see were dispatched by Cornelius while the modern versions omit that part. God wrote His word with specifics, not in nebulous terms that invite multiple and spurious interpretations.

Acts 10:30

> And Cornelius said, Four days ago I was *fasting* until this hour; and at the ninth hour I prayed in my house, and, behold, a man stood before me in bright clothing. (Acts 10:30, KJV)

Fasting is omitted.

In this verse, we read that Cornelius finally had met Peter, and he told him that he was fasting and praying concerning the vision that he saw. All the modern versions leave out the part where Cornelius was fasting. There is no reason given as to why the part about fasting was omitted; nevertheless, the modern-version editors and the manuscript defilers did not feel they needed a reason to omit this. The method of the modern-version editors is to chip away at the text of the scriptures, in some cases large chunks and in some cases very small pieces. No matter, large or small, it still constitutes an attack upon the scriptures. Let us never be fooled. If God places in the Bible even something so small, He has placed it there for a reason, and we must never think that anything written in scripture can be deleted without consequence. It is no doubt that fasting was repugnant to the intellectuals since they have omitted Matthew 17:21 in the modern versions.

> Howbeit this kind goeth not out but by prayer and fasting. (Matthew 17:21, KJV)

Acts 10:32

> Send therefore to Joppa, and call hither Simon, whose surname is Peter; he is lodged in the house

> of one Simon a tanner by the sea side: *who, when he cometh, shall speak unto thee.* (Acts 10:32, KJV)

"Who, when he cometh, shall speak unto thee" is omitted.

An angel had appeared to Cornelius and told him that his alms and his prayers came into remembrance in the sight of God. He was to send for Peter, and it was Peter himself who was going to come unto Cornelius and speak to him. Peter was not going to dispatch another to do it because God had specifically told Peter that what He named as clean must never be considered common or profane in preparation for his meeting with Cornelius. The modern versions omit the fact that it was Peter who was going to be the one who was to speak to Cornelius and not another. God was dealing with Peter on the subject of all in Christ being equal and clean before Him. There was no unclean Christians as God had cleansed them all, and Peter needed to realize that there were no second-class Christians at the cross.

Acts 12:4

> And when he had apprehended him, he put him in prison, and delivered him to four quaternions of soldiers to keep him; intending after *Easter* to bring him forth to the people. (Acts 12:4, KJV)

Easter is replaced by "Passover."

One of the accusations that is leveled at the King James Bible is the translation of the word *pascha* as "Easter." The word *pascha* is not a Greek word but is from the Aramaic *pascha*. The Herod in view here was Herod Agrippa, who was a grandson of Herod the Great and who was nephew to Herod Antipas, who beheaded John the Baptist. They were Idumaean, which was Edomite. This means that Herod Agrippa was not a Jew but an Edomite. The Edomites were descendants of Esau.

And Esau said to Jacob, Feed me, I pray thee, with that same red pottage; for I am faint: therefore was his name called Edom. (Genesis 25:30, KJV)

Now these are the generations of Esau, who is Edom. (Genesis 36:1, KJV)

Therefore, the Herod dynasty was not in the line of Jacob. It was the king of Edom, who did not allow Israel to pass through their land when they came out of the land of Egypt. "Thus Edom refused to give Israel passage through his border: wherefore Israel turned away from him" (Numbers 20:21, KJV).

Archaeology has dug up many clay figures in the area known as Edom. The main gods of the Edomites were the fertility gods of the region. According to Assyrian secular records, it is known that Edom had one national god named *Qos*; however, they were hardly monotheistic in that they had other gods. "Now it came to pass, after that Amaziah was come from the slaughter of the Edomites, that he brought the gods of the children of Seir, and set them up to be his gods, and bowed down himself before them, and burned incense unto them" (2 Chronicles 25:14, KJV).

If you notice, this verse speaks about gods in the plural. There was also evidence of Baal worship. The Bible does not mention any specific gods that the Edomites worshipped. In fact, in the early years, they had worshipped Jehovah; but after they refused passage to Israel, they started to descend into idolatry. Since they had taken up the local gods of the area, Astarte would have been one of the gods of the area. Normally, wherever Baal was, Astarte was also found. Astarte was a female deity of fertility. Astarte was known as Aphrodite to the Greeks. Astarte was also known as *Ishtar*, which was the goddess of fertility.

These false gods can be found in basically all these ancient pagan civilizations, so the region of Edom, which was south of Israel, would not have been a stranger to them. These false gods even crept into both Israel and Judah. "The children gather wood, and the fathers kindle the fire, and the women knead their dough, to make cakes to the queen of heaven, and to pour out drink offerings unto other gods, that they may provoke me to anger" (Jeremiah 7:18, KJV). The queen of heaven was also known as Ishtar, the fertility goddess. In our day, we are seeing a resurgence of goddess worship.

Now, back to Herod's declaration about Peter. Herod was going to wait until after Easter to bring Peter out to the people, and no doubt they would have pronounced the same sentence as the Lord Jesus Christ received. Now, there seems to be a difficulty because the word *pascha* should be translated "Passover," correct? Absolutely not. We owe a great debt to William Tyndale, who translated this verse correctly.

> And when he had caught him he put him in preson and delyvered him to .iiii. quaternios of soudiers to be kepte entendynge after ester to brynge him forth to the people. (Tyndale 1526)

The reason that Tyndale translated *pascha* as "Easter" in this verse was a question of timing.

> And in the fourteenth day of the first month is the passover of the LORD. And in the fifteenth day of this month is the feast: seven days shall unleavened bread be eaten. (Numbers 28:16–17, KJV)

> And the first day of unleavened bread, when they killed the passover, his disciples said unto him, Where wilt thou that we go and prepare that thou mayest eat the passover? (Mark 14:12, KJV)

As we can see, the Passover came first and was followed by the Feast of Unleavened Bread. So if we look at Acts 12:3, we see a very important phrase.

> And because he saw it pleased the Jews, he proceeded further to take Peter also. (Then were the days of unleavened bread.) (Acts 12:3, KJV)

Notice very carefully what it says in the last phrase. It states that these were the days of Unleavened Bread. The Passover was already complete. So therefore, in verse 4, it would not make sense if Herod was going to bring Peter out after Passover when Passover was already over, but Peter was still in prison. Since the days of Unleavened Bread was a feast lasting seven days, we are not told what day this was. It could have been day 6, when Peter was still in prison.

Now, enter the word *Easter*. Immediately, Christians think of the day the Lord Jesus Christ rose from the dead. However, the word *Easter* is a very pagan name. It is derived from *Eostra*, which is a pagan festival of spring. The Bible nowhere commands Christians to celebrate the resurrection or birth of Christ, so when Christianity was turned into a religion by the third century, these pagan holidays were incorporated in the church calendar year, but with Christian meanings. For example, Christmas was really the feast of Saturnalia, but the church wanted to cover this pagan festival and therefore instituted Christmas as Christ's birth being on December 25.

Herod, being an Edomite and a pagan, would not care the least about what festival was taking place. After all, they crucified the Lord Jesus Christ on the preparation day for the High Sabbath and Passover. Why would a pagan king concern himself with the holidays of the Jews? He could have had Peter executed any time he wanted to and during any holiday in the Jewish calendar.

Since Herod was a pagan, he would have been celebrating a feast of Ishtar, the fertility god. This was his "Easter" as he would have been too busy celebrating Ishtar under the name *Easter* that he would wait until after his pagan festival was over, and then he would get back to his duties and have Peter executed. Easter was a pagan spring festival that occurred simultaneously with Passover, and therefore *Easter* is the proper word for Acts 12:4 and not *Passover*. So the *Easter* in Acts 12:4 is not the Christian Easter but it is the pagan Easter.

Acts 13:33

God hath fulfilled the same unto us their children,
in that he hath raised up Jesus again; as it is also

written in the second psalm, Thou art my Son,
this day have I begotten thee. (Acts 13:33, KJV)

"this day have I begotten thee" is changed to "today I have become your father" in the CEB, CEV, GNB, HCSB, NCV, NET, NIRV, NIV, NLV, NLT, VOICE.

One of the main arguments from those who favor the modern versions is that no doctrines are affected. Well, they have not looked at Acts 13:33. Since when did Jesus only become the Son of God at His resurrection? "But when the fulness of the time was come, God sent forth his Son, made of a woman, made under the law" (Galatians 4:4, KJV). Notice that Galatians 4:4 states that God "sent forth His Son," which means Jesus was already the Son of God. God had fulfilled the promise to their present generation because they were the ones who lived to see the seed of Abraham and the fulfillment of the promise physically walk on earth. It was their generation that saw Jesus die and be raised from the dead.

Paul then reaches into Psalm 2 and brings up the following verse: "I will declare the decree: the LORD hath said unto me, Thou art my Son; this day have I begotten thee" (Psalm 2:7, KJV). This does not mean that Christ became the Son of God upon the resurrection because He is the eternal Son of God, but it carries with it the meaning that because He conquered death, it confirmed His deity and who He stated that He was. God is giving testimony that Jesus is exactly who He stated He was, even though the world hated and rejected Him. His true testimony came from the Father. "And declared to be the Son of God with power, according to the spirit of holiness, by the resurrection from the dead" (Romans 1:4, KJV). If Jesus would have remained dead, then His testimony would have been proven false and the Pharisees correct, but we all know that is not what happened.

Acts 13:42

And when *the Jews* were gone out of the synagogue, *the Gentiles* besought that these words

might be preached to them the next sabbath.
(Acts 13:42, KJV)

"The Jews" replaced by *"Paul and Barnabas."* *"The Gentiles"* is omitted.

No doubt these were Gentiles who were proselytes (v. 43) who heard the words of Paul and desired that they would bring this message again the following Sabbath. "Now when the congregation was broken up, many of the Jews and religious proselytes followed Paul and Barnabas: who, speaking to them, persuaded them to continue in the grace of God" (Acts 13:43, KJV). In verse 43, we are informed that many of the Jews and the Gentiles had followed Paul and Barnabas, so the conversation could be continued as we read that the subject must have been the grace of God. There is no reason that the words *Jews* and *Gentiles* should be omitted in verse 42 since salvation was being accomplished among both the Jews and Gentiles. Paul was the apostle to the Gentiles, and it seemed that here he was fulfilling that ministry by preaching the grace of God, and the Gentiles were responding to that message.

Acts 15:11

But we believe that through the grace of the Lord Jesus *Christ* we shall be saved, even as they. (Acts 15:11, KJV)

Christ is omitted.

Once again, one of the names of the Lord Jesus Christ has met the scissors of the Gnostics. *Christ* is His title of deity, which is omitted in the modern versions.

Acts 15:18

Known *unto God are all his works* from the beginning of the world.

"Unto God are all his works" is omitted.

This verse has been corrupted in two ways in the modern versions as we have seen. In some versions, it states that God has made known all His works; and in others, it just states the works were known from old. When we read the verse in the King James Version, we read the correct rendering where the verse states that all the works of the Lord are known unto Him. This does not mean that He has revealed all His works to us.

> The secret things belong unto the LORD our God: but those things which are revealed belong unto us and to our children for ever, that we may do all the words of this law. (Deuteronomy 29:29, KJV)

The verse gives us an assurance that even though we do not know the reason for things that are happening in our lives or in the world, it does not mean that events are not under God's control. God is under no obligation to reveal to us everything that He does. Since God's ways are not our ways and His thoughts are not our thoughts, we would be hard-pressed to understand what God is doing. God does choose to reveal some of His works to us but not all, for we would be unable to fathom the depths of His wisdom. Once again, we see the modern versions giving confusion rather than a proper interpretation.

> Here is this verse in the Holman Christian Standard Bible: "known from long ago" (Acts 15:18, HCSB).

Compare that to the King James verse above and tell me which one makes sense.

Acts 15:23

> And they wrote letters by them *after this manner;* The apostles and elders and brethren send greeting unto the brethren which are of the Gentiles in Antioch and Syria and Cilicia. (Acts 15:23, KJV)

"After this manner" is omitted.

When the letters were written, they were written "after this manner" with the apostles and elders. It meant that these letters were authoritative, and that is why the letters were sent in the manner of an official capacity. They probably used Silas and Judas Barsabas to pen the letters, both being scribes and well educated. The modern versions make it sound like a casual correspondence.

Acts 15:24

Forasmuch as we have heard, that certain *which went out* from us have troubled you with words, subverting your souls, *saying, Ye must be circumcised, and keep the law*: to whom we gave no such commandment. (Acts 15:24, KJV)

"Which went out" and *"saying ye must be circumcised, and keep the law"* are omitted.

Here is another verse that has been mutilated going from the specific to the nebulous. Paul was a staunch fighter against those who believed that you must keep the law and be circumcised to be saved. Paul knew that these false teachers were spiritually seducing the people by claiming that they came from the apostle Paul and his entourage. Paul always believed that a person was saved by grace alone without keeping the law. The false teachers in the Jerusalem church had attempted to bring their hearers back under the law by convincing them they needed to be circumcised and to keep the tenets of the law. There is no reason that these specific warnings should be omitted unless those unbelievers in the early church who butchered the manuscripts wanted to avoid the teachings of grace alone and amalgamate the keeping of the law with grace for salvation so they would be able to keep their hearers in bondage. Paul faced the false teachers and their works gospel until he was taken home. It seems like we are going to face the same situation, confronting the false teachers and their counterfeit versions until we go home.

Acts 15:34

Notwithstanding it pleased Silas to abide there still. (Acts 15:34, KJV)

The entire verse omitted or placed in brackets

There is no reason as to why this verse was omitted. Hort and Westcott had omitted it from their version, but they retained the verse in the margin, which is the same as a total omission. Theoretically, the omission is dated back to the fourth century. Silas chose to stay in Antioch, and he became a companion with Paul as they had ventured into Philippi. When the narrative progresses into chapter 16, we find that it was Paul and Silas who were the two principal prisoners in the Philippian jail when the earthquake happened at midnight while they sang songs of praise. This led to the conversion of the Philippian jailer. Obviously, this was a divine appointment for Silas to stay behind in Antioch so he could become Paul's partner in ministry as they went to Philippi. It is still a mystery as to why this verse was omitted in the corrupt manuscripts, but then again, that is why they are called corrupt manuscripts. Once again, the King James Bible gives us an ongoing flow of a very important event.

Acts 16:31

And they said, Believe on the Lord Jesus *Christ*, and thou shalt be saved, and thy house. (Acts 16:31, KJV)

Christ is omitted.

If there was one thing the Gnostics hated, it was the idea that salvation only came by the Lord Jesus Christ, so they did what they could to neutralize or lower the true testimony of the Lord Jesus Christ. One way was to break up His three-word name. In this verse, the modern versions removed *Christ*. The name *Christ* appears 555 times in the New Testament in 522 verses. There are 7,959 verses in the New Testament, which means the name appears about every 15 verses. This means that it is a very important title if God chose to include it 555 times. The name *Christ* means "Anointed One" or "Messiah." It specifically points to Jesus as the Savior and the promised Messiah so there is no mistaking who Jesus is.

Acts 17:5

> But the Jews *which believed not*, moved with envy, took unto them certain lewd fellows of the baser sort, and gathered a company, and set all the city on an uproar, and assaulted the house of Jason, and sought to bring them out to the people. (Acts 17:5, KJV)

"*Which believed not*" is omitted.

When Paul came to Thessalonica, he had gone to the local synagogue, and he preached and reasoned with the Jews for three weeks. Some of the Jews believed, and also many Greeks had believed. Then if you notice in verse 5, it was those Jews who did not believe that caused the great uproar. The modern versions leave this portion out and make it sound like all the Jews had attacked Paul and the house of Jason, but it was only those who were still unbelievers. This is important to know because the modern versions indict all the Jews in attendance, and the ones who gave Paul the biggest problem were those who remained in unbelief. The King James Bible does not indict the believing Jews with the unbelieving Jews but rightly makes a clear distinction that it was those in unbelief who descended upon Paul and the house of Jason. Once again, the modern versions inject confusion into a passage where there is none to begin with.

Acts 17:18

> Then certain philosophers of the Epicureans, and of the Stoicks, encountered him. And some said, What will this babbler say? other some, He seemeth to be a setter forth of strange gods: because he preached *unto them* Jesus, and the resurrection. (Acts 17:18, KJV)

"Unto them" is omitted.

Here is an omission that concerns itself about a direct witness to the philosophers. The Gnostics would definitely want this out because it speaks of Paul directly witnessing to them about the Lord Jesus Christ and the resurrection. The Gnostics did not believe that Jesus was divine and that He only was raised in spirit and not in body. This belief is present today with the Jehovah's Witnesses and New Age beliefs where they equate Jesus with other teachers like Buddha or Confucius. They see Him as an ascended master. Paul was directly challenging the philosophy of the Epicureans and stoics. The Epicureans followed Epicurus (342–270 BC) who taught that nature is the supreme teacher by supplying feelings, sensations, and anticipations for the testing of truth. Later, his followers saw sensual pleasures as the goal of life. Stoics followed Zeno of Citium (335–263 BC), and he believed in a creative power and saw duty, reason, and self-sufficiency as goals of life. He also encouraged his followers to follow the laws of nature. We can see why they would have called Paul a babbler concerning the resurrection because their philosophy was totally tied to this earth.

The modern versions make it sound like Paul was having an evangelism crusade, but he was directly challenging the beliefs of these two philosophical systems that teach us that the Gospel can go up against any form of philosophy. We need not shrink back simply because these philosophical systems seem to be so intense; instead, we hit them head-on and let the Holy Spirit do the convicting. These systems seem to bring much wisdom, but in reality, they are Satanism couched in big words and fantasies.

Acts 17:26

And hath made of one *blood* all nations of men for to dwell on all the face of the earth, and hath determined the times before appointed, and the bounds of their habitation. (Acts 17:26, KJV)

Blood is omitted.

In this verse, we are taught that it was of one blood that God created all the people of the world. There is a deeper reason why God uses this term *blood* instead of just using the term "from one man," and that is because *blood* has a much deeper meaning. "For the life of the flesh is in the blood: and I have given it to you upon the altar to make an atonement for your souls: for it is the blood that maketh an atonement for the soul" (Leviticus 17:11, KJV). Just as the blood holds the life of the flesh and makes atonement for the soul, as it states in Leviticus 17:11, it is the blood of Christ that gives eternal life for all the believers.

"Much more then, being now justified by his blood, we shall be saved from wrath through him. For if, when we were enemies, we were reconciled to God by the death of his Son, much more, being reconciled, we shall be saved by his life" (Romans 5:9–10, KJV). Just as the blood of man makes up all the nations of the world, the blood of Christ makes up the one eternal nation that reaches throughout the entire world. "Therefore say I unto you, The kingdom of God shall be taken from you, and given to a nation bringing forth the fruits thereof" (Matthew 21:43, KJV).

This eternal nation or kingdom was prophesied by Daniel the prophet. "And there was given him dominion, and glory, and a kingdom, that all people, nations, and languages, should serve him: his dominion is an everlasting dominion, which shall not pass away, and his kingdom that which shall not be destroyed" (Daniel 7:14, KJV). The modern versions completely miss the importance of the word *blood* in the text.

Acts 17:30

And the times of this ignorance God winked at; but now *commandeth* all men every where to repent. (Acts 17:30, KJV)

Commandeth is omitted in some versions.

God is commanding repentance and not making it a declaration or a suggestion. There is a big difference between a declaration and a command. A declaration is something that dispenses information to people, but a command is required obedience to what is declared. Repentance is not an option but a command.

Acts 18:7

> And he departed thence, and entered into a certain man's house, named *Justus*, one that worshipped God, whose house joined hard to the synagogue. (Acts 18:7, KJV)

Justus is replaced with "Titius Justus."

This verse has been corrupted with someone's imagination. In Acts 18:7, you will see that the modern versions all use the name *Titius* or *Titus Justus*. The problem is that this man does not exist. Justus exists, but not Titius Justus. In the Textus Receptus, Luke wrote only one name, and that was *Justus*. This is why these modern versions are dangerous because it seems that not one of the modern translators will ever check anything out.

Acts 18:21

> But bade them farewell, saying, *I must by all means keep this feast that cometh in Jerusalem*. but I will return again unto you, if God will. And he sailed from Ephesus. (Acts 18:21, KJV)

"*I must by all means keep this feast that cometh in Jerusalem*" is omitted.

This verse shows the missionary heart of Paul. He was not required to keep the feast, which would have been the Passover, because he was under grace. He wanted to keep the feast because he knew there would be a vast number of people in attendance, which would constitute a great opportunity for evangelizing with the true Gospel. The modern versions leave out this part, which is the reason the Apostle Paul left Ephesus and stated he would be back if God willed. The modern versions just have him leaving for no reason. The

King James teaches us that Paul left for the purpose of taking advantage of a great opportunity to bring the true Gospel to those Jews who were still in bondage under the law. Once again, the modern versions truncate the heart of a verse and leave the readers wondering, if they wonder at all, why Paul left. This verse is a great example for the believer that we are to take advantage of as many opportunities as we can to bring the true Gospel.

Acts 19:4

> Then said Paul, John verily baptized with the baptism of repentance, saying unto the people, that they should believe on him which should come after him, that is, on *Christ* Jesus. (Acts 19:4, KJV)

Christ is omitted.

Here is another attack upon the deity of the Lord Jesus Christ by omitting His deity.

Acts 19:10

> And this continued by the space of two years; so that all they which dwelt in Asia heard the word of the Lord *Jesus*, both Jews and Greeks. (Acts 19:10, KJV)

Jesus is omitted.

One of the main teachings of the New Testament is that in these last days, which began at the ascension of Christ, God will speak to us by His Son. "God, who at sundry times and in divers manners spake in time past unto the fathers by the prophets, Hath in these last days spoken unto us by his Son, whom he hath appointed heir of all things, by whom also he made the worlds" (Hebrews 1:1–2, KJV). No longer would we have to wait for a prophet to bring the word as it is complete.

Acts 19:10 tells us that the apostle Paul had been preaching in Asia for two full years and he was preaching the word of the Lord Jesus. It is through Christ that we receive salvation and not through any works. Paul's ministry was devoted to the propagation of the Gospel of Christ. Paul was not just teaching the word of the Lord, which could be Habakkuk or Obadiah; he was specifically preaching Christ, who was his whole life. It is the same with us: that we are to be teaching Christ to the world because it is only through Him that we can have salvation. It is not as though the word of God as found in Habakkuk or Obadiah is any less scripture than John or Acts, but Paul's ministry was Christ-centered and not Mosaic-law centered. Acts 19:10 is giving us a specific message to teach, and that is the Lord Jesus Christ, which is omitted in the modern versions as usual.

Acts 19:35

And when the townclerk had appeased the people, he said, Ye men of Ephesus, what man is there that knoweth not how that the city of the Ephesians is a worshipper of the great goddess Diana, and of the image which fell down from *Jupiter*? (Acts 19:35, KJV)

Jupiter is changed to "heaven."

By changing *Jupiter* to "heaven," the modern versions make it sound like the image of Diana came down from heaven meaning that God was endorsing false gods. Jupiter was the chief god of the pantheon of gods of the Greeks. Heaven condemns all idols and all idolatry. This verse in the modern versions is making a very serious accusation against heaven, as if the Lord in heaven is the one who sent down the image of Diana.

Acts 20:24

But none of these things move me, neither count I my life dear unto myself, so that I might finish my course with joy, and the ministry, which

I have received of the Lord Jesus, to testify the
gospel of the grace of God. (Acts 20:24, KJV)

"But none of these things move me" is omitted.

Here is another anomaly of the modern versions. If you look at
the Hort-Westcott text for the words in question, you will see that
they exist in both the WH and TR with the one-word variation. The
anomaly is that in the King James Bible, they are translated as "But
none of these things move me," and in the modern versions, *omitted!*
They do not translate anything for these first four Greek words. Why?
I have no idea other than, like water, corruption seeks its own level.

Acts 20:25

And now, behold, I know that ye all, among
whom I have gone preaching the kingdom *of God,*
shall see my face no more. (Acts 20:25, KJV)

"Of God" is omitted.

This verse stands in the midst of the final farewell of Paul to
the Ephesians. Here, he states that he had proclaimed the kingdom
of God. When the modern versions omit "of God," they are leaving
out a very important part of the message. If you recall, Ephesus was
the place where the heathens taught that Diana fell down from the
false god Jupiter. (Diana was a forerunner of the cult of the Virgin
Mary taught by the Roman Catholic Church.) Therefore, the center
of Diana worship was found to be in the city of Ephesus. Paul had
made it clear that he was proclaiming the kingdom of God to the
Ephesians.

The kingdom of Diana was at Ephesus, and without the clear
teaching from scripture, any cultist or occultist can change the
meaning of Paul's declaration. Without "of God," they could make
it say that Paul was a teacher and follower of Diana. Now we know
that Paul taught no such thing, but with the gullibility factor of the
masses, it could happen. This is why God placed in the scriptures "of
God," so there would be no mistake as to which kingdom Paul was

a representative of. Now, you may say I am stretching it a little bit, but given the times we live in and the way people believe anything, God was making sure that none of His true children would ever be confused. Thank the Lord today for the clearness of the King James Bible.

Acts 20:32

And now, *brethren*, I commend you to God, and to the word of his grace, which is able to build you up, and to give you an inheritance among all them which are sanctified. (Acts 20:32, KJV)

Brethren is omitted.

When the modern versions remove the word *brethren*, they removed a pivotal word. When we read the rest of the verse, it speaks of the body of believers in terms of an inheritance and being sanctified. The unbeliever is not sanctified unto the Lord, nor do they have an inheritance in heaven, nor are they under grace. By removing *brethren*, it makes the verse seem like it is stating that Paul is commending even the unbelievers unto God.

The word *brethren* is making it very specific that only true believers are included in Paul's salutation. This is important to know because it gives the believer true hope while it removes false hope for the unbeliever. Paul had commended (entrusted) the believers unto God because, previously, he had warned them that there would be false teachers coming into the church immediately upon his departure. It was the unbelievers whom Paul was warning the true believers of; he was not coddling them nor compromising with them. Once again, the King James Bible gives us the truth while showing us that the modern versions are the welcome versions of the unbelievers.

Acts 20:34

Yea, ye yourselves know, that these hands have ministered unto my necessities, and to them that were with me. (Acts 20:34, KJV)

Yea is omitted.

The word *yea* in English is a conjunction. It is translated from *de* in the Greek, which is a conjunction. In this case, because it connects contrasting thought in two sentences, it is an important word. The apostle Paul in verse 33 is telling his hearers that he has never coveted anyone's gold, silver, or anything, and then uses the conjunction to contrast coveting with the fact that he physically worked to provide for his needs and also those who worked with him. When Paul preached in new areas, he worked with his hands to show the people he was not there to covet or desire their goods but to make a proper show of the Gospel by not seeking material gain as the false teachers did.

Acts 21:8

> And the next day we *that were of Paul's company* departed, and came unto Caesarea: and we entered into the house of Philip the evangelist, which was one of the seven; and abode with him. (Acts 21:8, KJV)

"That were of Paul's company" is omitted.

Luke then states that they (Paul's company, including himself) went from Ptolemias to Caesarea. Paul's company would have included the following: "And there accompanied him into Asia Sopater of Berea; and of the Thessalonians, Aristarchus and Secundus; and Gaius of Derbe, and Timotheus; and of Asia, Tychicus and Trophimus" (Acts 20:4, KJV). Philip the evangelist must have been blessed mightily by God since he was able to have Paul and his company stay with him.

Philip, as you may recall, was one of the seven deacons who served in the church of Jerusalem. "And the saying pleased the whole multitude: and they chose Stephen, a man full of faith and of the Holy Ghost, and Philip, and Prochorus, and Nicanor, and Timon, and Parmenas, and Nicolas a proselyte of Antioch" (Acts 6:5, KJV). His home may have been the chief Christian center in Caesarea as a group of believers met there. There is no reason that the section that specifically points to the members of Paul's entourage should be omitted. Luke was an eyewitness to much of Paul's ministry, and maybe that is why this portion is cut out because it gives a specific name to the witness, who was Luke.

Acts 21:25

> As touching the Gentiles which believe, we have written *and concluded that they observe no such thing, save only* that they keep themselves from things offered to idols, and from blood, and from strangled, and from fornication. (Acts 21:25, KJV)

"And concluded that they observe no such thing, save only" is omitted.

The portion that is omitted in the modern versions pertains to the Gentiles who have become saved and that they are not required to keep any aspects of the law. If they have been saved by grace, then keeping any aspects of the law would be useless since you cannot add to grace. Circumcision was not necessary under grace, and this is what Paul had told them, and it was also the conclusion of the Jerusalem Council. The modern versions want to keep people in bondage to the law even if one is saved under grace. This is why the modern versions are dangerous because they can help any cult place Christians under bondage to rules and regulations that are nonexistent in scripture.

Acts 22:9

> And they that were with me saw indeed the light, *and were afraid*; but they heard not the voice *of him* that spake to me. (Acts 22:9, KJV)

"And were afraid" is omitted. *"Of him"* is replaced with "the One."

When the apostle Paul was on the road to Damascus to cause more trouble for the church, he was met by the Lord Jesus Christ, who told him that he was persecuting Him through His children. When the Lord Jesus spoke with Paul, those who were with him had seen the light from heaven, and the scripture stated that "they were afraid." In fact, the word in Greek for "afraid" carries with it the idea of being frightened or terrified. So these men were not just afraid; they were in raw terror.

But the modern versions remove this part, which is basically removing a phrase that deals with fearing the Lord because those who are unbelievers, when they go to the great white throne judgment, will also be in terror. This phrase gives good insight into the terror that awaits the unbeliever while the believer will feel at home in the presence of the Lord. The unbelievers with Paul were terrified, but Paul spoke with the Lord and did not suffer the terror the others did. Acts 9 states that he trembled and was astonished at the light and the voice that spoke to him, but the scripture does not state he was in terror.

If you will notice, some of the versions exchange "of him" for "the one." This is an erroneous translation. The word in the Greek underlying "spake" is in the masculine gender that would necessitate the translation "of him" as being proper. "The one" is neutered, which would be an erroneous translation. If you recall, we saw that the term *the One* is never used in the Bible as a reference to God the Father or God the Son.

Acts 22:16

And now why tarriest thou? arise, and be baptized, and wash away thy sins, calling on the name *of the Lord*. (Acts 22:16, KJV)

"Of the Lord" is omitted.

And it shall come to pass, that whosoever shall call on the name of the LORD shall be delivered:

for in mount Zion and in Jerusalem shall be deliverance, as the LORD hath said, and in the remnant whom the LORD shall call. (Joel 2:32, KJV)

And it shall come to pass, that whosoever shall call on the name of the Lord shall be saved. (Acts 2:21, KJV)

For whosoever shall call upon the name of the Lord shall be saved. (Romans 10:13, KJV)

Here, we have three verses, one in the Old Testament and two in the New Testament, where we are specifically told that those who call upon the name of the Lord shall be saved. Yet in this verse, we have seen how the modern versions remove that vital piece of information. The Lord is the only one who can give a person salvation. Removal of "the name of the Lord" would play perfectly into Roman Catholic belief, for their adherents call on the name of many dead saints. It is important for all to know that there is no other name under heaven for a person to be saved.

The pronoun *him* can be applied to anybody the reader wishes to apply it to. This is why it is so vital to keep "the name of the Lord" in this verse. But with the various belief systems tied to the modern versions, it is not surprising why they kept the Gnostic mutilation alive. The Lord has preserved His Word in the King James Bible and given us the true rendering. Let us stay with the King James Bible, and we will never have to worry about Gnostic mutilations of any verse. What a great legacy to hand down to our children.

Acts 22:20

And when the blood of thy martyr Stephen was shed, I also was standing by, and consenting *unto his death*, and kept the raiment of them that slew him. (Acts 22:20, KJV)

"Unto his death" is omitted.

Before the apostle Paul became the apostle Paul, he was a murderer of Christians, doing what he could to destroy the church and Christians in general. In Acts 22:20, the King James Bible tells us in no uncertain terms that Paul had consented or given approbation to the murder of Stephen. Now, the word that has been removed from this passage in the modern versions is a most important word and found here and only in Acts 8:1 in connection only with the stoning of Stephen. It is only used twice in the New Testament. It is the word *anairesis*, and it not only means "death or killing" but has a special meaning of "a taking up or raising of a life." It is like there is a Christian in your life who has a special place or meaning to you, and that person is taken in death. We do not view them as being taken in death, but we view them as having their life taken up or raised to glory. While they were with us, they had great impact, but now they are home with the Lord, just as Stephen was.

The modern versions leave this out, and those who use them miss out on such a tremendous lesson; plus, it removes the murderous intent of Saul, which is the same attitude that unbelievers have toward us. Even if it is not physical murder, unbelievers love to murder the reputation of Christians.

Acts 23:9

> And there arose a great cry: and *the scribes* that were of the Pharisees' part arose, and strove, saying, We find no evil in this man: but if a spirit or an angel hath spoken to him, *let us not fight against God.* (Acts 23:9, KJV)

"Let us not fight against God" is omitted. *"The scribes"* is changed to "teachers of the law," and some versions omit it.

In this section of scripture, the apostle Paul was once again involved in a major theological debate with the Pharisees and the Sadducees. The Pharisees believed in the resurrection, angels, and spirits, but the Sadducees did not believe in these. Paul knew that both sects were present, and he then went on to proclaim that he believed in the resurrection. This created a great commotion between the two sects. The multitude that was present was also divided, which made this an even greater commotion. However, the scribes, who had sided with the Pharisees, had deemed Paul to have nothing evil about him, and they were obviously following the advice given by Gamaliel in a previous situation. The Pharisees had believed that if an angel or spirit from heaven had spoken to Paul, then if they harmed him, they would be found fighting against God. "But if it be of God, ye cannot overthrow it; lest haply ye be found even to fight against God" (Acts 5:39, KJV).

The great principle found in this verse is very important because every time unbelievers or even believers fight against the very truth of God in the Bible, they are, in reality, fighting against God. This important truth in this verse has been omitted from the modern versions. That is because the modern translators, along with their second- and third-century Gnostic counterparts, are fighting against God by severely tampering with the word of God. This results in those who use the modern versions are also fighting against God, and that is why they cannot grow in the faith. God can only grow a Christian when they have the true word of God and not a counterfeit. "Can two walk together, except they be agreed?" (Amos 3:3, KJV).

God cannot produce growth in a believer unless they have the true word of God. How can God bless what He did not say? How can God bless corruption? How can God bless a version that is hostile to His Son and friendly and acceptable to sodomy? (NIV). Yes, by using the modern versions, the Christian can also be found fighting against God, but the modern versions will never admit this. Stay with the King James Bible and walk in accordance with God!

Acts 23:15

Now therefore ye with the council signify to the chief captain that he bring him down unto you *tomorrow*, as though ye would inquire something more perfectly concerning him: and

we, or ever he come near, are ready to kill him.
(Acts 23:15, KJV)

Tomorrow is omitted.

Here is another case of confusion in the modern versions. The Jews had planned to kill Paul, so they plotted against him. They were going to summon him, and then while he was being transported, they would ambush him and the squad of soldiers who were protecting him. This was to take place the following day after the plans were made. "And he said, The Jews have agreed to desire thee that thou wouldest bring down Paul to morrow into the council, as though they would inquire somewhat of him more perfectly" (Acts 23:20, KJV).

When Paul's nephew told the chief captain or centurion, he told them that this plot would take place tomorrow. The modern versions omit the word *tomorrow* in verse 15. It sounds like they were going to bring Paul out today and then ambush him tomorrow. However, the entire event was to take place on one day, which was the day after the chief captain received the information. So the chief captain took the necessary precautions and saved the life of Paul. The modern versions are sources of confusion, and we know who the author of confusion is!

Acts 24:6–8

Who also hath gone about to profane the temple: whom we took, *and would have judged according to our law. But the chief captain Lysias came upon us, and with great violence took him away out of our hands, Commanding his accusers to come unto thee*: by examining of whom thyself mayest take knowledge of all these things, whereof we accuse him. (Acts 24:6, KJV)

Verse 6, *"and would have judged according to our law,"* is omitted. The entire verse 7 is omitted, and many versions place it in footnotes with doubt. Verse 8, *"commanding his accusers to come unto thee,"* is omitted.

These verses are in the Peshitta (AD 150), the Italic (AD 157), and the Old Latin Vulgate (AD 157). As you can see with these verses included in these very early translations, they predate the corrupted versions by about two hundred years. This means that the true oldest and best manuscripts predate the corrupted "oldest and best," which are touted by modern-day scholars. The King James Bible is a descendant of the three listed versions, and that is why we have a Bible with purity because God would not allow every manuscript to be corrupted because He promised to preserve His word to all generations until the last one.

Paul was being falsely accused that he had profaned the temple, and because of his wanting to teach the true Gospel to the Jews, they wanted to kill him by means of a trumped-up charge. When the Roman tribune Lysias saw the trouble that was being stirred up, he intervened and saved the life of Paul and forced the accusers out into the open. I cannot see the reason that these three verses have been chopped up as they are. Maybe the twisted reason is lost in antiquity. If we stick to the King James Bible, then we will not have to worry about any reason the modern versions are chopped up.

Acts 24:14

> But this I confess unto thee, that after the way
> which they call heresy, so worship I the God of
> my fathers, believing all things which *are written*
> *in the law* and in the prophets. (Acts 24:14, KJV)

"Are written in the law" is replaced with "agrees or according to the law."

This is one of the subtleest changes in the English text. If you will notice, there are no corruptions in this verse. The word *gegrammenois* is a perfect-tense verb that may also be understood as "having been written." The perfect tense denotes a past action of which the results of that action are still in effect. If you will notice in the King James Bible, the words "are written" comes before "in the law and in the prophets." If you will notice, all the modern versions above place the word *written* only before "in the prophets." This is a subtle attack on the scriptures. "LAMED. For ever, O LORD, thy word is settled in heaven" (Psalm 119:89, KJV). God's word is forever settled in heaven, and He has preserved those words.

Both the written law and the written prophets are settled in heaven and are settled in the Bible on earth, except in the modern versions, where they are always changing. God gave us words and preserved those words for us. When the modern-version translators moved "it is written" to exclude the law, they do this without knowledge. This is because there was an oral law that was an administrative tool, which was used in religion and in the community.

Oral law was used much in rabbinic literature and held equal status to that of the written law. This is why Judaism is based more on the Talmud than the scriptures. By the English translators of the modern versions moving that phrase, they undermine the authority of the written law. The written law is still in effect today because those who are not under grace are under law and will be judged on the last day for all their transgressions of the law of God. "Whosoever committeth sin transgresseth also the law: for sin is the transgression of the law" (1 John 3:4, KJV). Keep in mind that 1 John 3:4 is in the New Testament and is speaking about transgressing the law, which was written about 1,600 years before 1 John, and transgressing the law is sin. On the last day, unbelievers are judged for their sins. We must never believe that the law is no longer in effect today.

Acts 24:15

And have hope toward God, which they themselves also allow, that there shall be a resurrection *of the dead*, both of the just and unjust. (Acts 24:15, KJV)

"Of the dead" is omitted.

Here is another attack on the resurrection from the dead. The second-century Gnostics did not believe in any type of resurrection except those who are resurrected from ignorance into knowledge.

Robert Schuller taught that being born again means going from low self-esteem to high self-esteem. I do not know if this was his only meaning for being born again. So we see that even in today's teachings, these terms are twisted to fit certain belief systems. There is no reason given as to why "of the dead" has been removed from the Greek text. It goes back to the second-century Gnostics who disbelieved in any type of resurrection, so it follows that they would remove a very important word from the Greek pointing to the specific resurrection from the dead.

Now, in today's society, many teach that a person is resurrected to life when they come out of some type of sin such as smoking, drunkenness, drugs, etc. Terms like *resurrection* and *born again* have been neutralized and inculcated into common terminology. However, in the Christian life, we believe deeply in the words of God and have hope that there is going to be a physical resurrection at the last day of both believers and unbelievers. The modern versions remove that hope by removing the words that point to that glorious day.

> Marvel not at this: for the hour is coming, in the which all that are in the graves shall hear his voice, And shall come forth; they that have done good, unto the resurrection of life; and they that have done evil, unto the resurrection of damnation. (John 5:28–29, KJV)

> Martha saith unto him, I know that he shall rise again in the resurrection at the last day. [Martha was speaking of Lazarus, who was a believer.] (John 11:24, KJV)

Acts 25:6

> And when he had tarried among them *more than ten days*, he went down unto Caesarea; and the next day sitting on the judgment seat commanded Paul to be brought. (Acts 25:6, KJV)

"More than ten days" is replaced with "eight or ten days."

Here, we have the modern versions changing a time reference. Festus had spent more than ten days in Jerusalem, probably becoming familiar with the city and ascertaining information about Paul. The modern versions change the time frame to eight to ten days. There is a vast difference eight to ten days and more than ten days. It is about a distance of sixty miles one way as the crow flies between Jerusalem and Caesarea, which could mean eighty miles each way with the dirt roads. You are probably talking about a two- or three-day trip in each direction, especially if Festus had a large entourage with him. So eight days would not be enough time for the kind of visit that Festus needed. The time frame of "more than ten days" would be more accommodating to the task at hand.

Acts 25:16

To whom I answered, It is not the manner of the Romans to deliver any man *to die*, before that he which is accused have the accusers face to face, and have licence to answer for himself concerning the crime laid against him. (Acts 25:16, KJV)

"To die" is omitted.

History does repeat itself as the new generation of chief priests and elders tried the same tactic on Paul that the previous leaders did on Jesus. They were trying to get King Agrippa and Festus to order a summary execution of Paul, but King Agrippa was very familiar with Roman law and custom and knew that it was Paul's right to face his accusers. They wanted to put Paul to death, but the king knew better than to order a summary judgment.

The modern versions leave out this important fact. Paul would not have appealed to Caesar if it was just for a misdemeanor. Paul knew that the Jews wanted him dead, and it was not just a case of a few accusations. The modern versions leave out the phrase "to die," which also shows the believer that being a witness for Christ can put our lives on the line. The modern versions seem to mollify this situation, making it a blame game, but the King James Bible puts it in perfect perspective and gives us the real situation Paul faced with the events leading up to His martyrdom.

Acts 26:30

And when he had thus spoken, the king rose up, and the governor, and Bernice, and they that sat with them. (Acts 26:30, KJV)

"And when he had thus spoken" is omitted.

The apostle Paul had just witnessed to all those who were in attendance in the court of King Agrippa. In verse 29, Paul had stated that his desire was that all those in attendance would become saved but not to have chains placed upon them. Once Paul went into the part about them all becoming Christians, that is when King Agrippa, Festus, and Bernice rose up. It was probably those words about becoming a Christian that caused them to rise up abruptly.

The words for *rose up* in the Greek have as its cognate the same word used for "resurrection." This would tell us that the words that Paul spoke in verse 29 had caused them to rise up from their thrones very quickly, as quickly as someone being resurrected. Then they had the meeting where they found no fault in Paul, but since he appealed to Caesar, he had to be taken to Rome.

The modern versions omit the phrase "and when he had thus spoken," which emphasized Paul's desire for them to become Christians. This is what caused them consternation, and they wanted the examination to end because Paul took the dialogue and turned it around from him to them. They would now have to face spiritual questions, and this they feared, so when unbelievers do not wish to face any questions about salvation, they quickly end the conversation. The modern versions make it a casual conversation, but the King James emphasizes the urgency of salvation and the expected response many believers will experience.

Acts 27:14

But not long after there arose *against it* a tempestuous wind, called Euroclydon. (Acts 27:14, KJV)

"Against it" is omitted.

The text of the modern versions omit the words "against it." There is no reason for those words to be omitted. This is just another case of the modern versions omitting English words without any reason given—a very dangerous practice of the modern versions.

Acts 28:16

And when we came to Rome, *the centurion delivered the prisoners to the captain of the guard: but* Paul was suffered to dwell by himself with a soldier that kept him. (Acts 28:16, KJV)

"The centurion delivered the prisoners to the captain of the guard: but" is omitted.

This passage describes Paul's arrival with the rest of the prisoners, and it tells us how all the prisoners were handed over to the captain of the guard. But Paul was allowed to dwell in his own place with a guard. Paul had dwelled in this place for two years, and no doubt it became a center of evangelism in Rome as Paul was allowed to have visitors. Why these twelve words have been omitted from the Hort-Westcott text remains a mystery lost in antiquity, but it is a shame how the modern translators do not question these omissions and reinstate them.

We do know that Paul was told by the Lord that he would be a witness in Rome. "And the night following the Lord stood by him, and said, Be of good cheer, Paul: for as thou hast testified of me in Jerusalem, so must thou bear witness also at Rome" (Acts 23:11, KJV). This would no doubt be the reason that Paul was separated from the rest of the prisoners in fulfillment of the Lord's command that he would be a witness in Rome, and maybe the Gnostics left out this portion of the passage because they did not believe the prophecy about Paul.

Acts 28:29

> And when he had said these words, the Jews departed, and had great reasoning among themselves. (Acts 28:29, KJV)

The entire verse is omitted or placed in brackets.

The apostle Paul had just finished telling the Jews that the Gospel is now being sent to the Gentiles because of the hardness of the heart of the Jews. Those who heard Paul's statements had great trouble with these words, and that is why they had great reasoning among them concerning what Paul had taught them. The word for *reasoning* may also be understood as "dispute or discussion." No doubt Paul had really stirred the pot and gave his visitors some things to think about. The way these people left Paul is the way that all should leave a good Bible study or sermon, and that is with great discussion.

The modern churches have adopted such an innocuous Gospel that no one discusses it anymore; instead, everyone feels good about themselves. A good message should always leave someone questioning and searching. "Examine yourselves, whether ye be in the faith; prove your own selves. Know ye not your own selves, how that Jesus Christ is in you, except ye be reprobates?" (2 Corinthians 13:5, KJV). Why this verse has been omitted in the modern versions remains a mystery, but we can be sure that the modern versions leave no place for discussion since those who use them believe they have instant understanding because of the so-called "updated language." But how can one have understanding of a passage when it is missing?

Romans 1:16

> For I am not ashamed of the gospel *of Christ*: for it is the power of God unto salvation to every one

that believeth; to the Jew first, and also to the Greek. (Romans 1:16, KJV)

"Of Christ" is omitted.

"Of Christ" is only two small words, but they project the essence of Paul's entire ministry and that also of the Christian throughout the ages. There are many "gospels" out in the world today, and for the last two thousand years, there have been an abundance of them. Without the qualifier "of Christ" in this verse, the religious unbeliever can claim they are not ashamed of their gospel. The Roman Catholic can proclaim they are not ashamed of the gospel of Mary. The Jehovah's Witnesses can claim they are not ashamed of their gospel. Any false church can claim they are not ashamed of their social gospel.

The words "of Christ" are very important because there is only one true Gospel that can save, and that is the Gospel of Christ. This is why the modern versions fit perfectly into false churches and cults because they do not proclaim the Gospel of Christ. This is why the King James Version is superior because it does not shrink back from giving the true Gospel in contrast to the false versions.

Romans 1:20

For the invisible things of him from the creation of the world are clearly seen, being understood by the things that are made, even his eternal power and *Godhead*; so that they are without excuse. (Romans 1:20, KJV)

Godhead is replaced by "divine nature."

"For in him dwelleth all the fulness of the Godhead bodily" (Colossians 2:9, KJV). The Godhead represents the one God in three Persons, and as we see in Colossians 2:9, all the fulness of the Godhead was in Christ. It was not just a divine nature, but it was the totality of the attributes of all three Persons. If it was just the divine nature, then it would reduce His authority.

Romans 1:22

Professing *themselves* to be wise, they became fools. (Romans 1:22, KJV)

Themselves is omitted.

This group claims themselves to be wise in their own eyes. They brag about their intellects, especially the Gnostics, who thought they were the chief minds among the people. "Woe unto them that are wise in their own eyes, and prudent in their own sight!" (Isaiah 5:21, KJV). God warns them in Isaiah about a woe pronounced on them who are wise in their own eyes, which is what Romans 1:22 is speaking of. In other words, their wisdom was their own assessment.

Romans 1:29

Being filled with all unrighteousness, *fornication*, wickedness, covetousness, maliciousness; full of envy, murder, debate, deceit, malignity; whisperers. (Romans 1:29, KJV)

Fornication is omitted.

Out of the entire list of sins, the one that is omitted in the modern versions is the sin of fornication. There are two types of fornication: First, there is spiritual fornication, where a true believer may go after a strange doctrine or partake in a false gospel. One of the most blatant and accepted forms of spiritual fornication is the modern versions, with their attacks on the Lord Jesus Christ and the cardinal doctrines of the faith. Christians who accept anything but a pure Bible are committing spiritual fornication because they are not getting the whole truth. The second type of fornication is physical fornication. It is having sex outside of marriage. Obviously, the original Bible corrupters had no problem with this, and the modern translators and publishers have no problem with it either since they allowed the omission to stand. "Even as Sodom and Gomorrha, and the cities about them in like manner, giving themselves over to fornication, and going after strange flesh, are set forth for an example, suffering the vengeance of eternal fire" (Jude 1:7, KJV). God had something to say about it when He destroyed Sodom and Gomorrha. He will have something to say about it on the last day. Once again, the modern versions omit a very important warning.

A blatant example of spiritual fornication is as follows. October 31, to the world, it is Halloween; but to the Christian, it is Reformation Day. It is a shame that many Christian parents dress their children up in costumes and take them or let them go trick-or-treating. Halloween for a Christian is spiritual fornication because it is emulating Satan and his fallen devils. Costumes are representing the demons as they come in deception to deceive people. Dressing up like ghouls, witches, vampires, etc., is all satanic, and Christians should have nothing to do with the occult. Let me be blunt, your children are not cute because God does not want His children playing with the occult.

Let me share a personal testimony that happened to me just prior to becoming saved. I had many books on the occult in my library, and one night, while I was sleeping, I felt I was being compressed from my shoulders. It was like my shoulders were being squeezed inward from the outside. It was a wake-up call. When I became saved shortly thereafter, I got rid of all the occult materials. The occult books were the highway that the devils used to come into my home. The occult is real, and there are real evil spirits who wish to deceive and destroy.

One more testimony about this subject. This comes from Harold Camping, the late president of Family Radio in Oakland, California. When he was much younger, he was doing research on Satan and the occult. He had purchased books and materials including a Ouija board. He had six children. He and his wife, Shirley, had gone out one evening and came home a little late to find all the lights in the house on. He wondered what happened, so he asked his children. While he was out, the children told him that doors and windows were opening and closing, and no one was there. So the children became extremely frightened and put all the lights on. It was then that he got rid of all occult materials in the house, and that never happened again.

Everything we need to know about the occult and Satan and his kingdom, we have in the Bible, which is protected by God for us. Once we go outside the Bible and start looking for these things on our own, we will get into serious trouble. Keep yourselves away from all things connected with the occult. Don't even fool with them. Past TV shows like *Ghost Hunters* do not realize they are really being tricked by Satan's demons as they pretend to be the dead people the hunters are seeking. Keep in mind that it is from Satan's kingdom that we have been delivered, and we have no business going back. The modern versions remove the warning about fornication.

Romans 1:31

> Without understanding, covenantbreakers, without natural affection, *implacable*, unmerciful. (Romans 1:31, KJV)

Implacable is omitted.

This omission is a mystery because there is no logical reason that the word *aspondous* (*implacable*) should have been omitted in the Greek. The word means "irreconcilable, unappeasable, or something which is unable to be mollified or assuaged." This word fits perfectly into the list of characteristics of those who hate God and oppose Him. However, there may be one reason the Gnostics left it out. "And all things are of God, who hath reconciled us to himself by Jesus Christ, and hath given to us the ministry of reconciliation" (2 Corinthians 5:18, KJV).

In Romans 1:24 and 26, the verses teach us that God gave up these vile people unto their own evil affections. If God gave them up, then maybe what the Lord is teaching us here is that they can no longer have the opportunity to be saved, which is the essence of reconciliation, since God gave them up. Since our omitted word has a meaning of the inability to be reconciled, that may be the confirmation that when God gives someone up, the door of salvation is no longer open to them, and maybe this is what the Gnostics tried to hide and the modern versions continue to hide.

Romans 3:3

For what if some did not believe? shall their
unbelief make the *faith* of God without effect?
(Romans 3:3, KJV)

Faith is exchanged for "faithfulness."

The word *faithfulness* appears nineteen times in the King James
Bible, but only in the Old Testament. Romans 3:3 is not speaking of
God's faithfulness, but it is speaking of the faith that God gives; that
is, salvation. It is speaking about the effectual calling of God. Just
because some do not believe does not mean that the effectual calling
of God is not operational in others. The elect of God will respond to
the effectual calling of God while the unbeliever will hear the Gospel
but will not respond, owing to the fact that they are not elect. The
modern versions have once again mistranslated the word and caused
the meaning to be totally different. The word *faithful* appears fifty
times in the New Testament, but the Greek word behind it is *pistos*,
a different word than *pistis*.

Romans 3:22

Even the righteousness of God which is by faith of
Jesus Christ unto all *and upon all* them that believe:
for there is no difference. (Romans 3:22, KJV)

"And upon all" is omitted.

Here is another example of a vital teaching omitted in the modern versions. The phrase "and upon all" is a very important part of
this verse. The first phrase "unto all" means that the righteousness of
God is for or toward those who believe in Christ. Now, the omitted
phrase teaches us that not only is the righteousness of God for those
who believe but it is upon those who believe. The root word for *upon*
in the Greek is *epi*, and it implies contact with its object and does not
imply resting above or over. In other words, this verse is teaching that
not only is the righteousness of God for the ones who believe, but it

is given to those who believe. The righteousness of God is imputed to the believer upon salvation.

The modern versions omit the part where we are told that the righteousness of God is not only for us but is given to us. Let me give a quick analogy. You work all week, and the boss comes up to you and says this paycheck is for you and then walks away. What good is it him telling you that the check is for you unless he gives it to you? To tell us that the righteousness of God is for us without telling us that it is given to us completely destroys the meaning of this passage and denies a cardinal truth of the Christian faith.

Romans 5:2

> By whom also we have access *by faith* into this grace wherein we stand, and rejoice in hope of the glory of God. (Romans 5:2, KJV)

"By faith" is omitted.

Faith is one of the fruits of the Holy Spirit, and we receive faith when we become saved and the Holy Spirit indwells us. The only way we can get to the Father is by being saved, and thus, having faith, which is a prime tenet of the Christian life. "For therein is the righteousness of God revealed from faith to faith: as it is written, The just shall live by faith" (Romans 1:17, KJV). It was Romans 1:17 and its teaching on faith that opened the door to the Reformation through Martin Luther.

Romans 6:11

> Likewise reckon ye also yourselves to be dead indeed unto sin, but alive unto God through Jesus Christ *our Lord*. (Romans 6:11, KJV)

"Our Lord" is omitted.

Here, we have another attack on the Lord Jesus Christ. The modern versions leave off the phrase "our Lord." "For there are certain men crept in unawares, who were before of old ordained to this

condemnation, ungodly men, turning the grace of our God into las-
civiousness, and denying the only Lord God, and our Lord Jesus
Christ" (Jude 1:4, KJV). The phrase "our Lord," in reference to the
Lord Jesus Christ, is used eighty times in the New Testament. Jude
4 gives a usage of the phrase "our Lord" and is a good description
of those who deny the Lord Jesus Christ, like the modern-version
editors. He is called "our Lord" because it was He who died for His
people and therefore has earned the right to be called "our Lord."

The word *our* is in the genitive case, which means not only
do we belong to Christ, but He also belongs to us. "I am the good
shepherd, and know my sheep, and am known of mine" (John 10:14,
KJV). It is amazing how the modern versions claim to be God's word
and do everything they can to attack the Son of God.

Romans 8:1

> There is therefore now no condemnation to them
> which are in Christ Jesus, *who walk not after the
> flesh, but after the Spirit.* (Romans 8:1, KJV)

"Who walk not after the flesh, but after the Spirit" is omitted.

The Jehovah's Witnesses version and the Roman Catholic version have absolute agreement with five major versions used in the
Protestant Church and by most Christians. This portion of scripture
is missing in both Vaticanus and Sinaiticus. In the footnotes of the
United Bible Societies fourth revised edition, the names of *Marcion*
and *Origen* appear as those who are the ones responsible for removing the above part of this verse. As previously mentioned, both were
heretics and Gnostics. It is interesting to note that a fifth-century
(maybe earlier in date) manuscript titled Alexandrinus (A) contains
the removed portion, yet the modern scholars of today have chosen
to leave it omitted since it does not appear in the two crowning manuscripts of modern scholarship.

The Roman Catholic institution would love nothing more than
to leave out that portion because if a person is walking according to
the Spirit, it means they are saved and indwelled by the Holy Spirit.

If a person is walking after the flesh, it means they are unsaved, but it also means they are able to be brought under the bondage of works gospels, such as Roman Catholicism, who keep their adherents fastened to a system of rituals and works. A person who is in the flesh will continue to work for their salvation according to the dictates of their church or institution. They may work for it but will never attain it.

"That the righteousness of the law might be fulfilled in us, who walk not after the flesh, but after the Spirit" (Romans 8:4, KJV). The fulfillment of God's righteous law comes by being indwelled with the Holy Spirit through salvation. Christ fulfilled the requirements of God's holy law for all His people, so those who are walking in the Spirit through salvation have also, in Christ, fulfilled the demands of God's holy law. To remove that part of scripture gives a person who is involved with false gospels a false assurance that just because they are doing religious works, they are in Christ Jesus. This is one of the grave dangers of tampering with the word of God because those who use these versions do not have the entire word, which means they are being deceived by a corrupted version. God gave every word in the Bible for a purpose, and for someone to remove anything is to endanger the eternal souls of people.

By removing that part of verse 1, it conveys to those working for salvation that they are not under condemnation. Every person who is not born again is under the wrath of God. No human being can work themselves out from under the wrath of God.

> He that believeth on him is not condemned: but he that believeth not is condemned already, because he hath not believed in the name of the only begotten Son of God. (John 3:18, KJV)

> He that believeth on the Son hath everlasting life: and he that believeth not the Son shall not see life; but the wrath of God abideth on him. (John 3:36, KJV)

The next time you get a letter from some Bible society or ministry asking for money to help send Bibles abroad, find out what manuscripts or what version they are using before you send money. Why would any Christian want to help foster corruption and deception upon unknowing Christians in other lands? We have a responsibility to other Christians, whether we see them face-to-face or never see them till eternity.

Romans 8:15

> For ye have not received the spirit of bondage again to fear; but ye have received *the Spirit* of adoption, whereby we cry, Abba, Father. (Romans 8:15, KJV)

"The Spirit" is changed to "a spirit" in the NASV, NRSV, NABRE.

> For you have not received a spirit of slavery leading to fear again, but you have received *a* spirit of adoption as sons by which we cry out, "Abba! Father!" (NASV)

> For you did not receive a spirit of slavery to fall back into fear, but you have received *a* spirit of adoption. When we cry, "Abba! Father!" (NRSV)

The Holy Spirit is the way we are adopted into the kingdom of God. He is the only way to become saved once we are indwelled by Him. The modern versions make it sound like there are many spirits by using the indirect article *a*. The King James uses the direct article *the*, teaching there is only one way we are adopted into the kingdom of God, and that is through the Holy Spirit.

Romans 8:16

> The Spirit *itself* beareth witness with our spirit, that we are the children of God. (Romans 8:16, KJV)

Itself is changed to "himself."

The word *auto* is written the same in both the Textus Receptus and the Hort-Westcott text. In the 1881 Revised Version, the word is also translated "himself." Now, it does not sound like a big change but it really is. If you notice, the King James Version translates the word *auto* as "itself" while the rest of them translate it "himself." The word *auto* is in the neuter gender, which means that the Holy Spirit has no sexual category; in other words, the Holy Spirit is neither male nor female. This is why the King James translated it correctly by applying no sexual gender to the Holy Spirit. The modern versions change this in the English from a neuter gender to the masculine gender without any grammatical reason; instead, they take grammatical license in doing it. Spirit has no gender. "For in the resurrection they neither marry, nor are given in marriage, but are as the angels of God in heaven" (Matthew 22:30, KJV).

Romans 8:28

And we know that all things work together for good
to them that love God, to them who are *the* called
according to his purpose. (Romans 8:28, KJV)

The is omitted.

Here is a case where the modern-version editors ignored a very important word in this verse. It is the Greek word *tois*, which is translated "to the." It is a definite article in the dative case. The dative case is the case of "for whom the action is being done for." The King James rightly translates it as *the* because it is showing for whom all things work together. The verse states that the condition is that those who love God, and who are the ones who love God? They are the true believers, and they are the specific group in view being known as *the called*. In Matthew 22:14, Jesus states, "For many are called, but few are chosen." This verse states that the Gospel call goes out to the world, and within that call are those who are chosen to be saved. So this is a generic call to the world, and only those who respond are those who are qualified to respond.

So by the modern versions omitting *the*, they are basically stating that all things work together for good to those who love God, and they would include the unbelievers in that. This is erroneous as *the called* is referring only to the body of believers. Based on John 15:18, I seriously doubt that God is going to work things out for the unbeliever, seeing that they hate Him. "If the world hate you, ye know that it hated me before it hated you" (John 15:18, KJV).

Romans 9:28

> For he will finish the work, *and cut it short in righteousness*: because a short work will the Lord make upon the earth. (Romans 9:28, KJV)

"And cut it short in righteousness" is omitted.
This verse is taken from Isaiah 10:22–23.

> For though thy people Israel be as the sand of the sea, yet a remnant of them shall return: the consumption decreed shall overflow with righteousness. For the Lord GOD of hosts shall make a consumption, even determined, in the midst of all the land. (Isaiah 10:22–23, KJV)

The work of salvation will be cut short, which means it will be a quick termination. When the Lord Jesus Christ went to the cross, He finished the work of salvation. "When Jesus therefore had received the vinegar, he said, It is finished: and he bowed his head, and gave up the ghost" (John 19:30, KJV). Now, the only part left is the calling and sealing of those who would be born in the future until the last one is saved. From the viewpoint of eternity, the work is already finished; and if you notice, the work was cut short in righteousness. The righteousness is the righteousness that was imputed to every believer. By omitting this portion from the verse, it removes the type of work that will be done on the earth, and that is salvation by grace, which imputes righteousness. The Mosaic law was in use for 1,500 years, but the sacrifice of Christ—and thus, the sealing of all the elect—was done in six hours on Calvary and confirmed by His resurrection on Sunday. The modern versions omit this fact, which affects all Christians.

Romans 9:31

> But Israel, which followed after the law of righteousness, hath not attained to the law *of righteousness.* (Romans 9:31, KJV)

"Of righteousness" is omitted.

Israel had rejected the Lord Jesus Christ as their Messiah, and it was only through Him that salvation could be attained. Instead of embracing the Lord Jesus Christ, they had attempted to attain salvation by keeping the law of righteousness. Now, there is no one on this earth who could keep the law perfectly. If there was a way to keep the law perfectly, then the cross would not have been needed. However, we know that keeping the law right down to the most minute detail is impossible for any human. This verse teaches that Israel had set before itself the impossible mission of keeping the law of righteousness to attain righteousness, which would be salvation. Their goal had eluded them with every sin they committed and were never able to attain the law of righteousness. Without the imputed righteousness of Christ, there would be no way a person could stand righteous before God.

The modern versions omit the goal that was the law of righteousness and just leave a nebulous law on the end of their verse. One could ask, what law? The King James Bible keeps the specific law in the text, and we know that trying to attain the law of righteousness by keeping the law of righteousness is an impossible task. There are many laws in God's law that a person can attain, but they must keep every single law, and therein lies the inability of any person to be able to do so. The only way we can attain the law of righteousness is in Christ, who fulfilled the demands of God's holy law in its entirety. The King James Bible once again shows it deals with specifics and does not keep a person guessing as to the meaning of a verse.

Romans 9:32

Wherefore? Because they sought it not by faith, but as it were by the works *of the law*. For they stumbled at that stumblingstone. (Romans 9:32, KJV)

"Of the law" is omitted.

The modern versions leave out a very important piece of information "of the law." The argument of grace versus law for salvation is a major theme in the New Testament. When the portion "of the law" is omitted, it could cause confusion about the works that a Christian does after salvation. "For we are his workmanship, created in Christ Jesus unto good works, which God hath before ordained that we should walk in them" (Ephesians 2:10, KJV). Salvation can never be attained by keeping the law. Good works are a part of the responsibility of those who have already become saved as we read in Ephesians 2:10. Once again, the King James gives us the specific truth.

Romans 10:1

Brethren, my heart's desire and prayer to God for *Israel* is, that they might be saved. (Romans 10:1, KJV)

Israel was changed to "them."

Romans 10:1 falls right in the middle of the discourse Paul is having concerning his desire to see Israel saved. Paul was also the apostle to the Gentiles, which means when the specific name *Israel* was changed to the generic "them," it took away the specific meaning of the passage. As we have noted in the past, God always speaks in specifics. The modern versions could make it seem like Paul was hoping that all the Gentiles would be saved when he was speaking of Israel. That would have been out of context for this passage.

Romans 10:15

And how shall they preach, except they be sent? as it is written, How beautiful are the feet of them

that preach the gospel *of peace*, and bring glad
tidings of good things! (Romans 10:15, KJV)

"*Of peace*" is omitted.

One of the greatest aspects of the true Gospel is that it not only
saves an individual for eternity, but it causes a cessation of hostility between God and the saved person. "Therefore being justified
by faith, we have peace with God through our Lord Jesus Christ"
(Romans 5:1, KJV). Before a person becomes saved, they are at
war with God because of them being in sin; but once that person is
saved, the war is over, and that is why it is called the Gospel of peace.
However, the modern versions omit those two little words that carry
with them an immense teaching as we just saw.

The modern versions just about change that truth from the
Gospel of peace to good news. What is the difference? The Gospel
always speaks about the saving power of the Lord Jesus Christ, but
when these words are reduced to only "good news," it can take on
the meaning of someone is blessed because they bring good news.
Now, "good news" can mean that some anchor on a news show is
bringing good news (for a change), but does that mean they are
blessed for doing so? The answer is no! If God wanted to use the
term *good news* instead of *gospel*, He could have done so, but He
chose to separate the Gospel from any intimation or association
with worldly news. Once again, the King James keeps a proper
separation between the two while the modern versions make no
distinctions.

Romans 10:17

So then faith cometh by hearing, and hearing by
the word of *God*. (Romans 10:17, KJV)

God is changed to "Christ."

The word in the Greek text is *theos*, which is translated "God."
The Hort-Westcott text changes it to *christos*, which is translated
"Christ." It was the Lord Jesus Christ who inspired His authors of

the Bible, and He was the one at Sinai who gave Moses the law. By changing *God* to "Christ," what they are doing is removing the fact that Christ is God when He gave the words of scripture.

Romans 11:6

> And if by grace, then is it no more of works: otherwise grace is no more grace. *But if it be of works, then is it no more grace: otherwise work is no more work.*

"*But if it be of works, then is it no more grace: otherwise work is no more work*" is omitted

"Even so then at this present time also there is a remnant according to the election of grace" (Romans 11:5, KJV). Here, Paul points out the great differences between grace and works. He continues the thoughts from verse 5 that, at present, there is a remnant who is saved by grace. The works-grace battle has been going on for thousands of years, but the bottom line is that works can never save anyone. What is presented here is an either-or situation. Either you are under a covenant of works as Israel was for many years, or you are saved and under the covenant of grace, which means you have become saved. You are part of the seven thousand (vs. 4). However, if you insist on trying to keep the law, then you will not be under grace. The Judaizers who followed Paul had tried to get the people to keep the law while under grace. They added that and claimed that keeping the law of Moses was a necessary part of salvation, and without it, one could not be saved.

The Gnostics of the second century would have fallen right in line in believing that works were necessary for salvation. They believed they were saved by increasing their knowledge. Grace came through the Lord Jesus Christ. "For the law was given by Moses, but grace and truth came by Jesus Christ" (John 1:17, KJV). Since the Gnostics did not believe that Christ had come from heaven and that He was the Son of God, God incarnate, they would have removed anything that would remotely connect Him with salvation. The

Gnostics believed that He had become Christ while He was here on Earth.

The change in this verse has Origen's name attached to it in the UBS fourth edition of the Greek. Origen was definitely a Pagan and a Gnostic and would have deleted the second half of this verse because it did not fit in with his belief system. Keep in mind that Origen was just one of the Gnostics at Alexandria, and any of them could have made any of the changes. There is no reason given why the last part of this verse was removed, so we may safely conclude that it was removed because works is an integral part of all religions outside of true Christianity and was removed because of the systematic prejudices of the Gnostics.

Romans 12:8

> Or he that exhorteth, on exhortation: he that giveth, let him do it with *simplicity*; he that ruleth, with diligence; he that sheweth mercy, with cheerfulness. (Romans 12:8, KJV)

Simplicity is changed to liberality or generosity.

The word we must look at is *haploteti*. It does carry with it the idea of being "liberal or generous" when used in its proper context. However, in Romans 12:8, the word is translated properly by the King James translators as "simplicity," which carries with it the meaning of "singleness or sincere without self-seeking." In other words, the giving is done with a single mind-set; that is, to further the kingdom of God without the giver looking for some type of payback in favors or anything. In today's terms, we would call it pay for play. This is why the word *simplicity* is used because it speaks of a person giving without making any demands on the one who is being given the money. Millions of dollars are given to political campaigns with the giver expecting favors in return. Millions of Christians all around the world give to further the kingdom of God without any expectation of a favor from the one or the ministry receiving the donation.

Romans 13:9

> For this, Thou shalt not commit adultery, Thou
> shalt not kill, Thou shalt not steal, *Thou shalt not
> bear false witness,* Thou shalt not covet; and if there
> be any other commandment, it is briefly compre-
> hended in this saying, namely, Thou shalt love thy
> neighbour as thyself. (Romans 13:9, KJV)

"Thou shalt not bear false witness" is omitted.

This is another one of those deletions where no reason is given as to why it was removed. However, the name of Origen does appear beside the commentary in the UBS fourth edition of the Greek. Origen was a pagan and not a Christian and had much to do with the corruption of the true Antiochan manuscripts. Romans 13:9 is a borrowed quotation from the episode of the rich young ruler from Matthew 19:19, when Jesus told him that he would have to keep the commandments to inherit eternal life. The commandments Jesus gave this ruler were the part of the Decalogue, which deals with one another. The first four deals with our relationship to God, and the other six deals with our relationship to one another.

Why they would leave out "Thou shalt not bear false witness" is another mystery. They keep the other ones in and delete this one, which makes no sense; and as I have already stated, there is no rea-son given as to why this was done. It was just another attack on the words of the Lord Jesus Christ. It just shows how untrustworthy the modern versions are since they follow the corruptions of the second century Alexandrian Gnostics.

Romans 14:6

> He that regardeth the day, regardeth it unto the
> Lord; *and he that regardeth not the day, to the Lord
> he doth not regard it.* He that eateth, eateth to
> the Lord, for he giveth God thanks; and he that
> eateth not, to the Lord he eateth not, and giveth
> God thanks. (Romans 14:6, KJV)

"And he that regardeth not the day, to the Lord he doth not regard it" is omitted

Let us continue the thought from verse 5. "One man esteemeth one day above another: another esteemeth every day alike. Let every man be fully persuaded in his own mind" (Romans 14:5, KJV). A Christian who celebrates Christmas and Easter may do so for the purpose of using it as a testimony of the Gospel because these are the only two times in a year that unbelievers become a little religious, and Christians can capitalize on it by using these days as evangelistic tools. The ones who do not celebrate them may tell others that these are pagan festivals and that Christians should not celebrate anything linked to pagan festivals. Do you see how both views can be used to the glory of God? That is why there should be no divisions in the body over these matters since both sides can capitalize on them for witnessing purposes.

It is the same thing with food. There are Christians who eat questionable foods yet see it as coming from the hand of the Lord, and therefore, they are thankful for those provisions. The one who is weak continues to eat the herbs and gives thanks for those herbs since he knows that is from the hand of God that those herbs come from. The one who does not eat certain foods does not eat those foods unto the Lord. In other words, as the one who eats those questionable foods eats them unto the Lord, those who do not eat those questionable foods are not eating them unto the Lord. If there is a steak and a vegetable platter on the table and two Christians approach that table, one who eats steak will take the steak, but the one who eats vegetables will take the vegetable platter. So if I believe that we should not be eating meat, then I would not be eating the steak unto the honor of the Lord. There is obedience in both camps in the realm of food.

When the modern versions leave out this large portion of scripture, they leave out half the account. There is much validity in Christians partaking of things lawful as there is of those who do not partake. The Roman Catholic Church has created many different days with many different feasts, which they want their adherents to celebrate; and if anyone studies their methods, these days were created to collect money from the parishioners. This is why false churches would want to leave out the fact that those who do not celebrate these days would be doing it to the glory of God, but a person must be saved before they can do anything to the glory of God. False churches and teachers want to only emphasize that celebrating certain days are to the glory of God and not the other way around. These false versions give too much leeway to the leaders of false religions. It is better to stay with the King James and get the entire thought from the word of God and not the mind of man.

Romans 14:9

> For to this end Christ both died, *and rose*, and revived, that he might be Lord both of the dead and living. (Romans 14:9, KJV)

"And rose" is omitted.

This is one of the subtlest yet blatant attacks on the bodily resurrection of Christ. The King James Bible specifically states that Christ "both died and rose." This tells us in no uncertain terms that Christ rose physically from the dead. By omitting "and rose," it can give credence to the long-held belief that Christ did not rise physically from the grave but rose spiritually. The Discovery Channel aired a program trying to convince the world that the earthly tomb of Jesus was discovered and that He did not bodily rise from the dead. This would add weight to the belief that he only rose spiritually. There are many cults that believe this. The great hope of the Christian is that if we die physically before the return of the Lord Jesus Christ, we will experience the resurrection of our bodies unto eternal life.

When the modern versions omit the fact that Jesus bodily rose from the dead, they are also removing the great hope of every Christian. Sure, in this verse, the modern versions say He lived again, but they neglect to say that He lived again by His resurrection from the dead. It can be easily interpreted that He lived again spiritually instead of in His fleshly body.

Romans 14:10

But why dost thou judge thy brother? or why dost thou set at nought thy brother? for we shall all stand before the judgment seat of *Christ*. (Romans 14:10, KJV)

Christ is changed to "God."

In this verse, we read that the Lord Jesus Christ is going to be the judge of all the unsaved on the last day. We see in the two verses below how Romans 14:10 is in concert with 2 Corinthians 5:10 and John 5:22, where the Lord Jesus tells us that the Father will judge no one but all final judgment has been committed to the Son.

For we must all appear before the judgment seat of Christ; that every one may receive the things done in his body, according to that he hath done, whether it be good or bad. (2 Corinthians 5:10, KJV)

For the Father judgeth no man, but hath committed all judgment unto the Son. (John 5:22, KJV)

Once again, the modern versions break continuity on a cardinal doctrine of the faith. The Lord Jesus Christ is not only Savior of the elect but the judge of the unsaved. In the Gnostic text, we read that "Christ" has been changed to "God." There is no reason given for this change, but again, when we understand that the Gnostics taught that Jesus was not born Christ but became Christ in his lifetime, we will understand that this is nothing more than another attack on the deity of Christ.

And I saw the dead, small and great, stand before God; and the books were opened: and another book was opened, which is the book of life: and the dead were judged out of those things which were written in the books, according to their works. (Revelation 20:12, KJV)

When we look at Revelation 20:12 in a description of the great white throne judgment, we read that all the unsaved will be standing before God. We know that the Lord Jesus Christ is God and that He is the one who will do the judging. We see this especially when we compare scripture with scripture as we have done. The Gnostics and the modern theologians question and attack the deity of Christ and therefore have left this verse as the second-century Gnostics had corrupted it.

Romans 14:21

It is good neither to eat flesh, nor to drink wine, nor any thing whereby thy brother stumbleth, *or is offended, or is made weak.* (Romans 14:21, KJV)

"Or is offended, or is made weak" is omitted.

This verse warns believers that our actions can have three consequences in the lives of other believers. The first is that a weaker brother can stumble. The word is in the present, active, indicative, which means that our actions may cause a weaker brother to "strike or beat against." If a brother sees us committing a sinful action without any remorse, then they might also begin to act sinfully and worse than the one who is offending. They would be striking out against the teachings of scripture. The mushrooming effect of sin is devastating in the life of any believer, but it is worse in a weaker brother or sister. The second consequence that is omitted from the modern versions is a weaker brother will be offended. The word *offended* in the Greek is where we get our word *scandal.* When a weaker brother sins without remorse, it can create a great scandal in the body of Christ and can also cause a scandal from the unbelievers who see these actions. The third effect that is omitted from the modern versions is that a brother or sister is weakened. If we act sinfully in front of a weaker brother or sister, they will become weaker in their Christian walk, especially if they adopt the habits we are exhibiting in front of them.

God warns that Christians must be attuned to those weaker brethren all around us because we can convey the wrong attitude and thereby create dreadful circumstances in the life of a younger believer. It is a shame that the modern versions do not seem to care about the nurturing responsibility of mature believers. Then again, it is hard to mature when using a false version. I personally knew a minister who used the NKJV and believed that drinking highballs, beer, and women wearing short skirts are a part of Christian liberty. Need I say more?

Romans 14:22

Hast thou faith? have it to thyself before God.
Happy is he that condemneth not himself in that
thing which he alloweth. (Romans 14:22, KJV)

"Hast thou faith?" is changed to "the faith that you have." A question is changed to a statement.

Here, the question is asked if you have faith? Now, the subject here is not of salvation, but do you have faith in what you are eating or doing? If you do, then if your brother or sister stumbles with what you are doing, then you need to keep the faith to yourself so there will be no stumbling on part of the weaker brethren. If you are doing something that does not cause a rift in your own conscience because it is something that is not causing another to stumble, then you are happy. The word *happy* is the same word used for "blessed."

One of the great blessings of the Christian walk is the capability of helping another Christian grow. "Train up a child in the way he should go: and when he is old, he will not depart from it" (Proverbs 22:6, KJV). We have seen this verse from Proverbs used many times concerning the training of children, but we can widen the meaning in that when we help train a new Christian in the proper way, then they will not depart when they are older in the faith, as many have done already. So training for a new Christian is very important, and it is not only book training but practical training as well. That is why we are to never cast a stumbling block before any Christian, even those who are in the faith longer. A Christian who is saved for a long time does not necessarily mean they have matured commensurate with the years of being saved. Even a Christian who is saved for many years can be an immature believer. We never know, and that is why we must walk according to the scriptures. The modern versions turn this question into a declarative statement. It needs to be kept as a question to challenge the one who is doing introspection, which is basically commanded in the scriptures. "Examine yourselves, whether ye be in the faith; prove your own selves. Know ye not your own selves, how that Jesus Christ is in you, except ye be reprobates?" (2 Corinthians 13:5, KJV).

Romans 15:8

Now I say that *Jesus* Christ was a minister of the circumcision for the truth of God, to confirm the promises made unto the fathers. (Romans 15:8, KJV)

Jesus is omitted.

Every once in a while, I like to include verses where the divine name of the Lord Jesus Christ has been tampered with, always keeping before us the hatred the modern versions have for Him. As we get closer to a single world religion, the title *Christ* will be stolen by many who believe they are the coming *One*. It is imperative that we keep the name of the Lord Jesus Christ intact because it separates the generic title from the specific title naming Jesus as the true Messiah.

Romans 15:24

Whensoever I take my journey into Spain, *I will come to you*: for I trust to see you in my journey, and to be brought on my way thitherward by you, if first I be somewhat filled with your company. (Romans 15:24, KJV)

"*I will come to you*" is changed to "I hope to see you in passing by or passing through."

Paul had sent word to the Roman Christians that when he journeys to Spain, he will make it a priority to stop and come to them for a time. He was hoping to meet these Christians and to be refreshed by their company. The King James Bible teaches that Paul was going to make an intentional visit to them. The modern versions omit this and make it sound like, as Paul passed by, he would only be able to see them quickly in passing and would have no time of fellowship with them, which is not what the scriptures teach. Paul loved to visit the Christians wherever he was and to fellowship with them. He had intimate fellowship with Christians wherever he visited.

Romans 15:29

> And I am sure that, when I come unto you, I shall come in the fulness of the blessing *of the gospel* of Christ. (Romans 15:29, KJV)

"*Of the gospel*" is omitted.

This verse conveys a very important truth. The blessings from Christ comes through the true Gospel and not just indiscriminately. By the modern versions omitting this great fact, false preachers can claim they have the blessing of Christ on their ministries just because they have a big church. A Catholic priest may think he has the blessing of Christ on him because he has a big parish or because he has many converts. When we compare the false religions that think they have the blessing of Christ on them to the scriptures, we find they have the curse of Christ upon them. The true blessings of God come through the true Gospel, and it is a travesty that the modern versions omit this fact. It is really an amazing fact to me that many men in media ministry are big proponents of the ESV. They claim to know so much Gospel yet accept the horrible butchering of the Bible. It is obvious that all these "geniuses" really do not know the Bible. Jesus had it so right when He said, "At that time Jesus answered and said, I thank thee, O Father, Lord of heaven and earth, because thou hast hid these things from the wise and prudent, and hast revealed them unto babes" (Matthew 11:25, KJV). We can be so thankful that God has preserved His word in the King James Bible and has not left us at the mercy of the "intellectual elite."

Romans 16:18

> For they that are such serve not our Lord *Jesus* Christ, but their own belly; and by good words and fair speeches deceive the hearts of the simple.

Jesus is omitted.

Once again, we see the name of the Lord Jesus Christ broken up. In this particular verse, the name of *Jesus* is omitted, and they use the term "Lord Christ." The name *Jesus* is important because it gives specific identity of who the Lord is and who Christ is. Otherwise, in the day we live in, the identity can be changed to a New Age teacher such as Maitreya, who claimed to be the Christ who has returned.

Romans 16:24

> The grace of our Lord Jesus Christ be with you all. Amen. (Romans 16:24, KJV)

The entire verse is omitted or placed in brackets.

This verse is a reoccurring benediction in the New Testament. For example, in 1 Corinthians 16:23, "The grace of our Lord Jesus Christ be with you" (1 Corinthians 16:23, KJV). There is no reason given as to why this verse has been removed and no reason given as to why it remains omitted. One of the greatest teachings in the Bible is the grace of God whereby we are saved, so it would fit the belief system of the Gnostics and other unbelievers to remove it since so many false belief systems are rooted in works. Once again, the King James Bible proves that it retains all the truth that God wrote in it and is not subjected to the whims of the unbeliever as the modern versions are.

1 Corinthians 1:14

I thank God that I baptized none of you, but
Crispus and Gaius. (1 Corinthians 1:14, KJV)

"I thank God" is changed to "I am thankful" in the ERV, JB
PHILLIPS, LB, THE MESSAGE, NIRV, NLV, RSV, VOICE.

Here is another case where Paul is thanking God, who is the
object of his thankfulness. When somebody states they are thankful
without an object of that thanks, then they are not thankful. These
eight modern versions omitted God, which is just another attack on
God the Father as the recipient of our thankfulness for what He has
done in our lives. "Theo" (God) is definitely written in the Textus
Receptus.

1 Corinthians 1:21

For after that in the wisdom of God the world
by wisdom knew not God, it pleased God by the
foolishness of preaching to save them that believe.
(1 Corinthians 1:21, KJV)

"Foolishness of preaching" is omitted and calls the Gospel
"foolishness."

Here is one of those verses that have words added to them in the
English that should not be there. The King James Version teaches us
that it is through the proclamation of the Gospel how God saves a
person. "So then faith cometh by hearing, and hearing by the word of
God" (Romans 10:17, KJV). The modern versions call the message
of the Gospel foolish. The wording no way implies that the message
that is preached is foolish, but the method whereby a person is saved
will seem like foolishness. The world thinks they can do works to
please God and make it to heaven, but the foolish aspect is that God
saves through the proclaiming of His Word and to the world that
would seem foolish. "For I am not ashamed of the gospel of Christ:
for it is the power of God unto salvation to every one that believeth;
to the Jew first, and also to the Greek" (Romans 1:16, KJV).

The gospel is the power of God unto salvation, and therefore, the message would not be considered foolishness, only the method of delivery, because it completely excludes any kind of works. Once again, the modern versions completely destroy the biblical message in this verse while making an attack on the Gospel by labeling it as "foolishness."

1 Corinthians 2:4

> And my speech and my preaching was not with enticing words of *man's* wisdom, but in demonstration of the Spirit and of power. (1 Corinthians 2:4, KJV)

"Man's" is omitted.

"Howbeit we speak wisdom among them that are perfect: yet not the wisdom of this world, nor of the princes of this world, that come to nought" (1 Corinthians 2:6, KJV). One of the great gifts that God gives every true believer is the wisdom of God Himself. In this verse, we have another confusing situation. The modern versions omit the word "man's" when speaking about the wisdom, which we are not to use when we bring the Gospel. The modern versions make it sound like we are not to use any wisdom. First Corinthians 2:6 above teaches us that we are to use the wisdom of God whenever we bring the Gospel. The wisdom of man likes to adulterate the gospel with many worldly teachings such as psychology, sociology, or other man-made disciplines that neutralize the true Gospel. That your faith should not stand in the wisdom of men, but in the power of God (1 Corinthians 2:5, KJV).

Our faith is not to stand or abide in the wisdom of man but the power of God, which is the unadulterated Gospel. When the Gospel is not mixed with anything worldly, it is the power of God unto salvation. "For I am not ashamed of the gospel of Christ: for it is the power of God unto salvation to every one that believeth; to the Jew first, and also to the Greek" (Romans 1:16, KJV). This is why the modern versions confuse the issue concerning wisdom. We must use the wisdom of God and not the wisdom of man. This distinction is lost in the modern versions.

1 Corinthians 2:13

> Which things also we speak, not in the words which man's wisdom teacheth, but which the *Holy* Ghost teacheth; comparing spiritual things with spiritual. (1 Corinthians 2:13, KJV)

Holy is omitted.

Jesus told the disciples that when He went back to heaven, He would send the Holy Spirit, and part of the ministry of the Holy Spirit will be to bring to remembrance what the Lord Jesus taught and to open up the scriptures to us. He is the third Person of the Godhead and is as Holy as the Father and the Son. This is why He can be grieved when we sin. The modern versions omit the important adjective of *holy*. That omission is just another attack upon the cardinal doctrine of the Holy Spirit. We see omissions like this, and then we are told that the modern versions do not affect any cardinal doctrines. Yeah, right!

1 Corinthians 3:3

> For ye are yet carnal: for whereas there is among you envying, and strife, *and divisions*, are ye not carnal, and walk as men? (1 Corinthians 3:3, KJV)

"And divisions" is omitted.

The mark of an immature Christian or congregation is the level of strife it sustains. If there is a consistent squabbling in the church, there will never be any type of Christian growth. In fact, if the church does not come into biblical guidelines, Christ may remove the candlestick from it and will go apostate. One of the marks of an apostate church is the glorification of the people who do the most "good works." When that happens, you know they are a works-based church and are completely void of what the church is supposed to be.

Paul mentions the same problem in the church at Galatia, when he chides them for having the same type of problems. Jealousy, rivalry, and divisions are not the traits of a true Christian church.

The modern versions omit the fact of "divisions" in the church at Corinth, which is also a warning to the modern church that divisions can also occur because of infighting. The word for *division* in the Greek carries with it the idea of dissension. The word *dissension* carries with it the meaning of "strife, quarreling, discord and contention in words." When these things are present in any congregation, it basically sounds the death knell for that particular church. This is why God placed it in the Bible to warn congregations when there are divisions beginning to form so they can be extinguished before the church suffers a split or dissolution. In either case, it is not a good testimony to the world. The modern versions offer no warnings against divisions, but the King James does in hope to save any church struggling from that problem.

1 Corinthians 5:1

> It is reported commonly that there is *fornication* among you, and such *fornication* as is not so much as named among the Gentiles, that one should have his father's wife. (1 Corinthians 5:1, KJV)

Both usages of *fornication* has been omitted and replaced with "sexual immorality."

Here is a case where the modern versions have softened the meaning of this verse. In this chapter, Paul is dealing with the church at Corinth for not disciplining a man who has committed fornication with his father's wife. The specific charge against this man is fornication. The modern versions changed it to "sexual immorality," which can have a wide meaning, but Paul is being specific about the church as he speaks of fornication in verses 9, 10, and 11.

Sexual immorality does not necessarily mean a person having sex with someone who is not their spouse but can have a number of meanings such as suggestive speech, being nude, or just evil thoughts, etc. In Corinth, there were a number of pagan temples that featured prostitution as a part of their religion, and the Bible calls it fornication. There is no difference between having sex with a prostitute or another woman who is not a spouse since both are specifically considered fornication. One of the main features of the modern versions is that they reduce the severity of sin, as in this case.

1 Corinthians 5:4

In the name of our Lord Jesus *Christ*, when ye are gathered together, and my spirit, with the power of our Lord Jesus *Christ*. (1 Corinthians 5:4, KJV)

Christ is omitted.

This verse received two hits with the Gnostic scissors. Both times, the name *Christ* is removed from the text. The name *christos* in the Greek is written both times in the verse in the Textus Receptus.

1 Corinthians 5:5

To deliver such an one unto Satan for the destruction of the flesh, that the spirit may be saved in the day of the Lord *Jesus*. (1 Corinthians 5:5, KJV)

Jesus is omitted.

The Lord Jesus is going to judge this world when He returns. This verse removes the name of *Jesus*, thus making only the day of the Lord, omitting the fact that it is the specific day of the Lord Jesus.

1 Corinthians 5:7

Purge out therefore the old leaven, that ye may be a new lump, as ye are unleavened. For even Christ our passover is sacrificed *for us*. (1 Corinthians 5:7, KJV)

"For us" is omitted.

If there is one thing that God deals in, it is specifics, as we have seen many times before. Man deals in the nebulous. The two words that are omitted are very important because they specifically state who the Lord Jesus Christ died for. He died only for His people. "And she shall bring forth a son, and thou shalt call his name JESUS: for he shall save his people from their sins" (Matthew 1:21, KJV). The Matthew verse states that Jesus came to save *His* people from their sins. Who are His people? Those whom He has saved.

The modern versions just state that Jesus was sacrificed, but the reason for His sacrifice is open for interpretation by anyone and any system. Christ died for His elect chosen from the foundation of the world. "According as he hath chosen us in him before the foundation of the world, that we should be holy and without blame before him in love" (Ephesians 1:4, KJV). The modern versions leave Christ's sacrifice without reason, and therefore, many believe they are saved when they are not. Once again, the King James Bible does not leave us without the proper understanding of the atonement of Christ.

1 Corinthians 6:20

For ye are bought with a price: therefore glorify God in your body, *and in your spirit, which are God's.* (1 Corinthians 6:20, KJV)

"And in your spirit, which are God's" is omitted

The omitted part is definitely a Gnostic attack on the doctrine of the Holy Spirit. The omitted part teaches us that the Holy Spirit indwells the true believer. The Gnostics did not believe that the Spirit of God could dwell in filthy flesh, so they rejected the idea of the indwelling of the Holy Spirit. The omission in this verse is another proof of their rejection of the spirit world. Alexandria, Egypt, was the hotbed of Gnosticism, and the first manuscript to reject this part of the scripture was the Alexandrinus manuscript, which came from Alexandria, Egypt, in AD fifth century. Two of the most famous Alexandrian Gnostics were Clement of Alexandria and Adamantius

Origen. No way was Origen a great church father because it was under his tutelage that the manuscripts from Antioch were corrupted. Yet the modern scholar believes and teaches that Origen was a great Christian and church father, and because of that, they base their modern versions on his work.

Once again, by using the King James Bible, we avoid all the corruption that Satan's minions have thrown into the mix. There is no one more confused in the body of Christ than a Christian who believes they can use a few modern versions to understand God's word. How many of us would like to undergo surgery by a surgeon who reads books in school according to the same way they corrupt the Bible? Would it give you confidence in that surgeon knowing that the part of the book that describes your problem was omitted? He who has ears to hear!

1 Corinthians 7:1

> Now concerning the things whereof ye wrote unto me: It is good for a man not to *touch* a woman. (1 Corinthians 7:1, KJV)

Touch is changed to "marry" or "sexual relations."

One of the mutilations of this verse comes when some of the modern versions state that it is not good to have sexual relations with a woman. If I was a sodomite, I would definitely buy that version to prove that even God is against men having sex with women. If men do not have sexual relations with women, then please tell me, where does the next generation come from? This verse is not implying total abstention from sexual relations in marriage.

Another mutilation of this verse comes when some of the modern versions state that it is good for a man not to get married. This, of course, would fit perfectly into Roman Catholic theology concerning the priesthood. The Bible in 1 Timothy 4:3 lumps the idea of "forbidding to marry" with doctrines of demons. This verse does not speak of marriage, but marriage is mentioned in the next verse. To prevent fornication, the Bible is stating that marriage should take place. Some of the modern versions state that it is good if a man does not marry, but in the next verse, it states they should be married. It sets up a confusing scenario. "Nevertheless, to avoid fornication, let every man have his own wife, and let every woman have her own husband" (1 Corinthians 7:2, KJV).

1 Corinthians 7:5

> Defraud ye not one the other, except it be with consent for a time, that ye may give yourselves to *fasting and* prayer; and come together again, that Satan tempt you not for your incontinency. (1 Corinthians 7:5, KJV)

"Fasting and" is omitted.

Fasting can be an integral part of one's personal devotion to the Lord. Fasting is not necessarily a time where one deprives themselves of food and water. What if a person decides to physically fast while praying for a spouse? What would happen to them if God willed them to be single? They would never eat or drink again.

> Is not this the fast that I have chosen? to loose the bands of wickedness, to undo the heavy burdens, and to let the oppressed go free, and that ye break every yoke? (Isaiah 58:6, KJV)

Isaiah 58:6 speaks of a fast but it is a fast whereby spiritual activity is replacing other activities. It speaks of giving out the Gospel. There must be harmonious consent on both partners to come apart for a while. Now when this verse speaks of fasting and prayer, it is speaking that within the confines of marriage, there must also be set aside time for spiritual work as well. Christian marriage is not all physical bliss but there must be time for spiritual things such as church attendance, Bible study, teaching the children, etc. Now this verse also tells us that after these spiritual activities, you may go back to being intimate again. Sometimes religious couples get so religious that they begin to think that sex is dirty, and that opens the door for Satan to tempt the deprived spouse. God is saying that He knows very well that because we are in the flesh, it has an intense enticement on us and He is saying that we are once again allowed to be intimate so Satan does not attempt to tempt and adulterate the marriage. So by the modern versions omitting fasting in this context, they are omitting a great spiritual lesson.

1 Corinthians 7:34

> *There is difference also between a wife and a virgin.* The unmarried woman careth for the things of the Lord, that she may be holy both in body and in spirit: but she that is married careth for the things of the world, how she may please her husband. (1 Corinthians 7:34, KJV)

"There is difference also between a wife and a virgin" is omitted.

Here, the Bible is teaching us that there is a difference between a married woman and a virgin. What is in view here is the marriage relationship as it relates to ministry. We are being told that those who are unmarried will have more time for ministry, and those who are married will have less time for ministry. This is in no way stating that those who are unmarried and are able to spend more hours in ministry are somehow holier and more obedient to the Lord. The Bible here is stating that there is a difference between the married woman and the unmarried woman concerning the arena of ministry.

Why the modern versions left out that leading sentence is a mystery. It gives an introduction into the subject of marriage. Those who want to get married must realize that their ministry time will be cut down. If one chooses not to marry, then they will be able to continue unabated in ministry.

The unmarried woman cares more for the things of the Lord. She is able to be holy (separated unto) in both body and spirit in dedication of herself to the work of the Lord without division or diversion in her walk. She is able to dedicate more time and resources for the work of the Lord.

She who is married must dedicate herself to her marriage. The married woman must commit herself to her marriage and the responsibilities of that marriage. While her heart's desire is to be fully dedicated unto the Lord, yet because of family responsibilities, she is unable to dedicate as much time as a single woman can. However, there is one thing that must be realized: that God did not give the family as an excuse to evade ministry. Families can have wonderful ministries if the parents rule the children instead of the other way around.

1 Corinthians 7:39

> The wife is bound *by the law* as long as her husband liveth; but if her husband be dead, she is at liberty to be married to whom she will; only in the Lord. (1 Corinthians 7:39, KJV)

"By the law" is omitted.

The modern versions omit the fact that marriage is a covenant by removing the phrase "by the law." When we were unbelievers we were under the law but when we became saved, we were freed from that law by the death of Christ who became our new husband. Previously, we were married to the law, but when Christ went to the cross and died for His people, then we became dead to our first husband, the law, because Christ fulfilled all the requirements of God's holy law, and we became known as the bride of Christ. Like the wife who is bound by the law to her first husband—and then, when her husband dies, she is free to marry in the Lord—all are bound to the law of God. But when one becomes saved, they are freed from the demands of the law because Christ already fulfilled it. So the first marriage is a marriage of bondage to the law, but the second marriage is a marriage of freedom in grace. Not only must we born again, we must also be married again. Great truths are compromised because of one omitted phrase.

1 Corinthians 8:4

> As concerning therefore the eating of those things that are offered in sacrifice unto idols, we know that *an idol is nothing in the world*, and that there is none other God but one. (1 Corinthians 8:4, KJV)

"An idol is nothing in the world" is changed to "there is no such thing as an idol in the world" in the NASV.

> Therefore concerning the eating of things sacrificed to idols, we know that there is no such thing as an idol in the world, and that there is no God but one. (NASV)

Someone reading this verse for the first time, especially a new Christian, will be very confused since idolatry is mentioned quite frequently throughout the Bible.

1 Corinthians 9:1

> Am I not an apostle? am I not free? have I not seen Jesus *Christ* our Lord? are not ye my work in the Lord? (1 Corinthians 9:1, KJV)

Christ is omitted.

Here is another Gnostic attack on the Lord Jesus Christ. The Gnostics did not believe that Jesus was the Messiah, nor was He God manifest in the flesh. What the Gnostics have done is to separate the name of the Lord Jesus from His divine title of Christ. This is why the modern versions have kept the truncated form of the divine name because the modern versions espouse Gnosticism. Gnosticism was alive and well even in the first century.

1 Corinthians 9:18

> What is my reward then? Verily that, when I preach the gospel, I may make the gospel *of Christ* without charge, that I abuse not my power in the gospel. (1 Corinthians 9:18, KJV)

"Of Christ" is omitted.

Here is another case of the nebulous gospel being offered in the modern versions. They omit "of Christ," which tells us specifically which Gospel Paul is speaking of. This same omission was also done to Romans 1:16.

> For I am not ashamed of the gospel *of Christ*: for it is the power of God unto salvation to every one that believeth; to the Jew first, and also to the Greek. (Romans 1:16, KJV)

> I am not ashamed of the gospel, because it is the power of God for the salvation of everyone who believes: first for the Jew, then for the Gentile. (Romans 1:16, NIV)

> What then is my reward? That, when I preach the gospel, I may make the gospel without charge, so as not to use to the full my right in the gospel. (1 Corinthians 9:18, ASV)

By omitting "of Christ" the modern versions attempt to detach the true Gospel from the living Gospel, who is Christ Himself. There are many gospels in this world, but only the Gospel of the Lord Jesus Christ can save. The modern versions are almost a "you fill in the blank and make it say what you want." We must only be concerned with what God said, and it is apparent from all these corruptions that you will not find it in the modern versions.

Paul then went on to explain the reward he received. He rejoiced in the fact that he could bring the Gospel of Christ without requesting any funds to do so, which means that he was not abusing his power. Basically, what he is saying is that he can bring the Gospel with pure motives. He also did not have to be concerned with the anxious thoughts of something like, "How much are they going to give me, or will it be enough to live on?" Paul makes what he knows he needs, and that frees him up to bring the Gospel without any shackles on it in the area of money.

1 Corinthians 9:22

> To the weak became I *as* weak, that I might gain the
> weak: I am made all things to all men, that I might
> by all means save some. (1 Corinthians 9:22, KJV)

As is omitted.

Paul now reminds these Corinthians of the weak brethren he spoke of in the previous chapter, plus many who are new Christians and still weak in the faith. He identified with these people to be able to grow them in the faith. Paul did not overwhelm those who are new in the faith, and neither should we. Then Paul states that he chose to identify himself with all people for the purpose of bringing the true Gospel to them. The sign of a great missionary is to place themselves on the same level as those who are being witnessed to.

Whenever we go out to the streets to witness, we always try to identify with the people whom we are trying to reach. We must keep in mind that at one time, we were all unbelievers holding to some type of worldly philosophy. By identifying with the group we are witnessing to, it keeps our pride from flaring up. This is why the scripture uses the word *as*. In the Greek, the word *hos* is a relative adverb that is a particle of comparison. Let us look at two examples from the scriptures:

> But, beloved, be not ignorant of this one thing,
> that one day is with the Lord *as* a thousand years,
> and a thousand years as one day. (2 Peter 3:8, KJV)

In 2 Peter 3:8, we see the word *as*, which is making a comparison of one thousand years and one day. The verse does not say that a day is a thousand years or a thousand years is a day. It is making a comparison to eternity that time is of no value in eternity because there is no measurement of time as we know it.

> When I was a child, I spake *as* a child, I understood as a child, I thought as a child: but when I became a man, I put away childish things.
> (1 Corinthians 13:11, KJV)

Here, Paul speaks about when he was child, he spake as a child would speak. Then he stated that he understood as a child understands. He makes another comparison. When he was a child, he spoke as a child speaks, but when he grew up, he put away childish things. Now back to 1 Corinthians 9:22. The modern versions claim that he became weak to reach the people who are weak. So according to the modern versions, if someone had a weakness with drinking alcohol, then Paul became a drunk to reach them, which is ridiculous. The King James Bible places *as* in that verse according to the true text, and it instead does not say Paul became a sinner to reach sinners, but he identified with them and understood where they were and reached them at that level. If I know someone with a gambling problem, do I become a gambler to reach them, or try to understand the motivations behind gambling and then reach them? A very big difference indeed.

1 Corinthians 9:27

> But I *keep under my body*, and bring it into subjection: lest that by any means, when I have preached to others, I myself should be a castaway.
> (1 Corinthians 9:27, KJV)

"Keep under my body" is changed to "buffet or beat my body" (teaches self-abuse).

Here is another example of the modern versions using the wrong words to convey the wrong idea. The apostle Paul is telling his readers that he keeps his body under subjection, so he would not obey the fleshly impulses and sin, which could cause him to be a hypocrite and a castaway. If he is sinning in his life, then he loses the right to instruct others. So Paul is conveying the idea of tough discipline to keep his body in line with his Christian testimony.

The modern versions in this list are giving a false idea as to how a Christian should keep their body disciplined. One of the words is *buffet*, which carries with it the meaning of "a slap, a blow with the fist, or to beat." Another word they use is *pummel* or *pommel*, which carries with it the meaning of "pound or beat." The Douay Rheims edition uses the term *chastise*, and when we look at the biblical use of that word, we find it used twice in the New Testament, both in reference to the scourging of Jesus.

It must also be noted that this type of chastisement was a common practice in the Catholic monasteries in the Middle Ages. Martin Luther flogged himself many times trying to tame the fleshly lust of the body. Then the other two words are *striking a blow* and *punishing*. The ideas of self-flagellation is present in these modern version verses. Nowhere in the Bible is the believer supposed to physically hurt themselves to gain greater spirituality. The believer buffets their body through the power of the indwelling Holy Spirit. There is a danger in these modern versions when they proclaim physical beating because someone may do this and cause death to themselves or others.

1 Corinthians 10:9

> Neither let us tempt *Christ*, as some of them
> also tempted, and were destroyed of serpents.
> (1 Corinthians 10:9, KJV)

Christ is changed to "Lord."

This is one of the biggest attacks on the Lord Jesus Christ. What is being recounted in this section is that fact that Israel had angered the Lord, and He sent serpents among the people, and those who were bitten had died. Israel had partaken in idolatry, and that is what the Corinthians did. Paul brought up the serpent event to show the Corinthians that it is a short distance from sensuality and compromise to full idolatry. In 1 Corinthians 10:9, we are also being told that they tempted or tried the Lord, and the "Lord" in this case is told to us as Jesus Himself. He is the Great I Am of Sinai. This is why in Matthew 23:37–38, Jesus laments over Jerusalem concerning them killing the prophets. Jesus is looking at their entire history and not just the present.

> O Jerusalem, Jerusalem, thou that killest the prophets, and stonest them which are sent unto thee, how often would I have gathered thy children together, even as a hen gathereth her chickens under her wings, and ye would not! Behold, your house is left unto you desolate. (Matthew 23:37–38, KJV)

Then a few verses before in Matthew 23:34, we read that it was Jesus who sent the prophets, which means that He is confirming that He is the Great I Am who directed the wanderings of Israel in the desert. "Wherefore, behold, I send unto you prophets, and wise men, and scribes: and some of them ye shall kill and crucify; and some of them shall ye scourge in your synagogues, and persecute them from city to city" (Matthew 23:34, KJV). When the modern versions remove *Christ* and replace His name with the generic *kurion* or *Lord*, they are denying an important teaching that Christ was the one who guided Israel and brought them through the wilderness. It is another attack on the doctrine of Christ. When they remove this information, they are removing Christ's involvement with the nation of Israel in the Old Testament. Christ came through the nation of Israel, and therefore He was guiding His own lineage.

1 Corinthians 10:11

> Now *all* these things happened unto them for ensamples: and they are written for our admoni-

tion, upon whom the ends of the world are come.
(1 Corinthians 10:11, KJV)

All is omitted.

God is giving warning to the Christians living in the last days, which commenced from the time of the cross. God is making sure we know that all the things that happened to Israel were for examples for us because if we too walk in the flesh, then we can expect the same situations to occur. The modern versions omit the word *all* and make it sound like only those few things in this chapter happened to Israel when, in reality, everything that happened to Israel in their entire history is a warning to the church. Just as Israel suffered some defeats in their history such as at AI, many churches today think that they can do things their way and have suffered defeats by means of being weakened and the blessing of God off them. This is because the modern-day church does not take the warning of the consequences that happened to apostate Israel.

One example is that when they went into Babylon, they had basically exchanged the scriptures for the Talmud. It is akin to the King James Bible being taken out of the church and replaced with the ESV. Once the true scriptures are removed from any milieu, the only thing that can be expected is weakness and judgment on that establishment, and this we have copiously seen in almost every church where they chose to replace the true scriptures with a counterfeit. When God tells us that *all* these things happened to them as examples to us, then we better investigate things before we make any moves in the church, or that church will suffer the same things Israel did, and that is to be removed from the faithful churches on earth.

Below, we read that if a church does not remain faithful, then the Lord Jesus Christ will remove their candlestick, as we read in Revelation 2:5. And when we look at Revelation 1:20, we see that the candlestick is the church itself and not just a part of it.

> Remember therefore from whence thou art
> fallen, and repent, and do the first works; or else I
> will come unto thee quickly, and will remove thy

candlestick out of his place, except thou repent.
(Revelation 2:5, KJV)

The mystery of the seven stars which thou sawest in
my right hand, and the seven golden candlesticks.
The seven stars are the angels of the seven churches:
and the seven candlesticks which thou sawest are
the seven churches. (Revelation 1:20, KJV)

1 Corinthians 10:28

But if any man say unto you, This is offered in sacrifice unto idols, eat not for his sake that shewed it,
and for conscience sake: *for the earth is the Lord's,
and the fulness thereof.* (1 Corinthians 10:28, KJV)

"For the earth is the Lord's, and the fulness thereof" is omitted.

The omitted part of this verse is taken from Psalm 24. "A Psalm
of David. The earth is the LORD's, and the fulness thereof; the world,
and they that dwell therein" (Psalm 24:1, KJV). The psalmist is assuring the true believer that the world belongs to the Lord by reason of
Him being the Creator. If someone offers a Christian food that was
offered to idols, then for a testimony, we are not to eat of it. We know
that the world belongs to the Lord and that idols are nothing more
than man's imagination, yet they can hold influence over any person
involved in a false religion. Just look at India where there are many
millions of gods that are worshipped. Our testimony is to avoid what
is sacrificed to idols.

The Thessalonian Christians had a great testimony concerning
the turning away from idols. "For they themselves show of us what
manner of entering in we had unto you, and how ye turned to God
from idols to serve the living and true God" (1 Thessalonians 1:9,
KJV). Now, let us bring the idols down to today. When we go to
work, there are no idols in front of the company, but are idols still
present? The answer is yes. Let's mention a few. The idol of greed
worshipped through office pools or group-lottery purchases. The idol

of sex worshipped through the eyes of lust when looking at someone in the office. The idol of laziness worshipped through slacking off when the boss is not looking. I think you get the picture. We, as the Thessalonians, must put off all forms of idolatry, no matter how subtle they may be. Idolatry is a learned lifestyle. Why the modern versions left off the part of the verse that deals with the Lord as the owner of the earth is a mystery. Nevertheless, they left it out, and it is an important part of understanding the verse.

1 Corinthians 11:24

> And when he had given thanks, he brake it, and said, *Take, eat*: this is my body, which is *broken* for you: this do in remembrance of me. (1 Corinthians 11:24, KJV)

"Take eat" and *"broken"* are omitted.

The Greek words for "take," "eat," and "broken" are omitted in the following corrupted manuscripts: p46, Aleph, A, and B. The omission of these three vital words removes the heart out of this verse; plus, it attacks the sacrifice of Christ for His people. During the Last Supper, the Lord symbolically broke bread and told His disciples that this represented His body, which was going to be broken for them the next day. Breaking bread is not just Christian fellowship, but it celebrates the relationship that the true Christian has with the Lord Jesus Christ. That word *broken* was showing that the Lord Jesus was going to suffer much physical pain and suffering, and to remove that word was to remove the reality and severity of what was going to take place.

He also made His disciples partakers in His suffering by means of giving them the broken bread. The Bible teaches that we are so intimate with Christ that we are members of His flesh and bones. "For we are members of his body, of his flesh, and of his bones" (Ephesians 5:30, KJV). When Christ gave them the bread, it was telling them that in order for them to become saved, it was necessary for Him to suffer. And just as each of them tore a piece of the bread, His body would be torn in like manner. "And said unto them, Thus it is written, and thus it behoved Christ to suffer, and to rise from the dead the third day:" (Luke 24:46, KJV).

For the modern versions to omit the fact that Christ's body was going to be broken for us is to omit the crucifixion. Of course, it follows that the Gnostics of the second century would not believe that the crucifixion of Christ purchased the salvation for all the elect, so they and their modern counterparts had to exclude this from the text.

This verse is normally read along with the rest of 1 Corinthians 11:23–34 on the day when the church celebrates communion. We are remembering the death and resurrection of the Lord Jesus Christ and His anticipated return on the last day. In the marriage ceremony, the Bible teaches that the husband's body belongs to the wife, and the wife's body belongs to the husband. "The wife hath not power of her own body, but the husband: and likewise also the husband hath not power of his own body, but the wife" (1 Corinthians 7:4, KJV). They are given to each other wholly, but the Lord Jesus Christ, in taking His bride, was required to have His body broken according to the scriptures. So when the word *broken* is omitted, it omits a great spiritual lesson and lessens the sacrifice of Christ. When the words "take," "eat" are left out, they remove the intimacy that the believer has with the Lord Jesus Christ. "For we being many are one bread, and one body: for we are all partakers of that one bread" (1 Corinthians 10:17, KJV).

So the next time your pastor uses a modern version at communion, you will see the emptiness of those words versus the reality of what took place. You can give your body to someone without suffering. You can give it to them in service, or a husband or wife can give it to each other in pleasure. But the word *broken* brings a special meaning to a special relationship between Christ and His church. If Christ's body was not broken, then we are still in our sins.

1 Corinthians 11:29

For he that eateth and drinketh *unworthily*, eateth and drinketh damnation to himself, not discerning the *Lord's* body. (1 Corinthians 11:29, KJV)

Unworthily and *Lord's* are omitted.

In this verse, the Gnostic hit squads removed two very important words: *unworthily* and *Lord's*. This verse deals with the Lord's Supper and teaches a very important principle. Those who are unworthy to take the Lord's Supper are those who are unsaved. "Thou hast a few names even in Sardis which have not defiled their garments; and they shall walk with me in white: for they are worthy" (Revelation 3:4, KJV). We read in the letter to Sardis that those who have not defiled their garments were worthy. Those who are in Christ are made worthy because of the sacrifice of Christ.

First Corinthians 11:29 gives a stern warning to those who are unsaved that they drink damnation to themselves simply because they think they are partaking of the Lord's supper, and this somehow makes them worthy for heaven. This could not be any further from the truth. When a person becomes saved, they are made worthy and are permitted to take the Lord's Supper. Unbelievers should never partake in the Lord's Supper, and that is why churches must only give communion to those who are saved. By removing the word *unworthily*, they are opening the door for the belief that all may partake of the Lord's Supper and that it could be considered some kind of ritual rather than a remembering of the Lord's sacrifice and looking forward to His return. A great deception takes place when the unworthy are led to believe they are worthy.

Then they removed the word *Lord's*, and this once again takes away the specific nature of this verse. The body that is in view is the Lord's body and no one else's. Without the word *Lord's*, anybody can be in view. It could be the body of any belief system. It could be the body of believers. It could be the church body with unbelievers in it. The Corinthian Christians were guilty of making the Lord's Supper a common feast instead of looking at the solemnity of it. If a person is a true believer, they will never suffer damnation of hell since all their sins have been paid for.

The word *damnation* in this verse may also be understood as "judgment." Unbelievers already have the wrath of God abiding on them, but the true believer can bring temporal judgment upon themselves by living a life in opposition to the principles of scripture. Any

Christian who does not understand the deep spiritual and solemn nature of the Lord's supper is in danger of being judged by God. Yes, a believer can suffer the judging hand of God. Remember David when he sinned with Bathsheba? The consequence of his sin was the death of his child. This is why we are never to treat communion as something common. By removing *Lord's*, they once again attack the Lord Jesus Christ by removing a specific allusion to His body.

1 Corinthians 12:13

> For by one Spirit are we all baptized into one body, whether we be Jews or Gentiles, whether we be bond or free; and have been all made to drink *into one Spirit*. (1 Corinthians 12:13, KJV)

"Into one spirit" is changed to "of one Spirit."

The word *into* as used in the King James Bible is a preposition that carries the meaning of "toward, to, unto." It is the Greek word *eis*.

> A bruised reed shall he not break, and smoking flax shall he not quench, till he send forth judgment *unto* victory. (Matthew 12:20, KJV)

> And while they looked stedfastly *toward* heaven as he went up, behold, two men stood by them in white apparel. (Acts 1:10, KJV)

> Now concerning the collection for the saints, as I have given order *to* the churches of Galatia, even so do ye. (1 Corinthians 16:1, KJV)

The word *into* in English is a very strong word that carries with it the meaning of "some type of motion which will terminate once the toward or unto has been achieved." In other words, the word denotes finality or goal reached.

> Know ye not, that so many of us as were baptized
> into Jesus Christ were baptized into his death?
> (Romans 6:3, KJV)

In Romans 6:3, we read that the Christian has been baptized into Christ. In other words, once we are in Christ and united with Him in spiritual baptism, the goal has been reached because we can never lose that unity with Christ, to wit, our salvation. When we drink into one Spirit as our verse teaches, we have reached the pinnacle of wisdom and salvation. Our lives as Christians are always geared toward the Holy Spirit. He is the one we seek for wisdom and understanding.

> Howbeit when he, the Spirit of truth, is come,
> he will guide you *into* all truth: for he shall not
> speak of himself; but whatsoever he shall hear,
> that shall he speak: and he will shew you things
> to come. (John 16:13, KJV)

The modern versions lose this great teaching by making it sound like we drink from the Spirit as we drink water. Our focus must be on the Spirit and the understanding He gives to the Christian.

> For by one Spirit are we all baptized into one
> body, whether we be Jews or Gentiles, whether
> we be bond or free; and have been all made to
> drink into one Spirit. (1 Corinthians 12:13, KJV)

1 Corinthians 14:25

> *And thus* are the secrets of his heart made man-
> ifest; and so falling down on his face he will
> worship God, and report that God is in you of a
> truth. (1 Corinthians 14:25, KJV)

"And thus" is omitted.

This is a very important omission because it connects verse 24 with 25. In verse 24, Paul is speaking about prophesying, which is the preaching of the true Gospel, and that it is superior to the speaking in tongues. If a person comes into the assembly and hears the true preaching of the Gospel, he will be convicted in his heart and will then worship God. Now, the omission of "and thus" is what separates the two verses when, in essence, they need to be connected by the conjunction and adverb. In the Greek text, the words that are missing are *kai houtos*, which means "in this manner, in this way, without further ado." Now let us connect the verses using these important words.

> But if all prophesy, and there come in one that
> believeth not, or one unlearned, he is convinced
> of all, he is judged of all: And thus [in this man-
> ner] are the secrets of his heart made manifest;
> and so falling down on his face he will worship
> God, and report that God is in you of a truth.
> (1 Corinthians 14:24–25, KJV)

Here, we see that the proclamation of the true Gospel will bring about repentance in a person. So what God is telling us here is that, in this manner, when the true Gospel is proclaimed or preached, it will then have the desired effect of convicting a person of sin. The idea of just having a band, repetitive choruses, and a watered-down sermon will never bring about the convicting of a person of their sin. God is telling us straight that the true Gospel is the only way a person can become convicted. He is also telling us that it is only "in this way" that the proclamation of the Gospel will be effective. The modern versions omit these words and makes it sound like there is no catalyst for a person to become convicted in their hearts about their sin. The catalyst is the true preaching of the convicting Gospel, and in this manner, people will become saved.

1 Corinthians 14:34

Let *your* women keep silence in the churches: for
it is not permitted unto them to speak; but they
are commanded to be under obedience, as also
saith the law. (1 Corinthians 14:34, KJV)

Your is changed to "the."

Here, the apostle Paul is laying down some principles of obedience in the church. When this verse is looked at in the light of verse 35, he is specifically speaking to the women who were married. They are to learn from their husbands at home. This is why he uses a word *your*, which is a genitive case, the case of possession. By using the word *your*, he is in keeping with the principle found in Genesis 3:16. "Unto the woman he said, I will greatly multiply thy sorrow and thy conception; in sorrow thou shalt bring forth children; and thy desire shall be to thy husband, and he shall rule over thee" (Genesis 3:16, KJV). The principle that the wife is in subjection to the husband is now carried over into the church. This is why Paul uses a specific word like *your* instead of the generic term *the*, which is found in the modern versions, thus causing a disconnect in the context with verse 35. In the case of an unmarried woman, she is to be under the authority of the elders; or if she is too young to be married, under the authority of her father.

1 Corinthians 14:38

But if any man be *ignorant*, let him be *ignorant*.
(1 Corinthians 14:38, KJV)

Ignorant is changed to "recognize or accept" (both instances).

Here, Paul is beginning his summation that if someone is ignorant, not understanding the word of the Lord, then let him remain that way. The church must never change the rules for those who do not wish to grow in the faith. The word *ignorant* means "not understanding." If a person wants to understand and grow, then the elders should teach them; but if they choose to remain ignorant, as many do today, then let them remain that way to their own shame. The modern versions use words like *recognize*, which means "seeing something a second time." It is a different meaning than ignorant.

The phrase "let him be ignorant" is in the present tense, active voice, imperative mood. The present tense means the ignorance is always present in a person. The active voice means they are doing something to fight against knowledge or understanding. The imperative mood in this case is not a command because Paul would never command someone to remain ignorant because his whole ministry was bringing understanding of the mystery of the Gospel. In this case, it is basically a request or entreaty, as if Paul is entreating a superior. He is stating that if a person wants to remain ignorant, then let them, and others should progress in the Christian walk.

1 Corinthians 15:3

> For I delivered unto you first of all that which I also received, *how* that Christ died for our sins according to the scriptures. (1 Corinthians 15:3, KJV)

How is omitted.

How is a conjunction where Paul is stating that he delivered to the Corinthians what he received, and then the conjunction joins the two parts of the sentence where he gives them the information how Christ died for our sins according to the scriptures.

1 Corinthians 15:47

> The first man is of the earth, earthy: the second man is *the Lord* from heaven. (1 Corinthians 15:47, KJV)

"The Lord" is omitted.

There is no reason given as to why the words *the Lord* was removed from the above manuscripts. By removing these words, they have removed the heavenly testimony of the Lord Jesus Christ because these words specifically identify Him as the second Adam who came from heaven to redeem His elect. The removal of these words also attacks the deity of Christ because He is the Lord from heaven. This way, they make the Lord Jesus just another man without any divine attributes.

1 Corinthians 15:55

O death, where is thy sting? O *grave*, where is thy victory? (1 Corinthians 15:55, KJV)

Grave is changed to "death."

One of the greatest promises in the Bible for the Christian is that just as the Lord Jesus Christ rose from the dead, the Christian will be raised from the dead on the last day. "I will ransom them from the power of the grave; I will redeem them from death: O death, I will be thy plagues; O grave, I will be thy destruction: repentance shall be hid from mine eyes" (Hosea 13:14, KJV). The apostle Paul and Hosea had much in common when they both wrote jubilantly about the abolition of death. The sting of death has disappeared because of the resurrection of Christ and the future resurrection of His followers. The grave may have a temporary victory on this side because it holds the people we love and it stops many ministries from continuing, but in the light of the resurrection, where does the grave hold any victory? The grave had no power over Christ, and it will have no power over the believers. Hosea mentioned the grave, but the modern versions try to make the connection by omitting the term *grave* and replacing it with "death." Once again, the King James Bible shows good harmony among passages.

1 Corinthians 16:22–23

If any man love not the Lord *Jesus Christ*, let him be Anathema Maran-atha. The grace of our Lord Jesus *Christ* be with you. (1 Corinthians 16:22–23, KJV)

Verse 22, *"Jesus Christ,"* is omitted. Verse 23, *"Christ,"* is omitted.

The omissions in these verses are nothing more than another attack upon the divine character of the Lord Jesus Christ. In verse 22, the Gnostics omitted the full identity of who the Lord is. In verse 23, the Gnostics, omitted the divine title of the Lord Jesus Christ. The modern versions show a continuing hostility to the Lord Jesus Christ throughout their pages. Since the Bible is about the Lord Jesus Christ and the plan of salvation, I do not know how anyone can call their modern version a Bible since they vilify the very central figure of the Bible. Staying with the King James avoids all the heresies and attacks by the ancient Gnostics and their modern adherents.

2 Corinthians 1:10

> Who delivered us from so great a death, *and doth* deliver: in whom we trust that he will yet deliver us. (2 Corinthians 1:10, KJV)

"And doth" is changed to "he will."

The word *doth* in the King James Bible is in the present tense. It is replaced in the modern versions with a future tense. Paul gives glory to God that he rescued him out of all the afflictions that came his way. At this point, Paul is also trusting God that He will deliver him from both present and future tribulations that may threaten his life. A great principle emerges here in that God will continue to deliver His people out of these tribulations until the time that a Christian's life and work on earth is done. Paul still had some years to go in service to God, and that is why God kept delivering him from tribulations until, one day, Paul was on the chopping block. God did not deliver him from that because Paul's work on earth was done, and now it was time for his eternal rest.

2 Corinthians 2:15

> For we are unto God a sweet savour of Christ, in them that *are* saved, and in them that perish. (2 Corinthians 2:15, KJV)

Are is changed to "are being."

Here is another example of the modern versions questioning the salvation status of every believer. The Greek word *sodzomenois*, which is translated for "are," is in the present tense. This means that it is speaking of those who are already saved, and although this word can possess a future tense, it is not designated here. Many in religion see salvation as an ongoing process and must be accomplished over time. However, the Bible tells us that each one who has become saved has been saved at one point in time. It is sanctification that is a life-long journey and not salvation. We become saved at one point in life, and then we begin to become sanctified. "For this is the will of God, even your sanctification, that ye should abstain from fornication" (1 Thessalonians 4:3, KJV). The New Age movement sees salvation as something that takes years to accomplish, but their salvation is much different from the salvation given by God.

In 2 Corinthians 2:15, we are a sweet savour to those who are saved already. The modern versions make it sound like we are a sweet savour to those "being saved." If they are being saved, then we are not a sweet savour to them because they are still unsaved, and we are a savour unto death to them as verse 16 states. The big issue here is that the modern versions are teaching that salvation is a process and not a single event. This is a false teaching because if salvation is a process, then how many works must we do? How long must we do them? How would we know they would be accepted by God? And probably a string of other questions that would have to be posed. It is good that we have the King James Bible to give us the truth about salvation and not make us think that salvation is a process.

2 Corinthians 2:17

> For we are not as many, which *corrupt* the word of God: but as of sincerity, but as of God, in the sight of God speak we in Christ. (2 Corinthians 2:17, KJV)

Corrupt is changed to "peddle."

This is another situation concerning a word meaning. The KJV, 1611 KJV, Tyndale, and Bishop's Bible understood the meaning to be a corruption of God's word. Tyndale and the Bishop's Bible both have the correct idea of this word when they translated it "chop and change." The Greek word behind *corrupt* does come from a merchandising term, but it took on the meaning of "someone who sells goods deceitfully." The word is *kapeleuo*, which carries with it the idea of "peddling, hawk, trade, or corrupt." It is like someone in a market who puts the best produce on top and the bad on the bottom. It is a deceitful sales gimmick. The bad product will eventually corrupt the good product.

The term *corrupt* would be a problem for the new-version editors since they have been corrupting the word of God since 1881, so it was necessary for them to give it a surface meaning and turn it into a meaning of someone who peddles the word of God for profit. Paul did fight against the idea of financial profit from preaching, and he did what he could to avoid any accusations in that area. However, the subject in view goes deeper than just financial hawking. It is the corruption of God's word that is the subject of this verse. This why the Bishop's Bible and Tyndale had it right when they translated it "chop and change" because this is what is happening to the word of God, especially in our day.

> For we are not as many are which choppe and chaunge with the worde of God: but even oute of purenes and by the power of God and in the sight of God so speake we in Christ. (Tyndale Bible 1526)

> For we are not as many are, whiche chop & chaunge with the word of God: but as of purenesse of God, in the syght of God, so speake we in Christe. (Bishops Bible 1568)

Modern-version editors are chopping up the word of God, and this chopping causes massive changes that result in substantial corruption. It goes way beyond a simple financial gain from God's word to the actual corruption of it. By replacing the word *corruption* with words that deal with financial gain in the modern versions, it removes any suspicion of someone using a corrupted modern version.

Second Corinthians 2:17 is a warning about the corrupting of God's word. There are two basic ways to corrupt God's word: The first is by actually deleting and omitting verses or phrases from the text. The second is subtler, and that is to skew an interpretation away from a core truth and replace it with conjecture favorable to the false teacher or teaching.

2 Corinthians 4:6

> For God, who commanded the light to shine out of darkness, hath shined in our hearts, to give the light of the knowledge of the glory of God in the face of *Jesus* Christ. (2 Corinthians 4:6, KJV)

Jesus is omitted.

Quite a number of the modern versions have omitted the name of Jesus in this verse, thus "chopping" His name in two to remove the name of Jesus from being associated with His deity.

2 Corinthians 4:10

> Always bearing about in the body the dying of *the Lord* Jesus, that the life also of Jesus might be made manifest in our body. (2 Corinthians 4:10, KJV)

"The Lord" is omitted.

The modern versions omit "the Lord," which is a divine title of the Lord Jesus Christ. The Gnostics did not believe that Christ was God or even divine, so they did what they could to lessen the fact that He was the incarnate Son of God. The King James Bible glorifies the Son by preserving all the divine titles that were penned by the holy men of old under the inspiration of the Holy Spirit.

2 Corinthians 4:14

Knowing that he which raised up the Lord Jesus
shall raise up us also *by* Jesus, and shall present us
with you. (2 Corinthians 4:14, KJV)

By is changed to "with." (The change gives the implication
that Christ will be raised on the last day when the Christians will be
raised. It denies the resurrection of Christ on the third day.)

Here is one of the craftier changes in the modern versions. If
you notice in the King James, it states that God is going to raise us
up from the dead by Jesus Christ. If you notice in the modern versions, it states that God is going to raise us up with Jesus. The Jesus
of the modern versions is still dead in His tomb if God is going to
raise Him up with us. The King James portrays Christ in truth that
He is alive, and it is by Him that God is going to raise us up on the
last day. This verse teaches us that Christ is going to be the means by
which the true believers are raised to eternal life.

The modern versions change the Greek preposition from *dia*,
which means "by or through," to *sun*, which means "with, together
with, or besides." This means the modern versions are teaching that
Christ is going to be raised along with all the other believers on the
last day. This would fit perfectly into Roman Catholic beliefs since
their Jesus is still hanging dead on a cross. Once again, the King James
Bible gives us the true teaching about the Lord Jesus Christ while the
modern versions attack Him. Let us stay with the King James Bible
and know truth so we can be stable in our Christian walk.

2 Corinthians 5:12

For we commend not ourselves again unto you,
but give you occasion *to glory* on our behalf,
that ye may have somewhat to answer them
which *glory* in appearance, and not in heart.
(2 Corinthians 5:12, KJV)

"To glory" and *"glory"* is changed to "proud" and "pride."

Paul here defends his ministry, but he states that he is not going to recommend himself to them again as this was not necessary because there were those at Corinth who knew of his integrity. As Paul spoke of persuading men of the terror of the Lord, he had no other reasons at heart than to see people become saved and avoid the final judgment. Paul's integrity of heart and ministry was allowing the Corinthian Christians an opportunity to boast in the honest ministry of Paul, especially to those who were his detractors. Paul identifies these false teachers as having glory in appearance but not in heart. In other words, there were people in Corinth following these false teachers because of outward appearance, but their heart was spiritually dead. The Corinthian Christians could boast in Paul's heart because it was focused on the salvation of souls.

How many today are following preachers because of their outward appearance? The megachurches draw thousands of people, but they do not preach the stinging message of the true Gospel. They are ear-tickling gospels that minister to the flesh and keep a person in unsaved bondage. This mind-set was in total opposition to the true Gospel that Paul preached and what is preached by true Christians, who are normally removed from megachurches for being a troublemaker. The words behind both usages of *glory* never speak of pride or being proud. Paul would never advocate something like that, knowing it was pride that caused Lucifer to become Satan. Paul wanted the Corinthians to use his life as a comparison against those who are false teachers, and this way, they would glory in the ministry of Paul, knowing there was nothing false about it. The second usage of the word *glory* indicates that Paul and his honest ministry was the object of that glorying being in the accusative case.

2 Corinthians 5:17

> Therefore if any man be in Christ, he is a new *creature*: old things are passed away; behold, all things are become new. (2 Corinthians 5:17, KJV)

Creature is changed to "creation."

Here is a subtle change. The word *creature* is the correct rendering since the new heart was placed in our bodies, making us new creatures with the same body. The modern versions change it to "creation," but there is nothing new about our bodies being a new creation. A new creation would include a new body, but this will not happen until the last day therefore creature is the correct rendering.

2 Corinthians 5:18

> And all things are of God, who hath reconciled us to himself by *Jesus* Christ, and hath given to us the ministry of reconciliation. (2 Corinthians 5:18, KJV)

Jesus is omitted.

This is another attack upon the name of the Lord Jesus Christ. By chopping up His name they are, in essence, attacking the doctrine of Christ since His deity is a major part of that doctrine.

2 Corinthians 6:5

> In stripes, in imprisonments, in tumults, in labours, in watchings, *in fastings*. (2 Corinthians 6:5, KJV)

"In fastings" is omitted.

Here is another case of a wrong English word being used to convey the Greek. The word behind "fastings" is the word *nesteia*, which is translated "fasting" in its nine uses in the New Testament. "And when they had ordained them elders in every church, and had prayed with *fasting*, they commended them to the Lord, on whom they believed" (Acts 14:23, KJV). There is a perfectly good word for hunger that the Lord could have used, and that is *limos*. "And when he came to himself, he said, How many hired servants of my father's have bread enough and to spare, and I perish with *hunger*!" (Luke 15:17, KJV)

Second Corinthians 11:27 gives us both uses of both words and shows that they are different and how the modern versions botched this. "In weariness and painfulness, in watchings often, in hunger

[*limos*] and thirst, in fastings [*nesteia*] often, in cold and nakedness"
(2 Corinthians 11:27, KJV). So we see that the correct rendering
should be *fastings* and not *hunger*.

2 Corinthians 6:9

> As unknown, and yet well known; as dying, and,
> behold, we live; as *chastened*, and not killed.
> (2 Corinthians 6:9, KJV)

Chastened is changed to "beaten or punished."

Here is another case of the modern-version editors redefining
a word with an erroneous definition. Modern-version publishers
must exhibit enough change to warrant a new copyright and thus
to be able to publish a new version. The word in question is *paide-
umoneoi*, and it carries with it the meaning of "train, teach, correct,
or chastise." It never carries with it the meaning of "punishment"
or "being beaten with an inch of our life." Training and teaching
does not mean one is being beaten to make them learn. God creates
chastisement to fit each Christian to grow them in the faith, not to
beat them into an unhealthy submission like someone being tied to
a post and whipped. God trains us and teaches us to make us better
Christians and witnesses.

The modern versions have made it sound like God is a very evil
taskmaster with only a desire to beat us if we err. He is our Heavenly
Father, and He only desires the best for His children. Sometimes
He may have to chastise us intensely, but it is never in the judicial
or vengeful sense. Here is another example of the modern versions
giving us the wrong impression of God's dealings with His children.
They must change words and their meanings, even if it is blatantly
wrong, to get that copyright so they can sell because profit is their
goal, not truth.

2 Corinthians 7:4

> *Great is my boldness of speech toward you, great
> is my glorying of you*: I am filled with comfort,

I am exceeding joyful in all our tribulation.
(2 Corinthians 7:4, KJV)

"Great is my boldness of speech toward you, great is my glorying of you" is changed to "I have confidence in you or great is my pride in you."

Here is a verse where the modern-version translators have taken a Greek word and completely mistranslated it for this verse. The word behind "boldness" in the King James Bible is *parrhesia*, which is translated as "boldness, frankness, openly, fearlessness, or outspokenness." In several verses in the King James Bible, the word is translated as "confidence." They are Hebrews 3:6, Hebrews 10:35, 1 John 2:28, 1 John 3:21, and 1 John 5:14. The five uses of "confidence" in these verses are all aimed toward our confidence in the Lord Jesus Christ.

In Hebrews 4:16, we are told: "Let us therefore come boldly unto the throne of grace, that we may obtain mercy, and find grace to help in time of need" (Hebrews 4:16, KJV). Hebrews 4:16 uses the same word for *boldly*, and that is why we can have such confidence because of the salvation that is wrought in Christ. The modern versions twist the use of "confidence" and use it in a way that Paul has confidence in man. Paul's confidence was always in Christ and not men. "For we are the circumcision, which worship God in the spirit, and rejoice in Christ Jesus, and have no confidence in the flesh" (Philippians 3:3, KJV). There were times when Paul did have confidence in the Christians who were walking with Christ in obedience.

Our verse is focused upon the fact that Paul spoke with them in boldness when he was absent from them. "For his letters, say they, are weighty and powerful; but his bodily presence is weak, and his speech contemptible" (2 Corinthians 10:10, KJV). Paul had spoken very frankly to the Corinthians because of their continual disobedience, yet because of the fact that they had become obedient, Paul was now glorying in them. Paul knew that his relationship with the Corinthians was such that he could use great boldness of speech without fear of being misunderstood or rejected by them. Paul boasts in them because, as he has stated in the past, they were his crown as they would someday be in heaven with him. Paul was completely comforted because he had drawn much inspiration from their lives, and this resulted in Paul being joyful in times of tribulation.

Notice that Paul stated he was joyful and not happy. Joy is something that comes from inside because of our relationship to Christ, but happiness is determined by outward circumstances. Happiness can change in a moment while joy is a stable tenet of Christianity. To change "boldness of speech" to "confidence" constitutes a very bad translational error and changes the meaning of the passage.

2 Corinthians 8:4

> Praying us with much intreaty *that we would receive* the gift, and take upon us the fellowship of the ministering to the saints. (2 Corinthians 8:4, KJV)

"That we would receive" is omitted.

Here, we have the true essence of Christian giving. Paul did not beg the Macedonians to give a gift; rather, it was the Christians of Macedonia who had urged Paul to receive the gift. The Macedonian Christians had so willingly given a gift because they wanted to share in the helping of the needy brethren. These Christians had caught on to the idea of ministering to the needs of the saints. They had insisted that Paul take the money with him to the needy saints in Jerusalem. These Macedonian Christians were poor themselves, so they knew what that hardship was all about and could well identify with it. The modern versions omit the fact that the Macedonian church wanted Paul to take the offering with him. It shows the eagerness of this church to be obedient and compassionate to the Jerusalem church. The modern versions omit this great testimony of this church.

2 Corinthians 8:24

> Wherefore shew ye to them, *and* before the churches, the proof of your love, and of our boasting on your behalf. (2 Corinthians 8:24, KJV)

And between "them" and "before the churches" is omitted.

Paul is commending Titus and his entourage to the men of Corinth. Titus was in charge of the finances, and Paul was giving his approbation to their character. Paul then tells these men that they need to show their love to them as fellow brethren on a missionary journey but also to show their love and acceptance of them before the church. So there are two groups in view: the men who are accepting them and the church. But the modern versions reduce it to only group, the church.

2 Corinthians 9:10

> Now he that ministereth seed to the sower both *minister* bread for your food, and *multiply* your seed sown, and *increase* the fruits of your righteousness. (2 Corinthians 9:10, KJV)

Minister, multiply, increase omitted.

Here is a case of all three words being changed from the optative mood to the future tense, indicative mood. The optative mood is used only sixty-seven times in the New Testament, and it is used as a mood of possibility. In some instances, it may be used as a remote possibility. Paul uses it three times in this one passage, and the reason for that is because he is basically praying an obtainable prayer; that is, that God may supply, multiply, and increase their individual ministries. The modern versions take those three prayers and turn them into future tenses, which means that they will not receive the blessings of God today in their ministries. Then they change the word to the indicative mood, which means that the modern versions are stating that God will supply, multiply, and increase.

No one knows the will of God for each individual Christian, and that is why Paul uses the optative mood, which is a prayer that God may minister, may multiply, and may increase their ministry. Once again, the King James Bible gives us a real scenario in the area of individual ministry. No one can force God's hands to supply, multiply, and increase, and that is why we pray with the word *may* and not in a dictatorial approach.

2 Corinthians 10:4

For the weapons of our warfare are not carnal,
but mighty *through God* to the pulling down of
strong holds. (2 Corinthians 10:4, KJV)

"Through God" is omitted.

Many of the modern versions retain the fact that it is through God that we have our weapons of warfare. Some versions take the name of God and remove it, then replace it with the word *divine*. The word *theos* is the name for God in the entire New Testament. *Theos* is never translated "divine." The word *divine* is used in two specific places in the New Testament:

According as his *divine* power hath given unto
us all things that pertain unto life and godliness,
through the knowledge of him that hath called
us to glory and virtue: Whereby are given unto
us exceeding great and precious promises: that by
these ye might be partakers of the *divine* nature,
having escaped the corruption that is in the world
through lust. (2 Peter 1:3–4, KJV)

In both instances, the word *divine* is taken from the Greek word *theios*, which is an adjective and modifies the word *power* in 2 Peter 1:3, and modifies the word *nature* in 2 Peter 1:4. The word *theos* is a noun and is the name of God. There is no reason that these versions should have replaced the proper name of God with an adjective. Sometimes I seriously wonder if these Greek scholars can actually read Greek. In the world of religions like New Age, the term *divine* takes on a whole new meaning that humans are divine, or they are achieving divinity. This is why these versions that replaced the name of God with "divine" would fit right into New Age philosophy. So we are seeing how compatible some of these modern versions are with New Age thinking! Hold on, folks, it is only going to get worse!

2 Corinthians 10:7

Do ye look on things after the outward appearance? If any man trust to himself that he is Christ's, let him of himself think this again, that, as he is Christ's, even so are we *Christ's*. (2 Corinthians 10:7, KJV)

Christ's in the third usage is omitted.

Some of the Corinthians had judged Paul according to his appearance. They accused him of walking in the flesh, being weak in body, being bold in the flesh when he was absent from them, and that he was teaching falsely. These accusers were looking at the outward appearance instead of looking at the person himself. In 2 Corinthians 5:16, Paul stated that no longer do we see anyone after the flesh, but we see them as new creatures in Christ. Paul was chiding these false accusers because if they claim to be in Christ and they treat a fellow brother like they treated Paul, then they need to look at themselves to see if they really do belong to Christ. Having a very accusatory and censorious spirit does not exude the Christian personality.

Paul is reminding them that if they belong to Christ, so does He and his band, and they at least deserve the benefit of the doubt, if someone is doubting them rather than public excoriation. If there are any questions, it should be brought to them in private so the unbelievers would have nothing to accuse the body of. Unbelievers love it when Christians fight because it feeds their cause. The modern versions omit the third instance of Christ where Paul was stating specifically that he and his band were of Christ. That word *Christ* is in the genitive case, meaning *possession*—that is, Paul and his band were possessed by Christ.

2 Corinthians 11:6

But though I be *rude* in speech, yet not in knowledge; but we have been throughly made manifest among you in all things. (2 Corinthians 11:6, KJV)

Rude is changed to "unskilled or untrained."

Here is a good example of the superior English of the King James Bible. The translators picked the perfect word for this particular verse. The word *rude* comes from the Latin word *rudis*, which means "raw or rough." It is used only once in the New Testament. The Greek word behind it is *idiotes*, which carries with it the meaning of "unlearned or unskilled." It is translated as

"Ignorant" (Acts 4:13)
"Unlearned" (1 Corinthians 14:16; 1 Corinthians 14:23; 1
 Corinthians 14:24)

So we see that the word *idiotes* does carry with it the meaning of "unlearned, unskilled, or ignorant." Then why would the translators use the word *rude* in 2 Corinthians 11:6? The word *rude* in one of its lesser meanings does carry with it the idea of "unlearned," but the primary meaning is "coarse or rough." The answer is simple and obvious. Can anyone really claim that the apostle Paul was unlearned or ignorant? He had a history of great ability of speech since he had spoken to many crowds and before many dignitaries. Here are some examples:

The Synagogue at Antioch of Pisidia (Acts 13)
Paul addressing the mob at Jerusalem (Acts 21:40–22:22)
Paul before the Sanhedrin (Acts 23)
Paul before King Agrippa (Acts 26)

These are just four examples of the fact that Paul was a very capable speaker, so the word *unskilled* or *unlearned* would definitely have been a false description of Paul's ability for public speaking. Yet the modern versions accuse Paul of being unskilled and incapable of bringing the message. Now, the reason that the word *rude* was used in 2 Corinthians 11:6 is because many times, the behavior of the Corinthian church required Paul to be more coarse with them than normal while not insulting them or offending them. He was rude in speech with the desire to build them up and to bring them back on course. Sometimes it is necessary to be rougher than normal to cause Christians to think and to bring them back from a possible trek down the apostasy highway. "For I have not shunned to declare unto you all the counsel of God" (Acts 20:27, KJV).

Do you think the full counsel of God requires only soft soap and rose petals? The full counsel of God is a rough teaching to us because it requires us to be obedient to the point of death, and when we start straying, God has to bring us back. Many times, it is not a pleasant U-turn but a necessary one. By using the word *rude*, the KJV translators gave us a tremendous insight into Paul's dealings with a very rebellious church. This is just one instance that shows how God guided the translators of the KJV to give us really good understanding in English while the modern versions continue to translate words ambiguously.

2 Corinthians 11:31

> The God and Father of *our* Lord Jesus *Christ*, which is blessed for evermore, knoweth that I lie not. (2 Corinthians 11:31, KJV)

Our is changed to "the." *Christ* is omitted.

This verse has taken a double hit. First, the Gnostics removed the word *our* and replaced it with "the." The word *our* in Greek is in the genitive case, which is the case of possession. The apostle Paul was speaking about God the Father and then went on to state that He is the God and Father of *our* Lord Jesus Christ. The word *our* would reveal a double possession. Since God is the Father of our Lord Jesus Christ, this would make Him our Father also. It creates a family connection between the believer, God the Father, and God the Son. Replacing the word *our* with "the" removes the family connection we have with the Father and the Son. This is a great encouraging truth for the believer. When we become saved, we are taken into the family of God.

> Blessed be the God and Father of our Lord Jesus
> Christ, who hath blessed us with all spiritual

blessings in heavenly places in Christ: According
as he hath chosen us in him before the foundation
of the world, that we should be holy and without
blame before him in love: Having predestinated
us unto the adoption of children by Jesus Christ
to himself, according to the good pleasure of his
will. (Ephesians 1:3–5, KJV)

The second hit this verse took is the divine title of the Lord
Jesus, which is *Christ*. The Gnostics did not believe Christ was God
manifest in the flesh, so they have removed many references to Jesus
being Christ. The modern versions show how inferior they are by
belittling the Lord Jesus Christ and removing encouragement for the
true believer.

2 Corinthians 12:11

I am become a fool *in glorying*; ye have compelled
me: for I ought to have been commended of you:
for in nothing am I behind the very chiefest apostles,
though I be nothing. (2 Corinthians 12:11, KJV)

"In glorying" is omitted.

Paul had told the Corinthians that he was playing the fool when
he had boasted concerning himself and his ministry. It was unfortunate that the situation at the Corinthian church had forced him to
boast openly about his ministry, which was an apologetic boast and
not self-aggrandizement. Instead of the Corinthians commending
Paul and embracing him as a brother, they attached themselves to the
false teachers who constantly puffed themselves up. Paul states here
that he was not inferior to those great apostles who took Corinth
by storm with all their false teachings and self-promotion. If those
false apostles in Corinth would have been true apostles, then they
would have agreed with Paul about being "nothing," which means
that without Christ, he could have done nothing, nor could he have
done so much for the church at Corinth.

The modern versions omit the phrase "in glorying," which is exactly what Paul had in view. Without that phrase, it reads as if Paul had become a fool, a buffoon, in general, and in no way was Paul a fool like a court jester. He felt foolish that he had to give a dissertation on his qualifications and his sacrifices, which he made as a true apostle of Christ. He did this to show that the false apostles had not suffered at all, which means they lined up their message with the world system and told people what they wanted to hear. Paul suffered because he told people what they needed to hear, and that in no way makes him some kind of fool.

2 Corinthians 13:2

I told you before, and foretell you, as if I were present, the second time; and being absent now *I write* to them which heretofore have sinned, and to all other, that, if I come again, I will not spare. (2 Corinthians 13:2, KJV)

"I write" is omitted.

Here, Paul is basically saying that when he finally did come to Corinth, he was not going to spare any method to put to death the accusations that were made against him. Paul even had the right to use legal means. Paul desired to rid the church of all the evil that had invaded and then pervaded that church. Although there might have been some who did not believe the accusations against Paul, it always seems those who wreak havoc in churches always seem to get the preeminence instead of getting the boot. Paul is warning those who have sinned, but he wants everyone to know that if they follow in the footsteps of the false teachers and those who have sinned, then they will not be exempt from the punishment that the others will receive. This should also be a warning to all Christians that those who want to follow the wrong crowd in a church will face consequences. This was more than just a verbal promise; it became part of the written scriptures.

The modern versions omit that fact that Paul warned them by means of writing so that no words would be changed or softened or neglected. A written tract has the same words written in it, and it will not change over time. Take it off the shelf in one year, and it says the same thing when it was placed there. But words that are spoken verbally can be changed and made to fit the audience without any offense. Paul wanted to make sure his words were conveyed to all the people in the church at Corinth, and that is why the scriptures state that Paul wrote and not just made a verbal proclamation. In those days, there would have been no way for Paul to send a verbal message since everything had to be written and carried.

Galatians 1:3

> Grace be to you and peace from God the Father, and
> from *our* Lord Jesus Christ. (Galatians 1:3, KJV)

Our is changed to "the."

This verse shows how the relationship between the Lord Jesus Christ and His children are downgraded. In the text, the word *hêmôn* is a personal pronoun in the genitive case, which means that the child of God can legitimately claim the Lord Jesus Christ as our personal Savior. However, the modern versions once again distance that relationship as if we are introducing Christ as *the* Savior instead of *our* Savior. The modern versions tend to distance relationships whether between God and the Lord Jesus Christ or the Lord Jesus Christ and His children. This is why the modern versions are inferior because they take an eternal relationship and distance it. This is why the King James Bible is superior because it presents the relationships in their proper standing and does not make any attempt to separate.

Galatians 1:15

> But when it pleased *God*, who separated me from
> my mother's womb, and called me by his grace.
> (Galatians 1:15, KJV)

God is changed to "he" or "the one" in numerous versions.

Here is an interesting verse stating that God was pleased when He had separated Paul or selected him from his mother's womb. God knows who His elect are even before they are born. God had chosen all His elect before the foundations of the world. "According as he hath chosen us in him before the foundation of the world, that we should be holy and without blame before him in love" (Ephesians 1:4, KJV). Even though those of us who are saved became saved at different times in our lives, yet, all the elect of God were chosen before the foundation of the world. All the elect were set apart in our mother's womb, even if we do not get saved until later in life. This salvation is our calling by grace and grace alone.

It is interesting that Paul injects that he was saved from his mother's womb, and I believe the reason is that the Judaizers had emphasized works to coincide with grace for salvation. If a person is in the womb, then what works can they do to facilitate their salvation? The answer is obvious: they can do none, and this is why this verse is included because it shows that grace is the only vehicle by which a person can be saved, even in the womb where no works can be done. How could the Judaizers debate works with a person who was saved from the womb without works? This is the wisdom of the scriptures.

Some of the modern versions exchange *God* for "he," which leaves it open as to who "he" is. It is the Greek word *theos*, which means "God," not "the one" or "him." God is the one who sets the believer apart for salvation. "All that the Father giveth me shall come to me; and him that cometh to me I will in no wise cast out" (John 6:37, KJV). This is another attack on the doctrine of God concerning salvation.

Galatians 2:20

I am crucified with Christ: *nevertheless I live*; yet not I, but Christ liveth in me: and the life which I now live in the flesh I live by the faith of the Son of God, who loved me, and gave himself for me. (Galatians 2:20, KJV)

"Nevertheless I live" is changed to "I do not live" or "I no longer live."

This is one of those verses that has been worded in such a way as to cause confusion. The modern versions make it sound like Paul was crucified and was physically killed. Look at the NCV translation below.

> I was put to death on the cross with Christ, and I do not live anymore—it is Christ who lives in me. I still live in my body, but I live by faith in the Son of God who loved me and gave himself to save me. (NCV)

If we were reading this while living in the first century when crucifixion was the normal method of execution, we would automatically think that Paul was physically crucified with Christ. The modern versions leave out a very important phrase: "nevertheless I live." Paul was not speaking of him suffering a physical crucifixion but a spiritual crucifixion, which is borne by every single born-again believer. We no longer live the life of worldliness, but we now live the Christian walk where we are to crucify the lusts of the flesh and walk against the ways of the world. This is why Paul was saying that even though he was crucified with Christ, he still lives physically, but the life he now lives is totally dedicated unto the Lord. The modern versions insert such confusing language. It is really amazing that this type of wording exists since these modern versions all had professional linguists on the staff, especially the NIV, which makes that a major selling point, yet that version is as confusing as the rest of them. It is good to stay with the King James because it removes such confusing language, thus edifying us.

Galatians 3:1

> O foolish Galatians, who hath bewitched you, *that ye should not obey the truth*, before whose eyes Jesus Christ hath been evidently set forth, crucified *among you*? (Galatians 3:1, KJV)

"That ye should not obey the truth" is omitted. *"Among you"* is omitted.

In the Galatian church, Paul had to chide the Christians because it seemed they had been bewitched. The word *bewitched* in the Greek carries with it the meaning of "to mislead by hypnotizing or fascinating." These Galatians had the Gospel presented to them in such an intense manner, no doubt by the apostle Paul, that it was like Christ being crucified in their presence. These Galatians were not obeying the truth of the Gospel of grace. Galatians brings forth the great battle between law and grace. The Judaizers had attempted to teach that a person must keep the law along with grace to effect salvation. No doubt the false teachers were very eloquent and had placed the Galatian church in some kind of stupor, which caused them to drift from the truth of grace alone.

The Gnostics of the second century and the modern theologians are in agreement that grace and works should be mixed to effect salvation. This is why they omitted the part where the Galatians were not obeying the truth, the truth being the Gospel of grace alone. There are new movements occurring today that claim you must have works added to grace to effect your salvation. This is utter blasphemy since no works that anyone can do can help in any way to effect salvation. They are also teaching by this method that the sacrifice of Christ for His elect was insufficient to effect salvation alone. The idea that one needs works to complete salvation is a completely false teaching and must be rejected.

Paul also chides them because their reception of the Gospel was so intense and clear that it was like Christ was crucified among them. This is how clear the Gospel of grace alone was given to them, and they became corrupted with the Judaizers who taught they must keep the law too. The reason why "among you" was removed from the text is a mystery, but it probably goes to the fact that the Galatian Christians received the Gospel in a very intense manner, and Paul was driving home that fact. So in this verse, we see an attack upon the Gospel of grace alone.

Galatians 3:17

And this I say, that the covenant, that was confirmed before of God *in Christ*, the law, which
was four hundred and thirty years after, cannot
disannul, that it should make the promise of
none effect. (Galatians 3:17, KJV)

"In Christ" is omitted.

This is one of the subtlest yet serious deletions in the New
Testament. Galatians 3:17 is teaching us plainly that the covenant of
grace that God made with Abraham before the law was given would
never be affected by the law. God had already named those whom
He was going to save before the foundation of the world. "The beast
that thou sawest was, and is not; and shall ascend out of the bottomless pit, and go into perdition: and they that dwell on the earth
shall wonder, *whose names were not written in the book of life from the
foundation of the world*, when they behold the beast that was, and is
not, and yet is" (Revelation 17:8, KJV).

Therefore, grace would never be annulled by the law. Here is
the subtle omission. The modern versions leave out the name of the
Lord Jesus Christ. It was through Him that grace came. This also
gives us insight into the salvation of the Old Testament saints. Many
Christians get tripped up thinking that the Old Testament saints
were saved in a different manner than those on the New Testament
side of the cross. God saves only through grace, and that grace came
through the Lord Jesus Christ. The Bible teaches us that the Lord
Jesus Christ was slain in principle from before the foundations of
the world. This means that everyone who was saved from the Old
Testament and New Testament eras were saved only through the
grace of God, which came through the Lord Jesus Christ.

"And all that dwell upon the earth shall worship him, whose
names are not written in the book of life of *the Lamb slain from
the foundation of the world*" (Revelation 13:8, KJV). Revelation 13:8
teaches us plainly that Christ was crucified, in principle, before the
foundation of the world. "According as he hath chosen us in him

before the foundation of the world, that we should be holy and without blame before him in love" (Ephesians 1:4, KJV). Ephesians 1:4 confirms the fact that all God's believers were chosen in Christ before the foundation of the world. It is a shame that the modern versions omit the name of Jesus Christ as God's only channel of grace for the true believer. By mutilating this verse, the translators and editors of the modern versions show they have no understanding of God's salvation program and are only out to make money. Surely, their place is secure in hell!

Galatians 4:7

Wherefore thou art no more a servant, but a son;
and if a son, then an heir of God *through Christ*.
(Galatians 4:7, KJV)

"Through Christ" is changed to "through God."

The only way a person can become an heir of God is by becoming a child of God. The only way a person becomes a child of God is through the Lord Jesus Christ. "Jesus saith unto him, I am the way, the truth, and the life: no man cometh unto the Father, but by me" (John 14:6, KJV). These modern versions are all denying the Son, which means they do not have the Father. "Whosoever denieth the Son, the same hath not the Father: (but) he that acknowledgeth the Son hath the Father also" (1 John 2:23, KJV). Once you remove the Lord Jesus Christ as the only way to the Father, then that falsely opens up a plethora of ways to get to heaven.

The cry in today's religious world (and in many churches) is that there are many ways to get to heaven and also knowing that every major religion uses the term *God*, which means that this verse is giving credence to any heavenly path in any religion. Billions of people worship false gods, and by replacing *Christ* with "God" in this verse gives anyone the green light to instill a personal meaning on the term *God* according to their own belief system.

In 1997, Billy Graham and Robert Schuller claimed that there will be people in heaven who have never even heard of the name of

Christ. Billy Graham made that statement on Robert Schuller's program *Hour of Power*. This kind of omission plays right into the hands of the false teachers and unbelievers. "And if children, then heirs; heirs of God, and joint-heirs with Christ; if so be that we suffer with him, that we may be also glorified together" (Romans 8:17, KJV). Here, once again, the King James shows its superiority in delivering the truth in contrast to the modern versions, which are loaded with deception. The Roman Catholic Church teaches that salvation comes through their rituals and ceremonies. Wouldn't leaving out Christ as the only way of salvation play right into the hands of this false system?

Galatians 4:24

Which things are an allegory: for these are *the* two covenants; the one from the mount Sinai, which gendereth to bondage, which is Agar. (Galatians 4:24, KJV)

The before "two covenants" is omitted.

Here is a case of one small word changing the entire understanding of this verse and the section in view. God made only two covenants: the one from Sinai (which was the first) and the covenant of grace (which was the second and final one). The word *the* is a definite article that means that this verse is pointing to the fact that God had made only two covenants. This is important because some years ago, I heard Harold Camping on the radio claiming that God was dissatisfied with the second covenant and therefore made a third covenant. This is impossible since the final covenant of grace was to cover all the saved, and a third covenant was unnecessary. This would also be blasphemous because the second covenant was instituted by Christ via His sacrifice upon Calvary. God was pleased with that sacrifice, raised Him from the dead, and now every believer is covered by the grace of God.

This verse in the modern versions leaves room for a third covenant because there is no definite article emphasizing the fact that

God made only two covenants. The modern versions leave the door open for all kind of spurious additions and interpretations, and we wonder why the church is in such disarray.

Galatians 5:4

Christ is *become of no effect unto you*, whosoever of you are justified by the law; ye are fallen from grace. (Galatians 5:4, KJV)

"Become of no effect unto you" is changed to "severed, estranged, separated."

Here is a case where the modern versions make a wrong translation. The gist of this verse is that Christ and grace have no effect on the life of one who desires to keep the physical law. It does not speak about being estranged or cut off. "Cut off" in the Old Testament meant that a person could actually lose their life, and nothing like that is in view here. "Ye shall keep the sabbath therefore; for it is holy unto you: every one that defileth it shall surely be put to death: for whosoever doeth any work therein, that soul shall be cut off from among his people" (Exodus 31:14, KJV). The word behind "no effect" is the word *katargeo*, which carries with it the meaning of "make or render useless." It does not have a meaning of "being cut off or estranged."

Galatians 5:12

I would they were *even cut off which trouble you*. (Galatians 5:12, KJV)

"Even cut off which trouble you" is changed to "emasculate or castrate."

This verse has to be one of the sloppiest yet typical translations in the modern versions. If you will notice, the modern versions are advocating castration and mutilation. The CEV advocates the cutting off of the male organ. God strictly forbids mutilation of the human body in any form.

Ye are the children of the LORD your God: ye shall not cut yourselves, nor make any baldness between your eyes for the dead. (Deuteronomy 14:1, KJV)

Ye shall not make any cuttings in your flesh for the dead, nor print any marks upon you: I am the LORD. (Leviticus 19:28, KJV)

And it came to pass at noon, that Elijah mocked them, and said, Cry aloud: for he is a god; either he is talking, or he is pursuing, or he is in a journey, or peradventure he sleepeth, and must be awaked. And they cried aloud, and cut themselves after their manner with knives and lancets, till the blood gushed out upon them. (1 Kings 18:27–28, KJV)

Since the Gnostics believed in castration and mutilation of the body, it is not surprising that this teaching has been maintained by the modern translators and their bootleg versions. We can read in 1 Kings 18, when Elijah challenged the false prophets on Mount Carmel, that one of the responses the false prophets did to call upon their god was to cut themselves till the blood gushed out. The word *gushed* carries with it the meaning of "pouring out like a libation." Nowhere in the pages of scripture (real scripture, that is) do we find God advocating the mutilation of the human body. We were made in the image of God and are not to mar that image by any type of pagan slashing of the body.

Let us look at the Greek word behind "even cut off" to see if the modern translators are misunderstanding the meaning. It is the word *apokopto* that carries with it the meaning of "cut off or cut loose." Now, Classical Greek in the fourth to the fifth century BC added another meaning to this word, and that is "to castrate or make a eunuch of." In the Koine Greek, the style in which our

New Testament is written, the word maintained the definition of "castrate" from Classical Greek. Now the question remains, would God the Holy Spirit violate the scriptures He penned in the Old Testament by advocating bloodletting from the body? Also, would Paul, a trained Jew in the Hebrew scriptures, write something that would violate the scriptures? The answer, of course, to both these questions is no.

Galatians 5:19

> Now the works of the flesh are manifest, which are these; *Adultery*, fornication, uncleanness, lasciviousness. (Galatians 5:19, KJV)

Adultery is omitted.

It is apparent from this omission that the modern versions do not believe that adultery is a work of the flesh, or else why would they leave it out? There is enough manuscript evidence for it to be included even if the ancients were the ones who took it out. I find it amazing that the King James translators are always "condemned" by the modern-version-only cult for not having the amount of manuscripts we have today, and yet the modern-version editors continue to follow the corruptions that were made back in the third century by only two major manuscripts. Am I seeing a hint of hypocrisy here?

Galatians 5:21

> Envyings, *murders*, drunkenness, revellings, and such like: of the which I tell you before, as I have also told you in time past, that they which do such things shall not inherit the kingdom of God. (Galatians 5:21, KJV)

Murders is omitted.

Good news for unsaved murderers! The modern versions omit *murderers* in the lineup of Galatians 5:19–21, which is a list of sins that will keep a person out of the kingdom of God. I really had to laugh at the footnote on the NAB where they claim a similar-sounding word was added. They may be similar, but they are different words. One means *envy*, and the other means *murder*. If the reason that the Greek word for "murders" was omitted is because it sounded like the one for "envy," then excuse me, but that is an erroneous reason and makes no sense. Then again, we are dealing with the modern versions, which attack the Lord Jesus Christ without any fear. Just because two words sound alike or even look alike is no reason to delete any of them. This is a very good example of the type of extremely poor scholarship that prevails in the modern versions. How could anyone trust them when their translators remove words because they sound alike or look alike? I know I am glad that the Lord has preserved His word in the King James Bible because how could we trust any modern version that omits vital words just because they look or sound like?

Galatians 6:15

> For *in Christ Jesus* neither circumcision availeth
> any thing, nor uncircumcision, but a new crea-
> ture. (Galatians 6:15, KJV)

"In Christ Jesus" is omitted.

By removing "in Christ Jesus," they are removing the only way a person can become a new creature. "Therefore if any man be in Christ, he is a new creature: old things are passed away; behold, all things are become new" (2 Corinthians 5:17, KJV). The same Greek word *ktisis* is used in both Galatians 6:15 and 2 Corinthians 5:17, which means "creature or creation." The Gnostics would have deleted this phrase simply because their idea of salvation is to increase in knowledge of God. So their persistent attacks on the Lord Jesus show here that they disbelieved that the Lord Jesus Christ is the only way one can become a new creature.

In Galatians 6:15, with the removal "in Christ Jesus," the verse really makes no sense. The modern versions speak of a new creation in this verse but does not tell you how to be a new creation by being in Christ Jesus. By removing that pivotal phrase, a person may try to become a new creation through yoga, Eastern meditation, ritualistic religion, cult involvement, or many other ways. Many years ago, John Denver sang a song called "Rocky Mountain High" where he speaks of a man going to the Rocky Mountains, and the phrase was, "Might say he's born again." People are trying to become new creations in a thousand different ways, but God only has one way for a person to become a new creature, and that is being in Christ Jesus.

This deletion is an attack upon the Lord Jesus Christ as Savior. Once again, modern theologians and publishers agree with their second-century Gnostic counterparts. You know, it is interesting that these theologians keep telling us that we have much more manuscripts available to us today than the King James translators had, and yet it seems we have a smaller Bible with every new translation. More manuscripts, less Bible—go figure!

Galatians 6:17

From henceforth let no man trouble me: for I bear in my body the marks of *the Lord* Jesus. (Galatians 6:17, KJV)

"The Lord" is omitted.

Here is another attack on the deity and doctrine of the Lord Jesus Christ. The modern-version proponents claim that there are no doctrinal attacks. Here, they reduce the Lord Jesus to Jesus.

Ephesians 1:6

To the praise of the glory of his grace, wherein he hath *made us accepted* in the beloved. (Ephesians 1:6, KJV)

"Made us accepted" is changed to "freely bestowed or free gift."

The Bible states that before salvation, we are spiritually dead and at enmity with God, as attested to by these two verses:

> Even when we were dead in sins, hath quickened
> us together with Christ, (by grace ye are saved).
> (Ephesians 2:5, KJV)

> Ye adulterers and adulteresses, know ye not that
> the friendship of the world is enmity with God?
> whosoever therefore will be a friend of the world
> is the enemy of God. (James 4:4, KJV)

Therefore, since the believer would not have the ability to save themselves, it must come from an outside source, that source being God. This is why the verse states that He "made us accepted in the beloved." Just as Christ made Lazarus physically alive, He makes us spiritually alive; and when that happens, we are accepted in the beloved. "Made us accepted"—we did not make us accepted, but *He* made us accepted—really means he made us objects of grace. The beloved is the Lord Jesus Christ Himself (Matthew 12:18–21). The modern versions just state that He bestowed grace upon us, which He did, but this word goes deeper because it states that when grace was given to God's elect, they were "made accepted" because the grace was not only bestowed but applied to the believer, a very important step.

Ephesians 1:10

> That in the dispensation of the fulness of times he
> might gather together in one all things in Christ,
> *both* which are in heaven, and which are on earth;
> even in him. (Ephesians 1:10, KJV)

Both is omitted.

The first gathering or uniting together was done at the cross when the Lord Jesus died for His elect and broke down all the walls of social separation as all Christians are on an equal footing. "There is neither Jew nor Greek, there is neither bond nor free, there is neither male nor female: for ye are all one in Christ Jesus" (Galatians 3:28, KJV).

The second gathering will be on the last day when all the believers, both in heaven and on earth will be united in the great gathering of believers and ushered into the presence of God where our faith will become sight. "For the Lord himself shall descend from heaven with a shout, with the voice of the archangel, and with the trump of God: and the dead in Christ shall rise first: Then we which are alive and remain shall be caught up together with them in the clouds, to meet the Lord in the air: and so shall we ever be with the Lord" (1 Thessalonians 4:16–17, KJV).

The principle being taught in Ephesians 1:10 is the fact that all those believers who died and are in heaven and all those who are still alive on the earth, that when the Lord returns, the body of Christ shall be united as one, never to be separated from one another again. The principle that is being taught is that of marriage. Once the marriage is performed in front of witnesses, the bride and groom are now one flesh. This is why the Lord Jesus Christ had to die publicly because He was consummating the marriage (John 19:30) to the body of believers and witnesses were needed as with any marriage ceremony. "Wherefore they are no more twain, but one flesh. What therefore God hath joined together, let not man put asunder" (Matthew 19:6, KJV).

The principle carries over to Ephesians 2:15, where we read that the body of Christ is now one man instead of twain. "Having abolished in his flesh the enmity, even the law of commandments contained in ordinances; for to make in himself of twain one new man, so making peace" (Ephesians 2:15, KJV). That is the importance of the word *both* because it not only speaks of the combining of the Jewish and Gentile believers but speaks about the believers who are both in heaven and on earth before the Lord returns. The word *both* confirms the teaching of the unity of the body of Christ. It also teaches that all heaven and earth and everything it contains will be under the authority of Christ. The word *both* here is a conjunction and is used to stress the specific inclusion of the two places mentioned, heaven and earth.

Ephesians 1:18

> The eyes of your *understanding* being enlight-
> ened; that ye may know what is the hope of his
> calling, and what the riches of the glory of his
> inheritance in the saints. (Ephesians 1:18, KJV)

"Understanding" is changed to "heart."

The word for *understanding* carries with it the meaning of "mind, intellect, or disposition." It is the word *dianoia*. If you break down the word, you will have two Greek words *dia* (meaning "through or by") and *noia* (meaning "mind"). Have you ever heard someone say they are beside themselves? That would be the word *paranoia* made up of two Greek words. They are *para* (meaning "beside or called to be beside") and *noia* ("mind"). The word *dianoia* as used in Ephesians 1:18 carries with it the meaning of "the mind as the seat of emotions and desire." It is through the mind or the intellect in which we have our understanding. The mind is where the Holy Spirit illuminates the words of scripture and gives us understanding. In Ephesians 4:18, we see the same principle but opposite. "Having the understanding darkened, being alienated from the life of God through the ignorance that is in them, because of the blindness of their heart" (Ephesians 4:18, KJV). The unbeliever has a darkened understanding because they are unregenerate.

Part of our salvation inheritance is an enlightened mind that causes us to ponder things for two reasons: (1) to avoid sin and sinful situations and (2) to be obedient to God. Do not be intimidated by those who put down the enlightened intellects God gives us in salvation. I have had numerous conversations with people who claim the intellect is not needed. I see them in total error because they are very bad testimonies for Christianity. They cannot hold a decent biblical conversation, nor can they really give a reason for the hope that is within them. God is not glorified by Christians who choose to stay dumb thinking that is a form of humility.

We are to use every faculty God gave us to His glory and for the defense of the Gospel and the dissemination of that Gospel. It is so paradoxical for a Christian to be very astute in their worldly profession and then spiritually illiterate for the Lord. Let me just say that God does save apart from the intellect, as in the case of those who are mentally handicapped or a very young person; but if He gives us a good mind, we are to use it to His glory. "When I was a child, I spake as a child, I understood as a child, I thought as a child: but when I became a man, I put away childish things" (1 Corinthians 13:11, KJV).

Ephesians 3:9

> And to make all men see what is the fellowship of the mystery, which from the beginning of the world hath been hid in God, who created all things by *Jesus Christ*. (Ephesians 3:9, KJV)

"By *Jesus Christ*" is omitted.

Like many verses that are corrupted in the modern versions, this one also is an attack on the deity of the Lord Jesus Christ. This verse speaks of the Lord Jesus Christ as partaking of the creation of all things. Remember the footnote on John 9:38 in the 1901 Unitarian Edition of the 1901 ASV that tried to convey that the Lord Jesus is a created being. However, the true Bible teaches that the Lord Jesus is the Creator. Ephesians 3:9 speaks of the "fellowship of the mystery." Ephesians 3:4 tells us who that mystery is: "Whereby, when ye read, ye may understand my knowledge in the mystery of Christ" (Ephesians 3:4, KJV). Ephesians 5:32 gives further understanding of the mystery: "This is a great mystery: but I speak concerning Christ and the church" (Ephesians 5:32, KJV).

When they remove the words "by Christ Jesus," they are removing the essence of this verse. The Lord Jesus Christ is as much the Creator as God the Father and God the Holy Spirit. "For by him were all things created, that are in heaven, and that are in earth, visible and invisible, whether they be thrones, or dominions, or principalities, or powers: all things were created by him, and for him" (Colossians 1:16, KJV). God has withheld the mystery until

the time of the Lord Jesus Christ since Christ was the mystery. God created all things by Jesus Christ, and to remove this portion from the verse is to attack the attribute of Creator from the Lord Jesus Christ, thus denying His deity since only God can create ex nihilo. The Gnostics would have attacked this verse since they disbelieved that Jesus was deity and the Son of God. After 1,900 years, modern theologians and publishers are still attacking the person of the Lord Jesus Christ with the same ferocity as their second-century counterparts.

Ephesians 3:14

> For this cause I bow my knees unto the Father *of our Lord Jesus Christ*. (Ephesians 3:14, KJV)

"Of our Lord Jesus Christ" is omitted.

The omission of the last part of that verse removes the relationship between God the Father and the Lord Jesus Christ as the Son of God. When that verse is shortened after the word *Father*, it could be made to mean any father. In the Roman Catholic system, the term *pope* means "papa." Throughout the ages, adherents to the Roman Catholic system have bowed before the pope. The shortened version of Ephesians 3:14 would give credence to that action. The word *father* could also be made to say the father of any religion or system. It could also imply the universal fatherhood of God. This verse specifically states that God is the Father of the Lord Jesus Christ.

It also removes the specificity of who the Lord Jesus Christ belongs to. Notice it says "of our Lord Jesus Christ," which means that He is not the universal Savior of everyone but is the Savior of the elect of God only. The Gnostics would have chopped up this verse because they did not believe that the Lord Jesus Christ came from heaven as God's begotten Son. So naturally, they would want to remove anything that taught this truth. In the four Gospels, the Lord Jesus uses the term *my father* forty-seven times, plus three times in the book of Revelation.

Therefore doth *my Father* love me, because
I lay down my life, that I might take it again.
(John 10:17, KJV)

Jesus saith unto her, Touch me not; for I am not
yet ascended to *my_Father*: but go to my brethren, and say unto them, I ascend unto *my_Father*,
and your Father; and to my God, and your God.
(John 20:17, KJV)

Ephesians 3:14 also speaks of whom the apostle Paul prays to.
By bowing the knee, he was speaking of praying to God the Father
and also deference before God the Father. A person could supplant
that meaning and claim that we are to pray to the father of the saints
or the father of some religion as many do in the East, such as Buddha
or Confucius. There is also much ancestor worship that goes on
today, and the patriarch of the family may be worshipped. This is
why the ending of that verse is so important because it makes specific
what otherwise would be nebulous.

This verse is mutilated in P46 (c. AD 200), Aleph (Sinaiticus),
B (Vaticanus), C (fifth century), P (ninth century). So we can see
that this corruption dates back to the second century when the texts
were mutilated to fit the Gnostic heresy of the Alexandrian school in
Egypt. Something to think about here. When we see all these omissions, how does it affect us? Do we take it in stride, or do we cringe
at the realization that Christians are being lied to? To those who feel
the omissions and deletions are acceptable, let me ask you a question.
If you had to go to the hospital for an operation, such as a gallbladder
operation, would you feel confident if the surgeon and anesthesiol-
ogist both used textbooks in school that had as many omissions and
deletions as your Bible has? Well, if you won't trust your temporary
physical body to a surgeon who studied from inferior textbooks, why
would you trust your eternal soul to an inferior version with many
omissions and deletions?

Ephesians 4:6

One God and Father of all, who is above all, and
through all, and in *you* all. (Ephesians 4:6, KJV)

You is omitted.

Before we look at the seriousness of this one-word omission and
what it proclaims, let us look at the following 100 percent comparison of three versions that hold complete agreement with the Roman
Catholic Bible, the NAB. The next time someone tries to claim that
the modern versions do not agree with the Roman Catholic Bible,
show them this word-for-word agreement found in the NIV, NASB,
TNIV, ESV, and the 1901 ASV.

> NIV: "One God and Father of all, who is over all
> and through all and in all."

> NASV: "One God and Father of all who is over
> all and through all and in all."

> 1901 ASV: "One God and Father of all, who is
> over all, and through all, and in all."

Pantheism and Hinduism teach that God is in everything. By
omitting the word *you* in Ephesians 4:6, the modern versions are
teaching that God is in everything and everyone, which gives credence to the New Age tenet that God is in everyone; therefore, everyone is God. Many years ago, in a movie, Shirley MacLaine claimed
that she was God. What Paul was focusing on in this verse is that
God dwells only in the true believers and not everyone in the entire
world. The word *you* is a qualifying word telling us whom God truly
indwells. When left out, as in the modern versions, it augments New
Age teaching, and that is why New Agers have no problems with the
modern versions since they were translated out of manuscripts by
two of their own, Hort and Westcott, who were necromancers and
occultists.

God is the God of all people, but He is not the Father of all people. "Ye are of your father the devil, and the lusts of your father ye will do. He was a murderer from the beginning, and abode not in the truth, because there is no truth in him. When he speaketh a lie, he speaketh of his own: for he is a liar, and the father of it" (John 8:44, KJV). Unbelievers, of whom the majority of people are, do not have God as their Father but Satan. Therefore, God is not the Father of the unbelievers, only the believers.

First of all, this verse also teaches pantheism and Hinduism by stating that God is in all. Secondly, it also claims that God is the Father of all people in the world, but we saw John 8:44 quash that belief very quickly. Thirdly, the second sentence in this verse has extreme New Age connotation as we read that everything you are and think is permeated with "Oneness." Probably the most noticeable teaching of the New Age movement is that a person can become one with the godhead and become god themselves. The New Age adherents are looking for "the Coming One," who is their avatar or "the Christ," which is so prevalent in their teaching. The "Christ" that they are looking for is not the Lord Jesus Christ but an ascended master from the seventh plane who is going to come back and put all of humanity on the right path, according to their beliefs. According to New Age teachings, the Lord Jesus Christ is an ascended master who is equal with Buddha and Confucius and others.

The more new versions that come out, the more they are leading toward New Age and one-world beliefs. Look at the word *universal—*uNIVersal. Coincidence? There is no such thing as a chance coincidence.

The New King James Version uses the term *Coming One* and has a satanic Mobius on its cover, which should send caution into the minds of every true Christian who has one. It also seems that with every new version that appears, it shows the King James Bible to be the great stabilizer of Christian beliefs, and stability is a core tenet of the true Christian faith. Why? God does not change, and neither should we!

Ephesians 4:9

Now that he ascended, what is it but that he also
descended *first* into the lower parts of the earth?
(Ephesians 4:9, KJV)

First is omitted.

This has to be one of the subtlest attacks on the resurrection of
Christ. This verse is speaking of the resurrection of Christ. It speaks
of the fact that the same Christ who ascended into heaven is the very
same one who was crucified and buried. This verse tells us that Christ
was physically buried after His death, which signified that His death
was real. It states that He was *first* buried in the ground, and then He
arose from the dead and ascended into heaven. By using the word
first, it shows a progression that He was crucified and then buried
first, and after He was buried, He was then resurrected. The modern
versions, omitting the word *first*, just make a statement that He came
into our world from heaven above and completely shroud the real
meaning of this verse.

Ephesians 4:17

This I say therefore, and testify in the Lord, that
ye henceforth walk not as *other* Gentiles walk, in
the vanity of their mind. (Ephesians 4:17, KJV)

Other is changed to "the."

Here, the apostle Paul is addressing the Gentile believers in
Ephesus. They were saved out of the Gentile lifestyle that contained
much debauchery. Paul was admonishing them that they must not
live like the other Gentiles who were not regenerated. There might
have been those at Ephesus who were doing nothing but vain things
that were of no spiritual value, and this might have been what pre-
cipitated the letter of Ephesians and this portion about becoming
Christians who are in concert with the word of God and the body of
Christ to help build it and not hinder its growth. There are Christians
in every congregation who are of no value to the body of Christ. I

mean, if they would move to an uninhabited island in the South Pacific, things would go on as usual. We are being admonished that we need to get busy for the kingdom of Christ.

Too many times, Christians are more skillful in the ways of the world rather than the ways of Christ. Their walk seems to reflect that they are not even Christians, and the great distinction between unbelievers and Christians is that the Christian is to be sold out to the Lord Jesus Christ and the unbeliever is sold out to the things of the world. Our jobs or social position can never be used to define who we are. If we belong to Christ, then we are to identify with His kingdom, even if it brings persecution here on earth. Christians cannot have mental affinity with unbelievers because our minds have been regenerated. When the modern versions exchange *other* for "the," it looks like Paul was addressing the Jews, but he was addressing the Gentile converts in Ephesus, reminding them that they must not live like their past lifestyle.

Ephesians 5:1

Be ye therefore *followers* of God, as dear children. (Ephesians 5:1, KJV)

Followers is changed to "imitators."

Here is another case of the modern versions instilling confusion instead of harmonious biblical truth. The Greek word in question is *mimetes*, which is translated seven times in the King James as "followers." The word is very close to being that of a disciple. One can easily imitate someone else or even imitate God up to a certain point, but that imitation will never bring a person to salvation or a deeper Christian walk. The King James has it correct in that one must be a follower of God. The only way one can be a true follower of God is if they are saved. To imitate the works of God such as benevolence or compassion can instill a false belief in a person that they are saved because they are exuding those things. If I imitate Christian characteristics, does that make me a Christian? The answer is no. I must be saved; then I will be a true follower of God because of the indwelling of the Holy Spirit that implants in me Christian characteristics. False religions are the great imitators, and so are the modern versions because many unbelievers in false churches use them, giving them the false idea that they are saved.

Ephesians 5:9

For the fruit of the *Spirit* is in all goodness and righteousness and truth. (Ephesians 5:9, KJV)

Spirit is changed to "light."

One of the most popular tenets of Gnosticism is their rejection of spirit, especially the Holy Spirit, so we see in this verse that they changed the word *Spirit* to "light." Since they disregard God's thoughts, they probably changed the words to reflect the usage of "light" in verse 8 in belief they are continuing the thought. However, this is a very subtle but major change. Verse 9 is speaking of the fruit of the Spirit that gives goodness, righteousness, and truth. These are all tenets of the born-again Christian, and the light that is in view in verse 8 is really speaking of the true Gospel. The children of light in verse 8 are the true children of God by regeneration.

There is a second danger of changing *spirit* to "light," and that is the New Age tenet of "inner light." The inner light of the New Age movement is actually demon possession. Many in the New Age movement have trance-channeled demons, believing they were walking in inner light given by the ascended masters. The New Age movement puts Jesus in the same category as Confucius, Buddha, and other false teachers whom the New Age movement touts as giving light for a new age.

When you read Ephesians 5:9 with the word *light*, it makes for a great New Age teaching and proof text. This is why the modern versions fit perfectly into false teachings, including the New Age. We can thank the Lord that He has preserved His word in the King James Bible because it does not send us into false teachings but protects us from them.

Ephesians 5:21

Submitting yourselves one to another in the fear
of *God.* (Ephesians 5:21, KJV)

God is changed to "Christ."

I do not have a solid reason as to why the text was changed from
God to "Christ." I can only offer a speculation. Since the Gnostics
did not believe that Christ could be fully man and fully God, they
may have wanted to reduce the fear of people in their assemblies by
removing God and placing in Christ, whom they thought was only a
man. Nevertheless, the change was made.

Ephesians 5:22

Wives, *submit yourselves* unto your own husbands, as unto the Lord. (Ephesians 5:22, KJV)

"Submit yourselves" is changed to "be in subjection" or "yield."

The words "submit yourself" is a verb in the imperative mood,
making it a command and not a suggestion as in the CEB, CEV,
ERV. Just as we are to be in subjection to the Lord Jesus Christ, wives
are commanded to submit themselves to their own husbands. The
ERV makes it a choice when it uses the word "be willing," and there
is no choice in the Greek—it is a specific command.

Ephesians 5:30

For we are members of his body, *of his flesh, and
of his bones.* (Ephesians 5:30, KJV)

"Of his flesh, and of his bones" is omitted.

Now, the Bible is teaching us that those who are in Christ are
members of His body. This we understand, but of his flesh and
bones? When the Lord Jesus Christ rose from the dead, He came
out of the grave bodily, not a spirit. Some teach that Christ only rose
in Spirit. If that is the case, then His grave would be with us today,

and believe me, the enemies of Christ would have definitely handed down the location of His grave to every generation, but they can't because wherever it was, it is now empty.

When Eve was formed from Adam's rib, the scripture teaches: "And Adam said, This is now bone of my bones, and flesh of my flesh: she shall be called Woman, because she was taken out of Man" (Genesis 2:23, KJV). God took Eve from the rib of Adam, and when the church was formed, the side of the Lord Jesus was punctured by the soldier with the spear, and out came water and blood. The church was formed the same way Eve was. We are one flesh with Christ as we are married to Him, just as Eve was one flesh with Adam when they were married. It is the principle that we have seen in this chapter. There is such an intimacy between Christ and the church that it is symbolized as us being a member of his physical body. Remember in John 6, when the Lord Jesus Christ was speaking of eating His flesh and drinking His blood? This was also symbolic of being such an intimate part of the Lord Jesus. The church as the wife of Christ is enjoined with Him as one, which is symbolized by the marriage relationship.

When the modern versions remove the portion of the verse concerning the flesh and bones, they remove the intimacy between the believer and the Lord Jesus Christ. By ending the verse with *body*, it can be made to sound like the believer is just part of a large body. That large body can be a large body of believers of which the true believer is a part, but the portion about flesh and bones explains and enhances the first portion of the verse and teaches us that we are as close to the Lord Jesus Christ as the flesh and bones of His body. Once again, the King James Bible gives us a very thorough teaching whereas the new versions make it a nebulous one.

Ephesians 6:10

Finally, *my brethren*, be strong in the Lord, and in the power of his might. (Ephesians 6:10, KJV)

"My brethren" is omitted.

Verse 10 begins the great section of Ephesians 6, which teaches that the brethren are to rely solely upon the Lord and His might. This is why the message is directed specifically to the saved, a.k.a. brethren. When the modern versions omit "my brethren," it is making it sound as if anyone can be strong in the Lord. This would include the religious and the disconnected unsaved. Only those who are truly saved will be able to be strong in the Lord because the Holy Spirit dwells in the saved and not in the unsaved. The spiritually dead will never become strong in the Lord until they become saved. False religions will love this type of omission because then they can fill the breach with their religious rhetoric and attempt to make their adherents believe they can be strong in the Lord. Just ask Goliath if that is possible. Once again, the King James Bible proves its superiority by giving us the whole story and not forcing us to rely upon clerical hooey to fill in the spaces.

Ephesians 6:18

> Praying always with *all prayer* and supplication in the Spirit, and watching thereunto with all perseverance and supplication for all saints. (Ephesians 6:18, KJV)

"All prayer" is omitted.

Here is another case of the translators creating confusion and portraying the wrong message. In the King James, the phrase "all prayer" is singular and not plural. It points to the fact that Christians pray with singleness of purpose. The three modern versions that pervert this verse expand this phrase to a plural one and add a very dangerous word. The NIV and NCV add *kinds*. The AMP inserts "manner of." The reason these additions are very dangerous is because they open the door for different types of false prayers and types of praying. Do you remember the contest on Mount Carmel between Elijah and the prophets of Baal? For many hours, they called upon their false god to answer them, and then we read this verse: "And they cried aloud, and cut themselves after their manner with knives and lancets, till the blood gushed out upon them" (1 Kings 18:28, KJV). They began to cut themselves in their praying until they bled.

Now let us bring this up to today. Praying the rosary is a form of prayer! Praying with beads is a form of prayer! Vain repetitions is a manner of prayer! The modern versions leave open the capacity for someone in a false gospel to pray any way they like and think that God hears their prayer. This is why it is dangerous to take a singular word and translate it in a plural form because you make praying some type of all-inclusive system whereby any prayer is acceptable when that is biblically incorrect and can lead to catastrophic events when a person believes they are right with God when they are not. Ephesians 6:18 tells us that we are to pray in the Spirit, which means that those who are indwelled by the Holy Spirit, the redeemed of God, are the ones whom God hears. Religion-based prayers by the unsaved are an abomination unto God. "He that turneth away his ear from hearing the law, even his prayer shall be abomination" (Proverbs 28:9, KJV). The modern versions make the unsaved comfortable in their religion and allow them to set the method of prayer and worship. That is a very dangerous scenario.

Philippians 1:16-17

> The one preach Christ of contention, not sincerely, supposing to add affliction to my bonds: But the other of love, knowing that I am set for the defence of the gospel. (Philippians 1:16–17, KJV)

Order is reversed in the modern versions: verse 16 is 17, and verse 17 is 16.

Philippians 2:6

> Who, being in the form of God, thought it not robbery to be equal with God. (Philippians 2:6, KJV)

"To be grasped" was added to the English text.

This verse shows us that three words were added to verse 6, "to be grasped." These words are not found in any manuscripts. It seems it was added between the 1881 RV, which does not contain it, and the 1901 ASV, which does contain it.

> Who, existing in the form of God, counted not
> the being on an equality with God a thing to be
> grasped. (Philippians 2:6, ASV)

By adding these words, the modern versions seem to be claiming that Jesus was grasping after the attributes of God after He came to earth instead of Him having them with Him when He came to earth.

The Lord Jesus Christ came to earth, and He had the form of God. This does not specifically denote outward appearance but, in this case, means that He had the nature and essence of God. The verse states that Jesus did not believe He was robbing anything, such as glory or attributes from God. He was the Son of God, which means that He was also God because, as the Bible states, like begets like.

So God sent His Son, and His Son could be no less deity than the Father. If Christ lacked one divine attribute, then He was not God, but He had all the attributes of God, such as being the Creator. At the wedding of Cana, Jesus turned the water into wine. This was an act of creation because there was water in the pots, and wine was created. So Jesus being God in the flesh did not rob any attribute of God because they were already in Him, being deity in the flesh. It is just that He set many of these aside to come to earth. If He would have come to earth in full glory, He would have consumed this earth.

Philippians 3:3

> For we are the circumcision, which *worship God
> in the spirit*, and rejoice in Christ Jesus, and have
> no confidence in the flesh. (Philippians 3:3, KJV)

"Worship God in the Spirit" is changed to "worship in or by the Spirit of God."

There is a change of an inflection in the word for God. The Hort-Westcott text changed the word for God from a dative to a genitive. The difference is like night and day. The genitive case is the case of possession, and that is why their text reads "the spirit of God." The word for God in the Hort-Westcott Text is *theou*. The ending of the word *ou* reveals that it is a genitive case. In the Textus Receptus, it is correctly rendered *theow*, which is in the dative case. The dative case is the case that is called the "case of personal interest or reference" and is normally used to indicate the noun to whom something is given. It is also called the case of the indirect object, which involves a person.

In Philippians 3:3, we are reading that we worship God, who is the indirect object because the worship of God is the catalyst for rejoicing in Christ and having no confidence in the flesh. The words *worship* and *rejoice* are in the nominative case, which is the case of revealing the subject of the sentence or a clause. So by making just one small change, they change the entire meaning of the passage. It is good that God gave us His preserved word in the King James Bible. "God is a Spirit: and they that worship him must worship him in spirit and in truth" (John 4:24, KJV). Philippians 3:3 is a fulfillment of the Lord's method of true worship.

Philippians 3:16

> Nevertheless, whereto we have already attained, let us walk by the same rule, *let us mind the same thing.* (Philippians 3:16, KJV)

"Let us mind the same thing" is omitted.

One of the most precious teachings of scripture is that Christians be of the same mind. That is what this portion of the scripture is teaching. Christians do not attain unity by just following rules and regulations, but the idea of unity begins in the mind.

> Let us therefore, as many as be perfect, be thus
> minded: and if in any thing ye be otherwise
> minded, God shall reveal even this unto you.
> (Philippians 3:15, KJV)

> Fulfil ye my joy, that ye be likeminded, having
> the same love, being of one accord, of one mind.
> (Philippians 2:2, KJV)

Paul uses the terms for Christians to be like-minded seven times in the book of Philippians because being like-minded is a major theme permeating this book. Paul does not stop at Christians walking by the same rule, which is the rule of equality among Christians because of the new birth.

> For in Christ Jesus neither circumcision availeth
> any thing, nor uncircumcision, but a new crea-
> ture. And as many as walk according to this rule,
> peace be on them, and mercy, and upon the Israel
> of God. (Galatians 6:15–16, KJV)

Paul teaches us that equality begins in the mind, and true understanding of scripture begins in the mind because Christians have the mind of Christ. We need to be in unity, not in disunity. By the modern-version editors leaving off the part of scripture that deals with being like-minded, they have cut off the source whereby a person can walk in the rule of equality. If a person thinks him or herself to be better than others, then they violate the rule of equality among Christians. This principle is taught in Romans 12:3:

> For I say, through the grace given unto me, to
> every man that is among you, not to think of him-
> self more highly than he ought to think; but to
> think soberly, according as God hath dealt to every
> man the measure of faith. (Romans 12:3, KJV)

Christians may be at different spiritual levels in their walk, but none is more equal than the other, and that is why this portion of scripture is very important. When we separate the regenerated mind from actions, we will fall into all kinds of sin. That is why Paul stresses the fact that we must be like-minded as we walk in our Christian walk.

Philippians 4:13

I can do all things through *Christ* which strengtheneth me. (Philippians 4:13, KJV)

Christ is omitted and replaced with "him."

Once again, we see the name of Christ removed from the Greek. The name *christoo* exists in the Textus Receptus but is totally omitted in the Hort-Westcott text. It was just taken out without any reason given. Instead of the modern translators placing *Christ* back into the text, they replaced the proper name *Christ* with the pronoun *him*.

In the Message, we see the words *the One*. Remember a while back we spoke about the term *the One* or *One* and how it has New Age connotations? The words *the One* is not a translation of the word *christoo*. This was a personal choice on behalf of the translator. Instead of giving Christ His rightful place as the one who strengthens the believers, this man would rather give it to a New Age avatar. An avatar is an incarnation of a Hindu deity and is used quite extensively in the New Age movement. By using the pronoun *him*, anyone can place any specific false god or saint in there. A Roman Catholic might claim that St. Anthony strengthens them. By removing the specific name of Christ from this passage, they remove the true revealed source of the believer's strength and rob Christ of His glory within the body of Christ. Once again, the modern versions engender confusion and make themselves agreeable to false religions when they should be countering false religions.

Philippians 4:23

The grace of *our* Lord Jesus Christ be with *you all. Amen.* (Philippians 4:23, KJV)

"Our" is changed to "the." *"You all"* is changed to "your spirit." *"Amen"* is omitted.

This verse received the penknife of Jehoiakim in three places (read Jeremiah 36 for the whole story of Jehoiakim's penknife). The first place the Gnostics chopped is where Paul states in the possessive that the Lord Jesus Christ is ours; that is, He is Lord of the believers, and since we are saved, we can claim him as *our* Lord and not "the" Lord, as if we were speaking about Him in the third person. The second place the penknife hit was the phrase "you all" being replaced with "your spirit." In the Textus Receptus, the words for "you all" are both in the genitive case (possessive), and the word for "you" is second person, plural.

Paul was speaking to a specific group of people, and that is the believers. If he included the unbelievers, he could have used the third-person plural, but his focus was on the believers in the Philippian church. His desire was for the grace of God to undergird them, especially when there would be weaknesses that would engender a compromise. Paul prayed that they would be strengthened in that grace.

I do not pretend to know why the modern versions changed this phrase to "your spirits." Apparently, their faulty reasoning has been lost to time, or it could be that Paul prayed for the strength of the Philippians that they would not compromise in body or mind. Since the Holy Spirit indwells them, their spirits cannot fall back, but the flesh can, and maybe Paul had their strengthening in mind. Basically speaking, whatever ministry is done, is done through our bodies, which are totally imperfect and very susceptible to sinning and getting off-track.

The next attack of the penknife was the word *amen*, which means "truly, surely, so let it be." Since the text of the Gnostics (modern versions) are always in flux, they would disdain any word that speaks of finality or something that is sure.

Colossians 1:2

> To the saints and faithful brethren in Christ which are at Colosse: Grace be unto you, and peace, from God our Father *and the Lord Jesus Christ*. (Colossians 1:2, KJV)

"And the Lord Jesus Christ" is omitted.

Here is another example of the Gnostic faction at work. They have retained the greeting from God the Father, but they have omitted the greeting from the Lord Jesus Christ. The omitted part would make this greeting a direct greeting to all the believers down through history, not only the Colossians. This omission would play perfectly into the beliefs of the New Age and false religions. The majority of the world's false religions teach a fatherhood of God but, of course, reject the Lord Jesus Christ, who is the only way to salvation. The fatherhood-of-God belief keeps people who are in false religions believing that they are on the correct path to heaven when, in reality, they are on the correct path to hell.

Back around June 2007, three brave Christians were removed and arrested from the US Senate because a Hindu opened up the session with a prayer to his false gods. What really is so sad about this is that many have commented on this, and it seems more Christians would rather stand with the Hindu than with the Christians who brought truth to the Satan-worshipping senate of our country. It seems that the modern versions have done their job because no longer do we have "thus saith the Lord." Instead, we have "thus says any god we prefer." Woe unto us!

As we continue to forget about the Lord Jesus Christ in this country—and many Christians are doing just that—we are already seeing a gradual forsaking of this country by God, and this forsaking will continue to escalate until we finally become a third-world, false-god-worshipping country.

Colossians 1:14

In whom we have redemption *through his blood,*
even the forgiveness of sins. (Colossians 1:14, KJV)

"Through his blood" is omitted.

This verse is another that has met the ax of the corruptors. The portion "through his blood" has been eliminated from this verse, which eradicates God's method of salvation. All the blood sacrifices of the Old Testament were looking forward to the sacrifice the Lord Jesus was going to make on Calvary. He came in the flesh and was to die for His people so they may gain eternal life. His death involved the shedding of His blood, and it was through that shedding of blood that we gained eternal life. "And almost all things are by the law purged with blood; and without shedding of blood is no remission" (Hebrews 9:22, KJV).

There are many liberals and apostates, even within the church, who have no problem with the removal of the sacrifice of Christ since many apostate churches seek their salvation by works. This phrase is eliminated in Aleph (Sinaiticus) and B (Vaticanus), the two crowning glories of the modernist. Satan will not assail the verses on a large scale but will use thousands of small corruptions so they will easily escape the eye. Colossians 1:14 is one of those verses. If you will look at Ephesians 1:7, we see the phrase "through his blood" is left intact.

Ephesians 1:7

In whom we have redemption *through his blood,*
the forgiveness of sins, according to the riches of
his grace. (KJV)

In him we have redemption *through his blood,* the
forgiveness of sins, in accordance with the riches
of God's grace. (NIV)

In whom we have our redemption *through his
blood,* the forgiveness of our trespasses, accord-

ing to the riches of his grace, in whom we have our redemption, the forgiveness of our sins. (1901 ASV)

In Him we have redemption *through His blood,* the forgiveness of our trespasses, according to the riches of His grace. (NASV)

How could leaving out such an important phrase enhance the meaning of Colossians 1:14? Now, if they left this phrase in Ephesians 1:7, what could possibly be the reason to remove it from Colossians 1:14? The answer is simple: the attack upon the scriptures is massive but done subtlly. They leave one in and take one out, knowing full well that the majority of Christians will defend the fact that they left this phrase in Ephesians 1:7 and will not concern themselves with the omission in Colossians 1:14. We must never forget that the scriptures teach that *all* scripture is given by inspiration of God, which means that tampering with just even one letter makes it an evil practice and places one under the judgment of God. *"And if any man shall take away from the words* of the book of this prophecy, God shall take away his part out of the book of life, and out of the holy city, and *from* the things which are written in this book" (Revelation 22:19, KJV). It states clearly that if we take away from "the words," then we are under God's judgment. Colossians 1:14 is definitely an example of taking away words. Why would any Christian want or defend a Bible version that removes the teaching of cardinal doctrines of the faith such as the blood of Christ?

Colossians 1:28

Whom we preach, warning every man, and teaching every man in all wisdom; that we may present every man perfect in Christ *Jesus.* (Colossians 1:28, KJV)

Jesus is omitted.

This verse is another separation of the names of the Lord Jesus Christ. In this particular verse, they have removed the name *Jesus*, leaving the name *Christ* to stand alone. Now I want to focus on the implications of separating the name of Jesus from Christ. When the name *Christ* stands alone, it opens it up for an infusion of a New Age meaning. Back in 1978, there was a New Age woman named Alice Bailey who authored the book called *The Reappearance of the Christ*. In 1980, a man named Benjamin Crème authored a book called *The Reappearance of the Christ and the Masters of Wisdom*. His book was about a man named "Lord Maitreya" who was touted as the Christ. Jews await Him as the Messiah, Hindus look for the coming of Krishna, Buddhists expect Him as Maitreya Buddha, and Muslims anticipate the Imam Mahdi or Messiah.

In the King James Bible, the Lord Jesus is always identified as Christ. The modern versions separate Christ from Jesus. This must be done if you are going to create a Bible that can be accepted by all world religions. I remember the following in an interview with Gail Riplinger on *Actions Sixties* program concerning Ephesians 3:9:

> And to make all men see what is the fellowship of the mystery, which from the beginning of the world hath been hid in God, who created all things *by Jesus Christ*. (Ephesians 3:9, KJV)

In the modern versions, "by Jesus Christ" is omitted. Gail made a very profound statement. She said, "If they left Jesus Christ in, it would be too Christian." This basically shows how the modern Bibles are increasingly pulling away from being Christian and allowing New Age and ecumenical world beliefs to prevail. Isn't that amazing to think that a Bible is too Christian? The Bible and its specific teachings must be neutralized so it can be accepted by different religions. When you look at Ephesians 3:9 without Jesus Christ in it, it would be acceptable to almost all religions because they all mention God in their belief systems. Once you add Jesus Christ, you have completely excluded all world religions; but if you remove Him, it becomes world-religions inclusive, and there would be nothing to offend a Buddhist, Hindu, or even a Muslim.

I think it is absolutely amazing and appalling how these modern versions are playing right into the hands of the kingdom of Satan and all its tentacles of false religion. This situation will become more Satanic with every false version that will be created. It is high time Christians start using spiritual discernment concerning their Bibles. If they continue to use the modern versions, they will profit nothing and remain spiritually neutered. God gave us one Bible and preserved it in the King James Bible.

Colossians 2:2

> That their hearts might be comforted, being knit together in love, and unto all riches of the full assurance of understanding, to the acknowledgement of the mystery of God, *and of the Father*, and of Christ. (Colossians 2:2, KJV)

"And of the Father" is omitted.

Paul desired that the Colossians would have complete confidence in their understanding of the mystery of Christ dwelling within them. Paul had desired that they continue to grow in understanding these mysteries. As a Christian grows in their understanding of the Gospel, they begin to better understand the mysteries found in the scriptures, and probably there is no greater mystery than Christ indwelling the Christian. As young Christians, we know of the relationship that Christ has with His people; but as we mature, we begin to understand the greater intimacies of that relationship.

The mystery of Christ is also deeply entwined with the mystery of the Father. This relationship is not something we learn outside the scriptures but under the illumination of the Holy Spirit. God the Father is so intently involved in the salvation of the Christian that to leave Him out of this verse is a travesty. If one goes verse by verse through the book of John, they would see that the Father is totally involved in every step of the ministry of the Lord Jesus and is totally involved with ours too because He has a great love for His children. To omit the mystery of the Father is to omit a vital portion of scripture relating heavily to the believer. But then again, why would we expect something different from the modern versions?

Colossians 2:7

Rooted and built up in him, and stablished in the faith, as ye have been taught, abounding *therein* with thanksgiving. (Colossians 2:7, KJV)

Therein is omitted.

Rooted and *built up* in him, and *stablished* in the faith, as ye have been taught, *abounding* therein with thanksgiving. (Colossians 2:7)

Here is a very encouraging verse for every Christian. First of all, the believer is rooted in Christ. Now, the word *rooted* is actually "having been rooted" because the word is in the perfect tense, which is the tense of completion but means that its effects are still in operation. For example, a person plants a tree in his backyard. How many times does he plant that tree? He plants it only once. This is the same effect for the Christian. We are rooted in Christ at the moment of salvation, which is a single act, but its effects are operational throughout our entire lives.

"Built up" "stablished" and "abounding" are in the present tense, which means a continuing action. First, we are being built up; that is, as we continue to walk in Christ, we will see our spiritual quality continue to grow. We will desire more of Christ and less of the world; plus, we will be more spiritually minded—that is, we will concern ourselves with missions, training the next generation, evangelism, etc. Then we are stablished in the faith; that is, we are confirmed or established in the faith. This too is an ongoing process because as we continue to grow in Christ, we become more established in the faith.

The world and all its entrapments are easily spotted by the Christian, and they are avoided. "A prudent man foreseeth the evil, and hideth himself: but the simple pass on, and are punished" (Proverbs 22:3, KJV). As a result of being rooted and continually being established in the faith, we will experience an abundance of thanksgiving, which is what should permeate all activities of the Christian. This is why the Bible uses the word *therein* because it is the Christian faith that we are to be abounding in, not just a generic thanksgiving that the modern versions give. The King James Bible gives a specific in naming the Christian faith *the faith*, which we are to abound in.

Colossians 2:9

For in him dwelleth all the fulness of the *Godhead* bodily. (Colossians 2:9, KJV)

Godhead is changed to "deity."

The Gnostics had totally disbelieved that Christ was of the Godhead. They had believed that Christ came into being at His birth. Some Gnostics believed Christ was only pure Spirit and had a specter-type body, not a physical one. This heresy is known as Docetism. The Gnostics basically believed that if a true being came from God, there was no way they could be overcome by the world and be killed as Christ was. They also believed that the resurrection of Christ was when His spirit left His body. In this verse, Paul is stating that all the fullness of the Godhead—that is, all the attributes of the Godhead—are in Christ. When He was on this earth, He emptied himself of His glory, but not His position as second Person of the Godhead as evidenced by His miracles. He never ceased to be God while on the earth, and He continues to be God throughout all eternity.

The word *Godhead* when replaced by the word *deity* can denote a generic term. The word *deity* is not found in the King James Bible because the Holy Spirit wanted to point the believer to the fact that Jesus is in the Godhead and is not some detached deity.

> For the invisible things of him from the creation of the world are clearly seen, being understood by the things that are made, even his eternal power and Godhead; so that they are without excuse. (Romans 1:20, KJV)

> Forasmuch then as we are the offspring of God, we ought not to think that the Godhead is like unto gold, or silver, or stone, graven by art and man's device. (Acts 17:29, KJV)

The word *Godhead* in Colossians 2:9 is in harmony with the other two uses of the word in Romans 1:20 and Acts 17:29.

Here is a paragraph from a New Age website speaking of solar deities:

> A solar deity is a deity who represents the sun, or an aspect of it. People have worshipped the sun and solar deities for all of recorded history; sun worship is also known as heliolatry. Hence, many beliefs and legends have been formed around this worship, most notably the various myths containing the "missing sun" motif from around the world. Although many sources contend that solar deities are generally male, and the brother, father, husband and/or enemy of the lunar deity (usually female), this is not cross-culturally upheld, as sun goddesses are found on every continent. (Taken from: http://www.new-age-guide.com/new_age/solar_deity.htm)

As you can see, it is important that we keep the term *Godhead* instead of relinquishing it to "deity." It is one thing that sets Christianity apart from worldly satanic religions and the King James Bible from New Age Bible versions.

Colossians 2:11

In whom also ye are circumcised with the circumcision made without hands, in putting off the body *of the sins* of the flesh by the circumcision of Christ. (Colossians 2:11, KJV)

"Of the sins" is omitted.

One of the greatest aspects of being a Christian is the fact that God has removed our sins from us.

As far as the east is from the west, so far hath he removed our transgressions from us. (Psalm 103:12, KJV)

And David said unto Nathan, I have sinned against the LORD. And Nathan said unto David, The LORD also hath put away thy sin; thou shalt not die. (2 Samuel 12:13, KJV)

And they shall teach no more every man his neighbour, and every man his brother, saying, Know the LORD: for they shall all know me, from the least of them unto the greatest of them, saith the LORD: for I will forgive their iniquity, and I will remember their sin no more. (Jeremiah 31:34, KJV)

For I will be merciful to their unrighteousness, and their sins and their iniquities will I remember no more. (Hebrews 8:12, KJV)

This is the covenant that I will make with them after those days, saith the Lord, I will put my laws into their hearts, and in their minds will I write them; And their sins and iniquities will I remember no more. (Hebrews 10:16–17, KJV)

The new nature that we have since salvation coexists with the sinful nature in this body of death until either we are taken home or the Lord returns. The sinful nature has not been removed from us because it is ingrained in our flesh, as Colossians 2:11 in the KJV shows us. God has removed our sins, and those sins include the ones we have not committed yet. This is total redemption of the believer because every sin past, present, and future has been removed from the believer by the sacrifice of Christ on Calvary. If only one sin remains, then no one can ever get into heaven.

The modern versions remove this tremendous truth and try to tell us that God has removed our body of flesh. If that was the case, then no believer would be alive since we must abide in our physical bodies until our last day or the last day of history. This is just another example of poor scholarship. If God removed our body of flesh, then we would be dead. Instead, He removed the sins that were attached to that body, and that is a big difference in understanding. Christians face having two natures in one body, and the apostle Paul had that great struggle too as evidenced in Romans 7.

Colossians 2:18

Let no man beguile you of your reward in a voluntary humility and worshipping of angels, intruding into those things which he hath *not* seen, vainly puffed up by his fleshly mind. (Colossians 2:18, KJV)

Not is omitted (reverses meaning of passage).

This is one of those reverse-meaning verses that the modern versions are famous for. In the KJV, you will notice that we are being warned that those who worship angels and believe they have seen visions of heaven will be trying to lead astray as many people as they can, especially the Christians. We are being informed that these people did *not* see anything of the sort, but they are false teachers and deceivers. However, when we look at the modern versions, you will see they have left out the important word *not* and claim these people have seen what they claim they have seen. No wonder the modern versions are well-accepted in the Charismatic movement, because they believe and teach visions and heavenly visitations.

One of their biggest false prophets in this area is Jesse Duplantis, who claims he was in heaven for five hours. Well, the verse in the King James tells us he didn't go there, nor did he really see anything. If he did, then he was happily deceived by Satan in believing he went there. The modern versions would sanction this heresy of heavenly visitations and visions. God warns us against these false teachers in the last days. The modern versions are welcome tools in the hands of the false teachers, and we must be well-warned about their fallaciousness.

Colossians 2:20

Wherefore if ye be dead with Christ from the rudiments of the world, why, as though living in the world, are ye subject to ordinances. (Colossians 2:20, KJV)

Wherefore is omitted.

"And not holding the Head, from which all the body by joints and bands having nourishment ministered, and knit together, increaseth with the increase of God" (Colossians 2:19, KJV). If one begins to think they can use angels or anything or anyone else as a mediator, they will begin to set Christ aside, and it is He who upholds the body of Christ, which is the body of believers. Just as the human body is held together by ligaments and other joints and requires nourishment to grow and be healthy, so the body of Christ must exist the same way. The Lord Jesus Christ nourishes the body, and that results in spiritual growth.

When the Lord Jesus Christ is replaced and someone else is made the focus, whatever that focus is can never nourish the body as Christ can, and that results in becoming weaker and eventually getting to the point of being so weak, it becomes useless. The Lord Jesus causes every part of the body to function properly. Believers have different callings and different ministries, but the goal is always the same, and that is building up the body. Christ supplies all the necessary strength to every believer to keep the body strong and functioning properly.

Paul then connects the truth of verse 19 to 20 by means of the word *wherefore*, which itself is basically a question. The word *wherefore* carries with it the meaning of "for which reason or for what reason?" Paul was asking them a very strong question. If they are embracing Christ as their Savior, then what would be the reason they were subjecting themselves to something like the ceremonial law since Christ had delivered the believer from having to keep the law for salvation? He wanted to get them to think about their actions and to assess if keeping the law or being involved in the pagan aspects of worldly religion would in any way increase their salvation. The Colossians were falling prey to some aspects of pagan religion such as the worship of angels, and Paul wanted to cut them off from any involvement in such false religions because they have no place in Christianity.

Colossians 3:6

For which things' sake the wrath of God cometh *on the children of disobedience*. (Colossians 3:6, KJV)

"On the children of disobedience" is omitted.

This omission in the modern versions attempts to hide the fact that the wrath of God will come upon the unbelievers, who are described in this verse as "children of disobedience." If I was a Bible mutilator, I would definitely not want a verse like this kept in its entirety. This verse teaches that every unbeliever will come under the wrath of God. This verse and the previous one is a warning to Christians to forsake the sins of the flesh because it is these sins that cause the wrath of God to come upon the unbelievers. Once again, the modern versions omit needed truth, but the King James Bible does not leave us wondering.

Colossians 3:10

And have put on the new man, which is renewed
in knowledge after the image of him that created
him. (Colossians 3:10, KJV)

The second use of *"him"* is omitted.

Here, Paul is basically saying that we are saved, and we need
to live within the confines of the life from God. This means that
sinful actions and lifestyle are not part of that new life. "And that
ye put on the new man, which after God is created in righteousness
and true holiness" (Ephesians 4:24, KJV). Paul told the Ephesians
the same thing that they were not to only put off the old man, but
they were to put on the new man. The new man is the Christian life,
and it is being renewed on a constant basis. "For which cause we
faint not; but though our outward man perish, yet the inward man
is renewed day by day" (2 Corinthians 4:16, KJV). In 2 Corinthians
4:16, we are told that the inward man—that is, our new life—is
being renewed daily.

In Colossians 3:10, we are told that this renewal is made in
knowledge and that knowledge begins with the fact of what we were
before salvation. But then we are given knowledge concerning the
person and work of the Lord Jesus Christ; plus, we are increasing our
knowledge by practical Christianity and the understanding of the
scriptures that the Holy Spirit gives us. Further, that knowledge is
according to the image of Christ in man, which was created in man
by Christ through salvation. Now, the reason why we are to live in
the new man and reject the ways of the old man is because we are
made in the image of Christ or according to Christ.

If you notice, whenever the Bible speaks of the new man, it
calls it the *new man*. The word *him* in Colossians 3:10 is a masculine
personal pronoun. Therefore, words like *it* and *its* are incorrect. They
would be correct if the word was neuter, but it is not. Some of the
versions even refer to God as "the one," which is a New Age term.
The words in the Greek for "him" and "one" are totally different. If
you look at the CEV, ERV, and NCV, you will notice a very subtle

theme. They include a statement that "you are becoming more and more like him." The NCV even states that "you are becoming like the One who made you." These statements are prevalent in the New Age movement as they seek to progress toward godhood. Their desire is to be more like God until they finally reach their goal. These statements are not in the Greek text; they were added.

Colossians 3:13

> Forbearing one another, and forgiving one another, if any man have a quarrel against any: even as *Christ* forgave you, so also do ye. (Colossians 3:13, KJV)

Christ is changed to "Lord."

As with any other group in this world, Christians are not exempt from quarrels. From time to time, there will be disagreements that will crop up. The difference is how these are attended to. There are two ways that Paul is saying that the Christians should handle this, and they are forbearing—that is, to have patience within the disagreement—and to forgive one another when needed. We are not to hold any grudges or any lingering hatred toward a brother or a sister. As we read in the previous verse, "Put on therefore, as the elect of God, holy and beloved, bowels of mercies, kindness, humbleness of mind, meekness, longsuffering" (Colossians 3:12, KJV). "Put on" means "to clothe someone."

The basic garments of the new life includes the ability to forgive an erring brother or sister. Christ has forgiven every sin that we ever committed. We read this in Colossians 2:13–14. Therefore, how can we hold anything against a brother or sister whom Christ has totally forgiven? The modern versions omit the fact that it is Christ who forgives us our sins and takes His name and changes it to a title. God the Father is also known as Lord, but we cannot bypass Christ and go directly to Him for forgiveness of sins. The sacrifice of Christ is the way a sinner becomes a child of God. The King James Version keeps this truth in plain sight by naming Christ.

Colossians 3:22

> Servants, obey in all things your masters according to the flesh; not with eyeservice, as menpleasers; but in singleness of heart, fearing *God*. (Colossians 3:22, KJV)

God is changed to "Lord" or "Him."

It was estimated that one-third of all those who lived in the Roman Empire were slaves. Now, many of the slaves were very educated and held good positions in many households. Paul was telling them that they needed to do their work in purity of heart; that is, they should not just do their work in front of the master, putting on a charade. Paul is teaching that they must perform their duties in obedience to their masters, whether the master sees them or not. This is like the employee who works very hard when the boss is around, and then as soon as the boss leaves, they begin to slack off. Then there are those who try to be menpleasers, which is trying to please their boss at any expense. They do not do it because they are doing it from the heart; they are doing it to hopefully gain some kind of advantage.

"These are murmurers, complainers, walking after their own lusts; and their mouth speaketh great swelling words, having men's persons in admiration because of advantage" (Jude 1:16, KJV). Jude wrote something similar that there are those who flatter to get something for themselves. Many of us have seen this situation on the job, where the best employee is never promoted and the worst is always elevated to a higher position. Paul then went on to state that the slave must work for their master with singleness of heart; that is, they are to do their work for the purpose of accomplishing the task at hand, whether the master is present or not. The Christian slave was to work in the fear of God, which meant that he or she was to do their work heartily unto the Lord. "And whatsoever ye do, do it heartily, as to the Lord, and not unto men" (Colossians 3:23, KJV).

If one was looking for an example of this attitude, it would be Joseph. He worked heartily unto God and did not look at his situation. God rewarded him with a good position in both the house of

Potiphar and in the prison, and finally, Joseph became governor of Egypt. Joseph's heart was stayed upon the Lord, and the Lord prospered him. "Submitting yourselves one to another in the fear of God" (Ephesians 5:21, KJV). Colossians 3:22 is very specific that the servant needs to work in the fear of God. Now, this would be pointing to the believers who were servants because the unbeliever has no fear of God. "There is no fear of God before their eyes" (Romans 3:18, KJV). The term "fear of the Lord" is used 110 times in scripture, but in this verse, it specifically states "fear of God." There was no logical reason for the modern versions to make that change.

Colossians 3:24

> Knowing that of the Lord ye shall receive the reward of the inheritance: *for* ye serve the Lord Christ. (Colossians 3:24, KJV)

For is omitted.

Here is where Paul was stating that the saved slave will receive their reward. On earth, a slave was the lowest social class, and it was totally rare that they would receive any tangible recompense for their service. Paul was encouraging them that since they were serving the Lord Jesus Christ, they too would receive that reward of the inheritance.

> Blessed be the God and Father of our Lord Jesus Christ, which according to his abundant mercy hath begotten us again unto a lively hope by the resurrection of Jesus Christ from the dead, To an inheritance incorruptible, and undefiled, and that fadeth not away, reserved in heaven for you. (1 Peter 1:3–4, KJV)

When we look at what the inheritance is, we see that it is the inheritance of heaven. No longer would the slave be a slave but instead they would be kings and priests in the kingdom of God.

"And hath made us kings and priests unto God and his Father; to him be glory and dominion for ever and ever. Amen" (Revelation 1:6, KJV). Revelation 1:6 makes this abundantly clear. On earth, the Christian who works for a living or was a slave to a master would receive very little or no compensation; but in heaven, all that will change, and that is why Paul wanted them to keep their eye focused on Christ because He is the one who gives out the true reward, which is eternal life. "And he said unto them, Verily I say unto you, There is no man that hath left house, or parents, or brethren, or wife, or children, for the kingdom of God's sake, Who shall not receive manifold more in this present time, and in the world to come life everlasting" (Luke 18:29–30, KJV).

The modern versions, by omitting *for*, break the continuity of thought that the conjunction provides. The modern versions create a second sentence and make it sound like they need to start serving Christ instead of acknowledging the fact that the Colossian believers are already serving Christ.

Colossians 4:8

> Whom I have sent unto you for the same purpose, *that he might know your estate*, and comfort your hearts. (Colossians 4:8, KJV)

"He might know your estate" is changed to "know things about us or our circumstances," thus reversing the meaning of this passage

Here is another example of a verse reversed in the modern versions. In the King James, we read that Paul is sending Tychicus and Onesimus, who would both bring the Colossians news of Paul, but they were also to bring Paul information about them and how they were faring in their Christian walk. The modern versions take Paul's concern for the Colossians and wipes it out. Paul was always interested in how the churches were doing. "Beside those things that are without, that which cometh upon me daily, the care of all the churches" (2 Corinthians 11:28, KJV).

Paul was not interested in just telling everyone how he was doing, but he wanted to know if there were any problems arising that would hinder the growth of the churches. The modern versions state that when these brothers arrived, they would encourage your hearts by telling them about Paul's condition, and they leave it at that. Paul was in prison when he penned the book of Colossians, so he was unable to come to them personally. The mission of the two brethren was to bring the Colossians information about Paul and to bring Paul information about the Colossians. Gnosticism was alive and well when the book of Colossians was written, and this book was to be a defense against it creeping into the church. There is no reason why the modern versions reversed the wording, but once again, it shows how corrupt and Gnostic they are.

Colossians 4:15

Salute the brethren which are in Laodicea, and
Nymphas, and the church which is in *his* house.
(Colossians 4:15, KJV)

Nymphas and *his* are changed to "Nympha" and "her" (a masculine name in the Greek is changed to feminine name in the modern English texts).

Here is a very troubling change. The name *Nymphas* is a male name and means "bridegroom," making it a male name. However, in the modern versions, it is changed to *Nympha*, making it a feminine name. In the Critical text, the personal pronoun was changed to feminine, making the word *her*. Instead of the pronoun following the noun, they made the noun follow the pronoun and changed the name of *Nymphas* to *Nympha*. The name *Nymphas* is found in both the Textus Receptus and the Critical text. The name *Nympha* does not appear in the Critical text but was changed in the English translation to conform to the feminine pronoun *her*. The corruption in these modern versions is horrendous when they start changing the genders, and no one even questions it.

1 Thessalonians 1:1

> Paul, and Silvanus, and Timotheus, unto the church of the Thessalonians which is in God the Father and in the Lord Jesus Christ: Grace be unto you, and peace, *from God our Father, and the Lord Jesus Christ.* (1 Thessalonians 1:1, KJV)

"From God our Father, and the Lord Jesus Christ" is omitted.

By omitting this part of the verse, the modern versions leave out the fact that grace and peace are sourced out of God the Father and the Lord Jesus Christ. Grace and peace do not come by words of a prophet or Bible teacher, but they come by the indwelling of the Holy Spirit. By omitting this part of the verse, it looks like Paul was giving his personal greeting when that greeting was coming from God the Father and the Lord Jesus Christ. Once again, the modern versions bring the word of God down to man's words. Once again, the King James Version gives us the truth in a very serious teaching. The greeting in verse 1 is much more than a greeting because it contains biblical truth concerning grace, which is the only way a person becomes saved.

1 Thessalonians 2:3

> For our exhortation was not of *deceit*, nor of uncleanness, nor in guile. (1 Thessalonians 2:3, KJV)

Deceit is changed to "error."

Here is a question of a word change in the English that gives the verse a different meaning. The Greek word is *planês*, which means "a wandering away from the truth, a delusion, deceit, or error." In this verse, Paul was stating that the exhortation he gave the Thessalonians was not from deceit. Deceit is an intentional plan or attempt to deceive somebody or to trick them. The apostle Paul had faced many such false teachers who taught a false gospel and deceived the people. Paul was stating that his Gospel was not based upon deceit but upon truth. He had no desire to trick or defraud anybody out of anything.

The false teachers had attempted to gain a foothold wherever they went for the purpose of making themselves wealthy and to contradict the true gospel. They had no concern for the souls of the people they were defrauding. On the other hand, Paul came to them in sincerity and not in any form of deceit. The modern versions use the word *error* here, but it does not fit the context. Error can be an innocent mistake or understanding, but Paul faced the false teachers wherever he went, and their mode of operation was intentional deceit, not a mistaken understanding of the Gospel—a very big difference!

1 Thessalonians 2:15

Who both killed the Lord Jesus, and *their own* prophets, and have persecuted us; and they please not God, and are contrary to all men. (1 Thessalonians 2:15, KJV)

"Their own" is changed to "the."

Here, the apostle Paul spoke candidly about the Jews. He stated that they both killed the Lord Jesus and the prophets whom God sent to them. This is not only speaking about the leaders but is speaking about those who are unsaved and followed the unsaved leaders. All one has to do is read the Old Testament and you will see how they killed their own prophets. Their rejection of the word of God brought by these prophets resulted in them going into captivity. The northern kingdom went into captivity with Assyria and was never heard from again. Judah, the southern kingdom, went into Babylon for seventy years, and then some came back to the land. But after the Lord Jesus went back to heaven, Judah was dispersed when General Titus razed Jerusalem in AD 70. That judgment was yet to happen when 1 Thessalonians was written. They continued to persecute the apostle Paul and all the apostles. The unsaved Jews showed tremendous hostility toward the true word of God, and they still do to this day.

Their main religious book is the Babylonian Talmud. God's chosen people are only those in Christ (see scriptures below). God had a special relationship with Israel for a limited time because the Lord Jesus Christ came from their lineage through the tribe of Judah. Once Jesus died and rose and went back to heaven, that spelled the end of the Mosaic system, and now God is not dealing with only one nation anymore. He is now dealing with the entire world. The Jews are as much of a mission field as any other people group. The modern versions make it a very vague statement when it speaks about "the prophets," but God is specifically stating that Israel put to death the prophets whom God raised up from their own people.

The Chosen People Are Those in Christ

> According as he hath *chosen* us in him before the foundation of the world, that we should be holy and without blame before him in love. (Ephesians 1:4, KJV)

> But we are bound to give thanks always to God for you, brethren beloved of the Lord, because God hath from the beginning *chosen* you to salvation through sanctification of the Spirit and belief of the truth. (2 Thessalonians 2:13, KJV)

> But ye are a *chosen* generation, a royal priesthood, an holy nation, a peculiar people; that ye should show forth the praises of him who hath called you out of darkness into his marvellous light. (1 Peter 2:9, KJV)

> These shall make war with the Lamb, and the Lamb shall overcome them: for he is Lord of lords, and King of kings: and they that are with him are called, and *chosen*, and faithful. (Revelation 17:14, KJV)

1 Thessalonians 2:19

For what is our hope, or joy, or crown of rejoicing? Are not even ye in the presence of our Lord Jesus *Christ* at his coming? (1 Thessalonians 2:19, KJV)

1 Thessalonians 3:11

Now God himself and our Father, and our Lord Jesus *Christ*, direct our way unto you. (1 Thessalonians 3:11, KJV)

1 Thessalonians 3:13

To the end he may stablish your hearts unblameable in holiness before God, even our Father, at the coming of our Lord Jesus *Christ* with all his saints. (1 Thessalonians 3:13, KJV)

Here are three verses where the divine title of the Lord Jesus Christ has been omitted. The Gnostic pen must have really been busy in this section. With every modern version produced, the name of the Lord Jesus Christ will be attacked even more.

1 Thessalonians 5:27

I charge you by the Lord that this epistle be read unto all the *holy* brethren. (1 Thessalonians 5:27, KJV)

Holy is omitted.

According as he hath chosen us in him before the foundation of the world, that we should be *holy* and without blame before him in love. (Ephesians 1:4, KJV)

> Put on therefore, as the elect of God, *holy* and beloved, bowels of mercies, kindness, humbleness of mind, meekness, longsuffering. (Colossians 3:12, KJV)

One of the main results of true salvation is that it takes a sinner and makes them a holy person before God. True Christians are holy in the Lord. The modern versions omit this fact in 1 Thessalonians 5:27. The King James keeps it in; plus, it is also a reminder that there will be false brethren in the church. "And that because of false brethren unawares brought in, who came in privily to spy out our liberty which we have in Christ Jesus, that they might bring us into bondage" (Galatians 2:4, KJV). The true brethren are the ones in Christ who are made holy, but the false brethren are still in the kingdom of Satan. The modern versions make no distinction in this verse.

2 Thessalonians 1:2

> Grace unto you, and peace, from God *our* Father and the Lord Jesus Christ. (2 Thessalonians 1:2, KJV)

Our is changed to "the."

The modern versions remove the personal pronoun *hemon* in the Greek text, which is in the genitive case. The modern versions replace it with the article *the* in English, just stating that God is "the" Father. The personal pronoun teaches that God is our Father; that is, the Father of all the believers. The modern versions remove that personal teaching and replace it with a generic teaching. The modern versions remove that familial reality.

2 Thessalonians 1:8

> *In flaming fire* taking vengeance on them that know not God, and that obey not the gospel of our Lord Jesus *Christ*. (2 Thessalonians 1:8, KJV)

"*Christ*" is omitted. "*In flaming fire*" is changed to "retribution or punishment."

This verse received the ax twice from its detractors. First, some of the modern versions remove the reality that hell is going to be a place of eternal fire. The modern versions want to make it sound like a place of only justice without severe and eternal consequences for sin. The second ax hit the title of the Lord Jesus Christ by removing *Christ*, which is His title of deity.

2 Thessalonians 1:12

> That the name of our Lord Jesus *Christ* may be glorified in you, and ye in him, according to the grace of our God and the Lord Jesus Christ.
> (2 Thessalonians 1:12, KJV)

Christ is omitted.

Looks like the same Gnostic who hit the first letter to the Thessalonians hit this one too by removing the divine title of *Christ*.

2 Thessalonians 2:2

> That ye be not soon shaken in mind, or be troubled, neither by spirit, nor by word, nor by letter as from us, as that the day of *Christ* is at hand.
> (2 Thessalonians 2:2, KJV)

"*Day of Christ*" is changed to "day of the Lord."

The name of *Christos* is found in the Byzantine text, and the name *Christ* was changed in the Vaticanus, Sinaiticus, and Alexandrian texts. These three manuscripts are the three chief corrupted Gnostic texts. It is possible they want to hide the fact that on the last day, all the unbelievers will stand before Christ to be judged for their sins.

1 Timothy 1:1

> Paul, an apostle of Jesus Christ by the command-
> ment of God our Saviour, and *Lord* Jesus Christ,
> which is our hope. (1 Timothy 1:1, KJV)

Lord is omitted.

Here is another attack upon the deity of the Lord Jesus Christ. By removing the title of *Lord*, they are reducing the Lord Jesus Christ to just another man. It took His full deity to pay for the sins of all the elect down through the ages until the last one is saved.

1 Timothy 1:2

> Unto Timothy, my own son in the faith: Grace,
> mercy, and peace, from God *our* Father and Jesus
> Christ our Lord. (1 Timothy 1:2, KJV)

"Our Father" is changed to "the Father."

Once again, we see the change from the possessive case to the generic *the*. It removes that great relationship we have with God the Father through the Lord Jesus Christ. Modern versions seem to desire a distancing of family relationships.

1 Timothy 1:17

> Now unto the King eternal, immortal, invisible,
> the only *wise* God, be honour and glory for ever
> and ever. Amen. (1 Timothy 1:17, KJV)

Wise is omitted.

Wisdom is a great part of the gift that God gives His children, but for someone to give wisdom, they must be wise themselves. The modern versions omit the word *wise*, and there is absolutely no reason given why it was omitted. It is just another attack upon the character of God. In fact, the Gnostics and the modern versions have also done this in Jude 1:25, which you will see for yourself. One of the chief characteristics of God is His wisdom. The book of Proverbs attests to this. The King James Bible honors God as a wise God, but the modern versions do not.

1 Timothy 2:7

> Whereunto I am ordained a preacher, and an apostle, (I speak the truth *in Christ*, and lie not;) a teacher of the Gentiles in faith and verity. (1 Timothy 2:7, KJV)

"In Christ" is omitted.

The words "in Christ" are used seventy-seven times in the New Testament, and out of those seventy-seven times, the apostle Paul uses it seventy-four times. It is the testimony of the apostle Paul that he is in Christ. In other words, it is through the Lord Jesus Christ that Paul had attained his salvation. In 1 Timothy 2:7, Paul affirmed his earthly offices of preacher and apostle. These two offices were given to him by Christ upon his salvation, which he described by being *in Christ*. He also tells his readers that the truth that he tells them is sourced in Christ. When the modern versions leave out "in Christ," then the statement is just focusing on Paul telling the truth. That truth is not based on Christ, but it is based on Paul. It moves the focus from Christ to Paul. It goes from being Christ-centered to being man-centered.

We all know what God says about the verity of man. "God forbid: yea, let God be true, but every man a liar; as it is written, That thou mightest be justified in thy sayings, and mightest overcome when thou art judged" (Romans 3:4, KJV). God is true, and every man a liar. Just like some self-appointed preachers today who call themselves "apostles," anyone can claim the title, but Paul is affirming that his calling came from Christ and not men. "Paul, an apostle, (not of men, neither by man, but by Jesus Christ, and God the Father, who raised him from the dead)" (Galatians 1:1, KJV). Paul's appointment is confirmed in Galatians 1:1. Removing "in Christ" also removes the reality that it is Christ who is the head of the church and can place anyone in any position He deems proper. The removal of His name disassociates Him from being the head of the church. It is another attack on the Lord Jesus Christ.

1 Timothy 3:3

> Not given to wine, no striker, *not greedy of filthy lucre*; but patient, not a brawler, not covetous. (1 Timothy 3:3, KJV)

"Not greedy of filthy lucre" is omitted.

They must not be men who are greedy of dishonest gain. If they see evil people prospering, they must never be envious and desire to make money or any type of gain by any other manner than legally. They must not pursue anything dishonest. "Filthy lucre" is a phrase that means not only money but also a gain in goods by means of evil methods. The Roman Catholic Church would not want that phrase in their Bibles because they were heavily engaged in the acquisition of property around the world. As we see, many preachers in the Charismatic movement today take the donations of their people and use it on themselves to build their empires. Many TV preachers, both charismatic and noncharismatic, are living on exorbitant incomes from their ministries. So many people use "religion" to become rich, and that is "filthy lucre." It has a much wider meaning than just "lover of money."

1 Timothy 3:16

> And without controversy great is the mystery of godliness: *God* was manifest in the flesh, justified in the Spirit, seen of angels, preached unto the Gentiles, believed on in the world, received up into glory. (1 Timothy 3:16, KJV)

God is changed to "he."

First Timothy 3:16 is one of the clearest teachings on the incarnation of Christ and His deity. The Gnostics had removed *Theos,* which is translated "God" (a noun), and changed it to "Hos," which is translated "He" (a pronoun). This is a glaring attack upon the Lord Jesus Christ by removing the fact that He was and is God, and specifically as God being the Savior. "I, *even* I, *am* the LORD; and beside me *there is* no saviour" (Isaiah 43:11, KJV).

If Christ, as God, did not die upon that cross for His children, then we are still in our sins. For no mere man can die for another and have their sins removed, for who will remove the sins of the one sacrificing himself? Sinner cannot redeem sinner!

Gnostic teaching did not allow for any deity to dwell in sinful flesh, so they removed the name of God and changed it to "He," which can now make room to substitute anyone else's name. The problem here is that this attack is answered by another verse of scripture: "And every spirit that *confesseth not that Jesus Christ is come in the flesh is not of God*: and this is that spirit of antichrist, whereof ye have heard that it should come; and even now already is it in the world" (1 John 4:3, KJV).

Let us look at 1 John 4:3 in the NIV, and you will see a pattern emerge. "But every spirit that does not acknowledge Jesus is not from God. This is the spirit of the antichrist, which you have heard is coming and even now is already in the world" (1 John 4:3, NIV). What is missing from that verse? The part about Jesus coming in the flesh! Do you see the underlying spirit of Satan that permeates these modern versions? They remove *God* in 1 Timothy 3:16, and so no one will question it. They remove the reference of Christ coming in the flesh in 1 John 4:3. It is a shame that so many churches and Christians are doing the work of Satan by proliferating these evil books under the name of Christianity.

By removing the name of God, in reference to the incarnation of the Lord Jesus Christ, the authors of the modern Bibles are admitting their books are not from God but from the Antichrist, who is Satan himself. They are not confessing that Jesus Christ came in the flesh, which makes these counterfeit versions as rooted in Satan and not in God. Christians must begin to realize that these modern versions are not the Bible and will not yield any fruit in the lives of any Christian or church that uses them. In fact, if we use a version that is hostile to biblical truth, we are, in essence, in rebellion against God, simply because we are accepting the false teachings in the false versions. Some Christians go so far as to defend these Gnostic books, simply because they refuse to do any research into the versions they use. They will research the stock market for investments, yet their spiritual life seems very unimportant to them.

There is a footnote in the original 1881 Revised Version, which also appears verbatim in the American Standard Version of 1901, stating that they claim that "God" appearing in this verse "rests on no sufficient ancient evidence." This is probably one of the biggest lies attached to these versions. The truth is that *God* is missing from only four of the manuscripts. Of course, the main one that *God* is missing from is Aleph (Sinaiticus). The word *God* is found in over three hundred cursives (manuscripts written in script) and many lectionaries. *Theos* in these lectionaries goes back as far as the first century with Ignatius, who died around AD 110. Lectionaries were used by the church for Bible lessons. This means that *God* was in the original manuscripts but was removed by Satan's intellects in Alexandria. And the horror of it is that the modern scholar agrees wholeheartedly with Satan's second-century intellects. If your Bible reduces the Lord Jesus Christ to a mere man, then you do not have the Bible. You have an inferior impostor.

1 Timothy 4:10

> For therefore we both labour and *suffer reproach*, because we trust in the living God, who is the Saviour of all men, specially of those that believe. (1 Timothy 4:10, KJV)

"Suffer reproach" is changed to "strive or struggle."

Paul is stating that for the truth of the Gospel and seeing people saved, they continually labored. They did not only labor by doing hard work in establishing churches and helping Christians grow, they were also wearied by the many persecutions they went through. They went through hunger, whippings, shipwrecks, jail, and many other things that weaken the physical body but strengthen the inner man. They were constantly reviled wherever they went. All one has to do is read the trouble Paul had in Ephesus when he threatened the merchants who sold idols of Diana. All these things they suffered, and the reason was because they trusted in the living God.

All Christians who labor in the Gospel will face the hostilities of this world because we are believers in the living God. The modern versions turn this tremendous truth into a personal work by stressing *striving*. The reality is that Christians will suffer persecution, and all one has to do is look around today, and that will be obvious. The modern versions seem to want to mollify the reality that Christians will suffer by omitting that fact in this verse.

1 Timothy 4:12

> Let no man despise thy youth; but be thou an example of the believers, in word, in conversation, in charity, *in spirit*, in faith, in purity.
> (1 Timothy 4:12, KJV)

"In spirit" is omitted.

The modern versions remove an encouraging aspect of the Christian walk. It is the spirit in which we do things. It is making sure that we have the correct motivations in doing the Lord's work. It is speaking of the motivation in the believer's life to effect holy and spiritually fruitful works to the glory of God. If we approach our Christian walk with the wrong spirit, it will ruin our testimony and will cause all the works we do to become of noneffect for the kingdom of God. Timothy was being encouraged by Paul to be a good example of the believers, but this could not happen if his motivations were wrong. This is why when the modern versions omit that phrase, they omit a very necessary part of the Christian walk. In fact, that correct spirit separates us from the religious crowd. Once again, the King James Bible gives the believer a full picture of the true Christian walk that separates us from religious behavior.

1 Timothy 5:4

But if any widow have children or nephews, let them learn first to shew piety at home, and to requite their parents: for that is *good and* acceptable before God. (1 Timothy 5:4, KJV)

"Good and" is omitted.

Not only does God see requiting ones parents as an acceptable practice; He also condones it by calling it "good." The word *good* may be understood as a "beautiful or worthy thing." There should have been no reason for this to be left out of the modern versions since it shows God giving approval for children helping out their parents in time of need. If there is one thing the family needs, it is encouragement to do the right thing. "Honour thy father and thy mother: that thy days may be long upon the land which the LORD thy God giveth thee" (Exodus 20:12, KJV). The fifth commandment has never been rescinded.

1 Timothy 5:16

If any *man or* woman that believeth have widows, let *them* relieve them, and let not the church be charged; that it may relieve them that are widows indeed. (1 Timothy 5:16, KJV)

"Man or" is omitted. *"Them"* is changed to "her."

In this verse, Paul had summarized his instructions concerning the care of widows. The modern versions have completely removed this responsibility from the men and placed it totally on the women. In fact, the modern versions take the word *them* and change it into "her." They take a third-person plural word and turn it into a second-person singular. The Greek text expressly states both men and women are to partake in the responsibility. When the Lord Jesus Christ was on the cross, He committed the care of His earthly mother, Mary, to the apostle John. Jesus had half-brothers and sisters, but they had probably abandoned Mary and Jesus in fear of the Romans and the Pharisees.

If a man loses his father to death, thus making his mother a widow, the modern versions absolve him from all responsibility to care for her, and this chapter in Timothy is expressing family relationships. The family is to take care of a widow so the church is not burdened. The church was to care for widows who had no family at all, but if there was family still living, then they were to care for the widow. The modern versions have ruined the real meaning of this verse too.

1 Timothy 5:21

> I charge thee before God, and the *Lord* Jesus Christ, and the elect angels, that thou observe these things without preferring one before another, doing nothing by partiality. (1 Timothy 5:21, KJV)

Lord is omitted.

Here is another verse that has removed the ruling title of the Lord Jesus Christ. They have changed it to "Christ Jesus."

1 Timothy 6:5

> Perverse disputings of men of corrupt minds, and destitute of the truth, supposing that gain is godliness: *from such withdraw thyself.* (1 Timothy 6:5, KJV)

"From such withdraw thyself" is omitted.

This verse ends a three-verse warning to the believer concerning the unbeliever and their false teachings. Not only are we warned to be on guard for false teachings and teachers, but we must heed the warning in verse 5 commanding us to withdraw or leave such a person. The word for "withdraw" in this verse is *aphistaso*, which is in the imperative mood. This means it is a command for us to leave and depart from those who teach false teachings; it is not a suggestion. Listening to false teachers is actually a sin for the believer since God commands us to depart from those who hold not to the true doctrine of the Bible. These false teachers have an agenda to draw you away from the truth.

God even commands the believer to withdraw from other believers who are walking disorderly and not according to the scriptures. The word for "withdraw" in this verse carries with it the meaning of "shunning." We are to actually shun the disobedient believer. Normally, disobedience begins with adapting to false doctrine.

> Now we command you, brethren, in the name of our Lord Jesus Christ, that ye withdraw yourselves from every brother that walketh disorderly, and not after the tradition which he received of us. (2 Thessalonians 3:6, KJV)

Now, why does God want us to withdraw and shun false teachings?

> Be not deceived: evil communications corrupt good manners. (1 Corinthians 15:33, KJV)

God reminds us that if we allow any evil teachings or teachers into our lives, we will become corrupted. You also cannot allow evil or corrupt teachings to linger in any church, or they will begin to chip away at the true teachings. The word *manners* carries with it the meaning of "habits." Once false teachings begin to pervade a church, the acting out of habits in concert with those false teachings begin to happen, and any false teaching will cause people to walk differently from the biblical norm. You cannot associate yourself with bad teachings and expect to walk a solid Christian walk. We see this today as many Christians are carried away by false teachings that sound good.

This is why God gave the command in 1 Timothy 6:5 for believers to disassociate themselves from false teachings and teachers. No wonder the false teachers love the new versions. The phrase to withdraw ourselves from them has been deleted. When we look at 1 Timothy 6:5, we can see that the TV hucksters of today, especially those of the Charismatic movement, who view wealth and health as a blessing from God. This verse warns us that those who think gain is godliness are severely deceived. If this world goes on for another one hundred years, who do you think will be remembered, the poor widow who gave her two mites or the ugly one-thousand-dollar tailored suits of some of the media preachers? Believe me, gain does not represent godliness, or else 99.9 percent of the Christians in the world, even the suffering Christians, would be considered ungodly, and this is nowhere taught in scripture. Let us stay with the King James Bible, and let the dead bury their dead!

1 Timothy 6:7

> For we brought nothing into this world, and *it is certain* we can carry nothing out. (1 Timothy 6:7, KJV)

"It is certain" is omitted.

The scripture here makes a great truth that is normally neglected by people. The truth is that it is a great certainty that we came into this world with absolutely nothing, and it is also a great certainty that we will carry nothing out. The word that is missing in the Hort-Westcott text is *dêlos*, which carries the meaning of "evident or clear." Every person who has died, including believers, leave all their worldly goods behind. Paul wanted to make this clear so Christians who had wealth or even decent wages would not try to hoard and build up their finances. There is nothing wrong with saving, but when we begin to hoard, it becomes an obsession.

A few years ago, I heard Dr. Charles Stanley on the radio make a really good statement, and I am repeating it from memory. "God is blessed by us being funnels." This means that God gives us finances and material goods for the purpose of glorifying God and advancing the kingdom of God on earth. Paul is stressing the fact that not a penny or a material good will ever go with us, and that is why Paul wants us to use what the Lord has given us for the sake of the Gospel. There is no reason for the Gnostics to have left out this important word, unless they believe that they will somehow take their treasures with them. Once again, the King James Bible emphasizes a great cardinal truth.

1 Timothy 6:19

> Laying up in store for themselves a good foundation against the time to come, that they may lay hold on *eternal* life. (1 Timothy 6:19, KJV)

Eternal is omitted.

> That they do good, that they be rich in good works, ready to distribute, willing to communicate; Laying up in store for themselves a good foundation against the time to come, that they may lay hold on eternal life. (1 Timothy 6:18–19, KJV)

This continues the thread from the previous verse that those who are willing to give according to their means are laying up a good foundation that is in heaven. The foundation in view is the stable and enduring foundation of heaven in contrast to the unstable foundations here on the earth. The "time to come" will be when they enter the gates of heaven. They are using their wealth wisely in investing in the kingdom of God because they have become saved and have obeyed the commandment to be liberal in their giving. Then Paul finishes this verse by stating that they may hold on to eternal life. This is not speaking of buying one's salvation, but it is stating that these people who give liberally for the sake of the Gospel have laid hold or grasped the reality of eternal life in that this life is only transitory and the next life is permanent. It shows they grasped the understanding of the difference in the transitory life and eternal life.

It seems the modern versions do not want you to know this as they seem to be focusing on a better life in this life. They speak of the future that could mean "ten years from today," but the King James Bible is very to the point that this verse is pointing to eternal life and not a life on this earth sometime in the future. I guess if one reads

Joel Osteen's book *Your Best Life Now*, it would match up perfectly with the idea in this verse as found in the modern versions. However, I would agree with the King James Bible that our best life will be eternal in heaven with the Lord Jesus Christ.

2 Timothy 1:11

> Whereunto I am appointed a preacher, and an apostle, and a teacher *of the Gentiles.* (2 Timothy 1:11, KJV)

"Of the Gentiles" is omitted.

In many places in the Old Testament, God had promised that the Gospel was going to be preached to the Gentiles. The Lord Jesus Christ even stated that the Gospel was going to the entire world. "And he said unto them, Go ye into all the world, and preach the gospel to every creature" (Mark 16:15, KJV). At the time the Lord Jesus Christ made that statement, the scriptures had been written for the Jews (yet applicable to all Christians); but when God saved the apostle Paul, He made him the teacher of the Gentiles, which became his primary ministry, especially concerning the founding of the churches in various areas. The Gentiles would continue the churches up until the last day, and along with these churches was needed written guidance.

The apostle Paul, under the inspiration of the Holy Spirit, had penned thirteen books of the Bible (fourteen, if you believe Paul wrote Hebrews). Those thirteen books became the guidelines for Christian living, for church government, and discipline; plus, the guideline for the Lord's Supper. When the section of the verse "of the Gentiles" is removed, it eradicates the part of the verse, which is a specific fulfillment of the promise of God that the Gospel would be sent to the Gentiles. The appointment of the apostle Paul as an apostle and teacher of the Gentiles is part of the fulfillment of God's promise. Once again, the modern versions have attacked a vital doctrine of a promise of God to the Gentile world.

2 Timothy 2:19

Nevertheless the foundation of God standeth sure, having this seal, The Lord knoweth them that are his. And, Let every one that nameth the name of *Christ* depart from iniquity. (2 Timothy 2:19, KJV)

Christ is changed to "Lord."

Here is another case of the removal of the name of Christ and replaced with a generic "Lord." The point is that those who are Christians who name the name of Christ are supposed to depart from all evil, but the modern versions widen the meaning. With the use of the generic word *Lord*, this admonition can be applied to groups outside of Christianity.

2 Timothy 3:16

All scripture is given by *inspiration* of God, and is profitable for doctrine, for reproof, for correction, for instruction in righteousness. (2 Timothy 3:16, KJV)

Inspiration is changed to "God-breathed."

Theopneustos—the word is used only once in the New Testament. This means that the original manuscripts that God gave, which includes both the Hebrew scriptures and the Greek scriptures, were inspired by God as the Holy Ghost gave the scriptures to chosen vessels who wrote them down. "For the prophecy came not in old time by the will of man: but holy men of God spake as they were moved by the Holy Ghost" (2 Peter 1:21, KJV). They not only spoke the word of God; it was written down by them or by an amanuensis. Once the original manuscripts were completed with the book of Revelation, revelation had ended, and now God would preserve the inspired word so future generations would have access to the same words that were written by the old prophets and apostles.

Now, for us to understand the scriptures, God illuminates them through the indwelling of the Holy Spirit. This is why we say "the inspired word of God" because they are living scriptures, even in the English of our King James Bible.

2 Timothy 4:1

> I charge thee *therefore* before God, and *the Lord* Jesus Christ, who shall judge the quick and the dead at his appearing and his kingdom. (2 Timothy 4:1, KJV)

"Therefore" and *"the Lord"* are omitted.

The word *therefore* makes a connection between what was just previously taught and the next actions. Paul is stating that the scriptures, being given by inspiration of God, have the ability to make the believer perfect and thoroughly furnished for the ministry. This is what Paul was building on when he stated that he "therefore" charged Timothy to preach the word. It is because the scriptures are sufficient for the task of Gospel proclamation, owing to the personal effect it also has on the teacher or preacher bringing the Gospel. The modern versions omit *therefore*, and by doing that, they omit the link between the believer's source of strength and their ministry of teaching, both in and out of season.

We preach confidently and boldly because the scriptures are our foundation of truth and strength. The modern versions also omit the divine title of the Lord Jesus Christ, *the Lord*. It is linked to the fact that He is going to be the one to judge both the living and dead unbelievers when He returns on the last day. Once again, the King James Version keeps the continuity of scripture where the modern versions do not.

2 Timothy 4:22

> The Lord *Jesus Christ* be with thy spirit. Grace be with you. *Amen.* (2 Timothy 4:22, KJV)

Jesus Christ and *amen* are omitted.

The apostle Paul is giving this benediction in two parts: The first part is directed to Timothy concerning "the Lord Jesus Christ be with thy spirit." *Thy* is singular. The second part, "grace be with you," is addressed to all Christians because *you* is plural. If you notice in the first part of this verse, the full name *Jesus Christ* has been omitted in the counterfeit versions. Depends on what type of spirit a person has, whether it be New Age or false religion, this verse could be used to confirm someone's relationship with their false god. At least in the King James Bible, we know exactly who the *Lord* is. The modern versions leave the Lord Jesus Christ out of the very book that is supposed to be all about Him.

> Then said I, Lo, I come: in the volume of the book it is written of me. (Psalm 40:7, KJV)

> Then said I, Lo, I come (in the volume of the book it is written of me,) to do thy will, O God. (Hebrews 10:7, KJV)

Titus 1:2

> In hope of eternal life, which God, that *cannot lie*, promised before the world began. (Titus 1:2, KJV)

"Cannot lie" is changed to "does not lie," making it a question of ability versus choice to not lie.

Here is a case of the translators using the wrong English words. The word *cannot* as used in the King James Bible is the Greek word *apseudês*, which has a specific meaning of "free from falsehood, truthful." It is used only once in the New Testament. It conveys the fact that God is absolutely free from any and all falsehood, and as a result, He cannot lie. The words *can* and *cannot* are words of ability. This means that He does not have the ability to lie. The Greek word should never be translated "does not" or "never tells" because these

English words convey that lying is optional and that God chooses not to lie, leaving Him the ability to lie.

Let me use an illustration. I will use myself as the subject. Ken has trouble with his legs and therefore cannot run. Modern usage would write, "Ken has trouble with his legs and therefore does not run." Do you see the major difference? My leg problems make it impossible for me to run; it does not give me a choice. Once again, the modern versions leave a confusing thought instead of a definite truth like the King James Bible does in this verse.

Titus 1:4

> To Titus, mine own son after *the common faith*: Grace, *mercy*, and peace, from God the Father and *the Lord* Jesus Christ our Saviour. (Titus 1:4, KJV)

"The common faith" is changed to "a common faith," giving the suggestion there is more than one specific faith. *"Mercy"* is omitted. *"The Lord"* is omitted.

This verse was hit in three different places:

1) The definite article *the* has been replaced by the indefinite article *a*. The word *the* points to a specific thing. In this verse, it points to the common faith that is found among believers. When the word is removed and reduced to an indefinite article, it could carry the meaning of "one faith among many." There was only one faith that the apostle Paul focused on, and that was the Christian faith because it is the only one that saves.

2) The word *mercy* in the Greek was removed. Mercy in the book of Titus is directly related to God's mercy, who saves His Elect. "Not by works of righteousness which we have done, but according to his mercy he saved us, by the washing of regeneration, and renewing of the Holy Ghost" (Titus 3:5, KJV). To remove this word is to remove an attribute of God that is tied to salvation.

3) Another attack on the divine title of the Lord Jesus Christ is by removing "the Lord." The Gnostics did not believe that Jesus was divine, so they did what they could to reduce Him to the level of a man.

Titus 2:7

In all things shewing thyself a pattern of good works: in doctrine shewing uncorruptness, gravity, *sincerity*. (Titus 2:7, KJV)

Sincerity is omitted.

Here is a case similar to the one we saw in Titus 1:4, where they omitted the *mercy* of God. In this passage, they have omitted *sincerity*, which means a person must not be corruptible and to bring the true Gospel to people in a manner that is free from all corruption and false pretense. The Gnostics were doing just that, bringing a false gospel according to their belief system so they would not be able to claim sincerity, so they removed it. If we had more sincere preachers of the Gospel, we would not be in a position of every church having their own variety of Gospel; then there would be more unity among Christianity. Since the modern versions are corrupt, I guess it is not much of a leap to allow their users to be corrupt and corruptible.

Titus 2:13

Looking for that blessed hope, and the *glorious appearing* of the great God and our Saviour Jesus Christ. (Titus 2:13, KJV)

"Glorious appearing" is changed to "the appearing of the glory" in the NASV.

When the Lord Jesus Christ returns on the last day, will He be appearing Himself, or will only the glory be appearing? The NASV makes it sound like only His glory will be coming back and not Him.

Philemon 6

That the communication of thy faith may become effectual by the acknowledging of every good thing which is in you in Christ *Jesus*. (Philemon 6, KJV)

Jesus is omitted.

Here is another Gnostic attempt to separate the full name of Jesus. Even the New Age movement has a christ, and even some other false religions have a christ. The name *Jesus* must be attached to give it a specific personality and not one of some false teacher's choosing.

Thank You, Father, for Philemon. I pray that as he goes and tells his story of faith, *he would tell everyone so that* they will know for certain all the good that comes *to those who put their trust* in the Anointed One. (VOICE)

Notice "the Voice" above where it completely removes the name of Jesus Christ and replaces it with "the Anointed One." That is as new age as you can get!

Philemon 12

Whom I have sent again: *thou therefore receive him,* that is, mine own bowels. (Philemon 12, KJV)

"Thou therefore receive him" is omitted.

Paul makes an impassioned plea for Onesimus to Philemon. Onesimus, a slave, had left Philemon and met up with Paul. Onesimus became a Christian, and Paul was now sending him back to Philemon. In verse 12, Paul desires that Philemon receive Onesimus. The word that is removed from the modern versions in the Greek means not only to receive Onesimus back into the service of Philemon but means that Paul is desiring that Philemon would "accept, welcome, to take alongside, or to welcome with hospitality."

In the modern versions, Paul is seen as just sending him back to Philemon, and without the desire that Philemon accept him as a brother, it could be interpreted that Paul was sending him back, and Philemon can do what he wants to Onesimus. The modern versions leave out the element of mercy and compassion that Paul desires Philemon to show to Onesimus. The great lesson here is that we, before salvation, as servants of sin, return unto the Lord as children of God and that He has great compassion on us, not giving us the punishment we deserve. This is the great message of verse 12 that the Lord receives us as brethren and no longer as a slave because our relationship has changed.

Once again, the modern versions leave out a great lesson about the compassion of the Lord toward His children. This verse also teaches that when a child of God strays, He will receive us back as His children.

Philemon 25

> The grace of *our Lord Jesus Christ* be with your spirit. *Amen.* (Philemon 25, KJV)

"*Our Lord Jesus Christ*" is changed to "the Lord Jesus Christ." "Amen" is omitted.

This verse also received the ax twice. The first instance is the first part of the verse where it is addressing believers that the Lord Jesus Christ is *our* Lord Jesus Christ, which means only of the believer. Then the second instance is when the modern versions omit *amen*, which signifies the end of the verse and is a word of confirmation or establishment that there is a finality to what has been written, especially applying it to the word of God.

Hebrews 1:3

> Who being the brightness of his glory, and the express image of his person, and upholding all things by the word of his power, when he had

by himself purged *our* sins, sat down on the right
hand of the Majesty on high. (Hebrews 1:3, KJV)

"By himself" and *"our"* are omitted.

Here is a subtle attack on two of the most cardinal doctrines of
the Christian faith. In the first attack, the words "by himself" have
been omitted. Any true Christian knows that it was the Lord Jesus
Christ who went to the cross to pay for the sins of the elect. No one
helped Him, nor did anybody else have anything to add to the sacrifice of Christ. In fact, knowing what the Roman Catholics would
do with Peter, the Lord Jesus had to remove him to a different place,
or else they would teach that he assisted the Lord in His sacrifice.
Removing the words "by himself" removes the reality that Christ
Himself is the Savior of His people and that it was He who died.
"And she shall bring forth a son, and thou shalt call his name JESUS:
for he shall save his people from their sins" (Matthew 1:21, KJV).

When the fact that Jesus Himself was the sacrifice, the modern
versions convey that God had purged our sins by other methods. A
person who believes in works can claim that God accomplished their
salvation by giving them certain works to do. A Roman Catholic
can claim that God will accomplish their salvation by letting them
spend time in purgatory. So by removing those very important words
"by himself," it opens up the door for a host of belief systems that
attempt to circumvent the personal cross of Christ.

The second cardinal doctrine that is attacked is for whom Christ
died. Many believe He died for the sins of the whole world; that is, for
every single person who lives on earth. This can be taught when you
remove the word *our* because that word *our* points to a specific group
of people for whom Christ died, and that was His people. His people
are not the unregenerate nation of Israel, which the Premillennialists
teach. His people are those who are the truly redeemed of God by
free grace, chosen out of every nation on earth from before the foundation of the world, including both Jews and Gentiles. The word
our specifies for whom Christ died, and by removing it, you can
create another verse that seemingly would teach universal salvation.
Hebrews 1:3 is a long verse, and by removing those three words, it

changes the meaning of it. Once again, the King James Bible shows its doctrinal superiority and purity in comparison with the modern versions.

Hebrews 2:7

Thou madest him a little lower than the angels;
thou crownedst him with glory and honour,
and didst set him over the works of thy hands.
(Hebrews 2:7, KJV)

"And didst set him over the works of thy hands" is omitted.

When God first created man, He stated that he would have dominion over the earth. "And God said, Let us make man in our image, after our likeness: and let them have dominion over the fish of the sea, and over the fowl of the air, and over the cattle, and over all the earth, and over every creeping thing that creepeth upon the earth" (Genesis 1:26, KJV). Of course, when sin entered the picture, the entire situation changed. Nevertheless, the verse in Hebrews is speaking of the time when God first created man and gave him that dominion. The modern versions omit this extremely important fact. No reason is given why the Gnostics omitted it, but maybe they did not want to bring up the story of how man sinned in the Garden of Eden and bring him down to the status of a lowly sinner. Man loves to think of himself as being a king instead of a sinner. The King James leaves this verse intact so we will never forget from where we fell.

Hebrews 3:1

Wherefore, holy brethren, partakers of the heavenly calling, consider the Apostle and High Priest
of our profession, *Christ* Jesus. (Hebrews 3:1, KJV)

Christ is omitted.

The modern versions omit the divine name of Jesus from a very important description of Him in this verse.

Hebrews 3:6

But Christ as a son over *his own house*; whose house are we, if we hold fast the confidence and the rejoicing of the hope *firm unto the end.* (Hebrews 3:6, KJV)

"His own house" is changed to "God's house." *"Firm unto the end"* is omitted.

Here are two points concerning the superiority of Christ over Moses (v. 5): The first one is that Jesus is the *Son* and not a servant. The Son was always the heir of the estate, and the servants still continued to work for the son. The second point is that Christ is over His own house; He is not in the house. Christ rules over all the believers. He was not one of us. Instead, through His sacrifice, He made us believers in Him, resulting in all the true believers being His house.

The second part of this verse is a hint concerning those in the house being true believers. Some may claim to be believers but are not. "But he that shall endure unto the end, the same shall be saved" (Matthew 24:13, KJV). The key to knowing if you are a true believer is the fact that you continue to endure the hardships and challenges of the Christian life. This verse teaches us that we are the house of Christ if we hold fast with confidence and rejoicing of the hope, whether it be till the end of our life or the end of time. Many will claim to be saved, but when the time comes for a little boldness in the faith, they run away, and this is an indicator that they are not holding fast with confidence the hope. Those who are truly saved will have much confidence in the message of the Gospel because they know from where it comes and who the originator is. The false Christian has only enough confidence in themselves, and when that is exhausted, they flee. We are to hold firm our testimony till the end, and that is the indicator we have been truly saved.

Many of the modern versions use the name *God* in describing the house. The word *theos* does not appear in this verse in any form. They have, in essence, added to the word of God by doing this; plus, it makes Jesus out to be just a hireling, that He was equal with Moses in that He was faithful in God's house, when this verse is speaking of the fact that Christ is over His own house because of Calvary. The modern versions want to reduce Christ to just a prophet status. Moses did not build his house, but Jesus built His house because of His own sacrifice. Once again, the modern versions make subtle changes and omissions that are all violations of God's word.

Hebrews 3:16

For some, when they had heard, did provoke: *howbeit not all* that came out of Egypt by Moses. (Hebrews 3:16, KJV)

"Howbeit not all" is omitted.

This change causes the modern versions to tell a lie. If you will notice, the King James Bible teaches us that the children of Israel were rebellious, but the verse teaches us, according to all the information in the Old Testament, that not every Israelite who left Egypt with Moses was rebellious. However, the modern versions teach that every Israelite who left Egypt was rebellious. There was Joshua, Caleb, Eliezer, and probably a number of others who were unnamed who did not rebel against God. The number was definitely very small, but this shows a great foreshadowing of the number of true believers who will be in the world at any time. The modern versions tell us that all were rebellious, but even if you find only three or four who were not, that would negate the entire statement found in the modern versions and would cause it to be erroneous and would need to be retracted.

Hebrews 4:6

Seeing therefore it remaineth that some must enter therein, and they to whom it was first preached entered not in because of *unbelief*. (Hebrews 4:6, KJV)

Unbelief is changed to "disobedience."

Unbelief may lead to disobedience, but they are definitely two different things. One of the biggest problems with Israel was that she wreaked with unbelief, which led to her disobedience.

Hebrews 6:10

> For God is not unrighteous to forget your work and *labour of* love, which ye have shewed toward his name, in that ye have ministered to the saints, and do minister. (Hebrews 6:10, KJV)

"Labour of" is omitted.

The words "labour of" have been omitted in the Greek text as well as the English text. The word *labour* carries with the meaning of "toil, weariness, and trouble." The writer to the Hebrews is assuring his readers that those who toil and become weary in the service of the Lord, especially toward the household of faith, will not be forgotten by the Lord for all their work. In Galatians 6:10, the apostle Paul states: "As we have therefore opportunity, let us do good unto all men, especially unto them who are of the household of faith" (Galatians 6:10, KJV).

It is the believer's responsibility to not only do good to those outside the body of Christ, but we are to minister to the body of believers also. In other words, God is basically stating that we must not neglect those who are in the body of Christ. Sometimes in churches, those who have needs in the local congregation are neglected in favor of those who are unsaved. This is biased ministry in that the unbelievers are being ministered to but the believers are being neglected. We must always be prepared to evangelize the lost, but we must also continue to minister to those who are within the body of Christ.

Hebrews 6:10 teaches a great principle in that love is not just words or a state of mind, but true Christian love is action. When the Gnostics and their modern counterparts omitted the words "labour of," they were omitting the major standard of true love, and that is action and involvement. According to the modern versions, in this verse, love has no ingredients, and that is teaching a false notion of true Christian love. The word *labour* tells us that love contains action and that believers must not only love in word but also in deed. The apostle John sums up this principle: "My little children, let us not love in word, neither in tongue; but in deed and in truth" (1 John 3:18, KJV). Love is something that is way beyond words. Actions that we do for someone demonstrates the love we have for them and the love we have coming from our hearts because of our transformation in Christ. Nonaction and noninvolvement only shows apathy and not love. In fact, it may also show that a person is unsaved because our faith is confirmed by our works (James 2:14–26), and so is our love.

Hebrews 7:21

> For those priests were made without an oath;
> but this with an oath by him that said unto him,
> The Lord sware and will not repent, Thou art
> a priest for ever *after the order of Melchisedec*.
> (Hebrews 7:21, KJV)

"After the order of Melchisedec" is omitted.

The last part of the verse that is omitted in the modern versions is the reference to the priesthood of the Lord Jesus Christ having an eternal nature. It is a quote taken from Psalm 110:4: "The LORD hath sworn, and will not repent, Thou art a priest for ever after the order of Melchizedek" (Psalm 110:4, KJV). If you recall, Melchisedec is described in eternal terms in Hebrews 7:3: "Without father, without mother, without descent, having neither beginning of days, nor end of life; but made like unto the Son of God; abideth a priest continually" (Hebrews 7:3, KJV). It is a shame that the modern versions omit this significant fact about the Lord Jesus Christ. The Gnostics never believed that Jesus was eternal, so they did what they could to destroy the truth of His eternal nature.

Hebrews 8:12

For I will be merciful to their unrighteousness, and their sins *and their iniquities* will I remember no more. (Hebrews 8:12, KJV)

"And their iniquities" is omitted.

This great verse, Hebrews 8:12, carries two great promises: First, that God will forgive and forget all the sins that the believer has ever committed or will commit in the future. The other great promise in this verse is that God will also forgive and forget all our iniquities. The iniquities are basically "lawlessness," which means that all the transgressions of God's law will be forgiven because Christ had fulfilled all the righteous demands of the law. Therefore, the believer is no longer liable for not obeying the tenets of the law. Since Christ has completely fulfilled all the demands of the law and that was imputed to the believer, it is as if we never broke one of the laws of God.

For the modern versions to omit this section does a great disservice to the body of Christ and robs us of a great promise in scripture. Many Christians feel they have to do something in the way of works, but since Christ fulfilled all the demands of the law, we simply rest in the finished work of Calvary, and the modern versions omit this great truth.

Hebrews 10:9

Then said he, Lo, I come to do thy will, *O God*. He taketh away the first, that he may establish the second. (Hebrews 10:9, KJV)

"O God" is omitted.

This section of Hebrews describes the reason that the Lord Jesus came to earth, and that was to do the will of God in salvation. The King James Bible leaves no doubt that the Lord Jesus came to do the will of God, but the modern versions omit the direct reference to God and leave it open that the Lord Jesus came to do the will of someone. There is a New Age teaching that the Lord Jesus Christ did not go back to heaven but instead went to India. The modern version's omission of "O God" leaves the door open that Jesus went and did the will of someone. Who was that someone? Was it Krishna? Was it Maitreya? Was it the will of Caesar? The King James teaches us that Jesus came to do the will of God and not the will of anyone else. Once again, the King James leaves us no doubt as to the mission of the Lord Jesus Christ whereas the modern versions leave a serious fracture in their teachings, leaving it up to the reader to decide what is meant there.

Hebrews 10:14

For by one offering he hath perfected for ever them that *are sanctified*. (Hebrews 10:14, KJV)

"Are sanctified" is changed to "being made holy" in the NIV.

For by one sacrifice he has made perfect forever those who are being made holy. (NIV)

The Bible teaches that upon salvation, every believer becomes holy by means of their position in Christ. The NIV makes it sound like a person has to go through some process to become holy. This is absolutely erroneous. While "sanctified" and "holy" share a common word in the Greek, the English words are different. Sanctification is the progress a Christian makes in their Christian walk by eschewing the world and becoming closer to Christ. Holiness is something that happens instantly at salvation. "According as he hath chosen us in him before the foundation of the world, that we should be holy and without blame before him in love" (Ephesians 1:4, KJV).

Hebrews 10:19

Having therefore, brethren, boldness to enter into the *holiest* by the blood of Jesus. (Hebrews 10:19, KJV)

Holiest changed to "holy place" or just omitted.

Here is another subtle attack on the power of the blood of Christ. The King James uses the word *holiest*, which is a reference to the holy of holies in the tabernacle and temple. The word is an adjective, and it is in the genitive case. It is not a noun as the modern versions portray. A noun names a person, place, or thing. So they use the words "holy place" to translate the word. The word *holy* would be the adjective modifying the noun *place*. However, the word *place* is not in the text, so they add it in the English. Plus, the holy place was outside the holy of holies.

Basically, what the modern versions are saying is that the blood of Christ was not sufficient enough to bring us into the holy of holies, which represents God the Father, and that is false doctrine. Those who are truly in Christ have access to God the Father. That is the teaching of this verse that we are now qualified to enter the holy of holies or the presence of God the Father through the blood of Christ. This is a very egregious error in the modern versions, and they claim that no doctrines are affected. Here is an attack on the doctrine of Christ, atonement, and salvation all wrapped up in one modern-version verse.

Hebrews 10:30

> For we know him that hath said, Vengeance belongeth unto me, I will recompense, *saith the Lord*. And again, The Lord shall judge his people. (Hebrews 10:30, KJV)

"Saith the Lord" is omitted.
Verse 30 answers the question of verse 29!

> Of how much sorer punishment, suppose ye, shall he be thought worthy, who hath trodden under foot the Son of God, and hath counted the blood of the covenant, wherewith he was sanctified, an unholy thing, and hath done despite unto the Spirit of grace? (Hebrews 10:29, KJV)

The same God who spoke through Moses and the prophets is the same God of the new covenant. This means that He will dispense judgment to those who are deserving of it. Verse 30 is a quote from Deuteronomy 32:35–36:

> To me belongeth vengeance, and recompense;
> their foot shall slide in due time: for the day of
> their calamity is at hand, and the things that
> shall come upon them make haste. For the
> LORD shall judge his people, and repent him-
> self for his servants, when he seeth that their
> power is gone, and there is none shut up, or left.
> (Deuteronomy 32:35–36, KJV)

When the modern versions omit the phrase "saith the Lord," they are omitting the source of the statement. The modern versions soften the verse by making it sound like a commentary rather than the exact quotation of the Lord Himself. This is why the King James is superior because it retains the warning that God has given and does not lessen the severity of the consequences.

Hebrews 10:34

> For ye had compassion of me in my bonds, and
> took joyfully the spoiling of your goods, knowing
> in yourselves that ye have *in heaven* a better and
> an enduring substance. (Hebrews 10:34, KJV)

"In heaven" is omitted.

Here we are seeing an attack on the teachings of heaven. The King James teaches us that our better and enduring substance is in heaven. The modern versions leave out this vital phrase, which denies the existence of heaven. The true believer can lose everything on earth but will never lose their home in heaven. By removing the phrase "in heaven," it makes the verse in the modern versions have no sense. Notice the NIV:

You suffered along with those in prison and joyfully accepted the confiscation of your property,
because you knew that you yourselves had better
and lasting possessions. (NIV)

On one hand, we are told that our possessions were confiscated;
and on the other hand, we are told we have better and lasting possessions. So which is it? Were they confiscated, or do we still have them?

In the King James Bible, this verse teaches that even if every
earthly possession we have is taken from us, they can never remove
our heavenly possession. God has promised that the true redeemed
believer is going to live with Him in heaven for eternity, and that
is the better and enduring substance we have. It is a comparison
between the earthly possessions that can be lost and our heavenly
possession, which can never be lost. The modern versions remove
that comparison milieu, which is strategic for understanding that
verse.

Heaven is a spiritual place. "Now this I say, brethren, *that flesh
and blood cannot inherit the kingdom of God*; neither doth corruption inherit incorruption" (1 Corinthians 15:50, KJV). The Gnostics
would have attacked this biblical truth also. They did not believe
that Christ came from heaven, and that is why they have attacked 1
Corinthians 15:47 by removing the reference to Christ coming down
from heaven. If they did not believe that Christ came from heaven,
they would not believe that people go to heaven. In fact, reincarna-
tion is an accepted teaching by the Gnostics going back very far in
history. Yet the modern "Christian" scholars accept the corruptions
made by these Gnostics. No wonder the Bible teaches that the prostitutes will get into heaven before the religious leaders. "Whether of
them twain did the will of his father? They say unto him, The first.
Jesus saith unto them, Verily I say unto you, That the publicans and
the harlots go into the kingdom of God before you" (Matthew 21:31,
KJV). The Lord Jesus Christ stated at the Last Supper that He is
going to prepare a place for us. He went to the cross so that that place
would be in heaven. Why would any true Christian want a version
that denies heaven?

Hebrews 11:11

Through faith also Sara herself received strength to conceive seed, and *was delivered of a child* when she was past age, because she judged him faithful who had promised. (Hebrews 11:11, KJV)

"Was delivered of a child" is omitted.

And God said, Sarah thy wife shall bear thee a son indeed; and thou shalt call his name Isaac: and I will establish my covenant with him for an everlasting covenant, and with his seed after him. (Genesis 17:19, KJV)

But my covenant will I establish with Isaac, which Sarah shall bear unto thee at this set time in the next year. (Genesis 17:21, KJV)

For Sarah conceived, *and bare Abraham a son* in his old age, at the set time of which God had spoken to him. And Abraham called the name of his son that was born unto him, *whom Sarah bare to him*, Isaac. (Genesis 21:2–3, KJV)

The great promise that God made to Abraham concerning the fact that He would bring Isaac into the world through Sarah is omitted in this verse. The modern versions state that Sarah had conceived, but they omit the important part that she delivered that child. Many women conceive, but that does not always mean they deliver the baby. God specifically stated that Sarah would bear Abraham a son, and that child would be a covenant child through whom the Lord Jesus Christ would come. This was an important event since this child would carry the lineage of the eternal covenant.

By removing the part that Sarah was delivered of a child, they remove the very event that God Himself promised in that Sarah would deliver a covenant child. Once again, the Gnostics and the modern-version translators show their contempt for the Gospel of grace, which is the eternal covenant. In Genesis 21:2–3, we see the mention of the fact that Sarah brought forth a son. It is mentioned once in each verse because God is telling us that He fulfills what He decrees, and He mentions it twice so we would know this fact. If I butchered the scriptures the way these translators do, I personally would be afraid to go to sleep at night.

Hebrews 11:13

> These all died in faith, not having received the promises, but having seen them afar off, *and were persuaded of them*, and embraced them, and confessed that they were strangers and pilgrims on the earth. (Hebrews 11:13, KJV)

"And were persuaded of them" is omitted.

The word *peisthenes* that was omitted in the critical Greek text is very important because it states that those who received the promises but did not see them literally fulfilled yet were persuaded or convinced of the truth of those promises. They not only received the promises, but they were convinced in their heart through the Holy Spirit that they would come to pass in God's timing. As believers, there are promises we embrace from the scriptures, and we are convinced or persuaded that they will come to pass. We are persuaded or convinced that the Lord will return to earth, that the true believer will receive eternal life, that there will be a new heaven and new earth, that the believer will receive a new glorified body, etc. There are promises that you and I are convinced or persuaded of that have not come to pass yet, and we, like the patriarchs, are persuaded of the truth of these promises by the indwelling Holy Spirit. A great truth that is omitted in the modern versions.

Hebrews 11:37

They were stoned, they were sawn asunder, *were tempted*, were slain with the sword: they wandered about in sheepskins and goatskins; being destitute, afflicted, tormented. (Hebrews 11:37, KJV)

"Were tempted" is omitted.

"The LORD trieth the righteous: but the wicked and him that loveth violence his soul hateth" (Psalm 11:5, KJV). One thing the believer can count on in this life is not only that Satan is going to tempt us to sin, but God Himself is going to test us to see how faithful we are. For the modern versions to omit the fact that testing is a part in the believer's life is to remove a life's principle from scripture. In the Middle Ages, when the Roman Catholic Church was murdering Christians, before they would burn them, they would give them one more chance to recant, which would be their final test of faithfulness to God. So along with their martyrdoms came testing. If they recanted, they failed the test; if they refused, they passed.

In our day, testing comes all the time to the believer simply because of the sinful society we dwell in. The King James Bible leaves that important part in for us to know that not only are we Christians in the modern era tested; the earlier Christians were also subjected to it. In our day, many Christians allow themselves to succumb to temptation or testing; but when we read in the Bible that many of the early Christians suffered testing and passed, it can bolster us to live a more obedient life. This is why the King James is superior here also.

Hebrews 12:20

For they could not endure that which was commanded, And if so much as a beast touch the mountain, it shall be stoned, *or thrust through with a dart.* (Hebrews 12:20, KJV)

"Or thrust through with a dart" is omitted.

And thou shalt set bounds unto the people round
about, saying, Take heed to yourselves, that ye go
not up into the mount, or touch the border of
it: whosoever toucheth the mount shall be surely
put to death: There shall not an hand touch it,
but he shall surely be stoned, or shot through;
whether it be beast or man, it shall not live: when
the trumpet soundeth long, they shall come up
to the mount. (Exodus 19:12–13, KJV)

The part that is omitted in the modern versions is part of the
penalty attached to any man or animal that approached Mount Sinai.
If either had touched it, then they were to be stoned or shot through.
If the violator was close at hand, they could be stoned by the people;
but if they were at a distance, then the people would shoot arrows at
them so there would be no fear of another casualty by approaching
the mountain. The Greek word *bolidi* can refer to a javelin, spear,
arrow, or dart. There is no legitimate reason for this second penalty
to have been omitted.

James 1:26

If any man *among you* seem to be religious, and
bridleth not his tongue, but deceiveth his own
heart, this man's religion is vain. (James 1:26, KJV)

"Among you" is omitted.

James was addressing the brethren if any among them did not
seem to be able to bridle ("to restrain or curb") their tongue, which
may give an indication that the person is not saved. Now, James was
specifically addressing the brethren, but the modern versions make
it sound like this applies to any religion, making it a universal application. Those in false religions, whether they have bridled tongues
or big mouths, are not saved. False religion does not save, no matter how pious or reserved one lives their life. "Examine yourselves,
whether ye be in the faith; prove your own selves. Know ye not your

own selves, how that Jesus Christ is in you, except ye be reprobates?" (2 Corinthians 13:5, KJV).

One way the true Christian can examine their Christian walk is by how they handle their tongue. If their words are vicious and attacking, then they may not be saved. This would be on a steady basis because being in the flesh, we all lose our tempers once in a while and let the words fly; but those who consistently speak nastily, it is a definite indicator that salvation never took place in their hearts. Normally, the transformation that inwardly took place by means of being saved is manifested outwardly. If that testimony is missing, then probably salvation is too. This is why it is important that we check our speech because it is a very simple salvation test.

James 2:19

Thou believest that *there is one God*; thou doest well: the devils also believe, and tremble. (James 2:19, KJV)

"There is one God" is changed to "God is one."

Here is another case of a reversed meaning in the English text. The King James Bible states that "there is one God." The Christian believes there is one God in three Persons, which is a belief in the tri-unity of the Godhead. The modern versions have the meaning reversed. First, the way the modern versions have it translated, it is stating that "God is one," which would deny the Trinity. This is what caused the Jews to stumble when Christ claimed to be the Son of the Heavenly Father; they only believed in one God as one person. Secondly, when it says "God is one," does it speak as God being one with the universe, being one person, one unity, one pantheon? "God is one" leaves an open door for anyone to add some kind of spurious ending and makes it say what they want. "There is one God" closes the subject because in the time James was written, there were many false gods, but James rejects those gods by claiming that there is only one God and no others.

James 2:20

> But wilt thou know, O vain man, that faith with-
> out works is *dead*? (James 2:20, KJV)

Dead is changed to "useless."

The word *vain* here is "empty" or "worthless." The word in the Greek for "dead" is *nekros*. James is driving home the reality that a life of verbal faith is not evidence of salvation. Faith without works is like a lightbulb that is off. If the lightbulb is off in the dark, it does not light the way and is as lifeless as a bulb that is bad. But if that lightbulb claims it is a lightbulb and then lights the way, the lightbulb has proven that it is a lightbulb by being lit. A Christian proves they are a Christian by working for the kingdom of God. The difference between true and false works is that false works are tied to this world and the glory of the doer. The true works are tied to the kingdom of God and the glory of God.

The modern versions remove the word *nekros*, which definitely means "dead," and replaces it with *argê*, which severely lessens the reality of the verse. Faith without works is dead, and something that is dead is dead. *Argê*" means "inactive, idle, or lazy" and does not speak of being dead. Something that is inactive can be made active, something that is idle may be employed, and something that is lazy can be made to be industrious. However, something that is dead is dead and lifeless. Once again, the King James Bible brings the truth while the modern versions sidestep it.

James 4:4

> Ye *adulterers and* adulteresses, know ye not that
> the friendship of the world is enmity with God?
> whosoever therefore will be a friend of the world
> is the enemy of God. (James 4:4, KJV)

"Adulterers and" is omitted.

In this verse, God is specifically charging both men and women with committing spiritual adultery. We are spiritually married to

Christ, and God is pointing out that if we start acting like the world in our erroneous prayer expectations, then we are as those who adulterate the relationship with Christ by disobedience. He reminds us that if we are acting like the world, then we are making friends with the world; and if we do that, we become the enemy of God, the position from which we were delivered. "Love not the world, neither the things that are in the world. If any man love the world, the love of the Father is not in him. For all that is in the world, the lust of the flesh, and the lust of the eyes, and the pride of life, is not of the Father, but is of the world" (1 John 2:15–16, KJV).

We must have holy motives in our praying and have no desire for camaraderie with the world. "For they that are after the flesh do mind the things of the flesh; but they that are after the Spirit the things of the Spirit" (Romans 8:5, KJV). Spiritual adultery is not only committed by women but men too. The modern versions omit the masculine gender and only keep the feminine gender. Some of the modern versions just combine both words and say "adulterous people." It is probably because they are doing away with specific genders and going toward that one unisex Bible.

James 4:12

There is one lawgiver, who is able to save and
to destroy: who art thou that judgest another?
(James 4:12, KJV)

"There is one lawgiver" is changed by adding to the text in the Greek to, "There is one Lawgiver and Judge."

Here is a case of adding to the word of God. The corrupted manuscripts added *kai kritês*, which is translated "and judge." They probably tried to copy the verse Isaiah 33:22: "For the LORD is our judge, the LORD is our lawgiver, the LORD is our king; he will save us" (Isaiah 33:22, KJV). However, even if this is what they attempted to do, they are still in violation of Revelation 22:18 because God did not place the words *and judge* in the text. The CEV, ERV, GNB, THE MESSAGE, NCV, and the NLT all insert the name *God*. Here is another example of false teaching. "For the Father judgeth no man, but hath committed all judgment unto the Son" (John 5:22, KJV). The Bible teaches in John 5:22 that Jesus will be the judge of mankind and not God the Father. These six versions remove that truth. Once again, the King James Bible proves its superiority in accuracy.

James 5:16

> Confess your *faults* one to another, and pray one for another, that ye may be healed. The effectual fervent prayer of a righteous man availeth much. (James 5:16, KJV)

Faults is changed to "sins."

James 5:16 has been changed from *faults* to "sins" in the modern versions. Hort and Westcott were both Roman Catholics, and for them to change the wording to read "sins" gives credence to the Roman Catholic system of confession. Nowhere in the Bible are we ever commanded to confess our sins to one another. We are to confess our sins to God, for it is only He who can forgive sins based upon whether a person is truly saved. "Why doth this man thus speak blasphemies? who can forgive sins but God only?" (Mark 2:7, KJV). The Pharisees were absolutely correct in that only God can forgive sins. In the Roman Catholic system, there is a very false belief that the priest can give absolution for sins. In other words, they believe they hold the power to forgive sins. The bigger question is, who forgives the sins of the priest?

The word for "faults" in the Greek is *paraptomata*, which carries with it the meaning of "a misfall or a mishap." It basically carries the meaning of referencing a subjective weakness of a person. It does not necessarily mean a person is sinning. For example, a person may come upon a car accident and see blood, and instead of getting involved, they remain in the car when they could have helped. Now, they could not stand to see the sight of blood, and that is where they have a weakness that caused them not to be involved because of their weakness in that area, and that does not mean they are sinning.

The word that replaced *paraptomata* in the modern versions is *hamartias*, which is translated "sin" in the rest of the New Testament, and it references a transgression of God's law. It can be adultery, lying, stealing, or any violation of God's law, and this is very different from a person having a weakness in a certain area. A person having a weakness in a certain area will not be the reason an unbeliever goes to hell, but the transgression of God's law will condemn a person eternally. This is a very important difference and shows how the modern versions once again placate Roman Catholicism and proclaim a very false teaching.

1 Peter 1:16

> Because it is written, *Be ye holy*; for I am holy.
> (1 Peter 1:16, KJV)

"Be ye holy" is changed to "ye shall be holy." (This change makes it to be a future action when the Christian is made holy at the moment of salvation.)

This a very subtle change to the text because in the King James Bible, the verse is a command for the believer to be holy; and the moment a person becomes saved, they are made holy. The modern versions abolish that command and make it a future tense, as if God does not require holiness of his children in the present. God expects a change of living from the profane to the holy as soon as a person becomes saved, not at some future date. He expects us to grow in holiness and not grow unto it—a very big difference.

1 Peter 1:22

> Seeing ye have purified your souls in obeying the truth *through the Spirit* unto unfeigned love of the brethren, see that ye love one another with a *pure* heart fervently. (1 Peter 1:22, KJV)

"Through the Spirit" and *"pure"* are omitted.

This verse has been corrupted in two places: The first place where there is corruption is where the Greek words *dia pneumatos* have been removed. These words are translated "through the Spirit," which is a reference to the Holy Spirit. This deletion attacks the work of the Holy Spirit in the life of a true believer. Removing this phrase makes it look like a person has the ability to obey God on their own, without the regenerating power of the Holy Spirit. The fact is that if a person does not have the Holy Spirit indwelling them, they are unsaved. "But ye are not in the flesh, but in the Spirit, if so be that the Spirit of God dwell in you. Now if any man have not the Spirit of Christ, he is none of his" (Romans 8:9, KJV). The Romans verse confirms that if a person does not have the Holy Spirit living in them, they do not belong to Christ.

The only way a person can ever be obedient to the truth is when the Holy Spirit is dwelling in them. In other words, we see a very important tenet of salvation being omitted here. No person who is in the flesh can ever please God. "So then they that are in the flesh cannot please God" (Romans 8:8, KJV). Therefore, when the Gnostics removed this portion of the verse, they were keeping in line with their disbelief of a spirit world, especially the Holy Spirit. Their idea of salvation is to be pumped up with more and more knowledge.

The second place of corruption in this verse is the word *katharas*, which means "pure." It is omitted in Sinaiticus and P72 but is found in Vaticanus and Alexandrinus of the fifth century. It has been included in the text of the United Bible Societies fourth edition but is in brackets.

Omits "pure": NIV, NASB, 1901 ASV, RSV, NRSV, NAB, NWT
Includes "pure": ESV, HCSB

What does the rest of the Bible say about the necessity of a pure heart?

Who shall ascend into the hill of the LORD? or who shall stand in his holy place? He that hath clean hands, *and a pure heart*; who hath not lifted up his soul unto vanity, nor sworn deceitfully. (Psalm 24:3–4, KJV)

Now the end of the commandment is charity *out of a pure heart*, and of a good conscience, and of faith unfeigned. (1 Timothy 1:5, KJV)

Flee also youthful lusts: but follow righteousness, faith, charity, peace, with them that call on the Lord out *of a pure heart*. (2 Timothy 2:22, KJV)

Blessed are the *pure in heart*: for they shall see God. (Matthew 5:8, KJV)

When we read about a person's true salvation, it always comes through the Spirit, for it is the Holy Spirit who creates a pure heart, and that pure heart means it has been cleansed by the sacrifice of the Lord Jesus Christ. When we have been cleansed, only then are we ready for heaven. However, if you do not believe in heaven, then you will see no reason to be cleansed. It is obvious from the perversions in the modern versions that there is very little belief in anything truly spiritual. Once again, the King James Bible proves itself absolutely superior to the modern quagmire of "fielder's choice" modern versions. I would much rather have God decide what to put in my Bible rather than unbelieving theologians. Seven out of the nine modern versions omit "pure," and they all omit "through the Spirit." What kind of a stability can a Christian build upon when they use a modern-version Bible that changes every year?

1 Peter 1:23

Being born again, not of corruptible seed, but of incorruptible, by the word of God, which liveth and abideth *for ever*. (1 Peter 1:23, KJV)

Forever is omitted.

This verse shows an attack on the eternal word of God in the modern versions by omitting the words *for ever*. Apparently, these Gnostics do not believe that the word of God is eternal and have removed the words in the Greek texts, and the modern-version editors have followed obediently. Do these false-version editors actually think they will not be held accountable for mutilating the word of God? The sorry thing is that majority of Christians look up to these people. What does the word of God say about the word of God?

> LAMED. For ever, O LORD, thy word is settled in heaven. (Psalm 119:89, KJV)

> He hath remembered his covenant for ever, the word which he commanded to a thousand generations. (Psalm 105:8, KJV)

> The grass withereth, the flower fadeth: but the word of our God shall stand for ever. (Isaiah 40:8, KJV)

The word of God is forever settled in heaven and shall stand forever. It is not just for some temporary time period. God's word is eternal and must be treated as such. Maybe the Gnostics felt that if the word is not eternal, then there will be no accountability?

1 Peter 2:2

> As newborn babes, desire the sincere milk of the word, *that ye may grow thereby*. (1 Peter 2:2, KJV)

"That ye may grow thereby" is changed to "grow into salvation." (This makes the verse teach that a person is saved by studying the scriptures instead of grace.)

This is one of the most devious changes in the modern versions. First, if you notice, the King James states that by the milk of the word of God, we will grow. When we look at the modern versions, they are stating that a person will grow unto salvation. They are teaching that by following the word of God, we can become saved. Now, that seems to be a proper method. However, a person is not saved by studying the word of God; we are saved only by the grace of God. We can read the word of God until we are blue in the face, and if God does not save us, then we can never grow unto salvation. This is a works gospel to the max. No one can grow into salvation. Salvation is a gift from God, and we grow in the faith after we are saved and not before.

Before we are saved, we are spiritually dead. "And you hath he quickened, who were dead in trespasses and sins" (Ephesians 2:1, KJV). Nothing that is dead can grow; only something that is alive can grow. Ephesians 2:1 states that God quickens us (makes us alive), and that is contrasted in the same verse with the fact that before we were saved, we were dead in sins and trespasses. Nowhere does the Bible ever teach that we are saved by reading and keeping the sayings in the word of God.

A spiritually dead person may read the word of God and reform some of their ways, but that is a moral salvation and not an eternal salvation. Many churches and organizations teach a moral salvation based upon works, but that type of salvation only causes people to end up in hell. It is when we are saved by the grace of God for eternal salvation based upon the merits of Christ and not upon our merits that true salvation takes place. After true salvation takes place, then we grow in the faith with the scriptures as our guide. Once again, the modern versions introduce a false gospel, but the King James teaches us correctly that we grow in the faith after we are truly saved and not deceived into thinking that we are saved while remaining in a spiritually dead state.

1 Peter 3:15

But sanctify the Lord *God* in your hearts: and be ready always to give an answer to every man that asketh you a reason of the hope that is in you with meekness and fear. (1 Peter 3:15, KJV)

God is changed to "Christ."

Peter continues from verse 14 that we are not to be afraid of those who would terrorize us, but we are to set apart the Lord God in our hearts. "But and if ye suffer for righteousness' sake, happy are ye: and be not afraid of their terror, neither be troubled; If we allow fear to take over, then that fear becomes the master" (1 Peter 3:14, KJV). If God reigns in our hearts, we will not only elude the fear but we'll then be able to give an answer to everyone concerning the hope we have in our hearts.

The word in the Greek for "answer" is *apologia*, where we derive our English word *apologetics* from, and it just means "a reasoned defense." Every believer should be able to give a reasoned defense of the true Christian faith, especially now in the day we live in when so many false religions exist and so many false branches of Christianity exist. We must be able to give a reason why we believe what we do, and we must do it in gentleness and fear—that fear being an awe of God in which we show dependence upon Him during these times. "For the Holy Ghost shall teach you in the same hour what ye ought to say" (Luke 12:12, KJV).

It is important to realize our dependence upon God, but it also strengthens our witness if we study and learn the scriptures because they are the word of God, and many times, our defense of the faith will come directly out of the scriptures. When we read the history of the martyrs, we would read that they knew the scriptures and were able to give a strong reasoned defense for the true faith. First Peter 3:15 is basically a quote from Isaiah 8:13: "Sanctify the LORD of hosts himself; and let him be your fear, and let him be your dread" (Isaiah 8:13, KJV). We are not to fear man but to fear the Lord. By changing *God* to "Christ," they remove the venue that is transferred from Isaiah to 1 Peter.

1 Peter 4:1

Forasmuch then as Christ hath suffered *for us* in the flesh, arm yourselves likewise with the same mind: for he that hath suffered in the flesh hath ceased from sin. (1 Peter 4:1, KJV)

"For us" is omitted.

The question that has been plaguing the church down through the ages is, for whom did Christ die? Well, if we go to the scriptures, we will get a firm answer to that question. Christ died for His elect and no other. When the intellectual hit squads deleted the words "for us," what they did was turn this verse from a specific into an abstract. In other words, they took the specific salvation plan of God and turned it into an abstract formula. In this verse, Peter is stating definitely that Christ died *for us* and not for the entire population of the world. The apostle Paul used this term many times to show that Christ died for His people.

> For God hath not appointed *us* to wrath, but to obtain salvation by our Lord Jesus Christ, Who died *for us*, that, whether we wake or sleep, we should live together with him. (1 Thessalonians 5:9–10, KJV)

> And walk in love, as Christ also hath loved *us*, and hath given himself *for us* an offering and a sacrifice to God for a sweetsmelling savour. (Ephesians 5:2, KJV)

> But God commendeth his love *toward us*, in that, while we were yet sinners, Christ died *for us*. (Romans 5:8, KJV)

God's salvation plan is not open for the spiritually dead, sinful man to accept or reject. Christ died for a specific group of people, and that is His eternal church or the redeemed of God. "And she shall bring forth a son, and thou shalt call his name JESUS: for he shall save his people from their sins" (Matthew 1:21, KJV). Since Christ died for His elect, this means that universal salvation is a total myth. By leaving out "for us" in 1 Peter 4:1, the verse tends to exalt universal salvation. As you can plainly see in the three verses from the writings of the apostle Paul, the phrase "for us" in 1 Peter 4:1 harmonizes perfectly. God speaks in specifics and never leaves anything open-ended.

Once again, the King James Bible gives us the specific truth, but the modern versions leave us guessing to make up our own interpretations that will end up in error.

1 Peter 4:14

If ye be reproached for the name of Christ, happy are ye; for the spirit of glory and of God resteth upon you: *on their part he is evil spoken of, but on your part he is glorified.* (1 Peter 4:14, KJV)

"On their part he is evil spoken of, but on your part he is glorified" is omitted.

This verse has been mutilated by removing eight words in the Greek and fifteen words in English. The reference in this verse is to the Holy Spirit: "for the spirit of glory and of God resteth upon you." The Gnostics did not believe in the Holy Spirit, so to prevent themselves from being judged by the scriptures for their blasphemy against Him, they removed the part that states that they speak evil against Him. The Holy Spirit, by indwelling the true believer, brings glory to Himself in the manner of salvation of God's elect. The glory of the Holy Spirit is the way He guides and indwells the believer forever without ever leaving them for any sin they commit.

Obviously, the modern translators of the modern versions tend to agree with the Gnostics because they have allowed this part to remain deleted. The doctrine of the Holy Spirit is a cardinal doctrine of the Christian faith. By removing these eight Greek and fifteen English words, they are attacking the doctrine of the Holy Spirit, which is a direct attack upon the Trinity, which the Gnostics and many modern theologians deny. So for anyone to claim that the modern versions do not attack doctrine is to boldly lie, and all liars will have their place in the lake of fire. "But the fearful, and unbelieving, and the abominable, and murderers, and whoremongers, and sorcerers, and idolaters, and all liars, shall have their part in the lake which burneth with fire and brimstone: which is the second death" (Revelation 21:8, KJV).

1 Peter 5:8

Be sober, be vigilant; *because* your adversary the
devil, as a roaring lion, walketh about, seeking
whom he may devour. (1 Peter 5:8, KJV)

Because is omitted.

First Peter 5:8 is a verse of warning to the believer. We are
to remain well balanced in mind and not easily thrown about by
every wind of doctrine, nor are we to be quickly upset. We know
that Satan goes around as a roaring lion, just as a physical lion goes
about after prey. The Christian is the devil's prey. "Therefore rejoice,
ye heavens, and ye that dwell in them. Woe to the inhabiters of the
earth and of the sea! for the devil is come down unto you, having
great wrath, because he knoweth that he hath but a short time"
(Revelation 12:12, KJV). When Satan was cast out of heaven, he
was cast to the earth where he will, until the last day, cause all kinds
of havoc in the world. But his primary target is the Christian. He
knows that he cannot attack the Lord Jesus as he tried when the
Lord was here on earth, so instead he mounts programs of persecution against the Christians. This is why Peter tells the Christians to
remain sober, so they will not be ignorant of Satan's methods. "Lest
Satan should get an advantage of us: for we are not ignorant of his
devices" (2 Corinthians 2:11, KJV).

The word *because* is a conjunction connecting us to the reason
why we must be sober and vigilant. It brings to the sentence a sense
of personalization that Satan is *our enemy* as it reveals to the Christian
that he is "your adversary." He is not the adversary of the unsaved
because they are in his camp, but his enemy is the true child of God,
and he goes about attempting to derail the Christian in their daily
walk. So by omitting the word *because*, the modern versions separate
the reality that Satan is our personal adversary.

1 Peter 5:10

But the God of all grace, who hath called us unto
his eternal glory by Christ *Jesus*, after that ye

have suffered a while, make you perfect, stablish, strengthen, settle you. (1 Peter 5:10, KJV)

Jesus is omitted.

Here is another example of the name of Jesus being separated from His divine title.

1 Peter 5:11

To him be *glory and* dominion for ever and ever. Amen. (1 Peter 5:11, KJV)

"Glory and" is omitted.

Whether therefore ye eat, or drink, or whatsoever ye do, do all to the glory of God. (1 Corinthians 10:31, KJV)

For all the promises of God in him are yea, and in him Amen, unto the glory of God by us. (2 Corinthians 1:20, KJV)

To the chief Musician, A Psalm of David. The heavens declare the glory of God; and the firmament showeth his handiwork. (Psalm 19:1, KJV)

The glory of God is a major theme throughout the entire Bible. According to 1 Corinthians 10:31, everything the believer does is to be to the glory of God. In 1 Peter 5:11, Peter is declaring that God is to be glorified forever and ever, and also to Him belongs the power or dominion. The modern versions omit the fact of God's eternal glory, and also some omit the second *ever*, which emphasizes the eternality of God. It is a great comfort to the Christian that because of salvation in Christ, we will live eternally in the glory of God.

1 Peter 5:12

By Silvanus, a faithful brother unto you, as I suppose, I have written briefly, exhorting, and testifying that this is the true grace of God *wherein ye stand.* (1 Peter 5:12, KJV)

"Wherein ye stand" is changed to "stand ye fast therein." (The believer stands or abides in the true grace because that is where God has placed us, but the verse in the modern versions is reversed, making it a suggestion to stand therein.)

The modern versions remove a very powerful principle from this verse. The last word in the verse in the Textus Receptus is in the perfect tense. The perfect tense denotes a past onetime action with the results still in effect. The last word speaks about the grace of God wherein we stand. This means that when a person becomes saved, they are already standing in the grace of God. The word *stand* means "established, set, place firmly." The King James Bible tells us that it is God who firmly establishes us in His grace. The modern versions make it sound like an option. In fact, if the word was in the imperative mood, it would at least be a command, but it is not. The believer is kept by the power of God by means of being established in His grace at the moment of salvation. The modern versions make fickle man as the one who stands firm, but the King James Bible removes all and any doubt that it is God Himself who firmly establishes us in His grace for eternity.

1 Peter 5:14

Greet ye one another with a kiss of charity. Peace be with you all that are in Christ *Jesus. Amen.* (1 Peter 5:14, KJV)

"Jesus. Amen" is omitted.

The word *amen* in scripture gives finality and confirmation to what has just been written. When the word is left out, it gives the idea that there is still a continuation instead of an ending. It leaves the door open for addition to the text.

When the name of Jesus is omitted in connection with the title *Christ*, it leaves the door open for a person to name their own Messiah. The New Age movement speaks heavily of "the Christ." If we did not know that Jesus is the Christ, we could fall prey to the New Age definition and be totally deceived. The modern versions open the door for deception to easily happen.

2 Peter 1:21

> For the prophecy came not in old time by the will of man: but *holy* men of God spake as they were moved by the Holy Ghost. (2 Peter 1:21, KJV)

Holy is omitted before "men of God."

The omitting of the word *holy* in the modern versions opens the door for anybody to claim they can hear from God. The holy men of old who penned the word of God were saved men, which means they rightly held to the appellation of holy. When any person becomes saved, they are made holy by means of the Holy Spirit dwelling in them. "According as he hath chosen us in him before the foundation of the world, that we should be holy and without blame before him in love" (Ephesians 1:4, KJV). God would not trust His Holy Word to just anyone but only those whom He qualified by means of salvation.

To be holy does not mean some cleric dresses up in a cassock. Dressing religiously is not an indication of holiness. Religious garb is nothing more than an attempt to supplant true holiness. One is made truly holy only by means of salvation. The problem we have today is that there are many unholy hands involved in modern translations. Many of the translators of some of the modern versions do not even believe what they are translating. Hort and Westcott themselves disbelieved the first three chapters of Genesis. Robert Bratcher, chief translator of the Good News Version, also disbelieved the first three chapters of Genesis. Would a holy God trust His word to men like this? There is no way that God would ever do that. When we read the lives of the King James translators, they were all exemplary Christians in contrast to the money grubbers who corrupt God's word today. This is why the removal of the word *holy* in this verse is a subtle but extremely important omission. God would never trust His word to anyone who is not saved. In fact, one cannot rightly preach the word unless they are saved. Once again, the King James Bible proves its faithfulness.

2 Peter 2:4

> For if God spared not the angels that sinned, but cast them down to hell, and delivered them *into chains* of darkness, to be reserved unto judgment. (2 Peter 2:4, KJV)

"Into chains" is changed to "pits or gloomy."

When Satan's rebellion took place, many of the angels had rebelled with him. God then sent them to hell to chains of darkness. The word *chain* is very important because it teaches us that these angels will never be allowed to leave since they are chained. Now we know that the word *chain* is speaking figuratively, which means they were consigned to hell and were unable to leave, as if they were literally chained there. The modern versions just state that they were thrown into pits of darkness. Now, someone can climb the side of a pit and escape, but if someone is chained, they are unable to leave, and that chain means they have been intentionally assigned there without the possibility of escape. Satan's rebellion against God caused Him to take action against these evil angels and permanent consignment in hell with no possibility of escape is their plight. Thankfully, the King James Bible teaches that it is absolutely useless to rebel against God because anyone who does loses eternally.

2 Peter 2:17

These are wells without water, clouds that are
carried with a tempest; to whom the mist of
darkness is reserved *for ever*. (2 Peter 2:17, KJV)

"For ever" is omitted.

When we look at this verse, we immediately see what is under
attack. It is the doctrine of hell. Unbelievers will be spending an eternity in hell, and 2 Peter 2:17 speaks of the destination of the false
teachers. It speaks of them spending an eternity in hell, which is symbolized by the phrase "to whom the mist of darkness is reserved forever." The Gnostics who changed this verse obviously believed that
hell was a nonexistent place, and if it did exist, then there would be no
one spending an eternity there. By the modern versions removing the
term *forever*, they are attacking the doctrine of eternal punishment.
By removing *forever*, it can be misconstrued that those unbelievers
will be in darkness only for a while and not forever. This omission
plays perfectly into the belief of purgatory. Just as the true believer
has eternal life in heaven, the unbeliever has eternal punishment in
hell.

2 Peter 3:2

That ye may be mindful of the words which were
spoken before by the holy prophets, and of the
commandment of *us the* apostles of the Lord and
Saviour. (2 Peter 3:2, KJV)

"Us the" is changed to "your" (this removes the authority of
Peter and the other eleven apostles and shifts the focus to someone
else).

Here is a verse in which the modern versions remove the authority of the apostles. The apostles were in a class equal to those of the
Old Testament prophets, where they received a word from the Lord
and passed it on. Peter is stating that they have received the commandment of the Lord and were passing it on to their hearers. Peter

makes the intentional identification that they are the apostles of the Lord by using the phrase "of us."

If you notice, the modern versions completely remove that divine identification and place it on the hearers. The way the modern versions word it, it sounds like Peter is stating that they are hearing the word through their apostles. When it states "through your apostles," it sounds like there are more than just the commissioned apostles of which Peter is identified with. The Lord had only fourteen apostles, the original twelve, and then Matthias and Paul came later. The modern versions are opening the door for those who claim to be apostles and will use this verse as proof that there were more than just the fourteen. It is also implying that the Lord was bringing the word through these other apostles. In our time, there are many who claim to be apostles and prophets who still claim the Lord is giving them a word when He is not. Once again, the modern versions are in error and opens the door for any self-appointed apostle to make ridiculous claims.

2 Peter 3:9

The Lord is not slack concerning his promise, as some men count slackness; but is longsuffering to *us-ward*, not willing that any should perish, but that all should come to repentance. (2 Peter 3:9, KJV)

Us-ward is omitted.

"And all that dwell upon the earth shall worship him, whose names are not written in the book of life of the Lamb slain from the foundation of the world" (Revelation 13:8, KJV). Before the foundation of the world was laid, God already knew whom He was going to save. If you are a Christian, your name was written in the Lamb's book of life before you were even born. Second Peter 3:9 is teaching that God is being very patient with those who have not yet become saved, and he is long-suffering in this matter. This means that God will wait to end this world when the last one to be saved becomes saved.

The word *us-ward* is telling us that God is specifically speaking of the body of believers. This is why the Bible uses the word *us-ward* because it has the body of believers in view. The modern versions remove this word and use the word *you*. Instead of it focusing on the body of believers, it reverses that focus to anyone. Before a person is saved, they are spiritually dead, and this is why God is the one who has to do the saving because He takes our dead souls and makes them alive. No amount of saying the sinner's prayer can ever regenerate a person. Only God can take a spiritually dead person and make them spiritually alive. This is why when the focus is shifted to the unbelievers through the word *you*, it gives a false hope since the majority of people die in their sins and are not saved. God's long-suffering is not waiting for sinners to turn their lives around, but it is for Him to save the last one on the last day of earth's history, whenever that will be. The King James Bible keeps its focus on the body of believers while the modern versions keep its eye on the unbelievers as usual.

2 Peter 3:10

> But the day of the Lord will come as a thief *in the night*; in the which the heavens shall pass away with a great noise, and the elements shall melt with fervent heat, the earth also and the works that are therein shall be *burned up.* (2 Peter 3:10, KJV)

"In the night" is omitted. *"Burned up"* is replaced with "laid bare or judgment" in some of the versions.

"For yourselves know perfectly that the day of the Lord so cometh as a thief in the night" (1 Thessalonians 5:2, KJV). The King James Bible states that the return of the Lord is going to be a very swift event. One moment, we will be walking on earth; and the next moment, we will be in heaven in the presence of the Lord. Second Peter 3:10 and 1 Thessalonians 5:2 both speak of the Lord's return as a thief in the night. The nighttime speaks of people being in spiritual darkness, or in other words, they are unsaved. "For they that sleep sleep in the night; and they that be drunken are drunken in the night" (1 Thessalonians 5:7, KJV). It is for these people that the Lord will return as a thief in the night because they are unprepared. "But ye, brethren, are not in darkness, that that day should overtake you as a thief" (1 Thessalonians 5:4, KJV). The true believer is not in darkness, so the Lord will not be coming as a thief in the night for us. We are prepared by means of our salvation.

The second portion that was attacked by the modernist was the fact that not only will the world and universe be burned up, but all the works that are contained in them will also be burned up. Every work that has been sin, cursed, will be done away with, not discovered as the modern versions put it. He describes the end as a great conflagration that will signal an end to the present heaven and earth. It will be burned up right down to the smallest particles, which will be total destruction. It will be done with great heat that will consume the earth and universe.

The words "shall be burned up" is in the future tense and passive voice. This means that the universe and the earth will be burned up from an outside source, which will be God Himself. Some try to take this passage and make it say nuclear war, but there is no way an atom bomb on earth could melt the horse head or crab nebulae in deep space. All the universe and the earth will be subjected to the final purging by fire on the last day, and it will not be anything that man does but what God does as He promised to remake the new heavens and the new earth.

2 Peter 3:12

> Looking for and *hasting* unto the coming of the day of God, wherein the heavens being on fire shall be dissolved, and the elements shall melt with fervent heat? (2 Peter 3:12, KJV)

Hasting is replaced by "hastening."

The understanding of this verse has been distorted in many of the modern versions. The word in question is the Greek word *speudo*, which carries with it the meaning of "desire earnestly, hasten, or hurry up." "And they came with *haste*, and found Mary, and Joseph, and the babe lying in a manger" (Luke 2:16, KJV). "And when Jesus came to the place, he looked up, and saw him, and said unto him, Zacchaeus, make *haste*, and come down; for to day I must abide at thy house" (Luke 19:5, KJV). It is also used in Luke 19:6 and Acts 20:16 and 22:18. The word is basically peculiar to Luke as we read in his epistle and the book of Acts. In each of the usages in Luke and Acts, it is used in the sense of "hurry."

In 2 Peter 3:12, the meaning is not "to hurry along or speed up," but it means to "desire earnestly." The reason that the meaning would follow this understanding is because no matter what any Christian does, it can never hasten or speed up the day of the Lord's return. That is simply bad interpretation and understanding. "Because he hath appointed a day, in the which he will judge the world in righteousness by that man whom he hath ordained; whereof he hath given assurance unto all men, in that he hath raised him from the dead" (Acts 17:31, KJV). Acts 17:31 states that God has already appointed a day when the world will be judged, and since that day is set, it means that no matter what we do, we can never move that date. God is the one who set that date, which means it is a firm date.

I have heard numerous times that we need to get the Gospel out so we can speed up the Lord's return. This places undue stress on Christians when they think they can affect the timing of the Lord's return by their actions. The modern versions want to place Christians in a panic mode, having them believe they can hasten the Lord's return. The King James Bible gives us the true interpretation that we are to "desire earnestly" the return of the Lord Jesus Christ, and that desire compels us to work until that day arrives.

1 John 1:4

And these things write we *unto you*, that *your* joy may be full. (1 John 1:4, KJV)

"Unto you" is omitted, and *"your"* is changed to "our."

John writes to this group of Christians so that their joy may be made full. The King James Bible use the term "unto you" while the modern versions omit this important word in the Greek. The word in the Greek is in the dative case, which expresses an act given toward an object. In this case, the act is the writing of these deeper truths of the scriptures to the object that is the Christians. This is why the word *your* is used instead of *our*, which is used in the modern versions. John is desiring that the joy be focused on the ones he is writing to.

The way the modern versions word it, it sounds like the group that is sending the letter will be the joyful ones based on the action of sending the letter. No doubt that John would have been joyful in sending these truths, but the focus here is that John wanted these Christians he was writing to, to be filled with joy upon reading and understanding these truths. This is also a small figure of the entire Bible that was given to the Christians for the purpose of making their joy complete. Once again, the King James Version brings out the truth of this passage while the modern versions muddy the waters.

1 John 1:7

But if we walk in the light, as he is in the light, we have fellowship one with another, and the blood of Jesus *Christ* his Son cleanseth us from all sin. (1 John 1:7, KJV)

Christ is omitted.

Here is another verse that attempts to separate the divine name of Jesus from his other name, which is especially important in this verse since there is a direct correlation to Jesus being God's Son.

1 John 2:7

Brethren, I write no new commandment unto you, but an old commandment which ye had from the beginning. The old commandment is

the word which ye have heard *from the beginning*.
(1 John 2:7, KJV)

"From the beginning" is omitted.

One of the main teachings of the Bible is that all things started with the Lord Jesus Christ. "In the beginning was the Word, and the Word was with God, and the Word was God" (John 1:1, KJV). So when the modern versions remove the quotation concerning the beginning, they are removing a reference to Christ. "That which was from the beginning, which we have heard, which we have seen with our eyes, which we have looked upon, and our hands have handled, of the Word of life" (1 John 1:1, KJV). John spoke much of the beginning being identified with Christ. Christ had no beginning because He is eternal God, but the beginning of the Gospel that John is speaking about is referencing Christ.

John goes on to say that the old commandment remains the same. Christ is identified with the old commandment; in other words, He is the Great I Am of Sinai where the law was given. To remove the phrase "from the beginning" removes the fact that Christ was the great lawgiver. As John pens this Gospel under the inspiration of the Holy Spirit, the Jews in attendance would have known immediately what was in view here as the Jews were brought up in the knowledge of the Old Testament. John is connecting the Old and New Testament, and Christ is that connecting person between the two testaments. This is why that phrase "from the beginning" is very important. Once again, the modern versions mutilate this truth.

1 John 3:5

And ye know that he was manifested to take away
our sins; and in him is no sin. (1 John 3:5, KJV)

Our is omitted (making the verse sound like universal salvation).

One of the greatest errors taught in Christendom is that Christ went to the cross to pay for the sins of every human being that would ever live. Nowhere in scripture do we read that He did this. If He did, then there would not be one unsaved person in the world today.

> And she shall bring forth a son, and thou shalt call his name Jesus: for he shall save his people from their sins. (Matthew 1:21, KJV)

> For this people's heart is waxed gross, and their ears are dull of hearing, and their eyes they have closed; lest at any time they should see with their eyes and hear with their ears, and should understand with their heart, and should be converted, and I should heal them. (Matthew 13:15, KJV)

> But as many as received him, to them gave he power to become the sons of God, even to them that believe on his name: Which were born, not of blood, nor of the will of the flesh, nor of the will of man, but of God. (John 1:12–13, KJV)

> I pray for them: I pray not for the world, but for them which thou hast given me; for they are thine. (John 17:9 KJV)

The way the modern versions omit the word *our* makes it look like Christ went to the cross to give universal salvation. However, when we look at some verses closely, we will see that Christ came to pay for the sins of His people only. God applies the atonement to those who were named for salvation before the foundation of the world (Revelation 13:8 and 17:8). This is why the King James Bible has it correct when it uses the word *our*. It shows the proper perspective on the sacrifice of Christ and that it was for His people that He died. *Our* shows us that it was for a specific group that Christ died, and that was His elect. Or else, in John 17:9, why was He only praying for those whom the Father gave Him, and why wasn't He praying for the world? It is an important question that must be broached. The King James gives us the correct rendering as the other versions attempt to show a universal salvation that is not taught in scripture.

1 John 3:14

We know that we have passed from death unto life, because we love the brethren. He that loveth not *his brother* abideth in death. (1 John 3:14, KJV)

"His brother" is omitted.

Here is another case of going from the specific to the nebulous. The second part of this verse specifically states that if you do not love your brother, then you are abiding in death, which basically means you are giving evidence you are unsaved. One of the major tests of being a true Christian is that we have genuine love for the brethren. It is a love that is proactive and has no hidden agendas. The world hates Christians, but true Christians will love one another despite the hatred the world has for them. The modern versions state that you must have love, or you are abiding in death. What type of love? For the environment? For whales? It leaves the door wide open so someone can inject any type of love and think they are on their way to heaven.

In fact, the books of 1, 2, and 3 John are all basically speaking about loving the brethren as giving evidence of a person's salvation. Vague love means nothing. A husband can love a wife or a wife can love a husband, but that does not give evidence of salvation. When we love the brethren, we are showing a spiritual affinity to other Christians. This type of love supersedes the love of the world, which has only a physical aspect. True love based in salvation is much deeper and more caring than the surface dimension of love that can change in a moment. True spiritual love is a fruit of the Holy Spirit, given only to the believer. "But the fruit of the Spirit is love, joy, peace, longsuffering, gentleness, goodness, faith" (Galatians 5:22, KJV)

1 John 3:19

And hereby *we know* that we are of the truth, and
shall assure our hearts before him. (1 John 3:19, KJV)

"We know," in present tense, is changed to "shall we know," in
the future tense.

"My little children, let us not love in word, neither in tongue;
but in deed and in truth. And hereby we know that we are of the
truth, and shall assure our hearts before him" (1 John 3:18–19, KJV).
The King James Bible teaches that true believers are of the truth
the moment they become saved. The modern versions change that
present-tense word "we know" to a future tense "we shall" or "we will
know." But it never states when we would know, just leaving believers
guessing as to what future time we would be of the truth. The King
James Bible removes all guessing and states that Christians are in the
truth at present and not some future undesignated time. Once again,
the King James Bible removes doubt.

1 John 4:3

And every spirit that confesseth not that Jesus
Christ is come in the flesh is not of God: and this
is that spirit of antichrist, whereof ye have heard
that it should come; and even now already is it in
the world. (1 John 4:3, KJV)

"Christ is come in the flesh" is omitted.
This verse has been affected in two major ways: First, they
remove the name of *Christ*, which is the title for the Lord Jesus. Then
they remove the portion of text that deals with His incarnation. One
of the major tests of a true believer is their firm belief in the incarnation of Christ. Anyone can say that they believe that Jesus is from
God. You do not even need to acknowledge Him as God's Son. You
can just view Him as a prophet, a good teacher, a good man, or
any way you want and still say He came from God. Herein lies the
great deception. There are countless millions who see Christ as just a

prophet or good man, and by doing this, they think they are in the right relationship with God.

The importance of the incarnation cannot be overstressed because the Son of God left His throne in heaven and took on a human body to die for the sins of the elect. If one does not believe this, then they are not of God, as the rest of the verse teaches. The Gnostics did not believe that anything holy could ever exist in human flesh, and therefore, they completely deny any belief in the incarnation of the Son of God. They also disbelieve the indwelling of the Holy Spirit in a true believer. This unbelief of the Gnostics has been carried through to the modern versions of scripture. It is so sad that the Bible that is written about the Lord Jesus Christ should so vilify Him in the modern versions, and what compounds it is that the majority of Christians accept them as real Bibles.

1 John 4:9

In this was manifested the love of God toward us, because that God sent his only *begotten* Son into the world, that we might live through him. (1 John 4:9, KJV)

Begotten is omitted.

The word *monogene* is in both the Textus Receptus and Hort-Westcott Greek texts. What we have in this verse is just another case of translators attacking the Lord Jesus Christ. The word carries with it the meaning of "unique or one of a kind." The word is used to denote the difference between the Lord Jesus Christ, who is in unique relationship with the Father, and the born-again Christian, who is also called son or daughter of God. The importance of the word *begotten* shows the difference between those who have become sons and daughters of God by adoption ("To redeem them that were under the law, that we might receive the adoption of sons" [Galatians 4:5, KJV]) and the Lord Jesus Christ, who has always been with the Father throughout all eternity.

1 John 4:19

We love *him*, because he first loved us.
(1 John 4:19, KJV)

Him is omitted.

This is a very subtle yet significant omission. The Bible is telling us that we love God because He first loved us. Man, in his unsaved condition, is spiritually dead and unable to love or even gravitate toward God. What is in view here is that the love of God bestowed upon us is really a biblical synonym for the salvation of God being bestowed upon His children. Once salvation is given, we are then qualified to love God because we are now alive unto God. "And we know that all things work together for good to them that love God, to them who are the called according to his purpose" (Romans 8:28, KJV).

The modern versions omit this great truth. Our love must first be toward God, and then we will have the ability to love others. By the modern versions omitting *Him*, they state that we love because God loved us. But the question remains, love what or who? I love the Grand Canyon because God loved me? I love my children because God loved me? No, because God loved me first—in other words, bestowed salvation upon me—I now can love Him with all my heart. "And thou shalt love the LORD thy God with all thine heart, and with all thy soul, and with all thy might" (Deuteronomy 6:5, KJV). Since God loved me, the relationship between God and myself is one of intimate love and not just superficial love that can change in an instant.

The King James conveys this by keeping the word intact, but the modern versions remove this great truth and make it a nebulous love that can be abused grammatically by anyone wanting to make it a verse of private interpretation. The love of God toward His children is eternal and never-changing.

1 John 5:7–8

For there are three that bear record *in heaven, the Father, the Word, and the Holy Ghost: and these*

> *three are one. And there are three that bear witness*
> *in earth*, the spirit, and the water, and the blood:
> and these three agree in one. (1 John 5:7–8, KJV)

Verse 7, *"in heaven, the Father, the Word, and the Holy Ghost: and these three are one,"* is omitted. Verse 8, *"And there are three that bear witness in earth,"* is omitted.

Aleph - Sinaiticus (nineteenth-century counterfeit)
B, Vaticanus (fourth century)
A, Alexandrinus (fifth century)

These three manuscripts are the primary manuscripts where 1 John 5:7–8 have been corrupted. There are many other later manuscripts that are ancillary to these three because they were copied from them. Like begets like, and when you copy from a corrupted manuscripts, the lineage of corruption will continue. First John 5:7–8 has been attacked by the pro-modern-version crowd as being a scribal addition later on in years. However, 1 John 5:7–8 is found in the Old Latin Vulgate and Greek Vulgate (AD 90–150), plus the Syriac Peshiito (AD 150). It is also found in many first-century church lectionaries. Lectionaries were used in churches for readings and liturgy for church services, especially for special days of the year. They are akin to the responsive readings that we find in today's hymnbooks. Tatian's Diatessaron was a harmony of the four gospels written about AD 150. When Tatian was writing the book of John, he had referenced 1 John 5:7, which proves that 1 John 5:7 antedates Vaticanus by two hundred years, where the verse is omitted.

Dr. John Overall, who was one of the King James translators, was a scholar in the teachings of the early church fathers. His contribution concerning 1 John 5:7 was vital since manuscript evidence was lacking because of the Alexandrian school where it was mutilated. He knew that the early church fathers had referenced those verses quite frequently. The modern-version proponents only look to Vaticanus and Sinaiticus as their authorities and reject the massive amount of other evidences such as the church lectionaries. If 1

John 5:7–8 was not in the originals, then how could they have been quoted by the church fathers if it was nonexistent? A simple question of logic.

Erasmus was a Greek scholar who was used by the Lord mightily as a precursor to the Reformation. He printed a Greek New Testament in 1516, and the Reformation took place in 1517. There is no such thing as a coincidence in the kingdom of God, only a God-incident. Now, Erasmus in reference to 1 John 5:7, originally did not want to include that portion unless a Greek manuscript could be found as evidence of its authenticity. He claimed that Greek manuscripts and even some Latin manuscripts did not have this verse in it. In due time, Erasmus was presented with Codex Montfortianus (Manuscript 61, which is in Dublin, Ireland) and Codex Britannicus, both containing 1 John 5:7. With this proof, he confidently placed these verses in his third edition of the Greek in 1522 and his last one in 1535. Erasmus died in 1536, but God had set the stage for the translation of the final true Bible in the English language that would be used by Christians until the Lord returned on the last day.

Some of the other evidences where 1 John 5:7-8 can be found are as follows:

- John Calvin, in his *Institutes of the Christian Religion* (mid-sixteenth century) in book 3,chapter 1, section 1, mentions 1 John 5:7–8 without any doubt.
- Some Syriac Peshitto manuscripts
- The Syriac Edition at Hamburg
- Bishop Uscan's Armenian Bible
- The Armenian Edition of John Zohrob
- The first printed Georgian Bible

Early Latin Witnesses

1) Tertullian, who died in AD 220
2) Cyprian of Carthage, who died in AD 258
3) Priscillan, who died in AD 358
4) The Speculum (fifth century)

5) A creed called Esposito Fidei (fifth or sixth century)
6) Old Latin (fifth or sixth century)
7) The confession of faith by Eugenius, bishop of Carthage (AD 484)
8) Cassiodoris of Italy (AD 480–570)

The evidence is overwhelming for the authenticity of 1 John 5:7–8. Keep in mind that it was Origen who was the father of the false manuscripts who removed this verse, as he did with verses like Acts 8:37 and Luke 24:40. The Alexandrian school was no friend of the true manuscripts, which were taken from Antioch and mutilated according to Gnostic beliefs.

The mutilation of 1 John 5:7–8 in the second century was an attack upon the Trinity. The rejection of the Trinity is alive and well today in the Jehovah's Witnesses camp and is alive and well in the modern versions that agree totally with their New World translation. Trinitarian theology is totally disbelieved by the Gnostics and many cult groups, including the Jews. For any theologian, pastor, or Christian to endorse a version that attacks the Trinity means they too disbelieve the Trinity; or else, they would not be defending the Gnostic view.

These verses are the most hotly contested by the modern-version proponents simply because they disregard all the evidence that is available. This section of scripture has been named the "Johannine comma." First John 5:7–8 is as much a part of the original autographs as Jesus Himself was. Therefore, we can claim these verses as authentic without hesitation.

I would suggest that you print this information out (which is available at http://www.scionofzion.com/1 john 5 78.htm) and keep it as part of your library since 1 John 5:7–8 is a major bone of contention that the pro-modern-version people tend to throw at us. If you have this information at hand, you will disarm them and cause them to go on the defensive; and since most Christians are ignorant and refuse to do any research to combat their ignorance, you will have succeeded in proving your case and maybe winning over another Christian to the truth.

1 John 5:13

These things have I written unto you that believe
on the name of the Son of God; that ye may know
that ye have eternal life, *and that ye may believe on
the name of the Son of God.* (1 John 5:13, KJV)

"And that ye may believe on the name of the Son of God" is omitted.

First John 5:13 is being written to all those who are believers
already. This verse is a verse of encouragement because then, as now,
there are people who teach that a person can lose their salvation; plus,
there are many Christians who really believe they are not saved but
are truly saved. This verse is encouraging and assuring Christians that
if they have truly become saved, then the things written in the scriptures are there so a Christian may know and not continually be guessing as to whether they have eternal life or not. Not being sure of our
salvation can really cause a Christian to spend their life in fear, and
that will result in them not being a suitable witness for the Gospel.
Fear of loss of salvation has many Christians in bondage trying to do
better in their Christian walk. We all want to do better, but we must
realize that once we are saved, we can never increase our salvation by
any type of works; nor can we lose that salvation by decreasing works.
All true Christians desire to grow in sanctification, and that means
growing closer to Christ and growing farther from the world.

The part of the verse that is omitted is a portion of encouragement. When Christians are going through rough times or even
persecution, the fact that the scriptures are written assuring us of
eternal life enables us not to lose heart. Those who are true believers
already are being encouraged that if they really take the scriptures
to heart, no matter what their present predicament is, they will be
able to continue believing on the Lord Jesus in the manner that He
is able to bring us through all the hard times in our life. It is an
essential portion of scripture to keep the Christian from becoming
discouraged in their Christian walk. It seems that the modern versions attempt to discourage encouragement in the Lord Jesus Christ,
who brings us through the hard times in life. The removal of this

portion of scripture is another attack on the Lord Jesus Christ and His keeping power over His children. "Who are kept by the power of God through faith unto salvation ready to be revealed in the last time" (1 Peter 1:5, KJV).

1 John 5:19

And we know that we are of God, and the whole world *lieth in wickedness*. (1 John 5:19, KJV)

"*Lieth in wickedness*" is changed to "lies in the power of the evil one or devil."

Here is a great example where the modern-version editors have interpolated this passage. According to the 1828 *Webster's Dictionary*, the word interpolate has the following meaning:

> 2. To foist in; to insert, as a spurious word or passage in a manuscript or book; to add a spurious word or passage to the original.

In 1 John 5:19, the modern-version editors have placed Satan in a position equal to that of God, and that cannot happen. In the Textus Receptus, we have the following words *to ponero keitai* translated as "lieth in wickedness." This is the proper translation from the Greek. It is the same three words in the Hort-Westcott Critical Text, yet in some of the modern versions, they have added words via interpolation, which makes Satan appear to be the ruler of the world.

NASV: "lies in the power of the evil one"
NCV: "Evil One controls the whole world"
NIV: "the whole world is under the control of the evil one"
ASV: "the whole world lieth in the evil one"
HCSB: "the whole world is under the sway of the evil one"
NRSV: "that the whole world lies under the power of the evil one"
RSV: "the whole world is in the power of the evil one"

If you notice the words that have been added to the text such as *power, control,* and *one,* none of these words are found in the Textus Receptus or the Hort-Westcott Critical Text. These words were added, and because they have been added, it conveys the idea that Satan is in absolute control of the world. While the world is nothing but a cesspool of sin, Satan does not have absolute control over it. God still controls this world, and Satan is just a created being whom God has allowed to exist to bring about His plan to fruition. Satan is called the "god of this world" in 2 Corinthians 4:4, but that does not mean he is ruling in the world. It means that when people commit evil acts, they are, in essence, doing obeisance to Satan because he is the architect of evil.

The modern-version editors have added words where they do not belong, and that has resulted in the belief that Satan rules this world, and he doesn't. The term *evil one* is not even intimated in the Greek text. The word *ponero* may be translated "evil," but not "evil one." The word is an adjective without a noun attached, so the modern-version translators thought they would help the text along and add "one" to "evil" or "wicked." The bottom line is that these modern versions are teaching serious error when they teach that the world is under the power or control of Satan because God is still in control and is working out His plan of redemption in the midst of a wicked world.

Here is what the modern-version editors did. In 1 John 5:18, we read "We know that whosoever is born of God sinneth not; but he that is begotten of God keepeth himself, and that wicked one toucheth him not." The word in the Greek for "wicked" is also *ponero,* as in verse 19. However, in verse 18, it is the masculine gender and the nominative case, which is the subject of either the complete sentence or a portion of it. You can see that the words "wicked one" fits the context of the passage perfectly because the masculine gender is focusing on a person, and in this case, it is Satan. In verse 19, it is the same word *ponero,* but it is a dative without gender, which is a different inflection than in verse 18. So the Greek experts in the modern versions translated a different word the same way as they did in verse 18.

We know that anyone born of God does not continue to sin; the One who as born of God keeps them safe, and the *evil one* cannot harm them. (1 John 5:18, NIV)

We know that we are children of God, and that the whole world is under the control of the *evil one*. (1 John 5:19, NIV)

This is why the modern versions cannot be counted on for accuracy.

A Psalm of David. The earth is the LORD's, and the fulness thereof; the world, and they that dwell therein. (Psalm 24:1, KJV)

Psalm 24:1 settles the question as to who owns and rules the world!

2 John 3

Grace be with you, mercy, and peace, from God the Father, and from *the Lord* Jesus Christ, the Son of the Father, in truth and love. (2 John 3, KJV)

"The Lord" is omitted.

Here is another attack on the deity of the Lord Jesus Christ. He is specifically called the Son of the Father, carrying with it the title of *Lord*, which the modern versions omit.

2 John 9

Whosoever transgresseth, and abideth not in the doctrine of Christ, hath not God. He that abideth in the doctrine *of Christ*, he hath both the Father and the Son. (2 John 9, KJV)

"Of Christ" second usage is omitted.

Here is another example of the modern versions taking a specific doctrine and turning it into a vague doctrine. The specific is the "doctrine of Christ" while the modern versions omit the second usage of "of Christ." They open a door for inserting whatever anyone wants to.

3 John 7

Because that for *his* name's sake they went forth, taking nothing of the Gentiles. (3 John 7, KJV)

"His name" is changed to "the Name."

Here is another subtle change. The Christians went from the church in Judea in the name of Christ, which is written in His name, alluding specifically to the name of Christ but changed in the modern versions to the generic *the*, which means they can insert any name in there, replacing the allusion to Christ. This is one of the reasons that these brethren needed and deserved help. They had been proclaiming the true Gospel as missionaries and evangelists, and like the apostle Paul, they took no money from those they preached to. They wanted to show that their motives were not the same as the false teachers. There were religious hucksters in those days who peddled religion for profit, just as we see the religious hucksters today on TV and hear them on radio.

3 John 11

Beloved, follow not that which is evil, but that which is good. He that doeth good is of God: *but* he that doeth evil hath not seen God. (3 John 11, KJV)

But is omitted.

There may have been a problem on the part of Gaius where he might have stopped helping the missionaries in hopes that he would not get thrown out of the church, and it seems that John is addressing Gaius that he should not follow the evil ways of Diotrephes. John points out that there is a great difference between those who do good and those who don't. Those who do not do good are giving evidence they are unsaved, which would be the case of Diotrephes because he did what he could to hinder or stop the spread of the Gospel. John contrasts that mind-set with those who do good, which would have been the case of Gaius, who did what he could to further the Gospel. John wants to make sure that if Gaius fell prey to the works of Diotrephes, then John wanted to warn Gaius not to follow the evil works of the unsaved but continue the course he was on.

The word *but* in the Greek is *de*, which is a conjunction. In fact, it is something called a coordinating conjunction, which joins words, phrases, clauses, or sentences of equal elements or equal ranks. In this case, John is elevating the fact that he who does good is of God, but equally important is the fact that those who do not do good have not seen God or are unsaved. This is a very important omission in the modern versions.

Jude 1

Jude, the servant of Jesus Christ, and brother of James, to them that are *sanctified* by God the Father, and preserved in Jesus Christ, and called. (Jude 1, KJV)

Sanctified is omitted.

This word switch is probably one of the subtlest switches in the Bible. The King James word uses the root *hagios*, which means "sanctified, holy, or set apart." The Gnostics changed this word to the root word *agapao*, which means "love." Agapao is a term used in the New Testament, which teaches that God cares for His people and the world. This word change is an attack on the doctrine of sanctification. When a person becomes saved, they are instantly set apart or sanctified as one of God's children. The word *hagios* describes that action. When the word *agapao* is substituted, it completely changes the meaning of this passage. The passage teaches that we are sancti-fied and preserved. It does not say we are loved and preserved.

Now, it is true that the love of God is qualified and that He loves His own. "Now before the feast of the passover, when Jesus knew that his hour was come that he should depart out of this world unto the Father, having loved his own which were in the world, he loved them unto the end" (John 13:1, KJV). We read in the John 13:1 passage that Jesus loved His own in the world and does not say that He loved everyone in the world. The word *loved* is the Greek word *agapao*. While the love of God and the action of sanctification by God are linked, they are two different entities that are both enjoyed by the elect of God. To substitute love for sanctification does a disservice to this verse and eliminates the doctrine of sanctification from it. The sanctification of the believer is a major biblical doctrine, and this attack on it shows that these modern versions do have an effect on doctrinal teaching, even though their supporters claim otherwise.

Jude 4

> For there are certain men crept in unawares, who were before of old ordained to this condemna-tion, ungodly men, turning the grace of our God into lasciviousness, and denying the only *Lord God*, and our Lord Jesus Christ. (Jude 4, KJV)

"*Lord God*" is omitted.

Here is an omission concerning God the Father. The book of Jude deals with apostasy. God the Father is the only Lord God; this does not take away from the Lord Jesus Christ or the Holy Spirit. In a time of great apostasy, which Jude dealt with, there were many false gods, and God the Father stood in truth, which is opposite of the false gods, who were at the root of apostasy in the lives of false teach-ers. These false teachers had crept into the church with their belief systems and had not only denied the Lord Jesus Christ but God the Father also. The modern versions hide the fact that God the Father was also rejected by these false teachers along with the Lord Jesus

Christ. Any time someone brings a false gospel, they are, in essence, denying the Trinity in its entirety.

Jude 25

> To the only *wise* God our Saviour, be glory and majesty, dominion and power, both now and ever. Amen. (Jude 25, KJV)

"Wise" is omitted. "Before all time" and "through Jesus Christ our Lord" are added to the text.

> To the only God our Saviour, *through Jesus Christ our Lord*, be glory, majesty, dominion and power, *before all time*, and now, and for evermore. Amen. (Jude 25, ASV)

Jude 25 has received three hits by the Gnostic and intellectual hit squads:

1) With the removal of the Greek word *sophoo*, they have removed a description of God as being wise. "Now unto the King eternal, immortal, invisible, the only wise God, be honour and glory for ever and ever. Amen" (1 Timothy 1:17, KJV). The Gnostics must have felt that God is not wise, yet they themselves felt they were wise. When we look at the creation, we see the wisdom of God before our eyes; and when we read the scriptures, we read the wisdom of God. In fact, the first eight chapters of the book of Proverbs deals with the subject of wisdom. This removal of the description of the wise nature of God is just another attack upon the doctrine of God because when you remove any portion of His description, then you are attacking His character, and wisdom is definitely one of the main characteristics of God.

2)   Here is another major attack upon the Lord Jesus Christ. What is attacked here is His deity and the fact that He is our Savior. Jude 25 teaches that Jesus, who is God, is the only wise God, our Savior. By adding the phrase "through Jesus Christ our Lord," it refocuses the passage on God the Father. Then it is only through the Lord Jesus Christ that God is our Savior, completely removing the fact that Jesus is the Savior and making Him only a conduit.

3)   The corrupted manuscripts added "before all time" to this verse. I do not know for what reason it was added and by whom.

Revelation 1:5

> And from Jesus Christ, who is the faithful witness, and the first begotten of the dead, and the prince of the kings of the earth. Unto him that loved us, and *washed* us from our sins in his own blood, (Revelation, 1:5, KJV)

"Washed" is changed to "loosed."

Here is another attack on a cardinal doctrine of the faith. The true believer has been washed by the blood of Christ from their sins, which resulted in all the sins of the believer forgiven and removed.

> And such were some of you: but ye are washed, but ye are sanctified, but ye are justified in the name of the Lord Jesus, and by the Spirit of our God. (1 Corinthians 6:11, KJV)

> That he might sanctify and cleanse it with the washing of water by the word. (Ephesians 5:26, KJV)

> Not by works of righteousness which we have done, but according to his mercy he saved us, by the washing of regeneration, and renewing of the Holy

Ghost; Which he shed on us abundantly through
Jesus Christ our Saviour. (Titus 3:5–6, KJV)

The results of the washing of the Lord Jesus is how the true
believer is freed from their sins.

But now being made free from sin, and become
servants to God, ye have your fruit unto holiness,
and the end everlasting life. (Romans 6:22, KJV)

The problem is that the modern versions exchange the method
of how the believer, which is the washing by Christ with His blood,
attains the result of being free from sin. The blood has to be applied
to a person for them to become saved and have all their sins removed.
However, we must keep in mind that the freeing of the believer from
their sins is not in view in this particular verse, but the washing by
the blood of Christ is. So in essence, the modern versions have omitted this cardinal truth of the Christian faith.

Revelation 1:6

And hath made us *kings* and priests unto God
and his Father; to him be glory and dominion for
ever and ever. Amen. (Revelation 1:6, KJV)

Kings is changed to "kingdom."
See full commentary at Revelation 5:10, which has the same
change as this verse.

Revelation 1:8

I am Alpha and Omega, *the beginning and the ending,*
saith the Lord, which is, and which was, and which is
to come, the Almighty. (Revelation 1:8, KJV)

"The beginning and the ending" is omitted.

The alpha and omega are the first and last letters of the Greek alphabet. The phrase "beginning and the ending" is the definition of the alpha and omega. God is telling us that the Lord Jesus Christ is the beginning and the end. Both of these words are dealing with time since there is no beginning nor end in eternity; hence the term *eternity*. The Lord Jesus Christ was the Creator of this world and universe, which envelops the word *beginning*. There is going to come a point in history where time will be no more. "And sware by him that liveth for ever and ever, who created heaven, and the things that therein are, and the earth, and the things that therein are, and the sea, and the things which are therein, that there should be time no longer" (Revelation 10:6, KJV). This means the Lord Jesus, who created the world, will also bring the world and universe to an end at the time appointed from the foundation of the world.

"Because he hath appointed a day, in the which he will judge the world in righteousness by that man whom he hath ordained; whereof he hath given assurance unto all men, in that he hath raised him from the dead" (Acts 17:31, KJV). I guess the Gnostics and the modern Bible translators disbelieve that there is going to be an end to this world, but the biggest disbelief they would have on this subject would be the end by the Lord Jesus Christ since the Gnostics did not believe that Christ was God. And sadly, the modern versions have perpetuated that belief. Let us stay with the King James Bible until that last day of earth's existence, knowing that we have truth that will keep us from believing a false doctrine.

Revelation 1:9

I John, who also am your brother, and companion in tribulation, and in the kingdom and patience of Jesus *Christ*, was in the isle that is called Patmos, for the word of God, and for the testimony of Jesus *Christ*. (Revelation 1:9, KJV)

Christ is omitted twice in this verse.

This verse suffered the knife of the Gnostic by omitting the divine title of the Lord Jesus Christ, which is *Christ*, twice. The Gnostics did not believe in Christ's divinity, so they did what they could by removing these two references to His deity.

Revelation 1:11

Saying, *I am Alpha and Omega, the first and the last*: and, What thou seest, write in a book, and send it unto the seven churches which are in Asia; unto Ephesus, and unto Smyrna, and unto Pergamos, and unto Thyatira, and unto Sardis, and unto Philadelphia, and unto Laodicea. (Revelation 1:11, KJV)

"I am Alpha and Omega, the first and the last: and" is omitted.

Textus Receptus Traditional Text

λεγουσης <u>εγω ειμι το α και το ω ο πρωτος και ο εσχατος και</u> ο βλεπεις γραψον εις βιβλιον και πεμψον ταις εκκλησιαις ταις εν ασια εις εφεσον και εις σμυρναν και εις περγαμον και εις θυατειρα και εις σαρδεις και εις φιλαδελφειαν και εις λαοδικειαν

Hort-Westcott Critical Text

λεγουσης ο βλεπεις γραψον εις βιβλιον και πεμψον ταις επτα εκκλησιαις εις εφεσον και εις σμυρναν και εις περγαμον και εις θυατειρα και εις σαρδεις και εις φιλαδελφειαν και εις λαοδικειαν

The highlighted section in the Textus Receptus Greek is the part that is left out of the modern versions undergirded by the Westcott-Hort Alexandrian Text of 1881. In the Greek NT of the United Bible Societies, which I have in my possession, there is not even a notation as to why this was omitted. This section is omitted in the Sinaiticus and is completely omitted in the Vaticanus; in fact, the entire book of Revelation is omitted in the Vaticanus. After all, if your church was labeled the great whore in that book and the leader of that church called the Antichrist, wouldn't you want to leave it out too?

The part that is left out of Revelation 1:11 witnesses to the divinity of the Lord Jesus Christ; plus, it shows His eternality. Gnostic influence disbelieves the reality of eternal life, so here too they chopped up another divine title of the Lord Jesus in an attempt to make Him just a mere man. This portion of scripture shows that everything begins with the Lord Jesus Christ and ends with Him.

In fact, the Hebrew manuscript that underlies the King James Version is the 1525 Bomberg edition of the Masoretic text also known as the Ben Chayyim text. That manuscript witnesses harmony with Revelation 1:11 in Micah 5:2.

> But thou, Bethlehem Ephratah, though thou be little among the thousands of Judah, yet out of thee shall he come forth unto me that is to be ruler in Israel; whose goings forth have been from of old, *from everlasting*. (Micah 5:2, KJV)

But notice how the Hebrew text in the modern versions witness to the eternality of the Lord Jesus. This is because in 1937, Rudolph Kittel changed the Hebrew text from the Ben Chayyim text to the corrupted Ben Asher text, which they based on the Leningrad Manuscript dated AD 1008 (older is better error). The NIV, NASV, and the NKJV use this corrupted Hebrew text and therefore differs from the reading in the KJB. In 1967/77 there was a revision of Kittel's Biblia Hebraica, which became known as the Biblia Hebraica Stuttgartensia text. This new revision is used in the modern versions such as the NIV and NASV and others. Notice how they change the everlasting character of the Lord Jesus to one who is within the confines of time.

> But you, O Bethlehem Eph'rathah, who are little to be among the clans of Judah, from you shall

come forth for me one who is to be ruler in Israel, whose origin is from of old, *from ancient days*. (Micah 5:2, RSV)

But you, Bethlehem Ephrathah, though you are small among the clans of Judah, out of you will come for me one who will be ruler over Israel, whose origins are from of old, *from ancient times*. (Micah 5:2, NIV)

Notice how the King James Bible creates a beautiful witness to the everlasting nature of the Lord Jesus while the modern versions abort His eternal testimony in Revelation 1:11 and Micah 5:2. Yet pastors all over this country and around the world insist these modern versions are more accurate than the KJB. When these megalomaniac pastors start taking their calling seriously and bring their churches back to the real word of God in the KJB, then the churches will once again be a place of power and reverence. When power is preached from the pulpits once again, then unbelievers will fear the church instead of the church fearing them.

Revelation 1:17

And when I saw him, I fell at his feet as dead. And he laid his right hand upon me, saying *unto me*, Fear not; I am the first and the last. (Revelation 1:17, KJV)

"Unto me" is omitted.

Here is another example of the modern versions turning a specific into a general statement. John was in heaven and saw the Lord Jesus Christ. Verse 16 states that His countenance was as the sun. "And he had in his right hand seven stars: and out of his mouth went a sharp twoedged sword: and his countenance was as the sun shineth in his strength" (Revelation 1:16, KJV). John saw Jesus and immediately fell at His feet as if he were dead. John said that Jesus laid His right hand on John and spoke unto him. Jesus did not speak generally or to a crowd. He spoke specifically to John in this awesome vision. The word *moi* in the Greek is in the dative case, which means John was receiving the action; that is, Jesus was speaking specifically to him, and John was receiving the action of that speech. Without *moi*, it turns into a general statement.

Revelation 1:20

The mystery of the seven stars which thou sawest in my right hand, and the seven golden candlesticks. The seven stars are the angels of the seven churches: and the seven candlesticks *which thou sawest* are the seven churches. (Revelation 1:20, KJV)

"Which thou sawest" is omitted.

The Lord Jesus Christ is telling John specifically that the seven candlesticks he saw were the seven churches of Revelation. The modern versions omit "which thou sawest," making that portion of the statement an open-ended statement. Jesus is showing John specifically what He means by the seven golden candlesticks and what they represent, but the modern versions turn it into a general statement, putting the meaning outside of the vision. John was seeing a specific thing, which was the seven candlesticks, which have a specific meaning, which are the seven churches of Revelation chapters 2–3.

Revelation 2:9

I know thy *works, and* tribulation, and poverty, (but thou art rich) and I know the blasphemy of them which say they are Jews, and are not, but are the synagogue of Satan. (Revelation 2:9, KJV)

"Works and" is omitted.

A very important teaching has been omitted from this verse. Notice it starts out by the Lord saying, "I know thy works." The church at Smyrna was working hard for the Lord to send forth the Gospel, and as a result, they were suffering much persecution for their deeds. The Lord Jesus Christ was acknowledging the fact that these Christians were working very hard on kingdom business, but their testimony and works had reduced them to a state of poverty because of the persecution. "For God is not unrighteous to forget your work and labour of love, which ye have showed toward his name, in that ye have ministered to the saints, and do minister" (Hebrews 6:10, KJV).

This is a very important principle because no matter what works we do for the kingdom of God, they never go unnoticed by the Lord Jesus Christ, regardless of how small the task may be. The reason that the Christians were being persecuted was because they were active in the Lord's work. Satan does not care how much you know as long as you do nothing with it. Uninvolved Christians make no impact for the kingdom of God and are no threat to the kingdom of Satan.

The moment you begin to invade Satan's kingdom with the Gospel, you will be persecuted. The modern versions omit the fact that the Lord Jesus Christ is fully cognizant of the works we do after salvation because we can never work for salvation. They omit this great encouraging principle that harmonizes beautifully with Hebrews 6:10. Works are an important part of every Christian's life. Polycarp lived from AD 69–155 and became the bishop of Smyrna. He was discipled by the apostles themselves. In AD 155, as he faced martyrdom, he was asked to renounce Christianity, and they would spare his life. In his martyrdom, Polycarp is recorded as saying on the day of his death, "Eighty and six years I have served Him, how then can I blaspheme my King and Savior? Bring forth what thou wilt." Polycarp was burned at the stake for refusing to burn incense to the Roman emperor.

Revelation 2:13

I know thy works, and where thou dwellest, even where Satan's seat is: and thou holdest fast my name, and hast not denied my faith, even in those days wherein Antipas was my faithful mar-

tyr, who was slain among you, where Satan dwelleth. (Revelation 2:13, KJV)

"I know thy works" is omitted.

Here at the outset, God is commending the church at Pergamos
for upholding His name correctly. God knows the works of this
church. This principle also applies to the individual believer. God
knows all of our works, and if we compare our lives to the scriptures,
God would definitely have a few things against us too. I guess the
Gnostics and the modern-day translators did not feel that this commendation was worthy to be placed in scripture, so they omitted it
for no reason given. Maybe they were afraid that God knew their
works too, and you can be sure He knows the works of the modern
translators and publishers who corrupt His word for profit. Let us
stay with the King James Bible and allow God to refine our Christian
walk by letting us compare our walk to the complete scriptures and
not the *doctored* portions.

Revelation 2:15

So hast thou also them that hold the doctrine of the Nicolaitans, *which thing I hate.*
(Revelation 2:15, KJV)

"Which thing I hate" is omitted.

In this verse, God is specifically telling us that he hates the doctrine of the Nicolaitans. Now, this doctrine has been debated over by
many scholars as to what this doctrine may have been. Some believe
they were a sect of the Gnostics. The part that the Hort-Westcott
leaves out is "which thing I hate." The word *misoo* ("I hate") is in
the present tense. This means that whatever this doctrine was, is still
around in present times and is still hated by God today because it
remains present tense. The word *Nicolaitian* comes from two Greek
words *nikos* (which means "conqueror") and *laos* (which means "people"). So in essence, this word means "conqueror of the people." In
many churches, the pastor is in charge of the church, and they nor-

mally take absolute control of the congregation, which is against the biblical teachings for the spiritual gift of pastor. They are to be under the authority of the elders and the bishop of the congregation, who is the chief or ruling elder.

In the Roman Catholic Church, the priest is the head of their particular parish. They are looked on as God's personal representative in that assembly, and this deception has been taught and accepted for 1,800 years. When the Reformation came and Protestant denominations began to form, they followed the Roman Catholic system. They ordained one man to be head of each church. Ordination is a Roman Catholic tradition and is not found in the Bible. In the majority of churches, one man stands as absolute authority, and if he is teaching error and is confronted, the truth bearer is castigated and normally thrown out of the church. This may be the error that God hates simply because He has given every Christian spiritual gifts that are to be used for the furtherance of the kingdom and the building up of other Christians. There is nothing found in scripture that teaches that seminaries and Bible colleges create pastors. Being a pastor is a spiritual gift, not a ruling gift.

"And he gave some, apostles; and some, prophets; and some, evangelists; and some, pastors and teachers" (Ephesians 4:11, KJV) If you notice, in Ephesians 4:11, the spiritual gift of "pastor" is not a superior office but is listed along with the other spiritual gifts that also bring the word of God. The pastor has spiritual authority over the congregation, and as a shepherd watches the flocks of his master, the pastor watches over the spiritual well-being of the congregation of the Lord. He is not to be elevated to god status in the congregation, and he is not to be looked upon as the final and only authority in the congregation.

> And he said unto them, The kings of the Gentiles exercise lordship over them; and they that exercise authority upon them are called benefactors. But ye shall not be so: but he that is greatest among you, let him be as the younger;

THE MODERN VERSION INCURSION

and he that is chief, as he that doth serve. (Luke 22:25–26, KJV)

Feed the flock of God which is among you, taking the oversight thereof, not by constraint, but willingly; not for filthy lucre, but of a ready mind; *Neither as being lords over God's heritage, but being ensamples to the flock.* (1 Peter 5:2–3, KJV)

Now, back to Revelation 2:15. God specifically says that He hates this doctrine; however, the Hort-Westcott text removes "which thing I hate" and replaces it with the word *likewise.* This means nothing. By removing "which thing I hate" and lopping off the verse, we cannot tell whether God endorses that teaching or loathes it. Verse 16 commands the church at Pergamos to repent of that pernicious doctrine, but when "which thing I hate" is removed from the verse, we are not sure what God is requiring the church at Pergamos to repent of. In my United Bible Societies fourth edition of the Hort-Westcott text, there is no reason given as to why this section was removed.

Yet we can give a real reason why it was removed. If God was referring to some superspiritual class of clergy that tries to exalt themselves over the flock of God, then it would make perfect sense to remove that from the text. So if you are one of those exalted clergy, as the Gnostics thought they were, as well as the seminary-trained clergy of today, then the people will have no idea that God hates that idea of a class of exalted clergy that sets themselves up as rulers instead of examples to the flock as 1 Peter 5:3 states. No wonder so many Protestant churches have thrown the King James Bible out and replaced them with the Gnostic versions. It keeps the clergy exalted and the sheep in their rightful place, sitting at their feet. This is nothing more than the spiritual abuse of Christians, and the sorry part is that the majority of Christians still choose to remain biblically ignorant, which paves the way for this situation in the church.

Revelation 2:20

Notwithstanding I have a few things against thee, because thou sufferest that woman Jezebel, which calleth herself a prophetess, to teach and to seduce my servants to commit *fornication*, and to eat things sacrificed unto idols. (Revelation 2:20, KJV)

Fornication changed to "sexual immorality."

The modern versions all focus in on sexual immorality while that is not initially in view. What is in view is spiritual fornication, which is a departure from the teachings of scripture. The Lord Jesus Christ brings to their attention the things that are causing the church to become weak. Then the name *Jezebel* is introduced into the text as one who was causing the people of God to seduce the Christians and compromise their church by mixing the true Christianity with false religion.

And it came to pass, as if it had been a light thing for him to walk in the sins of Jeroboam the son of Nebat, that he took to wife Jezebel the daughter of Ethbaal king of the Zidonians, and went and served Baal, and worshipped him. And he reared up an altar for Baal in the house of Baal, which he had built in Samaria. And Ahab made a grove; and Ahab did more to provoke the LORD God of Israel to anger than all the kings of Israel that were before him. (1 Kings 16:31–33, KJV)

In 1 Kings 16:31 and following, we are introduced to King Ahab and his wife, Jezebel. Jezebel was the daughter of Ethbaal II, who was king of the Sidonians. When she came into power, her husband had made an altar to Baal and worshipped that false god. The allusion in Revelation 2:20 to the Jezebel of Israel tells us that they were permitting an unsaved woman to teach, and that teaching had seduced many in that church. The word *seduced* carries with it the meaning of "lead astray, delude, or mislead." Whatever this woman

was teaching was misleading the Christians to commit spiritual fornication, which may have led to sexual fornication. Whatever her
teachings were, they were definitely of a false religion and had no
business inside the church.

She was also in violation of God's rules about women teaching
in a church. "Let the woman learn in silence with all subjection. But I
suffer not a woman to teach, nor to usurp authority over the man, but
to be in silence" (1 Timothy 2:11–12, KJV). We see the same thing
in modern churches where women are now teaching in churches and
even large crowds. Many women in the Charismatic movement are
teaching and leading people astray with their emotion and prosperi-
ty-based gospels. These would not exist if men would not attend their
meetings in droves. "As for my people, children are their oppressors,
and women rule over them. O my people, they which lead thee cause
thee to err, and destroy the way of thy paths" (Isaiah 3:12, KJV). The
problem in Thyatira was the church was permitting this woman to
teach, and obviously, no one had opposed her teachings.

Spiritual fornication is when one diverts from the true Gospel.
We see spiritual fornication widely spread in the majority of modern
churches. Just look at things like the Charismatic movement with its
prosperity and barking and laughter. Then you have the emergent
church movement with all its Roman Catholic mystics and its rejection of the Bible. Then there is the acceptance of sodomites in the
pulpit. I could go on, but I think you get the message that the message in view in Revelation 2:20 is not sexual immorality but spiritual
fornication, which leads to eternal damnation.

Revelation 2:22

> Behold, I will cast her into a *bed*, and them
> that commit adultery with her into great trib-
> ulation, except they repent of their deeds.
> (Revelation 2:22, KJV)

Bed is changed to "sickbed" or "suffering."

573

The modern versions add the word *sick* to the word *bed*. In Greek, the word for "bed" just means "bed." It could mean a bed of sickness, a bed of affliction, a place to sit, or a place to sleep. There is no intimation of the word being a bed of sickness in this verse. That interpretation does not even keep with the meaning of the verse. It is not speaking about sickness but about those who sin with the false teachings of the world system.

This was added by the translators in another violation of Revelation 22:18.

> For I testify unto every man that heareth the words of the prophecy of this book, If any man shall add unto these things, God shall add unto him the plagues that are written in this book. (Revelation 22:18, KJV)

> And when her sister Aholibah saw this, she was more corrupt in her inordinate love than she, and in her whoredoms more than her sister in her whoredoms. (Ezekiel 23:11, KJV)

> And the Babylonians came to her into the bed of love, and they defiled her with their whoredom, and she was polluted with them, and her mind was alienated from them. (Ezekiel 23:17, KJV)

In Ezekiel 23:11–17, we read that Aholibah (Judah and Benjamin) had seen the wickedness that the northern ten tribes had partaken in; plus, they also saw that the Lord had punished them by sending them into the Assyrians as punishment for their idolatry. This punishment did not even faze Judah and Benjamin because they did not mend their ways. So the Lord sent the Babylonians to take Judah captive for seventy years. In Ezekiel 23:17, the Bible tells us that the Babylonians came to Judah in the bed of love. In other words, they came to them as a husband comes to a wife or a wife comes to a husband in the bedroom. It is the height of intimacy, but the Babylonians were not showing real love but seduced Judah with their false religion and caused them to commit whoredom, which resulted in their punishment.

God is basically saying the same thing to the Thyatira church, that He is going to cast her into a bed, and those who commit spiritual fornication with her will go into great tribulation. Those who followed her pernicious teachings would suffer great affliction and distress in their lives. It is like Christians today who follow the false teachings of any false teacher. The passage is speaking about Jezebel who represented Baal worship in the Old Testament, and here, the warning went out to this church, that they were to eschew false teachings that crept into the church.

They became very spiritually dry, and their spiritual life came apart by being in great affliction. It is not beyond the means of God to remove a person's material goods or even loved ones to get the attention of the one who has slid into spiritual fornication. However, God is also telling them that they could avoid this if they repent and turn from those false teachings. This is why He sent the prophets to Judah to try and get them to turn from their spiritual harlotry. This is why He sent this letter to Thyatira to get them to repent of the same type of evil.

Revelation 3:3

> Remember therefore how thou hast received and heard, and hold fast, and repent. If therefore thou shalt not watch, I will come *on thee* as a thief, and thou shalt not know what hour I will come upon thee. (Revelation 3:3, KJV)

"On thee" is omitted.

Christ is now commanding them to remember not the fact that they heard but how they received and heard. They received the truth in much hardship and persecution. They also received the Gospel through faith. The Lord is telling them to hold fast to the things they had when they first became a church. Christ is commanding them to repent and abide in those things that make for a solid spiritual church. Worldly things in the church does not grow Christians in the faith. If this church refuses to remain vigilant in those things that still remain, then the Lord is going to come upon them as a thief; and when a thief comes, you do not know what hour he comes.

There are two scenarios in view in the second half of this verse: The first one is that if they do not repent, the Lord will come swiftly and uncompromisingly upon this church and remove them from being a living church among the congregations of the Lord. The second scenario is that the return of the Lord at His second coming will be as a thief in the night. It will come upon all churches, and if they are not found faithful, they will suffer the consequences of the unsaved world. The Lord is specifically telling this to the church at Sardis, making it a personal warning instead of the generic warning the modern versions give by omitting "on thee."

Revelation 3:4

> Thou hast a few names *even* in Sardis which have not defiled their garments; and they shall walk with me in white: for they are worthy. (Revelation 3:4, KJV)

Even is omitted.

There were some in the church at Sardis who did not defile their garments; that is, they did not go the way of the world and cling to false teachings or unbelieving works, which is what secular works are. Any time a Christian adopts any false teachings or false ways, it is like defiling the pure garments we were given at the moment of salvation. All true believers wear the robe of Christ's righteousness.

> I will greatly rejoice in the LORD, my soul shall be joyful in my God; for he hath clothed me with the garments of salvation, he hath covered me with the robe of righteousness, as a bridegroom deck-

eth himself with ornaments, and as a bride adorneth herself with her jewels. (Isaiah 61:10, KJV)

However, those Christians who continue to persevere in the true
teachings of the Lord shall walk with Him in white, which means
they will be with Him throughout all eternity because these are the
truly redeemed. Walking with Christ in white means they are pure
before the eyes of God. We are made worthy only through the shed
blood of Christ and the fact that His righteousness was imputed to
us. When the Lord uses the conjunction *even*, He is basically stating
that even within the sinful atmosphere of Sardis, the church has not
been infected with the sins totally. There were some *even* in Sardis
who did not forsake the true Gospel and still walk with the Lord.
It would be like saying, "*Even* in Las Vegas, there are some believers
who do not gamble." The Lord is stating that a Christian does not
have to become blemished with the world's sin, and in this case, He
is pointing to that fact within Sardis.

Revelation 3:11

Behold, I come quickly: hold that fast which
thou hast, that no man take thy crown.
(Revelation 3:11, KJV)

Behold is omitted.

The word *behold*, which is missing in the modern versions, is
the word in the Greek for "see, perceive, or look." In this usage of
the word, it is in the imperative mood, which means the Lord Jesus
Christ is giving a command to the church at Philadelphia. He is not
merely giving some type of information that is not important, but
He is commanding them to look—that is, to attend to, direct, or
fix their mind upon the fact that the Lord Jesus Christ is coming
quickly, and they are to remain faithful until He does come back.
They were to avoid false teachers and not to let their spiritual guard
down. What the Lord is charging here is not an option but a command to remain faithful.

The modern versions omit this fact that the Lord desires His church to remain faithful and is commanding them to be vigilant. They skip this fact and focus upon the return of Christ, but what is the Christian to be during that time? They are to be faithful. This is why the Lord commands them in the rest of the verse to hold fast or hold on to what they have. The words *hold fast* is one word in the Greek, and it is also in the imperative mood, which is a command and not an option.

Revelation 5:1

And I saw in the right hand of him that sat on the throne a *book* written *within* and on the backside, sealed with seven seals. (Revelation 5:1, KJV)

Book and *within* are omitted.

The modern versions above speak about the word of God being written on "both sides" and "front and back." These are both very erroneous interpretations because if one looks at their Bible, the words of God are not written on the front and back or "both sides." I have to ask, both sides of what? The scroll? The word in the Greek as we read in the King James Bible is *biblion*, where we get the word *book* or *bible* from. In both the Textus Receptus and Hort-Westcott text, the word *Biblion* is capitalized, which means it is speaking about the word of God. The reason it is not speaking of a scroll is the Greek word *esothen*, which is also highlighted above. It carries only one meaning, and that is "inside." A scroll has two sides, and that is where the modern versions get "front and back" and "both sides." However, with the word *esothen*, it is speaking about writing "inside," which excludes a scroll because there is no inside, just a front and back. The only item that has writing "within or inside" is a book, not a scroll. Revelation 5:1–10 speaks about a book, and verse 10 speaks about Christ making the believers kings and priests.

The modern versions who substitute "scroll" for "book" are AMP, ESV, HCSB, ISV, LEB, LB, MESSAGE, NKJV, NLT, NRSV, RSV, THE VOICE.

Revelation 5:4

And I wept much, because no man was found worthy to open *and to read* the book, neither to look thereon. (Revelation 5:4, KJV)

"And to read" is omitted.

It does no good to open a book if you are not going to read its contents. The word *anagnonai* is used thirty-three times in the New Testament and occurs in the context of a literal reading such as in the following verses:

When ye therefore shall see the abomination of desolation, spoken of by Daniel the prophet, stand in the holy place, (whoso *readeth*, let him understand). (Matthew 24:15, KJV)

Was returning, and sitting in his chariot *read* Esaias the prophet. (Acts 8:28, KJV)

As we see in these two verses, they speak of a literal reading. The Ethiopian eunuch in Acts 8 and the reader of Matthew 24. John had realized that the revelation contained in the book was of utmost importance, and believing that there was no one found worthy to open the book, he wept bitterly. In Revelation 4:1, he was told that he was going to be shown the things that were to happen; and if the book could not be opened nor read, then the revelation would be at an impasse. John was saddened because the end of the world and the judgments that were to come seemed to now be thwarted unless the book could be opened and read. The modern versions omit this serious situation.

Revelation 5:5

And one of the elders saith unto me, Weep not: behold, the Lion of the tribe of Juda, the Root of

David, hath prevailed to open the book, and *to loose* the seven seals thereof. (Revelation 5:5, KJV)

"To loose" is omitted.

The portion of scripture omitted in the modern versions is a very important part of this verse. The Lord Jesus will not only open the book but will loose the seven seals. The word *lusai* in the Greek is in the *infinitive aorist active*, which means that the action is punctiliar and without time duration. It is not just a question of opening the book, but Jesus will have a specific timetable when the seals are to be opened. The punctiliar action is an action that has taken place in the past, and with the aorist tense, the action has no specific duration.

Revelation 5:6

And I beheld, *and, lo*, in the midst of the throne and of the four beasts, and in the midst of the elders, stood a Lamb as it had been slain, having seven horns and seven eyes, which are the seven Spirits of God sent forth into all the earth. (Revelation 5:6, KJV)

"And, lo" is omitted.

Here is another case of a removal of a word that is very important to the verse. The Greek words behind "and I beheld" and "and lo" are the same root word but are different inflections. In the first instance, John is stating that he is seeing the Lamb; but in the second instance "and lo," it is in the imperative mood, which means John is being commanded to look in such a manner as not just a glance but an intense looking. John was in the throne room of God and was to look intently at the Lamb of God and the fact that He is the one who will send out the Holy Spirit to all parts of the earth, having all power, which is represented by the seven horns. "And Jesus came and spake unto them, saying, All power is given unto me in heaven and in earth" (Matthew 28:18, KJV).

Revelation 5:10

And hast made *us* unto our God *kings* and priests: and *we* shall reign on the earth. (Revelation 5:10, KJV)

"*Us*" is changed to "them." "*Kings*" is changed to "kingdom." "*We*" is changed to "they." The modern versions take away the reality that the Christians will be made kings in God's kingdom. By changing "us" and "we" to third-person plural words, it gives the idea that someone else rather than *us* is going to be the kings.

This is one of those verses that has seen the apostates' knife in three places. To gain the context of this verse, we need to back up to verse 9.

And they sung a new song, saying, Thou art worthy to take the book, and to open the seals thereof: for thou wast slain, and hast redeemed us to God by thy blood out of every kindred, and tongue, and people, and nation. (Revelation 5:9, KJV)

In Revelation 5:9, we read of the saints in heaven singing praises to the Lord Jesus Christ for their salvation. John is describing the fact that the redeemed are singing a new song, and then he goes on to quote the words of that song. The believers are praising Christ for redeeming them to God by His blood—"thou has redeemed us." Then the context is picked up in verse 10:

And hast made us unto our God kings and priests: and we shall reign on the earth. (Revelation 5:10, KJV)

Not only was the believer redeemed unto God, He made us kings and priests, and we will reign in those positions on the earth. In both verse 9 and 10, we see that they are referring to themselves in the song by the word *us* in both verses and the word *we* in verse 10.

In the modern versions, we will look at the NIV and the 1901 ASV as representative.

> And they sang a new song: "You are worthy to take the scroll and to open its seals, because you were slain, and with your blood you purchased men for God from every tribe and language and people and nation." (Revelation 5:9, NIV)

> And they sing a new song, saying, Worthy art thou to take the book, and to open the seals thereof: for thou was slain, and didst purchase unto God with thy blood men of every tribe, and tongue, and people, and nation. (Revelation 5:9, ASV)

If you will notice in just these two versions, the personal nature of salvation by those who are singing the song is removed. The modern versions make it sound like those in Revelation 5:9 and 10 are singing about another group of individuals by using the word *they* and removing the fact that the redeemed are the ones praising Christ. The redeemed are thankful that they are redeemed and are made kings and priests. They are not singing this song on behalf of another group because only they are the redeemed from the earth.

Not only do the modern versions remove the personal-praise aspect of these verses, but they also remove the fact that Christ has made us kings. "And hath made us kings and priests unto God and his Father; to him be glory and dominion for ever and ever. Amen" (Revelation 1:6, KJV). Revelation 1:6 is a confirmation of this fact and vice versa. The modern versions turn our kingship into a king-dom. They take a plural word *kings* and replace it with a singular word *kingdom*. Now, it is true that when we become saved, we are in the kingdom of God, but that is not what is in view here. What is in view is that we are made kings and priests within the kingdom of God. The English words "we shall reign" is one word in the Greek, and it is in the future tense and probably points to our positions in the new heaven and new earth. The fact that God has made us kings and priests along with a ruling position is why these believers are singing and praising Christ. These verses are important because it shows an aspect of salvation that is much more than just being saved from hell. The modern versions divert the believer from the reality that is ours and focus them on some other mythical group that does not exist, except only in the minds of Hort and Westcott.

Revelation 5:14

And the four beasts said, Amen. And the *four and twenty* elders fell down and worshipped *him that liveth for ever and ever.* (Revelation 5:14, KJV)

"Four and twenty" and *"him that liveth forever and ever"* are omitted.

And every creature which is in heaven, and on the earth, and under the earth, and such as are in the sea, and all that are in them, heard I saying, Blessing, and honour, and glory, and power, be unto him that sitteth upon the throne, and unto the Lamb *for ever and ever.* And the four beasts said, Amen. And the four and twenty elders fell down and worshipped him that liveth *for ever and ever.* (Revelation 5:13–14, KJV)

Verse 14 is tied directly to verse 13 by the phrase "for ever and ever." We read in verse 13 that every human and creature in both heaven and earth is paying homage to the Lamb who lives forever and ever. This is a statement about the eternality of the Lord Jesus Christ and the fact that He is receiving worship as God. When the phrase "him that liveth for ever and ever" is omitted in verse 14, it makes the verses in the modern versions approve the worship of whatever god they want. That phrase gives a specific identity of the person who is receiving the worship, and that is the Lord Jesus Christ. There is absolutely no reason given why this verse was truncated in the Aleph manuscript except that it is just another Gnostic attack on the deity of the Lord Jesus Christ.

Another omission that was done without reason was the number "twenty and four," which gave the specific number of elders that is listed five times in the book of Revelation (Revelation 4:4; 4:10; 5:8; 5:14; 11:16). In Revelation 11:16, it specifically states that the twenty-four elders fell down and worshipped God. If you notice, one major characteristic about the modern versions is that they always turn specific into nonspecific. The modern versions are so written that they can be used in any form of any religion. Without any specifics, any version can be made to fit into any belief system. This is why it is very important to have a Bible that is specific in nature rather than nebulous, and that is the good ole' King James Bible.

Revelation 6:1, 3, 5, 7

> And I saw when the Lamb opened one of the seals, and I heard, as it were the noise of thunder, one of the four beasts saying, Come *and see*.... And when he had opened the second seal, I heard the second beast say, Come *and see*.... And when he had opened the third seal, I heard the third beast say, Come *and see*. And I beheld, and lo a black horse; and he that sat on him had a pair of balances in his hand....And when he had opened the fourth seal, I heard the voice of the fourth beast say, Come *and see*. (Revelation 6:1–7, KJV)

"And see" is omitted in all four verses.

Four times, the apostle John is told by one of the four living creatures to come and see. The word "see" in the Greek is *blepe* in the majority of New Testament usage, which means to "physically see." This is how it is used in Revelation 6:1, 3, 5, and 7. John is being called to heaven as a witness of things to come, and he could not be a witness if he is unable to physically see. In a court of law, an eyewitness who did not see something could not be an eyewitness; he would be dismissed as pure hearsay. But if he sees something physically, then he becomes a credible eyewitness. The modern versions take away his credibility because they leave out the fact that John is not only told to come but to come and see. The purpose for John to see has been extinguished from the modern versions, making him a hearsay witness instead of an eyewitness. It is another blatant attack on the clarity of scripture.

Revelation 6:17

> For the great day of *his* wrath is come; and who
> shall be able to stand? (Revelation 6:17, KJV)

His is changed to "their" (denying the wrath is emanating from the Lamb).

This is one of the subtle changes that you can easily overlook if you are not looking for it.

> And said to the mountains and rocks, Fall on us,
> and hide us from the face of him that sitteth on
> the throne, and from the wrath of the Lamb: For
> the great day of his wrath is come; and who shall
> be able to stand? (Revelation 6:16–17, KJV)

In Revelation 6:17, we are being told that the wrath of the Lamb has come. We see this in the preceding verse (16), where it plainly speaks about the wrath of the Lamb. Verse 17 then goes on to say that this wrath is sourced in the Lord Jesus Christ, and it is He who is sending this wrath upon the earth. The Gnostics changed the word in the Greek from the singular *his* to the plural *their*. This is highly erroneous because verse 17 has changed the focus from the Lord Jesus Christ, the sender of the wrath, to those who are receiving it. This is the wrong focus of this verse. The focus is on the Lord Jesus Christ and not man. Once again, we see the modern versions removing the readers' focus from the Lord Jesus Christ to man. This change is an attack on the doctrine of the Lord Jesus Christ and the doctrine of eschatology.

Revelation 7:5–8

> Of the tribe of Juda were *sealed* twelve thousand. Of the tribe of Reuben were *sealed* twelve thousand. Of the tribe of Gad were *sealed* twelve thousand. Of the tribe of Aser were *sealed* twelve thousand. Of the tribe of Nepthalim were *sealed* twelve thousand. Of the tribe of Manasses were *sealed* twelve thousand. Of the tribe of Simeon were *sealed* twelve thousand. Of the tribe of Levi were *sealed* twelve thousand. Of the tribe of Issachar were *sealed* twelve thousand. Of the tribe of Zabulon were *sealed* twelve thousand. Of the tribe of Joseph were *sealed* twelve thousand. Of the tribe of Benjamin were *sealed* twelve thousand. (Revelation 7:5–8, KJV)

Sealed is omitted ten, eleven, or twelve times out of twelve readings.

Some of the modern versions omit all twelve of the words *sealed*, and some of them omit only ten, and some omit eleven. This means that this omission of the word *sealed* can be found in every modern version.

> Not as though the word of God hath taken none effect. For they are not all Israel, which are of Israel. (Romans 9:6, KJV)

Here, Paul reveals that there are two Israels. In the past few verses, Paul was speaking of his kinsman according to the flesh and the coming of the Lord Jesus Christ according to the flesh. The Bible is now revealing that there are two different Israels. There is Israel according to the flesh and Israel according to the Spirit. This is a very important verse as Paul begins by stating that the word of God was effective in doing what it was supposed to do. When we look back at the history of the nation of Israel from the time they came out of Egypt, we will see two distinct populations. One of them were the people who built the golden calf and were the ones who disobeyed God right down through their entire history (men such as Korah, King Saul, Baalam, etc.). Then you also have the history of the men who obeyed God during their history such as Moses, Joshua, David, Nehemiah, etc. What Paul is saying here is that God's word reached His elect among the ancient nation of Israel, even though it looked more like it failed in keeping the nation of Israel as a holy people. Nothing could be further from the truth.

The word of God made a distinction between the Israel in the flesh, which was disobedient, and the Israel of God, which was in the Spirit, who were obedient of God. Thus, we see that Paul speaks of two Israels, one according to the flesh and one according to the Spirit. Those who are born again are of spiritual Israel, which is the eternal Israel. Paul is saying that just because a person was born in national Israel does not mean they are part of the eternal Israel. One enters the eternal Israel through redemption through the grace of the Lord Jesus Christ. The true chosen people of God are those chosen for salvation, and that is the only chosen people God has. "Which in time past were not a people, *but are now the people of God*: which had not obtained mercy, but now have obtained mercy" (1 Peter 2:10, KJV). Notice in this verse that it states "*the* people of God." The direct article means there is no other people of God. The people of God have been sealed by the Holy Spirit as we see in Revelation, where the names of the tribes are symbolic of the entire body of Christ. "And grieve not the holy Spirit of God, whereby ye are sealed unto the day of redemption" (Ephesians 4:30, KJV).

Revelation 8:7

The first angel sounded, and there followed hail and fire mingled with blood, and they were cast upon the earth: and the third part of trees

was burnt up, and all green grass was burnt up.
(Revelation 8:7, KJV)

"The third part of the earth" was added to the corrupt Greek text by means of Codex Sinaiticus and Alexandrinus, but it is not in the Textus Receptus.

> And the first sounded, and there followed hail
> and fire, mingled with blood, and they were cast
> upon the earth: *and the third part of the earth*
> was burnt up, and the third part of the trees
> was burnt up, and all green grass was burnt up.
> (Revelation 8:7, ASV)

If you look closely at the trumpet judgments in Revelation 8, you will see they are strategic judgments, and nowhere do we find that one-third of the earth was burned up. God is making specific judgments, not a general one, at this point. Below is a little commentary on Revelation 8:7 so we can gain a better understanding concerning the specific judgments in view.

The first trumpet judgment is patterned after Exodus 9:22–25, which was the plague of hail and fire. The mixing with blood is taken from Joel 2:31.

> And the LORD said unto Moses, Stretch forth
> thine hand toward heaven, that there may be hail
> in all the land of Egypt, upon man, and upon
> beast, and upon every herb of the field, through-
> out the land of Egypt. And Moses stretched
> forth his rod toward heaven: and the LORD sent
> thunder and hail, and the fire ran along upon
> the ground; and the LORD rained hail upon the
> land of Egypt. So there was hail, and fire min-
> gled with the hail, very grievous, such as there
> was none like it in all the land of Egypt since it
> became a nation. And the hail smote through-

> out all the land of Egypt all that was in the field, both man and beast; and the hail smote every herb of the field, and brake every tree of the field. (Exodus 9:22–25, KJV)

> The sun shall be turned into darkness, and the moon into blood, before the great and the terrible day of the LORD come. (Joel 2:31, KJV)

In the plague on Egypt, we read that this judgment had devastated all the vegetation in the land of Egypt, except that the wheat and rye were not smitten (Exodus 9:32). In the Revelation verse, we read that one-third of the trees were burnt up, and all the green grass were burnt up by reason of the prayers of the saints being answered by God in the judgments that are coming upon the unsaved world. The second set of judgments is showing more intensity than the previous seal judgments. The seal judgments spoke of one-fourth of the earth being affected.

> Whilst their children remember their altars and their groves by the green trees upon the high hills. (Jeremiah 17:2, KJV)

This first trumpet judgment is aimed primarily at the trees and the green grass as we see that one-third of all the trees were burned up, plus all the green grass. In the book of Jeremiah, God was also warning Judah about their idolatry. The trees were associated with the groves where Baal and other false religions were practiced by both Judah and Israel. In the judgments of the seven trumpets, there is mentioned that those on earth who were not killed had not repented of their sorceries and idolatries. While the first trumpet judgment may have a physical effect upon a limited part of the earth, we are also seeing that God will be sending judgment upon all those who are idolatrous and who are involved in false religions.

In our times, we are seeing the prostitution of true Christianity as it is increasingly turned into a social religion by having the sting of the Gospel removed and the teachings of salvation reinterpreted. The Lord Jesus Christ has been removed from the majority of churches, but there is still a remnant of faithful churches that have not embraced false gospels. As God judged Judah and Israel for their idolatrous ways, the churches that have embraced false gospels in our day will begin to feel the judging hand of God upon them.

> Yea, the hind also calved in the field, and forsook it, because there was no grass. And the wild asses did stand in the high places, they snuffed up the wind like dragons; their eyes did fail, because there was no grass. (Jeremiah 14:5–6 KJV)

In Jeremiah 14, God is telling us that Judah had suffered because of a great dearth. The fact that there was no grass for the animals to feed on had caused great damage to the livestock population. In Revelation, when God burns up all the green grass, He is telling us that the true Gospel, which feeds the believers, will become increasingly difficult to find. In Psalm 23, we are told that we will be beside green pastures. However, as God removes those pastures and burns them up in judgment, the true believer will also have a hard time in this world because of the scarcity or absence of the true Gospel. "Behold, the days come, saith the Lord GOD, that I will send a famine in the land, not a famine of bread, nor a thirst for water, but of hearing the words of the LORD" (Amos 8:11, KJV).

Revelation 8:13

> And I beheld, and heard an *angel* flying through the midst of heaven, saying with a loud voice, Woe, woe, woe, to the inhabiters of the earth by reason of the other voices of the trumpet of the three angels, which are yet to sound! (Revelation 8:13, KJV)

Angel is changed to "eagle."

In Revelation 8, we have a series of angels who are announcing the seven trumpet judgments of God upon the earth. Revelation 8 begins the second parallel vision that covers chapters 8–11. There we read about one-third of the earth being affected. This means that the second vision is parallel to the first, which covers chapters 4–7. Revelation 8–11 is showing an intensifying of the judgments that was revealed in the first vision of chapters 4–7. When we come to Revelation 8:13, we are told that this angel was announcing a woe to the earth because of the three trumpet judgments yet to come.

The modern versions replace the angel with an eagle. The word in the Greek for eagle could also be translated as "vulture." Now, they probably changed it to use the vulture as a symbol for judgment. However, God did not write an eagle or vulture in this passage. He wrote it with an angel. The real reason why the modern versions exchanged "eagle" for *angel* is unknown, but whatever their reason is for doing something like that is unacceptable. We learn from what God wrote in the Bible, and we do not change it out, whether we like it or not. Once again, the modern versions exchange a word in the Greek text for no apparent reason or one that is lost to antiquity. It is a shame that the modern translators continue to keep these false teachings in.

Revelation 10:4

> And when the seven thunders had uttered their voices, I was about to write: and I heard a voice from heaven saying *unto me*, Seal up those things which the seven thunders uttered, and write them not. (Revelation 10:4, KJV)

"Unto me" is omitted.

Here is a case of the modern versions turning a specific event into another nebulous episode. The word "unto me" in the Greek is in the Dative case which is the case of the one who is receiving the command or the one who the action is for. John was about to write what the seven thunders said. In the beginning of the book of

Revelation, John was given the command to write the things which he shall see that shall happen hereafter. However, after these seven thunders had uttered their voices, he was about to write what he heard but he was told that he was not to write them. In other words, at this time these judgments have been sealed up until an appointed time. Daniel was also told to seal up the words which he was given until the appointed time of the end.

> But thou, O Daniel, shut up the words, and seal the book, even to the time of the end: many shall run to and fro, and knowledge shall be increased. (Daniel 12:4, KJV)

> And he said, Go thy way, Daniel: for the words are closed up and sealed till the time of the end. (Daniel 12:9, KJV)

Whatever these seven thunders were, it is significant to know that something will happen in the end-times that is not being revealed to the people at present.

> The secret things belong unto the Lord our God: but those things which are revealed belong unto us and to our children for ever, that we may do all the words of this law. (Deuteronomy 29:29, KJV)

The Lord reserves the right to reveal to His people whatever He believes is necessary for them to know and at the right time. The seven thunders here in Revelation refer to the voice of God as written in Psalm 29.

> The *voice* of the Lord is upon the waters: *the God of glory thundereth*: the Lord is upon many waters. The *voice* of the Lord is powerful; the *voice* of the Lord is full of majesty. The *voice* of the Lord breaketh the cedars; yea, the Lord

breaketh the cedars of Lebanon. He maketh them
also to skip like a calf; Lebanon and Sirion like a
young unicorn. The *voice* of the LORD divideth
the flames of fire. The *voice* of the LORD shaketh
the wilderness; the LORD shaketh the wilderness
of Kadesh. The *voice* of the LORD maketh the
hinds to calve, and discovereth the forests: and
in his temple doth every one speak of his glory.
(Psalm 29:3–9, KJV)

Revelation 11:4

These are the two olive trees, and the two candlesticks standing before *the God* of the earth.
(Revelation 11:4, KJV)

"The God" is changed to "the Lord."

The Greek word *theos* was changed to *kurios* in the modern versions. The word *theos* has many synonyms in the Greek, but *kurios*
is not one of them. What the modern versions have done is bor-
row from Zechariah 6:5: "And the angel answered and said unto me,
These are the four spirits of the heavens, which go forth from standing before the Lord of all the earth" (Zechariah 6:5 KJV). The word
theos in the Greek speaks only of God Himself, but *kurios* has several
meanings such as "owner, master, lord." There is no valid reason for
the text to have been changed from *theos* to *kurios*.

Revelation 11:8

And their dead bodies shall lie in the street of
the great city, which *spiritually* is called Sodom
and Egypt, where also *our* Lord was crucified.
(Revelation 11:8, KJV)

Spiritually is changed to "mystically" or "figuratively."

The word *pneumatikôs* is used only twice in the New Testament
and only translated as "spiritually," an adverb. "But the natural man

receiveth not the things of the Spirit of God: for they are foolishness unto him: neither can he know them, because they are spiritually discerned" (1 Corinthians 2:14, KJV). If you notice in this verse, God is stating that the natural man does not understand the things of scripture because they are spiritually discerned or understood. The natural man does not have the Holy Spirit and therefore cannot understand spiritual things. The spiritual things in view are the scriptures.

The modern versions have replaced the word *spiritually* with words such as "mystical, allegorically, prophetically, symbolically, and figuratively." None of these words will give understanding as to what is in view. The answer is in scripture, which is why the word *spiritually* is used. It is pointing to the fact that the answer is found in other parts of scripture, and the question is, who is Sodom and Gomorrah in this verse? The modern versions will make it some type of mystical atmosphere or allegory that is applied to scripture from the outside, but the answer is found in the scriptures itself.

Once the witness of the true believer and the true church have been completed, the vestiges of the once-mighty church will still be seen, Unfortunately, it will be seen only as a dead body, an empty shell. The churches that once preached the true Gospel will now be filled with false gospels. The great media ministries that once preached the true Gospel will have been replaced by those false gospels. In Eastern thought, not to bury someone after death was a disgrace, not only to the deceased but to their families. Here, we are told that their bodies will lie in the street of the great city that is called Sodom and Egypt. If you notice, the city is "spiritually" called *Sodom and Egypt*. This is a reference to the world. The world is not only called *Babylon* but is known by other names also.

> Hear the word of the LORD, ye rulers of Sodom;
> give ear unto the law of our God, ye people of
> Gomorrah. (Isaiah 1:10, KJV)

In Isaiah, God had called the rulers and the people of Judah *Sodom and Gomorrah*. Now we know that these two cities had been destroyed many years prior, but God is still calling them Sodom and

Gomorrah. He does this because of the sinfulness of Judah and their affinity to the surrounding pagan nations. He also refers to them as Sodom in Ezekiel.

> And thine elder sister is Samaria, she and her daughters that dwell at thy left hand: and thy younger sister, that dwelleth at thy right hand, is Sodom and her daughters. Yet hast thou not walked after their ways, nor done after their abominations: but, as if that were a very little thing, thou wast corrupted more than they in all thy ways. As I live, saith the Lord GOD, Sodom thy sister hath not done, she nor her daughters, as thou hast done, thou and thy daughters. Behold, this was the iniquity of thy sister Sodom, pride, fulness of bread, and abundance of idleness was in her and in her daughters, neither did she strengthen the hand of the poor and needy. (Ezekiel 16:46–49, KJV)

The reference to the great city is a reference to the world. When the Lord was crucified in Jerusalem, the city had become so corrupt and embellished with false gospels that they did not even recognize Christ from the scriptures. The reference to Sodom is a reference to the degrading and base spiritual condition the city of Jerusalem had fallen into. The reference to Egypt was that of a city engrafted into idolatry and pagan worship. When Christ came on the scene, the money changers were corrupting the temple of God, just as the modern money changers are doing to the modern church. Jerusalem had become so much like the world that they are spoken of as being as bad as both Sodom and Egypt; both were typical representations of the world. This is why the great city where Christ was crucified can be identified with the world because Jerusalem became as corrupt as the world. Jerusalem had placed its faith in the world system in contrast to the heavenly Jerusalem of Galatians 4.

> For thus saith the LORD unto the king's house of Judah; Thou art Gilead unto me, and the head of Lebanon: yet surely I will make thee a wilderness, and cities which are not inhabited. And I will prepare destroyers against thee, every one with his weapons: and they shall cut down thy choice cedars, and cast them into the fire. And many nations shall pass by this city, and they shall say every man to his neighbour, Wherefore hath the LORD done thus unto this great city? Then they shall answer, Because they have forsaken the covenant of the LORD their God, and worshipped other gods, and served them. (Jeremiah 22:6–9, KJV)

John is giving a picture of the two witnesses who have been killed and that their bodies would lie in the street of the great city where *our* Lord was crucified. John is using a possessive personal pronoun showing that it was Jesus who was also his Lord as well as the Lord of all believers. The modern versions, by using the word *their*, are showing that John was pointing out that Jesus was Lord of only those two witnesses instead of showing that Jesus is the Lord of all believers.

Revelation 11:17

> Saying, We give thee thanks, O Lord God Almighty, which art, and wast, *and art to come*; because thou hast taken to thee thy great power, *and hast reigned.* (Revelation 11:17, KJV)

"And art to come" is omitted. *"And has reigned"* is changed to "begun to reign." (This change in the modern versions makes it sound like Christ was not already reigning).

The phrase "which art, and wast, and art to come" shows the eternality of God. The statement in effect is saying that God is at present, He was in the past, and He will be in the future. The modern versions omit "and art to come," which is vital to the book of Revelation. This is because John is seeing these visions of what is going to take place in the future, which is the span of the book of Revelation, from the cross to the second coming of Christ. By omitting the future return of the Lord Jesus Christ, the Gnostics place the book of Revelation as completed, if there is no future. There are some belief systems today that claim the book of Revelation was fulfilled by AD 70 with the destruction of Jerusalem. This is a totally erroneous view. The events in the book of Revelation will soon be completed, but from John's vantage point, it was all still in the future. This is why this omission is dangerous.

If you will notice, the second portion I have emphasized in the King James verse was "and hast reigned." In the modern versions, it states "begun to reign." This is a serious heresy since God's reign is from everlasting to everlasting, and there was never a time that God did not reign in this universe. This intentional addition by the translators fits in with their beliefs stemming from Micah 5:2:

> But you, Bethlehem Ephrathah, though you are small among the clans of Judah, out of you will come for me one who will be ruler over Israel, whose origins are from of old, from ancient times. (NIV)

> But you, O Bethlehem of Ephrathah, who are one of the little clans of Judah, from you shall come forth for me one who is to rule in Israel, whose origin is from of old, from ancient days. (NRSV)

> But you, O Bethlehem Eph'rathah, who are little to be among the clans of Judah, from you shall come forth for me one who is to be ruler in Israel, whose origin is from of old, from ancient days. (RSV)

If you will notice, the NIV, RSV, and the NRSV state that Christ had a beginning, but the KJB teaches us that Christ was from eternity. In Revelation 11:17, the words "hast reigned" are one word in the Greek, which is in the aorist tense. The aorist tense states a past action with no reference to time or duration of the action, which means God reigned in the past and continues to reign today and into eternity. If the modern-version translators did a better job, they would know this, but instead they used a future-tense term "begun to reign." I say "future tense" because when would God have begun to reign? At what point in time would that have occurred? You see, the modern versions once again change a very cardinal doctrine. If God was not reigning in the past, then what was He doing? We run into all kinds of problems when we use a modern version. The King James treats God's reign as a past action that continues because none of us know nor can fathom eternity, and that is why the King James Bible is superior to the modern versions.

Revelation 12:12

> Therefore rejoice, ye heavens, and ye that dwell in them. Woe to *the inhabiters of* the earth and of the sea! for the devil is come down unto you, having great wrath, because he knoweth that he hath but a short time. (Revelation 12:12, KJV)

"The inhabiters of" is omitted.

This is a warning verse given to the human race that Satan is on earth and he will be reaping havoc because he knows that his time is short and he will do everything to fight against God. Those that are in heaven are rejoicing that Satan has been cast out but the inhabiters of the earth must now face his wrath. The modern versions leave out the fact that Satan's target is the human race, instead, they say that the earth and the sea are the targets of Satan's wrath. This is a serious warning verse for the human race but the modern versions gut this warning as they do many others. Once again the King James keeps the verse intact so the warning is very clear that we are to be on the lookout for the deceptions of Satan as we head toward the last day.

Revelation 12:17

And the dragon was wroth with the woman, and went to make war with the remnant of her seed, which keep the commandments of God, and have the testimony of Jesus *Christ*. (Revelation 12:17, KJV)

Christ is omitted.

Here is another example of the separation of the name of Jesus from His divine name.

Revelation 13:1

And *I stood upon the sand of the sea*, and saw a beast rise up out of the sea, having seven heads and ten horns, and upon his horns ten crowns, and upon his heads the name of blasphemy. (Revelation 13:1, KJV)

"I stood upon the sand of the sea" is changed to "the dragon stood on the shore of the sea."

Here, we have one of those verses that have been mutilated in several ways. The HCSB, CEV, NLT, and NAB take the first part of the verse and create an eighteenth verse for chapter 12. Chapter 12 only has seventeen verses. Now, the verse addition is not inspired but will cause people to look at the other versions and think that verse 18 is missing. Now, that would be par for the course for the modern versions, but not for the King James, which ends the twelfth chapter at verse 17. In chapter 13, John was continuing to record the vision that God was giving him, and he stated that he was standing on the sand of the sea or something like a beach, and he was watching this beast rise out of the sea.

In the modern versions, it is kind of confusing because it states that "he stood" on the sand of the sea, which is pointing to the dragon of chapter 12, verse 17. This is incorrect because John was the one giving account and was telling us that it was he who was seeing this vision. By removing "I stood," the modern versions remove the witness being given to John.

Revelation 14:1

And I looked, and, lo, a Lamb stood on the mount Sion, and with him an hundred forty and four thousand, having his Father's name written in their foreheads. (Revelation 14:1, KJV)

And I saw, and behold, the Lamb standing on the mount Zion, and with him a hundred and forty and four thousand, having *his name*, and the name of his Father, written on their foreheads. (Revelation 14:1, ASV)

"His name" is added to the text both in Greek and English.

I have no idea why they added "his name" when it was not written originally in the Greek text—another addition that is a violation of Revelation 22:18–19.

Revelation 14:5

And in their mouth was found no guile: for they are without fault *before the throne of God*. (Revelation 14:5, KJV)

"Before the throne of God" is omitted.

The believers are so pure that not even guile (which is "craftiness or deceit") is found in their mouth; and because of them being redeemed by the blood of the Lamb, they are without any fault before the throne of God. "Who shall lay any thing to the charge of God's elect? It is God that justifieth" (Romans 8:33, KJV). The 144,000 in this chapter represent all the believers who have been saved throughout time, and as they are all assembled in heaven before the throne of God, they are declared absolutely pure. They have the right to be in heaven because the Lord Jesus Christ redeemed each one with His blood and washed them thoroughly clean.

The unbelievers will stand before the throne of God and will be judged for their sins, but here the believers are before the throne of God, not for judgment but for the fact that this is their eternal home. The throne of God represents the abode of heaven for the believers. The modern versions omit this glorious fact that they are standing in heaven completely blameless. Let's stay with the King James Bible as it contains all the glorious truths for the believer's future.

Revelation 14:6

> And I saw another angel fly in the midst of heaven, having *the* everlasting gospel to preach unto them that dwell on the earth, and to every nation, and kindred, and tongue, and people. (Revelation 14:6, KJV)

The is changed to "an."

If you notice, the King James is very specific in stating that the angel that is flying in the midst of heaven is bringing *the* everlasting Gospel. The word *the* denotes the fact that there is only one specific Gospel, and that is the gospel of salvation in Christ. The modern versions use the word *an* and even omit any word pointing to the Gospel. They make it look like there is more than one gospel. Once again, the King James Bible clarifies the verse by using a definite article instead of a nebulous word like *an*. The worst part of this is that the definite article is in the Critical text and is changed in the English instead of being translated properly.

Revelation 14:8

> And there followed another angel, saying, Babylon is fallen, is fallen, that great *city*, because

she made all nations drink of the wine of the
wrath of her fornication. (Revelation 14:8, KJV)

City is omitted.

We see more detail about Babylon in chapters 17 and 18, but here we are given a single statement that Babylon has fallen. It is a fulfillment of a vision that was given to Isaiah in chapter 21. There, it is speaking about the physical kingdom of Babylon that would eventually capture Judah for seventy years in 586 BC. "And, behold, here cometh a chariot of men, with a couple of horsemen. And he answered and said, Babylon is fallen, is fallen; and all the graven images of her gods he hath broken unto the ground" (Isaiah 21:9, KJV).

Here, the term *Babylon* is widened and is a synonym for the worldwide kingdom of Satan. As God judged Babylon in the Old Testament, God will swiftly judge the kingdom of Satan at the end of time. There is nowhere on earth that the kingdom of Satan has not touched. Every single nation of this world has been under the evil influence of the kingdom of Satan. The fornication that these nations have been seduced by is the evil beast and the false prophet that had been responsible for seducing both governments of the world and the religious systems by creating false religions that bring only destruction to a person's soul. When one drinks wine, it makes them feel good until they realize that wine has led to their eternal destruction, as in the case of the wine of the wrath of the fornication of Babylon. The unbeliever drinks the wine of Babylon, thinking that it will be only innocent, but he will realize too late that it has set him up for eternal damnation.

In Daniel 4:30, we read about Nebuchadnezzar, who looked over the city of Babylon and glorified himself as if it was he who built it himself. "The king spake, and said, Is not this great Babylon, that I have built for the house of the kingdom by the might of my power, and for the honour of my majesty?" (Daniel 4:30, KJV). He was looking over the great city, and that same principle is found in Revelation as Satan's kingdom has reached the entire world, and in his pride, he thought that he was untouchable. Yet, in this scenario, in the third parallel vision in Revelation, that great city would now be completely destroyed.

"And a mighty angel took up a stone like a great millstone, and cast it into the sea, saying, Thus with violence shall that great city Babylon be thrown down, and shall be found no more at all" (Revelation 18:21, KJV). There is no reason for the word *city* to be omitted. Maybe because the word *city* can be a synonym for a "kingdom," and the scripture corrupters could not see this in other parts of scripture.

Revelation 14:12

Here is the patience of the saints: *here are they* that keep the commandments of God, and the faith of Jesus. (Revelation 14:12, KJV)

"*Here are they*" is changed to "those who obey" or "those who keep."

This verse is speaking of the patience of the saints, and in this context, it is the fulfillment of that patience. The end has come, and the believers no longer need any patience because the faith has now become sight. With the destruction of Babylon (kingdom of Satan) and the judgment of the unbelievers completed, now John switches to the saints and their heavenly reward. No longer will the believer have to rely on faith and patience because the time has now come for them to completely inherit the new heaven and new earth. John is being shown the multitude of believers who did not bow to the world system, and it is a specific group of believers—that is, the entire number of Christians. This is why the words "here are they" are used because the group is now visible to John.

When the modern versions leave the words out, they replace them with words that seem to teach that they still have to keep faithful in the presence of apostasy. This would be an erroneous teaching since the end has come already, and the believers never have to face the kingdom of Satan anymore. Chapter 14 is in the third parallel vision where the earth is ready to be harvested of all the believers (v. 15).

Revelation 14:13

And I heard a voice from heaven saying *unto me*,
Write, Blessed are the dead which die in the Lord
from henceforth: Yea, saith the Spirit, that they
may rest from their labours; and their works do
follow them. (Revelation 14:13, KJV)

"Unto me" is omitted.

Here is a case of the modern versions turning a specific event
into another nebulous episode. The word "unto me" in the Greek is
in the dative case, which is the case of the one who is receiving the
command or the one whom the action is for. In the beginning of the
book of Revelation, John was given the command to write the things
that he shall see that shall happen hereafter. This word was given to
John and not a general announcement to everyone at that time.

Revelation 14:15

And another angel came out of the temple,
crying with a loud voice to him that sat on the
cloud, Thrust in thy sickle, and reap: for the time
is come *for thee* to reap; for the harvest of the
earth is ripe. (Revelation 14:15, KJV)

"For thee" is omitted.

And I looked, and behold a white cloud, and
upon the cloud one sat like unto the Son of man,
having on his head a golden crown, and in his
hand a sharp sickle. (Revelation 14:14, KJV)

In Revelation 14:14, we are seeing that the Lord Jesus Christ is
the one who is sitting on a cloud, and in his hand is the sharp sickle.
This sets up the scene for the next verse.

And another angel came out of the temple,
crying with a loud voice to him that sat on the
cloud, Thrust in thy sickle, and reap: for the time
is come for thee to reap; for the harvest of the
earth is ripe. (Revelation 14:15, KJV)

Here, an angel now approaches the Lord Jesus Christ and conveys to Him to put in the sickle, for the harvest is ripe. *Thrust* is in
the imperative mood, making it a command or instruction. Since no
angel ever has any authority over the Lord Jesus Christ, this angel is
no doubt bringing the command from God the Father, and he is just
relaying it.

Now, there is going to come a time right at the end when the
last one whom the Father named will be brought to the Lord Jesus
Christ, and then comes the harvest of the earth. Now, this harvest
does not only include the elect of God; the unbelievers will also be
harvested from the earth and will stand before the Lord Jesus Christ.
"When the Son of man shall come in his glory, and all the holy
angels with him, then shall he sit upon the throne of his glory: And
before him shall be gathered all nations: and he shall separate them
one from another, as a shepherd divideth his sheep from the goats"
(Matthew 25:31–32, KJV).

So here we have the sickle being cast into the harvest, and all
things in the fields will be harvested. "The field is the world; the
good seed are the children of the kingdom; but the tares are the children of the wicked one; The enemy that sowed them is the devil;
the harvest is the end of the world; and the reapers are the angels"
(Matthew 13:38–39, KJV). Matthew 13:38–39 teaches us what the
field is and what the harvest is so there can be no guesswork.

By the modern versions omitting the phrase "for thee," it takes
out the specific person who will be doing the reaping of the earth.
That person is the Lord Jesus Christ, who will be doing the reaping.
Revelation 12–14 is the third parallel vision that culminates in the
reaping of the world, which is the end of the world.

For the Lord himself shall descend from heaven with a shout, with the voice of the archangel, and with the trump of God: and the dead in Christ shall rise first: Then we which are alive and remain shall be caught up together with them in the clouds, to meet the Lord in the air: and so shall we ever be with the Lord. (1 Thessalonians 4:16–17, KJV)

Revelation 15:2

And I saw as it were a sea of glass mingled with fire: and them that had gotten the victory over the beast, and over his image, *and over his mark*, and over the number of his name, stand on the sea of glass, having the harps of God. (Revelation 15:2, KJV)

"And over his mark" is omitted.

The omission of the phrase "and over his mark" is a significant omission. Now, the beast causes all his people to have a mark, and if you will notice, the locations of this mark on the body are significant. First of all, we see this mark on the right hand. "Show thy marvellous lovingkindness, O thou that savest by thy right hand them which put their trust in thee from those that rise up against them" (Psalm 17:7, KJV). In Psalm 17:7, we see that the right hand is associated with salvation by the power of the Lord. The beast will imitate the things that the Lord does. The mark on the right hand is associated with those who work deceitfully, bringing a false salvation. The right hand will also be associated with those who do works for the beast; in other words, their life's work will be in concert with the deceit of the beast. They will do the works that deceive others.

Then the mark in their foreheads shows that their mind is given over to the work of the beast. So in this particular passage, we see that those who invent systems and then implement them in the world are those with the mark on the hands (works) and the mind (evil thoughts). "Perverse disputings of men of corrupt minds, and destitute of the truth, supposing that gain is godliness: from such withdraw thyself" (1 Timothy 6:5, KJV). The mind is Satan's playground, and he is very active with his people. It does not matter what a person's social status is; Satan will deceive all his people. Now, some people want to make this out to be some type of physical mark like a bar code, but this is not what it in view. Sensationalizing verses only clouds the real meaning but, of course, sells books.

Revelation 15:3

And they sing the song of Moses the servant of God, and the song of the Lamb, saying, Great and marvellous are thy works, Lord God Almighty; just and true are thy ways, thou King of *saints*. (Revelation 15:3, KJV)

Saints is changed to "ages or nations."

This verse is similar to Revelation 8:13, where they exchanged "eagle" for "angel." There is no reason why *saints* should be exchanged for "nations," unless the Gnostics decided they would rather attach the Lord Jesus Christ to the world rather than to salvation of His saints. They disbelieved His deity, so they would look for every possible way to reduce Him to nothing more than a mere human. Here, He is called the King of saints, which would make Him Savior of His people. The "king of nations" title would make Him king of the earth; this could be attained by a human but never King of saints. Once again, the King James Bible exalts the Lord Jesus Christ where the modern versions reduce Him to only a mere human.

Revelation 15:5

And after that I looked, and, *behold*, the temple of the tabernacle of the testimony in heaven was opened. (Revelation 15:5, KJV)

Behold is omitted.

The word *behold*, which is missing in the modern versions, is the word in the Greek for "see, perceive, or look." In this usage of the word, it is in the imperative mood, which means the Lord Jesus Christ is giving a command to John to behold the temple of the tabernacle being opened in heaven. The word *behold* in the Greek is in the imperative mood, which is a command and not an option. Now, it may seem trite concerning the omission of this one word, but it is an important word. "Saying, I am Alpha and Omega, the first and the last: and, What thou seest, write in a book, and send it unto the seven churches which are in Asia; unto Ephesus, and unto Smyrna, and unto Pergamos, and unto Thyatira, and unto Sardis, and unto Philadelphia, and unto Laodicea" (Revelation 1:11, KJV). John was given the command to write what he sees. If he does not behold something based on the definitions above and below, then how could he write what he has not seen? Plus, he is being directed as to what is seen, so what is written is exactly what God wants to be written in the book of Revelation.

The word *behold* is important. For example, I see a 1932 Duesenberg parked across the street, so I go up close and look at it and see that it is in beautiful condition. I saw it from a distance, but I beheld it when I got close to it, and I was able to gain information about it, something I could not do from a distance. The word *behold* in English means "to fix eyes upon, see with attention, or observe with care." This is why the word is very important because it tells us John was carefully watching the unfolding events so he could write them with all divine accuracy.

There is also another interesting fact about the Greek word *idou* being omitted in the modern versions. It is found in the 1550 Stephanus text, and the word was also in the 1382 Wycliffe New Testament. This means that the word was in the text 168 years before Stephanus made his Greek text. Wycliffe had used the Latin Vulgate of Jerome from the fourth century, translated from Latin to Middle English. This means that the Greek word *idou* was in that translation as far back as the fourth century—another evidence that Receptus readings are old and not recent.

Revelation 16:5

And I heard the angel of the waters say, Thou art righteous, *O Lord*, which art, and wast, and shalt be, because thou hast judged thus. (Revelation 16:5, KJV)

"O Lord" is omitted.

Here is a case of the modern versions omitting the title of *Lord* for the Lord Jesus Christ. The term "Holy One" can be a generic term, even speaking of a believer as a holy one because of salvation in Christ. Jesus is called the Holy One of God in a few places in the New Testament. "Saying, Let us alone; what have we to do with thee, thou Jesus of Nazareth? art thou come to destroy us? I know thee who thou art; the *Holy One* of God" (Luke 4:34). However, in Revelation 16:5, the word for "O Lord" in the Greek is *kurie*, which is from *kurios*, which means "lord, owner, or master." This is another attack on the Lord Jesus as Lord. The fact that an angel is speaking to Jesus in heaven shows that the angel was showing deference to the Lord Jesus by calling Him *Lord*. The angel surely would have known that Jesus was the Holy One since they were both in heaven.

Revelation 16:7

And I heard *another out of* the altar say, Even so, Lord God Almighty, true and righteous are thy judgments. (Revelation 16:7, KJV)

"Another out of" is omitted.

By removing the phrase "another out of," it makes it say that it was the altar that was doing the talking instead of another angel, who is praising the Lord. Don't these modern-version editors ever read their own products? Altars do not, talk but angels do.

Revelation 16:14

> For they are the spirits of devils, working mira-
> cles, which go forth unto the kings *of the earth*
> *and* of the whole world, to gather them to
> the battle of that great day of God Almighty.
> (Revelation 16:14, KJV)

"Of the earth and" is omitted.

The first part of this verse explains exactly what the unclean spirits are. These are the spirits of devils, and by means of miracles, they
go out and deceive not only the populations of the world but also
incite the leaders of the nations around the entire world. It is through
the political governments that Christianity has either been curtailed
or endorsed. In this verse, we are seeing that because of the nature
of these miracles as being unclean, this will be a worldwide crusade
against true Christianity. What are we seeing today? There will be no
nation that will not attempt some type of persecution for the purpose
of silencing the Gospel. God will be using this time of persecution
as the precursor for the great battle of God Almighty, which will be
Armageddon, the final battle between God and Satan. While the war
will be waged in the spiritual realm, it will also be waged here on earth
by the followers of the beast. The kings of the earth here are linked
also to the kings of the east in chapter 16, verse 12.

> And when ye shall see Jerusalem compassed with
> armies, then know that the desolation thereof is
> nigh. Then let them which are in Judaea flee to
> the mountains; and let them which are in the
> midst of it depart out; and let not them that are
> in the countries enter thereinto. For these be the
> days of vengeance, that all things which are writ-
> ten may be fulfilled. (Luke 21:20–22, KJV)

Luke 21:20–22 calls these the days of vengeance when Satan
will try to enact vengeance upon the body of Christ, but instead God

will bring vengeance upon the kingdom of Satan for its persecution of the true believers. The New Jerusalem, which is the body of believers, will definitely suffer a final persecution just before the return of Christ. By omitting "of the earth, and," the modern versions limit the final battle of Armageddon to only leaders of countries; but the fact is that all believers will be partakers of the final battle between God and Satan, which of course God ultimately wins on the last day, culminating in judgment day for Satan and all his followers.

Revelation 16:16

> And *he gathered them* together into a place called in the Hebrew tongue Armageddon. (Revelation 16:16, KJV)

"He gathered them" is changed to "they or evil spirits gathered them."

The word *sunegagen* is a third-person singular verb and not a plural verb. Therefore, the word *they* is an erroneous translation. Take a look at some of what was translated out of that word, which simply means "he gathered together": armies, evil spirits, frog demons, demons, and demonic spirits. None of these are even intimated in this verse, which means they did interpretations instead of translations, and the modern-version proponents complain about the King James translators? What hypocrisy in their camp! This verse teaches that it is the Lord Jesus Christ who is drawing the forces into Armageddon, but the modern versions make it sound like man is in control.

Revelation 16:17

> And the seventh angel poured out his vial into the air; and there came a great voice out of the temple *of heaven*, from the throne, saying, It is done. (Revelation 16:17, KJV)

"Of heaven" is omitted.

Once again, we see an attack on the place of heaven. The Gnostics did not believe in such a place, so they took out the location of this temple. By removing "of heaven," they are removing the fact that this judgment is coming from God, who is in heaven. Without "of heaven," this could refer to any temple that one wishes to make, whether in heaven or on earth. This is a matter of removing prophetic doctrine from the scriptures. "And the temple of God was opened in heaven, and there was seen in his temple the ark of his testament: and there were lightnings, and voices, and thunderings, and an earthquake, and great hail" (Revelation 11:19, KJV).

Revelation 17:1

And there came one of the seven angels which had the seven vials, and talked with me, saying *unto me*, Come hither; I will shew unto thee the judgment of the great whore that sitteth upon many waters. (Revelation 17:1, KJV)

"Unto me" is omitted.

The personal Greek pronoun *moi* for "unto me" is used twenty-two times in the book of Revelation, showing that John is the one being addressed. It is in the dative case, which is the case of "personal interest." In this instance, it is the indirect object that is used to express to whom or for whom the action of the verb is done. In this case, it is John being personally addressed to see the destruction of religious Babylon.

Revelation 17:10

And *there are* seven kings: five are fallen, and one is, and the other is not yet come; and when he cometh, he must continue a short space. (Revelation 17:10, KJV)

"There are" is changed to "they are."

Now, in this verse, many have been trying to attach ancient world leaders to these seven kings. Some have even tried to attach the series of kingdoms mentioned in scripture such as Babylon, Assyria,

Rome, Egypt, and others. Some prophetic preachers try to make this out to be a prophecy of a physical Antichrist who will rule the world in the future. However, what we have in this verse is a general description of leaders through whom the beast has worked his evil. We do not know who they are, but the numbers line up with the method of description we had in verse 8.

> The beast that thou sawest was, and is not; and shall ascend out of the bottomless pit, and go into perdition: and they that dwell on the earth shall wonder, whose names were not written in the book of life from the foundation of the world, when they behold the beast that was, and is not, and yet is. (Revelation 17:8, KJV)

The "beast that thou sawest was," "five fallen kings and is not," "one is and shall ascend out of the bottomless pit," "the other is not yet and will continue for a short time." These seven kings represent a continuing rulership by the beast of governments and religions that persecute the Christians, and this rulership will continue until the last day when the kingdom of Satan will be judged in its totality. Hence, the number seven as being the perfect number that represents the kingdom of Satan in its entirety and length of time of existence. "And here is the mind which hath wisdom. The seven heads are seven mountains, on which the woman sitteth" (Revelation 17:9, KJV). The modern versions tend to make the mountains the seven kings. In verse 10, the Greek word is *eisen*, translated "there are" and not "they are." The kings are a separate symbol than the seven mountains and need to remain separated.

Revelation 18:6

> Reward her even as she rewarded *you*, and double unto her double according to her works: in the cup which she hath filled fill to her double. (Revelation 18:6, KJV)

You is omitted.

Just as Babylon rewarded the true believer with persecution and death, Babylon will now receive the reward of death. This verse is telling us that Babylon is going to be paid back, and that payment is going to be doubled. Babylon is going to receive a full requital for the evil it performed on the body of Christ. "Call together the archers against Babylon: all ye that bend the bow, camp against it round about; let none thereof escape: recompense her according to her work; according to all that she hath done, do unto her: for she hath been proud against the LORD, against the Holy One of Israel" (Jeremiah 50:29, KJV).

Just as earthly Babylon was to be judged according to all her evil actions, the spiritual Babylon is also going to be judged in the same manner it doled out its evil, but it will receive double for her actions. Babylon is going to receive a severe form of punishment, and as we go on in Revelation 18, we will see that this form of punishment is going to be the complete judgment and destruction of it. Though it tried to destroy the body of Christ and had created many martyrs, the body of Christ continued to flourish. Yet Babylon will be destroyed in a final blow because of its attempt to destroy the body of Christ. What it tried to do will be repaid to it twofold, resulting in total destruction.

This is why the personal pronoun *you* is very important because spiritual Babylon did not go after the cults or false denominational religions, but Satan had targeted the body of Christ from Abel to the last martyr before the Lord returns. Just as the kingdom of Satan targeted the body of believers, the Lord Jesus Christ is now targeting the kingdom of Satan for total destruction. Some of the modern translations change *you* to "others." The word *you* in the Greek is in the dative case, making it the receiver of the action, so it specifically states that the Christians were the receivers of the persecution and not other groups. The modern versions tend to leave out the truth and make things universal.

Revelation 18:9

And the kings of the earth, who have committed *fornication* and lived deliciously with her, shall
bewail her, and lament for her, when they shall see
the smoke of her burning. (Revelation 18:9, KJV)

Fornication is changed to "immorality."

The modern versions replace this word *fornication* with "sexual
immorality, immorality, adultery, intercourse." The scene in view is
that the kingdom of Satan is now being judged at the end of time,
and those who committed fornication with her are being permitted to see this happen. What is in view here is spiritual fornication
and nothing sexual because how can you have sexual relations with
a kingdom? Sexual immorality requires two people, and that is not
what is in view. The kings of the earth are those who ruled nations
and held some type of authority on earth and had placed their trust
in the kingdom of Satan, but now that kingdom is being destroyed
forever.

The word for "fornication" in the Greek is *porneuô*, and it is
used only three times in 1 Corinthians and five times in Revelation.
In 1 Corinthians, Paul uses it to describe physical fornication. "Flee
fornication. Every sin that a man doeth is without the body; but
he that committeth fornication sinneth against his own body" (1
Corinthians 6:18, KJV). In Revelation, all the usages are used specifically to point out spiritual fornication. "But I have a few things
against thee, because thou hast there them that hold the doctrine
of Balaam, who taught Balac to cast a stumblingblock before the
children of Israel, to eat things sacrificed unto idols, and to commit
fornication" (Revelation 2:14, KJV).

The physical kings of the world are not the only ones who are
placing their trust in the kingdom of Satan. There are millions of
Christians who have dual allegiance. They are in the kingdom of God
and still place trust in the kingdom of Satan. How many are running after false preachers like the health and wealth preachers? How
many own and defend the modern versions of the Bible, which are

all Vatican versions? How many believe the lies of false preachers and send them millions of dollars? How many Christians have bought into the ecumenical movement by believing Roman Catholicism is a Christian denomination? How many Christians have bought into the belief that sodomy is acceptable? How many Christians are following the emergent church movement with all its false and esoteric teachings? "Ye cannot drink the cup of the Lord, and the cup of devils: ye cannot be partakers of the Lord's table, and of the table of devils" (1 Corinthians 10:21, KJV). Once many Christians renounce dual allegiance, God will once again bless the USA as it once was.

Revelation 18:20

> Revelation 18:20 (KJV) Rejoice over her, thou
> heaven, and ye *holy apostles and prophets*; for God
> hath avenged you on her.

"*Holy apostles and prophets*" is changed to "ye saints, ye apostles, and ye prophets." (This change removes the fact that the apostles and prophets were holy men.)

All throughout history, God had sent the prophets and apostles to the nations to warn them of impending judgment. Now God was specifically telling the holy apostles and prophets to rejoice over the fall of political Babylon. The vindication of their messages and their calling from God is at hand, and this also means that soon the new heavens and new earth will be made. The Hort-Westcott texts adds two words "and the" between *holy* and *apostles*.

> Rejoice over her, thou heaven, and ye saints, and
> ye apostles, and ye prophets; for God hath judged
> your judgment on her. (Revelation 18:20, ASV)

This verse also points out that heaven will be rejoicing, which means all the believers who are there will be rejoicing, so there is no need to place additional wording in the verse to include *saints*. The holy apostles and prophets had special callings, and now God was vindicating them as their warnings are now coming to pass. The modern versions remove the specifics of this verse.

Revelation 19:1

> And after these things I heard a great voice of much people in heaven, saying, Alleluia; Salvation, and glory, and honour, and power, unto *the Lord* our God. (Revelation 19:1, KJV)

"The Lord" is omitted.

Revelation 19:1 begins another vision of John. This verse begins with the many voices in heaven giving glory to God and praising Him because now the final judgment of the great whore of Babylon has been consummated and vengeance has been meted out because of the cry of all the martyrs. This rejoicing in heaven can be called a real hallelujah chorus. *Hallelujah* means "praise the Lord." These voices in heaven are praising the Lord for His redemption and the manner in which He kept all the saints throughout all the ages. The phrase "Lord our God" is referring to God the Father and is used ninety-eight times in the Old Testament. By leaving out this phrase in this verse, they are omitting it once out of the three times it appears in the New Testament: in Mark 12:29 and Acts 2:39. It is another attack on the doctrine of God the Father.

Revelation 19:2

> For true and righteous are his judgments: for he hath judged the great whore, which did corrupt the earth with her fornication, and hath avenged the blood of his servants *at her hand*. (Revelation 19:2, KJV)

"At her hand" is omitted.

"Dearly beloved, avenge not yourselves, but rather give place unto wrath: for it is written, Vengeance is mine; I will repay, saith the Lord" (Romans 12:19, KJV). Revelation 19:2 states that God is now taking vengeance on the kingdom of Satan for the shedding of blood of His saints. God is specifically pointing out the fact that it was by the hand of Satan's kingdom that untold numbers of Christians were murdered, and now judgment day has arrived, and He is taking vengeance on behalf of His children. The modern versions leave out the important phrase "at her hand," which specifies who was responsible for the martyrdom of many Christians. Of course, Satan does not want this portion left in because it is His kingdom that is going to face the fierce wrath of God, and that is why he has his theologians omit it from his versions.

Revelation 19:8

And to her was granted that she should be arrayed
in fine linen, clean and white: for the fine linen is
the *righteousness* of saints. (Revelation 19:8, KJV)

Righteousness is changed to "righteous acts" (this change gives the appearance that works will get a person to heaven).

The Greek text is the same, but the English wording has created a wrong picture in the modern versions. The word *dikaioma* may be translated as "righteous or equitable deed, commandment, and the act of justification brought about in and for the sinner" but must be translated according to the context. Now, all the modern versions translated this word as "righteous act or deed." What must be understood is how the word is to be translated in Revelation 19:8:

And to her was granted that she should be
arrayed in fine linen, clean and white: for
the fine linen is the righteousness of saints.
(Revelation 19:8, KJV)

Revelation 19:8 speaks of fine linen that is clean and white, and this linen is the righteousness of the saints. Isaiah 61:10 gives us a good understanding of what that fine linen is.

> I will greatly rejoice in the LORD, my soul shall be
> joyful in my God; for he hath clothed me with the
> garments of salvation, he hath covered me with
> the robe of righteousness, as a bridegroom deck-
> eth himself with ornaments, and as a bride ador-
> neth herself with her jewels. (Isaiah 61:10, KJV)

In Isaiah 61:10, we read that God has covered us in the robe of righteousness, which is the garment of salvation. Now, you will notice what is missing, and that is any type of works that the believer does to gain salvation. The believer is totally passive in this verse because it is God doing all the action. The body of believers is referred to as the *bride of Christ*, and we are seeing this clearly in this verse. The fine linen in Revelation 19:8 is not referring to any works the believer does simply because it is speaking of the imputed righteousness of Christ to His children. No work can ever gain the righteousness needed to become saved. There is a passage in Revelation that speaks of the works of the believers, not those working for salvation.

> And I heard a voice from heaven saying unto me,
> Write, Blessed are the dead which die in the Lord
> from henceforth: Yea, saith the Spirit, that they
> may rest from their labours; and their works do
> follow them. (Revelation 14:13, KJV)

If you notice in this verse, the works that are spoken of are those of the believers on earth, and there is no mention of any of those works causing a Christian to be righteous. The works we do on earth are those that the Lord has commanded us to do. "So likewise ye, when ye shall have done all those things which are commanded you, say, We are unprofitable servants: we have done that which was our duty to do" (Luke 17:10, KJV). The key to understanding Revelation 19:8 is found in Romans 5:16–18:

> And not as it was by one that sinned, so is the
> gift: for the judgment was by one to condemna-

tion, but the free gift is of many offences unto justification. For if by one man's offence death reigned by one; much more they which receive abundance of grace and of the gift of *righteousness* shall reign in life by one, Jesus Christ. Therefore as by the offence of one judgment came upon all men to condemnation; even so by the *righteousness* of one the free gift came upon all men unto justification of life. (Romans 5:16–18, KJV)

If you will notice, the term *righteousness* is used two times, and that is the same word in the Greek that is found in Revelation 19:8. You will notice in verse 17 that the gift of righteousness comes by Jesus Christ and not by any type of works that we do. It states that righteousness came by *one*, and that one is the Lord Jesus Christ apart from any works. Therefore, it is absolutely impossible for any type of works to be equated with the righteousness of Christ.

Righteousness is not something that is earned but something that is bestowed upon the believer upon the moment of their salvation. The Roman Catholic Church and many apostate Protestant churches teach that works are a necessary part of a person's salvation. However, we cannot find one verse in scripture that teaches that works are needed for salvation; all we find is that works are a result of salvation. People may think they are working for salvation, but the true Bible teaches the opposite. This creates a fearful situation in telling people that their righteousness is based upon their works. This is fallacious as stated in Isaiah 64:6: "But we are all as an unclean thing, and all our righteousness are as filthy rags; and we all do fade as a leaf; and our iniquities, like the wind, have taken us away" (Isaiah 64:6, KJV).

Yet the Bible is replete with the proclamation of the righteousness of the true believer. "Let thy priests be clothed with righteousness; and let thy saints shout for joy" (Psalm 132:9, KJV). The believers are a nation of priests and would be clothed with the righteousness of God, causing joy in the believers. "Though these three men, Noah, Daniel, and Job, were in it, they should deliver but their own souls by their righteousness, saith the Lord GOD" (Ezekiel 14:14, KJV).

When the Lord was speaking about the coming destruction of Judah, He makes a statement that if Noah, Daniel, and Job were in the land, then they would be delivered by their own righteousness. How could that be? It is because they have the imputed righteousness of Christ, and that is how the saved are delivered among an evil generation.

So the word in Revelation 19:8 should not have "acts or deeds" added on because it contradicts the entire Bible by making people believe that their works can gain enough righteousness to get them into heaven. Those works can never equate to the righteousness that the Lord Jesus Christ bestows upon a true believer. Once again, the modern versions give us a teaching that has eternal consequences for those who follow them. The King James gives us the true teaching. Revelation 19:8 in the modern versions is probably one of the subtlest change the translators have ever made.

Revelation 20:9

> And they went up on the breadth of the earth, and compassed the camp of the saints about, and the beloved city: and fire came down from *God out of* heaven, and devoured them. (Revelation 20:9, KJV)

"*God out of*" is omitted.

This verse teaches us that Satan will make one last great sweep of the earth in an attempt to deceive all the nations with his false religions and false gospels. His main point of attack will be the body of Christ, where he will attempt to separate the believer from the Lord Jesus Christ through false teachings. The camp of the saints and the beloved city are one and the same as both describe the body of believers. The camp is where the body of believers dwells on earth, but they are part of the beloved city, the New Jerusalem, which is the body of believers. Then comes the end for Satan. God then sends fire down from heaven and devours Satan and all his cohorts.

The word for *devoured* in the Greek carries with it the meaning of "destroy or consume." "For our God is a consuming fire" (Hebrews 12:29, KJV). It is the end for Satan and all of his evil. The modern versions remove the fact that this judgment is coming from God Himself and not someone else. By removing the source of the judgment, the modern versions remove the fact that God is personally vindicating His children and protecting them from Satan. The verse, as read in the modern versions, is an attack on the doctrines of God and the final judgment.

Revelation 20:12

> And I saw the dead, small and great, stand before *God*; and the books were opened: and another book was opened, which is the book of life: and the dead were judged out of those things which were written in the books, according to their works. (Revelation 20:12, KJV)

God is changed to "throne."

"For the Father judgeth no man, but hath committed all judgment unto the Son" (John 5:22, KJV). In John 5:22, we read that the Son of God, the Lord Jesus Christ, will be the one who will be doing all the judging. When we look at Matthew 25:31–46, we see that all nations of the world are gathered before the Lord Jesus Christ. When the Gnostics removed *God* from Revelation 20:12, they took away the identification of the deity of the Lord Jesus Christ. Revelation 20:12 states that God is going to be the judge, and when we compare that to other scriptures, we see that the Lord Jesus is the judge, and that means that Revelation 20:12 is calling Him *God*.

When they remove the name *God* and replace it with the word *throne*, they remove the reality of the deity of Christ and the fact that He is the judge of all mankind. This is another attack on the Lord Jesus Christ as deity and removes His name from final events of earth's history. Once again, the King James Bible proves superior in theology as this verse is definitely a matter of doctrine. The word *God* was changed to "the throne" without any explanation given.

Revelation 21:2

And I *John* saw the holy city, new Jerusalem, coming down from God out of heaven, prepared as a bride adorned for her husband. (Revelation 21:2, KJV)

John is omitted.

Here is another case of John specifically identifying himself as the one who was now seeing the New Jerusalem descending from heaven. John identified himself throughout the book of Revelation because it was he who was commissioned to see these events unfold. His self-identification gives authenticity and firsthand witness to the events in Revelation. The modern versions omit his name, thus making it a very nebulous statement without identifying the person who is seeing it.

Revelation 21:4

And *God* shall wipe away all tears from their eyes; and there shall be no more death, neither sorrow, nor crying, neither shall there be any more pain: for the former things are passed away. (Revelation 21:4, KJV)

God is changed to "he."

Here is another example of the modern versions changing a noun to a pronoun. God always writes in specifics, and that is why *God* has placed His name here. The problem with replacing a noun with a pronoun is that the verse then goes from specific to ambiguous. In fact, the name *theos* in the Greek is in the nominative case, which means God is the subject of the sentence. When you take His name out and replace it, then the subject of the sentence is removed. God is going to be the one who will completely wipe away all tears, and when you remove Him, you remove the source of the believer's joy. This is an attack on God the Father, and it is good we have the King James Bible to bring us the truth.

Revelation 21:24

> And the nations *of them which are saved* shall walk in the light of it: and the kings of the earth do bring their glory and honour into it. (Revelation 21:24, KJV)

"Of them which are saved" is omitted.

In this section of scripture, we are reading a description of the new heaven and the new earth. We come to Revelation 21:24, where we see the qualification for entrance into the heaven and the new earth. That requirement is salvation! The word *nations* is the Greek word *ethnos*, which is also translated "people." In the KJB, we read that only those who are saved will be in glory with the Lord. The modern versions remove the eternal qualification of salvation from the entrance into heaven. According to the modern versions, the Jehovah's Witness version, and the Roman Catholic version, salvation is not a requirement to get into heaven. The Jehovah's Witness Bible and Roman Catholic versions show the absolute agreement between them and the ones used by the churches, and Christians still think that God can bless a church who uses compatible versions with these two cults.

In the Hort-Westcott Greek text, the portion "of them which are saved" is removed from the text and not even a note as to why; it is just removed. It is left out of Aleph, which is Sinaiticus, while the entire book of Revelation is omitted from Sinaiticus. These two manuscripts are the foundation of all the modern versions. By removing the requirement for salvation, they are also denying the sacrifice of Christ as necessary.

> Nevertheless we, according to his promise, look for new heavens and a new earth, wherein dwelleth righteousness. (2 Peter 3:13, KJV)

If anyone who is unregenerate will be allowed to enter into the new heavens and new earth, then righteousness will not dwell. Then

sin will have existence in both these eternal abodes. If the unregenerate are allowed to enter, then who was judged at the white throne
judgment and cast into hell? Will only some unbelievers be judged
for their sin and others will be allowed to live in bliss? Of course not.
But you see what questions must be asked and answered if an omission of this magnitude is allowed to stand. Those who accept these
false versions must ask these questions. However, they just accept
them without any suspicion.

Revelation 22:6

> And he said unto me, These sayings are faithful and
> true: and the Lord God of the *holy* prophets sent
> his angel to shew unto his servants the things which
> must shortly be done. (Revelation 22:6, KJV)

Holy is omitted.

The King James Bible states specifically in this verse that God
is the God of the holy prophets. It shows that He has full authority
over the prophets of the Old Testament and the apostles in the New
Testament. By the modern versions changing the word *holy* to "spirits
of," it removes the harmony that the Bible teaches concerning the
prophets.

> For the prophecy came not in old time by the will
> of man: but holy men of God spake as they were
> moved by the Holy Ghost. (2 Peter 1:21, KJV)
> Rejoice over her, thou heaven, and ye holy apos-
> tles and prophets; for God hath avenged you on
> her. (Revelation 18:20, KJV)

God refers to both categories as holy, which means they were set
apart unto the Lord and by the Lord for those offices to receive revelation and inspiration. By the modern versions removing the specific
description of holy, they open the door for anyone to claim they are
a prophet.

Revelation 22:14

> Blessed are they that *do his commandments,*
> that they may have right to the tree of life, and
> may enter in through the gates into the city.
> (Revelation 22:14, KJV)

"Do his commandments" is changed to "wash their robes or cleanse their garments."

Here is a verse that has been mutilated to show that it is the believer who washes their robe or, in other words, does good works for salvation. The Christian does nothing to earn salvation, and that includes doing any type of work. As Christians, we are clothed in the robe of Christ's righteousness, and it is done by God and not by us. "I will greatly rejoice in the LORD, my soul shall be joyful in my God; for he hath clothed me with the garments of salvation, he hath covered me with the robe of righteousness, as a bridegroom decketh himself with ornaments, and as a bride adorneth herself with her jewels" (Isaiah 61:10, KJV). Isaiah 61:10 is dripping with salvation language, and if you notice, we are the ones who are clothed by the Lord, and we do nothing.

In the Textus Receptus, we read that we who do his commandments will have a right to the tree of life. What is the difference? It is a major difference. Those who wash their robes are doing so in a state of unbelief and are washing them to gain salvation. Those who do the commandments are those who are already saved. In the books of 1–3 John, we read many times that those who are saved will do the commandments of God. The commandments in view are not those who comprise the law of Sinai, or else that would be a works Gospel too.

> And this is his commandment, That we should
> believe on the name of his Son Jesus Christ, and
> love one another, as he gave us commandment.
> (1 John 3:23, KJV)

> He that hath my commandments, and keepeth
> them, he it is that loveth me: and he that loveth me
> shall be loved of my Father, and I will love him, and
> will manifest myself to him. (John 14:21, KJV)

> And whatsoever we ask, we receive of him, because
> we keep his commandments, and do those things
> that are pleasing in his sight. (1 John 3:22, KJV)

This verse points to the fact that a person must be saved because only saved people are pleasing in the sight of God because they are children of God. The children of God are the ones who are indwelled by the Holy Spirit and have the ability to obey God and His commandments. Those who are in the flesh cannot please God. "So then they that are in the flesh cannot please God" (Romans 8:8, KJV).

So we see that keeping His commandments are the commandments of the new life, and those are not the physical laws but the spiritual laws that Christ has given us for us to keep only after salvation. "If ye fulfil the royal law according to the scripture, Thou shalt love thy neighbour as thyself, ye do well" (James 2:8, KJV).

We can only truly love our neighbor if we are already saved. So we see once again that the modern versions turn salvation by grace into salvation by works.

Revelation 22:19

> And if any man shall take away from the words
> of the book of this prophecy, God shall take away
> his part out of the *book* of life, and out of the holy
> city, and from the things which are written in this
> book. (Revelation 22:19, KJV)

Book is changed to "tree."

Anyone who removes anything from His word will be subject to eternal damnation. Those who are unbelievers were never in the holy city nor in the Lamb's book of life. God is telling us that those who adulterate His word are not worthy to be in the book of life or the holy city. One of the most major attacks on the word of God today is the modern versions, which remove verses and the portions of many other verses. This is one way they are taking away from the word of God. Then another way that teachings are removed from the word of God is by preachers and teachers who cast doubt on parts of the word of God. Many preachers do not believe in hell, nor do they believe in the first three chapters of Genesis being literal. Those who take away from the word of God in any fashion are revealing that they are under the judgment of God and, unless they become saved, will suffer the same penalty as all the rest of the unbelievers. God records the name of everyone He has saved in the book of life and not in the tree of life.

The tree of life is symbolic of the Lord Jesus Christ. "Blessed are they that do his commandments, that they may have right to the tree of life, and may enter in through the gates into the city" (Revelation 22:14, KJV). Notice Revelation 22:14 states that they are blessed who do His commandments. Without the benefit of the rest of the Bible, we could look at this passage and claim that we are saved by works in keeping His commandments. Of course, we know that is impossible for anyone to do as no one can work for salvation. We do the commandments of the Lord through salvation by grace because Christ had satisfied all the demands of God's holy law on behalf of the believer, and we do the commandments as a result of salvation and not for salvation. Every saved person has their name written in the Lamb's book of life, and as a result, we have the right to the tree of life for eternity—that is, Christ. For the modern versions to remove the second usage of *book* in verse 19 is to remove continuity of the thread that is in view in verses 18 and 19, which is speaking about those who are saved and those who are not.

Revelation 22:21

The grace of *our* Lord Jesus Christ be with *you all. Amen.* (Revelation 22:21, KJV)

"Our" is changed to "the." "Christ" is omitted. *"You all"* is changed to "saints" or "holy people." *"Amen"* is omitted in some versions.

We end up this book revealing what the modern versions do best, and that is attacking the Lord Jesus Christ. First of all, they omit His title of deity *Christ*, and then they omit the personalization by calling Him *"the* Lord Jesus" instead of *our*. The word *our* is in the possessive case, which means that we claim Him as our Savior, and He claims us as His children. Then they remove the other personal message "be with you all." They change it to third-person "all the saints" or "the saints."

Let me use an analogy. A father has four children, and he is away on business but makes a call home and says to his children, "My love to all the children," or he says, "My love to all of you." Which one would mean more to the children? The second because he personalized his love toward his children, and that is exactly what God did. The modern versions make it very cold and distant, but God's true word, the King James Bible, makes it personal to each of us.

Multiple-Version Disorder
Is it God's Judgment on the Church?

> Now all these things happened unto them for
> ensamples: and they are written for our admoni-
> tion, upon whom the ends of the world are come.
> (1 Corinthians 10:11, KJV)

Are multiple Bible versions God's judgment on the church? What a question. How could the word of God be a judgment on the very establishment it proclaims? Very simple. Any version can call itself a Bible, but it is the content inside those versions that cause them to be a judgment rather than a blessing. Let us look at the precedent for this biblical principle. In 1 Corinthians 10:11, we are told that the things that happened to ancient Israel were recorded by God for the purpose of our admonition. The word *admonition* in the Greek carries with it the meaning of "instruction, warning, or counsel." It is the word *nouthesia* from which we derive the word *nouthetic*, which is a form of accountability counseling made popular by Jay Adams. In other words, God did not record those things that happened to Israel as something just to be read, but they are there to warn us to not fall into the same traps that they allowed themselves to fall into, which resulted in them being judged by God and eventually losing their nation forever in AD 70.

"For with stammering lips and another tongue will he speak to this people" (Isaiah 28:11, KJV). In Isaiah 28:11, God had already stated that He was going to bring a judgment on Judah, which happened in 586 BC. Here is the principle that we are able to carry over to the New Testament church. The prophecy that God is making through Isaiah is that of the coming of the Chaldeans or the Babylonians, who will eventually take Judah into captivity for seventy years. Notice how God reveals this fact. He tells them that He is going to speak to these people—that is Judah, with men of stammering lips and another tongue. The phrase "stammering lips" carries with it the meaning of "foreign lips." The English word *stammering* means "stopping or hesitating in the speaking of syllables and words." So this gives us a little insight about the way the Chaldean language was spoken.

For many years since the times of Moses, which would have been about seven hundred years before Isaiah was written, God had sent prophets and leaders to Israel, but the problem was that they were a very rebellious and recalcitrant people. Whenever God sent a prophet to them to guide them back into obedience, they had refused to listen. Now, the prophets came to them in their own language, speaking to them in no uncertain terms, so there was no problem in them understanding. We know this because they would hear the prophets and then afterward would become very angry with them to the point of persecuting and even killing them." O Jerusalem, Jerusalem, which killest the prophets, and stonest them that are sent unto thee; how often would I have gathered thy children together, as a hen doth gather her brood under her wings, and ye would not!" (Luke 13:34, KJV). Jesus Himself made that accusation against them, so the time of God's patience wore out, and He was now going to do something to Judah, which they would be unable to believe.

> Behold ye among the heathen, and regard, and wonder marvellously: for I will work a work in your days, which ye will not believe, though it be told you. For, lo, I raise up the Chaldeans, that bitter and hasty nation, which shall march through the breadth of the land, to possess the dwelling-places that are not theirs. (Habakkuk 1:5–6, KJV)

Habakkuk was written about 626–605 BC, which was about 150 years after Isaiah, and we can tell from this that Judah still remained in disobedience to God and the law. Now they refused to listen to those prophets who came to them in their own language to warn them and admonish them that if they did not become obedient, God was going to judge them with the Chaldeans. Remember, the Chaldeans were described by God as those "with stammering lips and another tongue." In other words, God was going to use a people whereby Judah would not be able to understand their language. Since they refused to listen in their own language, God was now going to judge them by a foreign language. That was the principle God was giving in Isaiah 28:11.

Now, how does that apply to the Christian and the church of today? Up until 1881, the church used one Bible, and that was the King James. You could go into any church, and you would hear that Bible being expounded. If you look at history, you will see that the church was a very powerful entity at that time, and because people in this country used the King James Bible, it spawned not only a powerful church but the greatest century of world missions. Then in 1881, the Revised Version of Hort and Westcott was released on the Christian world. It did not make the greatest impact at that time, but the fact that it was there meant that the source of corruption was just waiting to be used, and it was.

In 1872, Phillip Schaff chose thirty theologians from various denominations, including the Unitarian church, and began the translation from the 1881 RV Greek of Hort and Westcott into what would be called the 1901 American Standard Version. Satan now had his foot in the door with the corrupt Bible version. Then in 1906 came the "Azuza street revival," which it was called; but when one studies it, there was also much witchcraft involved in it. That lasted from 1906 to 1915. Just long enough for the Assemblies of God to form in 1914, whereby it started the Charismatic movement with all the tongues, signs, and wonders. The churches were beginning to accept the tongues, and because they did, they suffered the same fate as the people of Judah did in the time of Habakkuk.

Just as the message was being preached in the language of the people, they began to start accepting the tongues movement; and because of this, God was now judging them as He did Judah with other tongues that are totally gibberish. With the acceptance of the tongues movement, God was now judging every single church that adapted that satanic phenomenon. If a church accepts tongues, then that is not evidence of the Holy Spirit but evidence that church is under judgment. Individual Christians who accept tongues, if they are truly saved, will not lose their salvation but will be severely hindered in their Christian walk and will not grow beyond tongues, healing, miracles, and signs. In other words, these Christians will not grow because they are stagnating their own growth by accepting what is not of God.

Now, that principle has been transferred to every church that accepts the modern versions. Every single modern version says something different and therefore cannot get past "what does your version say?" Try to have a Bible study where there are ten different versions, and you will be at an impasse. When the church was using only one Bible, namely the King James Bible, there was a very powerful church. Now that we have many counterfeit versions in the churches, the church has become the weakest entity on earth. In fact, it has been downgraded to nothing but a religious social club where everyone is welcome, no matter what your belief system is.

With each modern version saying something different, if you have a church full of Christians with modern versions, then what you have is a situation of total confusion. The pastor is teaching from his ESV, you are sitting there with your NIV, your wife or husband has the NASV, and your child has the Message. It is just like the judgment of Judah with the foreign tongues. Each modern version is a tongue of its own, and since so many Christians have multiple versions in every church, it is not a place of growth but of confusion. Since God cannot speak to the church in the language of the King James Bible, He is now speaking to these churches with stammering lips. Remember what the stammering lips were. They were the hesitation and stopping of pronouncing syllables. Is that happening in the church? It sure is.

How many times does your pastor stop the sermon to quote another version, or how many times does he go to the Greek or the Hebrew and expound the word from his Nestle-Aland or UBS Greek New Testament? The reality is that multiple versions in a church is just like God speaking to Judah through the stammering lips of the Chaldeans. The Gospel needs continuity in its teaching and not confusion. If your church suffers from multiple-version disorder, then your church is under God's judgment. If the Bible that He gave us in 1611, which is bathed in the blood of the martyrs, is not good enough for you, then you are a traitor by embracing the Roman Catholic modern versions. Then you, like Judah, have become an enemy of Christ, and your Christian walk will be a total disappointment.

Manuscripts Mentioned in This Book

Byzantine Text (450–1450 AD)
Stephanus (1550 AD)

A 02, Alexandrinus (fifth century)
C 04, Ephraemi Rescriptus (fifth century)
D 05, Bezae Cantabrigiensis (fifth century)
K 017 (ninth century)
L 020 (ninth century)
M 021 (ninth century)
Q 026 (fifth century)
U 030 (ninth century)

W 032 (fourth/fifth century)
X 033 (tenth century)
Delta 037 (ninth century)
Theta 038 (ninth century)
PI-041 (ninth century)

28, Minuscule (eleventh century)
33, Minuscule (ninth century)
137, Minuscule (twelfth century)
138, Minuscule (eleventh century)
565, Minuscule (ninth century)
700, Minuscule (eleventh century)
892, Minuscule (ninth century)
1010, Minuscule (twelfth century)
1110, Minuscule (eleventh century)
1210, Minuscule (eleventh century)
1215, Minuscule (thirteenth century)
1216, Minuscule (ninth century)
1217, Minuscule (AD 1186)
1221, Minuscule (eleventh century)
1582, Minuscule (AD 948)
036, Majuscule (tenth century)

P 46 (c. AD 200)
P72 (third/fourth century)
P 75 (third century)

The Vaticanus Manuscript (B)

The word *Vatican* in Latin means "hill of divination." "There shall not be found among you any one that maketh his son or his daughter to pass through the fire, or that useth divination, or an observer of times, or an enchanter, or a witch" (Deuteronomy 18:10, KJV). The Vaticanus manuscript was found in the Vatican library in 1481. It was rejected by the King James translators because it was very corrupt and unreliable. The following portions of scripture are missing from the Vaticanus: Genesis 1:1–46; 28; Psalms 106–138; Matthew 16:2–3; Mark 16:9–20; the pastoral epistles (1 and 2 Timothy and Titus), and everything after Hebrews 9:14. These were intentional omissions because the manuscript was found in excellent condition with no pieces missing.

In the Gospels, it leaves out 237 words, 452 clauses, and 748 whole sentences. These omissions were intentional since there was room left on pages to write these in. The Vaticanus manuscript was written on expensive vellum and was in good condition when found, which means that the missing areas were not due to missing sections but intentional omission.

The Sinaiticus Manuscript (a) Aleph

Since this manuscript came into existence in 1844, it was thought to be a fourth-century document. In the late months of 2015 and early months of 2016, this manuscript has been proven to be a nineteenth-century counterfeit. The pages of this manuscript were purely white, but in a few short years, the pages turned brown, giving it the appearance of being old. The reality is that it was darkened by tea, giving it the appearance of age. It was a collusion between Constantine Tischendorf and Constantine Simonides. Tischendorf was blessed by the pope for this manuscript because he knew that it would be used to help displace the King James Version.

The Sinaiticus is a total fake! The sorry situation is that this is one the main forty-five manuscripts that underlie all the modern versions, which means that the modern versions are all based upon a counterfeit manuscript, making them all null and void. There are over six thousand manuscripts, but the modern versions are based on only forty-five, and some of them are very corrupt in nature, such as Sinaiticus, Vaticanus, Alexandrinus (A 02), Bezae Canatbrigiensis (D 05). Sinaiticus is one of the two manuscripts, Vaticanus being the other, where Mark 16:9–20 is omitted intentionally while it appears in 618 other manuscripts. It also contains the "Shepherd of Hermes" and "The Epistle of Barnabas." For more information on this, go to www.scionofzion.com/sinaiticus_fake.html. There, you will find an entire series of videos giving the details of this counterfeit manuscript and its Catholic connection.

Textual Variations Between Vaticanus and Sinaiticus

There are 3036 textual differences in the Gospels alone. 656 in Matthew - 567 in Mark - 791 in Luke - 1022 in John. With these amounts of disagreements in the Gospels alone, how could these 2 manuscripts ever be trusted for accuracy, yet all your modern versions rely heavily on these two manuscripts.

Summary

These two manuscripts are the foundational manuscripts of all the modern versions. When we see the characteristics of the two manuscripts as being inferior and loaded with false books, plus many scribal errors and writings (and now proof exists that Sinaiticus is a fake), we can see plainly why the modern versions lack integrity and why they are missing so much. The sad part is that the modern scholars claim these two manuscripts are the "oldest and best." This is such an outright lie that the publishers should be sued for false advertising. Just because something is old does not make it the best. Would you like to have an operation according to 1905 medical knowledge? After all, oldest is best! Would you like to drive across country in winter in a 1905 car? After all, oldest is best! That theory is nothing but a lie and should not and must not be believed. Just taking a look at these two manuscripts, we see how corrupted they are and how they completely violate the scriptures.

> For I testify unto every man that heareth the words of the prophecy of this book, If any man shall add unto these things, God shall add unto him the plagues that are written in this book: And if any man shall take away from the words of the book of this prophecy, God shall take away his part out of the book of life, and out of the

> holy city, and from the things which are written
> in this book. (Revelation 22:18–19, KJV)

These modern Bibles have definitely taken away the words of God to the tune of thousands in the Greek and thousands in the English, which means that all the modern Bibles are under the curse of God and in no way can ever be blessed. When we also factor in the fact that these translation committees all have unbelievers on them, we can know instantly that these modern Bibles are nothing more than false versions.

> But unto the wicked God saith, What hast thou
> to do to declare my statutes, or that thou shoul-
> dest take my covenant in thy mouth? Seeing thou
> hatest instruction, and castest my words behind
> thee. (Psalm 50:16–17, KJV)

The above verses teach that unbelievers hate the word of God. Why then would a holy God commit His holy word unto Satan's people for correction? The NIV had two sodomites working on it. The Revised Version of 1881 had a Unitarian working on it. The 1901 ASV had Philip Schaff as its committee head, and he was one who wanted reunification with Rome. The Good News Bible had Robert Bratcher, who was an unbeliever and disbelieved the first three chapters of Genesis as Westcott did. The Lockman Foundation refused to divulge the names of the translators of the New American Standard Bible. What have they got to hide?

When we look at the beliefs of men like Origen and Justin Martyr who tried to combine Greek philosophy with the Gospel, would God commit His holy word to unbelievers like that? We must ask those questions of the modern versions and demand an answer.

Well, I have done my part—the rest is up to you! May the Lord open your eyes very wide to this ongoing deception and then do something about it!

Bible Suggestions

If you have read this material and have realized your modern version is no longer trustworthy, then may I suggest two very fine Bibles:

- The Defined King James Bible is available from Bible for Today Ministries and can be located on line at www.bible-fortoday.org.
- The Reformation Heritage Bible is available from Reformation Heritage Books and can be located on line at www.heritagebooks.org.

Both these Bibles utilize the King James Cambridge Texts, which are the best in use today. I own two of each, one for the house and one for the car.

I am also a lifetime member of the Dean Burgon Society, which is dedicated to the truth about the false versions and the superiority of the King James Bible over these counterfeit versions. They sponsor a yearly meeting in different places around the country. They can be located online at www.deanburgonsociety.org.

ABOUT THE AUTHOR

The author's name is Ken Matto, and he lives in Whiting, New Jersey. He holds a doctor of ministry degree from Bethany Theological Seminary in Dothan, Alabama. He is reformed in theology and currently disabled since 2003, so his main ministry is on the Internet. The website "Scion of Zion" (www.scionofzion.com) has been online since November 20, 1997. It is viewed in over 170 countries each month.

He came to the Bible-version issue in this manner. In March 1986, he overheard two senior saints speaking about Bible versions but did nothing. In May 1986, he purchased a Chick tract entitled "The Attack," which was a capsulized version of the attack on the King James Bible. He corresponded with David Otis Fuller concerning the modern versions. At the time, he used the NASV and compared about fifty verses with the King James Bible and saw the corruption in the NASV. Then he went to the New King James Version, which also had problems in it. He finally purchased a King James Bible and has been blessed ever since.

Since 1986, he has done many studies in the area of the modern versions and have found them all to be wanting. His desire is to see other Christians come to the same conclusion he has by just making simple comparisons. He states that since he has come back to the King James Bible, he noticed more authority in ministry, and so will you!

CPSIA information can be obtained
at www.ICGtesting.com
Printed in the USA
LVHW041320220721
693405LV00001B/4